DELPHI
IN A NUTSHELL

A Desktop Quick Reference

DELPHI
IN A NUTSHELL

A Desktop Quick Reference

Ray Lischner

O'REILLY®

Beijing • Cambridge • Farnham • Köln • Paris • Sebastopol • Taipei • Tokyo

Delphi in a Nutshell
by Ray Lischner

Published by O'Reilly & Associates, Inc., 1005 Gravenstein Highway North,
Sebastopol, CA 95472.

Editor: Simon Hayes

Production Editor: Madeleine Newell

Cover Designer: Ellie Volckhausen

Printing History:

> March 2000:   First Edition.

Library of Congress Cataloging-in-Publication Data

Lischner, Ray, 1961–
    Delphi in a nutshell / by Ray Lischner.
      p. cm.
    ISBN 1-56592-659-5 (alk. paper)
      1. Delphi (Computer file) 2. Computer software--Development. I. Title.

QA76.76.D47 L56 2000

005.26'8--dc21   99-086244

ISBN: 1-56592-659-5
[M]   [7/03]

Table of Contents

Preface

Borland's Delphi is a combination of a modern programming language, an integrated development environment (IDE), and the visual component library (VCL). Delphi's IDE is readily familiar to anyone who has used similar tools. For example, a WYSIWYG form editor lets you design a window visually, with drag-and-drop ease. More important, the framework is object-oriented, extensible and customizable, due to the power and flexibility of the Delphi programming language.

The heart of Delphi is the Delphi Pascal programming language, which has key features to support the IDE and VCL. It has all the power of a modern object-oriented language, along with the elegance and simplicity of Pascal.

Delphi in a Nutshell is a comprehensive reference manual for Delphi Pascal. It covers the entire language, and it also highlights ways to use the language effectively. Experienced Delphi programmers can use this book as an alphabetical reference. Newcomers to Delphi should spend extra time with the first few chapters. I hope that everyone will find something of value in these pages.

Not Your Father's Pascal

Delphi Pascal is one of many object-oriented variants of Pascal. Over the years, Delphi has evolved and is no longer recognizable as the Pascal you used in school all those many years ago. In addition to unit-based modular programming and a robust class model, Delphi Pascal has a number of other modern language features, including the following:

- Interfaces (similar to Java™ and COM interfaces)
- Unicode strings
- Properties
- Exception handling

Delphi started as a Windows programming language and environment, and many Delphi programmers (myself included) consider Delphi to be the best Windows development tool available. Delphi includes full support for COM and ActiveX, an object-oriented widget library (called the Visual Component Library, or VCL), and a rapid-application development environment that is extensible and customizable.

Delphi for Linux

As I write this, Borland is hard at work porting Delphi to Linux. Perhaps when you read this, Delphi for Linux will be available, bringing its integrated development environment to X-Windows, including its WYSIWYG form editor, multi-tier database support, and full CORBA support.

Until Borland finishes this work and releases Delphi for Linux, I can only speculate about how the final product will look. (No, I don't get any special inside information.) You can rely on the core language being the same in both Delphi for Linux and Delphi for Windows, including classes, objects, interfaces, strings, dynamic arrays, exceptions, and the basic data types. Most of the built-in subroutines will work the same under Linux as under Windows.

Some language features described in this book are clearly Windows specific, such as the CmdShow and DllProc variables or the FindHInstance function. If you want to write code that is portable between Windows and Linux, you must avoid these Windows-specific features.

Delphi for Windows is the best development environment for writing Windows applications and libraries. To attain this premier position, Delphi has incorporated a number of Windows-specific features. Borland has a goal of making Delphi for Linux the best Linux development environment. To achieve that goal, we can expect Delphi to include some Linux-specific features.

I'm just guessing, but I believe it will be feasible to write code that is portable between Windows and Linux. However, you will have to sacrifice some features that are unique to each environment. Writing components that are easily portable, especially interactive controls, will probably be a daunting task. Making an application that is portable will most likely be easier.

About This Book

The first four chapters of this book present information on how to use Delphi effectively, and subsequent chapters form the language reference proper.

Chapter 1, *Delphi Pascal*, discusses the differences between Delphi Pascal and standard Pascal. If you have used Turbo Pascal or other variants of Object Pascal, you should give Chapter 1 a quick read to learn about the new features that are unique to Delphi Pascal. Similarly, if you haven't used Pascal since your college days (all those years ago), you must read Chapter 1 to learn about the new and nifty features in Delphi Pascal. You might be surprised at how far the language has come over the years.

Chapter 2, *The Delphi Object Model*, discusses classes and objects in greater depth. If you have used other variants of Object Pascal, you must read this chapter because Delphi's object model is quite different. If you have experience with other object-oriented programming languages, read Chapter 2 to learn the differences between Delphi and other languages, such as Java and C++.

Chapter 3, *Runtime Type Information,* covers the key to Delphi's integrated development environment. RTTI is not documented in Borland's official help files, but anyone writing or using components (that is, every Delphi programmer) should understand the nature of RTTI, including its limitations and proper uses. Chapter 3 tells you everything there is to know about RTTI, and then some.

Chapter 4, *Concurrent Programming,* is about using Delphi in a modern, multi-threaded, multiprocessor world. Delphi includes several language features to help you write multithreaded applications, but these features can be difficult to use if you do not have much experience with the tricks and traps of multithreaded programming. This chapter gets you started using Delphi effectively to write modern applications.

Chapter 5, *Language Reference,* is the bulk of the book. The alphabetical reference lists every keyword, directive, subroutine, type, and variable in the Delphi Pascal language and its system units. Full examples show you how to use the language correctly and effectively.

Chapter 6, *System Constants,* contains tables of related constants. Chapter 5 is large enough without adding these literals. Moving them to a separate chapter makes the complete reference easier to use.

Chapter 7, *Operators,* describes all the arithmetic and other operators in Delphi Pascal. Symbols do not alphabetize well, so listing the symbol operators in their own chapter makes it easier to find information about a particular operator.

Chapter 8, *Compiler Directives,* lists all the special comments that you can include in your source code to control how Delphi compiles and links your program.

Appendix A, *Command-Line Tools,* describes the usage and options for the various command-line tools that come with Delphi. These tools are not related to the Delphi Pascal language, but they are often overlooked and can be extremely useful for the Delphi professional.

Appendix B, *The SysUtils Unit,* lists all the subroutines, types, and variables in the SysUtils unit. This unit is not built into the compiler (as the System unit is). It is not part of the Delphi Pascal language, but is part of Delphi's runtime library. Nonetheless, many Delphi professionals have come to rely on SysUtils as though it were part of the language, and indeed, many subroutines in SysUtils are superior to their equivalents in the System unit (such as AnsiPos instead of Pos).

Conventions Used in This Book

The following typographical conventions are used in this book:

Constant width

> Used for Delphi identifiers and symbols, including all keywords and directives. In the language reference, constant width shows the syntax elements that must be used exactly as shown. For example, the array declaration

requires the square brackets and other symbols, and the `type`, `array`, and `of` keywords to be used as shown:

```
type Name = array[Index type, ...] of Base type;
```

Constant width italic
: Used in the language reference for syntax elements that must be replaced by your code. In the previous example, you must supply the type *Name*, the *Index type*, and the *Base type*.

Constant Width Bold
: Used in longer code examples to highlight the lines that contain the language element being described.

Italic
: Used to indicate variables, filenames, directory names, URLs, and glossary terms.

Note Icons

 The owl icon designates a tip, suggestion, or general note related to the surrounding text.

 The turkey icon designates a warning related to the surrounding text.

For More Information

When you have a question about Delphi, you should first consult the Delphi help files. Delphi also comes with numerous examples (in the *Demos* directory) that are often more helpful than the help files.

If you still cannot find the answer you seek, try posing your question to one of the many Delphi newsgroups. Several standard newsgroups exist, and Borland maintains its own newsgroups on its server, *forums.borland.com*. In particular, *borland.public.delphi.objectpascal* is the appropriate newsgroup for questions related to the Delphi Pascal language.

If you want to know about Delphi's integrated development environment, about the visual component library, or other topics on Delphi programming, the two most popular books are *Mastering Delphi 5*, by Marco Cantu (Sybex, 1999) and *Delphi 5 Developer's Guide*, by Steve Teixeira and Xavier Pacheco (Sams, 1999).

If you find errors or omissions in this book, please bring them to my attention by sending email to *nutshell@tempest-sw.com*. I receive too much email to answer every message individually, but be assured that I read everything (everything that makes it past my anti-spam filters, anyway).

How to Contact Us

The information in this book has been tested and verified, but you may find that features have changed (or you may even find mistakes!). You can send any errors you find, as well as suggestions for future editions, to:

O'Reilly & Associates, Inc.
101 Morris Street
Sebastopol, CA 95472
(800) 998-9938 (in the United States or Canada)
(707) 829-0515 (international or local)
(707) 829-0104 (fax)

There is a web page for this book, where we list any errata, examples, and additional information. You can access this page at:

http://www.oreilly.com/catalog/delphi/

To ask technical questions or to comment on the book, send email to:

bookquestions@oreilly.com

For more information about our books, conferences, software, Resource Centers, and the O'Reilly Network, see our web site at:

http://www.oreilly.com

Acknowledgments

I thank Tim O'Reilly for taking a chance with his first Delphi title. I look forward to reading and writing other Delphi books published by O'Reilly.

The technical editors—Allen Bauer and Hallvard Vassbotn—did an excellent job of spotting my mistakes. Hallvard's copious and detailed comments were invaluable. Any remaining mistakes are ones that I added after the editors finished their thorough work.

I thank my editor, Simon Hayes, and the entire team at O'Reilly—Bob Herbstman, Troy Mott, and the design and production staff—for turning my humble manuscript into this polished book you see now.

None of my books would be possible without the support of family. I thank my wife, Cheryl, and the once-and-future programmer, Arthur, who makes it all worthwhile.

CHAPTER 1

Delphi Pascal

Delphi Pascal is an object-oriented extension of traditional Pascal. It is not quite a proper superset of ISO standard Pascal, but if you remember Pascal from your school days, you will easily pick up Delphi's extensions. Delphi is not just a fancy Pascal, though. Delphi adds powerful object-oriented features, without making the language too complicated. Delphi has classes and objects, exception handling, multithreaded programming, modular programming, dynamic and static linking, OLE automation, and much, much more.

This chapter describes Delphi's extensions to Pascal. You should already be familiar with traditional Pascal or one of the other popular extensions to Pascal, such as Object Pascal. If you already know Borland's Object Pascal from the Turbo Pascal products, you will need to learn a new object model (detailed in Chapter 2, *The Delphi Object Model*), plus other new features.

Borland uses the name "Object Pascal" to refer to Delphi's programming language, but many other languages use the same name, which results in confusion. This book uses the name "Delphi Pascal" to refer to the Delphi programming language, leaving Object Pascal for the many other object-oriented variations of Pascal.

Units

Delphi Pascal is a modular programming language, and the basic module is called a *unit*. To compile and link a Delphi program, you need a program source file and any number of additional units in source or object form. The program source file is usually called a *project* source file because the project can be a program or a library—that is, a dynamically linked library (DLL).

When Delphi links a program or library, it can statically link all the units into a single *.exe* or *.dll* file, or it can dynamically link to units that are in packages. A *package* is a special kind of DLL that contains one or more units and some extra logic that enables Delphi to hide the differences between a statically linked unit and a dynamically linked unit in a package. See the section "Packages," later in this chapter, for more information about packages.

Forms and Files

Some units represent forms. A *form* is Delphi's term for a window you can edit with Delphi's GUI builder. A form description is stored in a *.dfm* file, which contains the form's layout, contents, and properties.

Every *.dfm* file has an associated *.pas* file, which contains the code for that form. Forms and *.dfm* files are part of Delphi's integrated development environment (IDE), but are not part of the formal Delphi Pascal language. Nonetheless, the language includes several features that exist solely to support Delphi's IDE and form descriptions. Read about these features in depth in Chapter 3, *Runtime Type Information*.

 A binary *.dfm* file is actually a 16-bit *.res* (Windows resource) file, which maintains compatibility with the first version of Delphi. Versions 2 and later produce only 32-bit programs, so Delphi's linker converts the *.dfm* resource to a 32-bit resource automatically. Thus, binary *.dfm* files are usually compatible with all versions of Delphi. Delphi 5 also supports textual *.dfm* files. These files are plain text and are not compatible with prior versions of Delphi, at least not without conversion back to the binary format. The only way to tell whether a *.dfm* file is binary or text is to open the file and check the contents. An easy way to do this programmatically is to test the first three bytes, which are always $FF $0A $00 in a binary *.dfm* file.

Table 1-1 briefly describes the files you are likely to find in Delphi and what they are used for. Files marked with "(IDE)" are not part of Delphi Pascal, but are used by the IDE.

Table 1-1: Delphi Files

Extension	Description
.bpg	Project group (IDE)
.bpl	Compiled package (special kind of DLL)
.cfg	Options for the command line compiler
.dcp	Compiled package information, needed to link with a package
.dcr	Component bitmap resource (IDE)
.dcu	Unit object code
.dfm	Form description (IDE)
.dof	Project options file (IDE)
.dpk	Source file for building a package
.dpr	Main source file for a program or library
.drc	Resource script for `resourcestring` declarations

Table 1-1: Delphi Files (continued)

Extension	Description
.dsk	Desktop layout (IDE)
.pas	Unit source code
.res	Windows resource (every .dpr has an associated .res file)

Separating Interface from Implementation

A unit has two parts: interface and implementation. The interface part declares the types, variables, constants, and routines that are visible to other units. The implementation section provides the guts of the routines declared in the interface section. The implementation section can have additional declarations that are private to the unit's implementation. Thus, units are Delphi's primary means of information hiding.

One unit can *use* another unit, that is, import the declarations from that other unit. A change to a unit's interface requires a recompilation of all units that use the changed declaration in the modified unit. Delphi's compiler manages this automatically, so you don't need to use makefiles to compile Delphi projects.

You can use a unit in the interface or implementation section, and the choice is important when building a project:

- If unit A uses unit B in its interface section, changes to unit B's interface are propagated as changes to unit A's interface. Delphi must recompile all the units that use unit A.

- If unit A uses unit B in its implementation section, only unit A must be recompiled to use the new declarations in unit B.

Units cannot have circular references in their interface sections. Sometimes, you will run into two class declarations that contain mutually dependent declarations. The simplest solution is to use a single unit, but if you have reasons to declare the classes in separate units, you can use an abstract base class in one or both units to eliminate the circular dependency. (See Chapter 2 for more information.)

Initializing and Finalizing

Every unit can have an initialization and a finalization section. Code in every initialization section runs before the program or library's main begin-end block. Code in the finalization section runs after the program terminates or when the library is unloaded. Delphi runs the initialization sections using a depth-first traversal of the unit dependency tree. In other words, before a unit's initialization code runs, Delphi runs the initialization section of every unit it uses. A unit is initialized only once. Example 1-1 demonstrates how Delphi initializes and finalizes units.

Example 1-1: Showing the Order of Unit Initialization

```
program Example1_1;
uses unitA;
{$AppType Console}
```

Example 1-1: Showing the Order of Unit Initialization (continued)

```
begin
  WriteLn('Example 1-1 main program');
end.

unit unitA;
interface
uses unitB;
implementation
initialization
  WriteLn('unitA initialization');
finalization
  WriteLn('unitA finalization');
end.

unit unitB;
interface
implementation
initialization
  WriteLn('unitB initialization');
finalization
  WriteLn('unitB finalization');
end.
```

When you compile and run Example 1-1, be sure to run it from a command prompt, not the IDE, or else the console will appear and disappear before you can see the output, which is shown as Example 1-2.

Example 1-2: The Output from Running Example 1-1

```
W:\nutshell>example1_1
unitB initialization
unitA initialization
Example 1-1 main program
unitA finalization
unitB finalization
```

The System and SysInit Units

The System and SysInit units are automatically included in every unit, so all of the declarations in these units are effectively part of the Delphi Pascal language, and the compiler has special knowledge about many of the functions and procedures in the System and SysInit units. Chapter 5, *Language Reference*, is a complete reference to the system routines and declarations meant for your use.

Programs

A Delphi program looks similar to a traditional Pascal program, starting with the program keyword and using a begin-end block for the main program. Delphi programs are usually short, though, because the real work takes place in one or more separate units. In a GUI application, for example, the main program usually calls an initialization procedure, creates one or more forms (windows), and calls a procedure for the Windows event loop.

For compatibility with standard Pascal, Delphi allows a parameter list after the program name, but—like most modern Pascal compilers—it ignores the identifiers listed there.

In a GUI application, you cannot use the standard Pascal I/O procedures because there is no input device to read from and no output device to write to. Instead, you can compile a *console application*, which can read and write using standard Pascal I/O routines. (See Chapter 8, *Compiler Directives*, to learn about the $AppType directive, which tells Delphi to build a console or a GUI application.)

A program's **uses** declaration lists the units that make up the program. Each unit name can be followed by an **in** directive that specifies a filename. The IDE and compiler use the filename to locate the units that make up the project. Units without an **in** directive are usually library units, and are not part of the project's source code. If a unit has an associated form, the IDE also stores the form name in a comment. Example 1-3 shows a typical program source file.

Example 1-3: A Typical Program File

```
program Typical;

uses
  Forms,
  Main in 'Main.pas' {MainForm},
  MoreStuff in 'MoreStuff.pas' {Form2},
  Utils in 'Utils.pas';

{$R *.RES}

begin
  Application.Initialize;
  Application.CreateForm(TMainForm, MainForm);
  Application.CreateForm(TForm2, Form2);
  Application.Run;
end.
```

The **Forms** unit is part of the standard Delphi library, so it does not have an **in** directive and source file. The other units have source filenames, so Delphi's IDE manages those files as part of the project. To learn about the $R compiler directive, see Chapter 8. The **Application** object is part of Delphi's visual component library and is not covered in this book. Consult Delphi's online help for information about the **Application** object and the rest of the VCL.

Libraries

A Delphi library compiles to a standard Windows DLL. A library source file looks the same as a program source file, except that it uses the **library** keyword instead of **program**. A library typically has an **exports** declaration, which lists the routines that the DLL exports. The **exports** declaration is optional, and if you intend to use a unit in a library, it's usually best to put the **exports** declaration in the unit, close to the subroutine you are exporting. If you don't use the unit in a library, the **exports** declaration has no impact.

The main body of the library—its **begin-end** block—executes each time the library is loaded into an application. Thus, you don't need to write a DLL procedure to handle the DLL_PROCESS_ATTACH event. For process detach and thread events, though, you must write a handler. Assign the handler to the DllProc variable. Delphi takes care of registering the procedure with Windows, and Windows calls the procedure when a process detaches or when a thread attaches or detaches. Example 1-4 shows a simple DLL procedure.

Example 1-4: DLL Attach and Detach Viewer

```
library Attacher;

uses Windows;

procedure Log(const Msg: string);
begin
  MessageBox(0, PChar(Msg), 'Attacher', Mb_IconInformation + Mb_OK);
end;

procedure AttachDetachProc(Reason: Integer);
begin
  case Reason of
  Dll_Process_Detach: Log('Detach Process');
  Dll_Thread_Attach:  Log('Attach Thread');
  Dll_Thread_Detach:  Log('Detach Thread');
  else                Log('Unknown reason!');
  end;
end;

begin
  // This code runs each time the DLL is loaded into a new process.
  Log('Attach Process');
  DllProc := @AttachDetachProc;
end.
```

Using Dynamic Memory

When using a DLL, you must be careful about dynamic memory. Any memory allocated by a DLL is freed when the DLL is unloaded. Your application might retain pointers to that memory, though, which can cause access violations or worse problems if you aren't careful. The simplest solution is to use the **ShareMem** unit as the first unit in your application and in every library the application loads. The **ShareMem** unit redirects all memory requests to a single DLL (*BorlndMM.dll*), which is loaded as long as the application is running. You can load and unload DLLs without worrying about dangling pointers.

Sharing Objects

ShareMem solves one kind of memory problem, but not another: class identity. If class **A** is used in the application and in a DLL, Delphi cannot tell that both modules use the same class. Although both modules use the same class name, this doesn't mean the classes are identical. Delphi takes the safest course and assumes the classes are different; if you know better, you have no easy way to inform Delphi.

Sometimes, having separate class identities does not cause any problems, but if your program tries to use an object reference across a DLL boundary, the is and as operators will not work the way you expect them to. Because the DLL thinks class A is different from the application's class A, the is operator always returns False.

One way to circumvent this problem is not to pass objects across DLL boundaries. If you have a graphic object, for example, don't pass a TBitmap object, but pass a Windows handle (HBITMAP) instead. Another solution is to use packages. Delphi automatically manages the class identities in packages to avoid this problem.

Setting the Image Base

When you create a library, be sure to set the Image Base option. Windows must load every module (DLL and application) at a unique image base address. Delphi's default is $00400000, but Windows uses that address for the application, so it cannot load a DLL at the same address. When Windows must move a DLL to a different address, you incur a performance penalty, because Windows must rewrite a relocation table to reflect the new addresses. You cannot guarantee that every DLL will have a unique address because you cannot control the addresses other DLL authors use, but you can do better than the default. You should at least make sure your DLLs use a different image base than any of the standard Delphi packages and Windows DLLs. Use Windows Quick View to check a file's image base.

Packages

Delphi can link a unit statically with a program or library, or it can link units dynamically. To link dynamically to one or more units, you must put those units in a package, which is a special kind of DLL. When you write a program or library, you don't need to worry about how the units will be linked. If you decide to use a package, the units in the package are not linked into your *.exe* or *.dll*, but instead, Delphi compiles a reference to the package's DLL (which has the extension *.bpl* for Borland Package Library).

Packages avoid the problems of DLLs, namely, managing memory and class identities. Delphi keeps track of the classes defined in each unit and makes sure that the application and all associated packages use the same class identity for the same class, so the is and as operators work correctly.

Design-Time Versus Runtime

Delphi's IDE uses packages to load components, custom forms, and other design-time units, such as property editors. When you write components, keep their design-time code in a design-time package, and put the actual component class in a runtime package. Applications that use your component can link statically with the component's *.dcu* file or link dynamically with the runtime package that contains your component. By keeping the design-time code in a separate package, you avoid linking any extraneous code into an application.

Note that the design-time package requires the runtime package because you cannot link one unit into multiple packages. Think of an application or library as a collection of units. You cannot include a unit more than once in a single program—it doesn't matter whether the units are linked statically or dynamically. Thus, if an application uses two packages, the same unit cannot be contained in both packages. That would be the equivalent of linking the unit twice.

Building a Package

To build a package, you need to create a *.dpk* file, or package source file. The *.dpk* file lists the units the package contains, and it also lists the other packages the new package requires. The IDE includes a convenient package editor, or you can edit the *.dpk* file by hand, using the format shown in Example 1-5.

Example 1-5: Sample Package Source File

```
package Sample;
{$R 'COMP.DCR'}
{$IMAGEBASE $09400000}
{$DESCRIPTION 'Sample Components'}

requires
  vcl50;

contains
  Comp in 'Comp.pas';

end.
```

As with any DLL, make sure your packages use unique addresses for their Image Base options. The other options are self-explanatory. You can include options as compiler directives in the *.dpk* file (as explained in Chapter 8), or you can let the package editor in the IDE write the options for you.

Data Types

Delphi Pascal supports several extensions to the standard Pascal data types. Like any Pascal language, Delphi supports enumerations, sets, arrays, integer and enumerated subranges, records, and variant records. If you are accustomed to C or C++, make sure you understand these standard Pascal types, because they can save you time and headache. The differences include the following:

- Instead of bit masks, sets are usually easier to read.

- You can use pointers instead of arrays, but arrays are easier and offer bounds-checking.

- Records are the equivalent of structures, and variant records are like unions.

Integer Types

The basic integer type is `Integer`. The `Integer` type represents the natural size of an integer, given the operating system and platform. Currently, `Integer` represents a 32-bit integer, but you must not rely on that. The future undoubtedly holds a 64-bit operating system running on 64-bit hardware, and calling for a 64-bit `Integer` type. To help cope with future changes, Delphi defines some types whose size depends on the natural integer size and other types whose sizes are fixed for all future versions of Delphi. Table 1-2 lists the standard integer types. The types marked with *natural* size might change in future versions of Delphi, which means the range will also change. The other types will always have the size and range shown.

Table 1-2: Standard Integer Types

Type	Size	Range in Delphi 5
Integer	*natural*	–2,147,483,648 .. 2,147,483,647
Cardinal	*natural*	0 .. 4,294,967,295
ShortInt	8 bits	–128 .. 127
Byte	8 bits	0 .. 255
SmallInt	16 bits	–32,768 .. 32,767
Word	16 bits	0 .. 65,535
LongInt	32 bits	–2,147,483,648 .. 2,147,483,647
LongWord	32 bits	0 .. 4,294,967,295
Int64	64 bits	–9,223,372,036,854,775,808 .. 9,223,372,036,854,775,807

Real Types

Delphi has several floating-point types. The basic types are `Single`, `Double`, and `Extended`. `Single` and `Double` correspond to the standard sizes for the IEEE-754 standard, which is the basis for floating-point hardware on Intel platforms and in Windows. `Extended` is the Intel extended precision format, which conforms to the minimum requirements of the IEEE-754 standard for extended double precision. Delphi defines the standard Pascal `Real` type as a synonym for `Double`. See the descriptions of each type in Chapter 5 for details about representation.

The floating-point hardware uses the full precision of the `Extended` type for its computations, but that doesn't mean you should use `Extended` to store numbers. `Extended` takes up 10 bytes, but the `Double` type is only 8 bytes and is more efficient to move into and out of the floating-point unit. In most cases, you will get better performance and adequate precision by using `Double`.

Errors in floating-point arithmetic, such as dividing by zero, result in runtime errors. Most Delphi applications use the `SysUtils` unit, which maps runtime errors into exceptions, so you will usually receive a floating-point exception for such errors. Read more about exceptions and errors in "Exception Handling," later in this chapter.

The floating-point types also have representations for infinity and not-a-number (NaN). These special values don't arise normally unless you set the floating-point control word. You can read more about infinity and NaN in the IEEE-754 standard, which is available for purchase from the IEEE. Read about the floating-point control word in Intel's architecture manuals, especially the *Pentium Developer's Manual*, volume 3, *Architecture and Programming Manual*. Intel's manuals are available online at *http://developer.intel.com/design/processor/*.

Delphi also has a fixed-point type, `Currency`. This type represents numbers with four decimal places in the range –922,337,203,685,477.5808 to 922,337,203,685,477.5807, which is enough to store the gross income for the entire planet, accurate to a hundredth of a cent. The `Currency` type employs the floating-point processor, using 64 bits of precision in two's complement form. Because `Currency` is a floating-point type, you cannot use any integer operators (such as bit shifting or masking).

 The floating-point unit (FPU) can perform calculations in single-precision, double-precision, or extended-precision mode. Delphi sets the FPU to extended precision, which provides full support for the `Extended` and `Currency` types. Some Windows API functions, however, change the FPU to double precision. At double precision, the FPU maintains only 53 bits of precision instead of 64.

When the FPU uses double precision, you have no reason to use `Extended` values, which is another reason to use `Double` for most computations. A bigger problem is the `Currency` type. You can try to track down exactly which functions change the FPU control word and reset the precision to extended precision after the errant functions return. (See the `Set8087CW` function in Chapter 5.) Another solution is to use the `Int64` type instead of `Currency`, and implement your own fixed-point scaling in the manner shown in Example 1-6.

Example 1-6: Using Int64 to Store Currency Values

```
resourcestring
  sInvalidCurrency = 'Invalid Currency string: ''%s''';
const
  Currency64Decimals = 4;    // number of fixed decimal places
  Currency64Scale = 10000;   // 10**Decimal64Decimals
type
  Currency64 = type Int64;

function Currency64ToString(Value: Currency64): string;
begin
  Result := Format('%d%s%.4d',
    [Value div Currency64Scale,
     DecimalSeparator,
     Abs(Value mod Currency64Scale)]);
end;
```

Example 1-6: Using Int64 to Store Currency Values (continued)

```
function StringToCurrency64(const Str: string): Currency64;
var
  Code: Integer;
  Fraction: Integer;
  FractionString: string[Currency64Decimals];
  I: Integer;
begin
  // Convert the integer part and scale by Currency64Scale
  Val(Str, Result, Code);
  Result := Result * Currency64Scale;

  if Code = 0 then
    // integer part only in Str
    Exit

  else if Str[Code] = DecimalSeparator then
  begin
    // The user might specify more or fewer than 4 decimal points,
    // but at most 4 places are meaningful.
    FractionString := Copy(Str, Code+1, Currency64Decimals);
    // Pad missing digits with zeros.
    for I := Length(FractionString)+1 to Currency64Decimals do
      FractionString[I] := '0';
    SetLength(FractionString, Currency64Decimals);

    // Convert the fractional part and add it to the result.
    Val(FractionString, Fraction, Code);
    if Code = 0 then
    begin
      if Result < 0 then
        Result := Result - Fraction
      else
        Result := Result + Fraction;
      Exit;
    end;
  end;

  // The string is not a valid currency string (signed, fixed point
  // number).
  raise EConvertError.CreateFmt(sInvalidCurrency, [Str]);
end;
```

Arrays

In additional to standard Pascal arrays, Delphi defines several extensions for use in special circumstances. *Dynamic arrays* are arrays whose size can change at runtime. *Open arrays* are array parameters that can accept any size array as actual arguments. A special case of open arrays lets you pass an array of heterogeneous types as an argument to a routine. Delphi does not support conformant arrays, as found in ISO standard Pascal, but open arrays offer the same functionality.

Dynamic arrays

A dynamic array is an array whose size is determined at runtime. You can make a dynamic array grow or shrink while the program runs. Declare a dynamic array without an index type. The index is always an integer, and always starts at zero. At runtime you can change the size of a dynamic array with the SetLength procedure. Assignment of a dynamic array assigns a reference to the same array. Unlike strings, dynamic arrays do not use copy-on-write, so changing an element of a dynamic array affects all references to that array. Delphi manages dynamic arrays using reference counting so when an array goes out of scope, its memory is automatically freed. Example 1-7 shows how to declare and use a dynamic array.

Example 1-7: Using a Dynamic Array

```
var
  I: Integer;
  Data: array of Double;    // Dynamic array storing Double values
  F: TextFile;              // Read data from this file
  Value: Double;
begin
  AssignFile(F, 'Stuff.dat');
  Reset(F);
  while not Eof(F) do
  begin
    ReadLn(F, Value);
    // Inefficient, but simple way to grow a dynamic array. In a real
    // program, you should increase the array size in larger chunks,
    // not one element at a time.
    SetLength(Data, Length(Data) + 1);
    Data[High(Data)] := Value;
  end;
  CloseFile(F);
end;
```

 Delphi checks array indices to make sure they are in bounds. (Assuming you have not disabled range checks; see the $R directive in Chapter 8.) Empty dynamic arrays are an exception. Delphi represents an empty dynamic array as a nil pointer. If you attempt to access an element of an empty dynamic array, Delphi dereferences the nil pointer, resulting in an access violation, not a range check error.

Open arrays

You can declare a parameter to a function or procedure as an *open array*. When calling the routine, you can pass any size array (with the same base type) as an argument. The routine should use the Low and High functions to determine the bounds of the array. (Delphi always uses zero as the lower bound, but the Low and High functions tell the maintainer of your code exactly what the code is doing. Hard-coding 0 is less clear.) Be sure to declare the parameter as const if the routine does not need to modify the array, or as var if the routine modifies the array contents.

The declaration for an open array argument looks like the declaration for a dynamic array, which can cause some confusion. When used as a parameter, an array declaration without an index type is an open array. When used to declare a local or global variable, a field in a class, or a new type, an array declaration without an index means a dynamic array.

You can pass a dynamic array to a routine that declares its argument as an open array, and the routine can access the elements of the dynamic array, but cannot change the array's size. Because open arrays and dynamic arrays are declared identically, the only way to declare a parameter as a dynamic array is to declare a new type identifier for the dynamic array type, as shown below:

```
procedure CantGrow(var Data: array of integer);
begin
  // Data is an open array, so it cannot change size.
end;
```

```
type
  TArrayOfInteger = array of integer; // dynamic array type
procedure Grow(var Data: TArrayOfInteger);
begin
  // Data is a dynamic array, so it can change size.
  SetLength(Data, Length(Data) + 1);
end;
```

You can pass a dynamic array to the CantGrow procedure, but the array is passed as an open array, not as a dynamic array. The procedure can access or change the elements of the array, but it cannot change the size of the array.

If you must call a Delphi function from another language, you can pass an open array argument as a pointer to the first element of the array and the array length minus one as a separate 32-bit integer argument. In other words, the lower bound for the array index is always zero, and the second parameter is the upper bound.

You can also create an open array argument by enclosing a series of values in square brackets. The open array expression can be used only as an open array argument, so you cannot assign such a value to an array-type variable. You cannot use this construct for a var open array. Creating an open array on the fly is a convenient shortcut, avoiding the need to declare a const array:

```
Avg := ComputeAverage([1, 5, 7, 42, 10, -13]);
```

The Slice function is another way to pass an array to a function or procedure. Slice lets you pass part of an array to a routine. Chapter 5 describes Slice in detail.

Type variant open arrays

Another kind of open array parameter is the *type variant open array*, or array of const. A variant open array lets you pass a heterogeneous array, that is, an array where each element of the array can have a different type. For each array element,

Delphi creates a TVarRec record, which stores the element's type and value. The array of TVarRec records is passed to the routine as a const open array. The routine can examine the type of each element of the array by checking the VType member of each TVarRec record. Type variant open arrays give you a way to pass a variable size argument list to a routine in a type-safe manner.

TVarRec is a variant record similar to a Variant, but implemented differently. Unlike a Variant, you can pass an object reference using TVarRec. Chapter 6, *System Constants*, lists all the types that TVarRec supports. Example 1-8 shows a simple example of a routine that converts a type variant open array to a string.

Example 1-8: Converting Type Variant Data to a String

```
function AsString(const Args: array of const): string;
var
  I: Integer;
  S: String;
begin
  Result := '';
  for I := Low(Args) to High(Args) do
  begin
    case Args[I].VType of
    vtAnsiString:
      S := PChar(Args[I].VAnsiString);
    vtBoolean:
      if Args[I].VBoolean then
        S := 'True'
      else
        S := 'False';
    vtChar:
      S := Args[I].VChar;
    vtClass:
      S := Args[I].VClass.ClassName;
    vtCurrency:
      S := FloatToStr(Args[I].VCurrency^);
    vtExtended:
      S := FloatToStr(Args[I].VExtended^);
    vtInt64:
      S := IntToStr(Args[I].VInt64^);
    vtInteger:
      S := IntToStr(Args[I].VInteger);
    vtInterface:
      S := Format('%p', [Args[I].VInterface]);
    vtObject:
      S := Args[I].VObject.ClassName;
    vtPChar:
      S := Args[I].VPChar;
    vtPointer:
      S := Format('%p', [Args[I].VPointer]);
    vtPWideChar:
      S := Args[I].VPWideChar;
    vtString:
      S := Args[I].VString^;
```

Example 1-8: Converting Type Variant Data to a String (continued)

```
vtVariant:
  S := Args[I].VVariant^;
vtWideChar:
  S := Args[I].VWideChar;
vtWideString:
  S := WideString(Args[I].VWideString);
else
  raise Exception.CreateFmt('Unsupported VType=%d',
                            [Args[I].VType]);
  end;
  Result := Result + S;
  end;
end;
```

Strings

Delphi has four kinds of strings: short, long, wide, and zero-terminated. A short string is a counted array of characters, with up to 255 characters in the string. Short strings are not used much in Delphi programs, but if you know a string will have fewer than 255 characters, short strings incur less overhead than long strings.

Long strings can be any size, and the size can change at runtime. Delphi uses a copy-on-write system to minimize copying when you pass strings as arguments to routines or assign them to variables. Delphi maintains a reference count to free the memory for a string automatically when the string is no longer used.

Wide strings are also dynamically allocated and managed, but they do not use reference counting. When you assign a wide string to a WideString variable, Delphi copies the entire string.

Delphi checks string references the same way it checks dynamic array references, that is, Delphi checks subscripts to see if they are in range, but an empty long or wide string is represented by a nil pointer. Testing the bounds of an empty long or wide string, therefore, results in an access violation instead of a range check error.

A zero-terminated string is an array of characters, indexed by an integer starting from zero. The string does not store a size, but uses a zero-valued character to mark the end of the string. The Windows API uses zero-terminated strings, but you should not use them for other purposes. Without an explicit size, you lose the benefit of bounds checking, and performance suffers because some operations require two passes over the string contents or must process the string contents more slowly, always checking for the terminating zero value. Delphi will also treat a pointer to such an array as a string.

For your convenience, Delphi stores a zero value at the end of long and wide strings, so you can easily cast a long string to the type PAnsiChar, PChar, or PWideChar to obtain a pointer to a zero-terminated string. Delphi's PChar type is the equivalent of char* in C or C++.

String literals

You can write a string literal in the standard Pascal way, or use a pound sign (#) followed by an integer to specify a character by value, or use a caret (^) followed by a letter to specify a control character. You can mix any kind of string to form a single literal, for example:

```
'Normal string: '#13#10'Next line (after CR-LF)'^I'That was a ''TAB'''
```

The caret (^) character toggles the sixth bit ($40) of the character's value, which changes an upper case letter to its control character equivalent. If the character is lowercase, the caret clears the fifth and sixth bits ($60). This means you can apply the caret to nonalphabetic characters. For example, ^2 is the same as 'r' because '2' has the ordinal value $32, and toggling the $40 bit makes it $72, which is the ordinal value for 'r'. Delphi applies the same rules to every character, so you can use the caret before a space, tab, or return, with the result that your code will be completely unreadable.

Mixing string types

You can freely mix all different kinds of strings, and Delphi does its best to make sense out of what you are trying to do. You can concatenate different kinds of strings, and Delphi will narrow a wide string or widen a narrow string as needed. To pass a string to a function that expects a PChar parameter, just cast a long string to PChar. A short string does not automatically have a zero byte at the end, so you need to make a temporary copy, append a #0 byte, and take the address of the first character to get a PChar value.

Unicode and multibyte strings

Delphi supports Unicode with its WideChar, WideString and PWideChar types. All the usual string operations work for wide strings and narrow (long or short) strings. You can assign a narrow string to a WideString variable, and Delphi automatically converts the string to Unicode. When you assign a wide string to a long (narrow) string, Delphi uses the ANSI code page to map Unicode characters to multibyte characters.

A multibyte string is a string where a single character might occupy more than one byte. (The Windows term for a multibyte character set is *double-byte character set*.) Some national languages (e.g., Japanese and Chinese) use character sets that are much larger than the 256 characters in the ANSI character set. Multibyte character sets use one or two bytes to represent a character, allowing many more characters to be represented. In a multibyte string, a byte can be a single character, a lead byte (that is, the first byte of a multibyte character), or a trailing byte (the second byte of a multibyte character). Whenever you examine a string one character at a time, you should make sure that you test for multibyte characters because the character that looks like, say, the letter "A" might actually be the trailing byte of an entirely different character.

Ironically, some of Delphi's string handling functions do not handle multibyte strings correctly. Instead, the SysUtils unit has numerous string functions that work correctly with multibyte strings. Handling multibyte strings is especially important for filenames, and the SysUtils unit has special functions for working with multibyte characters in filenames. See Appendix B, *The SysUtils Unit*, for details.

Windows NT and Windows 2000 support narrow and wide versions of most API functions. Delphi defaults to the narrow versions, but you can call the wide functions just as easily. For example, you can call CreateFileW to create a file with a Unicode filename, or you can call CreateFileA to create a file with an ANSI filename. CreateFile is the same as CreateFileA. Delphi's VCL uses the narrow versions of the Windows controls, to maintain compatibility with all versions of Windows. (Windows 95 and 98 do not support most Unicode controls.)

Boolean Types

Delphi has the usual Pascal Boolean type, but it also has several other types that make it easier to work with the Windows API. Numerous API and other functions written in C or C++ return values that are Boolean in nature, but are documented as returning an integer. In C and C++, any non-zero value is considered True, so Delphi defines the LongBool, WordBool, and ByteBool values with the same semantics.

For example, if you must call a function that was written in C, and the function returns a Boolean result as a short integer, you can declare the function with the WordBool return type and call the function as you would any other Boolean-type function in Pascal:

```
function SomeCFunc: WordBool; external 'TheCDll.dll';
...
if SomeCFunc then ...
```

It doesn't matter what numeric value SomeCFunc actually returns; Delphi will treat zero as False and any other value as True. You can use any of the C-like logical types the same way you would the native Delphi Boolean type. The semantics are identical. For pure Delphi code, you should always use Boolean.

Variants

Delphi supports OLE variant types, which makes it easy to write an OLE automation client or server. You can use Variants in any other situation where you want a variable whose type can change at runtime. A Variant can be an array, a string, a number, or even an IDispatch interface. You can use the Variant type or the OleVariant type. The difference is that an OleVariant takes only COM-compatible types, in particular, all strings are converted to wide strings. Unless the distinction is important, this book uses the term Variant to refer to both types.

A Variant variable is always initialized to Unassigned. You can assign almost any kind of value to the variable, and it will keep track of the type and value. To learn the type of a Variant, call the VarType function. Chapter 6 lists the values that VarType can return. You can also access Delphi's low-level implementation of Variants by casting a Variant to the TVarData record type. Chapter 5 describes TVarData in detail.

When you use a Variant in an expression, Delphi automatically converts the other value in the expression to a Variant and returns a Variant result. You can assign that result to a statically typed variable, provided the Variant's type is compatible with the destination variable.

The most common use for Variants is to write an OLE automation client. You can assign an IDispatch interface to a Variant variable, and use that variable to call functions the interface declares. The compiler does not know about these functions, so the function calls are not checked for correctness until runtime. For example, you can create an OLE client to print the version of Microsoft Word installed on your system, as shown in the following code. Delphi doesn't know anything about the Version property or any other method or property of the Word OLE client. Instead, Delphi compiles your property and method references into calls to the IDispatch interface. You lose the benefit of compile-time checks, but you gain the flexibility of runtime binding. (If you want to keep the benefits of type safety, you will need a type library from the vendor of the OLE automation server. Use the IDE's type library editor to extract the COM interfaces the server's type library defines. This is not part of the Delphi language, so the details are not covered in this book.)

```
var
   WordApp: Variant;
begin
   try
     WordApp := CreateOleObject('Word.Application');
     WriteLn(WordApp.Version);
   except
     WriteLn('Word is not installed');
   end;
end;
```

Pointers

Pointers are not as important in Delphi as they are in C or C++. Delphi has real arrays, so there is no need to simulate arrays using pointers. Delphi objects use their own syntax, so there is no need to use pointers to refer to objects. Pascal also has true pass-by-reference parameters. The most common use for pointers is interfacing to C and C++ code, including the Windows API.

C and C++ programmers will be glad that Delphi's rules for using pointers are more C-like than Pascal-like. In particular, type checking is considerably looser for pointers than for other types. (But see the $T and $TypedAddress directives, in Chapter 8, which tighten up the loose rules.)

The type Pointer is a generic pointer type, equivalent to void* in C or C++. When you assign a pointer to a variable of type Pointer, or assign a Pointer-type expression to a pointer variable, you do not need to use a type cast. To take the address of a variable or routine, use Addr or @ (equivalent to & in C or C++). When using a pointer to access an element of a record or array, you can omit the dereference operator (^). Delphi can tell that the reference uses a pointer, and supplies the ^ operator automatically.

You can perform arithmetic on pointers in a slightly more restricted manner than you can in C or C++. Use the Inc or Dec statements to advance or retreat a pointer value by a certain number of base type elements. The actual pointer value changes according to the size of the pointer's base type. For example, incrementing a pointer to an `Integer` advances the pointer by 4 bytes:

```
var
  IntPtr: ^Integer;
begin
  ...
  Inc(IntPtr); // Make IntPtr point to the next Integer, 4 bytes later
  Inc(IntPtr, 3); // Increase IntPtr by 12 bytes = 3 * SizeOf(Integer)
```

Programs that interface directly with the Windows API often need to work with pointers explicitly. For example, if you need to create a logical palette, the type definition of `TLogPalette` requires dynamic memory allocation and pointer manipulation, using a common C hack of declaring an array of one element. In order to use `TLogPalette` in Delphi, you have to write your Delphi code using C-like style, as shown in Example 1-9.

Example 1-9: Using a Pointer to Create a Palette

```
// Create a gray-scale palette with NumColors entries in it.
type
  TNumColors = 1..256;
function MakeGrayPalette(NumColors: TNumColors): HPalette;
var
  Palette: PLogPalette;        // pointer to a TLogPalette record
  I: TNumColors;
  Gray: Byte;
begin
  // TLogPalette has a palette array of one element. To allocate
  // memory for the entire palette, add the size of NumColors-1
  // palette entries.
  GetMem(Palette, SizeOf(TLogPalette) +
               (NumColors-1)*SizeOf(TPaletteEntry));

  try
    // In standard Pascal, you must write Palette^.palVersion,
    // but Delphi dereferences the pointer automatically.
    Palette.palVersion := $300;
    Palette.palNumEntries := NumColors;

    for I := 1 to NumColors do
    begin
      // Use a linear scale for simplicity, even though a logarithmic
      // scale gives better results.
      Gray := I * 255 div NumColors;
// Turn off range checking to access palette entries past the first.
{$R-}
      Palette.palPalEntry[I-1].peRed   := Gray;
      Palette.palPalEntry[I-1].peGreen := Gray;
      Palette.palPalEntry[I-1].peBlue  := Gray;
      Palette.palPalEntry[I-1].peFlags := 0;
{$R+}
    end;
```

Example 1-9: Using a Pointer to Create a Palette (continued)

```
    // Delphi does not dereference pointers automatically when used
    // alone, as in the following case:
    Result := CreatePalette(Palette^);
  finally
    FreeMem(Palette);
  end;
end;
```

Function and Method Pointers

Delphi lets you take the address of a function, procedure, or method, and use that address to call the routine. For the sake of simplicity, all three kinds of pointers are called *procedure pointers.*

A procedure pointer has a type that specifies a function's return type, the arguments, and whether the pointer is a method pointer or a plain procedure pointer. Source code is easier to read if you declare a procedure type and then declare a variable of that type, for example:

```
type
  TProcedureType = procedure(Arg: Integer);
  TFunctionType = function(Arg: Integer): string;
var
  Proc: TProcedureType;
  Func: TFunctionType;
begin
  Proc := SomeProcedure;
  Proc(42); // Call Proc as though it were an ordinary procedure
```

Usually, you can assign a procedure to a procedure variable directly. Delphi can tell from context that you are not calling the procedure, but are assigning its address. (A strange consequence of this simple rule is that a function of no arguments whose return type is a function cannot be called in the usual Pascal manner. Without any arguments, Delphi thinks you are trying to take the function's address. Instead, call the function with empty parentheses—the same way C calls functions with no arguments.)

You can also use the @ or Addr operators to get the address of a routine. The explicit use of @ or Addr provides a clue to the person who must read and maintain your software.

Use a nil pointer for procedure pointers the same way you would for any other pointer. A common way to test a procedure variable for a nil pointer is with the Assigned function:

```
if Assigned(Proc) then
  Proc(42);
```

Type Declarations

Delphi follows the basic rules of type compatibility that ordinary Pascal follows for arithmetic, parameter passing, and so on. Type declarations have one new trick, though, to support the IDE. If a type declaration begins with the type keyword,

Delphi creates separate runtime type information for that type, and treats the new type as a distinct type for **var** and **out** parameters. If the type declaration is just a synonym for another type, Delphi does not ordinarily create separate RTTI for the type synonym. With the extra **type** keyword, though, separate RTTI tables let the IDE distinguish between the two types. You can read more about RTTI in Chapter 3.

Variables and Constants

Unlike standard Pascal, Delphi lets you declare the type of a constant, and you can initialize a global variable to a constant value. Delphi also supports multi-threaded applications by letting you declare variables that have distinct values in each thread of your application.

Typed Constants

When you declare the type of a constant, Delphi sets aside memory for that constant and treats it as a variable. You can assign a new value to the "constant," and it keeps that value. In C and C++, this entity is called a static variable.

```
// Return a unique number each time the function is called.
function Counter: Integer;
const
  Count: Integer = 0;
begin
  Inc(Count);
  Result := Count;
end;
```

At the unit level, a variable retains its value in the same way, so you can declare it as a constant or as a variable. Another way to write the same function is as follows:

```
var
  Count: Integer = 0;
function Counter: Integer;
begin
  Inc(Count);
  Result := Count;
end;
```

The term "typed constant" is clearly a misnomer, and at the unit level, you should always use an initialized **var** declaration instead of a typed constant. You can force yourself to follow this good habit by disabling the $J or $WriteableConst compiler directive, which tells Delphi to treat all constants as constants. The default, however, is to maintain backward compatibility and let you change the value of a typed constant. See Chapter 8 for more information about these compiler directives.

For local variables in a procedure or function, you cannot initialize variables, and typed constants are the only way to keep values that persist across different calls to the routine. You need to decide which is worse: using a typed constant or declaring the persistent variable at the unit level.

Thread Variables

Delphi has a unique kind of variable, declared with **threadvar** instead of **var**. The difference is that a **threadvar** variable has a separate value in each thread of a multithreaded application. An ordinary variable has a single value that is shared among all threads. A **threadvar** variable must be declared at the unit level.

Delphi implements **threadvar** variables using thread local storage (TLS) in the Windows API. The advantage of using **threadvar** instead of directly using TLS is that Windows has a small number of TLS slots available, but you can declare any number and size of **threadvar** variables. More important, you can use **threadvar** variables the way you would any other variable, which is much easier than messing around with TLS. You can read more about **threadvar** and its uses in Chapter 4, *Concurrent Programming*.

Exception Handling

Exceptions let you interrupt a program's normal flow of control. You can raise an exception in any function, procedure, or method. The exception causes control to jump to an earlier point in the same routine or in a routine farther back in the call stack. Somewhere in the stack must be a routine that uses a **try-except-end** statement to catch the exception, or else Delphi calls **ExceptProc** to handle the exception.

Delphi has two related statements for dealing with exceptions. The **try-except** statement sets up an exception handler that gets control when something goes wrong. The **try-finally** statement does not handle exceptions explicitly, but guarantees that the code in the **finally** part of the statement always runs, even if an exception is raised. Use **try-except** to deal with errors. Use **try-finally** when you have a resource (such as allocated memory) that must be cleaned up properly, no matter what happens. The **try-except** statement is similar to try-catch in C++ or Java. Standard C++ does not have **finally**, but Java does. Some C++ compilers, including Borland's, extend the C++ standard to add the same functionality, e.g., with the **__finally** keyword.

Like C++ and Java, Delphi's **try-except** statement can handle all exceptions or only exceptions of a certain kind. Each **try-except** statement can declare many on sections, where each section declares an exception class. Delphi searches the on sections in order, trying to find an exception class that matches, or is a superclass of, the exception object's class. Example 1-10 shows an example of how to use **try-except**.

Example 1-10: Using try-except to Handle an Exception

```
function ComputeSomething:
begin
  try
    PerformSomeDifficultComputation;
  except
    on Ex: EDivideByZero do
      WriteLn('Divide by zero error');
```

Example 1-10: Using try-except to Handle an Exception (continued)

```
  on Ex: EOverflow do
    WriteLn('Overflow error');
  else
    raise; // reraise the same exception, to be handled elsewhere
  end;
end;
```

In a multithreaded application, each thread can maintain its own exception information and can raise exceptions independently from the other threads. See Chapter 4 for details.

When your code raises an exception, it must pass an object to the **raise** statement. Usually, a program creates a new exception object as part of the **raise** statement, but in rare circumstances, you might want to raise an object that already exists. Delphi searches the call stack to find **try** statements. When it finds a **try-finally**, it executes the code in the **finally** part of the statement, then continues to search the stack for an exception handler. When the stack unwinds to a **try-except** block, Delphi searches the **on** sections to find one that matches the exception object. If there are no **on** sections, Delphi runs the code in the **except** part of the statement. If there are **on** sections, Delphi tries to find a match, or it runs the code in the **else** part of the **except** block.

The variable that is declared in the **on** statement contains a reference to the exception object. Delphi automatically frees the object after the exception handler finishes. (See Chapter 2 for more information on objects.)

If Delphi reaches the end of the call stack without finding a matching exception handler, it calls **ExceptProc**. **ExceptProc** is actually a pointer variable, pointing to a procedure of two arguments: the exception object and the address where the exception occurred. For example, you might want to record unhandled exceptions in a special log file, as shown in Example 1-11.

Example 1-11: Logging Unhandled Exceptions to a File

```
var
  LogFileName: string = 'C:\log.txt';

procedure LogExceptProc(ExceptObject: TObject; ErrorAddr: Pointer);
const
  Size = 1024;
resourcestring
  Title = 'Internal error: Please report to technical support';
var
  Buffer: PChar[0..Size-1];
  F: TextFile;
begin
  ExceptionErrorMessage(ExceptObject, ExceptAddr, Buffer, Size);

  AssignFile(F, LogFileName);
  if FileExists(LogFileName) then
    AppendFile(F)
  else
    Rewrite(F);
```

Example 1-11: Logging Unhandled Exceptions to a File (continued)

```
  WriteLn(F, Buffer);
  CloseFile(F);

  MessageBox(0, Buffer, Title, Mb_IconStop);
end;
...
// Tell Delphi to use your exception procedure.
ExceptProc := @LogExceptProc;
```

Delphi also catches runtime errors, such as stack overflow, and calls `ErrorProc` for each one. Note that `ErrorProc` is actually a pointer variable whose value is a procedure pointer. To set up an error handler, declare a procedure and assign its address to `ErrorProc`.

The `System` unit deals with two kinds of error codes: internal and external. If you write an `ErrorProc` procedure, it must deal with internal error codes. These are small numbers, where each number indicates a kind of error. Chapter 6 lists all the internal error codes. Delphi's default `ErrorProc` maps internal error codes to external error codes. External error codes are documented in Delphi's help files and are visible to the user. Chapter 6 also lists the external error codes.

When Delphi calls `ErrorProc`, it passes two arguments: the error code and the instruction address where the error occurred. Your error handler might look like the following, for example:

```
  procedure DumbErrorProc(ErrorCode: Integer; ErrorAddr: Pointer);
  begin
    ShowMessage(Format('Runtime error %d at %p', [ErrorCode, ErrorAddr]));
  end;
  ...
  ErrorProc := @DumbErrorProc;
```

The `SysUtils` unit provides extra help for working with exceptions and runtime errors. In particular, it defines `ErrorProc` and `ExceptProc` procedures. `ErrorProc` turns a runtime error into an exception, such as `EStackOverflow` for a stack overflow error. The `ExceptProc` routine displays the exception message, then halts the program. In a console application, the exception message is written to the standard output, and in GUI applications, it is displayed in a dialog box.

The `SysUtils` unit sets up the `ErrorProc` and `ExceptProc` routines in its initialization section. If your application raises an exception or runtime error before the `SysUtils` unit is initialized, you won't get the benefit of its routines and exception handlers. Therefore, when your application reports a raw runtime error, not wrapped as an exception, your problem probably lies in an initialization or finalization section.

To raise an exception, use the **raise** statement, followed by an object reference. Usually, the **raise** statement creates a brand-new object. You can create an object of any class to use as the exception object, although most programs use SysUtils.Exception or one of its derived classes.

Delphi keeps track of information about an exception, where it was raised, the program's context when it was raised, and so on. You can access this information from various variables in the System unit. The full details are explained in Chapter 5, but Table 1-3 presents an overview of the relevant variables.

Table 1-3: Exception and Error-Related Variables

Declaration	Description
AbstractErrorProc	Abstract method error handler.
AssertErrorProc	Assertion error handler.
ErrorAddr	Address of runtime error.
ErrorProc	Error handler procedure.
ExceptClsProc	Map a Windows exception to a Delphi class.
ExceptionClass	Exception base class.
ExceptObjProc	Map a Windows exception to a Delphi object.
ExceptProc	Unhandled exception handler.
SafeCallErrorProc	Safecall error handler.

When an exception unwinds the call stack, Delphi calls the code in the **finally** part of each enclosing **try-finally** block. Delphi also cleans up the memory for dynamic arrays, long strings, wide strings, interfaces, and **Variants** that have gone out of scope. (Strictly speaking, it decreases the reference counts, so the actual memory is freed only if there are no other references to the string or array.)

If a **finally** block raises an exception, the old exception object is freed, and Delphi handles the new exception.

The most common use for a **try-finally** statement is to free objects and release other resources. If a routine has multiple objects to free, it's usually simplest to initialize all variables to **nil**, and use a single **try-finally** block to free all the objects at once. If an object's destructor is likely to raise an exception, though, you should use nested **try-finally** statements, but in most cases the technique shown in Example 1-12 works well.

Example 1-12: Using try-finally to Free Multiple Objects

```
// Copy a file. If the source file cannot be opened, or the
// destination file cannot be created, raise EFileCopyError,
// and include the original error message in the new exception
// message. The new message gives a little more information
// than the original message.
type
  EFileCopyError = class(EStreamError);

procedure CopyFile(const ToFile, FromFile: string);
var
```

Example 1-12: Using try-finally to Free Multiple Objects (continued)

```
  FromStream, ToStream: TFileStream;
resourcestring
  sCannotRead = 'Cannot read file: %s';
  sCannotCreate = 'Cannot create file: %s';
begin
  ToStream := nil;
  FromStream := nil;
  try
    try
      FromStream := TFileStream.Create(FromFile, fmOpenRead);
    except
      // Handle EFopenError exceptions, but no other kind of exception.
      on Ex: EFOpenError do
        // Raise a new exception.
        raise EFileCopyError.CreateFmt(sCannotRead, [Ex.Message]);
    end;
    try
      ToStream := TFileStream.Create(ToFile, fmCreate);
    except
      on Ex: EFCreateError do
        raise EFileCopyError.CreateFmt(sCannotCreate, [Ex.Message]);
    end;
    // Now copy the file.
    ToStream.CopyFrom(FromStream, 0);
  finally
    // All done. Close the files, even if an exception was raised.
    ToStream.Free;
    FromStream.Free;
  end;
end;
```

File I/O

Traditional Pascal file I/O works in Delphi, but you cannot use the standard Input and Output files in a GUI application. To assign a filename to a File or TextFile variable, use AssignFile. Reset and Rewrite work as they do in standard Pascal, or you can use Append to open a file to append to its end. The file must already exist. To close the file, use CloseFile. Table 1-4 lists the I/O procedures Delphi provides.

Table 1-4: File I/O Procedures and Functions

Routine	Description
Append	Open an existing file for appending.
AssignFile or Assign	Assign a filename to a File or TextFile variable.
BlockRead	Read data from a file.
BlockWrite	Write data to a file.
CloseFile or Close	Close an open file.
Eof	Returns True for end of file.
Erase	Delete a file.

Table 1-4: File I/O Procedures and Functions (continued)

Routine	Description
FilePos	Return the current file position.
FileSize	Return the size of a file, in records.
Read	Read formatted data from a file or text file.
ReadLn	Read a line of data from a text file.
Rename	Rename a file.
Reset	Open a file for reading.
Rewrite	Open a file for writing, erasing the previous contents.
Seek	Change the file position.
Write	Write formatted data.
WriteLn	Write a line of text.

When you open a file with Reset, the FileMode variable dictates the mode for opening the file. By default, FileMode is 2, which allows read and write access. If you just want to read a file, you should set FileMode to 0 before calling Reset. (Set FileMode to 1 for write-only access.)

Delphi's runtime library has a better way to do file I/O using streams. Streams are object oriented and offer much more flexibility and power than traditional Pascal I/O. The only time not to use streams is when you cannot use the library and must stick to the Delphi Pascal language only. Chapter 5 presents all the file I/O procedures. Read about TStream and related stream classes in Delphi's online help files.

 Delphi does not support the standard Pascal procedures Get and Put.

Functions and Procedures

Delphi supports several extensions to standard Pascal functions and procedures. You can overload routines by declaring multiple routines with the same name, but different numbers or types of parameters. You can declare default values for parameters, thereby making the parameters optional. Almost everything in this section applies equally to functions and procedures, so the term *routine* is used for both.

Overloading

You can overload a routine name by declaring multiple routines with the same name, but with different arguments. To declare overloaded routines, use the overload directive, for example:

```
function AsString(Int: Integer): string; overload;
function AsString(Float: Extended): string; overload;
```

```
function AsString(Float: Extended; MinWidth: Integer):string; overload;
function AsString(Bool: Boolean): string; overload;
```

When you call an overloaded routine, the compiler must be able to tell which routine you want to call. Therefore, the overloaded routines must take different numbers or types of arguments. For example, using the declarations above, you can tell which function to call just by comparing argument types:

```
Str := AsString(42);      // call AsString(Integer)
Str := AsString(42.0);    // call AsString(Extended)
Str := AsString(42.0, 8); // call AsString(Extended, Integer)
```

Sometimes, unit A will declare a routine, and unit B uses unit A, but also declares a routine with the same name. The declaration in unit B does not need the overload directive, but you might need to use unit A's name to qualify calls to A's version of the routine from unit B. A derived class that overloads a method from an ancestor class should use the overload directive.

Default Parameters

Sometimes, you can use default parameters instead of overloaded routines. For example, consider the following overloaded routines:

```
function AsString(Float: Extended): string; overload;
function AsString(Float: Extended; MinWidth: Integer):string; overload;
```

Most likely, the first overloaded routine converts its floating-point argument to a string using a predefined minimum width, say, 1. In fact, you might even write the first AsString function so it calls the second one, for example:

```
function AsString(Float: Extended): string;
begin
  Result := AsString(Float, 1)
end;
```

You can save yourself some headaches and extra code by writing a single routine that takes an optional parameter. If the caller does not provide an actual argument, Delphi substitutes a default value:

```
function AsString(Float: Extended; MinWidth: Integer = 1): string;
```

Judicious use of default parameters can save you from writing extra overloaded routines. Be careful when using string-type parameters, though. Delphi must compile the string everywhere the routine is called with the default parameter. This isn't a problem if the string is empty (because Delphi represents an empty string with a nil pointer), but if the string is not empty, you should use an initialized variable (or typed constant). That way, Delphi can store a reference to the variable when it needs to use the default parameter. The alternative is to let Delphi waste space storing extra copies of the string and waste time creating a new instance of the string for each function call.

Result Variable

Delphi borrows a feature from the Eiffel language, namely the Result variable. Every function implicitly declares a variable, named Result, whose type is the function's return type. You can use this variable as an ordinary variable, and when the function returns, it returns the value of the `Result` variable. Using `Result` is more convenient than assigning a value to the function name, which is the standard Pascal way to return a function result. Because `Result` is a variable, you can get and use its value repeatedly. In standard Pascal, you can do the same by declaring a result variable explicitly, provided you remember to assign the result to the function name. It doesn't make a big difference, but the little niceties can add up in a large project. Delphi supports the old way of returning a function result, so you have a choice. Whichever approach you choose, be consistent. Example 1-13 shows two different ways to compute a factorial: the Delphi way and the old-fashioned way.

Example 1-13: Using the Result Variable

```
// Computing a factorial in Delphi.
function Factorial(Number: Cardinal): Int64;
var
  N: Cardinal;
begin
  Result := 1;
  for N := 2 to Number do
    Result := Result * N;
end;

// Computing a factorial in standard Pascal.
function Factorial(Number: Integer): Integer;
var
  N, Result: Integer;
begin
  Result := 1;
  for N := 2 to Number do
    Result := Result * N;
  Factorial := Result;
end;
```

 Delphi usually initializes string and dynamic array variables, but `Result` is special. It's not really a local variable, but is more like a hidden `var` parameter. In other words, the caller must initialize it. The problem is that Delphi does *not* always initialize `Result`. To be safe, if your function returns a string, interface, dynamic array, or `Variant` type, initialize the `Result` variable to an empty string, array, or `Unassigned`.

CHAPTER 2

The Delphi Object Model

Delphi's support for object-oriented programming is rich and powerful. In addition to traditional classes and objects, Delphi also has interfaces (similar to those found in COM and Java), exception handling, and multithreaded programming. This chapter covers Delphi's object model in depth. You should already be familiar with standard Pascal and general principles of object-oriented programming.

Classes and Objects

Think of a class as a record on steroids. Like a record, a class describes a type that comprises any number of parts, called *fields*. Unlike a record, a class can also contain functions and procedures (called *methods*), and *properties*. A class can inherit from another class, in which case it inherits all the fields, methods, and properties of the ancestor class.

An *object* is a dynamic instance of a class. An object is always allocated dynamically, on the heap, so an object reference is like a pointer (but without the usual Pascal caret operator). When you assign an object reference to a variable, Delphi copies only the pointer, not the entire object. When your program finishes using an object, it must explicitly free the object. Delphi does not have any automatic garbage collection (but see the section "Interfaces," later in this chapter).

For the sake of brevity, the term *object reference* is often shortened to *object*, but in precise terms, the object is the chunk of memory where Delphi stores the values for all the object's fields. An object reference is a pointer to the object. The only way to use an object in Delphi is through an object reference. An object reference usually comes in the form of a variable, but it might also be a function or property that returns an object reference.

A class, too, is a distinct entity (as in Java, but unlike C++). Delphi's representation of a class is a read-only table of pointers to virtual methods and lots of information about the class. A *class reference* is a pointer to the table. (Chapter 3,

Runtime Type Information, describes in depth the layout of the class tables.) The most common use for a class reference is to create objects or to test the type of an object reference, but you can use class references in many other situations, including passing class references as routine parameters or returning a class reference from a function. The type of a class reference is called a *metaclass*.

Example 2-1 shows several class declarations. A class declaration is a type declaration that starts with the keyword **class**. The class declaration contains field, method, and property declarations, ending with the **end** keyword. Each method declaration is like a forward declaration: you must implement the method in the same unit (except for abstract methods, which are discussed later in this chapter).

Example 2-1: Examples of Classes and Objects

```
type
  TAccount = class
  private
    fCustomer: string;   // name of customer
    fNumber: Cardinal;   // account number
    fBalance: Currency;  // current account balance
  end;
  TSavingsAccount = class(TAccount)
  private
    fInterestRate: Integer; // annual percentage rate, scaled by 1000
  end;
  TCheckingAccount = class(TAccount)
  private
    fReturnChecks: Boolean;
  end;
  TCertificateOfDeposit = class(TSavingsAccount)
  private
    fTerm: Cardinal;   // CD maturation term, in days
  end;

var
  CD1, CD2: TAccount;
begin
  CD1 := TCertificateOfDeposit.Create;
  CD2 := TCertificateOfDeposit.Create;
  ...
```

Figure 2-1 depicts the memory layout of the objects and classes from Example 2-1. The variables and their associated objects reside in read-write memory. Classes reside in read-only memory, along with the program code.

Delphi's object model is similar to those in other object-oriented languages, such as C++ and Java. Table 2-1 shows a quick comparison between Delphi and several other popular programming languages.

The following sections explain each of these language features in more detail.

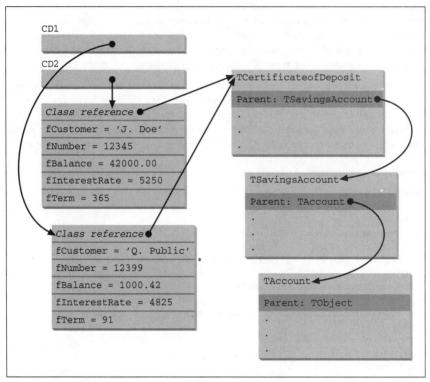

Figure 2-1: The memory layout of objects and classes

Table 2-1: Delphi Versus the World

Language Feature	Delphi	Java	C++	Visual Basic
Inheritance	✓	✓	✓	
Multiple inheritance			✓	
Interfaces	✓	✓	a	✓
Single root class	✓	✓		
Metaclasses	✓	✓		
Class (static) fields		✓	✓	
Virtual methods	✓	✓	✓	
Abstract (pure) virtual methods	✓	✓	✓	
Class (static) methods	✓	✓	✓	
Dynamic methods	✓			
Garbage collection	b	✓		b
Variant types	✓			✓
OLE automation	✓			✓
Static type-checking	✓	✓	✓	
Exception handling	✓	✓	✓	✓

Table 2-1: Delphi Versus the World (continued)

Language Feature	Delphi	Java	C++	Visual Basic
Function overloading	✓	✓	✓	
Operator overloading			✓	
Non-class functions	✓		✓	✓
Non-object variables	✓		✓	✓
Properties	✓			✓
Runtime type information	✓	✓	c	
Generic types (templates)			✓	
Built-in support for threads	✓	✓		
Message passing	✓			
Built-in assembler	✓		d	
Inline functions			✓	

a C++ can emulate interfaces with abstract classes.
b Interfaces use reference counting to manage lifetimes.
c RTTI in C++ is limited to comparing and casting types.
d A built-in assembler is not part of the C++ language standard, but most C++ compilers, including Borland's, support a built-in assembler as a language extension.

Classes

A class declaration is a kind of type declaration. A class declaration describes the fields, methods, and properties of the class. You can declare a class in an interface or implementation section of a unit, but the methods—like any other function or procedure—are defined in the implementation section. You must implement a class's methods in the same unit as the class declaration.

A class declaration has one or more sections for different access levels (private, protected, public, published, or automated). Access levels are discussed later in this chapter. You can mix sections in any order and repeat sections with the same access level.

Within each section, you can have any number of fields, followed by method and property declarations. Method and property declarations can be mixed together, but all fields must precede all methods and properties within each section. Unlike Java and C++, you cannot declare any types nested inside a class declaration.

A class has a single base class, from which it inherits all the fields, properties, and methods. If you do not list an explicit base class, Delphi uses TObject. A class can also implement any number of interfaces. Thus, Delphi's object model most closely resembles that of Java, where a class can extend a single class and implement many interfaces.

 The convention in Delphi is that type names begin with the letter T, as in TObject. It's just a convention, not a language rule. The IDE, on the other hand, always names form classes with an initial T.

A class reference is an expression that refers to a specific class. A class reference is not quite a first class object, as it is in Java or Smalltalk, but is used to create new objects, call class methods, and test or cast an object's type. A class reference is implemented as a pointer to a table of information about the class, especially the class's virtual method table (VMT). (See Chapter 3 for the complete details of what's inside a VMT.)

The most common use for a class reference is to create instances of that class by calling a constructor. You can also use a class reference to test the type of an object (with the **is** operator) or to cast an object to a particular type (with the **as** operator). Usually, the class reference is a class name, but it can also be a variable whose type is a metaclass, or a function or property that returns a class reference. Example 2-2 shows an example of a class declaration.

Example 2-2: Declaring a Class and Metaclass

```
type
  TComplexClass = class of TComplex; // metaclass type
  TComplex = class(TPersistent)
  private
    fReal, fImaginary: Double;
  public
    constructor Create(Re: Double = 0.0); overload;
    constructor Create(Re, Im: Double); overload;
    destructor Destroy; override;
    procedure Assign(Source: TPersistent); override;
    function AsString: string;
  published
    property Real: Double read fReal write fReal;
    property Imaginary: Double read fImaginary write fImaginary;
  end;
```

Objects

An object is a dynamic instance of a class. The dynamic instance contains values for all the fields declared in the class and all of its ancestor classes. An object also contains a hidden field that stores a reference to the object's class.

Objects are always allocated dynamically, on the heap, so an object reference is really a pointer to the object. The programmer is responsible for creating objects and for freeing them at the appropriate time. To create an object, use a class reference to call a constructor, for example:

```
Obj := TSomeClass.Create;
```

Most constructors are named **Create**, but that is a convention, not a requirement of Delphi. You will sometimes find constructors with other names, especially older classes that were written before Delphi had method overloading. For maximum compatibility with C++ Builder, which does not let you name constructors, you should stick with **Create** for all your overloaded constructors.

To get rid of the object when your program no longer needs it, call the **Free** method. To ensure that the object is properly freed, even if an exception is raised, use a try-finally exception handler. (See Chapter 1, *Delphi Pascal*, for more information about try-finally.) For example:

```
Obj := TSomeOtherClass.Create;
try
  Obj.DoSomethingThatMightRaiseAnException;
  Obj.DoSomethingElse;
finally
  Obj.Free;
end;
```

When freeing a global variable or field, always set the variable to nil when freeing the object so you are not left with a variable that contains an invalid pointer. You should take care to set the variable to nil *before* freeing the object. If the destructor, or a method called from the destructor, refers to that variable, you usually want the variable to be nil to avoid any potential problems. An easy way to do this is to call the FreeAndNil procedure (from the SysUtils unit):

```
GlobalVar := TFruitWigglies.Create;
try
  GlobalVar.EatEmUp;
finally
  FreeAndNil(GlobalVar);
end;
```

Each object has a separate copy of all of its fields. A field cannot be shared among multiple objects. If you need to share a variable, declare the variable at the unit level or use indirection: many objects can hold separate pointers or object references that refer to common data.

Inheritance

A class can inherit from another class. The derived class inherits all the fields, methods, and properties of the base class. Delphi supports only single inheritance, so a class has one base class. That base class can have its own base class, and so on, so a class inherits the fields, properties, and methods of every ancestor class. A class can also implement any number of interfaces (which are covered later in this chapter). As in Java, but not C++, every class inherits from a single root class, TObject. If you do not specify an explicit base class, Delphi automatically uses TObject as the base class.

 A *base* class is a class's immediate parent class, which you can see in the class declaration. An *ancestor* class is the base class or any other class in the inheritance chain up to TObject. Thus, in Example 2-1, TCertificateOfDeposit has a base class of TSavingsAccount; its ancestor classes are TObject, TAccount, and TSavingsAccount.

The TObject class declares several methods and one special, hidden field to store a reference to the object's class. This hidden field points to the class's virtual method table (VMT). Every class has a unique VMT and all objects of that class share the class's VMT. Chapter 5, *Language Reference*, covers the other details of the `TObject` class and its methods.

You can assign an object reference to a variable whose type is the object's class or any of its ancestor classes. In other words, the declared type of an object reference is not necessarily the same as the actual type of the object. Assignments that go the other way—assigning a base-class object reference to a derived-class variable—are not allowed because the object might not be of the correct type.

Delphi retains the strong type-checking of Pascal, so the compiler performs compile-time checks based on the declared type of an object reference. Thus, all methods must be part of the declared class, and the compiler performs the usual checking of function and procedure arguments. The compiler does not necessarily bind the method call to a specific method implementation. If the method is virtual, Delphi waits until runtime and uses the object's true type to determine which method implementation to call. See the section "Methods," later in this chapter for details.

Use the `is` operator to test the object's true class. It returns True if the class reference is the object's class or any of its ancestor classes. It returns False if the object reference is `nil` or of the wrong type. For example:

```
if Account is TCheckingAccount then ... // tests the class of Account
if Account is TObject then ...          // True when Account is not nil
```

You can also use a type cast to obtain an object reference with a different type. A type cast does not change an object; it just gives you a new object reference. Usually, you should use the `as` operator for type casts. The `as` operator automatically checks the object's type and raises a runtime error if the object's class is not a descendant of the target class. (The `SysUtils` unit maps the runtime error to an `EInvalidCast` exception.)

Another way to cast an object reference is to use the name of the target class in a conventional type cast, similar to a function call. This style of type cast does not check that the cast is valid, so use it only if you know it is safe, as shown in Example 2-3.

Example 2-3: Using Static Type Casts

```
var
  Account: TAccount;
  Checking: TCheckingAccount;
begin
  Account  := Checking;                      // Allowed
  Checking := Account;                       // Compile-time error
  Checking := Account as TCheckingAccount;   // Okay
  Account as TForm;                          // Raises a runtime error
  Checking := TCheckingAccount(Account);     // Okay, but not recommended
  if Account is TCheckingAccount then        // Better
    Checking := TCheckingAccount(Account)
  else
    Checking := nil;
```

Fields

A *field* is a variable that is part of an object. A class can declare any number of fields, and each object has its own copy of every field declared in its class and in every ancestor class. In other languages, a field might be called a data member, an instance variable, or an attribute. Delphi does not have class variables, class instance variables, static data members, or the equivalent (that is, variables that are shared among all objects of the same class). Instead, you can usually use unit-level variables for a similar effect.

A field can be of any type unless the field is published. In a published section, a field must have a class type, and the class must have runtime type information (that is, the class or an ancestor class must use the $M+ directive). See Chapter 3 for more information.

When Delphi first creates an object, all of the fields start out empty, that is, pointers are initialized to nil, strings and dynamic arrays are empty, numbers have the value zero, Boolean fields are False, and Variants are set to Unassigned. (See NewInstance and InitInstance in Chapter 5 for details.)

A derived class can declare a field with the same name as a field in an ancestor class. The derived class's field hides the field of the same name in the ancestor class. Methods in the derived class refer to the derived class's field, and methods in the ancestor class refer to the ancestor's field.

Methods

Methods are functions and procedures that apply only to objects of a particular class and its descendants. In C++, methods are called "member functions." Methods differ from ordinary procedures and functions in that every method has an implicit parameter called Self, which refers to the object that is the subject of the method call. Self is similar to this in C++ and Java. Call a method the same way you would call a function or procedure, but preface the method name with an object reference, for example:

```
Object.Method(Argument);
```

A *class method* applies to a class and its descendants. In a class method, Self refers not to an object but to the class. The C++ term for a class method is "static member function."

You can call a method that is declared in an object's class or in any of its ancestor classes. If the same method is declared in an ancestor class and in a derived class, Delphi calls the most-derived method, as shown in Example 2-4.

Example 2-4: Binding Static Methods

```
type
  TAccount = class
  public
    procedure Withdraw(Amount: Currency);
  end;
  TSavingsAccount = class(TAccount)
  public
```

Example 2-4: Binding Static Methods (continued)

```
    procedure Withdraw(Amount: Currency);
  end;
var
  Savings: TSavingsAccount;
  Account: TAccount;
begin
  ...
  Savings.Withdraw(1000.00);    // Calls TSavingsAccount.Withdraw
  Account.Withdraw(1000.00);    // Calls TAccount.Withdraw
```

An ordinary method is called a *static method* because the compiler binds the method call directly to a method implementation. In other words, the binding is static. In C++ this is an ordinary member function, and in Java it's called a "final method." Most Delphi programmers refrain from using the term *static method*, preferring the simple term, *method* or even *non-virtual method*.

A *virtual method* is a method that is bound at runtime instead of at compile time. At compile time, Delphi uses the declared type of an object reference to determine which methods you are allowed to call. Instead of compiling a direct reference to any specific method, the compiler stores an indirect method reference that depends on the object's actual class. At runtime, Delphi looks up the method in the class's runtime tables (specifically, the VMT), and calls the method for the actual class. The object's true class might be the compile-time declared class, or it might be a derived class—it doesn't matter because the VMT provides the pointer to the correct method.

To declare a virtual method, use the `virtual` directive in the base class, and use the `override` directive to provide a new definition of the method in a derived class. Unlike in Java, methods are static by default, and you must use the `virtual` directive to declare a virtual method. Unlike in C++, you must use the `override` directive to override a virtual method in a derived class.

Example 2-5 uses virtual methods.

Example 2-5: Binding Virtual Methods

```
type
  TAccount = class
  public
    procedure Withdraw(Amount: Currency); virtual;
  end;
  TSavingsAccount = class(TAccount)
  public
    procedure Withdraw(Amount: Currency); override;
  end;
var
  Savings: TSavingsAccount;
  Account: TAccount;
begin
  ...
```

Example 2-5: Binding Virtual Methods (continued)

```
Savings.Withdraw(1000.00);      // Calls TSavingsAccount.Withdraw
Account := Savings;
Account.Withdraw(1000.00);      // Calls TSavingsAccount.Withdraw
```

Instead of using the **virtual** directive, you can also use the **dynamic** directive. The semantics are identical, but the implementation is different. Looking up a virtual method in a VMT is fast because the compiler generates an index directly into a VMT. Looking up a dynamic method is slower. Calling a dynamic method requires a linear search of a class's dynamic method table (DMT). If the class does not override that method, the search continues with the DMT of the base class. The search continues with ancestor classes until TObject is reached or the method is found. The tradeoff is that in a few circumstances, dynamic methods take up less memory than virtual methods. Unless you are writing a replacement for the VCL, you should use virtual methods, not dynamic methods. See Chapter 3 for a complete explanation of how dynamic and virtual methods are implemented.

A virtual or dynamic method can be declared with the **abstract** directive, in which case the class does not define the method. Instead, derived classes *must* override that method. The C++ term for an abstract method is a "pure virtual method." If you call a constructor for a class that has an abstract method, the compiler issues a warning, telling you that you probably made a mistake. You probably wanted to create an instance of a derived class that overrides and implements the abstract method. A class that declares one or more abstract methods is often called an *abstract class*, although some people reserve that term for a class that declares only abstract methods.

 If you write an abstract class that inherits from another abstract class, you should redeclare all abstract methods with the **override** and **abstract** directives. Delphi does not require this, but common sense does. The declarations clearly inform the maintainer of the code that the methods are abstract. Otherwise, the maintainer must wonder whether the methods should have been implemented or should have remained abstract. For example:

```
type
  TBaseAbstract = class
    procedure Method; virtual; abstract;
  end;
  TDerivedAbstract = class(TBaseAbsract)
    procedure Method; override; abstract;
  end;
  TConcrete = class(TDerivedAbstract)
    procedure Method; override;
  end;
```

A class method or constructor can also be virtual. In Delphi, class references are real entities that you can assign to variables, pass as parameters, and use as references for calling class methods. If a constructor is virtual, a class reference can have a static type of the base class, but you can assign to it a class reference for a derived class. Delphi looks up the virtual constructor in the class's VMT and calls the constructor for the derived class.

Methods (and other functions and procedures) can be overloaded, that is, multiple routines can have the same name, provided they take different arguments. Declare overloaded methods with the `overload` directive. A derived class can overload a method it inherits from a base class. In that case, only the derived class needs the `overload` directive. After all, the author of the base class cannot predict the future and know when other programmers might want to overload an inherited method. Without the overload directive in the derived class, the method in the derived class hides the method in the base class, as shown in Example 2-6.

Example 2-6: Overloading Methods

```
type
  TAuditKind = (auInternal, auExternal, auIRS, auNasty);
  TAccount = class
  public
    procedure Audit;
  end;
  TCheckingAccount = class(TAccount)
  public
    procedure Audit(Kind: TAuditKind); // Hides TAccount.Audit
  end;
  TSavingsAccount = class(TAccount)
  public
    // Can call TSavingsAccount.Audit and TAccount.Audit
    procedure Audit(Kind: TAuditKind); overload;
  end;
var
  Checking: TCheckingAccount;
  Savings: TSavingsAccount;
begin
  Checking := TCheckingAccount.Create;
  Savings := TSavingsAccount.Create;
  Checking.Audit;              // Error because TAccount.Audit is hidden
  Savings.Audit;               // Okay because Audit is overloaded
  Savings.Audit(auNasty);      // Okay
  Checking.Audit(auInternal);  // Okay
```

Constructors

Every class has one or more constructors, possibly inherited from a base class. By convention, constructors are usually named `Create`, although you can use any name you like. Some constructor names start with `Create`, but convey additional information, such as `CreateFromFile` or `CreateFromStream`. Usually, though, the simple name `Create` is sufficient, and you can use method overloading to define multiple constructors with the same name. Another reason to overload the name `Create` is for compatibility with C++ Builder. C++ does not permit different constructor names, so you must use overloading to define multiple constructors.

Calling a constructor

A constructor is a hybrid of object and class methods. You can call it using an object reference or a class reference. Delphi passes an additional, hidden parameter to indicate how it was called. If you call a constructor using a class reference, Delphi calls the class's NewInstance method to allocate a new instance of the class. After calling NewInstance, the constructor continues and initializes the object. The constructor automatically sets up a try-except block, and if any exception occurs in the constructor, Delphi calls the destructor.

When you call a constructor with an object reference, Delphi does not set up the try-except block and does not call NewInstance. Instead, it calls the constructor the same way it calls any ordinary method. This lets you call an inherited constructor without unnecessary overhead.

 A common error is to try to create an object by calling a constructor with an object reference, rather than calling it with a class reference and assigning it to the object variable:

```
var
   Account: TSavingsAccount;
begin
   Account.Create;                        // wrong
   Account := TSavingsAccount.Create; // right
```

One of Delphi's features is that you have total control over when, how, and whether to call the inherited constructor. This lets you write some powerful and interesting classes, but also introduces an area where it is easy to make mistakes.

Delphi always constructs the derived class first, and only if the derived class calls the inherited constructor does Delphi construct the base class. C++ constructs classes in the opposite direction, starting from the ancestor class and constructing the derived class last. Thus, if class C inherits from B, which inherits from A, Delphi constructs C first, then B, and A last. C++ constructs A first, then B, and finally C.

Virtual methods and constructors

Another significant difference between C++ and Delphi is that in C++, a constructor always runs with the virtual method table of the class being constructed, but in Delphi, the virtual methods are those of the derived class, even when the base class is being constructed. As a result, you must be careful when writing any virtual method that might be called from a constructor. Unless you are careful, the object might not be fully constructed when the method is called. To avoid any problems, you should override the AfterConstruction method and use that for any code that needs to wait until the object is fully constructed. If you override AfterConstruction, be sure to call the inherited method, too.

One constructor can call another constructor. Delphi can tell the call is from an object reference (namely, Self), so it calls the constructor as an ordinary method.

The most common reason to call another constructor is to put all the initialization code in a single constructor. Example 2-7 shows some different ways to define and call constructors.

Example 2-7: Declaring and Calling Constructors

```
type
  TCustomer = class ... end;
  TAccount = class
  private
    fBalance: Currency;
    fNumber: Cardinal;
    fCustomer: TCustomer;
  public
    constructor Create(Customer: TCustomer); virtual;
    destructor Destroy; override;
  end;
  TSavingsAccount = class(TAccount)
  private
    fInterestRate: Integer; // Scaled by 1000
  public
    constructor Create(Customer: TCustomer); override; overload;
    constructor Create(Customer: TCustomer; InterestRate: Integer);
        overload;
    // Note that TSavingsAccount does not need a destructor. It simply
    // inherits the destructor from TAccount.
  end;

var
  AccountNumber: Cardinal = 1;

constructor TAccount.Create(Customer: TCustomer);
begin
  inherited Create;              // Call TObject.Create.
  fNumber := AccountNumber;      // Assign a unique account number.
  Inc(AccountNumber);
  fCustomer := Customer;         // Notify customer of new account.
  Customer.AttachAccount(Self);
end;

destructor TAccount.Destroy;
begin
  // If the constructor fails before setting fCustomer, the field
  // will be nil. Release the account only if Customer is not nil.
  if Customer <> nil then
    Customer.ReleaseAccount(Self);
  // Call TObject.Destroy.
  inherited Destroy;
end;

const
  DefaultInterestRate = 5000;   // 5%, scaled by 1000
```

Example 2-7: Declaring and Calling Constructors (continued)

```
constructor TSavingsAccount.Create(Customer: TCustomer);
begin
  // Call a sibling constructor.
  Create(Customer, DefaultInterestRate);
end;

constructor TSavingsAccount(Customer: TCustomer; InterestRate:Integer);
begin
  // Call TAccount.Create.
  inherited Create(Customer);
  fInterestRate := InterestRate;
end;
```

Destructors

Destructors, like constructors, take an extra hidden parameter. The first call to a destructor passes True for the extra parameter. This tells Delphi to call **FreeInstance** to free the object. If the destructor calls an inherited destructor, Delphi passes False as the hidden parameter to prevent the inherited destructor from trying to free the same object.

A class usually has one destructor, called **Destroy**. Delphi lets you declare additional destructors, but you shouldn't take advantage of that feature. Declaring multiple destructors is confusing and serves no useful purpose.

Before Delphi starts the body of the destructor, it calls the virtual method, **BeforeDestruction**. You can override **BeforeDestruction** to assert program state or take care of other business that must take place before any destructor starts. This lets you write a class safely without worrying about how or whether any derived classes will call the base class destructor.

When writing a class, you might need to override the **Destroy** destructor, but you must not redeclare the **Free** method. When freeing an object, you should call the **Free** method and not the destructor. The distinction is important, because **Free** checks whether the object reference is **nil** and calls **Destroy** only for non-nil references. In extraordinary circumstances, a class can redefine the **Free** method (such as **TInterface** in the seldom-used **VirtIntf** unit), which makes it that much more important to call **Free**, not **Destroy**.

If a constructor or **AfterConstruction** method raises an exception, Delphi automatically calls the object's destructor. When you write a destructor, you must remember that the object being destroyed might not have been completely constructed. Delphi ensures that all fields start out at zero, but if the exception occurs in the middle of your constructor, some fields might be initialized and some might still be zero. If the destructor just frees objects and pointers, you don't need to worry, because the Free method and FreeMem procedure both check for nil pointers. If the destructor calls other methods, though, always check first for a nil pointer.

Object Life Cycle

For most objects, you call a constructor to create the object, use the object, and then call Free to free the object. Delphi handles all the other details for you. Sometimes, though, you need to know a little more about the inner mechanisms of Delphi's object model. Example 2-8 shows the methods that Delphi calls or simulates when it creates and frees an object.

Example 2-8: The Life Cycle of an Object

```
type
  TSomething = class
    procedure DoSomething;
  end;
var
  Ref: TSomething;
begin
  Ref := TSomething.Create;
  Ref.DoSomething;
  Ref.Free;
end;

// The hidden code in the constructor looks something like this:
function TSomething.Create(IsClassRef: Boolean): TSomething;
begin
  if IsClassRef then
  try
    // Allocate the new object.
    Self := TSomething.NewInstance;

    // NewInstance initializes the object in the same way that
    // InitInstance does. If you override NewInstance, though,
    // and do not call the inherited NewInstance, you must call
    // InitInstance. The call is shown below, so you know what
    // happens, but remember that ordinarily Delphi does not
    // actually call InitInstance.
    InitInstance(Self);

    // Do the real work of the constructor, but without all the
    // class reference overhead. Delphi does not really call the
    // constructor recursively.
    Self.Create(False);

    Self.AfterConstruction;
  except
    // If any exception occurs, Delphi automatically calls the
    // object's destructor.
```

Example 2-8: The Life Cycle of an Object (continued)

```
      Self.Destroy;
  end
  else
    Self.Create(False);
  Result := Self;
end;

// The hidden code in the destructor looks something like this:
procedure TSomething.Destroy(Deallocate: Boolean);
begin
  if Deallocate then
    Self.BeforeDestruction;

  // Delphi doesn't really call the destructor recursively, but
  // this is where the destructor's real work takes place.
  Self.Destroy(False);

  if Deallocate then
  begin
    // Delphi doesn't really call CleanupInstance. Instead, the
    // FreeInstance method does the cleanup. If you override
    // FreeInstance and do not call the inherited FreeInstance,
    // you must call CleanupInstance to clean up strings,
    // dynamic arrays, and Variant-type fields.
    Self.CleanupInstance;
    // Call FreeInstance to free the object's memory.
    Self.FreeInstance;
  end;
end;
```

Access Levels

Like C++ and Java, Delphi has different access levels that determine which objects can access the fields, methods, and properties of another object. The access levels are as follows:

private

>   Declarations that are declared private can be accessed only by the class's own methods or by any method, procedure, or function defined in the same unit's implementation section. Delphi does not have C++-style friend declarations or Java-style package level access. The equivalent in Delphi is to declare package or friend classes in the same unit, which gives them access to the private and protected parts of every class defined in the same unit.

protected

>   A protected declaration can be accessed from any method of the class or its descendants. The descendent classes can reside in different units.

public

>   Public methods have unrestricted access. Any method, function, or procedure can access a public declaration. Unless you use the $M+ compiler directive (see Chapter 8, *Compiler Directives*, for details), the default access level is public.

published

Published declarations are similar to public declarations, except that Delphi stores runtime type information for published declarations. Some declarations cannot be published; see Chapter 3 for details. If a class or a base class uses the $M+ directive, the default access level is published.

 Delphi's IDE declares fields and methods in the initial unnamed section of a form declaration. Because TForm inherits from TPersistent, which uses the $M+ directive, the initial section is published. In other words, the IDE declares its fields and methods as published. When Delphi loads a form description (*.dfm* file), it relies on the published information to build the form object. The IDE relies on the initial, unnamed section of the form class. If you modify that section, you run the risk of disabling the IDE's form editor.

automated

Automated declarations are similar to public declarations, except that Delphi stores additional runtime type information to support OLE automation servers. Automated declarations are obsolete; you should use Delphi's type library editor instead, but for now, they remain a part of the language for backward compatibility. A future release of Delphi might eliminate them entirely. Chapter 3 describes automated declarations in more depth.

A derived class can increase the access level of a property by redeclaring the property under the new access level (e.g., change protected to public). You cannot decrease a property's access level, and you cannot change the visibility of a field or method. You can override a virtual method and declare the overridden method at the same or higher access level, but you cannot decrease the access level.

Properties

A property looks like a field but can act like a method. Properties take the place of accessor and mutator methods (sometimes called getters and setters), but have much more flexibility and power. Properties are vital to Delphi's IDE, and you can also use properties in many other situations.

A property has a reader and writer to get and set the property's value. The reader can be the name of a field, a selector for an aggregate field, or a method that returns the property value. The writer can be a field name, a selector for an aggregate field, or a method that sets the property value. You can omit the writer to make a read-only property. You can also omit the reader to create a write-only property, but the uses for such a beast are limited. Omitting both the reader and the writer is pointless, so Delphi does not let you do so.

Most readers and writers are field names or method names, but you can also refer to part of an aggregate field (record or array). If a reader or writer refers to an array element, the array index must be a constant, and the field's type cannot be a dynamic array. Records and arrays can be nested, and you can even use variant

Hiding a Constructor

Sometimes, a class is not for public use, but is a helper class whose use is entirely subservient to another class. In that case, you probably want to make the constructors for the helper class private or protected, but this is tricky. TObject declares a public constructor: Create. Even though the helper class's constructors are private or protected, you can call the public Create constructor inherited from TObject.

Although you cannot change the access level of the inherited Create constructor, you can hide it with another public constructor. Because the derived constructor should not be called, it can raise an exception. For example:

```
type
  TPublic = class;
  TPrivateHelper = class
  private
    // TPublic is the only class allowed to
    // call the real constructor:
    constructor Create(Owner: TPublic);
      overload;
  public
    // Hide TObject.Create, in case someone
    // accidentally tries to create a
    // TPrivateHelper instance.
    constructor Create;
      reintroduce; overload;
  end;
  TPublic = class
  private
    fHelper: TPrivateHelper;
  public
    constructor Create;
    destructor Destroy;
  end;

constructor TPrivateHelper.Create;
begin
  raise Exception.Create('Programming error')
end;

constructor TPublic.Create;
begin
  // This is the only place where
  // TPrivateHelper is created.
  fHelper := TPrivateHelper.Create(Self);
end;
```

records. Example 2-9 shows an extended rectangle type, similar to the Windows
TRect type, but because it is a class, it has properties and methods.

Example 2-9: Properties Readers and Writers

```
TRectEx = class(TPersistent)
  private
    R: TRect;
    function GetHeight: Integer;
    function GetWidth: Integer;
    procedure SetHeight(const Value: Integer);
    procedure SetWidth(const Value: Integer);
  public
    constructor Create(const R: TRect); overload;
    constructor Create(Left, Top, Right, Bottom: Integer); overload;
    constructor Create(const TopLeft, BottomRight: TPoint); overload;

    procedure Assign(Source: TPersistent); override;

    procedure Inflate(X, Y: Integer);
    procedure Intersect(const R: TRectEx);
    function IsEmpty: Boolean;
    function IsEqual(const R: TRectEx): Boolean;
    procedure Offset(X, Y: Integer);
    procedure Union(const R: TRectEx);

    property TopLeft: TPoint read R.TopLeft write R.TopLeft;
    property BottomRight: TPoint read R.BottomRight write R.BottomRight;
    property Rect: TRect read R write R;
    property Height: Integer read GetHeight write SetHeight;
    property Width: Integer read GetWidth write SetWidth;
  published
    property Left: Integer read R.Left write R.Left default 0;
    property Right: Integer read R.Right write R.Right default 0;
    property Top: Integer read R.Top write R.Top default 0;
    property Bottom: Integer read R.Bottom write R.Bottom default 0;
  end;
```

Array properties

Properties come in scalar and array flavors. An array property cannot be
published, but they have many other uses. The array index can be any type, and
you can have multidimensional arrays, too. For array-type properties, you must
use read and write methods—you cannot map an array-type property directly to
an array-type field.

You can designate one array property as the default property. You can refer to the
default property by using an object reference and an array subscript without
mentioning the property name, as shown in Example 2-10.

Example 2-10: Using a Default Array Property

```
type
  TExample = class
```

Example 2-10: Using a Default Array Property (continued)

```
    ...
    property Items[I: Integer]: Integer read GetItem write SetItem;
    property Chars[C: Char]: Char read GetChar write SetChar; default;
  end;
var
  Example: TExample;
  I: Integer;
  C: Char;
begin
  Example := TExample.Create;
  I := Example.Items[4];     // Must mention property name explicitly
  C := Example['X'];         // Array property is default
  C := Example.Chars['X'];   // Same as previous line
```

Indexed properties

You can map many properties to a single read or write method by specifying an index number for each property. The index value is passed to the read and write methods to differentiate one property from another.

You can even mix array indices and an index specifier. The reader and writer methods take the array indices as the first arguments, followed by the index specifier.

Default values

A property can also have **stored** and **default** directives. This information has no semantic meaning to the Delphi Pascal language, but Delphi's IDE uses this information when storing form descriptions. The value for the **stored** directive is a Boolean constant, a field of Boolean type, or a method that takes no arguments and returns a Boolean result. The value for the **default** directive is a constant value of the same type as the property. Only enumerated, integer, and set-type properties can have a default value. The **stored** and **default** directives have meaning only for published properties.

To distinguish a default array from a default value, the default array directive comes after the semicolon that ends the property declaration. The default value directive appears as part of the property declaration. See the **default** directive in Chapter 5 for details.

Using properties

A common approach to writing Delphi classes is to make all fields private, and declare public properties to access the fields. Delphi imposes no performance penalty for properties that access fields directly. By using properties you get the added benefit of being able to change the implementation at a future date, say to add validation when a field's value changes. You can also use properties to enforce restricted access, such as using a read-only property to access a field whose value should not be changed. Example 2-11 shows some of the different ways to declare and use properties.

Example 2-11: Declaring and Using Properties

```
type
  TCustomer = record
    Name: string;
    TaxIDNumber: string[9];
  end;
  TAccount = class
  private
    fCustomer: TCustomer;
    fBalance: Currency;
    fNumber: Cardinal;
    procedure SetBalance(NewBalance: Currency);
  published
    property Balance: Currency read fBalance write SetBalance;
    property Number: Cardinal read fNumber; // Cannot change account #
    property CustName: string read fCustomer.Name;
  end;
  TSavingsAccount = class(TAccount)
  private
    fInterestRate: Integer;
  published
    property InterestRate: Integer read fInterestRate
        write fInterestRate default DefaultInterestRate;
  end;
  TLinkedAccount = class(TObject)
  private
    fAccounts: array[0..1] of TAccount;
    function GetAccount(Index: Integer): TAccount;
  public
    // Two ways for properties to access an array: using an index
    // or referring to an array element.
    property Checking: TAccount index 0 read GetAccount;
    property Savings:  TAccount read fAccounts[1];
  end;
  TAccountList = class
  private
    fList: TList;
    function GetAccount(Index: Integer): TAccount;
    procedure SetAccount(Index: Integer; Account: TAccount);
    function GetCount: Integer;
  protected
    property List: TList read fList;
  public
    property Count: Integer read GetCount;
    property Accounts[Index: Integer]: TAccount read GetAccount
        write SetAccount; default;
  end;

procedure TAccount.SetBalance(NewBalance: Currency);
begin
  if NewBalance < 0 then
    raise EOverdrawnException.Create;
  fBalance := NewBalance;
```

Example 2-11: Declaring and Using Properties (continued)

```
end;

function TLinkedAccount.GetAccount(Index: Integer): TAccount;
begin
  Result := fAccounts[Index]
end;

function TAccountList.GetCount: Integer;
begin
  Result := List.Count
end;

function TAccountList.GetAccount(Index: Integer): TAccount;
begin
  Result := List[Index]
end;

procedure TAccountList.SetAccount(Index: Integer; Account: TAccount);
begin
  fList[Index] := Account
end;
```

Class-type properties

Properties of class type need a little extra attention. The best way to work with class-type properties is to make sure the owner object manages the property object. In other words, don't save a reference to other objects, but keep a private copy of the property object. Use a write method to store an object by copying it. Delphi's IDE requires this behavior of published properties, and it makes sense for unpublished properties, too.

 The only exception to the rule for class-type properties is when a property stores a reference to a component on a form. In that case, the property must store an object reference and *not* a copy of the component.

Delphi's IDE stores component references in a *.dfm* file by storing only the component name. When the *.dfm* is loaded, Delphi looks up the component name to restore the object reference. If you must store an entire component within another component, you must delegate all properties of the inner component.

Make sure the property's class inherits from **TPersistent** and that the class overrides the **Assign** method. Implement your property's write method to call **Assign**. (**TPersistent**—in the **Classes** unit—is not required, but it's the easiest way to copy an object. Otherwise, you need to duplicate the **Assign** method in whatever class you use.) The read method can provide direct access to the field. If the property object has an **OnChange** event, you might need to set that so your object is notified of any changes. Example 2-12 shows a typical pattern for using a class-type property. The example defines a graphical control that repeatedly displays a bitmap throughout its extent, tiling the bitmap as necessary. The Bitmap property stores a TBitmap object.

Example 2-12: Declaring and Using a Class-type Property

```
unit Tile;

interface

uses SysUtils, Classes, Controls, Graphics;

type
  // Tile a bitmap
  TTile = class(TGraphicControl)
  private
    fBitmap: TBitmap;
    procedure SetBitmap(NewBitmap: TBitmap);
    procedure BitmapChanged(Sender: TObject);
  protected
    procedure Paint; override;
  public
    constructor Create(Owner: TComponent); override;
    destructor Destroy; override;
  published
    property Align;
    property Bitmap: TBitmap read fBitmap write SetBitmap;
    property OnClick;
    property OnDblClick;
    // Many other properties are useful, but were omitted to save space.
    // See TControl for a full list.
  end;

implementation

{ TTile }

// Create the bitmap when creating the control.
constructor TTile.Create(Owner: TComponent);
begin
  inherited;
  fBitmap := TBitmap.Create;
  fBitmap.OnChange := BitmapChanged;
end;

// Free the bitmap when destroying the control.
destructor TTile.Destroy;
begin
  FreeAndNil(fBitmap);
  inherited;
end;

// When the bitmap changes, redraw the control.
```

Example 2-12: Declaring and Using a Class-type Property (continued)

```
procedure TTile.BitmapChanged(Sender: TObject);
begin
  Invalidate;
end;

// Paint the control by tiling the bitmap. If there is no
// bitmap, don't paint anything.
procedure TTile.Paint;
var
  X, Y: Integer;
begin
  if (Bitmap.Width = 0) or (Bitmap.Height = 0) then
    Exit;

  Y := 0;
  while Y < ClientHeight do
  begin
    X := 0;
    while X < ClientWidth do
    begin
      Canvas.Draw(X, Y, Bitmap);
      Inc(X, Bitmap.Width);
    end;
    Inc(Y, Bitmap.Height);
  end;
end;

// Set a new bitmap by copying the TBitmap object.
procedure TTile.SetBitmap(NewBitmap: TBitmap);
begin
  fBitmap.Assign(NewBitmap);
end;

end.
```

Interfaces

An *interface* defines a type that comprises abstract virtual methods. Although a class inherits from a single base class, it can implement any number of interfaces. An interface is similar to an abstract class (that is, a class that has no fields and all of whose methods are abstract), but Delphi has extra magic to help you work with interfaces. Delphi's interfaces sometimes look like COM (Component Object Model) interfaces, but you don't need to know COM to use Delphi interfaces, and you can use interfaces for many other purposes.

You can declare a new interface by inheriting from an existing interface. An inter-face declaration contains method and property declarations, but no fields. Just as all classes inherit from TObject, all interfaces inherit from IUnknown. The IUnknown interface declares three methods: _AddRef, _Release, and QueryInterface. If you are familiar with COM, you will recognize these methods. The first two methods manage reference counting for the lifetime of the object that implements the interface. The third method accesses other interfaces an object might implement.

When you declare a class that implements one or more interfaces, you must provide an implementation of all the methods declared in all the interfaces. The class can implement an interface's methods, or it can delegate the implementation to a property, whose value is an interface. The simplest way to implement the _AddRef, _Release, and QueryInterface methods is to inherit them from TInterfacedObject or one of its derived classes, but you are free to inherit from any other class if you wish to define the methods yourself.

A class implements each of an interface's methods by declaring a method with the same name, arguments, and calling convention. Delphi automatically matches the class's methods with the interface's methods. If you want to use a different method name, you can redirect an interface method to a method with a different name. The redirected method must have the same arguments and calling convention as the interface method. This feature is especially important when a class implements multiple interfaces with identical method names. See the class keyword in Chapter 5 for more information about redirecting methods.

A class can delegate the implementation of an interface to a property that uses the implements directive. The property's value must be the interface that the class wants to implement. When the object is cast to that interface type, Delphi automatically fetches the property's value and returns that interface. See the implements directive in Chapter 5 for details.

For each non-delegated interface, the compiler creates a hidden field to store a pointer to the interface's VMT. The interface field or fields follow immediately after the object's hidden VMT field. Just as an object reference is really a pointer to the object's hidden VMT field, an interface reference is a pointer to the interface's hidden VMT field. Delphi automatically initializes the hidden fields when the object is constructed. See Chapter 3 to learn how the compiler uses RTTI to keep track of the VMT and the hidden field.

Reference counting

The compiler generates calls to _AddRef and _Release to manage the lifetime of interfaced objects. To use Delphi's automatic reference counting, declare a variable with an interface type. When you assign an interface reference to an interface variable, Delphi automatically calls _AddRef. When the variable goes out of scope, Delphi automatically calls _Release.

The behavior of _AddRef and _Release is entirely up to you. If you inherit from TInterfacedObject, these methods implement reference counting. The _AddRef method increments the reference count, and _Release decrements it. When the reference count goes to zero, _Release frees the object. If you inherit from a different class, you can define these methods to do anything you want. You should implement QueryInterface correctly, though, because Delphi relies on it to implement the as operator.

Typecasting

Delphi calls QueryInterface as part of its implementation of the as operator for interfaces. You can use the as operator to cast an interface to any other interface type. Delphi calls QueryInterface to obtain the new interface reference. If QueryInterface returns an error, the as operator raises a runtime error. (The SysUtils unit maps the runtime error to an EIntfCastError exception.)

You can implement QueryInterface any way you want, but you probably want to use the same approach taken by TInterfacedObject. Example 2-13 shows a class that implements QueryInterface normally, but uses stubs for _AddRef and _Release. Later in this section, you'll see how useful this class can be.

Example 2-13: Interface Base Class Without Reference Counting

```
type
  TNoRefCount = class(TObject, IUnknown)
  protected
    function QueryInterface(const IID:TGUID; out Obj):HResult; stdcall;
    function _AddRef: Integer; stdcall;
    function _Release: Integer; stdcall;
  end;

function TNoRefCount.QueryInterface(const IID:TGUID; out Obj): HResult;
begin
  if GetInterface(IID, Obj) then
    Result := 0
  else
    Result := Windows.E_NoInterface;
end;

function TNoRefCount._AddRef: Integer;
begin
  Result := -1
end;

function TNoRefCount._Release: Integer;
begin
  Result := -1
end;
```

Interfaces and object-oriented programming

The most important use of interfaces is to separate type inheritance from class inheritance. Class inheritance is an effective tool for code reuse. A derived class easily inherits the fields, methods, and properties of a base class, and thereby avoids reimplementing common methods. In a strongly typed language, such as Delphi, the compiler treats a class as a type, and therefore class inheritance becomes synonymous with type inheritance. In the best of all possible worlds, though, types and classes are entirely separate.

Textbooks on object-oriented programming often describe an inheritance relationship as an "is-a" relationship, for example, a TSavingsAccount "is-a" TAccount.

You can see the same idea in Delphi's is operator, where you test whether an Account variable is TSavingsAccount.

Outside of textbook examples, though, simple is-a relationships break down. A square is a rectangle, but that doesn't mean you want to derive TSquare from TRectangle. A rectangle is a polygon, but you probably don't want to derive TRectangle from TPolygon. Class inheritance forces a derived class to store all the fields that are declared in the base class, but in this case, the derived class doesn't need that information. A TSquare object can get away with storing a single length for all of its sides. A TRectangle object, however, must store two lengths. A TPolygon object needs to store many sides and vertices.

The solution is to separate the type inheritance (a square is a rectangle is a polygon) from class inheritance (class C inherits the fields and methods of class B, which inherits the fields and methods of class A). Use interfaces for type inheritance, so you can leave class inheritance to do what it does best: inheriting fields and methods.

In other words, ISquare inherits from IRectangle, which inherits from IPolygon. The interfaces follow the "is-a" relationship. Entirely separate from the interfaces, the class TSquare implements ISquare, IRectangle, and IPolygon. TRectangle implements IRectangle and IPolygon.

 The convention in COM programming is to name interfaces with an initial I. Delphi follows this convention for all interfaces. Note that it is a useful convention, but not a language requirement.

On the implementation side, you can declare additional classes to implement code reuse. For example, TBaseShape implements the common methods and fields for all shapes. TRectangle inherits from TBaseShape and implements the methods in a way that make sense for rectangles. TPolygon also inherits from TBaseShape and implements the methods in a way that make sense for other kinds of polygons.

A drawing program can use the shapes by manipulating IPolygon interfaces. Example 2-14 shows simplified classes and interfaces for this scheme. Notice how each interface has a GUID (Globally Unique Identifier) in its declaration. The GUID is necessary for using QueryInterface. If you need the GUID of an interface (in an explicit call to QueryInterface, for example), you can use the interface name. Delphi automatically converts an interface name to its GUID.

Example 2-14: Separating Type and Class Hierarchies

```
type
  IShape = interface
  ['{50F6D851-F4EB-11D2-88AC-00104BCAC44B}']
    procedure Draw(Canvas: TCanvas);
    function GetPosition: TPoint;
    procedure SetPosition(Value: TPoint);
    property Position: TPoint read GetPosition write SetPosition;
  end;
```

Example 2-14: Separating Type and Class Hierarchies (continued)

```
IPolygon = interface(IShape)
['{50F6D852-F4EB-11D2-88AC-00104BCAC44B}']
  function NumVertices: Integer;
  function NumSides: Integer;
  function SideLength(Index: Integer): Integer;
  function Vertex(Index: Integer): TPoint;
end;
IRectangle = interface(IPolygon)
['{50F6D853-F4EB-11D2-88AC-00104BCAC44B}']
end;
ISquare = interface(IRectangle)
['{50F6D854-F4EB-11D2-88AC-00104BCAC44B}']
  function Side: Integer;
end;

TBaseShape = class(TNoRefCount, IShape)
private
  fPosition: TPoint;
  function GetPosition: TPoint;
  procedure SetPosition(Value: TPoint);
public
  constructor Create; virtual;
  procedure Draw(Canvas: TCanvas); virtual; abstract;
  property Position: TPoint read fPosition write SetPosition;
end;
TPolygon = class(TBaseShape, IPolygon)
private
  fVertices: array of TPoint;
public
  procedure Draw(Canvas: TCanvas); override;
  function NumVertices: Integer;
  function NumSides: Integer;
  function SideLength(Index: Integer): Integer;
  function Vertex(Index: Integer): TPoint;
end;
TRectangle = class(TBaseShape, IPolygon, IRectangle)
private
  fRect: TRect;
public
  procedure Draw(Canvas: TCanvas); override;
  function NumVertices: Integer;
  function NumSides: Integer;
  function SideLength(Index: Integer): Integer;
  function Vertex(Index: Integer): TPoint;
end;
TSquare = class(TBaseShape, IPolygon, IRectangle, ISquare)
private
  fSide: Integer;
public
  procedure Draw(Canvas: TCanvas); override;
  function Side: Integer;
```

Example 2-14: Separating Type and Class Hierarchies (continued)

```
    function NumVertices: Integer;
    function NumSides: Integer;
    function SideLength(Index: Integer): Integer;
    function Vertex(Index: Integer): TPoint;
  end;
```

A derived class inherits the interfaces implemented by the ancestors' classes. Thus, TRectangle inherits from TBaseShape, and TBaseShape implements IShape so TRectangle implements IShape. Inheritance of interfaces works a little differently. Interface inheritance is merely a typing convenience, so you don't have to retype a lot of method declarations. When a class implements an interface, that does not automatically mean the class implements the ancestor interfaces. A class implements only those interfaces that are listed in its class declaration (and in the declaration for ancestor classes). Thus, even though IRectangle inherits from IPolygon, the TRectangle class must list IRectangle and IPolygon explicitly.

To implement a type hierarchy, you might not want to use reference counting. Instead, you will rely on explicit memory management, the way you do for normal Delphi objects. In this case, it's best to implement the _AddRef and _Release methods as stubs, such as those in the TNoRefCount class in Example 2-13. Just be careful not to have any variables that hold stale references. A variable that refers to an object that has been freed can cause problems if you use the variable. An interface variable that refers to an object that has been freed will certainly cause problems, because Delphi will automatically call its _Release method. In other words, you never want to have variables that contain invalid pointers, and working with interfaces that do not use reference counting forces you to behave.

COM and Corba

Delphi interfaces are also useful for implementing and using COM and Corba objects. You can define a COM server that implements many interfaces, and Delphi automatically manages the COM aggregation for you. The runtime library contains many classes that make it easier to define COM servers, class factories, and so on. Because these classes are not part of the Delphi Pascal language, they are not covered in this book. Consult the product documentation to learn more.

Reference Counting

The previous section discusses how Delphi uses reference counting to manage the lifetime of interfaces. Strings and dynamic arrays also use reference counting to manage their lifetimes. The compiler generates appropriate code to keep track of when interface references, strings, and dynamic arrays are created and when the variables go out of scope and the objects, strings, and arrays must be destroyed.

Usually, the compiler can handle the reference counting automatically, and everything works the way the you expect it to. Sometimes, though, you need to give a hint to the compiler. For example, if you declare a record that contains a reference counted field, and you use GetMem to allocate a new instance of the record, you must call Initialize, passing the record as an argument. Before calling FreeMem, you must call Finalize.

Sometimes, you want to keep a reference to a string or interface after the variable goes out of scope, that is, at the end of the block where the variable is declared. For example, maybe you want to associate an interface with each item in a TListView. You can do this by explicitly managing the reference count. When storing the interface, be sure to cast it to IUnknown, call _AddRef, and cast the IUnknown reference to a raw pointer. When extracting the data, type cast the pointer to IUnknown. You can then use the as operator to cast the interface to any desired type, or just let Delphi release the interface. For convenience, declare a couple of subroutines to do the dirty work for you, and you can reuse these subroutines any time you need to retain an interface reference. Example 2-15 shows an example of how you can store an interface reference as the data associated with a list view item.

Example 2-15: Storing Interfaces in a List View

```
// Cast an interface to a Pointer such that the reference
// count is incremented and the interface will not be freed
// until you call ReleaseIUnknown.
function RefIUnknown(const Intf: IUnknown): Pointer;
begin
  Intf._AddRef;              // Increment the reference count.
  Result := Pointer(Intf);   // Save the interface pointer.
end;

// Release the interface whose value is stored in the pointer P.
procedure ReleaseIUnknown(P: Pointer);
var
  Intf: IUnknown;
begin
  Pointer(Intf) := P;
  // Delphi releases the interface when Intf goes out of scope.
end;

// When the user clicks the button, add an interface to the list.
procedure TForm1.Button1Click(Sender: TObject);
var
  Item: TListItem;
begin
  Item := ListView1.Items.Add;
  Item.Caption := 'Stuff';
  Item.Data := RefIUnknown(GetIntf as IUnknown);
end;

// When the list view is destroyed or the list item is destroyed
// for any other reason, release the interface, too.
procedure TForm1.ListView1Deletion(Sender: TObject; Item: TListItem);
begin
  ReleaseIUnknown(Item.Data);
end;

// When the user selects the list view item, do something with the
// associated interface.
procedure TForm1.ListView1Click(Sender: TObject);
```

Example 2-15: Storing Interfaces in a List View (continued)

```
var
  Intf: IMyInterface;
begin
  Intf := IUnknown(ListView1.Selected.Data) as IMyInterface;
  Intf.DoSomethingUseful;
end;
```

You can also store strings as data. Instead of using **_AddRef**, cast the string to a **Pointer** to store the reference to the string, then force the variable to forget about the string. When the variable goes out of scope, Delphi will not free the string, because the variable has forgotten all about it. After retrieving the pointer, assign it to a string variable that is cast to a pointer. When the subroutine returns, Delphi automatically frees the string's memory. Be sure your program does not retain any pointers to memory that is about to be freed. Again, convenience subroutines simplify the task. Example 2-16 shows one way to store strings.

Example 2-16: Storing Strings in a List View

```
// Save a reference to a string and return a raw pointer
// to the string.
function RefString(const S: string): Pointer;
var
  Local: string;
begin
  Local := S;                 // Increment the reference count.
  Result := Pointer(Local);   // Save the string pointer.
  Pointer(Local) := nil;      // Prevent decrementing the ref count.
end;

// Release a string that was referenced with RefString.
procedure ReleaseString(P: Pointer);
var
  Local: string;
begin
  Pointer(Local) := P;
  // Delphi frees the string when Local goes out of scope.
end;

// When the user clicks the button, add an item to the list view
// and save an additional, hidden string.
procedure TForm1.Button1Click(Sender: TObject);
var
  Item: TListItem;
begin
  Item := ListView1.Items.Add;
  Item.Caption := Edit1.Text;
  Item.Data := RefString(Edit2.Text);
end;

// Release the string when the list view item is destroyed
// for any reason.
procedure TForm1.ListView1Deletion(Sender: TObject; Item: TListItem);
```

Example 2-16: Storing Strings in a List View (continued)

```
begin
  ReleaseString(Item.Data);
end;

// Retrieve the string when the user selects the list view item.
procedure TForm1.ListView1Click(Sender: TObject);
var
  Str: string;
begin
  if ListView1.Selected <> nil then
  begin
    Str := string(ListView1.Selected.Data);
    ShowMessage(Str);
  end;
end;
```

Messages

You should be familiar with Windows messages: user interactions and other events generate messages, which Windows sends to an application. An application processes messages one at a time to respond to the user and other events. Each kind of message has a unique number and two integer parameters. Sometimes a parameter is actually a pointer to a string or structure that contains more complex information. Messages form the heart of Windows event-driven architecture, and Delphi has a unique way of supporting Windows messages.

In Delphi, every object—not only window controls—can respond to messages. A message has an integer identifier and can contain any amount of additional information. In the VCL, the **Application** object receives Windows messages and maps them to equivalent Delphi messages. In other words, Windows messages are a special case of more general Delphi messages.

A Delphi message is a record where the first two bytes contain an integer message identifier, and the remainder of the record is programmer-defined. Delphi's message dispatcher never refers to any part of the message record past the message number, so you are free to store any amount or kind of information in a message record. By convention, the VCL always uses Windows-style message records (**TMessage**), but if you find other uses for Delphi messages, you don't need to feel so constrained.

To send a message to an object, fill in the message identifier and the rest of the message record and call the object's **Dispatch** method. Delphi looks up the message number in the object's message table. The message table contains pointers to all the message handlers that the class defines. If the class does not define a message handler for the message number, Delphi searches the parent class's message table. The search continues until Delphi finds a message handler or it reaches the **TObject** class. If the class and its ancestor classes do not define a message handler for the message number, Delphi calls the object's **DefaultHandler** method. Window controls in the VCL override **Default-Handler** to pass the message to the window procedure; other classes usually ignore unknown messages. You can override `DefaultHandler` to do anything you want, perhaps raise an exception.

Use the `message` directive to declare a message handler for any message. See Chapter 5 for details about the `message` directive.

Message handlers use the same message table and dispatcher as dynamic methods. Each method that you declare with the `dynamic` directive is assigned a 16-bit negative number, which is really a message number. A call to a dynamic method uses the same dispatch code to look up the dynamic method, but if the method is not found, that means the dynamic method is abstract, so Delphi calls `AbstractErrorProc` to report a call to an abstract method.

Because dynamic methods use negative numbers, you cannot write a message handler for negative message numbers, that is, message numbers with the most-significant bit set to one. This limitation should not cause any problems for normal applications. If you need to define custom messages, you have the entire space above `WM_USER` ($0F00) available, up to $7FFF. Delphi looks up dynamic methods and messages in the same table using a linear search, so with large message tables, your application will waste time performing method lookups.

Delphi's message system is entirely general purpose, so you might find a creative use for it. Usually, interfaces provide the same capability, but with better performance and increased type-safety.

Memory Management

Delphi manages the memory and lifetime of strings, `Variants`, dynamic arrays, and interfaces automatically. For all other dynamically allocated memory, you—the programmer—are in charge. It's easy to be confused because it seems as though Delphi automatically manages the memory of components, too, but that's just a trick of the VCL.

Memory management is thread-safe, provided you use Delphi's classes or functions to create the threads. If you go straight to the Windows API and the `CreateThread` function, you must set the `IsMultiThread` variable to `True`. For more information, see Chapter 4, *Concurrent Programming*.

Ordinarily, when you construct an object, Delphi calls `NewInstance` to allocate and initialize the object. You can override `NewInstance` to change the way Delphi allocates memory for the object. For example, suppose you have an application that frequently uses doubly linked lists. Instead of using the general-purpose memory allocator for every node, it's much faster to keep a chain of available nodes for reuse. Use Delphi's memory manager only when the node list is empty. If your application frequently allocates and frees nodes, this special-purpose allocator can be faster than the general-purpose allocator. Example 2-17 shows a simple implementation of this scheme. (See Chapter 4 for a thread-safe version of this class.)

Components Versus Objects

The VCL's TComponent class has two fancy mechanisms for managing object lifetimes, and they often confuse new Delphi programmers, tricking them into thinking that Delphi always manages object lifetimes. It's important that you understand exactly how components work, so you won't be fooled.

Every component has an owner. When the owner is freed, it automatically frees the components that it owns. A form owns the components you drop on it, so when the form is freed, it automatically frees all the components on the form. Thus, you don't usually need to be concerned with managing the lifetime of forms and components.

When a form or component frees a component it owns, the owner also checks whether it has a published field of the same name as the component. If so, the owner sets that field to nil. Thus, if your form dynamically adds or removes components, the form's fields always contain valid object references or are nil. Don't be fooled into thinking that Delphi does this for any other field or object reference. The trick works only for published fields (such as those automatically created when you drop a component on a form in the IDE's form editor), and only when the field name matches the component name.

Example 2-17: Custom Memory Management for Linked Lists

```
type
  TNode = class
  private
    fNext, fPrevious: TNode;
  protected
    // Nodes are under control of TLinkedList.
    procedure Relink(NewNext, NewPrevious: TNode);
    constructor Create(Next: TNode = nil; Previous: TNode = nil);
    procedure RealFree;

  public
    destructor Destroy; override;
    class function NewInstance: TObject; override;
    procedure FreeInstance; override;
    property Next: TNode read fNext;
    property Previous: TNode read fPrevious;
end;

// Singly linked list of nodes that are free for reuse.
// Only the Next fields are used to maintain this list.
var
  NodeList: TNode;

// Allocate a new node by getting the head of the NodeList.
// Remember to call InitInstance to initialize the node that was
// taken from NodeList.
```

Example 2-17: Custom Memory Management for Linked Lists (continued)

```
// If the NodeList is empty, allocate a node normally.
class function TNode.NewInstance: TObject;
begin
  if NodeList = nil then
    Result := inherited NewInstance
  else
  begin
    Result := NodeList;
    NodeList := NodeList.Next;
    InitInstance(Result);
  end;
end;


// Because the NodeList uses only the Next field, set the Previous
// field to a special value. If a program erroneously refers to the
// Previous field of a free node, you can see the special value
// and know the cause of the error.
const
  BadPointerValueToFlagErrors = Pointer($F0EE0BAD);


// Free a node by adding it to the head of the NodeList. This is MUCH
// faster than using the general-purpose memory manager.
procedure TNode.FreeInstance;
begin
  fPrevious := BadPointerValueToFlagErrors;
  fNext := NodeList;
  NodeList := Self;
end;


// If you want to clean up the list properly when the application
// finishes, call RealFree for each node in the list. The inherited
// FreeInstance method frees and cleans up the node for real.
procedure TNode.RealFree;
begin
  inherited FreeInstance;
end;
```

You can also replace the entire memory management system that Delphi uses. Install a new memory manager by calling SetMemoryManager. For example, you might want to replace Delphi's suballocator with an allocator that performs additional error checking. Example 2-18 shows a custom memory manager that keeps a list of pointers the program has allocated and explicitly checks each attempt to free a pointer against the list. Any attempt to free an invalid pointer is refused, and Delphi will report a runtime error (which SysUtils changes to an exception). As a bonus, the memory manager checks that the list is empty when the application ends. If the list is not empty, you have a memory leak.

Example 2-18: Installing a Custom Memory Manager

```
unit CheckMemMgr;

interface
```

Example 2-18: Installing a Custom Memory Manager (continued)

```
uses Windows;

function CheckGet(Size: Integer): Pointer;
function CheckFree(Mem: Pointer): Integer;
function CheckRealloc(Mem: Pointer; Size: Integer): Pointer;

var
  HeapFlags: DWord; // In a single-threaded application, you might
                    // want to set this to Heap_No_Serialize.
implementation

const
  MaxSize = MaxInt div 4;
type
  TPointerArray = array[1..MaxSize] of Pointer;
  PPointerArray = ^TPointerArray;
var
  Heap: THandle;            // Windows heap for the pointer list
  List: PPointerArray;      // List of allocated pointers
  ListSize: Integer;        // Number of pointers in the list
  ListAlloc: Integer;       // Capacity of the pointer list

// If the list of allocated pointers is not empty when the program
// finishes, that means you have a memory leak. Handling the memory
// leak is left as an exercise for the reader.
procedure MemoryLeak;
begin
  // Report the leak to the user, but remember that the program is
  // shutting down, so you should probably stick to the Windows API
  // and not use the VCL.
end;

// Add a pointer to the list.
procedure AddMem(Mem: Pointer);
begin
  if List = nil then
  begin
    // New list of pointers.
    ListAlloc := 8;
    List := HeapAlloc(Heap, HeapFlags, ListAlloc * SizeOf(Pointer));
  end
  else if ListSize >= ListAlloc then
  begin
    // Make the list bigger. Try to do it somewhat intelligently.
    if ListAlloc < 256 then
      ListAlloc := ListAlloc * 2
    else
      ListAlloc := ListAlloc + 256;
    List := HeapRealloc(Heap, HeapFlags, List,
                        ListAlloc * SizeOf(Pointer));
  end;
  // Add a pointer to the list.
```

Example 2-18: Installing a Custom Memory Manager (continued)

```
    Inc(ListSize);
    List[ListSize] := Mem;
end;

// Look for a pointer in the list, and remove it. Return True for
// success, and False if the pointer is not in the list.
function RemoveMem(Mem: Pointer): Boolean;
var
  I: Integer;
begin
  for I := 1 to ListSize do
    if List[I] = Mem then
    begin
      MoveMemory(@List[I], @List[I+1], (ListSize-I) * SizeOf(Pointer));
      Dec(ListSize);
      Result := True;
      Exit;
    end;

  Result := False;
end;

// Replacement memory allocator.
function CheckGet(Size: Integer): Pointer;
begin
  Result := SysGetMem(Size);
  AddMem(Result);
end;

// If the pointer isn't in the list, don't call the real
// Free function. Return 0 for success, and non-zero for an error.
function CheckFree(Mem: Pointer): Integer;
begin
  if not RemoveMem(Mem) then
    Result := 1
  else
    Result := SysFreeMem(Mem);
end;

// Remove the old pointer and add the new one, which might be the
// same as the old one, or it might be different. Return nil for
// an error, and Delphi will raise an exception.
function CheckRealloc(Mem: Pointer; Size: Integer): Pointer;
begin
  if not RemoveMem(Mem) then
    Result := nil
  else
  begin
    Result :=SysReallocMem(Mem, Size);
    AddMem(Result);
  end;
end;
```

Example 2-18: Installing a Custom Memory Manager (continued)

```
procedure SetNewManager;
var
  Mgr: TMemoryManager;
begin
  Mgr.GetMem := CheckGet;
  Mgr.FreeMem := CheckFree;
  Mgr.ReallocMem := CheckRealloc;
  SetMemoryManager(Mgr);
end;

initialization
  Heap := HeapCreate(0, HeapFlags, 0);
  SetNewManager;
finalization
  if ListSize <> 0 then
    MemoryLeak;
  HeapDestroy(Heap);
end.
```

If you define a custom memory manager, you must ensure that your memory manager is used for all memory allocation. The easiest way to do this is to set the memory manager in a unit's initialization section, as shown in Example 2-18. The memory management unit must be the first unit listed in the project's **uses** declaration.

Ordinarily, if a unit makes global changes in its initialization section, it should clean up those changes in its finalization section. A unit in a package might be loaded and unloaded many times in a single application, so cleaning up is important. A memory manager is different, though. Memory allocated by one manager cannot be freed by another manager, so you must ensure that only one manager is active in an application, and that the manager is active for the entire duration of the application. This means you must not put your memory manager in a package, although you can use a DLL, as explained in the next section.

Memory and DLLs

If you use DLLs and try to pass objects between DLLs or between the application and a DLL, you run into a number of problems. First of all, each DLL and EXE keeps its own copy of its class tables. The **is** and **as** operators do not work correctly for objects passed between DLLs and EXEs. Use packages (described in Chapter 1) to solve this problem. Another problem is that any memory allocated in a DLL is owned by that DLL. When Windows unloads the DLL, all memory allocated by the DLL is freed, even if the EXE or another DLL holds a pointer to that memory. This can be a major problem when using strings, dynamic arrays, and **Variants** because you never know when Delphi will allocate memory automatically.

The solution is to use the **ShareMem** unit as the first unit of your project and every DLL. The **ShareMem** unit installs a custom memory manager that redirects all memory allocation requests to a special DLL, *BorlndMM.dll*. The application doesn't unload *BorlndMM* until the application exits. The DLL magic takes place transparently, so you don't need to worry about the details. Just make sure you use the ShareMem unit, and make sure it is the first unit used by your program and libraries. When you release your application to your clients or customers, you will need to include *BorlndMM.dll*.

If you define your own memory manager, and you need to use DLLs, you must duplicate the magic performed by the ShareMem unit. You can replace ShareMem with your own unit that forwards memory requests to your DLL, which uses your custom memory manager. Example 2-19 shows one way to define your own replacement for the ShareMem unit.

Example 2-19: Defining a Shared Memory Manager

```
unit CheckShareMem;

// Use this unit first so all memory allocations use the shared
// memory manager. The application and all DLLs must use this unit.
// You cannot use packages because those DLLs use the default Borland
// shared memory manager.

interface

function CheckGet(Size: Integer): Pointer;
function CheckFree(Mem: Pointer): Integer;
function CheckRealloc(Mem: Pointer; Size: Integer): Pointer;

implementation

const
  DLL = 'CheckMM.dll';

function CheckGet(Size: Integer): Pointer; external DLL;
function CheckFree(Mem: Pointer): Integer; external DLL;
function CheckRealloc(Mem: Pointer; Size: Integer): Pointer;
    external DLL;

procedure SetNewManager;
var
  Mgr: TMemoryManager;
begin
  Mgr.GetMem := CheckGet;
  Mgr.FreeMem := CheckFree;
  Mgr.ReallocMem := CheckRealloc;
  SetMemoryManager(Mgr);
end;

initialization
  SetNewManager;
end.
```

The CheckMM DLL uses your custom memory manager and exports its functions so they can be used by the CheckShareMem unit. Example 2-20 shows the source code for the CheckMM library.

Example 2-20: Defining the Shared Memory Manager DLL

```
library CheckMM;

// Replacement for BorlndMM.dll to use a custom memory manager.

uses
  CheckMemMgr;

exports
  CheckGet, CheckFree, CheckRealloc;

begin
end.
```

Your program and library projects use the **CheckShareMem** unit first, and all memory requests go to *CheckMM.dll*, which uses the error-checking memory manager. You don't often need to replace Delphi's memory manager, but as you can see, it isn't difficult to do.

The memory manager that comes with Delphi works well for most applications, but it does not perform well in some cases. The average application allocates and frees memory in chunks of varying sizes. If your application is different and allocates memory in ever-increasing sizes (say, because you have a dynamic array that grows in small steps to a very large size), performance will suffer. Delphi's memory manager will allocate more memory than your application needs. One solution is to redesign your program so it uses memory in a different pattern (say, by preallocating a large dynamic array). Another solution is to write a memory manager that better meets the specialized needs of your application. For example, the new memory manager might use the Windows API (**HeapAllocate**, etc.).

Old-Style Object Types

In addition to class types, Delphi supports an obsolete type that uses the **object** keyword. Old-style objects exist for backward compatibility with Turbo Pascal, but they might be dropped entirely from future versions of Delphi.

Old-style **object** types are more like records than new-style objects. Fields in an old-style **object** are laid out in the same manner as in records. If the **object** type does not have any virtual methods, there is no hidden field for the VMT pointer, for example. Unlike records, **object** types can use inheritance. Derived fields appear after inherited fields. If a class declares a virtual method, its first field is the VMT pointer, which appears after all the inherited fields. (Unlike a new-style object, where the VMT pointer is always first because **TObject** declares virtual methods.)

An old-style object type can have private, protected, and public sections, but not published or automated sections. Because it cannot have a published section, an old object type cannot have any runtime type information. An old object type cannot implement interfaces.

Constructors and destructors work differently in old-style object types than in new-style class types. To create an instance of an old object type, call the New procedure. The newly allocated object is initialized to all zero. If you declare a constructor, you can call it as part of the call to New. Pass the constructor name and arguments as the second argument to New. Similarly, you can call a destructor when you call Dispose to free the object instance. The destructor name and arguments are the second argument to Dispose.

You don't have to allocate an old-style object instance dynamically. You can treat the object type as a record type and declare object-type variables as unit-level or local variables. Delphi automatically initializes string, dynamic array, and Variant fields, but does not initialize other fields in the object instance.

Unlike new-style class types, exceptions in old-style constructors do not automatically cause Delphi to free a dynamically created object or call the destructor.

Runtime Type Information

Runtime Type
Information

Delphi's Integrated Development Environment (IDE) depends on information provided by the compiler. This information, called Runtime Type Information (RTTI), describes some aspects of classes and other types. It's not a full reflection system such as you find in Java, but it's more complete than type identifiers in C++. For ordinary, everyday use of Delphi, you can ignore the details of RTTI and just let Delphi do its thing. Sometimes, though, you need to look under the hood and understand exactly how RTTI works.

The only difference between a published declaration and a public declaration is RTTI. Delphi stores RTTI for published fields, methods, and properties, but not for public, protected, or private declarations. Although the primary purpose of RTTI is to publish declarations for the IDE and for saving and loading *.dfm* files, the RTTI tables include other kinds of information. For example, virtual and dynamic methods, interfaces, and automated declarations are part of a class's RTTI. Most types also have RTTI called *type information*. This chapter explains all the details of RTTI.

Virtual Method Table

The Virtual Method Table (VMT) stores pointers to all the virtual methods declared for a class and its base classes. The layout of the VMT is the same as in most C++ implementations (including Borland C++ and C++ Builder) and is the same format required for COM, namely a list of pointers to methods. Each virtual method of a class or its ancestor classes has an entry in the VMT.

Each class has a unique VMT. Even if a class does not define any of its own virtual methods, but only inherits methods from its base class, it has its own VMT that lists all the virtual methods it inherits. Because each VMT lists every virtual method, Delphi can compile calls to virtual methods as quick lookups in the VMT. Because each class has its own VMT, Delphi uses the VMT to identify a class. In fact, a class reference is really a pointer to a class's VMT, and the ClassType method returns a pointer to the VMT.

In addition to a table of virtual methods, the VMT includes other information about a class, such as the class name, a pointer to the VMT for the base class, and pointers to many other RTTI tables. The other RTTI pointers appear before the first virtual method in the VMT. Example 3-1 shows a record layout that is equivalent to the VMT. The actual list of virtual methods begins after the end of the TVmt record. In other words, you can convert a TClass class reference to a pointer to a TVmt record by subtracting the size of the record, as shown in Example 3-1.

Example 3-1: Structure of a VMT

```
type
  PVmt = ^TVmt;
  TVmt = record
    SelfPtr:            TClass;          // Points forward to the start
                                         //   of the VMT
    // The following pointers point to other RTTI tables. If a class
    // does not have a table, the pointer is nil. Thus, most classes
    // have a nil IntfTable and AutoTable, for example.
    IntfTable:          PInterfaceTable; // Interface table
    AutoTable:          PAutoTable;      // Automation table
    InitTable:          PInitTable;      // Fields needing finalization
    TypeInfo:           PTypeInfo;       // Properties & other info
    FieldTable:         PFieldTable;     // Published fields
    MethodTable:        PMethodTable;    // Published methods
    DynMethodTable:     PDynMethodTable; // List of dynamic methods

    ClassName:          PShortString;    // Points to the class name
    InstanceSize:       LongInt;         // Size of each object, in bytes
    ClassParent:        ^TClass;         // Immediate base class

    // The following fields point to special virtual methods that
    // are inherited from TObject.
    SafeCallException:  Pointer;
    AfterConstruction:  Pointer;
    BeforeDestruction:  Pointer;
    Dispatch:           Pointer;
    DefaultHandler:     Pointer;
    NewInstance:        Pointer;
    FreeInstance:       Pointer;
    Destroy:            Pointer;

    // Here begin the virtual method pointers.
    // Each virtual method is stored as a code pointer, e.g.,
    // VirtualMethodTable: array[1..Count] of Pointer;
    // But the compiler does not store the count of the number of
    // method pointers in the table.
  end;
var
  Vmt: PVmt;
begin
  // To get a PVmt pointer from a class reference, cast the class
```

Example 3-1: Structure of a VMT (continued)

```
// reference to the PVmt type and subtract the size of the TVmt
// record. This is easily done with the Dec procedure:
Vmt := PVmt(SomeObject.ClassType);
Dec(Vmt);
```

As you can see, the VMT includes pointers to many other tables. The following sections describe these tables in more detail.

Published Declarations

The only difference between a published declaration and a public one is that a published declaration tells the compiler to store information in the VMT. Only certain kinds of information can be stored, so published declarations face a number of restrictions:

- In order to declare any published fields, methods, or properties, a class must have RTTI enabled by using the $M+ directive or by inheriting from a class that has RTTI. (See Chapter 8, *Compiler Directives*, for details.)

- Fields must be of class type (no other types are allowed). The class type must have RTTI enabled.

- Array properties cannot be published. The type of a published property cannot be a pointer, record, or array. If it is a set type, it must be small enough to be stored in an integer. In the current release of Delphi, that means the set can have no more than 32 members.

- The published section cannot contain more than one overloaded method with each name. You can overload methods, but only one of the overloaded methods can be published.

The Classes unit declares TPersistent with the $M+ directive. TPersistent is usually used as a base class for all Delphi classes that need published declarations. Note that TComponent inherits from TPersistent.

Published Methods

Delphi stores the names and addresses of published methods in a class's RTTI. The IDE uses this information to store the values of event properties in a *.dfm* file. In the IDE, each event property is either nil or contains a method reference. The method reference includes a pointer to the method's entry point. (At design time, the IDE has no true entry point, so it makes one up. At runtime, your application uses the method's real entry point.) To store the value of an event property, Delphi looks up the method address in the class's RTTI, finds the corresponding method name, and stores the name in the *.dfm* file. To load a *.dfm* file, Delphi reads the method name and looks up the corresponding method address from the class's RTTI.

A class's RTTI stores only the published methods for that class, and not for any ancestor classes. Thus, to look up a method name or address, the lookup might fail for a derived class, in which case, the lookup continues with the base class. The MethodName and MethodAddress methods of TObject do the work of searching a class's RTTI, then searching the base class's RTTI, and so on, up the inheritance chain. (See the TObject type in Chapter 5, *Language Reference*, for details about these methods.) The published method table contains only the method name and address.

You can declare any method in the published section of a class declaration. Usually, though, Delphi's IDE creates the methods for you. When you double-click an event property, for example, the IDE creates a method in the initial, unnamed section of the form class. Because a form class has RTTI enabled, the initial, unnamed section is published. (Form classes have RTTI because TPersistent is an ancestor class.)

The method table starts with a 2-byte count of the number of published methods, followed by a record for each method. Each method record starts with a 2-byte size of the method record, followed by the method address (4 bytes), and then followed by the method name as a short string, that is, as a 1-byte string length followed by the text of the string.

More Method RTTI

The record size for a method is usually 2 + 4 + 1 + Length(Name), but some method records have additional information. The additional information is not part of the official RTTI for the class. Future versions of the compiler might not generate this information, so you should not write any code that relies on it. The information is interesting, though, so take a look at what Delphi hides in its method records.

Delphi stores additional information for methods that use the stdcall calling convention and that have parameter and return types for which Delphi ordinarily stores type information. The extra information is stored after the method name and includes the names and types of the parameters. You can tell this extra information is present when the size of the method record is larger than it needs to be to store the record size, method address, and method name. If the size is 4 bytes larger than it needs to be, that means the method takes no parameters. The extra 4 bytes are always zero.

If the size is more than 6 bytes larger than it needs to be, the information for the method's parameters is stored following the sixth byte. (The extra 2 bytes do not seem to serve any useful purpose, but they are not always zero.) Each parameter has a pointer to a TTypeInfo record for the parameter's type, followed by the parameter name (as a short string), followed by a trailing #0 byte. (See "The TypInfo Unit," later in this chapter, to learn about the TTypeInfo record.)

Example 3-2 depicts the logical structure of the method table. Note that Delphi cannot use these declarations verbatim because the record size varies to fit the size of the strings.

Example 3-2: The Layout of the Published Method Table

```
type
  TMethodParam = packed record
    TypeInfo: PPTypeInfo;
    Name: ShortString;
    // The name is followed by a trailing #0 byte.
  end;
  TMethod = packed record
    Size: Word;                  // Size of the TVmtMethod record.
    Address: Pointer;            // Pointer to the method entry point.
    Name: packed ShortString;    // Name of the published method.
    // Some methods have an additional 4 zero bytes, which means the
    // method takes no parameters.
    // Some methods have an additional 6 bytes, followed by a series of
    // TMethodParam records, for each parameter.
    // It seems that only stdcall methods have this extra information.
    // You can identify the extra info by the TMethod.Size value being
    // too big for just the Size, Address, and Name members. The only
    // way to know how many parameters are stored here is to check
    // each parameter until you reach the record size.
    ExtraStuff: array[1..FourOrSix] of Byte;
    Params: array[1..ParamCount] of TMethodParam;
  end;
  { Published method table }
  TMethodTable = packed record
    Count: Word;
    Methods: array[1..Count] of TMethod;
  end;
```

Published Fields and Field Types

Each published field has a name, a type, and an offset. The type is a class reference for the field's type. (Published fields must be of class type.) The offset is an offset (in bytes) into the object's storage, where the field is stored.

The published field table starts with a 2-byte count of the number of fields, followed by a 4-byte pointer to a class table, followed by the field definitions. Each field definition is a record containing a 4-byte offset, and a 2-byte index into the class table, followed by the field name as a short string.

The class table lists all the classes used by the published fields. Each field contains an index into this table. The class table starts with a 2-byte count, followed by a list of class references where each class reference is 4 bytes. A class reference is a pointer to the class's VMT.

Example 3-3 shows the logical layout of the field table. Because the records are variable length, you cannot use these declarations in a Delphi program.

Example 3-3: Layout of the Published Field Table

```
type
  { Field class table }
  PFieldClassTable = ^TFieldClassTable;
  TFieldClassTable = packed record
```

Example 3-3: Layout of the Published Field Table (continued)

```
    Count: Word;
    Classes: packed array[1..Count] of ^TClass;
end;

{ Published field record }
TField = packed record
    Offset: LongWord;     // Byte offset of field in the object. }
    ClassIndex: Word;     // Index in the FieldClassTable of the
                          // field's type.
    Name: packed ShortString;  // Name of the published field. }
end;

{ Published field table }
TFieldTable = packed record
    Count: Word;
    FieldClassTable: PFieldClassTable;
    Fields: packed array [1..Count] of TField;
end;
```

Published Properties

Published properties have lots of information stored about them: name, type, reader, writer, default value, index, and stored flag. The type is a pointer to a **TTypeInfo** record (discussed in the next section). The reader and writer can be fields, methods, or nothing. The default value is an ordinal value; non-ordinal properties don't have default values. The stored flag can be a constant, a field, or a method reference. The Object Inspector in Delphi's IDE relies on published properties, and Delphi uses the default and stored information when saving and loading *.dfm* files.

The reader, writer, and stored fields can be pointers to static methods, byte offsets of virtual methods, or byte offsets of fields. Dynamic methods are not allowed, and static or virtual methods must use the **register** calling convention (which is the default). Additionally, the **stored** value can be a constant True or False. Delphi stores these different kinds of values as follows:

- A constant True or False is stored as a literal zero or 1. Only the **stored** directive can have a constant True or False. If a reader or writer is zero, that means the property does not have that particular directive, that is, the property is write-only or read-only, respectively.

- A field offset is stored with $FF in the most significant byte. For example, a field stored at offset 42 ($2A) would have the value $FF00002A. Note that published fields are rarely used to store property values, so it is unlikely that you could look up the name of the field in the published field table.

- A virtual method is stored with $FE in the most significant byte and the byte offset of the method as a **SmallInt** in the low order 2 bytes. For example, the third virtual method is stored as $FE000008. (The first virtual method has offset 0.)

Published Fields and Components

When you drop a component on a form in Delphi's IDE, the IDE creates a published field declaration for that component. Delphi takes advantage of published fields in the form class when saving and loading .*dfm* files, but the mechanisms Delphi uses are common to any component because they are implemented as methods of the TComponent class. These tricks are not part of the Delphi language, but they affect most Delphi programs.

When a component (call it Owner) becomes the owner of another component (call it Child), the child looks up its name (that is, the value of the Name property) in the owner. If Owner has a published field with the same name as Child, the owner sets the value of its field to be a reference to the child object. When Child is destroyed, Owner checks again for a published field of the same name, and if it finds a match, it sets the field to nil.

Usually, the only time a Delphi programmer encounters this behavior is for the published fields of a form. When Delphi loads a .*dfm*, it creates the child components. The form class (which is the owner) notices that a component's name matches that of a published field and automatically sets the field to refer to the newly created component.

In other words, the Delphi language does not treat components or forms specially. Instead, the TComponent class knows about published fields and uses that information to manage the components it owns. Don't be fooled into thinking that Delphi automatically manages the lifetime of all components just because it manages some components.

The published field table is especially important when loading a .*dfm*. When Delphi loads a component from a .*dfm*, it reads the name of the component's type as a string. Delphi needs a class reference for the class name, which it can look up in the field class table. If you write a component that stores a subcomponent and that subcomponent is not declared in a published field, you will need to register its class explicitly by calling RegisterClass or RegisterClasses (both in the Classes unit). Registering classes is not a feature of the Delphi language.

- A static method is stored as an address, e.g., $00401E42. The memory architecture of Windows prevents any method from having an address with $FF or $FE in the most significant byte, so there is no danger of conflicts or ambiguities.

The default value can be stored only for integer, character, enumeration, or set types. If the programmer declares a property with the nodefault directive (which is the same as omitting the default directive), Delphi stores the most negative integer ($80000000 or –2,147,483,648) as the default value. In other words, you cannot have an integer property whose default value is –2,147,483,648 because Delphi would interpret that as being the same as nodefault.

String, floating-point, Int64, Variant, and class-type properties cannot have default values, and the nodefault directive has no effect. (Delphi always uses an empty string, zero, Unassigned, or nil as the default value for these types when reading and writing .dfm files.) If you want the effect of defining a default value for these kinds of properties, you can play a trick in the class's constructor: set the property's value when the user drops the component on a form, and not when Delphi loads the component from the .dfm file. What makes this tricky is that the ComponentState property is not set until after the constructor returns. (Read about ComponentState in Delphi's help files.) Thus, you need to test the owner's ComponentState, as follows:

```
constructor TStringDefault.Create(Owner:
   TComponent);
begin
  inherited;
  if (Owner = nil) or
     (([csReading, csDesigning] *
       Owner.ComponentState) = [csDesigning])
  then
    StringProperty := 'Default value';
end;
```

This trick does not save any space in the .dfm file, but it achieves the goal of setting a default value for a property that does not ordinarily take a default value.

The primary purpose of a default value is to save space in a .dfm file. If a property's value is the same as the default value, Delphi doesn't store that value in the .dfm. If a property does not have a default value, Delphi always stores the value in the .dfm. Note that inherited forms get their default values from the ancestor form, which gets it from the default directive. It is the programmer's responsibility to initialize a property to its default value in the class's constructor—Delphi doesn't do that automatically. (See Example 3-5, later in this chapter, for help setting default property values.)

The index directive stores the index value for an indexed property. If the property is not indexed, Delphi stores the most negative integer as the index value.

The published property information also stores the name index, that is, the ordinal position of the property in the class declaration. The Object Inspector can sort properties into alphabetical order, which scrambles the declared order of a class's properties. The name index value gives you the original order.

Delphi makes it easy to access a class's published property information using the TypInfo unit, which is the subject of the next section.

The TypInfo Unit

The TypInfo unit declares several types and functions that give you easy access to the published properties of an object and other information. The Object Inspector relies on this information to perform its magic. You can obtain a list of the published properties of a class and get the name and type for each property. Given an object reference, you can get or set the value of any published property.

The TypeInfo function returns a pointer to a type information record, but if you don't use the TypInfo unit, you cannot access anything in that record and must instead treat the result as an untyped Pointer. The TypInfo unit defines the real type, which is PTypeInfo, that is, a pointer to a TTypeInfo record. The type information record contains a type kind and the name of the type. The type kind is an enumerated value that tells you what kind of type it is: integer, floating point, string, etc.

Type Data

Some types have additional type data, as returned by the GetTypeData function, which returns a PTypeData pointer. You can use the type data to get the names of an enumerated literal, the limits of an ordinal subrange, and more. Table 3-1 describes the data for each type kind.

Table 3-1: Type Kinds and Their Data

TTypeKind Literal	Associated Data
tkArray	No associated data.
tkChar	Limits of character subrange.
tkClass	Class reference, parent class, unit where class is declared, and published properties.
tkDynArray	No associated data for dynamic arrays.
tkEnumeration	If the type is a subrange of another type, the data includes a pointer to the base type and the limits of the subrange; otherwise, the data includes the limits of the subrange and a packed list of counted strings for the names of the enumerated literals.
tkFloat	Floating-point type: currency, comp, single, double, or extended (but not Real48).
tkInt64	Limits of integer subrange.
tkInteger	Limits of integer subrange.
tkInterface	Base interface, unit where the interface is declared, and the GUID.
tkLString	No associated data for a long string (AnsiString).
tkMethod	Return type, kind of method, and parameter names and type names.
tkRecord	No associated data.
tkSet	Pointer to the enumerated type of the set elements.
tkString	Maximum length of a short string.

Table 3-1: Type Kinds and Their Data (continued)

TTypeKind Literal	Associated Data
tkUnknown	No associated data.
tkVariant	No associated data.
tkWChar	Limits of wide character subrange.
tkWString	No associated data for a `WideString`.

Note that the primary purpose of type information is to support Delphi's IDE and for reading and writing *.dfm* files. A secondary purpose is for initialization and finalization of managed types. It is not a general-purpose reflection system, as you find in Java, so information about records and arrays, for example, is limited.

Published Properties

Many of the functions in the `TypInfo` unit make it easy for you to access the published properties of an object. Instead of accessing the type information directly, you can call some functions to get or set a property value, determine whether the property should be stored, get the property type and name, and so on.

To get or set a property value, you need to know what kind of property type you are dealing with: ordinal, floating point, string, `Variant`, method, or `Int64`. Each kind of type has a pair of subroutines to get and set a property value. If the property has methods for the reader or writer, the `TypInfo` routines call those methods, just as though you were getting or setting the property in the usual manner.

Integer-, character-, enumeration-, set-, and class-type properties are ordinal. They store their property values in an integer, so you must use an integer to get or set the property value. When you get the property value, cast it to the desired type. To set the property value, cast the value to an integer. Example 3-4 shows a procedure that takes any component as an argument and tests whether that component publishes a property called Font whose type is a class type. If so, the procedure sets the component's font to Arial, 10 pt.

Example 3-4: Setting an Ordinal Property

```
procedure SetFontToArial10pt(Component: TComponent);
var
  Font: TFont;
  PropInfo: PPropInfo;
begin
  // First find out if the component has a Font property.
  PropInfo := GetPropInfo(Component, 'Font');
  if PropInfo = nil then
    Exit;
  // Next see if the property has class type.
  if PropInfo.PropType^.Kind <> tkClass then
    Exit;
  Font := TFont.Create;
  try
    Font.Name := 'Arial';
    Font.Size := 10;
```

Example 3-4: Setting an Ordinal Property (continued)

```
    // Now set the component's Font property.
    SetOrdProp(Component, PropInfo, Integer(Font));
    // SetOrdProp is just like Component.Font := Font except that
    // the compiler doesn't need to know about the Font property.
    // The component's writer copies the TFont object, so this
    // procedure must free its Font to avoid a memory leak.
  finally
    Font.Free;
  end;
end;
```

You can get a list of PPropInfo pointers if you need to learn about all of an object's properties, or you can call GetPropInfo to learn about a single property. The GetPropList function gets only properties whose type kind matches a set of type kinds that you specify. You can use this to learn about events (tkMethod), string-valued properties only (tkString, tkLString, tkWString), and so on. Example 3-5 shows a procedure that takes an object as an argument and looks up all the ordinal-type properties, then gets the default values of those properties and sets the property values to the defaults. You can call this function from a constructor to guarantee that the properties are properly initialized, thereby avoiding a possible error where the property declaration has one default value, but the constructor has a different one.

Example 3-5: Setting Default Property Values

```
// Set the default value for all published properties.
procedure SetDefaultValues(Obj: TObject);
const
  tkOrdinal = [tkEnumeration, tkInteger, tkChar, tkSet, tkWChar];
  NoDefault = Low(Integer);
var
  PropList: PPropList;
  Count, I: Integer;
  Value: Integer;
begin
  // Count the number of ordinal properties that can have
  // default values.
  Count := GetPropList(Obj, tkOrdinal, nil);
  // Allocate memory to store the prop info & get the real prop list.
  GetMem(PropList, Count * SizeOf(PPropInfo));
  try
    GetPropList(Obj, tkOrdinal, PropList);
    // Loop through all the ordinal properties.
    for I := 0 to Count-1 do
      // If the property has a default value, set the property value
      // to that default.
      if PropList[I].Default <> NoDefault then
        SetOrdProp(Obj, PropList[I], PropList[I].Default)
  finally
    FreeMem(PropList);
  end;
end;
```

Runtime Type Information

The routines in the `TypInfo` unit, while not documented, are straightforward and easy to use. The following list describes all the subroutines in the `TypInfo` unit, for your convenience. Consult the *TypInfo.pas* source file for further details (provided you have at least the Professional edition of Delphi or C++ Builder). Note that these functions perform little or no error checking. It is your responsibility to ensure that you are calling the correct function for the property and its type. Changing the value of a read-only property or getting the value of a write-only property, for example, results in an access violation.

GetEnumName function

```
function GetEnumName(TypeInfo: PTypeInfo; Value: Integer): string;
```

Returns the name of an enumerated literal or an empty string if `Value` is out of range.

GetEnumProp function

```
function GetEnumProp(Instance: TObject; PropInfo: PPropInfo):
    string; overload;
function GetEnumProp(Instance: TObject; const PropName: string):
    string; overload;
```

Returns the name of the enumerated literal that is the property's value.

GetEnumValue function

```
function GetEnumValue(TypeInfo: PTypeInfo; const Name: string):Integer;
```

Returns the ordinal value of an enumerated literal or –1 if the type has no literal with the given name.

GetFloatProp function

```
function GetFloatProp(Instance: TObject; PropInfo: PPropInfo):
    Extended; overload;
function GetFloatProp(Instance: TObject; const PropName: string):
    Extended; overload;
```

Gets the value of a property with a floating-point type.

GetInt64Prop function

```
function GetInt64Prop(Instance: TObject; PropInfo: PPropInfo):
    Int64; overload;
function GetInt64Prop(Instance: TObject; const PropName: string):
    Int64; overload;
```

Gets the value of a property of type `Int64` or any subrange that requires more than 32 bits to represent.

GetMethodProp function

```
function GetMethodProp(Instance: TObject; PropInfo: PPropInfo):
    TMethod; overload;
function GetMethodProp(Instance: TObject; const PropName: string):
    TMethod; overload;
```

Gets the value of an event property.

GetObjectProp function

```
function GetObjectProp(Instance: TObject; PropInfo: PPropInfo;
    MinClass: TClass = nil): TObject; overload;
function GetObjectProp(Instance: TObject; const PropName: string;
    MinClass: TClass = nil): TObject; overload;
```

Gets the value of a class-type property. `MinClass` is the base class that you require for the property value; if the result is not of type `MinClass` or a descendant, `GetObjectProp` returns `nil`. The default is to allow an object of any class.

GetObjectPropClass function
```
function GetObjectPropClass(Instance: TObject; PropInfo: PPropInfo):
    TClass; overload;
function GetObjectPropClass(Instance: TObject; const PropName: string):
    TClass; overload;
```

Gets the class type from the property's type data. `Instance` is used only to look up the property information, so the first version of this function (which already has the property information in the `PropInfo` parameter) does not refer to `Instance`.

GetOrdProp function
```
function GetOrdProp(Instance: TObject; PropInfo: PPropInfo):
    Longint; overload;
function GetOrdProp(Instance: TObject; const PropName: string):
    Longint; overload;
```

Gets the value of any ordinal type property, or any property whose value fits in a 32-bit integer, e.g., object, set, character, enumerated, or integer subrange.

GetPropInfo function
```
function GetPropInfo(TypeInfo: PTypeInfo; const PropName: string):
    PPropInfo; overload;
function GetPropInfo(TypeInfo: PTypeInfo; const PropName: string;
    AKinds: TTypeKinds): PPropInfo; overload;
function GetPropInfo(Instance: TObject; const PropName: string;
    AKinds: TTypeKinds = []): PPropInfo; overload;
function GetPropInfo(AClass: TClass; const PropName: string;
    AKinds: TTypeKinds = []): PPropInfo; overload;
```

Returns the `PPropInfo` pointer for a published property or `nil` if the class does not have any such published property or if the named property does not have the correct type. The first argument can be an object reference, a class reference, or a class's type information (from the `TypeInfo` function or `ClassInfo` method).

GetPropInfos procedure
```
procedure GetPropInfos(TypeInfo: PTypeInfo; PropList: PPropList);
```

Gets a list of all the `PPropInfo` pointers for an object, in declaration order. Use the class's type data to learn how many published properties the class has, so you can allocate the `PropList` array.

GetPropList function
```
function GetPropList(TypeInfo: PTypeInfo; TypeKinds: TTypeKinds;
    PropList: PPropList): Integer;
```

Gets an alphabetized list of `PPropInfo` pointers for the matching properties of an object and returns a count of the number of properties stored in `PropList`. Pass `nil` for the `PropList` parameter to get a count of the number of matching properties.

GetPropValue function

```
function GetPropValue(Instance: TObject; const PropName: string;
    PreferStrings: Boolean = True): Variant;
```

Gets the value of a published property as a **Variant**. **GetPropValue** incurs more overhead than the other **Get...** functions, but is easier to use. If **PreferStrings** is True, **GetPropValue** will store the property value as a string, if this is possible.

GetSetProp function

```
function GetSetProp(Instance: TObject; PropInfo: PPropInfo;
    Brackets: Boolean = False): string; overload;
function GetSetProp(Instance: TObject; const PropName: string;
    Brackets: Boolean = False): string; overload;
```

Gets the value of a set-type property and returns the value as a string. The format of the string is a list of enumerated literals, separated by commas and spaces. You can optionally include square brackets. The format is the same as that used in the Object Inspector.

GetStrProp function

```
function GetStrProp(Instance: TObject; PropInfo: PPropInfo): string;
    overload;
function GetStrProp(Instance: TObject; const PropName: string): string;
    overload;
```

Gets the value of a string-type property. The property type can be **tkString**, **tkLString**, or **tkWString**. In all cases, the property value is automatically converted to **string**.

GetTypeData function

```
function GetTypeData(TypeInfo: PTypeInfo): PTypeData;
```

Returns a pointer to a type's **TTypeData** record, given its **PTypeInfo** pointer.

GetVariantProp function

```
function GetVariantProp(Instance: TObject; PropInfo: PPropInfo):
    Variant; overload;
function GetVariantProp(Instance: TObject; const PropName: string):
    Variant; overload;
```

Gets the value of a **Variant**-type property.

IsPublishedProp function

```
function IsPublishedProp(Instance: TObject; const PropName: string):
    Boolean; overload;
function IsPublishedProp(AClass: TClass; const PropName: string):
    Boolean; overload;
```

Returns True if the class has a published property of the given name.

IsStoredProp function

```
function IsStoredProp(Instance: TObject; PropInfo: PPropInfo):
    Boolean; overload;
function IsStoredProp(Instance: TObject; const PropName: string):
    Boolean; overload;
```

Returns the value of the **stored** directive. If the **stored** directive is a method, **IsStoredProp** calls the method; if it is a field, the field's value is returned.

PropIsType function

```
function PropIsType(Instance: TObject; const PropName: string;
   TypeKind: TTypeKind): Boolean; overload;
function PropIsType(AClass: TClass; const PropName: string;
   TypeKind: TTypeKind): Boolean; overload;
```

Returns True if the named property exists and has the given type.

PropType function

```
function PropType(Instance: TObject; const PropName: string):
   TTypeKind; overload;
function PropType(AClass: TClass; const PropName: string):
   TTypeKind; overload;
```

Returns the type kind of a published property or raises an **EPropertyError** exception if the class does not have a property with the given name.

SetEnumProp procedure

```
procedure SetEnumProp(Instance: TObject; PropInfo: PPropInfo;
   const Value: string); overload;
procedure SetEnumProp(Instance: TObject; const PropName: string;
   const Value: string); overload;
```

Sets the value of an enumerated-type property, given the name of an enumerated literal. If the **Value** is not the name of an enumerated literal, **SetEnumProp** raises the **EPropertyConvertError** exception. If you have the ordinal value instead of the literal name, call **SetOrdProp**.

SetFloatProp procedure

```
procedure SetFloatProp(Instance: TObject; PropInfo: PPropInfo;
   Value: Extended); overload;
procedure SetFloatProp(Instance: TObject; const PropName: string;
   Value: Extended); overload;
```

Sets the value of a property with a floating-point type.

SetInt64Prop procedure

```
procedure SetInt64Prop(Instance: TObject; PropInfo: PPropInfo;
   const Value: Int64); overload;
procedure SetInt64Prop(Instance: TObject; const PropName: string;
   const Value: Int64); overload;
```

Sets the value of a property whose type is **Int64** or a subrange that is larger than 32 bits.

SetMethodProp procedure

```
procedure SetMethodProp(Instance: TObject; PropInfo: PPropInfo;
   const Value: TMethod); overload;
procedure SetMethodProp(Instance: TObject; const PropName: string;
   const Value: TMethod); overload;
```

Sets the value of an event property.

SetObjectProp procedure

```
procedure SetObjectProp(Instance: TObject; PropInfo: PPropInfo;
   Value: TObject); overload;
procedure SetObjectProp(Instance: TObject; const PropName: string;
   Value: TObject); overload;
```

Sets the value of a class-type property. If `Value` is not of the correct type for the property, `SetObjectProp` silently ignores the attempt to set the property value.

SetOrdProp procedure
```
procedure SetOrdProp(Instance: TObject; PropInfo: PPropInfo;
  Value: Longint); overload;
procedure SetOrdProp(Instance: TObject; const PropName: string;
  Value: Longint); overload;
```

Sets the value of any ordinal-type property, including sets, objects, characters, and enumerated or integer properties.

SetPropValue procedure
```
procedure SetPropValue(Instance: TObject; const PropName: string;
  const Value: Variant);
```

Sets the value of a property from a `Variant`. `SetPropValue` must be able to convert the `Variant` value to the appropriate type for the property, or else it raises an `EPropertyConvertError` exception.

SetSetProp procedure
```
procedure SetSetProp(Instance: TObject; PropInfo: PPropInfo;
  const Value: string); overload;
procedure SetSetProp(Instance: TObject; const PropName: string;
  const Value: string); overload;
```

Sets the value of a set-type property by interpreting a string as a list of enumerated literals. `SetSetProp` recognizes the format that `GetSetProp` returns. If the format of `Value` is not valid, `SetSetProp` raises an `EPropertyConvertError` exception.

SetStrProp procedure
```
procedure SetStrProp(Instance: TObject; PropInfo: PPropInfo;
  const Value: string); overload;
procedure SetStrProp(Instance: TObject; const PropName: string;
  const Value: string); overload;
```

Sets the value of a string-type property. The property type can be `tkString`, `tkLString`, or `tkWString`.

SetVariantProp procedure
```
procedure SetVariantProp(Instance: TObject; PropInfo: PPropInfo;
  const Value: Variant); overload;
procedure SetVariantProp(Instance: TObject; const PropName: string;
  const Value: Variant); overload;
```

Sets the value of a `Variant`-type property.

Virtual and Dynamic Methods

The VMT stores a list of pointers for virtual methods and another table in the VMT, which this section refers to as the dynamic method table, lists both dynamic methods and message handlers.

The compiler generates a small negative number for each dynamic method. This negative number is just like a message number for a message handler. To avoid conflicts with message handlers, the compiler does not let you compile a message handler whose message number falls into the range of dynamic method numbers. Once the compiler has done its work, though, any distinction between dynamic methods and message handlers is lost. They both sit in the same table and nothing indicates whether one entry is for a dynamic method and another is for a message handler.

The dynamic method table lists only the dynamic methods and message handlers that a class declares; it does not include any methods inherited from ancestor classes. The dynamic method table starts with a 2-byte count of the number of dynamic methods and message handlers, followed by a list of 2-byte method numbers, followed by a list of 4-byte method pointers. The dynamic method table is organized in this fashion (instead of having a list of records, where each record has a method number and pointer) to speed up searching for a method number. Example 3-6 shows the logical layout of a dynamic method table. As with the other tables, you cannot compile this record, because it is not real Pascal, just a description of what a dynamic method table looks like.

Example 3-6: The Layout of a Dynamic Method Table

```
type
  TDynMethodTable = packed record
    Count: Word;
    Indexes: packed array[1..Count] of SmallInt;
    Addresses: packed array[1..Count] of Pointer;
  end;
```

Dispatching a message or calling a dynamic method requires a lookup of the method or message number in the **Indexes** array. The table is not sorted and the lookup is linear. Once a match is found, the method at the corresponding address is invoked. If the method number is not found, the search continues with the immediate base class.

 The only time you should even consider using dynamic methods is when all of the following conditions apply:

— You are creating a large framework of hundreds of classes.

— You need to declare many virtual methods in the classes near the root of the inheritance tree.

— Those methods will rarely be overridden in derived classes.

— Those methods never need to be called when speed is important.

The tradeoff between virtual and dynamic methods is that virtual method tables include all inherited virtual methods, so they are potentially large. Dynamic method tables do not list inherited methods, so they can be smaller. On the other hand, calling a virtual method is a fast index into a table, but calling a dynamic method requires a search through one or more tables.

In the VCL, dynamic methods are used only for methods that are called in response to user interactions. Thus, the slower lookup for dynamic methods will not impact overall performance. Also, the dynamic methods are usually declared in the root classes, such as TControl.

If you do not have a large class hierarchy, you will usually get smaller and faster code by using virtual methods instead of dynamic methods. After all, dynamic methods must store the method number in addition to the method address. Unless you have enough derived classes that do not override the dynamic method, the dynamic method table will end up requiring more memory than the virtual method table.

Initialization and Finalization

When Delphi constructs an object, it automatically initializes strings, dynamic arrays, interfaces, and Variants. When the object is destroyed, Delphi must decrement the reference counts for strings, interfaces, dynamic arrays, and free Variants and wide strings. To keep track of this information, Delphi uses initialization records as part of a class's RTTI. In fact, every record and array that requires finalization has an associated initialization record, but the compiler hides these records. The only ones you have access to are those associated with an object's fields.

A VMT points to an initialization table. The table contains a list of initialization records. Because arrays and records can be nested, each initialization record contains a pointer to another initialization table, which can contain initialization records, and so on. An initialization table uses a TTypeKind field to keep track of whether it is initializing a string, a record, an array, etc.

An initialization table begins with the type kind (1 byte), followed by the type name as a short string, a 4-byte size of the data being initialized, a 4-byte count for initialization records, and then an array of zero or more initialization records. An initialization record is just a pointer to a nested initialization table, followed by a 4-byte offset for the field that must be initialized. Example 3-7 shows the logical layout of the initialization table and record, but the declarations depict the logical layout without being true Pascal code.

Example 3-7: The Layout of the Initialization Table and Record

```
type
  { Initialization/finalization record }
  PInitTable = ^TInitTable;
  TInitRecord = packed record
    InitTable: ^PInitTable;
    Offset: LongWord;          // Offset of field in object
  end;
  { Initialization/finalization table }
  TInitTable = packed record
  {$MinEnumSize 1} // Ensure that TypeKind takes up 1 byte.
    TypeKind: TTypeKind;
    TypeName: packed ShortString;
    DataSize: LongWord;
```

```
  Count: LongWord;
  // If TypeKind=tkArray, Count is the array size, but InitRecords
  // has only one element; if the type kind is tkRecord, Count is the
  // number of record members, and InitRecords[] has a
  // record for each member. For all other types, Count=0.
  InitRecords: array[1..Count] of TInitRecord;
end;
```

The master `TInitRecord` for the class has an empty type name and zero data size. The type kind is always `tkRecord`. The `Count` is the number of fields that need initialization, and the `InitRecords` array contains a `TInitRecord` for each such member. Each initialization record points to an initialization table that contains the type kind and type name for the associated member. This organization seems a little strange, but you can soon grow accustomed to it.

Most types do not need initialization or finalization, but the following types do:

tkArray

> `DataSize` is the size of each array element, and the `Count` is the number of elements in the array. Every array element is the same, so the `InitRecords` array contains one `TInitRecord` that represents all the array elements. The `Offset` in the `TInitRecord` has no meaningful value.

tkDynArray

> `DataSize` and `Count` are not meaningful. Delphi decreases the reference count of the array and frees the array's memory if the reference count becomes zero.

tkInterface

> `DataSize` and `Count` are not meaningful. Delphi calls the `_Release` method, which frees the interface object if the reference count becomes zero.

tkLString

> `DataSize` and `Count` are not meaningful. Delphi decreases the reference count of the string and frees the string's memory if the reference count becomes zero.

tkRecord

> `DataSize` is the size of the record, and the `Count` is the number of members that need initialization. The `InitRecords` array contains a `TInitRecord` for each member that needs initialization.

tkVariant

> `DataSize` and `Count` are not meaningful. Delphi frees any memory associated with the `Variant` data.

tkWString

> `DataSize` and `Count` are not meaningful. Delphi frees the string.

Runtime Type Information

Automated Methods

The automated section of a class declaration is now obsolete because it is easier to create a COM automation server with Delphi's type library editor, using interfaces. Nonetheless, the compiler currently supports automated declarations for backward compatibility. A future version of the compiler might drop support for automated declarations.

The `OleAuto` unit tells you the details of the automated method table: The table starts with a 2-byte count, followed by a list of automation records. Each record has a 4-byte dispid (dispatch identifier), a pointer to a short string method name, 4-bytes of flags, a pointer to a list of parameters, and a code pointer. The parameter list starts with a 1-byte return type, followed by a 1-byte count of parameters, and ends with a list of 1-byte parameter types. The parameter names are not stored. Example 3-8 shows the declarations for the automated method table.

Example 3-8: The Layout of the Automated Method Table

```
const
  { Parameter type masks }
  atTypeMask = $7F;
  varStrArg  = $48;
  atByRef    = $80;
  MaxAutoEntries = 4095;
  MaxAutoParams = 255;

type
  TVmtAutoType = Byte;
  { Automation entry parameter list }
  PAutoParamList = ^TAutoParamList;
  TAutoParamList = packed record
    ReturnType: TVmtAutoType;
    Count: Byte;
    Types: array[1..Count] of TVmtAutoType;
  end;
  { Automation table entry }
  PAutoEntry = ^TAutoEntry;
  TAutoEntry = packed record
    DispID: LongInt;
    Name: PShortString;
    Flags: LongInt; { Lower byte contains flags }
    Params: PAutoParamList;
    Address: Pointer;
  end;

  { Automation table layout }
  PAutoTable = ^TAutoTable;
  TAutoTable = packed record
    Count: LongInt;
    Entries: array[1..Count] of TAutoEntry;
  end;
```

Interfaces

Any class can implement any number of interfaces. The compiler stores a table of interfaces as part of the class's RTTI. The VMT points to the table of interfaces, which starts with a 4-byte count, followed by a list of interface records. Each interface record contains the GUID, a pointer to the interface's VMT, the offset to the interface's hidden field, and a pointer to a property that implements the interface with the `implements` directive. If the offset is zero, the interface property (called `ImplGetter`) must be non-nil, and if the offset is not zero, `ImplGetter` must be nil. The interface property can be a reference to a field, a virtual method, or a static method, following the conventions of a property reader (which is described earlier in this chapter, under "Published Properties"). When an object is constructed, Delphi automatically checks all the interfaces, and for each interface with a non-zero `IOffset`, the field at that offset is set to the interface's `VTable` (a pointer to its VMT). Delphi defines the types for the interface table, unlike the other RTTI tables, in the `System` unit. These types are shown in Example 3-9.

Example 3-9: Type Declarations for the Interface Table

```
type
  PInterfaceEntry = ^TInterfaceEntry;
  TInterfaceEntry = record
    IID: TGUID;
    VTable: Pointer;
    IOffset: Integer;
    ImplGetter: Integer;
  end;

  PInterfaceTable = ^TInterfaceTable;
  TInterfaceTable = record
    EntryCount: Integer;
    // Declare the type with the largest possible size,
    // but the true size of the array is EntryCount elements.
    Entries: array[0..9999] of TInterfaceEntry;
  end;
```

`TObject` implements several methods for accessing the interface table. See Chapter 5 for the details of the `GetInterface`, `GetInterfaceEntry`, and `GetInterfaceTable` methods.

Exploring RTTI

This chapter introduces you to a class's virtual method table and runtime type information. To better understand how Delphi stores and uses RTTI, you should explore the tables on your own. The code that accompanies this book on the O'Reilly web site includes the *Vmt.exe* program. The `VmtInfo` unit defines a collection of interfaces that exposes the structure of all the RTTI tables. The `VmtImpl` unit defines classes that implement these interfaces. You can read the source code for the `VmtImpl` unit or just explore the *Vmt* program. See the `VmtForm` unit to add types that you want to explore, or to change the type declarations.

You can also use the VmtInfo interfaces in your own programs when you need access to the RTTI tables. For example, you might write your own object persistence library where you need access to a field class table to map class names to class references.

The interfaces are self-explanatory. Because they use Delphi's automatic reference counting, you don't need to worry about memory management, either. To create an interface, call one of the following functions:

```
function GetVmtInfo(ClassRef: TClass): IVmtInfo; overload;
function GetVmtInfo(ObjectRef: TObject): IVmtInfo; overload;
function GetTypeInfo(TypeInfo: PTypeInfo): ITypeInfo;
```

Use the IVmtInfo interface and its related interfaces to examine and explore the rich world of Delphi's runtime type information. For example, take a look at the TFont class, shown in Example 3-10.

Example 3-10: Declaration of the TFont Class

```
type
  TFont = class(TGraphicsObject)
  private
    FColor: TColor;
    FPixelsPerInch: Integer;
    FNotify: IChangeNotifier;
    procedure GetData(var FontData: TFontData);
    procedure SetData(const FontData: TFontData);
  protected
    procedure Changed; override;
    function GetHandle: HFont;
    function GetHeight: Integer;
    function GetName: TFontName;
    function GetPitch: TFontPitch;
    function GetSize: Integer;
    function GetStyle: TFontStyles;
    function GetCharset: TFontCharset;
    procedure SetColor(Value: TColor);
    procedure SetHandle(Value: HFont);
    procedure SetHeight(Value: Integer);
    procedure SetName(const Value: TFontName);
    procedure SetPitch(Value: TFontPitch);
    procedure SetSize(Value: Integer);
    procedure SetStyle(Value: TFontStyles);
    procedure SetCharset(Value: TFontCharset);
  public
    constructor Create;
    destructor Destroy; override;
    procedure Assign(Source: TPersistent); override;
    property FontAdapter: IChangeNotifier read FNotify write FNotify;
    property Handle: HFont read GetHandle write SetHandle;
    property PixelsPerInch: Integer read FPixelsPerInch
        write FPixelsPerInch;
  published
    property Charset: TFontCharset read GetCharset write SetCharset;
    property Color: TColor read FColor write SetColor;
```

Example 3-10: Declaration of the TFont Class (continued)

```
property Height: Integer read GetHeight write SetHeight;
property Name: TFontName read GetName write SetName;
property Pitch: TFontPitch read GetPitch write SetPitch
    default fpDefault;
property Size: Integer read GetSize write SetSize stored False;
property Style: TFontStyles read GetStyle write SetStyle;
end;
```

Notice that one field is of type `IChangeNotifier`. The `Changed` method is declared as dynamic in the base class, `TGraphicsObject`. `TFont` has no published fields or methods, but has several published properties. Example 3-11 shows the VMT and type information for the `TFont` class. You can see that the dynamic method table has one entry for `Changed`. The `Size` property is not stored, but the other published properties are. The *Vmt.exe* program can show you the same kind of information for almost any class or type.

Example 3-11: Runtime Type Information

```
Vmt: 40030E78
  Destroy: 4003282C
  FreeInstance: 400039D8
  NewInstance: 400039C4
  DefaultHandler: 40003CAC
  Dispatch: 40003CB8
  BeforeDestruction: 40003CB4
  AfterConstruction: 40003CB0
  SafeCallException: 40003CA4
  Parent: 40030DA4 (TGraphicsObject)
  InstanceSize: 32
  ClassName: 'TFont'
  Dynamic Method Table: 40030EE2
    Count: 1
    40032854 (-3)
  Method Table: 00000000
  Field Table: 00000000
  TypeInfo: 40030EF4
  InitTable: 40030ED0
  TypeName:
  TypeKind: tkRecord
  DataOffset: 0
  Count: 1
  RecordSize: 0
    [1]
    InitTable: 40030E44
    TypeName: IChangeNotifier
    TypeKind: tkInterface
    DataOffset: 28
  AutoTable: 00000000
  IntfTable: 00000000

type TFontCharset = 0..255; // otUByte
type TColor = -2147483648..2147483647; // otSLong
```

Runtime Type
Information

Example 3-11: Runtime Type Information (continued)

```
type Integer = -2147483648..2147483647; // otSLong
type TFontName; // tkLString
type TFontPitch = (fpDefault, fpVariable, fpFixed); // otUByte
type TFontStyle = (fsBold, fsItalic, fsUnderline, fsStrikeOut);
type TFontStyles = set of TFontStyle; // otUByte
type TObject = class // unit 'System'
end;
type TPersistent = class(TObject) // unit 'Classes'
end;
type TGraphicsObject = class(TPersistent) // unit 'Graphics'
end;
type TFont = class(TGraphicsObject) // unit 'Graphics'
published
  property Charset: TFontCharset read (static method 40032CD4)
    write (static method 40032CDC) nodefault stored True; // index 0
  property Color: TColor read (field 20) write (static method 400329AC)
    nodefault stored True; // index 1
  property Height: Integer read (static method 40032B8C)
    write (static method 40032B94) nodefault stored True; // index 2
  property Name: TFontName read (static method 40032BBC)
    write (static method 40032BD4) nodefault stored True; // index 3
  property Pitch: TFontPitch read (static method 40032CA4)
    write (static method 40032CAC) default 0 stored True; // index 4
  property Size: Integer read (static method 40032C30)
    write (static method 40032C4C) nodefault stored False; // index 5
  property Style: TFontStyles read (static method 40032C6C)
    write (static method 40032C78) nodefault stored True; // index 6
end;
```

CHAPTER 4

Concurrent Programming

The future of programming is concurrent programming. Not too long ago, sequential, command-line programming gave way to graphical, event-driven programming, and now single-threaded programming is yielding to multithreaded programming.

Whether you are writing a web server that must handle many clients simultaneously or writing an end-user application such as a word processor, concurrent programming is for you. Perhaps the word processor checks for spelling errors while the user types. Maybe it can print a file in the background while the user continues to edit. Users expect more today from their applications, and only concurrent programming can deliver the necessary power and flexibility.

Delphi Pascal includes features to support concurrent programming—not as much support as you find in languages such as Ada, but more than in most traditional programming languages. In addition to the language features, you can use the Windows API and its semaphores, threads, processes, pipes, shared memory, and so on. This chapter describes the features that are unique to Delphi Pascal and explains how to use Delphi effectively to write concurrent programs. If you want more information about the Windows API and the details of how Windows handles threads, processes, semaphores, and so on, consult a book on Windows programming, such as *Inside Windows NT*, second edition, by David Solomon (Microsoft Press, 1998).

Threads and Processes

This section provides an overview of multithreaded programming in Windows. If you are already familiar with threads and processes in Windows, you can skip this section and continue with the next section, "The TThread Class."

A *thread* is a flow of control in a program. A program can have many threads, each with its own stack, its own copy of the processor's registers, and related information. On a multiprocessor system, each processor can run a separate thread. On a uniprocessor system, Windows creates the illusion that threads are running concurrently, though only one thread at a time gets to run.

A *process* is a collection of threads all running in a single address space. Every process has at least one thread, called the *main* thread. Threads in the same process can share resources such as open files and can access any valid memory address in the process's address space. You can think of a process as an instance of an application (plus any DLLs that the application loads).

Threads in a process can communicate easily because they can share variables. Critical sections protect threads from stepping on each others' toes when they access shared variables. (Read the section "Synchronizing Threads" later in this chapter, for details about critical sections.)

You can send a Windows message to a particular thread, in which case the receiving thread must have a message loop to handle the message. In most cases, you will find it simpler to let the main thread handle all Windows messages, but feel free to write your own message loop for any thread that needs it.

Separate processes can communicate in a variety of ways, such as messages, mutexes (short for mutual exclusions), semaphores, events, memory-mapped files, sockets, pipes, DCOM, CORBA, and so on. Most likely, you will use a combination of methods. Separate processes do not share ordinary memory, and you cannot call a function or procedure from one process to another, although several remote procedure call mechanisms exist, such as DCOM and CORBA. Read more about processes and how they communicate in the section "Processes" later in this chapter.

Delphi has built-in support for multithreaded programming—writing applications and DLLs that work with multiple threads in a process. Whether you work with threads or processes, you have the full Windows API at your disposal.

In a multithreaded application or library, you must be sure that the global variable IsMultiThread is True. Most applications do this automatically by calling BeginThread or using the TThread class. If you write a DLL that might be called from a multithreaded application, though, you might need to set IsMultiThread to True manually.

Scheduling and States

Windows schedules threads according to their priorities. Higher priority threads run before lower priority threads. At the same priority, Windows schedules threads so that each thread gets a fair chance to run. Windows can stop a running thread (called *preempting* the thread) to give another thread a chance to run. Windows defines several different states for threads, but they fall into one of three categories:

Running
> A thread is running when it is active on a processor. A system can have as many running threads as it has processors—one thread per processor. A thread remains in the running state until it blocks because it must wait for some operation (such as the completion of I/O). Windows then preempts the thread to allow another thread to run, or the thread suspends itself.

Ready

> A thread is ready to run if it is not running and is not blocked. A thread that is ready can preempt a running thread at the same priority, but not a thread at a higher priority.

Blocked

> A thread is blocked if it is waiting for something: an I/O or similar operation to complete, access to a shared resource, and so on. You can explicitly block a thread by *suspending* it. A suspended thread will wait forever until you *resume* it.

The essence of writing multithreaded programming is knowing when to block a thread and when to unblock it, and how to write your program so its threads spend as little time as possible in the blocked state and as much time as possible in the running state.

If you have many threads that are ready (but not running), that means you might have a performance problem. The processor is not able to keep up with the threads that are ready to run. Perhaps your application is creating too many active threads, or the problem might simply be one of resources: the processor is too slow or you need to switch to a multiprocessor system. Resolving resource problems is beyond the scope of this book—read almost any book on Windows NT administration to learn more about analyzing and handling performance issues.

Synchronizing Threads

The biggest concern in multithreaded programming is preserving data integrity. Threads that access a common variable can step on each others' toes. Example 4-1 shows a simple class that maintains a global counter. If two threads try to increment the counter at the same time, it's possible for the counter to get the wrong value. Figure 4-1 illustrates this problem: Counter starts at 0 and should become 3 after creating three TCounter objects. The three threads compete for the shared variable, and as a result, Counter ends up with the incorrect value of 1. This is known as a *race condition* because each thread races to finish its job before a different thread steps in and bungles things.

Example 4-1: Simple Counter Class

```
var
  Counter: Integer;
type
  TCounter = class
  public
    constructor Create;
    function GetCounter: Integer;
  end;

constructor TCounter.Create;
begin
  inherited;
  Counter := Counter + 1;
end;
```

Example 4-1: Simple Counter Class (continued)

```
function TCounter.GetCounter: Integer;
begin
  Result := Counter;
end;
```

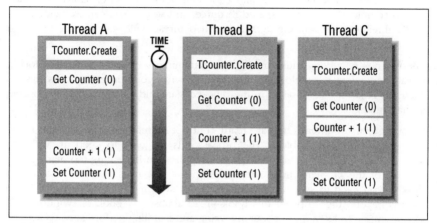

Figure 4-1: A race condition results in the wrong value of Counter

This example uses an integer counter because integers are simple. Reading an integer value is an *atomic* operation, that is, the operation cannot be interrupted by another thread. If the counter were, say, a Variant, reading its value involves multiple instructions, and another thread can interrupt at any time, so even reading the Variant counter is not safe in a multithreaded program without some way to limit access to one thread at a time

Critical sections

To preserve the integrity of the Counter variable, every thread must cooperate and agree that only one thread at a time should change the variable's value. Other threads can look at the variable and get its value, but when a thread wants to change the value, it must prevent all other threads from also trying to change the variable's value. The standard technique for ensuring single-thread access is a *critical section.*

A critical section is a region of code that is reserved for single-thread access. When one thread enters a critical section, all other threads are kept out until the first thread leaves the critical section. While the first thread is in the critical section, all other threads can continue to run normally unless they also want to enter the critical section. Any other thread that tries to enter the critical section blocks and waits until the first thread is done and leaves the critical section. Then the next thread gets to enter the critical section. The Windows API defines several functions to create and use a critical section, as shown in Example 4-2.

The new TCounter class is *thread-safe*, that is, you can safely share an object of that type in multiple threads. Most Delphi classes are not thread-safe, so you

Example 4-2: Counter Using a Critical Section

```
var
  Counter: Integer;
  CriticalSection: TRtlCriticalSection;

type
  TCounter = class
  public
    constructor Create;
    function GetCounter: Integer;
  end;

constructor TCounter.Create;
begin
  inherited;
  EnterCriticalSection(CriticalSection);
  try
    Counter := Counter + 1;
  finally
    LeaveCriticalSection(CriticalSection);
  end;
end;

function TCounter.GetCounter: Integer;
begin
  // Does not need a critical section because integers
  // are atomic.
  Result := Counter;
end;

initialization
  InitializeCriticalSection(CriticalSection);
finalization
  DeleteCriticalSection(CriticalSection);
end.
```

cannot share a single object in multiple threads, at least, not without using critical sections to protect the object's internal state.

One advantage of object-oriented programming is that you often don't need a thread-safe class. If each thread creates and uses its own instance of the class, the threads avoid stepping on each others' data. Thus, for example, you can create and use TList and other objects within a thread. The only time you need to be careful is when you share a single TList object among multiple threads.

Because threads wait for a critical section to be released, you should keep the work done in a critical section to a minimum. Otherwise, threads are waiting needlessly for the critical section to be released.

Multiple simultaneous readers

In the TCounter class, any thread can safely examine the counter at any time because the Counter variable is atomic. The critical section affects only threads that try to change the counter. If the variable you want to access is not atomic, you must protect reads and writes, but a critical section is not the proper tool. Instead, use the TMultiReadExclusiveWriteSynchronizer class, which is declared in the SysUtils unit. The unwieldy name is descriptive: it is like a critical section, but it allows many threads to have read-only access to the critical region. If any thread wants write access, it must wait until all other threads are done reading the data. Complete details on this class are in Appendix B, *The SysUtils Unit*.

Exceptions

Exceptions in a thread cause the application to terminate, so you should catch exceptions in the thread and find another way to inform the application's main thread about the exception. If you just want the exception message, you can catch the exception, get the message, and pass the message string to the main thread so it can display the message in a dialog box, for example.

If you want the main thread to receive the actual exception object, you need to do a little more work. The problem is that when a try-except block finishes handling an exception, Delphi automatically frees the exception object. You need to write your exception handler so it intercepts the exception object, hands it off to the main thread, and prevents Delphi from freeing the object prematurely. Modify the exception frame on the runtime stack to trick Delphi and prevent it from freeing the exception object. Example 4-3 shows one approach, where a thread procedure wraps a try-except block around the thread's main code block. The parameter passed to the thread function is a pointer to an object reference where the function can store an exception object or nil if the thread function completes successfully.

Example 4-3: Catching an Exception in a Thread

```
type
  PObject = ^TObject;
  PRaiseFrame = ^TRaiseFrame;
  TRaiseFrame = record
    NextFrame: PRaiseFrame;
    ExceptAddr: Pointer;
    ExceptObject: TObject;
    ExceptionRecord: PExceptionRecord;
  end;

// ThreadFunc catches exceptions and stores them in Param^, or nil
// if the thread does not raise any exceptions.
function ThreadFunc(Param: Pointer): Integer;
var
  RaiseFrame: PRaiseFrame;
begin
  Result := 0;
  PObject(Param)^ := nil;
  try
    DoTheThreadsRealWorkHere;
  except
```

Example 4-3: Catching an Exception in a Thread (continued)

```
    // RaiseList is nil if there is no exception; otherwise, it
    // points to a TExceptionFrame record.
    RaiseFrame := RaiseList;
    if RaiseFrame <> nil then
    begin
      // When the thread raises an exception, store the exception
      // object in the parameter's object reference. Then set the
      // object reference to nil in the exception frame, so Delphi
      // does not free the exception object prematurely.
      PObject(Param)^ := RaiseFrame.ExceptObject;
      RaiseFrame.ExceptObject := nil;
    end;
  end;
end;
```

Deadlock

Deadlock occurs when threads wait endlessly for each other. Thread A waits for thread B, and thread B waits for thread A, and neither thread accomplishes anything. Whenever you have multiple threads, you have the possibility of creating a deadlock situation. In a complex program, it can be difficult to detect a potential deadlock in your code, and testing is an unreliable technique for discovering deadlock. Your best option is to prevent deadlock from ever occurring by taking preventive measures when you design and implement the program.

A common source of deadlock is when a thread must wait for multiple resources. For example, an application might have two global variables, and each one has its own critical section. A thread might need to change both variables and so it tries to enter both critical sections. This can cause deadlock if another thread also wants to enter both critical sections, as depicted in Figure 4-2.

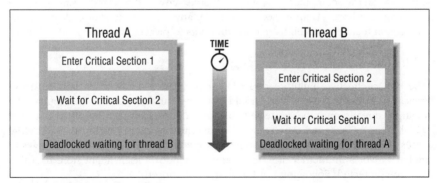

Figure 4-2: Deadlock prevents either thread from continuing

You can easily avoid deadlock in this situation by ensuring that both threads wait for the critical sections in the same order. When thread A enters critical section 1, it prevents thread B from entering the critical section, so thread A can proceed to enter critical section 2. Once thread A is finished with both critical sections, thread

B can enter critical section 1 and then critical section 2. Figure 4-3 illustrates how the two threads can cooperate to avoid deadlock.

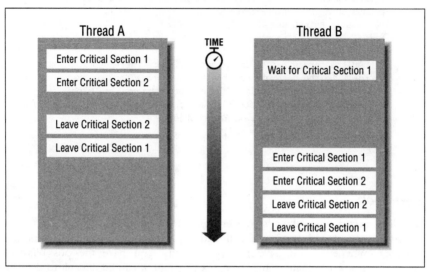

Figure 4-3: Avoiding deadlock by reordering critical sections

Another way to prevent deadlock when dealing with multiple resources is to make sure a thread gets all its required resources or none of them. If a thread needs exclusive access to two files, for example, it must be able to open both files. If thread A opens file 1, but cannot open file 2 because thread B owns file 2, then thread A closes file 1 and waits until both files are free.

Deadlock—causes and prevention—is a standard topic in computer science curricula. Many computer science textbooks cover the classic strategies for handling deadlock. Delphi does not have any special deadlock detection or prevention features, so you have only your wits to protect you.

Multithreaded Programming

The key to effective multithreaded programming is to know when you must use critical sections, and when you should not. Any variable that can be changed by multiple threads must be protected, but you don't always know when a global variable can be changed. Any composite data must be protected for read and write access. Something as simple as reading a property value might result in changes to global variables in another unit, for example. Windows itself might store data that must be protected. Following is a list of areas of concern:

- Any call to the Windows GDI (graphics device interface) must be protected. Usually, you will use Delphi's VCL instead of calling the Windows API directly.

- Some references to a VCL component or control must be protected. Each release of Delphi increases the thread safety of the VCL, and in Delphi 5, most of the VCL is thread-safe. Of course, you cannot modify a VCL object from multiple threads, and any VCL property or method that maps to the Windows GDI is not thread-safe. As a rule, anything visual is not thread-safe, but behind-the-scenes work is usually safe. If you aren't sure whether a property or method is safe, assume it isn't.

- Reading long strings and dynamic arrays is thread-safe, but writing is not. Referring to a string or dynamic array might change the reference count, but Delphi protects the reference count to ensure thread safety. When changing a string or dynamic array, though, you should use a critical section, just as you would when changing any other variable. (Note that Delphi 4 and earlier did not protected strings and dynamic arrays this way.)

- Allocating memory (with GetMem or New) and freeing memory (with FreeMem and Dispose) is thread-safe. Delphi automatically protects its memory allocator for use in multiple threads (if IsMultiThread is True, which is one reason to stick with Delphi's BeginThread function instead of using the Windows API CreateThread function).

- Creating or freeing an object is thread-safe only if the constructor and destructor are thread-safe. The memory-management aspect of creating and destroying objects is thread-safe, but the rest of the work in a constructor or destructor is up to the programmer. Unless you know that a class is thread-safe, assume it isn't. Creating a VCL control, for example, is not thread-safe. Creating a TList or TStringList object is thread-safe.

When you need to call a Windows GDI function or access the VCL, instead of using a critical section, Delphi provides another mechanism that works better: the TThread class and its Synchronize method, which you can read about in the next section.

The TThread Class

The easiest way to create a multithreaded application in Delphi is to write a thread class that inherits from TThread. The TThread class is not part of the Delphi language, but is declared in the Classes unit. This section describes the class because it is so important in Delphi programming.

Override the Execute method to perform the thread's work. When Execute finishes, the thread finishes. Any thread can create any other thread simply by creating an instance of the custom thread class. Each instance of the class runs as a separate thread, with its own stack.

When you need to protect a VCL access or call to the Windows GDI, you can use the Synchronize method. This method takes a procedure as an argument and calls that procedure in a thread-safe manner. The procedure takes no arguments. Synchronize suspends the current thread and has the main thread call the procedure. When the procedure finishes, control returns to the current thread. Because all calls to Synchronize are handled by the main thread, they are protected against race conditions. If multiple threads call Synchronize at the same time, they must wait in line, and one thread at a time gets access to the main thread. This process is often called *serializing* because parallel method calls are changed to serial method calls.

When writing the synchronized procedure, remember that it is called from the main thread, so if you need to know the true thread ID, read the `ThreadID` property instead of calling the Windows API `GetCurrentThreadID` function.

For example, suppose you want to write a text editor that can print in the background. That is, the user asks to print a file, and the program copies the file's contents (to avoid race conditions when the user edits the file while the print operation is still active) and starts a background thread that formats the file and queues it to the printer.

Printing a file involves the VCL, so you must take care to synchronize every VCL access. At first this seems problematic, because almost everything the thread does accesses the VCL's `Printer` object. Upon closer inspection, you can see that you have several ways to reduce the interaction with the VCL.

The first step is to copy some information from the `Printer` object to the thread's local fields. For example, the thread keeps a copy of the printer's resolution, so the thread does not have to ask the `Printer` object for that information. The next step is to break down the task of printing a file into basic steps, and to isolate the steps that involve the VCL. Printing a file involves the following steps:

1. Start the print job.
2. Initialize the margins, page number, and page position.
3. If this is a new page, print the page header and footer.
4. Print a line of text and increment the page position.
5. If the page position is past the end of the page, start a new page.
6. If there is no more text, end the print job; otherwise go back to step 2.

The basic operations that must be synchronized with the VCL are:

- Start the print job.
- Print a header.
- Print a footer.
- Print a line of text.
- Start a new page.
- End the print job.

Each synchronized operation needs a parameterless procedure, so any information these procedures need must be stored as fields in the thread class. The resulting class is shown in Example 4-4.

Example 4-4: Declaration of the TPrintThread Class

```
type
  TPrintThread = class(TThread)
  private
    fText: TStrings;            // fields to support properties
    fHeader: string;
    fExceptionMessage: string;
    fPrinter: TPrinter;
```

Example 4-4: Declaration of the TPrintThread Class (continued)

```
    PixelsPerInch: Integer;   // local storage for synchronized thunks
    LineHeight: Integer;
    YPos: Integer;
    Line: string;
    LeftMargin, TopMargin: Integer;
    PageNumber: Integer;
  protected
    procedure Execute; override;
    procedure PrintText;

    procedure EndPrinting;        // procedures for Synchronize
    procedure PrintLine;
    procedure PrintHeader;
    procedure PrintFooter;
    procedure StartPrinting;
    procedure StartNewPage;

    property Header: string read fHeader;
    property Printer: TPrinter read fPrinter;
    property Text: TStrings read fText;
  public
    constructor Create(const Text, Header: string;
                        OnTerminate: TNotifyEvent);
    destructor Destroy; override;
    property ExceptionMessage: string read fExceptionMessage;
  end;
```

If the print job raises an exception, the exception message is stored as the **ExceptionMessage** property. The main thread can test this property when the thread finishes.

The **TThread.Create** constructor takes a **Boolean** argument: if it is True, the thread is initially suspended until you explicitly resume it. If the argument is False, the thread starts immediately. Whenever you override the constructor, you usually want to pass True to the inherited constructor. Complete the initialization your constructor requires, and as the last step, call **Resume**. By starting the thread in a suspended state, you avoid race conditions where the thread might start working before your constructor is finished initializing the thread's necessary fields. Example 4-5 shows the **TPrintThread.Create** constructor.

Example 4-5: Constructing a TPrintThread Object

```
constructor TPrintThread.Create(const Text, Header: string;
                                 OnTerminate: TNotifyEvent);
begin
  inherited Create(True);
  fHeader := Header;

  // Save the text as lines, so they are easier to print.
  fText := TStringList.Create;
  fText.Text := Text;
```

Example 4-5: Constructing a TPrintThread Object (continued)

```
  // Save a reference to the current printer in case
  // the user prints a different file to a different printer.
  fPrinter := Printers.Printer;

  // Save the termination event handler.
  Self.OnTerminate := OnTerminate;

  // The thread will free itself when it terminates.
  FreeOnTerminate := True;

  // Start the thread.
  Resume;
end;
```

The overridden **Execute** method calls **PrintText** to do the real work, but it wraps the call to **PrintText** in an exception handler. If printing raises an exception, the exception message is saved for use by the main thread. The **Execute** method is shown in Example 4-6.

Example 4-6: The Thread's Execute Method

```
// Run the thread.
procedure TPrintThread.Execute;
begin
  try
    PrintText;
  except
    on Ex: Exception do
      fExceptionMessage := Ex.Message;
  end;
end;
```

The **PrintText** method manages the main print loop, calling the synchronized print procedures as needed. The thread manages the bookkeeping details, which do not need to be synchronized, as you can see in Example 4-7.

Example 4-7: The Main Print Loop in PrintText

```
// Print all the text, using the default printer font.
procedure TPrintThread.PrintText;
const
  Leading = 120;  // 120% of the nominal font height
var
  I: Integer;
  NewPage: Boolean;
begin
  Synchronize(StartPrinting);
  try
    LeftMargin := PixelsPerInch;
    TopMargin  := PixelsPerInch;
    YPos := TopMargin;
    NewPage := True;
```

Example 4-7: The Main Print Loop in PrintText (continued)

```
    PageNumber := 1;

    for I := 0 to Text.Count-1 do
    begin
      if NewPage then
      begin
        Synchronize(PrintHeader);
        Synchronize(PrintFooter);
        NewPage := False;
      end;

      // Print the current line.
      Line := Text[I];
      Synchronize(PrintLine);
      YPos := YPos + LineHeight * Leading div 100;

      // Has the printer reached the end of the page?
      if YPos > Printer.PageHeight - TopMargin then
      begin
        if Terminated then
          Printer.Abort;
        if Printer.Aborted then
          Break;
        Synchronize(StartNewPage);
        YPos := TopMargin;
        NewPage := True;
        PageNumber := PageNumber + 1;
      end;
    end;
  finally
    Synchronize(EndPrinting);
  end;
end;
```

PrintText seems to spend a lot of time in synchronized methods, and it does, but it also spends time in its own thread, letting Windows schedule the main thread and the print thread optimally. Each synchronized print method is as small and simple as possible to minimize the amount of time spent in the main thread. Example 4-8 gives examples of these methods, with PrintLine, StartNewPage, and StartPrinting. The remaining methods are similar.

Example 4-8: Synchronized Printing Procedures

```
// Save the printer resolution so the print thread can use that
// information without needing to access the Printer object.
procedure TPrintThread.StartPrinting;
begin
  Printer.BeginDoc;
  PixelsPerInch := Printer.Canvas.Font.PixelsPerInch;
end;
```

Example 4-8: Synchronized Printing Procedures (continued)

```
// Print the current line of text and save the height of the line so
// the work thread can advance the Y position on the page.
procedure TPrintThread.PrintLine;
begin
  Printer.Canvas.TextOut(LeftMargin, YPos, Line);
  LineHeight := Printer.Canvas.TextHeight(Line);
end;

// Start a new page. The caller resets the Y position.
procedure TPrintThread.StartNewPage;
begin
  Printer.NewPage;
end;
```

To start a print process, just create an instance of **TPrintThread**. As the last argument, pass an event handler, which the thread calls when it is finished. A typical application might display some information in a status bar, or prevent the user from exiting the application until the print operation is complete. One possible approach is shown in Example 4-9.

Example 4-9: Using the Print Thread Class

```
// The user chose the File>Print menu item, so print the file.
procedure TMDIChild.Print;
begin
  if PrintThread <> nil then
    MessageDlg('File is already being printed.', mtWarning, [mbOK], 0)
  else
  begin
    PrintThread := TPrintThread.Create(Editor.Text, FileName,
                                       DonePrinting);
    MainForm.SetPrinting(True);
  end;
end;

// When the file is done printing, check for an exception,
// and clear the printing status.
procedure TMDIChild.DonePrinting(Sender: TObject);
begin
  if PrintThread.ExceptionMessage <> '' then
    MessageDlg(PrintThread.ExceptionMessage, mtError, [mbOK], 0);
  PrintThread := nil;
  MainForm.SetPrinting(False);
end;
```

The BeginThread and EndThread Functions

If you don't want to write a class, you can use **BeginThread** and **EndThread**. They are wrappers for the Win32 API calls **CreateThread** and **ExitThread** functions, but you must use Delphi's functions instead of the Win32 API directly. Delphi keeps a global flag, **IsMultiThread**, which is True if your program calls

BeginThread or starts a thread using **TThread**. Delphi checks this flag to ensure thread safety when allocating memory. If you call the **CreateThread** function directly, be sure to set **IsMultiThread** to True.

Note that using the **BeginThread** and **EndThread** functions does not give you the convenience of the **Synchronize** method. If you want to use these functions, you must arrange for your own serialized access to the VCL.

The **BeginThread** function is almost exactly the same as **CreateThread**, but the parameters use Delphi types. The thread function takes a **Pointer** parameter and returns an **Integer** result, which is the exit code for the thread. The **EndThread** function is just like the Windows **ExitThread** function: it terminates the current thread. See Chapter 5, *Language Reference*, for details about these functions. For an example of using **BeginThread**, see the section "Futures" at the end of this chapter.

Thread Local Storage

Windows has a feature where each thread can store limited information that is private to the thread. Delphi makes it easy to use this feature, called *thread local storage*, without worrying about the limitations imposed by Windows. Just declare a variable using **threadvar** instead of **var**. Ordinarily, Delphi creates a single instance of a unit-level variable and shares that instance among all threads. If you use **threadvar**, however, Delphi creates a unique, separate instance of the variable in each thread.

You must declare **threadvar** variables at the unit level, not local to a function or procedure. Each thread has its own stack, so local variables are local to a thread anyway. Because **threadvar** variables are local to the thread and that thread is the only thread that can access the variables, you don't need to use critical sections to protect them.

If you use the **TThread** class, you should use fields in the class for thread local variables because they incur less overhead than using **threadvar** variables. If you need thread local storage outside the thread object, or if you are using the **BeginThread** function, use **threadvar**.

Be careful when using the **threadvar** variables in a DLL. When the DLL is unloaded, Delphi frees all **threadvar** storage before it calls the **DllProc** or the finalization sections in the DLL.

Processes

Delphi has some support for multithreaded applications, but if you want to write a system of cooperating programs, you must resort to the Windows API. Each process runs in its own address space, but you have several choices for how processes can communicate with each other:

Messages
> Any thread can send a message to any other thread in the same process or in a different process. A typical use for interprocess messages is when one application is trying to control the user interface of another application.

Events

An event is a trigger that one thread can send to another. The threads can be in the same or different processes. One thread waits on the event, and another thread *sets* the event, which wakes up the waiting thread. Multiple threads can wait for the same event, and you can decide whether setting the event wakes up all waiting threads or only one thread.

Mutexes

A mutex (short for mutual exclusion) is a critical section that can be shared among multiple processes.

Semaphores

A semaphore shares a count among multiple processes. A thread in a process waits for the semaphore, and when the semaphore is available, the thread decrements the count. When the count reaches zero, threads must wait until the count is greater than zero. A thread can release a semaphore to increment the count. Where a mutex lets one thread at a time gain access to a shared resource, a semaphore gives access to multiple threads, where you control the number of threads by setting the semaphore's maximum count.

Pipes

A pipe is a special kind of file, where the file contents are treated as a queue. One process writes to one end of the queue, and another process reads from the other end. Pipes are a powerful and simple way to send a stream of information from one process to another—on one system or in a network.

Memory-mapped files

The most common way to share data between processes is to use memory-mapped files. A memory-mapped file, as the name implies, is a file whose contents are mapped into a process's virtual address space. Once a file is mapped, the memory region is just like normal memory, except that any changes are stored in the file, and any changes in the file are seen in the process's memory. Multiple processes can map the same file and thereby share data. Note that each process maps the file to a different location in its individual address space, so you can store data in the shared memory, but not pointers.

Many books on advanced Windows programming cover these topics, but you have to map the C and C++ code examples given in these books to Delphi. To help you, this section presents an example that uses many of these features.

Suppose you are writing a text editor and you want a single process that can edit many files. When the user runs your program or text editor, it first checks whether a process is already running that program, and if so, forwards the request to the existing process. The forwarded request must include the command-line arguments so the existing process can open the requested files. If, for any reason, the existing process is slow to respond, the user might be able to run the program many times, each time adding an additional request to the existing process. This problem clearly calls for a robust system for communicating between processes.

The single application functions as client and server. The first time the program runs, it becomes the server. Once a server exists, subsequent invocations of the program become clients. If multiple processes start at once, there is a race condition to see who becomes the server, so the architecture must have a clean and simple way to decide who gets to be server. To do this, the program uses a mutex.

A *mutex* (short for mutual exclusion) is a critical section that works across processes. The program always tries to create a mutex with a specific name. The first process to succeed becomes the server. If the mutex already exists, the process becomes a client. If any error occurs, the program raises an exception, as you can see in Example 4-10.

Example 4-10: Create a Mutex to See Who Gets to Play Server

```
const
  MutexName = 'Tempest Software.Threaditor mutex';
var
  SharedMutex: THandle;

// Create the mutex that all processes share. The first process
// to create the mutex is the server. Return True if the process is
// the server, False if it is the client. The server starts out
// owning the mutex, so you must release it before any client
// can grab it.
function CreateSharedMutex: Boolean;
begin
  SharedMutex := CreateMutex(nil, True, MutexName);
  Win32Check(SharedMutex <> 0);
  Result := GetLastError <> Error_Already_Exists;
end;
```

The mutex also protects the memory-mapped file the clients use to send a list of filenames to the server. Using a memory-mapped file requires two steps:

1. *Create a mapped file.* The mapped file can be a file on disk or it can reside in the system page file.

2. *Map a view of the file into the process's address space.* The view can be the entire file or a contiguous region of the file.

After mapping the view of the memory-mapped file, the process has a pointer to a shared memory region. Every process that maps the same file shares a single memory block, and changes one process makes are immediately visible to other processes. The shared file might have a different starting location in each process, so you should not store pointers (including long strings, wide strings, dynamic arrays, and complex Variants) in the shared file.

The program uses the TSharedData record for storing and retrieving the data. Note that TSharedData uses short strings to avoid the problem of storing pointers in the shared file. Example 4-11 shows how to create and map the shared file.

Example 4-11: Creating a Memory-Mapped File

```
const
  MaxFileSize = 32768; // 32K should be more than enough.
  MaxFileCount = MaxFileSize div SizeOf(ShortString);
  SharedFileName = 'Tempest Software.Threaditor shared file';
```

Example 4-11: Creating a Memory-Mapped File (continued)

```
type
  PSharedData = ^TSharedData;
  TSharedData = record
    Count: Word;
    FileNames: array[1..MaxFileCount] of ShortString;
  end;
var
  IsServer: Boolean;
  SharedFile: THandle;
  SharedData: PSharedData;

// Create the shared, memory-mapped file and map its entire contents
// into the process's address space. Save the pointer in SharedData.
procedure CreateSharedFile;
begin
  SharedFile := CreateFileMapping($FFFFFFFF, nil, Page_ReadWrite,
                     0, SizeOf(TSharedData), SharedFileName);
  Win32Check(SharedFile <> 0);

  // Map the entire file into the process address space.
  SharedData := MapViewOfFile(SharedFile, File_Map_All_Access, 0, 0, 0);
  Win32Check(SharedData <> nil);

  // The server created the shared data, so make sure it is
  // initialized properly. You don't need to clear everything,
  // but make sure the count is zero.
  if IsServer then
    SharedData.Count := 0;
end;
```

The client writes its command-line arguments to the memory-mapped file and notifies the server that it should read the filenames from the shared data in the memory-mapped file. Multiple clients might try to write to the memory-mapped file at the same time, or a client might want to write when the server wants to read. The mutex protects the integrity of the shared data.

The client calls **EnterMutex**, which waits until the mutex is available, then grabs it. Once a client owns the mutex, no other thread in any process can grab the mutex. The client is free to write to the shared memory without fear of data corruption. The client copies its command-line arguments to the shared data, then releases the mutex by calling **LeaveMutex**. Example 4-12 shows these two functions.

Example 4-12: Entering and Leaving a Mutex

```
// Enter the critical section by grabbing the mutex.
// This procedure waits until it gets the mutex or it
// raises an exception.
procedure EnterMutex;
resourcestring
  sNotResponding = 'Threaditor server process is not responding';
  sNoServer = 'Threaditor server process has apparently died';
```

Example 4-12: Entering and Leaving a Mutex (continued)

```
const
  TimeOut = 10000; // 10 seconds
begin
  case WaitForSingleObject(SharedMutex, TimeOut) of
  Wait_Timeout:
    raise Exception.Create(sNotResponding);
  Wait_Abandoned:
    raise Exception.Create(sNoServer);
  Wait_Failed:
    RaiseLastWin32Error;
  end;
end;

// Leave the critical section by releasing the mutex so another
// process can grab it.
procedure LeaveMutex;
begin
  Win32Check(ReleaseMutex(SharedMutex));
end;
```

The client wakes up the server by setting an *event.* An event is a way for one process to notify another without passing any additional information. The server waits for the event to be triggered, and after a client copies a list of filenames into the shared file, the client sets the event, which wakes up the server. Example 4-13 shows the code for creating the event.

Example 4-13: Creating the Shared Event

```
const
  EventName = 'Tempest Software.Threaditor event';
var
  SharedEvent: THandle;

// Create the event that clients use to signal the server.
procedure CreateSharedEvent;
begin
  SharedEvent := CreateEvent(nil, False, False, EventName);
  Win32Check(SharedEvent <> 0);
end;
```

The server grabs the mutex so it can copy the filenames from the shared file. To avoid holding the mutex too long, the server copies the filenames into a string list and immediately releases the mutex. Then the server opens each file listed in the string list. Network latency or other problems might slow down the server when opening a file, which is why the server copies the names and releases the mutex as quickly as it can.

Everyone has run into the infinite wait problem at some time. You click the button and wait, but the hourglass cursor never disappears. Something inside the program is waiting for an event that will never occur. So what do you do? Do you press Ctrl-Alt-Del and try to kill the program? But the program might not have saved your data yet. It could be waiting for a response from the server. If you kill the program now, you might lose all your work so far. It's so frustrating to be faced with the hourglass and have no way to recover.

Such scenarios should never happen, and it's up to us—the programmers—to make sure they don't.

Windows will let your thread wait forever if you use `Infinite` as the time out argument to the wait functions, such as `WaitForSingleObject`. The only time you should use an `Infinite` time out, though, is when a server thread is waiting for a client connection. In that case, it is appropriate for the server to wait an indeterminate amount of time. In almost every other case, you should specify an explicit time out. Determine how long a user should wait before the program reports that something has gone wrong. If your thread is deadlocked, for example, the user has no way of knowing or stopping the thread, short of killing the process in the Task Manager. By setting an explicit time out, as shown in Example 4-12, the program can report a coherent message instead of leaving the bewildered user wondering what is happening.

The server opens each of these files as though the user had chosen File → Open in the text editor. Because opening a file involves the VCL, the server uses **Synchronize** to open each file. After opening the files, the server waits on the event again. The server spends most of its time waiting to hear from a client, so it must not let the waiting interfere with its normal work. The server does its work in a separate thread that loops forever: waiting for an event from a client, getting the filenames from the shared file, opening the files, then waiting again. Example 4-14 shows the code for the server thread.

Example 4-14: The TServerThread Class

```
type
  TServerThread = class(TThread)
  private
    fFileName: string;
    fFileNames: TStringList;
  public
    constructor Create;
    destructor Destroy; override;
    procedure OpenFile;
    procedure RestoreWindow;
    procedure Execute; override;
    property FileName: string read fFileName;
    property FileNames: TStringList read fFileNames;
```

Example 4-14: The TServerThread Class (continued)

```
  end;

var
  ServerThread: TServerThread;

{ TServerThread }

constructor TServerThread.Create;
begin
  inherited Create(True);
  fFileNames := TStringList.Create;
  FreeOnTerminate := True;
  Resume;
end;

destructor TServerThread.Destroy;
begin
  FreeAndNil(fFileNames);
  inherited;
end;

procedure TServerThread.Execute;
var
  I: Integer;
begin
  while not Terminated do
  begin
    // Wait for a client to wake up the server. This is one of the few
    // times where a wait with an INFINITE time out is appropriate.
    WaitForSingleObject(SharedEvent, INFINITE);

    EnterMutex;
    try
      for I := 1 to SharedData.Count do
        FileNames.Add(SharedData.FileNames[I]);
        SharedData.Count := 0;
    finally
      LeaveMutex;
    end;

    for I := 0 to FileNames.Count-1 do
    begin
      fFileName := FileNames[I];
      Synchronize(OpenFile);
    end;
    Synchronize(RestoreWindow);
    FileNames.Clear;
  end;
end;

procedure TServerThread.OpenFile;
begin
```

Example 4-14: The TServerThread Class (continued)

```
  // Create a new MDI child window
  TMDIChild.Create(Application).OpenFile(FileName);
end;

// Bring the main form forward, and restore it from a minimized state.
procedure TServerThread.RestoreWindow;
begin
  if FileNames.Count > 0 then
  begin
    Application.Restore;
    Application.BringToFront;
  end;
end;
```

The client is quite simple. It grabs the mutex, then copies its command-line arguments into the shared file. If multiple clients try to run at the same time, the first one to grab the mutex gets to run, while the others must wait. Multiple clients might run before the server gets to open the files, so each client appends its filenames to the list, as you can see in Example 4-15.

Example 4-15: The Threaditor Client

```
// A client grabs the mutex and appends the files named on the command
// line to the filenames listed in the shared file. Then it notifies
// the server that the files are ready.
procedure SendFilesToServer;
var
  I: Integer;
begin
  if ParamCount > 0 then
  begin
    EnterMutex;
    try
      for I := 1 to ParamCount do
        SharedData.FileNames[SharedData.Count + I] := ParamStr(I);
      SharedData.Count := SharedData.Count + ParamCount;
    finally
      LeaveMutex;
    end;
    // Wake up the server
    Win32Check(SetEvent(SharedEvent));
  end;
end;
```

When it starts, the application calls the StartServerOrClient procedure. This procedure creates or opens the mutex and so learns whether the program is the server or a client. If it is the server, it starts the server thread and sets IsServer to True. The server initially owns the shared mutex, so it can safely create and initialize the shared file. Then it must release the mutex. If the program is a client, it sends the command-line arguments to the server, and sets IsServer to False.

The client doesn't own the mutex initially, so it has nothing to release. Example 4-16 shows the `StartServerOrClient` procedure.

Example 4-16: Start the Application as the Server or a Client

```
procedure StartServerOrClient;
begin
  IsServer := CreateSharedMutex;
  try
    CreateSharedFile;
    CreateSharedEvent;
  finally
    if IsServer then
      LeaveMutex;
  end;

  if IsServer then
    StartServer
  else
    SendFilesToServer;
end;
```

To start the server, simply create an instance of **TServerThread**. To stop the server, set the thread's **Terminated** flag to True, and signal the event to wake up the thread. The thread wakes up, goes through its main loop, and exits because the **Terminated** flag is True. To make sure the thread is cleaned up properly, the main thread waits for the server thread to exit, but it doesn't wait long. If something goes wrong, the main thread simply abandons the server thread so the application can close. Windows will clean up the thread when the application terminates. Example 4-17 shows the **StartServer** and **StopServer** procedures.

Example 4-17: Starting and Stopping the Server Thread

```
// Create the server thread, which will wait for clients
// to connect.
procedure StartServer;
begin
  ServerThread := TServerThread.Create;
end;

procedure StopServer;
begin
  ServerThread.Terminate;
  // Wake up the server so it can die cleanly.
  Win32Check(SetEvent(SharedEvent));
  // Wait for the server thread to die, but if it doesn't die soon
  // don't worry about it, and let Windows clean up after it.
  WaitForSingleObject(ServerThread.Handle, 1000);
end;
```

To clean up, the program must unmap the shared file, close the mutex, and close the event. Windows keeps the shared handles open as long as one thread keeps them open. When the last thread closes a handle, Windows gets rid of the mutex, event, or whatever. When an application terminates, Windows closes all open handles, but it's always a good idea to close everything explicitly. It helps the person who must read and maintain your code to know explicitly which handles should be open when the program ends. Example 4-18 lists the unit's finalization section, where all the handles are closed. If a serious Windows error were to occur, the application might terminate before all the shared items have been properly created, so the finalization code checks for a valid handle before closing each one.

Example 4-18: Close All Shared Handles When Finalizing the Unit

```
finalization
  if SharedMutex <> 0 then
    CloseHandle(SharedMutex);
  if SharedEvent <> 0 then
    CloseHandle(SharedEvent);
  if SharedData <> nil then
    UnmapViewOfFile(SharedData);
  if SharedFile <> 0 then
    CloseHandle(SharedFile);
end.
```

The final step is to edit the project's source file. The first thing the application does is call StartServerOrClient. If the program is a client, it exits without starting the normal Delphi application. If it is the server, the application runs normally (with the server thread running in the background). Example 4-19 lists the new project source file.

Example 4-19: Project Source File to Run the Server or Client

```
program Threaditor;

uses
  Forms,
  Main in 'Main.pas' {MainForm},
  Childwin in 'ChildWin.pas' {MDIChild},
  About in 'About.pas' {AboutBox},
  Process in 'Process.pas';

{$R *.RES}

begin
  StartServerOrClient;
  if IsServer then
  begin
    Application.Initialize;
    Application.Title := 'Threaditor';
    Application.CreateForm(TMainForm, MainForm);
    Application.Run;
  end;
end.
```

The remainder of the application is the standard MDI project from Delphi's object repository, with only a few modifications. Simply adding the **Process** unit and making one small change to the project source file is all you need to do. Different applications might need to take different actions when the clients run, but this example gives you a good framework for enhancements.

Futures

Writing a concurrent program can be more difficult than writing a sequential program. You need to think about race conditions, synchronization, shared variables, and more. *Futures* help reduce the intellectual clutter of using threads. A future is an object that promises to deliver a value sometime in the future. The application does its work in the main thread and calls upon futures to fetch or compute information concurrently. The future does its work in a separate thread, and when the main thread needs the information, it gets it from the future object. If the information isn't ready yet, the main thread waits until the future is done. Programming with futures hides much of the complexity of multithreaded programming.

Define a future class by inheriting from **TFuture** and overriding the **Compute** method. The **Compute** method does whatever work is necessary and returns its result as a **Variant**. Try to avoid synchronization and accessing shared variables during the computation. Instead, let the main thread handle communication with other threads or other futures. Example 4-20 shows the declaration for the **TFuture** class.

Example 4-20: Declaration of the TFuture Class

```
type
  TFuture = class
  private
    fExceptObject: TObject;
    fExceptAddr: Pointer;
    fHandle: THandle;
    fTerminated: Boolean;
    fThreadID: LongWord;
    fTimeOut: DWORD;
    fValue: Variant;
    function GetIsReady: Boolean;
    function GetValue: Variant;
  protected
    procedure RaiseException;
  public
    constructor Create;
    destructor Destroy; override;
    procedure AfterConstruction; override;

    function Compute: Variant; virtual; abstract;
    function HasException: Boolean;
    procedure Terminate;

    property Handle: THandle read fHandle;
```

Example 4-20: Declaration of the TFuture Class (continued)

```
  property IsReady: Boolean read GetIsReady;
  property Terminated: Boolean read fTerminated write fTerminated;
  property ThreadID: LongWord read fThreadID;
  property TimeOut: DWORD read FTimeOut write fTimeOut;
  property Value: Variant read GetValue;
end;
```

The constructor initializes the future object, but refrains from starting the thread. Instead, **TFuture** overrides **AfterConstruction** and starts the thread after all the constructors have run. That lets a derived class initialize its own fields before starting the thread.

When the application needs the future value, it reads the **Value** property. The **GetValue** method waits until the thread is finished. If the thread is already done, Windows returns immediately. If the thread raised an exception, the future object reraises the same exception object at the original exception address. This lets the calling thread handle the exception just as though the future was computed in the calling thread rather than in a separate thread. If everything goes as planned, the future value is returned as a **Variant**. Example 4-21 lists the implementation of the **TFuture** class.

Example 4-21: The TFuture Class

```
// Each Future computes its value in ThreadFunc. Any number of
// ThreadFunc instances can be active at a time. Windows requires a
// thread to catch exceptions, or else Windows shuts down the
// application. ThreadFunc catches exceptions and stores them in the
// Future object.
function ThreadFunc(Param: Pointer): Integer;
var
  Future: TFuture;
  RaiseFrame: PRaiseFrame;
begin
  Result := 0;
  Future := TFuture(Param);
  // The thread must catch all exceptions within the thread.
  // Store the exception object and address in the Future object,
  // to be raised when the value is needed.
  try
    Future.fValue := Null;
    Future.fValue := Future.Compute;
  except
    RaiseFrame := RaiseList;
    if RaiseFrame <> nil then
    begin
      Future.fExceptObject := RaiseFrame.ExceptObject;
      Future.fExceptAddr   := RaiseFrame.ExceptAddr;
      RaiseFrame.ExceptObject := nil;
    end;
  end;
end;
```

Example 4-21: The TFuture Class (continued)

```pascal
{ TFuture }
// Create the Future and start its computation.
constructor TFuture.Create;
begin
  inherited;
  // The default time out is Infinite because a general-purpose
  // future cannot know how long any concrete future should take
  // to finish its task. Derived classes should set a different
  // value that is appropriate to the situation.
  fTimeOut := Infinite;
end;

// The thread is started in AfterConstruction to let the derived class
// finish its constructor in the main thread and initialize the TFuture
// object completely before the thread starts running. This avoids
// any race conditions when initializing the TFuture-derived object.
procedure TFuture.AfterConstruction;
begin
  inherited;
  // Start the Future thread.
  fHandle := BeginThread(nil, 0, ThreadFunc, Self, 0, fThreadID);
  Win32Check(Handle <> 0);
end;

// If the caller destroys the Future object before the thread
// is finished, there is no nice way to clean up. TerminateThread
// leaves the stack allocated and might introduce all kinds of nasty
// problems, especially if the thread is in the middle of a kernel
// system call. A less violent solution is just to let the thread
// finish its job and go away naturally. The Compute function should
// check the Terminated flag periodically and return immediately when
// it is true.
destructor TFuture.Destroy;
begin
  if Handle <> 0 then
  begin
    if not IsReady then
    begin
      Terminate; // Tell the thread to stop.
      try
        GetValue;  // Wait for it to stop.
      except
        // Discard any exceptions that are raised now that the
        // computation is logically terminated and the future object
        // is being destroyed. The caller is freeing the TFuture
        // object, and does not expect any exceptions from the value
        // computation.
      end;
    end;
    Win32Check(CloseHandle(Handle));
  end;
  inherited;
```

Example 4-21: The TFuture Class (continued)

```
end;

// Return true if the thread is finished.
function TFuture.GetIsReady: Boolean;
begin
  Result := WaitForSingleObject(Handle, 0) = Wait_Object_0;
end;

// Wait for the thread to finish, and return its value.
// If the thread raised an exception, reraise the same exception,
// but now in the context of the calling thread.
function TFuture.GetValue: Variant;
resourcestring
  sAbandoned = 'Future thread terminated unexpectedly';
  sTimeOut   = 'Future thread did not finish before timeout expired';
begin
  case WaitForSingleObject(Handle, TimeOut) of
  Wait_Abandoned: raise Exception.Create(sAbandoned);
  Wait_TimeOut:   raise Exception.Create(sTimeOut);
  else
    if HasException then
      RaiseException;
  end;
  Result := fValue;
end;

function TFuture.HasException: Boolean;
begin
  Result := fExceptObject <> nil;
end;

procedure TFuture.RaiseException;
begin
  raise fExceptObject at fExceptAddr;
end;

// Set the terminate flag, so the Compute function knows to stop.
procedure TFuture.Terminate;
begin
  Terminated := True;
end;
```

To use a future, derive a class from TFuture and override the Compute method. Create an instance of the derived future class and read its Value property when you need to access the future's value.

Suppose you want to add a feature to the threaded text editor: when the user is searching for text, you want the editor to search ahead for the next match. For example, the user opens the Find dialog box, enters a search string, and clicks the Find button. The editor finds the text and highlights it. While the user checks the result, the editor searches for the next match in the background.

This is a perfect job for a future. The future searches for the next match and returns the starting position of the match. The next time the user clicks the Find button, the editor gets the result from the future. If the future is not yet finished searching, the editor waits. If the future is done, it returns immediately, and the user is impressed by the speedy result, even when searching a large file.

The future keeps a copy of the file's contents, so you don't have to worry about multiple threads accessing the same file. This is not the best architecture for a text editor, but is demonstrates how a future can be used effectively. Example 4-22 lists the TSearchFuture class, which does the searching.

Example 4-22: Searching for Text

```
type
  TSearchFuture = class(TFuture)
  private
    fEditorText: string;
    fFindPos: LongInt;
    fFindText: string;
    fOptions: TFindOptions;
    procedure FindDown(out Result: Variant);
    procedure FindUp(out Result: Variant);
  public
    constructor Create(Editor: TRichEdit; Options: TFindOptions;
      const Text: string);
    function Compute: Variant; override;

    property EditorText: string read fEditorText;
    property FindPos: LongInt read FFindPos write fFindPos;
    property FindText: string read fFindText;
    property Options: TFindOptions read fOptions;
  end;

{ TSearchFuture }

constructor TSearchFuture.Create(Editor: TRichEdit;
  Options: TFindOptions; const Text: string);
begin
  inherited Create;
  TimeOut := 30000; // Expect the future to do its work in < 30 sec.
  // Save the basic search parameters.
  fEditorText := Editor.Text;
  fOptions := Options;
  fFindText := Text;
  // Start searching at the end of the current selection,
  // to avoid finding the same text over and over again.
  fFindPos := Editor.SelStart + Editor.SelLength;
end;

// Simple-minded search.
function TSearchFuture.Compute: Variant;
begin
  if not (frMatchCase in Options) then
  begin
```

Example 4-22: Searching for Text (continued)

```
    fFindText := AnsiLowerCase(FindText);
    fEditorText := AnsiLowerCase(EditorText);
  end;

  if frDown in Options then
    FindDown(Result)
  else
    FindUp(Result);
end;

procedure TSearchFuture.FindDown(out Result: Variant);
var
  Next: PChar;
begin
  // Find the next match.
  Next := AnsiStrPos(PChar(EditorText) + FindPos, PChar(FindText));
  if Next = nil then
    // Not found.
    Result := -1
  else
  begin
    // Found: return the position of the start of the match.
    FindPos := Next - PChar(EditorText);
    Result := FindPos;
  end;
end;
```

If the user edits the file, changes the selection, or otherwise invalidates the search, the editor frees the future because it is no longer valid. The next time the user starts a search, the editor must start up a brand-new future. Example 4-23 shows the relevant method for the TMDIChild form.

Example 4-23: Managing the Editor's Future

```
// If the user changes the selection, restart the background search.
procedure TMDIChild.EditorSelectionChange(Sender: TObject);
begin
  if Future <> nil then
    RestartSearch;
end;

// When the user closes the Find dialog, stop the background
// thread because it probably isn't needed any more.
procedure TMDIChild.FindDialogClose(Sender: TObject);
begin
  FreeAndNil(fFuture);
end;

// Restart the search thread after a search parameter changes.
procedure TMDIChild.RestartSearch;
begin
  FreeAndNil(fFuture);
```

Example 4-23: Managing the Editor's Future (continued)

```
   fFuture := TSearchFuture.Create(Editor, FindDialog.Options,
                                   FindDialog.FindText);
end;
```

When the user clicks the Find button, the `TFindDialog` object fires its `OnFind` event. The event handler first checks whether it has a valid future, and if not, it starts a new future. Thus, all searching takes place in a background thread. The `TSearchFuture` object returns the position of the next match or −1 if the text cannot be found. Most of the work of the event handler is scrolling the editor to make sure the selected text is visible—managing the search future is trivial in comparison, as you can see in Example 4-24.

Example 4-24: Performing a Text Search

```
// The user clicked the Find button in the Find dialog.
// Get the next match, which might already have been found
// by a search future.
procedure TMDIChild.FindDialogFind(Sender: TObject);
var
   FindPos: LongInt;
   SaveEvent: TNotifyEvent;
   TopLeft, BottomRight: LongWord;
   Top, Left, Bottom, Right: LongInt;
   Pos: TPoint;
   SelLine, SelChar: LongInt;
   ScrollLine, ScrollChar: LongInt;
begin
   // If the search has not yet started, or if the user changed
   // the search parameters, restart the search. Otherwise, the
   // future has probably already found the next match. In either
   // case the reference to Future.Value will wait until the search
   // is finished.
   if (Future = nil) or
      (Future.FindText <> FindDialog.FindText) or
      (Future.Options <> FindDialog.Options)
   then
      RestartSearch;

   FindPos := Future.Value;

   if FindPos < 0 then
      MessageBeep(Mb_IconWarning)
   else
   begin
      // Bring the focus back to the editor, from the Find dialog.
      Application.MainForm.SetFocus;
      // Temporarily disable the selection change event
      // to prevent the future from being restarted until after
      // the selection start and length have both been set.
      SaveEvent := Editor.OnSelectionChange;
      try
         Editor.OnSelectionChange := nil;
```

Example 4-24: Performing a Text Search (continued)

```
    Editor.SelStart := FindPos;
    Editor.SelLength := Length(FindDialog.FindText);
  finally
    Editor.OnSelectionChange := SaveEvent;
  end;

  // Start looking for the next match.
  RestartSearch;

  // Scroll the editor to bring the selection in view.
  // Start by getting the character and line index of the top-left
  // corner of the rich edit control.
  Pos.X := 0;
  Pos.Y := 0;
  TopLeft := Editor.Perform(Em_CharFromPos, 0, LParam(@Pos));
  Top := Editor.Perform(Em_LineFromChar, Word(TopLeft), 0);
  Left := Word(TopLeft) - Editor.Perform(Em_LineIndex, Top, 0);

  // Then get the line & column of the bottom-right corner.
  Pos.X := Editor.ClientWidth;
  Pos.Y := Editor.ClientHeight;
  BottomRight := Editor.Perform(Em_CharFromPos, 0, LParam(@Pos));
  Bottom := Editor.Perform(Em_LineFromChar, Word(BottomRight), 0);
  Right := Word(BottomRight) -
          Editor.Perform(Em_LineIndex, Bottom, 0);

  // Is the start of the selection in view?
  // If the line is not in view, scroll vertically.
  SelLine := Editor.Perform(Em_ExLineFromChar, 0, FindPos);
  if (SelLine < Top) or (SelLine > Bottom) then
    ScrollLine := SelLine - Top
  else
    ScrollLine := 0;
  // If the column is not visible, scroll horizontally.
  SelChar := FindPos - Editor.Perform(Em_LineIndex, SelLine, 0);
  if (SelChar < Left) or (SelChar > Right) then
    ScrollChar := SelChar - Left
  else
    ScrollChar := 0;
    Editor.Perform(Em_LineScroll, ScrollChar, ScrollLine);
  end;
end;
```

The major advantage to using futures is their simplicity. You can often implement the TFuture-derived class as a simple, linear subroutine (albeit one that checks Terminated periodically). Using a future is as simple as accessing a property. All the synchronization is handled automatically by TFuture.

Concurrent programming can be tricky, but with care and caution, you can write applications that use threads and processes correctly, efficiently, and effectively.

CHAPTER 5

Language Reference

This is the big chapter—the language reference. Here you can find every keyword, directive, function, procedure, variable, class, method, and property that is part of Delphi Pascal. Most of these items are declared in the System unit, but some are declared in SysInit. Both units are automatically included in every Delphi unit. Remember that Delphi Pascal is not case sensitive, with the sole exception of the Register procedure (to ensure compatibility with C++ Builder).

For your convenience, runtime error numbers in this chapter are followed by exception class names. The SysUtils unit maps the errors to exceptions. The exceptions are not part of the Delphi language proper, but the SysUtils unit is used in almost every Delphi project, so the exceptions are more familiar to Delphi programmers than the error numbers.

Each item falls into one of a number of categories, which are described in the following list:

Directive

A directive is an identifier that has special meaning to the compiler, but only in a specific context. Outside of that context, you are free to use directive names as ordinary identifiers. Delphi's source editor tries to help you by showing directives in boldface when they are used in context and in plain text when used as ordinary identifiers. The editor is not always correct, though, because some of the language rules for directives are more complex than the simple editor can handle.

Function

Not all functions are really functions; some are built into the compiler. The difference is not usually important because the built-in functions look and act like normal functions, but you cannot take the address of a built-in function. The descriptions in this chapter tell you which functions are built-in and which are ordinary.

Interface

A declaration of a standard `interface`.

Keyword

A keyword is a reserved identifier whose meaning is determined by the Delphi compiler. You cannot use the keyword as a variable, method, or type name.

Procedure

As with functions, some procedures are built into the compiler and are not ordinary procedures, so you cannot take their addresses. Some procedures (such as `Exit`) behave as though they were statements in the language, but they are not reserved keywords, and you use them the same way you would use any other procedure.

Type

You know what a type is. Some types are built into the compiler, but many are defined explicitly in the `System` unit.

Variable

Most of the variables defined in the Delphi language are ordinary variables in the `System` or `SysInit` units. The difference between these units is that the variables in the `System` unit are shared by all packages loaded into an application, but each package has its own copy of the `SysInit` unit. If you know what you are doing, you can change their values. If you aren't careful, though, you can wreak havoc with Delphi. Other variables (`Self` and `Result`) are built into the compiler, and have special uses.

Abs Function

Syntax

```
function Abs(Number: Numeric type): Numeric type;
```

Description

The `Abs` function computes and returns an absolute value. The function is built into the compiler.

Return Value

- If the number has an integer type, `Abs` checks whether the value is negative and if so, negates it. The return type is `Integer` or `Int64`, depending on the type of the argument.

- For a floating-point number, `Abs` clears the sign bit without altering any other bit. In other words, negative zero and negative infinity become positive zero and positive infinity. Even if the value is NaN, the result is the original number with a zero for the sign bit.

Argument	Return
–infinity	+infinity
< 0	–number

Argument	Return
−0.0	+0.0
+0.0	+0.0
> 0.0	number
+infinity	+infinity
quiet NaN	original value with sign bit set to zero
signaling NaN	original value with sign bit set to zero

- If the argument is a **Variant**, Delphi converts it to a floating-point number and then takes the absolute value, returning a floating-point result (even if the **Variant** value is an integer).

See Also

Double Type, Extended Type, Int64 Type, Integer Type, Single Type

---

Absolute Directive

Syntax

```
var Declaration absolute Constant expression;
var Declaration absolute Variable;
```

Description

The **absolute** directive tells Delphi to store a variable at a particular memory address. The address can be a numerical address or it can be the name of a variable, in which case the memory location is the same as that used for the **Variable**. You can use the **absolute** directive with local or global variables.

Tips and Tricks

- Don't use the **absolute** directive unless you absolutely have to. Instead, you should usually use variant records, which are less error-prone and easier to read and understand.

- Use **absolute** instead of variant records when you cannot reasonably change the variable's type. For example, a subroutine that must reinterpret its argument might use **absolute**.

- Using **absolute** with a numerical memory address is a holdover from Delphi 1 and has no real use in the newer 32-bit Windows operating systems.

Example

See the **Extended** type for an example of using **absolute**.

See Also

Record Keyword, Var Keyword

Abstract Directive

Syntax

```
Virtual method declaration; abstract;
```

Description

The **abstract** directive applies to a virtual or dynamic method and means the method has no implementation. The compiler reserves a place in the virtual method table or assigns a dynamic method number. A derived class must provide an implementation for the abstract method. The **abstract** directive must follow the **virtual**, **dynamic**, or **override** directive.

Tips and Tricks

- If a derived class does not override an abstract method, you can omit the method from the class declaration or declare the method with the **override** and **abstract** directives (in that order). The latter is preferable because it clearly documents the programmer's intention not to implement the method, and does not leave the reader wondering whether the omission was deliberate or an oversight.

- If you try to construct an object, and the compiler can tell that the class has abstract methods, the compiler issues a warning. Usually such a warning indicates one of two possible errors: (1) the programmer forgot to implement an abstract method in a derived class, or (2) you are trying to create an instance of a base class when you should be creating an instance of a derived class.

- If you create an instance of the base class and call one of its abstract methods, Delphi calls the **AbstractErrorProc** procedure or generates runtime error 210 (**EAbstractError**).

See Also

AbstractErrorProc Variable, Class Keyword, Dynamic Directive, Override Directive, Virtual Directive

AbstractErrorProc Variable

Syntax

```
var AbstractErrorProc: Pointer;

procedure YourProcedure;
begin ... end;
AbstractErrorProc := @YourProcedure;
```

Description

When an abstract method is called and the object reference is that of the base class so the class does not implement the method, Delphi calls the procedure that **AbstractErrorProc** points to. If **AbstractErrorProc** is **nil**, Delphi raises runtime error 210 (**EAbstractError**). If the pointer is not **nil**, the pointer value must be the entry point of a procedure that takes no arguments. Delphi calls the procedure, which must handle the error.

Tips and Tricks

The SysUtils unit sets AbstractErrorProc to a procedure that raises an EAbstractError exception, so most applications will never need to set AbstractErrorProc. If you define your own handler for abstract errors, remember to raise an exception; if the procedure returns normally, Delphi halts the program.

See Also

Abstract Directive, AssertErrorProc Variable, ErrorProc Variable, ExceptProc Variable, Halt Procedure

---

AddModuleUnloadProc Procedure

Syntax

```
procedure AddModuleUnloadProc(Proc: TModuleUnloadProc);

procedure YourProcedure(HInstance: THandle);
begin ... end;
AddModuleUnloadProc(YourProcedure);
```

Description

Delphi keeps a list of packages that comprise an application. When Delphi unloads a package, it calls a series of unload procedures, passing the package DLL's instance handle to each one. You can add your own unload procedure to the head of the list by passing its address to AddModuleUnloadProc. When the application exits, Delphi calls the module unload procedures for the application, too.

AddModuleUnloadProc is a real procedure.

Example

```
// The graphics server manages graphical resources.
// When the application loads a graphical resource, the server
// checks the color depth of the resource and if it is higher
// than the color depth of the display, it makes a new copy of
// the graphical object at the display's color depth, and returns
// the new graphical object. Using a high-quality renderer
// gives better results than letting Windows do the color matching.
//
// When a module is unloaded, free all of its resources.

type
  PResource = ^TResource;
  TResource = record
    Module: THandle;
    Resource: TGraphicsObject;
  case Boolean of
    True:  (Name: PChar;);
```

```
      False: (ID: LongInt;);
    end;
var
  List: TList;

procedure ByeBye(HInstance: THandle);
var
  I: Integer;
  Resource: PResource;
begin
  for I := List.Count-1 downto 0 do
  begin
    Resource := List[I];
    if Resource.Module = HInstance then
    begin
      List.Delete(I);
      Resource.Resource.Free;
      Dispose(Resource);
    end;
  end;
end;

initialization
  List := TList.Create;
  AddModuleUnloadProc(ByeBye);
finalization
  RemoveModuleUnloadProc(ByeBye);
  FreeAndNil(List);
end.
```

See Also

ModuleUnloadList Variable, PModuleUnloadRec Type,
RemoveModuleUnloadProc Procedure, TModuleUnloadRec Type,
UnregisterModule Procedure

Addr Function

Syntax

```
function Addr(var X): Pointer;

Addr(Variable)
Addr(Subroutine)
```

Description

The Addr function returns the address of a variable or subroutine. The return type
is Pointer, that is, an untyped pointer. Even if you use the $T or $TypedAddress
compiler directive, Addr always returns an untyped pointer.

The @ operator is similar to the Addr function, but the @ operator can return a
typed pointer if you use the $T or $TypedAddress directive.

The Addr function is built into the compiler.

See Also

Pointer Type, $T Compiler Directive, $TypedAddress Compiler Directive

AllocMemCount Variable

Syntax

```
var AllocMemCount: Integer;
```

Description

`AllocMemCount` stores the number of blocks allocated by Delphi's memory manager.

Tips and Tricks

- Delphi doesn't use the `AllocMemCount` variable for anything—it is purely for informational purposes. Changing its value, although pointless, is also harmless.

- If you write your own memory manager, check `AllocMemCount` before calling `SetMemoryManager`. `AllocMemCount` should be zero. If it is not, the default memory manager has allocated at least one block. The problem is that Delphi might try to free that block by calling your custom memory manager. Unless your memory manager can handle this situation, it is safest to halt the program.

- If you write your own memory manager, you can set `AllocMemCount` to reflect the number of blocks allocated by your memory manager.

- If you use DLLs, `AllocMemCount` might not reflect the blocks allocated in other modules. If you use the `ShareMem` unit, call its `GetAllocMemCount` function to count the number of blocks it has allocated for all the modules that use `ShareMem`.

See Also

AllocMemSize Variable, Dispose Procedure, FreeMem Procedure, GetHeapStatus Procedure, GetMem Procedure, GetMemoryManager Procedure, New Procedure, ReallocMem Procedure, SetMemoryManager Procedure

AllocMemSize Variable

Syntax

```
var AllocMemSize: Integer;
```

Description

`AllocMemSize` stores the total size in bytes of all the memory blocks allocated by Delphi's memory manager; that is, it represents the amount of dynamic memory in use by your application.

Tips and Tricks

- Delphi doesn't use the `AllocMemSize` variable for anything. Changing its value, although pointless, is also harmless.

- If you write your own memory manager, you can set `AllocMemSize` to reflect the amount of memory allocated by your memory manager.

- If you use DLLs, `AllocMemSize` might not reflect the blocks allocated in other modules. If you use the `ShareMem` unit, call its `GetAllocMemSize` function to find the size of the blocks it has allocated for all the modules that use `ShareMem`.

See Also

AllocMemCount Variable, Dispose Procedure, FreeMem Procedure, GetHeapStatus Procedure, GetMem Procedure, GetMemoryManager Procedure, New Procedure, ReallocMem Procedure, SetMemoryManager Procedure

---

And Keyword

Syntax

```
Boolean expression and Boolean expression
Integer expression and Integer expression
```

Description

The **and** operator performs a logical *and* if the operators are of Boolean type or a bitwise *and* if the operators are integers. Integer operands can be of any integer type, including `Int64`. A logical *and* is False if either operand is False and is True if both operands are True.

Tips and Tricks

- Unlike standard Pascal, if the left-hand operand is False, Delphi does not evaluate the right-hand operand because the result must be False. You can avoid this shortcut operation and return to standard Pascal with the `$BoolEval` or `$B` compiler directives.

- An integer **and** operates on each bit of its operands, setting the result bit to zero if either operand has a zero bit, and sets a bit to one if both operands have 1 bits. If one operand is smaller than the other, Delphi extends the smaller operand with zero in the leftmost bits. The result is the size of the largest operand.

Examples

```
var
  I, J: Integer;
  S: string;
begin
  I := $F0;
  J := $8F;
  WriteLn(I and J); // Writes 128 (which is $80)
```

```
// The short-circuit behavior of AND in the next example prevents
// Delphi from referring to the nonexistent string element, S[1].
S := '';
if (Length(S) > 0) and (S[1] = 'X') then
  Delete(S, 1, 1);
```

See Also

Boolean Type, ByteBool Type, LongBool Type, Not Keyword, Or Keyword,
Shl Keyword, Shr Keyword, WordBool Type,
Xor Keyword, $B Compiler Directive, $BoolEval Compiler Directive

---

AnsiChar Type

Syntax

```
type AnsiChar = #0..#255;
```

Description

The AnsiChar type represents an 8-bit extended ANSI character. In the current
release of Delphi, the generic Char type is the same as AnsiChar, but future
releases might redefine the Char type. AnsiChar will be an 8-bit type regardless
of the definition of Char.

See Also

AnsiString Type, Char Type, WideChar Type

AnsiString Type

Syntax

```
type AnsiString;
```

Description

The AnsiString type is a long, reference-counted string containing AnsiChar
characters. By default, Delphi treats the generic string type as synonymous with
AnsiString. If you use the $H- or $LongStrings compiler directives, though,
string becomes the same as ShortString.

Delphi stores an AnsiString as a pointer to a record, but instead of pointing to
the start of the record, the AnsiString pointer points to the start of the Data
member. The Length and RefCount members precede the string contents.

```
type
  // This is the logical structure of an AnsiString, but the
  // declaration below is descriptive and cannot be compiled.
  TAnsiString = record
    RefCount: LongWord;
    Length: LongWord;
    Data: array[1..Length+1] of AnsiChar;
  end;
```

Tips and Tricks

- Delphi manages the lifetime of **AnsiString** strings using reference counting. You can manipulate the reference count with the **Initialize** and **Finalize** procedures, should the need arise.

- Assigning a string to an **AnsiString**-type variable copies a pointer to the string and increments the reference count. You can still think of the new variable as having its own copy because Delphi uses copy-on-write semantics. If you change the contents of a string whose reference count is greater than one, Delphi automatically creates a unique copy of the string and modifies the copy.

- Each string also maintains its length as a separate integer. You can set the length of a string by calling **SetLength**. Delphi automatically keeps a #0 character at the end of the string (but does not include the #0 in the string's length), so you can easily cast the string to the **PChar** type, as needed by the Windows API and other C-style functions.

See Also

AnsiChar Type, Finalize Procedure, Initialize Procedure, Length Function, PChar Type, SetLength Procedure, SetString Procedure, ShortString Type, String Keyword, WideString Type, $H Compiler Directive, $LongStrings Compiler Directive

---

Append Procedure

Syntax

```
procedure Append(var F: TextFile);
```

Description

The **Append** procedure opens an existing text file for writing. The initial file position is the end of the file, so future writes append to the end of the file.

The **Append** procedure is built into the compiler. For an example, see the **AssignFile** Procedure.

Errors

- If you have not called **AssignFile** before **Append**, Delphi reports I/O error 102.

- If the file cannot be opened for any reason, **Append** reports the Windows error code as an I/O error.

Tips and Tricks

Note that you cannot open a typed or untyped binary file for appending—only text files. To append to a binary file, call **Reset** and seek to the end of the file.

AssignFile Procedure, CloseFile Procedure, Eof Function, IOResult Function, Reset Procedure, Rewrite Procedure, TextFile Type, $I Compiler Directive, $IOChecks Compiler Directive

ArcTan Function

Syntax

```
function ArcTan(Number: Floating-point type): Extended;
```

Description

The `ArcTan` function returns the arctangent in radians of `Number`. The `ArcTan` function is built-in.

Tips and Tricks

- Delphi automatically converts `Integer` and `Variant` arguments to floating-point. To convert an `Int64` argument to floating-point, add 0.0.

- If `Number` is positive infinity, the result is $\pi/2$ (or more accurately, Delphi's best approximation of $\pi/2$); if `Number` is negative infinity, the result is an approximation of $-\pi/2$.

- If `Number` is a quiet NaN, the result is `Number`.

- If `Number` is a signaling NaN, `Arctan` reports runtime error 6 (`EInvalidOp`).

See Also

Cos Function, Sin Function

Array Keyword

Syntax

```
type Name = array[Index type] of Base type;       // static array type
type Name = array[Index type, ...] of Base type;  // static array type
type Name = array of Base type;                    // dynamic array type
Name: array of Base type        // open array as a subroutine parameter
Name: array of const     // open variant array as a subroutine parameter
```

Description

Delphi has several different kinds of arrays: static arrays, dynamic arrays, and open arrays:

- A static array is a traditional Pascal array. You can use any ordinal type as an index, and an array can have multiple indices. The size of a static array cannot change at runtime.

- A dynamic array is an array whose index type is `Integer` and whose size can change while the program runs. The lower bound of the index is always zero, and the upper bound is set with the `SetLength` procedure. To copy a dynamic array, call the `Copy` procedure. Assigning a dynamic array assigns a reference to the array without assigning the array's contents. Delphi uses reference counting to manage the lifetime of dynamic arrays. Unlike strings, Delphi does not use copy-on-write for dynamic arrays.

- A subroutine parameter can be an open array. You can pass any static or dynamic array to the subroutine. Delphi passes an additional, hidden parameter that gives the upper bound of the array. The subroutine cannot change the size of a dynamic array that is passed as an open array. Regardless of the index type of the actual array, the open array parameter uses an Integer index type, with zero as the lower bound.

- A special kind of open array is a variant open array, which is declared as array of const. Each element of the array is converted to a TVarRec record. The most common use for a variant open array is to write a subroutine that takes a variable number of arguments (such as the Format function in the SysUtils unit).

- An array of AnsiChar, Char, or WideChar is special when the index is an integer range starting from zero. Delphi treats such an array as a string or wide string (unless you disable the $ExtendedSyntax or $X compiler directives), except that you cannot pass a character array to a subroutine that has a var string parameter. You can also pass an array reference as an argument to a subroutine that takes a parameter of type PChar or PWideChar. Delphi automatically passes the address of the first character in the array.

- Arrays are stored in column-major order, that is, the rightmost subscript varies fastest.

Examples

```
// Append a message to a log file.
// See the example with AssignFile for the other overloaded
// version of the Log procedure.
procedure Log(const Fmt: string; const Args: array of const);
overload;
begin
  Log(Format(Fmt, Args));
end;

// Append a random number to a dynamic array of integers.
// Because dynamic arrays and open arrays use the same syntax,
// you must use a named type for the dynamic array parameter.
type
  TIntArray = array of integer;

procedure AppendRandomInt(var Ints: TIntArray);
begin
  SetLength(Ints, Length(Ints) + 1);
  Ints[High(Ints)] := Random(MaxInt);
end;

var
  Counter: Integer;
  TestInfo: string;
  Ints: TIntArray;
```

```
   I: Integer;
begin
   ...
   Log('This is test #%d: %s', [Counter, TestInfo]);
   for I := 1 to 10 do
      AppendRandomInt(Ints);
end.
```

See Also

Copy Procedure, High Function, Length Function, Low Function, PAnsiChar Type, PChar Type, PWideChar Type, SetLength Procedure, Slice Function, Type Keyword, TVarRec Type, $ExtendedSyntax Compiler Directive, $X Compiler Directive

---

As Keyword

Syntax

```
Object reference as Class type
Object or interface reference as Interface type
```

Description

The as operator converts an object reference to a different class type or converts an interface reference to a different interface type. The type of the expression is the class or interface type on the right-hand side of the as operator.

Tips and Tricks

- If the object or interface reference is nil, the result is nil.

- The object's declared class must be a descendant or ancestor of the class type. If the object reference is not of a compatible type, the compiler issues an error. If the declared type is compatible, but the object's true type at runtime is not the class type or a descendant type, Delphi raises runtime error 10 (EInvalidCast).

- You should use the as operator instead of a type cast when typecasting an object reference. The only exception is when you know the type from an earlier use of the is operator.

- If the desired type is an interface, Delphi calls the QueryInterface method, passing the interface type's GUID as the first argument. If the object does not implement the interface, Delphi raises runtime error 23 (EIntfCastError).

Example

```
// When any check box is checked, enable the OK button.
// This event handler can be used for multiple check boxes.
procedure TForm1.CheckBox1Click(Sender: TObject);
begin
   if (Sender as TCheckBox).Checked then
      OkButton.Enabled := True;
end;
```

See Also

Interface Keyword, Is Keyword, TObject Type

Asm Keyword

Syntax

```
asm
  assembler instructions
end;
```

Description

The **asm** keyword starts a block of assembler instructions.

Tips and Tricks

- An **asm** block is a statement, and you can use it anywhere that calls for a Pascal statement or block, such as the body of a subroutine.

- You can refer to variable names within the assembly block and jump to labels declared elsewhere in the procedure. Do not jump into a loop unless you know what you are doing. A label that starts with an @ sign is local to the subroutine and does not need to be declared.

- Delphi's built-in assembler tends to lag behind the technology, so you cannot usually rely on having the latest and greatest instruction set. Instead, you can use DB, DW, or DD directives to compile the opcodes manually.

- An **asm** block can change the EAX, ECX, and EDX registers, but must preserve the values of EBX, ESI, EDI, EBP, and ESP. As a rule, you should not assume that any registers contain special values, but if you are careful, you can access a subroutine's parameters in their registers. See the calling convention directives (cdecl, pascal, register, safecall, and stdcall) to learn how arguments are passed to a subroutine.

- Writing assembly code by hand rarely gives you better performance. The most common reason to use an **asm** block is to use instructions that are not available in Delphi, such as the CPUID instruction shown in the example.

Example

```
unit cpuid;

// CPU identification.
// This unit defines the GetCpuID function, which uses the CPUID
// instruction to get the processor type. GetCpuID returns True if the
// processor supports the CPUID instruction and False if it does not.
// Older 486 and earlier processors do not support CPUID.

interface

const
  VendorIntel = 'GenuineIntel';
  VendorAMD   = 'AuthenticAMD';
  VendorCyrix = 'CyrixInstead';
```

```
type
  TCpuType = (cpuOriginalOEM, cpuOverdrive, cpuDual, cpuReserved);
  TCpuFeature = (cfFPU, cfVME, cfDE, cfPDE, cfTSC, cfMSR, cfMCE, cfCX8,
               cfAPIC, cfReserved10, cfReserved11, cfMTRR, cfPGE, cfMCA,
               cfCMOV, cfPAT, cfReserved17, cfReserved18, cfReserved19,
               cfReserved20, cfReserved21, cfReserved22, cfReserved23,
               cfMMX, cfFastFPU, cfReserved26, cfReserved27,
               cfReserved28, cfReserved29, cfReserved30, cfReserved31
               );
  TCpuFeatureSet = set of TCpuFeature;

  UInt4 = 0..15;
  TCpuId = packed record
    CpuType: TCpuType;
    Family: UInt4;
    Model: UInt4;
    Stepping: UInt4;
    Features: TCpuFeatureSet;
    Vendor: string[12];
  end;

// Get the CPU information and store it in Cpuid.
function GetCpuid(var Cpuid: TCpuid): Boolean; register;

implementation

function GetCpuid(var Cpuid: TCpuid): Boolean;
asm
  // GetCpuid uses the register calling convention, so
  // the Cpuid parameter is in EAX. Because it is a VAR parameter,
  // EAX contains a pointer to the record.
  // Test whether the processor supports the CPUID instruction.
  // The test changes ECX and EDX.
  pushfd
  pop ecx             // Get the EFLAGS into ECX.
  mov edx, ecx        // Save a copy of EFLAGS in EDX.
  xor ecx, $200000    // Toggle the ID flag.
  push ecx            // Try to set EFLAGS.
  popfd
  pushfd              // Now test whether the change sticks.
  pop ecx             // Get the new EFLAGS into ECX.
  xor ecx, edx        // Compare with EDX.
  je @NoCpuId         // If the bits are equal, the processor
                      // doesn't support the CPUID instruction.

  // Okay to use CPUID instruction. Restore original EFLAGS.
  push edx
  popfd

  // The CPUID instruction will trample EAX, so save the Cpuid argument
  // in ESI. Delphi requires ESI be preserved when the ASM block ends,
  // so save its previous value. Also save EBX, which CPUID will
  // trample, and which must be preserved.
  push esi
```

```
        push ebx
        mov esi, eax

        // Get the vendor name, which is the concatenation of the contents
        // of the EBX, EDX, and EAX registers, treated as three 4-byte
        // character arrays.
        xor eax, eax                        // EAX = 0 means get vendor name
        dw $a20f                            // CPUID instruction
        mov BYTE(TCpuid(esi).Vendor), 12        // string length
        mov DWORD(TCpuid(esi).Vendor+1), ebx    // string content
        mov [OFFSET(TCpuid(esi).Vendor)+5], edx
        mov [OFFSET(TCpuid(esi).Vendor)+9], ecx

        // Get the processor information.
        // Now EAX is not zero, so CPUID gets the processor info.
        dw $a20f                // CPUID instruction
        mov TCpuid(esi).Features, edx

        // The signature comes in parts, most of which are 4 bits long.
        // Delphi doesn't support bit fields, so the TCpuid record uses
        // bytes to store these fields. That means unpacking the nibbles
        // into bytes.
        mov edx, eax
        and al, $F
        mov TCpuid(esi).Stepping, al

        shr edx, 4
        mov eax, edx
        and al, $F
        mov TCpuid(esi).Model, al

        shr edx, 4
        mov eax, edx
        and al, $F
        mov TCpuid(esi).Family, al

        shr edx, 4
        mov eax, edx
        and al, $3
        mov TCpuid(esi).CpuType, al

        pop ebx              // Restore the EBX and ESI registers.
        pop esi
        mov al, 1            // Return True for success.
        ret

@NoCpuId:
      xor eax, eax          // Return False for no CPUID instruction.
    end;

  end.
```

CDecl Directive, Pascal Directive, Register Directive, SafeCall Directive, StdCall Directive

---

Assembler Directive

Syntax

```
Subroutine header; assembler;
```

Description

The `assembler` directive has no meaning. It exists for backward compatibility with Delphi 1.

See Also

Asm Keyword

Assert Procedure

Syntax

```
procedure Assert(Test: Boolean);
procedure Assert(Test: Boolean; const Message: string);
```

Description

Use the `Assert` procedure to document and enforce the assumptions you must make when writing code. `Assert` is not a real procedure. The compiler handles `Assert` specially and compiles the filename and line number of the assertion to help you locate the problem should the assertion fail.

If the `Test` condition is False, Delphi calls the procedure pointed to by the `AssertErrorProc` variable. The `SysUtils` unit sets this variable to a procedure that raises the `EAssertionFailed` exception. If `AssertErrorProc` is `nil`, Delphi raises runtime error 21 (`EAssertError`).

You can include an optional message that Delphi passes to the `AssertErrorProc` procedure. If you do not include the message, Delphi uses a default message, i.e., "Assertion failed."

Tips and Tricks

- The proper way to use `Assert` is to specify conditions that must be true in order for your code to work correctly. All programmers make assumptions—about the internal state of an object, the value or validity of a subroutine's arguments, or the value returned from a function. A good way to think about assertions is that they check for programmer errors, not user errors.

- Although you can turn off assertions with the `$Assertions` or `$C` compiler directives, you will rarely have any reason to do so. Receiving an "assertion failed" error is disconcerting to a user, but much less disconcerting than the user's data being corrupted.

Example

This chapter contains several examples of using **Assert**: see the **Move** procedure, **TypeInfo** function, **VarArrayLock** function, and **VarIsArray** function.

See Also

AssertErrorProc Variable, $Assertions Compiler Directive, $C Compiler Directive

---

AssertErrorProc Variable

Syntax

```
var AssertErrorProc: Pointer;

procedure ErrorProc(const Message, FileName: string;
    LineNumber: Integer; ErrorAddress: Pointer);
AssertErrorProc := @ErrorProc
```

Description

When an assertion fails, Delphi calls the procedure whose address is stored in the **AssertErrorProc** variable. The compiler passes the assertion message and the location of the **Assert** statement to the procedure.

Tips and Tricks

- You can implement this procedure to take any action, such as logging the failure, sending email to your QA staff, etc. Unlike the other error-handling procedures, the **AssertErrorProc** procedure can return, in which case the program continues with the statement following the **Assert** procedure call.

- If **AssertErrorProc** is **nil**, Delphi raises runtime error 21 (**EAssertError**).

- The **SysUtils** unit sets this variable to a procedure that raises an **EAssertError** exception.

See Also

AbstractErrorProc Variable, Assert Procedure, ErrorProc Variable, ExceptProc Variable

---

Assign Procedure

Syntax

```
procedure Assign(var F: File; const FileName: string);
procedure Assign(var F: TextFile; const FileName: string);
```

Description

The **Assign** procedure does the same thing as **AssignFile**, but you should use **AssignFile** in new code. **Assign** is a method name that is often used in Delphi, and the two names can result in confusion. **Assign** is not a real procedure.

See Also

AssignFile Procedure

Assigned Function

Syntax

```
function Assigned(P: Pointer): Boolean;
function Assigned(Obj: TObject): Boolean;
function Assigned(Method: TMethod): Boolean;
```

Description

The `Assigned` function returns True if the argument is not `nil`; it returns False if the argument is `nil`. `Assigned` is not a real function.

Tips and Tricks

- The argument can be a pointer, an object reference, or a method.

- Calling `Assigned` instead of comparing a pointer with `nil` incurs no performance penalty.

- If the pointer is a function pointer, using `Assigned` makes it clear that you do not intend to call the function and compare its result to `nil`. Thus, `Assigned` is often used to test function and method pointers.

- A method pointer has two parts: a code pointer and a data pointer. `Assigned` checks only the most significant word of the code reference: if the high-order word is zero, the method reference is `nil`. `Assigned` ignores the data pointer.

See Also

Nil Keyword

AssignFile Procedure

Syntax

```
procedure AssignFile(var F: File; const FileName: string);
procedure AssignFile(var F: TextFile; const FileName: string);
```

Description

Call `AssignFile` to assign a filename to a typed file, an untyped file, or a text file prior to opening the file. `AssignFile` is not a real procedure.

Tips and Tricks

- A subsequent call to `Append`, `Reset`, or `Rewrite` will open the file. If you do not call `AssignFile` first, a call to `Append`, `Reset`, or `Rewrite` causes Delphi to report I/O error 102.

- Delphi interprets an empty string as the console. In a console application, the `Input` and `Output` files are automatically assigned to the console. Trying to use a console file in a GUI application results in I/O error 105.

Example

```
var
  LogFile: string = 'c:\log.txt';

// Append a message to a log file. See the example with the Array
// Keyword for the other overloaded Log procedure.
procedure Log(const Msg: string); overload;
var
  F: TextFile;
begin
  AssignFile(F, LogFile);
  // Try to append to the file, which succeeds only if the file exists.
{$IoChecks Off}
  Append(F);
{$IoChecks On}
  if IOResult <> 0 then
    // The file does not exist, so create it.
    Rewrite(F);
  WriteLn(F, Msg);
  CloseFile(F);
end;
```

See Also

Append Procedure, CloseFile Procedure, Eof Function, File Type, IOResult Function, Reset Procedure, Rewrite Procedure, TextFile Type, $I Compiler Directive, $IOChecks Compiler Directive

---

At Directive

Syntax

```
raise Exception at Address;
```

Description

Use the at directive to raise an exception with a specific address as the origin of the exception. The *Address* can be any integer expression.

Tips and Tricks

The at directive is not used in most applications, but it can be helpful when writing certain libraries or generic error-handling packages.

Example

The following example is a subroutine that raises an exception that uses the caller's address as the exception address. Thus, you can call the example procedure anywhere in your application, and when the debugger stops the application, the position is not where the exception is truly raised, but where the RaiseExceptionInCaller procedure is called, which is much more useful and informative.

```
procedure RaiseExceptionInCaller;
  // Get the return address from the stack and save it in EAX,
```

```
// which is the function's result. The value at [ESP] is the
// address of RaiseExceptionInCaller; go back one more frame
// to [ESP+4] to get the caller of RaiseExceptionInCaller.
// If you need to add local variables to RaiseExceptionInCaller,
// you might want to get an offset from EBP instead.
function CallerAddress: Pointer;
asm
  mov eax, [esp+4]
end;
begin
  raise Exception.Create('Example') at CallerAddress;
end;

procedure Demo;
begin
  RaiseExceptionInCaller; // Debugger shows exception here.
end;
```

See Also

Raise Keyword

Automated Directive

Syntax

```
type Class declaration
automated
    Method and property declarations...
end;
```

Description

The automated directive denotes a section of a class declaration where subsequent method and property declarations are stored for use in COM automation servers. An automated method declaration is like a public declaration, but the compiler stores additional RTTI for the methods, namely, the type of each parameter and the return type if the method is a function. Chapter 3, *Runtime Type Information*, describes in detail the format of the RTTI tables that store the method signatures.

Automated declarations are obsolete. You should use type libraries and interfaces instead, which give you much more power and flexibility.

See Also

Class Keyword, Dispinterface Keyword, Interface Keyword, Public Directive

---

Begin Keyword

Syntax

```
begin
  Statement...
end
```

Description

The begin keyword starts a block. A block is the main body of a program, library, procedure, function, or unit. A block can enclose any number of statements and can be used anywhere a single statement is required, such as the body of a conditional or loop statement.

The begin keyword works the same way in Delphi as it does in standard Pascal. You can also write a block in assembly language, using the asm keyword instead of begin.

See Also

Asm Keyword, End Keyword, Initialization Keyword, Library Keyword, Program Keyword, Unit Keyword

---

BeginThread Function

Syntax

```
function BeginThread(SecurityAttributes: Pointer; StackSize: LongWord;
    ThreadFunc: TThreadFunc; Parameter: Pointer; CreationFlags: LongWord;
    var ThreadId: LongWord): Integer;
```

Description

Call BeginThread to start a thread in a multithreaded program. BeginThread calls the Windows API function CreateThread, which starts a new thread and calls the thread function (ThreadFunc) in the context of the new thread. When the thread function returns, the thread terminates. For more information about the security attributes or creation flags, see the Windows API documentation for the CreateThread function.

BeginThread returns the handle of the new thread or zero if Windows cannot create the thread. BeginThread is a real function.

Tips and Tricks

- You should use BeginThread instead of the Windows API function CreateThread because BeginThread sets the global variable IsMultiThread to True. BeginThread also defines the ThreadFunc and ThreadID parameters in Pascal style rather than C style.

- The thread function should catch and handle all exceptions. If the thread function raises an exception that it does not handle, BeginThread catches the exception and terminates the application.

- Refer to Chapter 4, *Concurrent Programming*, for more information about programming with threads.

- Like any Windows resource, you must call CloseHandle after the thread terminates to make sure Windows releases all the resources associated with the thread. Delphi has a small memory leak if you start a thread in the suspended state, then close it without ever resuming the thread. To avoid the leak, always resume the thread before closing it.

Example

The following example shows how a background thread can compute a Mandelbrot set and draw a depiction of the set on a bitmap. The thread notifies the foreground thread when the bitmap is complete, and the foreground thread can display the bitmap. The background thread uses the Scanline property because it provides fast, convenient access to the bitmap data without involving the Windows API. If a thread needs to use any Windows GDI function, it should use the TThread.Synchronize method (in the Classes unit).

```
const
    // Background thread sends this message to the main thread.
    Wm_Finished = Wm_User;

type
  TThreadInfo = class;
  TWmFinished = packed record
    Msg: Cardinal;
    Aborted: Boolean;
    Bitmap: TBitmap;
    Result: LongInt;
  end;
    // Pass a ThreadInfo object to each thread. The object
    // contains the bitmap where the thread draws the Mandelbrot set
    // and a flag that the thread checks periodically to see if it
    // should terminate early.
  TThreadInfo = class
  private
    fBitmap: TBitmap;
    fAborted: Boolean;
  public
    constructor Create(Width, Height: Integer);
    destructor Destroy; override;
    procedure Abort;

    property Bitmap: TBitmap read fBitmap;
    property Aborted: Boolean read fAborted;
  end;

// Use up to 360 iterations so it is easy to map iterations to a Hue
// in an HSV color scheme.
const
  MaxIterations = 360;

// See the example for the Exit Procedure to see the
// ComputeIterations functions.

// These starting points look nice. Feel free to change them
// to something different if you wish.
const
  XOffset = -0.03;
  YOffset = 0.78;
  Zoom = 450000.0;
  Background = clBlack;
```

```
// The bitmap uses a 24-bit pixel format, so each pixel
// occupies three bytes. The TRgb array makes it easier to access
// the red, green, and blue components of a color in a scanline.
type
  TRgb = array[0..2] of Byte;
  PRgb = ^TRgb;

function MandelbrotThread(Param: Pointer): Integer;
var
  Info: TThreadInfo;
  R, C: Integer;                       // Position on the bitmap.
  Color: TColor;                       // Color to paint a pixel.
  Count: Integer;                      // Number of iterations.
  X, Y: Double;                        // Position in the imaginary plane.
  XIncrement, YIncrement: Double;      // Increment X, Y for each pixel.
  Scanline: PRgb;                      // Access the bitmap one scanline
                                       // at a time.
begin
  Result := 0;
  Info := TThreadInfo(Param);

  XIncrement := Info.Bitmap.Width / Zoom;
  YIncrement := Info.Bitmap.Height / Zoom;

  Y := YOffset;
  for R := 0 to Info.Bitmap.Height-1 do
  begin
    X := XOffset;
    Scanline := Info.Bitmap.ScanLine[R];
    for C := 0 to Info.Bitmap.Width-1 do
    begin
      Count := ComputeIterations(X, Y); // See the Exit procedure.
      X := X + XIncrement;
      // Map the maximum number of iterations to a background color,
      // and turn the other iterations into a variety of colors
      // by using the count as the hue in a saturated color scheme.
      if Count = MaxIterations then
        Color := Background
      else
        Color := HSV(Count, 255, 255); // See the Case keyword for
      Scanline[0] := GetBValue(Color); // the definition of the
      Scanline[1] := GetGValue(Color); // HSV function.
      Scanline[2] := GetRValue(Color);
      Inc(Scanline);
    end;
    Y := Y + YIncrement;
    if Info.Aborted then
    begin
      PostMessage(Form1.Handle, Wm_Finished, 1, LParam(Param));
      Exit;
    end;
  end;
  // Tell the main thread that the background thread is finished.
  // Pass the thread info object as a message parameter.
```

```
      PostMessage(Form1.Handle, Wm_Finished, 0, LParam(Param));
    end;

    // When the background thread finishes, draw the bitmap and free
    // the thread info object.
    procedure TForm1.WmFinished(var Msg: TWmFinished);
    begin
      if not Msg.Info.Aborted then
        Image1.Picture.Bitmap := Msg.Info.Bitmap;
      FreeAndNil(Msg.Info);
      CloseHandle(Thread);
      Thread := 0;
    end;

    // Start a new thread to compute and draw a Mandelbrot set.
    // Info is a TThreadInfo record, which is a private field of TForm1.
    // Thread is a THandle, also a private field.
    procedure TForm1.StartThread;
    var
      Id: Cardinal;
    begin
      Info := TThreadInfo.Create(Image1.Width, Image1.Height);
      Thread := BeginThread(nil, 0, @MandelbrotThread, Info, 0, Id);
    end;

    // When the form closes, it aborts the thread. It is possible that
    // the Wm_Finished message will arrive after the form is destroyed,
    // but that should not be a major problem. Windows will clean up the
    // thread when the application terminates.
    procedure TForm1.FormClosed(Sender: TObject);
    begin
      if Info <> nil then
        Info.Abort;
    end;
```

See Also

IsMultiThread Variable, ThreadVar Keyword, TThreadFunc Type

BlockRead Procedure

Syntax

```
procedure BlockRead(var F: File; var Buffer; Count: Integer);
procedure BlockRead(var F: File; var Buffer; Count: Integer;
  var RecordCount: Integer);
```

Description

Call BlockRead to read Count records from a binary file into Buffer. If F is an untyped file, BlockRead uses the record size that you specified when opening the file with Reset. If you supply the RecordCount variable, BlockRead stores in it the number of records actually read. In the case of an error or end of file, RecordCount might be less than Count. BlockRead is not a real procedure.

Errors

- If you do not supply the RecordCount argument, and BlockRead encounters an error or end of file, it reports I/O error 100.

- If the file is not open, BlockRead reports I/O error 103.

Tips and Tricks

- The Buffer argument is not a pointer, but an untyped var parameter. Pass the actual variable, not its address. If you have a pointer to a dynamically allocated buffer, dereference the pointer when calling BlockRead.

- The two most common uses for BlockRead are to read many records at once and to read complex data structures that do not fit neatly into a simple typed file. For example, suppose a file contains a four-byte string length, followed by the string's contents, and you want to read the data into a long string. In that case, you need to read the length and the string contents separately, as shown in the example.

Example

```
// Read a string from a binary file.
// The string begins with a four-byte length.
function ReadString(var F: File): string;
var
   Len: LongInt;
begin
   BlockRead(F, Len, SizeOf(Len));
   SetLength(Result, Len);
   if Len > 0 then
      BlockRead(F, Result[1], Len);
end;
```

See Also

AssignFile Procedure, BlockWrite Procedure, CloseFile Procedure, IOResult Function, Reset Procedure, Rewrite Procedure, $I Compiler Directive, $IOChecks Compiler Directive

---

BlockWrite Procedure

Syntax

```
procedure BlockWrite(var F: File; const Buffer; Count: Integer);
procedure BlockWrite(var F: File; const Buffer; Count: Integer;
    var RecordCount: Integer);
```

Description

The BlockWrite procedure writes Count records from Buffer to a binary file. If you supply the RecordCount variable, BlockWrite stores in it the number of records actually written to the file. In the case of a disk-full or other error, RecordCount might be less than Count. BlockWrite is not a real procedure.

- If you do not supply the `RecordCount` argument, and `BlockWrite` encounters an error, it reports I/O error 101 or the Windows error code as an I/O error.

- If the file is not open, `BlockWrite` reports I/O error 103.

Tips and Tricks

- The `Buffer` argument is not a pointer, but an untyped `var` parameter. Pass the actual variable, not its address. If you have a pointer to a dynamically allocated buffer, dereference the pointer when calling `BlockWrite`.

- The two most common uses for `BlockWrite` are to write many records at once and to store complex data structures that do not fit neatly into a simple typed file. For example, to store a long string, you might want to write the string's length as a four-byte binary number, followed by the string's contents.

Example

```
// Write a string to a binary file. Preface the string with
// the string length, as a four-byte integer.
procedure WriteString(var F: File; const Str: string);
var
  Len: LongInt;
begin
  Len := Length(Str);
  BlockWrite(F, Len, SizeOf(Len));
  if Len > 0 then
    BlockWrite(F, Str[1], Len);
end;
```

See Also

Append Procedure, AssignFile Procedure, BlockRead Procedure, CloseFile Procedure, IOResult Function, Reset Procedure, Rewrite Procedure, $I Compiler Directive, $IOChecks Compiler Directive

---

Boolean Type

Syntax

```
type Boolean = (False, True);
```

Description

The `Boolean` type is an enumerated type with two values. All comparison and logical operators produce a `Boolean` result. Conditions for `if`, `while`, and `repeat-until` statements must be of type `Boolean` or one of the other logical types (`ByteBool`, `WordBool`, or `LongBool`).

Tips and Tricks

Do not cast an integer value to `Boolean`. If you want compatibility with C and C++, where any non-zero integer is considered `True`, use the `ByteBool`, `WordBool`, or `LongBool` type instead of `Boolean`. The three other types have the same semantics, but different sizes. Unlike `Boolean`, the other three types interpret any non-zero ordinal value as `True`.

See Also

And Keyword, ByteBool Type, LongBool Type, Not Keyword, Or Keyword, WordBool Type, Xor Keyword

Break Procedure

Syntax

```
Break;
```

Description

`Break` jumps out of a loop, similar to the following `goto` statement:

```
label BreakOut;
begin
  while Condition do
  begin
    DoSomething;
    if AnotherCondition then
      goto BreakOut;  // like Break;
  end;
  BreakOut:
  // Controls transfer to the statement after the loop
```

If you call `Break` from within nested loop statements, control transfers out of the innermost loop only. To break out of multiple loops at one time, you must use a goto statement.

`Break` is not a real procedure, but is handled specially by the compiler. If you try to use `Break` outside of a loop statement, the compiler issues an error message.

See Also

Continue Procedure, Exit Procedure, For Keyword, Repeat Keyword, While Keyword

Byte Type

Syntax

```
type Byte = 0..255;
```

Description

The `Byte` type is an integer subrange. In an array or packed record, `Byte` values occupy one byte (8 bits) of memory. See the `Integer` type for information about other integer types.

See Also

Integer Type, ShortInt Type

ByteBool Type

Syntax

```
type ByteBool;
```

Description

The `ByteBool` type is a logical type whose size is the same as the size of a `Byte`. A `ByteBool` value is `False` when its ordinal value is zero, and it is `True` when its ordinal value is any non-zero value. `ByteBool` uses –1 as the ordinal value for `True` constants, e.g., `ByteBool(True)`.

Tips and Tricks

- You can use a `ByteBool` value anywhere you can use a `Boolean`. It is most useful when interfacing with C and C++, where any non-zero integer is considered `True`.

- `WordBool` and `LongBool` are similar to `ByteBool`, but they have different sizes.

See Also

And Keyword, Boolean Type, LongBool Type, Not Keyword, Or Keyword, WordBool Type, Xor Keyword

Cardinal Type

Syntax

```
type Cardinal = 0..4294967295;
```

Description

The `Cardinal` type is an unsigned integer subrange whose size is the natural size of an integer. In Delphi 5, the size is 32 bits, but in future versions of Delphi, it might be larger. Use `LongWord` for an unsigned integer type that must be 32 bits, regardless of the natural size of an integer. See the `Integer` type for information about other integer types.

Tips and Tricks

- The most common use for `Cardinal` is calling Windows API or other external functions that take parameters of type `DWORD` (unsigned long in C or C++).

- If you need an integer type for natural or whole numbers, you should usually define your own subranges, as shown here:

```
// Better than Cardinal for use in computation
type
  Whole = 1..MaxInt;
  Natural = 0..MaxInt;
```

- Using `Cardinal` as an ordinary integer type often gives results different from what you expect because the result might be any `Integer` or `Cardinal` value. The range of values covered by each individual type is 32 bits, but the combination requires 33 bits. Thus, any arithmetic operation that combines `Integer` and `Cardinal` values forces the compiler to expand the operands to at least 33 bits—so Delphi converts the operands to the `Int64` type:

```
type
  I: Integer;
  C: Cardinal;
begin
  ReadLn(I, C);
  // Result of I+C can be Low(Integer)..High(Cardinal), which
  // requires 33 bits, so Delphi must use Int64 for the result type.
  WriteLn(I + C);

  // Comparing Integer and Cardinal requires changing I and C to
  // Int64 in order to compare the numbers correctly. For example,
  // consider what happens when I=Low(Integer) and C=High(Cardinal),
  // and you try to compare the values as 32-bit integers.
  if I < C then
    WriteLn('I < C');
end;
```

See Also

Int64 Type, Integer Type, LongWord Type

Case Keyword

Syntax

```
case Ordinal expression of
  Ordinal range: Statement;
  Ordinal range, Ordinal range, ...: Statement
  else Statements...;
end;

type Name = record
  Declarations...
case Ordinal type of
  Ordinal range: (Declarations...);
  Ordinal range, Ordinal range, ...: (Declarations...);
end;

type Name = record
  Declarations...
case MemberName: Ordinal type of
  Ordinal range: (Declarations...);
  Ordinal range, Ordinal range, ...: (Declarations...);
end;
```

Description

The **case** statement selects one branch out of many possible branches, depending on the value of an ordinal-type expression. Delphi's **case** statement extends that of standard Pascal by including the optional **else** condition. If no other case matches the expression, Delphi executes the **else** statements. The **else** clause is similar to the **otherwise** clause found in other Pascal extensions.

The **case** keyword can also be used in a record type declaration, to declare a variant record. See the **record** keyword for details.

The type of the case expression must be an ordinal type, that is, integer, character, or enumeration. Each case selector must be a constant expression of the appropriate type or a constant range (*constant..constant*). The cases can be in any order, but the **else** clause must be last. Case selectors must be unique. Each case must have a single statement, except that you can have many statements after the **else**.

Tips and Tricks

If the case expression is an enumerated type, and the cases cover all possible values of the type, you should still have an **else** clause to raise an exception. The catch-all exception notifies you immediately if something is wrong with the program, and protects you in case a future version of the program extends the type without also extending the **case** statement.

Example

The following function maps a hue, saturation, and value to a red, green, and blue color. The **Hue** is interpreted as a position on a color wheel, so it is mapped to the range 0..359. The division of **Hue** by 60 must always result in a number in the range 0..5. Nonetheless, the **case** statement has an **else** clause that raises an exception to report the error. This defensive programming has no runtime cost, but helps identify errors. (If you cannot see the error in this function, consider what happens if Hue < 0. In that case, **Hue div 60** will be in the range –5..0, and the HSV function will raise an exception.)

```
// Map Hue, Saturation, and Value to a TColor, that is, RGB color.
function HSV(Hue: Integer; Saturation, Value: Byte): TColor;
var
  P, Q, R, S: Byte;
begin
  if Saturation = 0 then
    Result := RGB(Value, Value, Value)
  else
  begin
    Hue := Hue mod 360;
    S := Round(Saturation * Frac(Hue / 60));
    P := MulDiv(Value, 255 - Saturation, 255);
    Q := MulDiv(Value, 255 - S, 255);
    R := MulDiv(Value, 255 - (Saturation-S), 255);
    case Hue div 60 of
    0: Result := RGB(Value, R, P);
    1: Result := RGB(Q, Value, P);
    2: Result := RGB(P, Value, R);
    3: Result := RGB(P, Q, Value);
    4: Result := RGB(R, P, Value);
    5: Result := RGB(Value, P, Q);
    else
```

```
                raise Exception.CreateFmt('Cannot happen: Invalid Hue = %d',
                                          [Hue]);
          end;
        end;
      end;
```

See Also

If Keyword, Record Keyword

CDecl Directive

Syntax

```
Subroutine declaration; cdecl;
```

Description

The **cdecl** directive tells the compiler to use C-style calling conventions for the function or procedure. The caller of the subroutine pushes arguments onto the stack, starting with the rightmost argument. After the subroutine returns, the caller pops the arguments from the stack.

Functions return ordinal values, pointers, and small records or sets in **EAX** and floating-point values on the FPU stack. Strings, dynamic arrays, **Variants**, and large records and sets are passed as a hidden **var** parameter. This hidden parameter is the first parameter, so it is pushed last onto the stack. If the subroutine is a method, **Self** is pushed just before the function's **var** result (if one is needed).

See Also

Function Keyword, Pascal Directive, Procedure Keyword, Register Directive, SafeCall Directive, StdCall Directive

---

ChangeAnyProc Variable

Syntax

```
var ChangeAnyProc: Pointer;

procedure ChangeAny(var V: Variant);
ChangeAnyProc := @ChangeAny;
```

Description

The **ChangeAnyProc** procedure changes a **varAny Variant** value to a **Variant** type that Delphi can use. A **varAny** value represents an opaque type Delphi cannot work with other than to assign and pass to subroutines.

The default value of **ChangeAnyProc** is a procedure that raises runtime error 15 (**EVariantError**).

Tips and Tricks

The CorbaObj unit sets this variable to point to a procedure that supports CORBA's Any type. If you are not using CORBA, you can use varAny values for your own purposes.

Example

Suppose you want to use Variants in an application, but you need to store Int64 values. Delphi's Variant does not support the Int64 type, but you can use varAny to store Int64 values. When Delphi needs a concrete value, the ChangeAnyProc procedure converts the Int64 to a string, which Delphi understands how to use. The VAny field is a pointer, so the SetVarInt64 procedure allocates dynamic memory to store the Int64 value, and saves the pointer in the Variant. The ClearAnyProc procedure frees the memory when Delphi is done using the Variant value.

```
// Change a varAny Int64 value to a known Variant type, specifically
// a string.
procedure ChangeVarInt64(var V: Variant);
var
  Value: Int64;
begin
  if TVarData(V).VType = varAny then
  begin
    Value := PInt64(TVarData(V).VAny)^;
    V := IntToStr(Value);
  end;
end;
...
ChangeAnyProc := @ChangeVarInt64;
```

See Also

ClearAnyProc Variable, RefAnyProc Variable, TVarData Type, Variant Type

---

Char Type

Description

The Char type represents a single character, just as it does in standard Pascal. You can cast any integer type to a character by using the Char type name in a type cast. Unlike some other type casts, the size of the integer value does not have to match the size of a Char.

You can write a character constant in several different ways:

- As a string of length 1, e.g., 'A' (best for printable characters)

- As a caret control character, e.g., ^A (good for ANSI control characters, but you should probably give the character a meaningful name, as shown here):

```
const
  TAB = ^I;
  CRLF = ^M^J;
```

- As # followed by an integer constant, e.g., #65 or #$41 (good for control characters, e.g., #0 or #255)

- By calling the Chr function, e.g., Chr(65) (best for converting integer variables to characters)

- By typecasting an integer, e.g., Char(65) (same as Chr)

Tips and Tricks

In the current release of Delphi, Char is the same as AnsiChar, but in future versions, the meaning of Char might change. For example, it might become synonymous with WideChar. Char is suitable for most uses, but do not assume that a Char and a Byte occupy the same amount of memory.

See Also

AnsiChar Type, Chr Function, PChar Type, String Keyword, WideChar Type

---

ChDir Procedure

Syntax

```
procedure ChDir(const Directory: string);
```

Description

The ChDir procedure changes the working directory and drive to the path specified in the Directory argument. If ChDir cannot set the directory for any reason, it reports an I/O error, using the error code returned by Windows. ChDir is not a real procedure.

See Also

GetDir Function, IOResult Function, MkDir Procedure, RmDir Procedure, $I Compiler Directive, $IOChecks Compiler Directive

---

Chr Function

Syntax

```
function Chr(IntValue: Integer): AnsiChar;
function Chr(IntValue: Integer): WideChar;
```

Description

The Chr function converts an integer to its equivalent character, either AnsiChar or WideChar, whichever is called for. Chr is not a real function, and calling Chr has no runtime impact. Delphi automatically maps IntValue into the range needed for the character type (#0..#255 for AnsiChar or #0..#65535 for WideChar).

Tips and Tricks

- The compiler treats the character expressions Chr(27), #27, and ^[identically, so choose the style you find most readable. For control characters, the caret notation is often best, e.g., ^M for a carriage return. For special

---

characters, a character constant usually works best, e.g., #0 to mark the end of a PChar string. Use Chr to convert variables.

- Calling Chr is identical to using a type cast, but Chr is more familiar to experienced Pascal programmers.

See Also

AnsiChar Type, Char Type, Ord Function, WideChar Type

Class Keyword

Syntax

```
type Name = class
  Declarations...
  class function ...;
  class procedure...;
end;

type Name = class(BaseClass)
  ...
end;

type Name = class(BaseClass);

type ForwardDeclaredName = class;

type Name = class(BaseClass, Interface name...)
  Declarations...
end;

type Name = packed class...

type MetaClass = class of Class type;
```

Description

The class keyword introduces a class declaration, and it starts the declaration of a class method. If a semicolon appears immediately after the class keyword, the declaration is a forward declaration: it tells the compiler that the type name is a class type, but provides no other information about the class. You must have a complete class declaration later in the same type declaration block.

The last example above shows the declaration of a metaclass type. A variable of metaclass type can store a class reference. You can use this variable in any expression that calls for a class reference, such as calling a constructor or class method, or as the right-hand argument to an is operator. (The as operator, on the other hand, requires a static class name, not a variable class reference because it performs a type cast, and the compiler must know the target type.)

A class declaration must have a single base class and can have any number of interfaces. If you omit the base class, Delphi uses TObject. If you want to list any interfaces, you must supply the name of a base class, even if that name is TObject.

A class declaration contains zero or more sections, where each section has a particular access level. The default access level is public unless a class has RTTI (by using the $M or $TypeInfo compiler directives or inheriting from a class that has RTTI), in which case the default is published.

Each section starts with zero or more field declarations. After all the field declarations come method and property declarations. You can have any number of sections, and you can repeat sections with the same access level. Sections can appear in any order.

If you supply a base class, and a semicolon appears immediately after the closing parenthesis, you can omit the **end** keyword.

By default, each field is aligned, but you can use the **packed** directive so fields start on byte boundaries. See the **packed** keyword for details. If you want every class and record to be packed, use the $A or $Align compiler directive.

Class Methods

A class method is similar to an ordinary method with the following differences:

- A class method declaration begins with the **class** keyword. You must use the **class** keyword in the class declaration and in the method's definition.

- You must call an ordinary method by invoking it from an object reference. You can call a class method by invoking it from an object reference or a class reference.

- Inside a class method, **Self** refers to the class and does not refer to an object. This means the method cannot use any fields because there is no object to store those fields.

Tips and Tricks

A class can implement any number of interfaces. Delphi matches interface method names with method names in the class. You can redirect interface methods to different methods in the class declaration with a method resolution clause, which has the following form:

```
procedure Interface.InterfaceMethod = MethodName;
function Interface.InterfaceMethod = MethodName;
```

The *MethodName* is the name of a method in the containing class declaration. Redirection is especially important when a class implements multiple interfaces, and two or more interfaces have methods with the same name and arguments.

Examples

```
type
  TSimpleStream = class;
  TSimpleClass = class        // Implicitly inherits from TObject.
  private                     // Sections can be in any order.  A
    fStream: TSimpleStream;   // common convention is to list sections
  public                      // in increasing order by access level.
    constructor Create(const FileName: string = '');
    destructor Destroy; override;
    property Stream: TSimpleStream read fStream;
  end;
```

```pascal
TSimpleStream = class(TPersistent, ISequentialStream)
private
  fHandle: THandle;
  fReadOnly: Boolean;
protected
  // method of ISequentialStream
  function Read(Data: Pointer; Count: LongInt; BytesRead: PLongInt):
    HResult; stdcall;
  function Write(Data: Pointer; Count: LongInt;
    BytesWritten: PLongint): HResult; stdcall;
public
  constructor Create(const FileName: string); overload;
  constructor Create(Handle: THandle); overload;
  destructor Destroy; override;
  procedure Assign(Source: TPersistent); override;
published
  property ReadOnly: Boolean read fReadOnly write fReadOnly;
end;


// In Delphi's Open Tools API, the IOTAWizard and IOTAFileSystem
// interfaces both have a method named GetIDString. The TVfsWizard
// class implements both interfaces, and uses method resolution
// clauses to select which method implements the interface methods.
TVfsWizard = class(TInterfacedObject, IOTAWizard, IOTAFileSystem)
private
// methods of IOTAFileSystem
  function DeleteFile(const FileName: string): Boolean;
  function FileAge(const FileName: string): LongInt;
  function FileExists(const FileName: string): Boolean;
  function GetBackupFileName(const FileName: string): string;
  function GetFileStream(const FileName: string; Mode: Integer):
      IStream;
  function GetFileSystemIDString: string;
  function IOTAFileSystem.GetIDString = GetFileSystemIDString;
  function GetTempFileName(const FileName: string): string;
  function IsFileBased: Boolean;
  function IsReadonly(const FileName: string): Boolean;
  function RenameFile(const OldName, NewName: string): Boolean;

// methods of IOTAWizard
  function GetWizardIDString: string;
  function IOTAWizard.GetIDString = GetWizardIDString;
  function GetName: string;
  function GetState: TWizardState;
  procedure Execute;

// The following function is a convenience function that anyone
// can call to get a reference to the global IOTAServices interface.
  class function Services: IOTAServices;
end;
```

See Also

Automated Directive, Constructor Keyword, Destructor Keyword, Function Keyword, Interface Keyword, Is Keyword, Packed Keyword, Private Directive,

Procedure Keyword, Property Keyword, Protected Directive, Public Directive, Published Directive, Self Variable, Type Keyword, $A Compiler Directive, $Align Compiler Directive, $M Compiler Directive, $TypeInfo Compiler Directive

ClearAnyProc Variable

Syntax

```
var ClearAnyProc: Pointer;

procedure ClearAny(var V: Variant);
ClearAnyProc := @ClearAny;
```

Description

When Delphi is finished using a **varAny Variant** value, it calls **ClearAnyProc** to free all memory associated with the opaque **varAny** value. The default value is a procedure that raises runtime error 16 (**EVariantError**).

Tips and Tricks

The **CorbaObj** unit sets this variable to point to a procedure that supports CORBA's Any type. If you are not using CORBA, you can use **varAny** values for your own purposes.

Example

See the **ChangeAnyProc** variable for an explanation of this example.

```
// Clear a varAny Variant that is holding a pointer to an Int64 value.
procedure ClearVarInt64(var V: Variant);
var
  Ptr: Pointer;
begin
  if TVarData(V).VType = varAny then
  begin
    Ptr := TVarData(V).VAny;
    TVarData(V).VType := varEmpty;
    FreeMem(Ptr);
  end;
end;
...
ClearAnyProc := @ClearVarInt64;
```

See Also

ChangeAnyProc Variable, RefAnyProc Variable, TVarData Type, Variant Type

Close Procedure

Syntax

```
procedure Close(var F: File);
procedure Close(var F: TextFile);
```

Description

`Close` exists for backward compatibility with Turbo Pascal and standard Pascal. New Delphi programs should call `CloseFile` to avoid conflicts with methods named `Close`. `Close` is not a real procedure.

See Also

CloseFile Procedure

CloseFile Procedure

Syntax

```
procedure CloseFile(var F: File);
procedure CloseFile(var F: TextFile);
```

Description

Call `CloseFile` to close a file that was opened with `Append`, `Reset`, or `Rewrite`. `CloseFile` is not a real procedure.

For an example, see the `AssignFile` procedure.

Errors

- If you call `CloseFile` for a file that is already closed, Delphi reports I/O error 103.

- If you try to close a file but have not yet called `AssignFile`, the results are unpredictable.

See Also

Append Procedure, AssignFile Procedure, IOResult Function, Reset Procedure, Rewrite Procedure

---

CmdLine Variable

Syntax

```
var CmdLine: PChar;
```

Description

The `CmdLine` variable stores the command line that was used to invoke the program. It is an empty string for libraries. The `ParamCount` and `ParamStr` functions parse the command line into separate arguments; it is usually more convenient to use these than to parse the entire command line yourself.

To check for switches on the command line, call the `FindCmdLineSwitch` function in the `SysUtils` unit.

See Also

CmdShow Variable, ParamCount Function, ParamStr Function

CmdShow Variable

Syntax

```
var CmdShow: Integer;
```

Description

The CmdShow variable determines how to show a program's initial window. For details, see the Windows API documentation for the ShowWindow function. If your application has a main form, Delphi automatically uses the CmdShow variable to start the application in a normal, minimized, or maximized state.

See Also

CmdLine Variable

Comp Type

Syntax

```
type Comp;
```

Description

The Comp type is a 64-bit signed integer type that uses the floating-point processor. The Comp type exists only for backward compatibility. New programs should use Int64 instead. The Int64 type is a true integer type and allows bitwise and shift operations, supports the full range of the 64-bit type, and is not dependent on the floating-point control word.

Tips and Tricks

- To use the full 64-bit precision of the Comp type, the floating-point control word must be set to extended precision. Some Microsoft and other DLLs change the floating-point control word to double or single precision, thereby reducing the Comp type to 53 or fewer bits.

- Delphi's I/O and the formatting routines in the SysUtils unit do not support the full range of the Comp type. Values near the limits of the Comp type are printed with less precision than is actually stored in the Comp variable. Most applications will not encounter this limitation.

See Also

CompToCurrency Function, CompToDouble Function, CurrencyToComp Procedure, DoubleToComp Procedure, Extended Type, Int64 Type

CompToCurrency Function

Syntax

```
function CompToCurrency(Value: Comp): Currency; cdecl;
```

Description

CompToCurrency converts a Comp value to Currency. It is a real function.

Tips and Tricks

- You can call CompToCurrency in a C++ Builder program. Delphi automatically converts Comp to Currency when it needs to, so you don't need to call this function in a Delphi program.

- Comp can represent numbers outside the range of Currency, so converting Comp to Currency can result in runtime error 6 (EInvalidOp).

See Also

Comp Type, CompToDouble Function, Currency Type, CurrencyToComp Procedure

---

CompToDouble Function

Syntax

```
function CompToDouble(Value: Comp): Double; cdecl;
```

Description

CompToDouble converts a Comp value to Double. It is a real function.

Tips and Tricks

- You can call CompToDouble in a C++ Builder program. Delphi automatically converts Comp to Double when it needs to, so you don't need to call this function in a Delphi program.

- Converting Comp to Double can lose precision.

See Also

Comp Type, CompToCurrency Function, Double Type, DoubleToComp Procedure

---

Concat Function

Syntax

```
function Concat(const S1, S2, ....: string): string;
```

Description

The Concat function concatenates all the strings given as arguments into a single string. It is the same as using the '+' operator: S1 + S2 + ... The Concat function is built into the compiler and is not a real function.

There is no performance difference between using the + operator and calling Concat.

Copy Function, Delete Function, Insert Procedure, SetLength Procedure, SetString Procedure

Const Keyword

Syntax

```
const
  Name = Expression;
  Name: Type = Expression;

Subroutine header(...; const Name: Type; const Name: array of const);
```

Description

Delphi extends the `const` keyword of standard Pascal by allowing you to specify any constant-valued expression as the value of a constant and by allowing you to give a specific type for a constant.

If you supply a type, you are creating a typed constant, which isn't really a constant, but rather is an initialized variable. The lifetime of a typed constant is that of the program or library, even if the typed constant is declared locally to a subroutine.

You can also declare a subroutine parameter as `const` or as an open array of `const`. A subroutine cannot modify a `const` parameter. This has several benefits:

- A `const` parameter clearly tells the reader that the subroutine does not change the parameter's value. This improves the readability and clarity of the code.

- The compiler enforces the restriction. If you accidentally try to assign a new value to a `const` parameter, the compiler issues an error message. Note that a `const` object reference means you cannot change the reference. The object itself is not `const`.

- Passing `const` strings, dynamic arrays, and interfaces is slightly more efficient because Delphi can avoid incrementing the reference count when it knows the subroutine will not modify the parameter.

Tips and Tricks

- One of the common uses for so-called typed constants is to declare a variable whose lexical scope is restricted to a subroutine, but whose value persists across subroutine calls.

- By default, typed constants can be modified. Some uses of typed constants are truly constant, so you can use the `$J` or `$WriteableConst` compiler directive to ensure that a typed constant is truly constant.

Example

```
// Silly example where the NextFruitName function returns the
// name of a different fruit each time it is called. The TFruit
// enumeration lists the available fruits. The example shows
```

```
// several ways of using constants. The first is an ordinary
// constant. The second is a typed constant where the values
// are truly constant. The third is a typed constant whose
// value changes, but the value persists across calls to
// the NextFruitName function.
type
  TFruit = (fKumquat, fMango, fStar, fStrawberry, fMarionberry);
function NextFruitName: string;
const
  InitialValue = fStar;
{$WriteableConst Off}
  FruitNames: array[TFruit] of string =
    ('Kumquat', 'Mango', 'Star Fruit', 'Strawberry', 'Marionberry');
{$WriteableConst On}
  Fruit: TFruit = InitialValue;
begin
  if Fruit = High(Fruit) then
    Fruit := Low(Fruit)
  else
    Inc(Fruit);
  Result := FruitNames[Fruit];
end;
```

See Also

AnsiString Type, Array Keyword, Interface Keyword, Out Directive, String Keyword, Var Keyword, $J Compiler Directive, $WriteableConst Compiler Directive

Constructor Keyword

Syntax

```
type Class declaration
...
  constructor Name;
  constructor Name(Arguments...);
end;
```

Description

A constructor is a special kind of method. If you call a constructor using a class reference, Delphi creates a new instance of that class, initializes the instance, and then calls the constructor proper. If you call a constructor using an object reference, Delphi calls the constructor as an ordinary method.

A natural consequence of Delphi's rules is that a constructor can call another constructor of the same class or call an inherited constructor. The call uses an object reference (namely, Self) so the constructor is called as an ordinary method.

When called using a class reference, Delphi calls the NewInstance method to create the instance. TObject.NewInstance allocates memory for the new object and fills that memory with all zeros, but you can override NewInstance to create the object in a different manner.

Tips and Tricks

- A common error for new Delphi programmers is to call a constructor using an object-type variable. Rather than creating the object, such a call invariably results in access violations because the object reference is most likely invalid. The compiler can warn you about such errors if you enable compiler warnings in the project options. For example:

```
var
  ObjRef: TSomething;
begin
  ObjRef.Create;                // wrong
  ObjRef := TSomething.Create;  // right
```

- If you are writing an abstract base class, and the constructor is virtual so you can write a class factory, do not make the constructor abstract. Derived classes should always call an inherited constructor, but if the constructor is abstract, that isn't possible. If the abstract base class has nothing to do in its constructor, you should supply a constructor that does nothing except call an inherited constructor. For example,

```
constructor TAbstractBaseClass.Create;
begin
  inherited Create;
end;
```

- Always call an inherited constructor. Even if you know that the inherited constructor does nothing (such as `TObject.Create`), you should call it. The overhead of calling the inherited constructor is small, but the potential payback is enormous. Imagine, for example, that a future revision to the class changes its base class. The new base class constructor might do something important. Even if the base class remains the same, the base class constructor might change from doing nothing to doing something. Changing a base class during code maintenance should be easy, and should not require a laborious search through all derived class constructors, checking to see whether they call an inherited constructor.

See Also

Class Keyword, Destructor Keyword, Inherited Keyword, TObject Type

---

Contains Directive

Syntax

```
package Name;
contains Unit, Unit in FileName;
  ...
```

Description

The **contains** directive heads a list of unit names that make up a package. The unit names are separated by commas, and each unit name can appear as just the name or the name followed by the name of the unit's file as a string.

Tips and Tricks

- All the units that are used by the units contained in a package must reside in the package itself or in one of the required packages. Delphi must know where to find every referenced unit so it can compile the package.

- You cannot list the same unit more than once, and all the units that a package contains must not be in any of the required packages. This rule prevents a unit from being included more than once in a project.

- Usually, you will use Delphi's package editor to add units to a package or remove units from a package. You can edit the package source manually, but doing so does not update the package editor. Close and reopen the project or project group to force Delphi to read the new package source file.

- Delphi's IDE does not always treat a package as a project. If you have difficulties with the IDE, try creating a new project group, then add the package to the project group.

See Also

Package Keyword, Requires Directive, Unit Keyword, Uses Keyword

---

Continue Procedure

Syntax

```
Continue;
```

Description

Continue jumps over the body of a loop, similar to the following goto statement:

```
label Continue;
begin
  while Condition do
  begin
    DoSomething;
    if AnotherCondition then
      goto Continue;
    DoSomeMore;
  Continue:
  end;
```

If you call Continue from within nested loop statements, control transfer within the innermost loop only. To continue multiple loops at one time, you must use a goto statement.

The Continue procedure is built into the compiler and is not a real procedure. If you try to use Continue outside of a loop statement, the compiler issues an error message.

See Also

Break Procedure, For Keyword, Repeat Keyword, While Keyword

Copy Function

Syntax

```
function Copy(Source: string; StartingIndex, Count: Integer): string;
function Copy(Source: array; StartingIndex, Count: Integer): array;
```

Description

The Copy function creates a copy of part of a string or dynamic array. The result is a new string or dynamic array. The new string or array starts with the element at StartingIndex in Source. The new string or array contains up to Count elements. If Count exceeds the number of items remaining in the source string or array, the elements from StartingIndex to the end of the string or array are copied.

Copy is not a real function.

Tips and Tricks

- If StartingIndex is less than zero or past the end of Source, the result is an empty string or array.

- The length of the new string or array is Count unless the Source has fewer than Count elements to copy, in which case Copy copies all the elements up to the end of the string or array.

- The first index of a string is 1. The first index of a dynamic array is 0.

- A convenient way to copy all the elements of Source from the starting index is to use MaxInt as the Count.

See Also

Delete Function, High Function, Insert Procedure, Length Function, Low Function, SetLength Procedure, SetString Procedure, Slice Function

---

Cos Function

Syntax

```
function Cos(Number: Floating-point type): Extended;
```

Description

The Cos function computes and returns the cosine of Number, which is an angle in radians. The Cos function is built-in.

Tips and Tricks

- Delphi automatically converts Integer and Variant arguments to floating-point. To convert an Int64 argument to floating-point, add 0.0.

- If Number is a signaling NaN, positive infinity, or negative infinity, Delphi raises runtime error 6 (EInvalidOp).

- If Number is a quiet NaN, the result is Number.

ArcTan Function, Sin Function

Currency Type

Syntax

```
type Currency;
```

Description

The Currency type is a 64-bit fixed-point type, with four places after the decimal point. The Currency type uses the floating-point processor, treating the Currency value as an integer. Input and output using the Currency type imposes the four-decimal place convention, and computation using Currency automatically adjusts the value by 10,000 to account for the implicit decimal places.

Tips and Tricks

- To use the full 64-bit precision of the Currency type, the floating-point control word must be set to extended precision. Some Microsoft and other DLLs change the floating-point control word to double or single precision, thereby reducing the Currency type to 54 or fewer bits.

- Delphi's I/O and the formatting routines in the SysUtils unit do not support the full range of the Currency type. Values near the limits of the Currency type are printed with less precision than is actually stored in the Currency variable. Most applications will not encounter this limitation.

See Also

Extended Type, Int64 Type, Set8087CW Procedure

CurrencyToComp Procedure

Syntax

```
procedure CurrencyToComp(Value: Currency; var result: Comp); cdecl;
```

Description

CurrencyToComp converts a Currency value to Comp. It is a real function.

Tips and Tricks

- You can call CurrencyToComp in a C++ Builder program. Delphi automatically converts Currency to Comp when it needs to, so you don't need to call this function in a Delphi program.

- Converting Currency to Comp can lose precision.

See Also

Comp Type, CompToCurrency Function, Currency Type

DataMark Variable

Syntax

```
unit SysInit;
var DataMark: Integer;
```

Description

DataMark is the first variable in the module's data segment. Its address is the virtual address where writable data begins.

DebugHook Variable

Syntax

```
var DebugHook: Byte;
```

Description

Delphi's debugger uses DebugHook to determine what to do with exceptions. When an application runs normally, DebugHook is 0. When you debug an application in Delphi's IDE, the IDE sets DebugHook to 1. When the IDE catches an exception or when you are single-stepping in the debugger, the IDE sets DebugHook to 2.

See Also

JITEnable Variable

Dec Procedure

Syntax

```
procedure Dec(var Variable);
procedure Dec(var Variable; Count: Integer);
```

Description

The Dec procedure decrements a variable. You can decrement any ordinal-type variable or pointer-type variable. You cannot use Dec to decrement a floating-point variable.

Decrementing a pointer adjusts the pointer by the size of the base type. For example, decrementing a pointer to AnsiChar decreases the pointer value by 1, and decrementing a pointer to WideChar decreases the pointer value by 2.

The default is to decrement the variable by 1 unit, but you can supply an integer to decrement by a different amount. When decrementing a pointer, Count is multiplied by the size of the base type.

The Dec procedure is built-in and is not a real procedure.

Tips and Tricks

- Count can be negative, in which case the variable's value increases.

- There is little performance difference between `Dec`, `Pred`, or subtraction. That is, the following all result in similar object code:

```
Dec(X);
X := Pred(X);
X := X - 1;      // if X is an integer or PChar type
```

- You cannot use a property for the variable because a property value cannot be used as a `var` parameter. Use a simple assignment instead.

See Also

High Function, Inc Procedure, Low Function, Pred Function, Succ Function

---

Default Directive

Syntax

```
property Declaration; default;
property Declaration default Ordinal constant;
```

Description

The `default` directive has two uses in property declarations:

- To make an array property the class's default property
- To supply a default value for an ordinal-type property

A class can declare one array property as the default property for the class. The default property lets you refer to an object reference as an array without mentioning the property name. For example, `TList` declares the `Items` property as its default array property. If `List` is a variable of type `TList`, you can refer to a list element as `List[Index]`, which is a shorthand for `List.Items[Index]`. A class can have only one default property. Derived classes can define a different default property from that of an ancestor class.

An ordinal-type property (integer, enumeration, set, or character type) can list a default value. The default value has no effect on the property's initial value. Instead, the default value is stored in the class's RTTI, and Delphi's design-time and runtime environments use the default value to reduce the size of a *.dfm* file or resource. Non-ordinal properties (e.g., floating-point, string, class) always use zero (empty string, `nil`, etc.) as the default value.

Tips and Tricks

- If you do not specify a `default` directive, Delphi assumes you mean `nodefault` and stores the smallest integer (–2,147,483,648) as the property's default value. A side effect is that you cannot use the smallest integer as a property's default value. If you do, Delphi interprets it as `nodefault`.

- Because the default directive affects only a class's RTTI, you must write your constructor to set the default value for each property. You can use RTTI to your advantage by reading the default values from the class's RTTI and setting the object's default values accordingly, as shown here:

```
// Set an object's default values by getting those values from
// the class's RTTI. Call this procedure from the constructor
```

```
    // of any class that uses the default directive.
    procedure SetDefaultValues(Obj: TObject);
    const
      tkOrdinal = [tkEnumeration, tkSet, tkInteger, tkChar, tkWChar];
      NoDefault = Low(Integer);
    var
      Count, I: Integer;
      PropList: PPropList;
    begin
      // Make sure the class has published properties & RTTI.
      if (Obj <> nil) and (Obj.ClassInfo <> nil) then
      begin
        // Get the number of ordinal-type properties
        Count := GetPropList(Obj.ClassInfo, tkOrdinal, nil);
        GetMem(PropList, Count * SizeOf(PPropInfo));
        try
          // Get the ordinal-type properties.
          GetPropList(Obj.ClassInfo, tkOrdinal, PropList);
          for I := 0 to Count-1 do
            // For each property, if the property has a default value,
            // set the property's value to the default.
            if PropList[I].Default <> NoDefault then
              SetOrdProp(Obj, PropList[I], PropList[I].Default);
        finally
          FreeMem(PropList);
        end;
      end;
    end;
```

Example

See the **property** keyword for examples of using the **default** directive.

See Also

Class Keyword, Dispinterface Keyword, Interface Keyword, Nodefault
Directive, Property Keyword, Read Directive, Stored Directive, Write Directive

---

Default8087CW Variable

Syntax

```
var Default8087CW: Word;
```

Description

Delphi sets the floating-point unit (FPU) control word to the value stored in
Default8087CW. You can set the control word by calling **Set8087CW**, and Delphi
automatically saves the new control word in **Default8087CW**.

Note that some DLLs change the FPU control word. You can call **SysUtils.
SafeLoadLibrary**, which ensures that the FPU control word is restored to
Default8087CW after loading the library.

See the **Set8087CW** procedure for more information about the floating-point
control word.

See Also

Set8087CW Procedure

Delete Procedure

Syntax

```
procedure Delete(var Str: string; StartingIndex, Count: Integer);
```

Description

The `Delete` procedure removes `Count` characters from a string, starting at `StartingIndex`. If `Count` is more than the number of characters remaining in the string, `Delete` deletes the rest of the string, starting from `StartingIndex`. `Delete` is not a real procedure.

Tips and Tricks

- The first character of a string has index 1.

- If `StartingIndex` is not positive or is greater than the length of the string, `Delete` does not change the string.

- If the `Count` is greater than the characters remaining after the starting index, the rest of the string is deleted.

- If you want to delete characters at the end of a string, `SetLength` is slightly faster than calling the more general purpose `Delete`.

Example

```
// Remove a drive letter from the front of a path.
procedure RemoveDriveLetter(var Path: string);
begin
   // First make sure the path has a drive letter in front.
   if (Length(Path) >= 2) and (Path[2] = ':') then
     // Delete the first two characters of the path.
     Delete(Path, 1, 2);
end;
```

See Also

Copy Function, Insert Procedure, SetLength Procedure, SetString Procedure

Destructor Keyword

Syntax

```
type Class declaration
   destructor Destroy; override;
end;
```

Description

A destructor cleans up an object and frees its memory. A destructor takes a hidden parameter. This parameter is 1 when the destructor is called from an ordinary method, which tells the destructor to call `BeforeDestruction`, then run the destructor proper, and finally call `FreeInstance` to free the object's memory. When a destructor calls an inherited destructor, the hidden parameter is zero.

Tips and Tricks

- To free an object, call its `Free` method. Do not call `Destroy`. `Free` checks whether the object reference is `nil`, and calls `Destroy` only for non-`nil` object references.

- Although you can declare a class destructor with any name and arguments, you should declare a single destructor named `Destroy`. Because `Destroy` is declared as a virtual method of `TObject`, you must declare it with the `override` directive in your class declaration.

- The reason you need to override the virtual `Destroy` directive is because the destructor will often be called polymorphically—where the type declaration of the object reference differs from the object's actual class.

- Delphi automatically calls `Destroy` if a constructor raises an exception. Therefore, you should program defensively. Fields might not be initialized when the destructor is called, so always check for a zero or `nil` value. Note that `Free`, `FreeMem`, and `Dispose` automatically check for `nil` before freeing the object or memory.

- If you are freeing an object reference that is stored in a global variable or a field of another object, call the `SysUtils.FreeAndNil` procedure instead of the `Free` method.

See Also

Class Keyword, Constructor Keyword, TObject Type

DispCallByIDProc Variable

Syntax

```
var DispCallByIDProc: Pointer;

type
  PDispRec = ^TDispRec;
  TCallDesc = packed record
    CallType: Byte;
    ArgCount: Byte;
    NamedArgCount: Byte;
    Args: array[0.255] of Byte;
  end;
  TDispDesc = packed record
    Dispid: Integer;
    ResultType: Byte;
    CallDesc: TCallDesc;
  end;
procedure CallProc(Result: Pointer; const Dispatch: IDispatch;
  DispDesc: PDispDesc; Params: Pointer); cdecl;

DispCallByIDProc := @CallProc;
```

Description

Delphi calls the `DispCallByIDProc` procedure to call a dispatch method that is identified by dispatch identifier in a `dispinterface`. Delphi fills the `DispDesc` record with the necessary information about the dispatch identifier and the method's formal parameters. `Params` points to the actual arguments for the method call. The procedure must store the result in the memory buffer pointed to by `Result`. The type of `Result`'s buffer is dictated by the dispatch descriptor.

The default value of `DispCallByIDProc` is a procedure that raises runtime error 17 (`EVariantError`).

Tips and Tricks

- The `ComObj` unit sets `DispCallByIDProc` to a procedure that implements the necessary code to call `IDispatch.Invoke`. `ComObj` also declares the `TCallDesc` and `TDispDesc` types.

- Writing your own `DispCallByIDProc` is a major undertaking. Consult the *ComObj.pas* source code to learn how.

See Also

Cdecl Directive, Dispid Directive, Dispinterface Keyword, IDispatch Interface, VarDispProc Variable

---

Dispid Directive

Syntax

```
Dispinterface declaration
  Method declaration; dispid Integer constant;
  Property declaration dispid Integer constant;
  ...
end;
```

Description

By default, Delphi assigns dispatch identifiers to methods and properties in a dispatch interface declaration, or you can specify them explicitly with the `dispid` directive. You cannot specify the index of a `dispid` that is already used in the enclosing `dispinterface`.

Example

See the `Dispinterface` keyword for examples.

See Also

Dispinterface Keyword, IDispatch Interface

Dispinterface Keyword

Syntax

```
type Name = dispinterface
  ['{Guid...}']
```

```
    Method and property declarations...
  end;
```

Description

The `dispinterface` keyword is similar to `interface` for declaring an interface type, but it declares a dispatch interface. Delphi uses a dispatch interface to access a COM automation server through the `Invoke` method of the `IDispatch` interface. A class cannot implement a dispatch interface, nor can a dispatch interface inherit from another interface (dispatch or normal).

Declarations can specify a dispatch identifier with the `dispid` directive. All the dispatch identifiers within a single `dispinterface` must be unique. No other method directives are allowed.

Property declarations do not include `read` or `write` specifiers. By default a property has read and write access, or you can declare the property with the `readonly` or `writeonly` directive. An array property can have a `default` directive. No other property directives are allowed.

Tips and Tricks

- The purpose of a `dispinterface` declaration is to make a dispatch interface available at compile time, so you don't have to wait until runtime to learn you misspelled a method name. The author of the COM server must provide the `dispinterface` declaration for the COM object. If you have a type library, you can use Delphi's type library editor to generate the source code and `dispinterface` declaration.

- A COM server can implement an ordinary interface, a dispatch interface, or both. Check the type library to learn what kind of interface it supports. An ordinary interface is faster than using a dispatch interface, but if you must use a dispatch interface, it is more convenient to use a `dispinterface` than to use a `Variant` to access the COM object.

- The COM server must create an object that implements the `dispinterface`, using a class factory or something similar, such as `CreateComObject` (in the `ComObj` unit). Consult the documentation for the COM server to learn exactly how to create the COM object.

Example

```
// Below is the IStrings dispatch interface from stdvcl.pas.
// When you create an ActiveX control from a Delphi control,
// IStrings is the COM interface for a TStrings-type property,
// such as TMemo.Lines or TListView.Items.
type
  IStringsDisp = dispinterface
    ['{EE05DFE2-5549-11D0-9EA9-0020AF3D82DA}']
    property ControlDefault[Index: Integer]: OleVariant dispid 0;
      default;
    function Count: Integer; dispid 1;
    property Item[Index: Integer]: OleVariant dispid 2;
    procedure Remove(Index: Integer); dispid 3;
    procedure Clear; dispid 4;
```

```
    function Add(Item: OleVariant): Integer; dispid 5;
    function _NewEnum: IUnknown; dispid -4;
  end;
```

See Also

Default Directive, Dispid Directive, Interface Keyword, Readonly Directive, Writeonly Directive

---

Dispose Procedure

Syntax

```
procedure Dispose(var P: Pointer-type);
procedure Dispose(var P: ^object; Destructor);
```

Description

Memory that you allocate with New must be freed with Dispose. Dispose quietly ignores an attempt to free a nil pointer. If you try to free a pointer that was already freed or was not allocated by New, the results are unpredictable. Dispose is not a real procedure.

When disposing of an old-style object instance, you can also pass a destructor call as the second argument. Use the destructor name and any arguments it requires.

Tips and Tricks

- Delphi calls Finalize for you before freeing the memory.

- After Dispose returns, the pointer P contains an invalid value. If the pointer is not a local variable, be sure to set it to nil.

- Call FreeMem to free memory allocated by GetMem. Call Dispose to free memory allocated by New.

Example

```
type
  PLink = ^TLink;
  TLink = record
    Info: string;
    Next: PLink;
    Previous: PLink;
  end;
const
  FreePattern = Pointer($BAD00BAD);

// Free a link in a doubly linked list.
procedure FreeLink(var Link: PLink);
var
  Tmp: PLink;
begin
  if Link.Previous <> nil then
    Link.Previous.Next := Link.Next;
  if Link.Next <> nil then
```

```
   Link.Next.Previous := Link.Previous;

   // Referring to Link or Link.Next, etc., after freeing Link would
   // be an error. Help detect such errors by storing a particular
   // pointer patter in Link. If the program raises an access
   // violation, and the erroneous pointer is this pattern, the
   // problem is probably caused by a dangling reference to Link.
   Link.Next := FreePattern;
   Link.Previous := FreePattern;
   Tmp := Link;
   Link := FreePattern;
   Dispose(Tmp);
end;
```

See Also

Finalize Procedure, FreeMem Procedure, IsMultiThread Variable, New
Procedure, Object Keyword

Div Keyword

Syntax

```
Dividend div Divisor
```

Description

The div operator performs integer division, which discards fractional results
without rounding. If the divisor is zero, Delphi reports runtime error 3
(EDivByZero).

See Also

Mod Keyword, / Operator

DllProc Variable

Syntax

```
unit SysInit;
var DllProc: Pointer;

procedure DllHandler(Reason: Integer);
begin ... end;
DllProc := @DllHandler;
```

Description

When Windows loads or unloads a DLL or when a thread starts or ends, Windows
call the DllProc procedure in the DLL, passing the reason for the call as the
Reason argument. Windows ordinarily calls the DLL procedure when the DLL is
first loaded in a process, but Delphi handles that situation by initializing every unit
and then executing the statement block in the library's project file. Thus, Delphi
calls DllProc only for the other three cases, that is, Reason is one of the
following constants (which are declared in the Windows unit):

Dll_Thread_Attach

A process that loaded the DLL has created a new thread. If more than one thread attaches to the DLL, be sure to set `IsMultiThread` to True.

Dll_Thread_Detach

A thread has terminated.

Dll_Process_Detach

A process is exiting or unloading the DLL.

Tips and Tricks

- Windows calls the `DLLProc` procedure in the context of the new thread, so you can use **threadvar** variables when attaching the DLL to a new thread. Do not use **threadvar** variables when detaching, though. Delphi cleans up all thread local storage before calling `DllProc`.

- The `Dll_Process_Detach` reason is most useful if the `DLLProc` procedure is in the library's project file. In a unit, you can use the unit's **finalization** section instead.

Example

```
// Keep track of the application's threads. Threads contains
// the thread IDs, but you can easily modify this example to
// store other information.
library ThreadMonitor;

uses Windows, SysUtils, Classes;

var
  Threads: TThreadList;

procedure DllHandler(Reason: Integer);
begin
  case Reason of
  Dll_Thread_Attach:
    with Threads.LockList do
      try
        IsMultiThread := Count >= 1;
        Add(Pointer(GetCurrentThreadID));
      finally
        Threads.UnlockList;
      end;
  Dll_Thread_Detach:
    with Threads.LockList do
      try
        Remove(Pointer(GetCurrentThreadID));
        IsMultiThread := Count <= 1;
      finally
        Threads.UnlockList;
      end;
  Dll_Process_Detach:
    FreeAndNil(Threads);

  // Else Windows might invent new reasons in the future. Ignore them.
```

```
    end;
  end;

begin
  Threads := TThreadList.Create;
  DllProc := @DllHandler;
end.
```

See Also

Finalization Keyword, Initialization Keyword, IsMultiThread Variable, Library Keyword, Threadvar Keyword

---

Do Keyword

Syntax

```
for Variable := Expression to Expression do Statement
while Expression do Statement
try Statement... except on ExceptionClass do Statement end;
with Expression do Statement
```

Description

The do keyword is part of Delphi's for and while statements, try-except exception handler, and with statement. See the explanations of these statements for details.

See Also

For Keyword, Try Keyword, While Keyword, With Keyword

Double Type

Syntax

```
type Double;
```

Description

The Double type is an IEEE standard floating-point type that uses 8 bytes to store a sign bit, an 11-bit exponent, and a 52-bit mantissa. The mantissa is usually normalized, that is, it has an implicit 1 bit before the most significant bit. If the exponent is zero, however, the mantissa is denormalized—without the implicit 1 bit. Thus, the numerical value of +0.0 is represented by all zero bits. An exponent of all 1 bits represents infinity (mantissa is zero) or not-a-number (mantissa is not zero).

The limits of the Double type are approximately 2.23×10^{-308} to 1.79×10^{308}, with about 15 decimal digits of precision. Table 5-1 shows the detailed format of finite and special Double values.

Tips and Tricks

* Double is a popular type that provides a good balance between performance and precision.

Table 5-1: Format of Double Floating-Point Numbers

Numeric class	Sign	Exponent Bits	Mantissa Bits
Positive			
Normalized	0	0...1 to 1...10	0...0 to 1...1
Denormalized	0	0...0	0...1 to 1...1
Zero	0	0...0	0...0
Infinity	0	1...1	0...0
Signaling NaN	0	1...1	0...1 to 01...1
Quiet NaN	0	1...1	1...0 to 1...1
Negative			
Normalized	1	0...1 to 1...10	0...0 to 1...1
Denormalized	1	0...0	0...1 to 1...1
Zero	1	0...0	0...0
Infinity	1	1...1	0...0
Signaling NaN	1	1...1	0...1 to 01...1
Quiet NaN	1	1...1	1...0 to 1...1

- The Double type corresponds to the double type in Java, C, and C++.

- Refer to the Intel architecture manuals (such as the *Pentium Developer's Manual*, volume 3, *Architecture and Programming Manual*) or IEEE standard 754 for more information about infinity and NaN (not a number). In Delphi, use of a signaling NaN raises runtime error 6 (EInvalidOp).

Example

```
type
  TDouble = packed record
    case Integer of
    0: (Float: Double;);
    1: (Bytes: array[0..7] of Byte;);
    2: (Words: array[0..3] of Word;);
    3: (LongWords: array[0..1] of LongWord;);
    4: (Int64s: array[0..0] of Int64;);
  end;
  TFloatClass = (fcPosNorm, fcNegNorm, fcPosDenorm, fcNegDenorm,
             fcPosZero, fcNegZero, fcPosInf, fcNegInf, fcQNaN, fcSNan);

// Return the class of a floating-point number: finite, infinity,
// not-a-number; also positive or negative, normalized or denormalized.
// Determine the class by examining the exponent, sign bit,
// and mantissa separately.
function fp_class(X: Double): TFloatClass; overload;
var
  XParts: TDouble absolute X;
  Negative: Boolean;
  Exponent: Word;
  Mantissa: Int64;
begin
  Negative := (XParts.LongWords[1] and $80000000) <> 0;
```

Language Reference

```
Exponent := (XParts.LongWords[1] and $7FF00000) shr 20;
Mantissa :=  XParts.Int64s[0] and $000FFFFFFFFFFFFF;

// The first three cases can be positive or negative.
// Assume positive, and test the sign bit later.
if (Mantissa = 0) and (Exponent = 0) then
  // Mantissa and exponent are both zero, so the number is zero.
  Result := fcPosZero
else if Exponent = 0 then
  // If the exponent is zero, but the mantissa is not,
  // the number is finite but denormalized.
  Result := fcPosDenorm
else if Exponent <> $7FF then
  // Otherwise, if the exponent is not all 1, the number is normalized.
  Result := fcPosNorm
else if Mantissa = 0 then
  // Exponent is all 1, and mantissa is all 0 means infinity.
  Result := fcPosInf

else
begin
  // Exponent is all 1, and mantissa is non-zero, so the value
  // is not a number. Test for quiet or signaling NaN.
  if (Mantissa and $8000000000000) <> 0 then
    Result := fcQNaN
  else
    Result := fcSNaN;
  Exit; // Do not distinguish negative NaNs.
end;

if Negative then
  Inc(Result);
end;
```

See Also

CompToDouble Function, DoubleToComp Procedure, Extended Type, Real Type, Single Type

---

DoubleToComp Procedure

Syntax

```
procedure DoubleToComp(Value: Double; var result: Comp); cdecl;
```

Description

DoubleToComp converts a Double value to Comp. It is a real function.

Tips and Tricks

- You can call DoubleToComp in a C++ Builder program. Delphi automatically converts Double to Comp when it needs to, so you don't need to call this function in a Delphi program.

- Double supports a wider range of values than Comp. Converting Double to Comp can result in runtime error 6 (EInvalidOp).

See Also

Comp Type, CompToDouble Function, Double Type

Downto Keyword

Syntax

```
for Variable := Expression downto Expression do Statement
```

Description

Use downto in a for loop to count down. See the explanation of the for loop for details.

See Also

For Keyword, To Keyword

Dynamic Directive

Syntax

```
Method declaration; dynamic;
```

Description

You can declare a virtual method in a base class by using the virtual directive or the dynamic directive. The semantics of both directives is the same. The only difference is the implementation of the method and how it is called. For details, see Chapter 3.

As with a virtual method, derived classes must use the override directive to override the method.

Tips and Tricks

- You should almost always use the virtual directive instead of dynamic. In most cases, virtual methods are faster and take up less memory than dynamic methods.
- The dynamic directive must follow the reintroduce and overload directives and precede the calling convention and abstract directives.

See Also

Abstract Directive, Class Type, Overload Directive, Override Directive, Reintroduce Directive, Virtual Directive

Else Keyword

Syntax

```
if Condition then Statement else Statement
try Statement... except Exception clauses... else Statements... end;
case Expression of Case clauses... else Statements... end;
```

Description

The else keyword introduces the catch-all part of several statements. See the sections describing those statements for details.

Note that the else part of an if statement is followed by a single statement, but the else part of the try-except and case statements can have multiple statements.

See Also

Case Keyword, If Keyword, Try Keyword

EmptyParam Variable

Syntax

```
var EmptyParam: OleVariant;
```

Description

Some COM servers have optional parameters, which you can omit from the method call. In Delphi, however, the interface and dispatch interface declarations do not support optional parameters. You can call a method with optional parameters by using a Variant or by passing EmptyParam as the parameter value. If you have an interface or dispatch interface, you should use the interface instead of using a Variant because you gain the advantage of compile-time checking.

The default value of EmptyParam is a varError, with an error code value of Disp_E_ParamNotFound. You can change the value, but you should have a good reason to do so.

Example

The ShellWindows COM object has the Item method, which takes an optional Index parameter. Delphi implements the optional parameter by declaring two overloaded methods. The implementation of one method passes EmptyParam as the index value:

```
// The following is an excerpt from shdocvw.pas
function  TShellWindows.Item: IDispatch;
begin
  Result := DefaultInterface.Item(EmptyParam);
end;

function  TShellWindows.Item(index: OleVariant): IDispatch;
begin
```

```
        Result := DefaultInterface.Item(index);
    end;
```

See Also

Dispinterface Keyword, Interface Keyword, OleVariant Type

End Keyword

Syntax

```
asm Statements... end;
begin Statements... end;
case Expression of Case clauses... else Statements... end;
library Name; ... end.
package Name; requires Packages... contains Units... end.
program Name; ... end.
try Statements... except Exception clauses... else Statements... end;
try Statements... finally Statements... end;
type Name = class Declarations... end;
type Name = object Declarations... end;
type Name = record Declarations... end;
type Name = interface Declarations... end;
type Name = dispinterface Declarations... end;
unit Name; interface ... implementation ... end.
```

Description

The end keyword ends just about anything that has multiple parts: blocks, class declarations, case statements, and so on. See the description of each keyword for details.

See Also

Asm Keyword, Begin Keyword, Case Keyword, Class Keyword, Dispinterface Keyword, Interface Keyword, Library Keyword, Object Keyword, Package Directive, Program Keyword, Record Keyword, Try Keyword, Unit Keyword

---

EnumModules Procedure

Syntax

```
procedure EnumModules(Func: TEnumModuleFuncLW; Data: Pointer);
```

Description

The EnumModules procedure calls a user-supplied callback function for each module in the application, that is, for the application's *.exe* module and for every package and DLL the application loads.

The callback function gets two arguments: the instance handle of each module and the Data argument. It returns True to continue enumerating modules or False to stop and cause EnumModules to return immediately.

EnumModules is a real procedure.

Tips and Tricks

For backward compatibility, EnumModules is overloaded and can use a callback function that declares its HInstance parameter with type Integer. For new code, however, you should use LongWord, or if you are using the Windows unit, THandle.

Example

```
// Display a list of modules in a string list. Data must be
// a TStrings reference.
function GetModules(Instance: THandle; Data: Pointer): Boolean;
var
  FileName: array[0..Max_Path] of Char;
begin
  if GetModuleFileName(Instance, FileName, SizeOf(FileName)) > 0 then
    TStrings(Data).Add(FileName)
  else
    RaiseLastWin32Error;
  Result := True;
end;
...
EnumModules(GetModules, ListBox1.Items);
```

See Also

EnumResourceModules Procedure, FindClassHInstance Function,
FindHInstance Function, LibModuleList Variable, PLibModule Type,
RegisterModule Procedure, TEnumModuleFuncLW Type, TLibModule Type,
UnregisterModule Procedure

EnumResourceModules Procedure

Syntax

```
procedure EnumResourceModules(Func: TEnumModuleFuncLW; Data: Pointer);
```

Description

The EnumResourceModules procedure calls a user-supplied callback function for each resource module in the application, that is, the resource DLL for the application's *.exe* file and for every package and DLL the application loads.

The callback function gets two arguments: the instance handle for each resource module and the Data argument. It returns True to continue enumerating modules or False to stop and cause EnumResourceModules to return immediately.

EnumResourceModules is a real procedure.

Tips and Tricks

- For backward compatibility, EnumResourceModules is overloaded and can use a callback function that declares its HInstance parameter with type Integer. For new code, however, you should use LongWord, or if you are using the Windows unit, THandle.

- If a module has no separate resource module, **EnumResourceModules** uses the module's instance handle. You can tell that a module has a resource module because its resource instance handle is different from the module's instance handle.

See Also

EnumModules Procedure, FindClassHInstance Function, FindHInstance Function, FindResourceHInstance Function, LoadResourceModule Function, RegisterModule Procedure, TEnumModuleFuncLW Type, UnregisterModule Procedure

---

Eof Function

Syntax

```
function Eof(var F: File): Boolean;
function Eof(var F: TextFile): Boolean;
```

Description

The **Eof** function returns True if the file **F** is at the end of the file. **Eof** is not a real function.

Errors

- If the file **F** is not open, **Eof** reports I/O error 103.

- The file **F** must have been opened by calling **Reset**. If the file was opened by calling **Rewrite** or **Append**, **Eof** reports I/O error 104.

See Also

Eoln Function, File Keyword, IOResult Function, Reset Procedure, SeekEof Procedure, TextFile Type, Truncate Procedure

---

Eoln Function

Syntax

```
function Eoln(var F: TextFile): Boolean;
```

Description

The **Eoln** function returns True if the text file **F** is at the end of a line or the end of the file. **Eoln** interprets a carriage return (#13) as the end of line. **Eoln** is not a real function.

Errors

- If the file **F** is not open, **Eof** reports I/O error 103.

- The file **F** must have been opened by calling **Reset**. If the file was opened by calling **Rewrite** or **Append**, **Eof** reports I/O error 104.

See Also

Eof Function, IOResult Function, Reset Procedure, SeekEoln Procedure, TextFile Type

---

Erase Procedure

Syntax

```
procedure Erase(var F: File);
procedure Erase(var F: TextFile);
```

Description

Erase deletes the file that is assigned to F. The file should be closed, but with a filename assigned to it. Erase is not a real procedure.

Errors

- If AssignFile has not been called, Erase raises I/O error 102.

- If the file cannot be deleted, Erase reports an I/O error using the Windows error code. In particular, if the file is open, the Windows error code is 32 (file in use), and if the file is read-only, the Windows error code is 5 (access is denied).

See Also

AssignFile Procedure, CloseFile Procedure, File Keyword, IOResult Function, Rename Procedure, TextFile Type

---

ErrorAddr Variable

Syntax

```
var ErrorAddr: Pointer;
```

Description

When Delphi raises a runtime error, it stores in ErrorAddr the code pointer where the error occurred. You can use this address in error messages, as the starting point for tracing the call stack, or whatever.

RunError sets ErrorAddr and then calls Halt. If ErrorAddr is not nil and you call Halt, the Halt procedure prints an error message.

See Also

ErrorProc Variable, Halt Procedure, NoErrMsg Variable, RunError Procedure

---

ErrorProc Variable

Syntax

```
var ErrorProc: Pointer;

procedure MyErrorProc(ErrorCode: Integer; ErrorAddr: Pointer);
```

```
begin
  ...
end;
ErrorProc := @MyErrorProc;
```

Description

When a runtime error occurs, and the `ErrorProc` variable is not `nil`, Delphi calls the procedure that `ErrorProc` points to. The procedure takes two arguments: the error number and the error address.

If `ErrorProc` is `nil`, Delphi calls `RunError` to issue an error message and halt the program. In a GUI application, Delphi shows the error message in a dialog box. In a console application, Delphi prints the error message to the console.

Delphi stores the error code for I/O errors separately. If `ErrorCode` is zero, most likely the error is an I/O error. Call `IOResult` to obtain the I/O error code.

Example

```
// Log errors in an application event log (in Windows NT).
procedure LogError(ErrorCode: Integer; ErrorAddr: Pointer);
var
  ApplicationName: string;
  Handle: THandle;
  Strings: array[0..0] of PChar;
begin
  // Change the application path to its base name, e.g., 'App'.
  // The application must have created the appropriate register key.
  ApplicationName := ChangeFileExt(ExtractFileName(ParamStr(0)), '');
  Handle := RegisterEventSource(nil, PChar(ApplicationName));

  if ErrorCode = 0 then
    ErrorCode := IOResult;

  // Get the exception message.
  Strings[0] := PChar('Runtime error #' + IntToStr(ErrorCode));

  // Define the Category elsewhere.
  ReportEvent(Handle, EventLog_Error_Type, Category, ErrorCode,
    nil, 0, 1, @Strings, nil);

  DeregisterEventSource(Handle);
end;
...
ErrorProc := @LogError;
```

See Also

ErrorAddr Variable, ExceptProc Variable, Halt Procedure, IOResult Function, RunError Procedure

Except Keyword

Syntax

```
try Statements... except Statements... end;
try Statements... except Exception handlers... end;
```

Description

The **except** keyword is part of a **try-except** block. The **try** part lists statements that Delphi executes, and the **except** part lists exception handlers, which Delphi executes only if a statement in the **try** part raises an exception.

The **try-except** statement has two varieties:

- The first kind has a list of statements in the **except** part. If any exception occurs, Delphi executes the statements in the **except** part. If the statements do not raise another exception, the program continues with the statement following the end of the **try-except** statement.

- The second kind has a list of exception handlers in the **except** part. Each exception handler starts with the **on** directive and specifies an exception class. The **except** part traps only the exceptions listed in the exception handlers. The last handler can be an **else** clause to trap all other exceptions. If an exception does not match any of the listed exception handlers, and the **except** part has no **else** clause, Delphi reraises the exception (just as though you had used **else raise** as the last exception handler).

For examples and more information about exception handlers, see the **try** keyword.

See Also

Finally Keyword, On Directive, Raise Keyword, Try Keyword

ExceptClsProc Variable

Syntax

```
var ExceptClsProc: Pointer;

function ExceptClassProc(var Rec: TExceptionRecord): TClass;
begin
  ...
end;
ExceptClsProc := @ExceptClassProc;
```

Description

Delphi calls the function that **ExceptClsProc** points to when a Windows exception occurs inside a **try-except** block that contains exception handlers (that is, where Delphi must test which exception handler matches the exception raised).

The sole argument to the **ExceptClsProc** function is a pointer to an exception record.

The class that `ExceptClsProc` returns must be the same type as the object that `ExceptObjProc` returns. Delphi uses the class from `ExceptClsProc` to identify which exception handler to use before it calls `ExceptObjProc` to create the exception object.

Tips and Tricks

- The `Windows` unit defines the `TExceptionRecord` type.
- The `SysUtils` unit sets `ExceptClsProc` to a function that maps all the Windows exceptions to appropriate Delphi exceptions, e.g., `Status_Integer_Overflow` becomes `EIntOverflow`.

Example

```
// Simple example of mapping Windows exceptions to custom exceptions.
class CustomException = class(Exception);
class CustomMathException = class(CustomException);
class CustomRangeException = class(CustomException);
function CustomExceptClsFunc(var Ex: TExceptionRecord): TClass;
begin
  case Ex.ExceptionCode of
    STATUS_ARRAY_BOUNDS_EXCEEDED,
    STATUS_INTEGER_OVERFLOW:
      Result := CustomRangeException;
    STATUS_INTEGER_DIVIDE_BY_ZERO,
    STATUS_FLOAT_INEXACT_RESULT,
    STATUS_FLOAT_INVALID_OPERATION,
    STATUS_FLOAT_STACK_CHECK,
    STATUS_FLOAT_DIVIDE_BY_ZERO,
    STATUS_FLOAT_OVERFLOW,
    STATUS_FLOAT_UNDERFLOW,
    STATUS_FLOAT_DENORMAL_OPERAND:
      Result := CustomMathException;
    else
      Result := CustomException;
  end;
end;

ExceptClsProc := @CustomExceptClsFunc;
```

See Also

ErrorProc Variable, Except Keyword, ExceptObjProc Variable, ExceptProc Variable, On Directive, Try Keyword

---

ExceptionClass Variable

Syntax

```
var ExceptionClass: TClass;
```

Description

Delphi's IDE uses the `ExceptionClass` variable to determine which exceptions the debugger handles. The IDE's integrated debugger stops only for exceptions that inherit from the base class stored in `ExceptionClass`. The `SysUtils` unit sets this variable to `Exception`.

Tips and Tricks

Delphi's IDE lets you control whether the debugger gains control when the program raises an exception. You can also control this behavior from within your program by setting `ExceptionClass`. In particular, setting the variable to `nil` prevents the debugger from stopping for any exception.

See Also

Raise Keyword, Try Keyword

ExceptObjProc Variable

Syntax

```
var ExceptObjProc: Pointer;

function ExceptProc(var Rec: TExceptionRecord): TObject;
begin ... end;
...
ExceptObjProc := @ExceptProc;
```

Description

When a Windows exception occurs, Delphi calls the procedure `ExceptObjProc` points to (if the variable is not `nil`). The `ExceptObjProc` function returns a new exception object that corresponds to the Windows exception. If `ExceptObjProc` is `nil` or if it returns `nil`, Delphi lets the Windows exception terminate the application.

The sole argument to the `ExceptObjProc` function is a pointer to an exception record.

Tips and Tricks

- The `Windows` unit defines the `TExceptionRecord` type. See the Windows Platform SDK documentation to learn about this record.

- The `SysUtils` unit sets `ExceptObjProc` to a function that maps all the Windows exceptions to appropriate Delphi exceptions, e.g., `Status_Integer_Overflow` becomes an `EIntOverflow` object.

Example

```
// Call the ExceptClsProc procedure to get the exception class,
// then create and return the exception object.
function CustomExceptObjFunc(var Rec: TExceptionRecord): TObject;
begin
  Result := CustomExceptClsFunc(Rec).Create;
end;

ExceptObjProc := @CustomExceptObjFunc;
```

ExceptClsProc Variable, ExceptProc Variable, TExceptionRecord Type

---

ExceptProc Variable

Syntax

```
var ExceptProc: Pointer;

procedure MyProc(ExceptObject: TObject; ExceptAddr: Pointer);
begin ... end;
...
ExceptProc := @MyProc;
```

Description

If an exception is not handled in a **try-except** block and **ExceptProc** is not nil, Delphi calls the procedure that **ExceptProc** points to, passing as arguments a reference to the exception object and the address where the exception originated. If **ExceptProc** is nil, Delphi raises runtime error 217.

Example

```
// Log exceptions in an application event log (in Windows NT).
procedure LogException(ExceptObject: TObject; ExceptAddr: Pointer);
var
  ApplicationName: string;
  Handle: THandle;
  Msg: string;
  Strings: array[0..0] of PChar;
begin
  ApplicationName := ChangeFileExt(ExtractFileName(ParamStr(0)), '');
  // Change the application path to its base name, e.g., 'App'.
  // The application must have created the appropriate register key.
  Handle := RegisterEventSource(nil, PChar(ApplicationName));

  // Get the exception message.
  if ExceptObject is Exception then
    Msg := Exception(ExceptObject).Message
  else
    Msg := ExceptObject.ClassName;
  Strings[0] := PChar(Msg);

  // Define the Category and Exception_ID elsewhere.
  ReportEvent(Handle, EventLog_Error_Type, Category, Exception_ID,
    nil, 0, 1, @Strings, nil);

  DeregisterEventSource(Handle);
end;
...
ExceptProc := @LogException;
```

See Also

ErrorProc Variable, Raise Keyword

Exclude Procedure

Syntax

```
procedure Exclude(var ASet: Set type; Value: Ordinal type);
```

Description

The **Exclude** procedure removes the element **Value** from the set variable **ASet**. The type of **Value** must be the base type of **ASet**. **Exclude** is not a real procedure.

Tips and Tricks

Note that you cannot use a property for the set reference because a property value cannot be used as a **var** parameter. Instead, use the – operator to remove the member from the set, as shown below:

```
Font.Style := Font.Style - [fsBold];
```

Example

```
// The TFontStyleProperty editor toggles the bold font style when
// the user double-clicks the TFont.Style property in the
// object inspector.
type
  TFontStyleProperty = class(TSetProperty)
  public
    procedure Edit; override;
  end;
...
procedure TFontStyleProperty.Edit;
var
  Style: TFontStyles;
begin
  Style := TFontStyles(Byte(GetOrdValue));// Get the current font style.
  if fsBold in Style then
    Exclude(Style, fsBold)
  else
    Include(Style, fsBold);
  SetOrdValue(Byte(Style));              // Set the component's font style.
end;
```

See Also

In Keyword, Include Procedure, Set Keyword

Exit Procedure

Syntax

```
Exit;
```

Description

Call the Exit procedure to return immediately from a function or procedure. If you call Exit from within a try-finally block, the finally parts runs before the subroutine returns.

The Exit procedure is built into the compiler and is not a real procedure. If you call Exit outside of a subroutine or method, Delphi exits the application.

Example

```
// Compute the number of iterations at the point (X, Y).
// Stop at MaxIterations, which is a crude approximation of infinity.
// This function is used in the BeginThread example.
function ComputeIterations(X, Y: Double): Integer;
const
  Threshold = 4.0;
var
  XNew, YNew: Double;
  XC, YC: Double;
begin
  XC := X;
  YC := Y;
  for Result := 0 to MaxIterations-1 do
  begin
    XNew := X * X - Y * Y + XC;
    YNew := 2 * X * Y + YC;
    if (XNew * XNew + YNew * YNew) > Threshold then
      Exit;
    X := XNew;
    Y := YNew;
  end;
  Result := MaxIterations;
end;
```

See Also

Break Procedure, Goto Keyword, Try Keyword

ExitCode Variable

Syntax

```
var ExitCode: Integer;
```

Description

ExitCode stores the exit code for an application. An exit procedure or finalization section can use ExitCode to take appropriate actions. The exit code is the argument to Halt.

Tips and Tricks

A batch or command file can use a program's exit code in an if statement. See the Windows help for "batch commands" for details.

See Also

Finalization Keyword, Halt Procedure, RunError Procedure

ExitProc Variable

Syntax

```
var ExitProc: Pointer;
```

Description

When an application exits, it calls the procedure that **ExitProc** points to. The procedure takes no arguments. **ExitProc** exists only for backward compatibility with older Delphi programs. New Delphi programs should use a finalization section instead. If you must use **ExitProc**, see the **AddExitProc** procedure in the **SysUtils** unit for a better way to set up an exit procedure.

See Also

Finalization Keyword

Exp Function

Syntax

```
function Exp(X: Floating-point type): Extended;
```

Description

The **Exp** function computes e^x. The **Exp** function is built-in.

Tips and Tricks

- Delphi automatically converts **Integer** and **Variant** arguments to floating-point. To convert an **Int64** argument to floating-point, add 0.0.

- If **X** is a signaling NaN, positive infinity, or negative infinity, Delphi reports runtime error 6 (**EInvalidOp**).

- If **X** is a quiet NaN, the result is **X**.

- If the result is too large, Delphi reports runtime error 8 (**EOverflow**).

See Also

Ln Function

Export Directive

Syntax

```
Subroutine declaration; export;
```

Description

Delphi ignores the **export** directive. This directive exists only for backward compatibility with Delphi 1.

See Also

Exports Keyword

Exports Keyword

Syntax

```
exports
  Subroutine,
  Subroutine name Identifier,
  Subroutine index Constant,
  Subroutine index Constant name Identifier,
  ...;
```

Description

The **exports** declaration lists the names or signatures of subroutines to be exported from a DLL. You can declare subroutines to export in any unit or in the library's project file.

If a subroutine is overloaded, you can specify which subroutine to export by including the subroutine's arguments in the **exports** declaration. You can export multiple overloaded subroutines, but make sure the caller is able to identify which one it wants to call by assigning a unique name to each one.

By default, the subroutine is exported under its own name, but you can specify a different name or an index number. If you do not supply an index, Delphi automatically assigns one.

Tips and Tricks

- You can use the **index** and **name** directives for the same exported routine (in that order).

- Delphi does not check for duplicate indices, so be careful.

- Delphi 5 does not allow the **index** directive for overloaded subroutines.

Example

```
unit Debug;
interface

  // Simple debugging procedures. Debug messages are written to
  // a debug log file. You can link this unit into an application,
  // or use in a DLL. See the External Directive for an example
  // of how an application can use these procedures from a DLL.
  procedure Log(const Msg: string); overload;
  procedure Log(const Fmt: string; const Args: array of const); overload;
  procedure SetDebugLog(const FileName: string);
  function GetDebugLog: string;

implementation

uses SysUtils;
```

```
var
  DebugLog: string = 'c:\debug.log';

procedure SetDebugLog(const FileName: string);
begin
  DebugLog := FileName;
end;

function GetDebugLog: string;
begin
 Result := DebugLog;
end;

procedure Log(const Msg: string); overload;
var
  F: Text;
begin
  AssignFile(F, DebugLog);
  if FileExists(DebugLog) then
    Append(F)
  else
    Rewrite(F);
  try
    WriteLn(F, '[', DateTimeToStr(Now), '] ', Msg);
  finally
    CloseFile(F);
  end;
end;

procedure Log(const Fmt: string; Args: array of const); overload;
begin
  WriteLn(Format(Fmt, Args));
end;

exports
  GetDebugLog,
  SetDebugLog,
  Log(const Msg: string) name 'Log',
  Log(const Fmt: string; const Args: array of const) name 'LogFmt';
end.
```

See Also

External Directive, Index Directive, Library Keyword, Name Directive

---

Extended Type

Syntax

```
type Extended;
```

Description

The Extended type is an Intel standard floating-point type that uses 10 bytes to store a sign bit, a 15-bit exponent, and a 64-bit mantissa. Extended conforms to the minimum requirements of the IEEE-754 extended double precision type.

The limits of the Extended type are approximately 3.37×10^{-4932} to 1.18×10^{4932}, with about 19 decimal digits of precision.

Unlike Single and Double, Extended contains all of its significant bits. Normalized values, infinity, and not-a-number have an explicit 1 bit as the most significant bit. Table 5-2 shows the detailed format of finite and special Extended values. Not all bit patterns are valid Extended values. Delphi raises runtime error 6 (EInvalidOp) if you try to use an invalid bit pattern as a floating-point number.

Table 5-2: Format of Extended Floating-Point Numbers

Numeric Class	Sign	Exponent Bits	Mantissa Bits
Positive			
Normalized	0	0...1 to 1...0	10...0 to 11...1
Denormalized	0	0...0	0...1 to 01...1
Zero	0	0...0	0...0
Infinity	0	1...1	10...
Quiet NaN	0	1...1	110...0 to 11...1
Signaling NaN	0	1...1	100...1 to 101...1
Negative			
Normalized	1	0...1 to 1...0	10...0 to 11...1
Denormalized	1	0...0	0...1 to 01...1
Zero	1	0...0	0...0
Infinity	1	1...1	10...
Quiet NaN	1	1...1	110...0 to 11...1
Signaling NaN	1	1...1	100...1 to 101...1

Tips and Tricks

- Use Extended when you must preserve the maximum precision or exponent range, but realize that you will pay a performance penalty because of its awkward size.

- Delphi sets the floating-point control word to extended precision, so intermediate computations are carried out with the full precision of Extended values. When you save a floating-point result to a Single or Double variable, Delphi truncates the extra bits of precision.

- Refer to the Intel architecture manuals (such as the *Pentium Developer's Manual*, volume 3, *Architecture and Programming Manual*) or IEEE standard 754 for more information about infinity and NaN (not a number). In Delphi, use of a signaling NaN raises runtime error 6 (EInvalidOp).

Example

```
type
  TExtended = packed record
    case Integer of
    0: (Float: Extended;);
    1: (Bytes: array[0..9] of Byte;);
    2: (Words: array[0..4] of Word;);
    3: (LongWords: array[0..1] of LongWord; LWExtra: Word;);
    4: (Int64s: array[0..0] of Int64; Exponent: Word;);
  end;
  TFloatClass = (fcPosNorm, fcNegNorm, fcPosDenorm, fcNegDenorm,
            fcPosZero, fcNegZero, fcPosInf, fcNegInf, fcQNaN, fcSNan);

// Return the class of a floating-point number: finite, infinity,
// not-a-number; also positive or negative, normalized or denormalized.
// Determine the class by examining the exponent, sign bit, and
// mantissa separately.
function fp_class(X: Extended): TFloatClass; overload;
var
  XParts: TExtended absolute X;
  Negative: Boolean;
  Exponent: LongWord;
  Mantissa: Int64;
begin
  Negative := (XParts.Exponent and $8000) <> 0;
  Exponent := XParts.Exponent and $7FFF;
  Mantissa := XParts.Int64s[0];

  // The first three cases can be positive or negative.
  // Assume positive, and test the sign bit later.
  if (Exponent = 0) and (Mantissa = 0) then
    // Mantissa and exponent are both zero, so the number is zero.
    Result := fcPosZero
  else if (Exponent = 0) and (Mantissa < 0) then
    // If the exponent is zero, and the mantissa has a 0 MSbit,
    // the number is denormalized. Note that Extended explicitly
    // stores the 1 MSbit (unlike Single and Double).
    Result := fcPosDenorm
  else if Exponent <> $7FFF then
    // Otherwise, if the exponent is not all 1,
    // the number is normalized.
    Result := fcPosNorm
  else if Mantissa = $8000000000000000 then
    // Exponent is all 1, and mantissa has 1 MSBit means infinity.
    Result := fcPosInf

  else
  begin
    // Exponent is all 1, and mantissa is non-zero, so the value
    // is not a number. Test for quiet or signaling NaN. MSBit is
    // always 1. The next bit is 1 for quiet or 0 for signaling.
    if (Mantissa and $4000000000000000) <> 0 then
      Result := fcQNaN
```

```
    else
      Result := fcSNaN;
    Exit; // Do not distinguish negative NaNs.
  end;

  if Negative then
    Inc(Result);
end;
```

See Also

Currency Type, Double Type, Real Type, Real48 Type, Set8087CW Procedure, Single Type

---

External Directive

Syntax

```
subroutine declaration; external;
subroutine declaration; external DllName;
subroutine declaration; external DllName name String;
subroutine declaration; external DllName index Constant;
```

Description

Every subroutine declared in a unit's **interface** section must be implemented in the same unit's **implementation** section. Subroutines can be implemented with the **external** directive, which means the actual implementation is in a separate object file or DLL. If no **DllName** is given, the external implementation must be linked from a compatible object file using the $L or $Link compiler directive.

A *DllName* must be a string constant. For maximum portability, be sure to include the *.dll* extension in the DLL's filename. (Windows NT, for example, requires the file's extension.) By default, Delphi looks up the subroutine name in the DLL, but you can specify a different name to look up or specify a numeric index.

Example

```
// Import the debugging procedures that were exported from
// the Debug library. (See the Exports Directive.)
procedure Log(const Msg: string); overload; external 'Debug.dll';
procedure Log(const Fmt: string; const Args: array of const); overload;
    external 'Debug.dll' name 'LogFmt';
```

See Also

Exports Directive, Index Directive, Name Directive, $L Compiler Directive, $Link Compiler Directive

---

Far Directive

Syntax

```
Subroutine declaration; far;
```

Description

Delphi ignores the **far** directive. It exists only for backward compatibility with Delphi 1.

See Also

Near Directive

File Keyword

Syntax

```
var
  BinaryFile: file;
  TypedFile: file of Some type;
```

Description

A **file** is a binary sequence of some type. A file's contents are usually stored in a persistent medium, such as a disk drive. If you do not specify a type, the untyped file is treated as a sequence of fixed-size records where the record size is determined when you open the file with **Reset** or **Rewrite**.

Internally, Delphi represents a binary file as a record. The **SysUtils** unit declares the **TFileRec** type for your convenience, or you can declare the record yourself:

```
type
  TFileRec = packed record
    Handle: Integer;              // Windows file handle
    Mode: Integer;            // fmInput, fmOutput, fmInOut, fmClosed
    RecSize: Cardinal;            // record size
    Private: array[1..28] of Byte;   // reserved by Delphi
    UserData: array[1..32] of Byte;  // you can use this
    Name: array[0..259] of Char;     // file path
  end;
```

Tips and Tricks

- The **file** type is for binary files. See the **TextFile** type for text files. Binary and text files often follow completely different rules in Delphi. Note also that the **TextFile** type is not the same as **file of Char**.

- The base type for a file can be a scalar type, an array type, or a record type. It should not be a pointer, dynamic array, or long string. Storing a pointer in a file serves no useful purpose because pointer values are ephemeral. Long and wide strings are pointers, so if you need to store strings in a file, use short strings or call **BlockRead** and **BlockWrite**.

- Call **Reset** to open an existing file or **Rewrite** to create a new file.

- Delphi does not buffer its file I/O, so reading and writing individual records can be slow. Call **BlockRead** and **BlockWrite** to handle many records at once to improve performance.

- Do not use **Integer**, **Cardinal**, or any other type whose size can vary from one release to another. Instead, choose a specific size, such as **Word** or

---

LongInt. That way, files that you create with one version can be read with another version.

- Alignment of fields within a record can change from one version of Delphi to another. Use packed records to minimize the chances that a record format will change from the version that creates a file to a version that reads a file.

- Delphi does not support the standard Pascal approach to file I/O: calling Get or Put, and dereferencing a file variable as a pointer. Instead, see the Read, Write, BlockRead, and BlockWrite procedures.

Example

```
type
  TStudent = packed record
    ID: string[9];
    Name: string[40];
    GPA: Single;
  end;
  TStudentFile = file of TStudent;
var
  F: TStudentFile;
  S: TStudent;
begin
  AssignFile(F, 'students.dat');
  Reset(F);
  try
    while not Eof(F) do
    begin
      Read(F, S);
      ProcessStudent(S);
    end;
  finally
    CloseFile(F);
  end;
end;
```

See Also

AssignFile Procedure, BlockRead Procedure, BlockWrite Procedure, Eof Function, FilePos Function, FileSize Function, IOResult Function, Packed Keyword, Read Procedure, Record Keyword, Seek Procedure, TextFile Type, Write Procedure

---

FileMode Variable

Syntax

```
var FileMode: Integer;
```

Description

When opening a binary file with Reset, Delphi always opens the file using the mode specified by FileMode. The possible values for FileMode are as follows:

0   Read only

1   Write only

2   Read and write

The default value is 2.

Tips and Tricks

- To open an existing file for read-only access, be sure to set `FileMode` to zero before calling `Reset`. If you do not set `FileMode`, `Reset` will fail when trying to open a read-only file, such as a file on a CD-ROM.

- To append to a binary file, set `FileMode` to 1 or 2, open the file with `Reset`, seek to the end of the file, and then begin writing.

- `FileMode` is not used when opening text files.

- `FileMode` is not used when opening a binary file with `Rewrite`.

See Also

Reset Procedure

FilePos Function

Syntax

```
function FilePos(var F: File): LongInt;
function FilePos(var F: TextFile): LongInt;
```

Description

`FilePos` returns the current position (as a record number) in the file `F`. The beginning of the file is position zero. If `F` is a `TextFile`, the record size is arbitrarily chosen as the buffer size, which defaults to 128. When `Eof(F)` is True, `FilePos` returns the number of records in the file. `FilePos` is not a real function.

Errors

- If the file `F` is not open, `FilePos` reports I/O error 103.

- Although you can get the file position in a text file, you cannot use it to seek to that position. The `Seek` procedure works only with binary files. To get a file position of a text file, use the Windows API:

```
// Return a byte position in a text file if its buffer is empty.
function TextFilePos(var F: TextFile): LongInt;
begin
  Result := SetFilePointer(TTextRec(F).Handle, 0, nil, File_Current);
end;
```

- `FilePos` does not support files larger than 2 GB. See the `FileSeek` function in the `SysUtils` unit, or call the Windows API for large files.

See Also

Eof Function, File Keyword, FileSize Function, IOResult Function, Seek Procedure, TextFile Type, Truncate Procedure

---

FileSize Function

Syntax

```
function FileSize(var F: File): LongInt;
function FileSize(var F: TextFile): LongInt;
```

Description

FileSize returns the size in records of the file F. If F is a TextFile, the record size is arbitrarily chosen as the buffer size, which defaults to 128. If F is an untyped binary file, the record size is determined when the file is opened. FileSize is not a real function.

Errors

- If the file F is not open, FileSize reports I/O error 103.

- Real text files don't have fixed-size records, so FileSize is useless for text files. Use streams or call the Windows API function GetFileSize instead of calling FileSize.

```
// Return the size in bytes of a text file or -1 for an error.
function TextFileSize(var F: TextFile): LongInt;
begin
  case TTextRec(F).Mode of
    fmInput, fmOutput: Result := GetFileSize(TTextRec(F).Handle, nil);
    else               Result := -1;
  end;
end;
```

- FileSize does not support files larger than 2 GB. See the FileSeek function in the SysUtils unit, or call the Windows API for large files.

See Also

Eof Function, File Keyword, FilePos Function, IOResult Function, Reset Procedure, Rewrite Procedure, Seek Procedure, TextFile Type, Truncate Procedure

---

FillChar Procedure

Syntax

```
procedure FillChar(var Buffer; Count: Integer; const Fill);
```

Description

FillChar fills a variable with Count bytes, copying Fill as many times as needed. Fill can be a Byte-sized ordinal value. FillChar is not a real procedure.

Tips and Tricks

- Note that Buffer is not a pointer. Do not pass the address of a variable, but pass the variable itself. If you dynamically allocate memory, be sure to dereference the pointer when calling FillChar.

- If the ordinal value of the Fill argument is out of the range of a Byte, Delphi silently uses only the least significant byte as the fill byte. Delphi does not report an error, even if you have overflow checking enabled.

- The most common use for FillChar is to fill a buffer with zeros. You can also call the SysUtils.AllocMem function, which calls GetMem and then FillChar to fill the newly allocated memory with all zeros.

- When allocating a new record or array that contains long strings, dynamic arrays, interfaces, or Variants, you must initialize those elements. The Initialize procedure is usually the best way to do this, but it does not initialize any other elements of the array or record. Instead, you can call FillChar to fill the new memory with all zeros, which is a correct initial value for strings, dynamic arrays, interfaces, and Variants. When you free the record, be sure to call Finalize to free the memory associated with the strings, dynamic arrays, interfaces, and Variants.

- If Count < 0, FillChar does nothing.

Example

```
// Create a dynamic array of Count integers, initialized to zero.
type
  TIntArray = array of Integer;
function MakeZeroArray(Count: Integer): TIntArray;
begin
  SetLength(Result, Count);
  if Count > 0 then
    FillChar(Result[0], Count*SizeOf(Integer), 0);
end;
```

See Also

GetMem Procedure, Initialize Procedure, New Procedure, StringOfChar Function

---

Finalization Keyword

Syntax

```
unit Name;
interface Declarations...
implementation Declarations...
initialization Statements...
finalization Statements...
end.
```

Description

The finalization section of a unit contains statements that run when the program exits or when Windows unloads a library. Finalization sections run in the opposite order of initialization.

Note that a unit must have an initialization section in order to have a finalization section. The initialization section can be empty.

Tips and Tricks

- Use a `finalization` section to clean up global memory allocation and other global settings, such as changes to global variables.

- Always free all memory and other resources used by the unit. The unit might be loaded into a package, and the package can be loaded and unloaded many times in a single application. Small memory or resource leaks can quickly grow to big problems if you aren't careful.

Example

```
procedure ErrorHandler(ErrorCode: Integer; ErrorAddr: Pointer);
begin
  ... // Handle runtime errors.
end;

// Set a new error handler, but save the old one. Restore the previous
// error handler when this unit finalizes (which might be when
// the application unloads the package that contains this unit,
// and the application will continue to run using the old
// error handler).
var
  OldErrorProc: Pointer;
initialization
  OldErrorProc := ErrorProc;
  ErrorProc := @ErrorHandler;
finalization
  ErrorProc := OldErrorProc;
end.
```

See Also

Initialization Keyword, Unit Keyword

Language
Reference

Finalize Procedure

Syntax

```
procedure Finalize(var Buffer);
procedure Finalize(var Buffer; Count: Integer);
```

Description

The `Finalize` procedure cleans up strings, dynamic arrays, interfaces, `Variants`, and records or arrays that contain these types. Delphi automatically finalizes variables of string, dynamic array, interface, or `Variant` type, but if you allocate such types dynamically, you need to finalize the memory before freeing it.

If you are finalizing more than one item in an array, pass the count of the number of array elements as the `Count` parameter. The `Count` is the number of array elements, not the number of bytes to be freed.

`Finalize` is not a real procedure.

Tips and Tricks

- Dispose calls Finalize for you, so you need to call Finalize only when you free memory by calling FreeMem.

- The first argument to Finalize is not a pointer, but the actual variable or dereferenced pointer.

- Finalize must know the type of the buffer so it can determine how to finalize array and record members. If you are casting a generic Pointer, be sure you cast it to the correct type. Typecasting pointers is a common source of hard-to-locate bugs.

Example

```
type
  TSample = record
    Str: string;
    List: array of Integer;
    Intf: IUnknown;
    V: Variant;
  end;
  TSampleArray = array[0..MaxInt div SizeOf(TSample)-1] of TSample;
  PSampleArray = ^TSampleArray;

// See the Initialize procedure to see how to allocate a TSample array.

procedure FreeSamples(Samples: PSampleArray; Count: Integer);
begin
  Finalize(Samples^, Count);
  FreeMem(Samples);
end;
```

See Also

FreeMem Procedure, Initialize Procedure

Finally Keyword

Syntax

```
try Statements... finally Statements... end;
```

Description

The finally keyword starts the finally part of a try-finally block. The statements in the finally block always run, no matter how control leaves the try block: exception, Exit or Break.

For more information and an example, see the try keyword.

See Also

Except Keyword, Raise Keyword, Try Keyword

FindClassHInstance Function

Syntax

```
function FindClassHInstance(ClassRef: TClass): LongInt;
```

Description

FindClassHInstance returns the instance handle of the module that contains the given class. The module might be the application or it might be a runtime package that the application loads. If you pass an invalid class reference, FindClassHInstance returns zero.

A class reference points to the class's VMT, which resides in the module's code segment, so FindClassHInstance calls FindHInstance. Feel free to call FindHInstance or FindClassHInstance, whichever is more convenient.

FindClassHInstance is a real function.

See Also

FindHInstance Function, HInstance Variable, MainInstance Variable

---

FindHInstance Function

Syntax

```
function FindHInstance(Ref: Pointer): LongInt;
```

Description

FindHInstance returns the instance handle of the module that contains the given code pointer. The module might be the application, a DLL, or a runtime package that the application or DLL loads. If the pointer is not a valid code pointer, FindHInstance returns zero.

Feel free to call FindHInstance or FindClassHInstance, whichever is more convenient. FindHInstance is a real function.

Tips and Tricks

Earlier releases of Delphi required you to call FindHInstance to get the instance handle for a package. The current release lets you use the HInstance variable, so there is little need for FindHInstance in most applications.

See Also

FindClassHInstance Function, FindResourceHInstance Function, HInstance Variable, MainInstance Variable

---

FindResourceHInstance Function

Syntax

```
function FindResourceHInstance(Instance: LongWord): LongInt;
```

Description

If you have resources that need translation, especially string resources, you can use Delphi's localization tools to build language-specific resource DLLs. Call FindResourceHInstance to obtain the instance handle of the resource DLL. Pass the instance handle of the module that contains the unit (usually HInstance). If the module has no resource module, FindResourceHInstance returns the module's instance handle. In either case, use the instance handle that FindResourceHInstance returns to load language-specific resources.

Delphi automatically loads localized resources from the language DLL, so you do not usually need to call FindResourceHInstance. If you have customized the language DLL and added other resources, you can call this function to load your extra resources.

FindResourceHInstance is a real function.

See Also

FindClassHInstance Function, FindHInstance Function, HInstance Variable, LoadResourceModule Function

---

Flush Procedure

Syntax

```
procedure Flush(var F: TextFile);
```

Description

The Flush procedure forces the output of buffered text to a text file that was opened for writing (with Append or Rewrite). By default, a text file accumulates a line of text before writing the text to the file. Flush is not a real procedure.

Tips and Tricks

Flush flushes Delphi's buffer, not the operating system's buffer. To make sure all data is safely stored, close the file.

Errors

- If the file is not open, Flush reports I/O error 103.
- If Flush cannot write the text, perhaps because the disk is full, it reports the Windows error code as an I/O error.
- You can call Flush on an input file (opened with Reset), but the function does nothing.

See Also

IOResult Function, Rewrite Procedure, TextFile Type, Write Procedure, WriteLn Procedure

For Keyword

Syntax

```
for Variable := Expr1 to Expr2 do Statement
for Variable := Expr1 downto Expr2 do Statement
```

Description

The for keyword introduces a for loop. A for loop evaluates the expressions that specify the limits of the loop, then performs the loop body repeatedly, assigning a new value to the loop control variable before each loop iteration. The loop control variable must be a local variable.

The types of *Variable*, *Expr1*, and *Expr2* must match and must be ordinal types: integer, character, or enumerated. Integer values outside the range of the Integer type are not supported. Instead, Delphi silently maps the *Expr1* and *Expr2* expressions into the range of Integer, giving results you might not expect.

Tips and Tricks

• Delphi optimizes the loop by computing the number of iterations before starting the loop. Changing the limits of the loop (*Expr1* and *Expr2*) inside the loop does not affect the number of times the loop executes.

• Because the for loop works only with values that fit in an Integer, if you want to iterate over Cardinal or Int64 values, you must use a while loop.

• After the loop terminates normally, the value of the loop control variable is not defined. If the loop exits because of a Break or goto statement, the loop control variable retains its last value.

See Also

Do Keyword, Integer Type, Repeat Keyword, While Keyword

Language Reference

Forward Directive

Syntax

```
Subroutine header; forward;
```

Description

In a unit's implementation section or in the body of a program or library, you can declare a function or procedure before you call it by declaring the header (name, parameters, and return type) with the forward directive.

Delphi compiles a file by reading from its beginning to the end. When it reaches a function or procedure call, it must already know the number and type of the subroutine or method parameters and the function's return type (the subroutine's *signature*). Using the forward directive is one way to declare a subroutine early in a file, and define the entire subroutine later.

Tips and Tricks

- A common use of the `forward` directive is for mutually recursive subroutines.

- All subroutine declarations in a unit's interface section are already forward declarations, so Delphi ignores the `forward` directive in a unit's interface section.

- A class declaration declares the signatures for all the methods of the class, so do not use the `forward` directive for methods.

- You can also declare a class type as a forward declaration, but you don't use the `forward` directive. See the `class` keyword for details.

Example

```
// The WalkDirectory procedure recursively iterates over the files
// in a directory and in its subdirectories. Each file is added to
// a TTreeView control, showing the directory and file hierarchy.

procedure WalkDirectory(const Dir: string; Node: TTreeNode); forward;

// Add a single file to the tree view. If the file is a directory,
// recursively walk the directory.
procedure WalkFile(const DirName, FileName: string;
      Attr: Integer; Parent: TTreeNode);
var
  Node: TTreeNode;
begin
  Node := Parent.Owner.AddChild(Parent, FileName);
  if (faDirectory and Attr) = faDirectory then
    WalkDirectory(DirName + FileName, Node);
end;

procedure WalkDirectory(const Dir: string; Node: TTreeNode);
var
  Rec: TSearchRec;
  Path: string;
begin
  Path := IncludeTrailingBackslash(Dir);
  if FindFirst(Path + '*.*', faAnyFile, Rec) = 0 then
    try
      repeat
        // Skip over the current and parent directories.
        if (Rec.Name = '.') or (Rec.Name = '..') then
          Continue;
        WalkFile(Path, Rec.Name, Rec.Attr, Node)
      until FindNext(Rec) <> 0;
    finally
      FindClose(Rec);
    end;
end;
```

See Also

Class Keyword, Function Keyword, Procedure Keyword

Frac Function

Syntax

```
function Frac(X: Floating-point type): Extended;
```

Description

Frac returns the fractional part of a floating-point number. It is not a real function.

Tips and Tricks

- If X is infinity or a signaling NaN, Frac raises runtime error 6 (EInvalidOp).

- If X is a quiet NaN, the result is X.

See Also

Int Function, Round Function, Trunc Function

FreeMem Procedure

Syntax

```
procedure FreeMem(P: Pointer);
```

Description

FreeMem frees the memory that P points to. FreeMem uses the installed memory manager to free the memory. FreeMem is not a real procedure.

Tips and Tricks

- P can be nil, in which case, FreeMem returns immediately.

- When freeing memory, always take care not to free a pointer more than once, and be sure not to refer to memory after freeing it.

- To help avoid mistakes, especially in a multithreaded program, be sure to set global variables or class fields to nil before freeing the memory. You want to avoid any windows—no matter how small—where a variable or field contains an invalid pointer. For example:

```
procedure FreeMemAndNil(var P);
var
  Tmp: Pointer;
begin
  Tmp := Pointer(P);
  Pointer(P) := nil;
  FreeMem(Tmp);
end;
```

- FreeMem in Delphi's default memory manager is thread-safe, that is, you can call FreeMem from multiple threads simultaneously, but only if IsMultiThread is True.

- Call FreeMem to free memory allocated by GetMem. Call Dispose to free memory allocated by New.

See Also

Dispose Procedure, IsMultiThread Variable, GetMem Procedure, ReallocMem Procedure, SetMemoryManager Procedure, SysFreeMem Function

FreeMemory Function

Syntax

```
function FreeMemory(P: Pointer): Integer; cdecl;
```

Description

FreeMemory calls SysFreeMem to free P using Delphi's built-in memory manager. It returns zero for success and non-zero for failure. If P is nil, FreeMemory returns zero.

FreeMemory is for use by C++ Builder. If you are writing a memory manager in Delphi, you should call SysFreeMem.

FreeMemory is a real function.

See Also

Dispose Procedure, FreeMem Procedure, GetMemory Function, IsMultiThread Variable, ReallocMemory Function, SysFreeMem Function

Function Keyword

Syntax

```
function Name: Return type; Directives...
function Name(Parameters...): Return type; Directives...

type Name = function(Parameters...): Return type;
type Name = function(Parameters...): Return type of object;
```

Description

A function is a subroutine that returns a value. In the interface section of a unit, only the function header (its name, parameters, return type, and directives, but not the body) can appear. You can also define a functional type.

In the implementation section, you must provide a complete function definition for every function declared in the interface section. (See the **external** directive to learn how to define a function without providing a body.) You can omit the parameters in the implementation section if the function is not overloaded. If you provide the parameters, they must match exactly (including the parameter names) with the function header in the interface section.

A function's implementation should not repeat the directives that appear first with the function header.

Tips and Tricks

- Although it seems like an additional maintenance burden to keep a copy of the header in the function's implementation, it is a great benefit to the person who maintains the code. It is inconvenient to have to jump to the function's declaration just to learn about the function's parameters.

- You can declare multiple functions with the same name but different arguments by using the overload directive.

- A function can be declared in a class declaration, in which case it is called a method. A method can be declared with the dynamic or virtual directives to declare a virtual method. A virtual method can be declared with the abstract directive, in which case you must not provide a function implementation.

- The default calling convention is register. You can choose a different calling convention with the cdecl, pascal, safecall, or stdcall directives.

- Directives are optional, but if you include them, you must use the following order for methods:
  - reintroduce
  - overload
  - virtual, dynamic, override
  - cdecl, pascal, register, safecall, stdcall
  - abstract (only if virtual, dynamic, or override appears earlier)

Examples

```
type
  TRandFunc = function(Min, Max: Integer): Integer;
  TRandMethod = function(Max: Integer): Integer of object;
  TRandClass = class
  private
    fMin: Integer;
  public
    constructor Create(Min: Integer);
    function IntFunc(Max: Integer): Integer;
    property Min: Integer read fMin;
  end;

function TestFunc(Min, Max: Integer): Integer;
begin
  Result := Random(Max - Min + 1) + Min;
end;

function TRandClass.IntFunc(Max: Integer): Integer;
begin
  Result := Random(Max - Min + 1) + Min;
end;

var
  F: TRandFunc;
  M: TRandMethod;
```

```
  O: TRandClass;
begin
  O := TRandClass.Create(10);
  try
    F := TestFunc;
    WriteLn(F(1, 6));
    M := O.IntFunc;
    WriteLn(M(50));
  finally
    O.Free;
  end;
end.
```

See Also

Abstract Directive, CDecl Directive, Class Keyword, External Directive, Object Keyword, Overload Directive, Pascal Directive, Procedure Keyword, Result Variable, SafeCall Directive, StdCall Directive, Type Keyword, Virtual Directive

---

GetDir Function

Syntax

```
procedure GetDir(Drive: Byte; var Directory: string);
```

Description

The `GetDir` procedure stores in `Directory` the default directory for the drive specified by `Drive`. If `Drive` is 1 (for *A:*) through 26 (for *Z:*), `GetDir` retrieves the default directory for that drive. If the drive is not valid or if `Drive` is any other value, `GetDir` retrieves the default drive and directory. The value stored in `Directory` always begins with the drive letter, e.g., `X:\Directory`.

`GetDir` is not a real procedure.

See Also

ChDir Procedure, MkDir Procedure, RmDir Procedure

GetHeapStatus Function

Syntax

```
function GetHeapStatus: THeapStatus;
```

Description

`GetHeapStatus` returns a record that contains the status of Delphi's memory manager. If a new memory manager has been installed and the new one does not use Delphi's built-in memory manager, all the values in the heap status will be zero. `GetHeapStatus` is a real function.

Tips and Tricks

Call `IsMemoryManagerSet` to learn whether a custom memory manager has been installed. If so, the value returned by `GetHeapStatus` is not necessarily valid.

```
procedure TForm1.Button1Click(Sender: TObject);
  procedure AddFmt(const Fmt: string; Args: array of const);
  begin
    Memo1.Lines.Add(Format(Fmt, Args));
  end;
var
  Status: THeapStatus;
begin
  Status := GetHeapStatus;
  AddFmt('TotalAddrSpace = %d', [Status.TotalAddrSpace]);
  AddFmt('TotalUncommitted = %d', [Status.TotalUncommitted]);
  AddFmt('TotalCommitted = %d', [Status.TotalCommitted]);
  AddFmt('TotalAllocated = %d', [Status.TotalAllocated]);
  AddFmt('TotalFree = %d', [Status.TotalFree]);
  AddFmt('FreeSmall = %d', [Status.FreeSmall]);
  AddFmt('FreeBig = %d', [Status.FreeBig]);
  AddFmt('Unused = %d', [Status.Unused]);
  AddFmt('Overhead = %d', [Status.Overhead]);
  AddFmt('HeapErrorCode = %d', [Status.HeapErrorCode]);
end;
```

See Also

AllocMemCount Variable, AllocMemFree Variable, IsMemoryManagerSet Function, SetMemoryManager Procedure, THeapStatus Type

GetMem Procedure

Syntax

```
procedure GetMem(var P: Pointer; Size: LongInt);
```

Description

GetMem allocates Size bytes of dynamic memory and stores a pointer to the memory in P. It does not initialize the allocated memory. GetMem is not a real procedure.

Tips and Tricks

- The memory that GetMem allocates is not initialized. If you are allocating strings, dynamic arrays, or Variants, you should call Initialize or set the memory to zero with FillChar.

- GetMem in Delphi's default memory manager is thread-safe, that is, you can call GetMem from multiple threads simultaneously, but only if IsMultiThread is True.

- If you are allocating a record or fixed-size array, call New instead of GetMem.

- A common use for GetMem is to allocate an array where you do not know the array size at compile time. Although dynamic arrays have largely replaced the need for this trick, it is still commonly found in legacy Delphi code.

Example

```
// Create a grayscale palette, and return the palette handle.
// Although you can create a palette with up to 255 shades of gray,
// many video adapters can display only 15 or 16 bits per pixel,
// which means 5 bits per gray shade, or 32 distinct shades of gray.
function CreateGrayScalePalette(NumShades: Bytes);
var
  LogPalette: PLogPalette;
  I: Integer;
begin
  // TLogPalette already has room for one palette entry, so allocate
  // room for NumShades-1 additional palette entries.
  GetMem(LogPalette,
         SizeOf(TLogPalette) + (NumShades-1)*SizeOf(TPaletteEntry));
  try
    LogPalette.palVersion := $300;
    LogPalette.palNumEntries := NumShades;
    // TLogPalette defines the palPalEntry array with bounds 0..0
    // so turn off range checking to set the other array entries.
{$R-}
    for I := 0 to NumShades-1 do
    begin
      LogPalette.palPalEntry[I].peRed   := I * 256 div NumShades;
      LogPalette.palPalEntry[I].peGreen := I * 256 div NumShades;
      LogPalette.palPalEntry[I].peBlue  := I * 256 div NumShades;
      LogPalette.palPalEntry[I].peFlags := 0;
    end;
{$R+}
    Result := CreatePalette(LogPalette);
  finally
    FreeMem(LogPalette)
  end;
end;
```

See Also

FillChar Procedure, FreeMem Procedure, GetMemory Function, Initialize Procedure, IsMultiThread Variable, ReallocMem Procedure, SysGetMem Function

---

GetMemory Function

Syntax

```
function GetMemory(Size: LongInt): Pointer; cdecl;
```

Description

GetMemory calls Delphi's default memory manager to allocate Size bytes of memory. It returns a pointer to the newly allocated memory or nil if the request could not be fulfilled.

GetMemory is for use by C++ Builder. If you are writing a memory manager in Delphi, you should call SysGetMem.

`GetMemory` is a real function.

See Also

FreeMemory Function, GetMem Procedure, IsMultiThread Variable, New Procedure, ReallocMemory Function, SysGetMem Function

GetMemoryManager Procedure

Syntax

```
procedure GetMemoryManager(var Mgr: TMemoryManager);
```

Description

`GetMemoryManager` retrieves pointers to the functions that Delphi uses to allocate and free memory, and stores those pointers in the `Mgr` record. `GetMemoryManager` is a real procedure.

Tips and Tricks

Ordinarily, it is good form when making a global change to save the old setting so you can restore it in a unit's finalization section. Setting a new memory manager is the exception. See `SetMemoryManager` for an explanation.

See Also

IsMemoryManagerSet Function, SetMemoryManager Procedure, TMemoryManager Type

GetPackageInfoTable Type

Syntax

```
type GetPackageInfoTable = function: PackageInfo;
```

Description

Every package exports a function named `@GetPackageInfoTable`. The function's type is `GetPackageInfoTable`. This function returns a pointer to the package's info table, which contains pointers to the initialization and finalization sections for all the units in the package. When Delphi loads a package, it calls `@GetPackageInfoTable` so it can initialize all the units in the package.

Tips and Tricks

Most programmers never need to concern themselves with this level of detail. Delphi handles all this automatically.

See Also

Finalization Keyword, Initialization Keyword, Package Directive, PackageInfo Type, PackageInfoTable Type, PUnitEntryTable Type, UnitEntryTable Type

Goto Keyword

Syntax

```
goto Label
```

Description

The goto statement transfers control to the given label. The label can be any identifier or a digit string with up to four digits. You cannot use an identifier used as a label as a local variable in the same block.

Tips and Tricks

- Indiscriminate use of the goto statement results in the classic problem of "spaghetti" code, that is, source code that is as tangled as a plate of spaghetti.

- The most common use for the goto statement is to jump out of deeply nested loops. When it is used in this way, you can think of it as a super-Break statement.

- The entire VCL source code contains only two goto statements. Both are used to break out of a nested loop. Consider this a guideline for the proper use of the goto statement.

- Jumping from outside a block (loop, conditional, or nested subroutine) into the block has unpredictable results. Delphi does not permit a jump into or out of any part of a try-except or try-finally statement.

- Unlike standard Pascal, Delphi does not permit a jump from a nested subroutine into an outer subroutine. Use the Exit procedure to return prematurely from a function or procedure.

Example

```
// Find the first non-blank cell in a grid, and return its
// contents, converted to all uppercase. If the entire grid
// is blank, return a default string. Skip over the fixed
// rows and columns because they are just identifying headers.
procedure UpcaseCell(Grid: TStringGrid; const Default: string): string;
var
  R, C: Integer;
label
  NestedBreak;
begin
  Result := Default;
  for R := Grid.FixedRows to Grid.RowCount-1 do
    for C := Grid.FixedCols to Grid.ColCount-1 do
      if Grid.Cells[C, R] <> '' then
      begin
        Result := Grid.Cells[C, R];
        goto NestedBreak;
      end;
NestedBreak:
  Result := UpperCase(Result);
end;
```

Break Procedure, Continue Procedure, Exit Procedure, Label Keyword

Halt Procedure

Syntax

```
procedure Halt(ExitCode: Integer);
```

Description

Halt terminates an application immediately, without giving it time to clean up after itself. Windows NT automatically releases any resources that the application was using, but Windows 95 and Windows 98 are less forgiving. Do not use Halt except in unusual circumstances, such as part of a last-ditch, catch-all exception handler.

Halt is not a real procedure.

Tips and Tricks

- Halt saves its argument in the global ExitCode variable.

- If the ErrorAddr variable is not nil, Halt prints an error message before it terminates the program.

- The ExitProc procedure and units' finalization sections get to run before the program terminates.

- Halt shuts down the program without freeing all objects and forms. A GUI application should close the main form to terminate the application instead of calling Halt.

Example

```
// Report a run-time error at a specific address.
procedure ReportError(ErrorCode: Integer; Addr: Pointer);
begin
  ErrorAddr := Addr;
  if ErrorProc <> nil then
    ErrorProc(ErrorCode, Addr);
  Halt(ErrorCode);
end;
```

See Also

ErrorProc Variable, ExceptProc Variable, ExitCode Variable, ExitProc Variable, Finalization Keyword, NoErrMsg Variable, RunError Procedure

HeapAllocFlags Variable

Syntax

```
var HeapAllocFlags: Word;
```

Description

The `HeapAllocFlags` variable exists for backward compatibility with Delphi 1, when it supplied the flags to use in calls to `GlobalAlloc`. It is no longer used.

Hi Function

Syntax

```
function Hi(Value: Integer): Byte;
```

Description

The `Hi` function returns the most significant byte of a 16-bit word, ignoring any bits higher than the 16th bit. The `Hi` function is not a real function, but is expanded inline by the compiler.

Tips and Tricks

The `Hi` function is equivalent to the following function:

```
function Hi(Value: Integer): Byte;
begin
  Result := (Value shr 8) and $FF;
end;
```

See Also

Lo Function

High Function

Syntax

```
function High(Type or variable): Ordinal type;
```

Description

The `High` function returns the largest value of an enumerated type, the upper bound of an array index, or the same information for a variable of ordinal or array type.

`High` is built into the compiler and is not a real function.

Tips and Tricks

- In a for loop, subrange type declaration, or any other situation where you use the limits of an ordinal or array type, always use the `High` function instead of referring explicitly to the high ordinal value. A future version of your code might extend the type, and you don't want to scramble through all your code looking for explicit references to an enumerated literal that should really have been calls to the `High` function.

- Calling `High` for a `ShortString` returns the highest index for the string type. You cannot call `High` for an `AnsiString` or `WideString`.

- High for an open array parameter is always the length of the array minus one, regardless of the type or range of the actual array argument.

Example

```
// See the example of the asm keyword for the GetCpuId function.

// Get the CPU identification, and write it to Output.
procedure WriteCpuId;
const
  CpuTypes: array[TCpuType] of string =
    ('Original', 'Overdrive', 'Dual', '?');
var
  ID: TCpuId;
  F:  TCpuFeature;
begin
  if not GetCpuId(ID) then
    WriteLn('No CPUID instruction')
  else
  begin
    WriteLn(ID.Vendor, ' ', CpuTypes[ID.CpuType]);
    WriteLn('Family: ', ID.Family);
    WriteLn('Model: ', ID.Model);
    WriteLn('Stepping: ', ID.Stepping);
    Write('Features:');
    for F := Low(TCpuFeature) to High(TCpuFeature) do
      if F in ID.Features then
        Write(' ', GetEnumName(TypeInfo(TCpuFeature), Ord(F)));
    WriteLn;
  end;
end;
```

See Also

Dec Procedure, Inc Procedure, Length Function, Low Function, Pred Function, Succ Function

---

HInstance Variable

Syntax

```
unit SysInit;
var HInstance: LongWord;
```

Description

The HInstance variable stores the instance handle for the module (application, library, or package) that contains the HInstance reference.

Tips and Tricks

- The most common use for a module's instance handler is to load resources from the module. A unit can use HInstance to load resources that are linked with that unit (using the $R compiler directive). To load resources that are linked with a different unit (which might reside in a different package), see the FindHInstance function.

- To load resources that must be localized (e.g., forms, strings), see `FindResourceHInstance`.

- The instance handle of the main application is stored in `MainInstance`.

- Earlier versions of Delphi stored the main instance handle in `HInstance`, requiring a call to `FindHInstance` to learn a module's instance handle. The current release stores the module's instance handle in `HInstance`.

Example

```
// Use the Image Editor to create a .RES file that
// contains the company logo as the resource named LOGO.
// The GetLogo procedure sets its Bitmap argument
// to the company logo bitmap.

{$R 'Logo.res'}

procedure GetLogo(Bitmap: TBitmap);
begin
  Bitmap.LoadFromResourceName(HInstance, 'LOGO');
end;
```

See Also

FindClassHInstance Function, FindHInstance Function, MainInstance Variable

---

HPrevInst Variable

Syntax

```
var HPrevInst: Integer;
```

Description

`HPrevInst` is always zero. It is an artifact from Delphi 1 and no longer serves any useful purpose.

Tips and Tricks

Most Delphi 1 programs use `HPrevInst` to determine whether the application is already running. Win32 has many ways of doing the same without using `HPrevInst`, but knowing whether the application is running is the easy part of the problem. More difficult is knowing what to do: should the new instance send its command line to the existing application? Should the application behave differently when running for the first time than when it is invoked at subsequent times? This book cannot answer these questions for you, but see Chapter 4 for one suggestion for handling this situation.

HResult Type

Syntax

```
type HResult = LongWord;
```

Description

HResult is the return type of most COM methods. The most significant bit is zero for success or one for an error. See the Windows API documentation to learn more about the HResult type and the standard error codes.

The SysUtils unit has several methods to help you use HResult values, such as Succeeded and Failed.

See Also

Safecall Directive

IDispatch Interface

Syntax

```
type
  IDispatch = interface(IUnknown)
  ['{00020400-0000-0000-C000-000000000046}']
    function GetTypeInfoCount(out Count: Integer): HResult; stdcall;
    function GetTypeInfo(Index, LocaleID: Integer; out TypeInfo):
      HResult; stdcall;
    function GetIDsOfNames(const IID: TGUID; Names: Pointer;
      NameCount, LocaleID: Integer; DispIDs: Pointer):
      HResult; stdcall;
    function Invoke(DispID: Integer; const IID: TGUID;
      LocaleID: Integer; Flags: Word; var Params;
      VarResult, ExcepInfo, ArgErr: Pointer): HResult; stdcall;
  end;
```

Description

IDispatch is a standard ActiveX interface that lets you call a COM method without knowing the method's name, arguments, or return type at compile time.

Tips and Tricks

- When you use a COM object that implements the IDispatch interface, Delphi automatically takes care of all the details involved in calling a method dynamically. You can store the object reference in a Variant variable or use a dispinterface type.

- To write a COM server that implements the IDispatch interface, simply derive your class from TAutoObject (in the ComObj unit) or one of its descendants. If you are using Delphi's type library editor, simply check the box for the Dual flag, and let Delphi handle the details for you.

- See the Windows Platform SDK documentation to learn more about the IDispatch interface.

See Also

Dispinterface Keyword, Interface Keyword, IUnknown Interface, VarDispProc Variable, Variant Type

If Keyword

Syntax

```
if Condition then Statement
if Condition then Statement else Statement
```

Description

Delphi's `if` statement is the same as the `if` statement in standard Pascal. The condition must be a Boolean expression. The `else` part is optional. If you have nested `if` statements, an `else` part binds with the nearest `if` statement. For example:

```
if X > Y then
  if A > B then
    WriteLn('A > B')
  else
    WriteLn('X > Y and A <= B');
```

Tips and Tricks

- C programmers are accustomed to using the semicolon as a statement terminator, but in Pascal a semicolon is a statement separator. In particular, no semicolon is allowed after the first statement and before the `else` keyword. Delphi Pascal loosens some of the restrictions on semicolons, so it is easy for C, C++, and Java programmers to be lulled into the misbelief that semicolons in Delphi can terminate statements.

- By default, Boolean operators in Delphi implement shortcut logic (just like their brethren in C, C++, and Java). See the `and` and `or` operators for details.

See Also

And Keyword, Begin Keyword, Boolean Type, Else Keyword, Or Keyword

Implementation Keyword

Syntax

```
unit Name;
interface Declarations...
implementation Declarations...
end.
```

Description

The `implementation` section of a unit is required, although it can be empty. The `implementation` section contains the definitions of all functions, procedures, and methods that are declared in the unit's `interface` section. You can also have additional type, subroutine, and variable declarations in the `implementation` section, in which case the declarations are private to the unit.

Changes to a unit's `implementation` section do not force dependent units to be recompiled.

Any used units not needed for the `interface` section should be listed in the `uses` declaration of the `implementation` section. This minimizes the amount of recompilation, should one of those units change. Changes to the interface—including changes to used units—force a recompilation of all dependent units. Changes to the implementation section, on the other hand, do not propagate to dependent units.

Example

See the `unit` keyword for an example.

See Also

Interface Keyword, Unit Keyword, Uses Keyword

Implements Directive

Syntax

```
Property declaration read Getter implements Interfaces...;
```

Description

A class can delegate the implementation of one or more interfaces to a property with the `implements` directive. The property's `Getter` must be a field or a simple method (no array or indexed properties allowed). The method can be virtual, but not dynamic or a message handler. The `Getter` field or method must have a class or interface type. If the property implements more than one interface, separate the interface identifiers with commas.

The listed interfaces must appear in the class declaration.

Tips and Tricks

- The `implements` directive is often used to implement COM-style aggregation. The `ComObj` unit declares the `TAggregatedObject` class as the base class for the inner object.

- If the `Getter` is of class type, you must be careful about the lifetime of the object. Once Delphi casts the object reference to an interface, Delphi's automatic reference counting manages the object's lifetime. Once the last interface is out of scope, the object will be freed automatically. The simplest way to manage this situation is for the `Getter` method to create a new object every time it is called.

- If the `Getter` is of class type, you can use method resolution clauses to redirect some of the interface methods to the containing class.

- If the `Getter` is of interface type, the returned interface must implement all the listed interfaces. You cannot use method resolution to alter the interfaces.

Example

```
interface
// In the interface section of a unit, declare the TWizardComponent
```

```
// class. The user drops this class on a form to create a wizard,
// that is, an extension to the Delphi IDE using the Open Tools API.
// The wizard must implement the IOTAWizard interface, but you want
// the details of the implementation to be private to the
// implementation section of the unit. Delegating the implementation
// to a property achieves this goal.
type
  TWizardComponent = class(TComponent, IOTAWizard)
  private
    fWizard: IOTAWizard;
    fOnExecute: TNotifyEvent;
    function GetIDString: string;
    procedure SetIDString(const Value: string);
    function GetWizardName: string;
    procedure SetWizardName(const Value: string);
    property Wizard: IOTAWizard read fWizard implements IOTAWizard;
  protected
    procedure Execute; virtual;
  public
    constructor Create(Owner: TComponent); override;
  published
    property IDString: string read GetIDString write SetIDString;
    property WizardName: string read GetWizardName write SetWizardName;
    property OnExecute: TNotifyEvent read fOnExecute write fOnExecute;
  end;


implementation

// The constructor for TWizardComponent creates a TWizard object
// and saves it as the fWizard field. The TWizard object provides
// the actual implementation of the IOTAWizard interface.
type
  TWizard = class(TInterfacedObject, IOTAWIzard)
  private
    fIndex: Integer;
    fOwner: TWizardComponent;
    function GetIDString: string;
    function GetName: string;
    function GetState: TWizardState;
    procedure Execute;
  public
    constructor Create(Owner: TWizardComponent);
    destructor Destroy; override;
  end;
```

See Also

Class Keyword, Interface Keyword, Property Keyword

In Keyword

Syntax

```
Ordinal expression in Set expression
```

Description

The in operator tests set membership. It returns True if the ordinal value is a member of the set, and it returns False otherwise.

Tips and Tricks

The base type for a set is limited to at most 256 members. The in operator tests only the least significant byte of the ordinal expression. The following example, therefore, always calls ShowMessage:

```
var
  X: set of 0..7;
begin
  X := [0];
  if 512 in X then
    ShowMessage('The in operator tests only the low byte of 512.');
```

Example

See the set keyword for an example.

See Also

Exclude Procedure, High Function, Include Procedure, Low Function, Set Keyword

---

Inc Procedure

Syntax

```
procedure Inc(var Variable);
procedure Inc(var Variable; Count: Integer);
```

Description

The Inc procedure increments a variable. You can increment any ordinal-type variable or pointer-type variable. You cannot use Inc to increment a floating-point variable.

Incrementing a pointer adjusts the pointer by the size of the base type. For example, incrementing a pointer to AnsiChar increases the pointer value by 1, and incrementing a pointer to WideChar increases the pointer value by 2. The default is to increment the variable by 1 unit, but you can supply an integer to increment by a different amount. When incrementing a pointer, Count is multiplied by the size of the base type.

The Inc procedure is built-in and is not a real procedure.

Tips and Tricks

- Count can be negative, in which case the variable's value decreases.

- There is little performance difference between Inc, Succ, or addition. That is, the following all result in similar object code:

```
Inc(X);
X := Succ(X);
X := X + 1;    // if X is an integer or PChar type
```

- You cannot use a property for the variable because a property value cannot be used as a **var** parameter. Use a simple assignment instead.

See Also

Dec Procedure, High Function, Low Function, Pred Function, Succ Function

---

Include Procedure

Syntax

```
procedure Include(var ASet: Set type; Value: Ordinal type);
```

Description

The **Include** procedure adds the element **Value** to the set variable **ASet**. The type of **Value** must be the base type of **ASet**. **Include** is not a real procedure.

Tips and Tricks

Note that you cannot use a property for the set reference because a property value cannot be used as a **var** parameter. Instead, use the + operator to add the member to the set, as shown below:

```
Font.Style := Font.Style + [fsBold];
```

Example

See the **Exclude** procedure for an example.

See Also

Exclude Procedure, In Keyword, Set Keyword

Index Directive

Syntax

```
function Getter(Index: Integer): Property type;
procedure Setter(Index: Integer; Value: Property type);
property Name: Property type index Constant read Getter write Setter;

function ArrayGet(Index: Integer; ArrayIndex: Index type): Prop. type;
procedure ArraySet(Index: Integer; ArrayIndex: Index type;
  Value: Property type);
property Name[ArrayIndex: Index type]: Property type index Constant
  read Getter write Setter;

exports
  Subroutine index Constant;

Subroutine header; external DllName index Constant;
```

Description

The index directive has three distinct uses: declaring indexed properties, exporting subroutines, and importing subroutines.

- Multiple properties can reuse a getter or setter method by specifying an **index** directive and a unique index value. The index value is passed as the first argument to the getter and setter methods. See the **property** keyword for more information.

- A unit or library can export subroutines with the **exports** declaration. Every exported subroutine has a unique index. If you do not supply an **index** directive, Delphi automatically assigns a unique index. See the **exports** keyword for more information.

- A subroutine declaration can use the **external** directive to import a subroutine from a DLL. By default, Delphi looks up the subroutine by name. If you supply an **index** directive, Delphi looks up the subroutine by index number, which is slightly faster (but subject to the possibility that the index number will change in a future revision of the DLL). See the **external** directive for more information.

Tips and Tricks

- A property that uses an **index** directive cannot use field names for the **read** and **write** directives.

- An array property can use the **index** directive. The index number is the first argument and the array indices are the second and subsequent arguments to the getter and setter methods.

- You can use the **index** and **name** directives for the same exported routine (in that order).

See Also

Exports Keyword, External Directive, Name Directive, Property Keyword

---

Inherited Keyword

Syntax

```
Subroutine header;
begin
   ...
   inherited;
   inherited Name(Arguments...);
```

Description

A method in a derived class can call a method of its base class by prefacing the method call with the **inherited** keyword instead of an object reference.

To call an inherited procedure with the same name and arguments, you can use the bare keyword (**inherited;**). To call an inherited function, to use different arguments, or to call a different method, you must supply the method name and arguments as in a normal method call.

Tips and Tricks

- Most constructors call the inherited constructor at the beginning of the method. Most destructors call the inherited destructor at the end.

- Be aware of the needs of your derived class. Some methods extend the behavior of the base class, and other methods replace the ancestor's behavior. The example below demonstrates both kinds of methods.

- In a message handler, using the bare keyword calls the message handler for the same message number in an ancestor class. If no ancestor class has a message handler for the same message number, `inherited` calls `DefaultHandler`. Note that the ancestor's message handler can have a different method name, and it might even be a private method.

- If you use the bare keyword, and no ancestor class has a method of the same name, Delphi ignores the `inherited` statement.

Example

```
// See the override directive for the class declaration.

// Create the bitmap when creating the control.
constructor TTile.Create(Owner: TComponent);
begin
  inherited;
  fBitmap := TBitmap.Create;
  fBitmap.OnChange := BitmapChanged;
end;

// Paint the control by tiling the bitmap. If there is no
// bitmap, don't paint anything. Does not call inherited
// because this Paint method replaces the ancestor's Paint method.
procedure TTile.Paint;
var
  X, Y: Integer;
begin
  if (Bitmap.Width = 0) or (Bitmap.Height = 0) then
    Exit;

  Y := 0;
  while Y < ClientHeight do
  begin
    X := 0;
    while X < ClientWidth do
    begin
      Canvas.Draw(X, Y, Bitmap);
      Inc(X, Bitmap.Width);
    end;
    Inc(Y, Bitmap.Height);
  end;
end;
```

See Also

Class Keyword, Dynamic Directive, Message Directive, Override Directive, Self Variable, Virtual Directive

Initialization Keyword

Syntax

```
unit Name;
interface Declarations...
implementation Declarations
initialization Statements...
end.
```

Description

The statements in a unit's `initialization` section run when Windows loads the module (application, DLL, or package) that contains the unit. Delphi first runs the `initialization` section for all the units the *Name* unit uses, in order of appearance, starting with the `interface` units, followed by the `implementation` units. A unit's initialization section runs after Delphi runs the initialization section for all used units.

Delphi keeps track of which units have been initialized, so a unit's `initialization` section never runs more than once.

Tips and Tricks

- Delphi initializes units in a depth-first manner. If you need your unit to be initialized first, make sure it is listed first in the project's *.dpr* file. Setting a new memory manager is a common example of a unit that must be initialized first.

- The order of unit initialization means you cannot know for certain when your unit will be initialized, but all the units used in the interface section will be initialized first.

- Units are finalized in reverse order of initialization.

- Even if a unit does not declare an initialization section, Delphi automatically creates one. For a large project, starting an application or loading a DLL can result in a lot of page faults as Windows pages in the initialization code for every unit.

- You can use the `begin` keyword instead of `initialization`, but if you do, the unit cannot have a `finalization` section.

Example

See the `unit` keyword for an example.

See Also

Begin Keyword, Finalization Keyword, Implementation Keyword, SetMemoryManager Procedure, Unit Keyword

---

Initialize Procedure

Syntax

```
procedure Initialize(var Value);
procedure Initialize(var Value; Count: Integer);
```

Description

The `Initialize` procedure initializes strings, dynamic arrays, interfaces, and Variants. `Value` can be a single variable or it can be a record or array that contains strings, dynamic arrays, interfaces, or `Variants`.

If you are initializing more than one item in an array, pass the count of the number of array elements as the `Count` parameter. The `Count` is the number of array elements, not the number of bytes allocated.

The `New` procedure automatically calls `Initialize`. Object fields are also initialized automatically (by the `NewInstance` method).

`Initialize` is not a real procedure.

Tips and Tricks

- `New` calls `Initialize` for you, so you need to call `Initialize` only when you allocate memory by calling `GetMem`.

- The first argument to `Initialize` is not a pointer, but the actual variable or dereferenced pointer.

- `Initialize` must know the type of the buffer so it knows about array and record members. If you are casting a generic `Pointer`, be sure you cast it to the correct type. Typecasting pointers is a common source of hard-to-locate bugs.

Example

```
type
  TSample = record
    Str: string;
    List: array of Integer;
    Intf: IUnknown;
    V: Variant;
  end;
  // The TSampleArray type is declared with the largest possible size.
  // At runtime, the program allocates only as many samples as it
  // needs. This is a common idiom in programs that must interface
  // with the Windows API or other C and C++ programs (which do not
  // support Delphi's dynamic arrays).
  TSampleArray = array[0..MaxInt div SizeOf(TSample)-1] of TSample;
  PSampleArray = ^TSampleArray;

  // See the Finalize procedure to see how to free a TSample array.

function AllocateSamples(Count: Integer): PSampleArray;
begin
  GetMem(Result, Count * SizeOf(TSample));
  Initialize(Result^, Count);
end;
```

See Also

Finalize Procedure, GetMem Procedure

InitProc Variable

Syntax

```
var InitProc: Pointer;

procedure MyInitProc;
begin ... end;
InitProc := @MyInitProc;
```

Description

The `InitProc` pointer points to a parameterless procedure that performs secondary initialization. The `TApplication.Initialize` method calls the `InitProc` procedure, for example.

If your unit needs to perform additional initialization, but it must wait until all units have been initialized, you can define a secondary initialization procedure.

Tips and Tricks

- Save the previous value of `InitProc`, and call that procedure when your initialization procedure is finished.

- Unlike an initialization section, Delphi does not guarantee that the `InitProc` procedure will be called. You are counting on the good graces of the other code. The VCL is well-behaved, and all of Delphi's GUI and server applications call `InitProc`. If you write your own application framework, be sure to call `InitProc`, because some units in Delphi's VCL depend on the secondary initialization.

- Use an initialization section whenever possible. Resort to `InitProc` only when you truly have no other way to perform the initialization.

- Take care of finalization in the unit's `finalization` section.

Example

```
...
procedure LocalInitProc;
begin
  SetUpUnit;              // Take care of unit's initialization.
  TProcedure(SaveInitProc); // Call the next InitProc in the chain.
end;

var
  SaveInitProc: Pointer;
initialization
  SaveInitProc := InitProc;
  InitProc := @LocalInitProc;
finalization
  CleanUpUnit;
end.
```

See Also

ExitProc Variable, Finalization Keyword, Initialization Keyword

Inline Keyword

Description

The inline keyword is reserved. Delphi 1 used inline, but Delphi 2 and subsequent versions do not use this keyword. Although it might be used in future versions of Delphi, the primary reason it is reserved is to catch errors when porting code from Delphi 1 to later versions.

Input Variable

Syntax

```
var Input: TextFile;
```

Description

The Input variable is a text file that Delphi automatically opens for reading, but only in console applications. The input file is usually the console, but the user can redirect input from the command shell.

Input is an ordinary TextFile, and you can close it or open a different file. If you open a file without a name, that is the same as opening the console file. For example, Delphi always performs the following when a console application starts running:

```
AssignFile(Input, '');
Reset(Input);
```

Calling Read or ReadLn without a file reference as the first argument is the same as calling Read or ReadLn using Input as the first argument.

See Also

AssignFile Procedure, Output Variable, Read Procedure, ReadLn Procedure, Reset Procedure, TextFile Type

Insert Procedure

Syntax

```
procedure Insert(const Ins: string; var Str: string; Index: Integer);
```

Description

The Insert procedure inserts the string Ins into the string Str at the position Index. If Index is ≤ 1, Ins is inserted at the beginning of Str. If Index is past the end of the string, Ins is appended to the end of Str.

Insert is not a real procedure.

Tips and Tricks

The first character of a string has index 1.

Example

```
// Insert a drive letter at the front of a path.
procedure InsertDriveLetter(var Path: string; const Drive: Char);
begin
  // First make sure the path does not have a drive letter in front.
  if (Length(Path) < 2) or (Path[2] <> ':') then
    // Insert the drive at the start of the path.
    Insert(Drive + ':', Path, 1);
end;
```

See Also

Copy Function, Delete Procedure, SetLength Procedure, SetString Procedure

---

Int Function

Syntax

```
function Int(X: Floating-point type): Extended
```

Description

The Int function truncates a floating-point number by discarding its fractional part (rounds toward zero). Note that Int returns a floating-point number. It is not a real function.

Tips and Tricks

- If X is a signaling NaN, Delphi reports runtime error 6 (EInvalidOp).

- If X is a quiet NaN, positive infinity, or negative infinity, the result is X.

- Call Trunc to truncate a floating-point number and obtain an integer-type result.

See Also

Frac Function, Round Function, Trunc Function

Int64 Type

Syntax

```
type Int64 = -9223372036854775808..9223372036854775807;
```

Description

The Int64 type is a 64-bit signed integer type.

Tips and Tricks

- Use Int64 instead of the Comp type. Int64 does not depend on the floating-point unit or the precision set in the floating-point control word. Also, Int64 supports integer operators such as shl or shr.

- An integer constant whose value is too large for the Integer type automatically has type Int64.

- All the usual integer functions (e.g., `IntToStr`) have overloaded versions to support `Integer` and `Int64` arguments.

- If you write your own routines that work with the `Integer` type, consider writing overloaded versions that use `Int64`. For example, if you write `IntToBinary` to convert an integer to a string of `'0'` and `'1'` characters, write two overloaded functions: one that takes an `Integer` argument and one that takes an `Int64` argument.

- There is no 64-bit unsigned integer type.

See Also

Integer Type

Integer Type

Syntax

```
type Integer = -2147483648..2147483647;
```

Description

The `Integer` type is the basic integer type. The size of an integer can vary with different versions of Delphi. Currently, `Integer` is a 32-bit type, but future versions might change the size.

Delphi defines a number of integer types of varying ranges. The predefined integer types are shown in the following table.

Type	Minimum	Maximum
Byte	0	255
ShortInt	−128	127
Word	0	65,535
SmallInt	−32,768	32,767
LongWord	0	4,294,967,295
LongInt	−2,147,483,648	2,147,483,647
Integer	natural	natural
Cardinal	0	natural
Int64	−9,223,372,036,854,775,808	9,223,372,036,854,775,807

Tips and Tricks

- Numeric constants are type `Integer` if they fall within the range of `Integer`; otherwise, they are of type `Int64`. Arithmetic expressions with at least one argument of type `Int64` yield a result of type `Int64`. If both arguments are integer types, the result type is `Integer`.

- The size of the `Cardinal` and `Integer` types can change from one release of Delphi to another. In Delphi 5, both are 32 bits, but a future version of Delphi will undoubtedly change the size to 64 bits.

- Whenever possible, you should use an explicit subrange. If you know that a value will always be positive, for example, declare the variable accordingly. The additional type safety helps catch mistakes (where you accidentally assign a nonpositive number to the variable), and it helps to document the program by giving the reader additional information about the variable.

- `Cardinal` is a subrange of `Int64`, so mixing `Cardinal` and `Integer` types in an expression forces Delphi to convert both arguments to type `Int64`. If you want to perform arithmetic with non-negative integers, use a subrange of `Integer`.

Example

```
// The Count can never be negative, so don't use Integer.
// Cardinal is not a good choice either because any arithmetic
// with Count and an integer might need to be expanded to Int64.
// Thus, declare a subrange that fits in an Integer, but restricts
// the type to values that are allowable for a count.
var Count: 0..MaxInt;

// If one must do this a lot, define useful names.
type
  WholeNumber = 1..MaxInt;
  Natural = 0..MaxInt;
```

See Also

Byte Type, Cardinal Type, Int64 Type, LongInt Type, LongWord Type, ShortInt Type, SmallInt Type, Word Type

Interface Keyword

Syntax

```
unit Name;
interface
  Declarations...
implementation
  Declarations...
end.

type Name = interface
  ...
end;

type Name = interface(BaseInterface, ...)
  ...
end;
```

Description

The `interface` keyword serves two entirely unrelated functions.

The most common use for `interface` is to start the interface section of a unit. Every unit must have an interface section, although it can be empty. Declarations in an interface section are exported and can be used by any other unit that uses the unit.

The second use is to declare an interface type. An interface defines an abstract protocol that can be implemented by a class. An interface can have method and property declarations, but no field declarations. All interface declarations are public.

Interface Section

- The uses declaration, if it is present, must be the first declaration in the interface section.

- Every function, procedure, and non-abstract method declared in the interface section must be defined in the implementation section. The parameter names and types in the definitions must match the declarations in the interface section.

Interface Types

- Although interfaces look and act like COM interfaces, you are not restricted to using COM. Interfaces are a powerful and underused technique for writing object-oriented code. Interfaces feature automatic memory management and increased polymorphism. Chapter 2, *The Delphi Object Model*, discusses this topic at length.

- Delphi automatically type casts an interface reference to a GUID when necessary. Thus, you can use an interface name in a call to QueryInterface, e.g.:

```
var
  Stream: IStream;
begin
  if Something.QueryInterface(IStream, Stream) = S_OK then
    Stream.Revert;
```

Example

See the unit keyword for an example of an interface section. See IDispatch and IUnknown for examples of interface types.

See Also

Class Keyword, Dispinterface Keyword, External Directive, IDispatch Interface, Implementation Keyword, IUnknown Interface, Type Keyword, Unit Keyword, Uses Keyword

---

IOResult Function

Syntax

```
function IOResult: Integer;
```

Description

Delphi has two ways to report an I/O error: runtime errors or the IOResult function. By default, Delphi reports I/O errors as runtime errors, and the SysUtils unit maps runtime errors to exceptions. If you use the $I- or $IOChecks Off directives to turn off I/O runtime errors, Delphi returns the status of input and output

---

operations in the IOResult function. It is the programmer's responsibility to call IOResult to test the success or failure of each I/O procedure or function call.

IOResult returns zero for success or an error code for failure. The error code might be a Windows error code, or one of the following Delphi error codes.

Error Number	Description
100	Read past end of file.
101	Disk is full.
102	AssignFile has not yet been called.
103	The file is closed.
104	File not open for input.
105	File not open for output.
106	Incorrectly formatted input for Read.

After you call IOResult, the I/O result code is reset to zero. IOResult is a real function.

Tips and Tricks

* Each thread keeps its own I/O result code, so be sure to call IOResult in the context of the correct thread.

* It is the programmer's responsibility to call IOResult after each I/O routine. If you don't check IOResult, a subsequent I/O call can overwrite the old error code with a new one.

* The SysUtils unit maps I/O errors to the EInOutError exception. This exception class maps only a few I/O error codes to strings. In a real application, you should catch EInOutError and map the error code yourself. For example, you might use the following as an application OnException handler:

```
procedure TForm1.AppEventsException(Sender: TObject; E: Exception);
resourcestring
  sEOF        = 'Attempt to read past end of file';
  sNotAssigned = 'File not assigned';
  sNotOpen    = 'File not open';
  sNotRead    = 'File not open for input';
  sNotWrite   = 'File not open for output';
  sBadRead    = 'Input format error';
begin
  if E is EInOutError then
    case EInOutError(E).ErrorCode of
    100: E.Message := sEOF;
    101: E.Message := SysErrorMessage(Error_Disk_Full);
    102: E.Message := sNotAssigned;
    103: E.Message := sNotOpen;
    104: E.Message := sNotRead;
    105: E.Message := sNotWrite;
    106: E.Message := SBadRead;
    else E.Message := SysErrorMessage(EInOutError(E).ErrorCode);
    end;
```

```
      Application.ShowException(E);
  end;
```

Example

```
// Create a directory. If the directory already exists, do nothing.
procedure CreateDir(const Dir: string);
type
  TErrorProc = procedure(Error: integer; Addr: Pointer);
var
  Error: Integer;
begin
  {$IOChecks Off}
  MkDir(Dir);
  {$IOChecks On}
  Error := IOResult;
  if (Error <> 0) and (Error <> Error_Already_Exists) then
    // Some error other than that the directory already exists.
    TErrorProc(ErrorProc)(Error, @CreateDir);
end;
```

See Also

Append Procedure, AssignFile Procedure, BlockRead Procedure, BlockWrite Procedure, ChDir Procedure, CloseFile Procedure, Eof Function, Eoln Function, Erase Procedure, FilePos Function, FileSize Function, Flush Procedure, MkDir Procedure, Read Procedure, ReadLn Procedure, Rename Procedure, Reset Procedure, Rewrite Procedure, RmDir Procedure, Seek Procedure, SeekEof Function, SeekEoln Function, SetTextBuf Procedure, Truncate Procedure, Write Procedure, WriteLn Procedure, $I Compiler Directive, $IOChecks Compiler Directive

---

Is Keyword

Syntax

```
Object reference is Class reference
```

Description

The is operator tests whether the type of an object reference is the same as a given class reference or is a descendant of that class. It returns True if the object has the same type or is derived from the class type; it returns False otherwise.

Tips and Tricks

- To test the type of an interface, call QueryInterface or the Supports function in the SysUtils unit.

- The is operator calls the object's InheritsFrom method.

- If you have tested an object's type with the is operator, you do not need to use the as operator. Use a plain type cast for better performance.

- The is operator requires an object reference as the left-hand operand. To test a class reference, call the InheritsFrom method of TObject.

Example

```
// Double-click any edit box to clear it. Set the OnDblClick handler
// for all edit boxes to this procedure.
procedure TForm1.EditDblClick(Sender: TObject);
begin
  if Sender is TCustomEdit then
    TCustomEdit(Sender).Clear;
end;
```

See Also

As Keyword, Class Type, TObject Type

IsConsole Variable

Syntax

```
var IsConsole: Boolean;
```

Description

Delphi sets IsConsole to True in a console application or False in a GUI application. You can test IsConsole before trying to read from Input or write to Output.

Example

```
// Report an error.
procedure ErrorHandler(Code: Integer; Addr: Pointer);
var
  ErrorMessage: string;
begin
  ErrorMessage := Format('Error %d at $%p', [Code, Addr]);
  if IsConsole then
    WriteLn(ErrorMessage)
  else
    ShowMessage(ErrorMessage);
  Halt(Code);
end;
```

See Also

Input Variable, Output Variable, $AppType Compiler Directive

IsLibrary Variable

Syntax

```
var IsLibrary: Boolean;
```

Description

Delphi sets IsLibrary to True in a library project (DLL) or False in a program (EXE).

Tips and Tricks

- In most cases, you should use `ModuleIsLib` instead of `IsLibrary` to avoid complications caused by packages.

- If a library uses the *vcl50* package, and that library is loaded into an application that also uses the *vcl50* package, the library and the program will share a single instance of the *vcl50* package. The application sets `IsLibrary` to False, so the library sees the same False value for `IsLibrary` in the *vcl50* package. Any unit you write can also be loaded simultaneously by an application and a library in the same process, so the value of `IsLibrary` is limited. `ModuleIsLib` does not have this problem.

See Also

Library Keyword, ModuleIsLib Variable, ModuleIsPackage Variable

---

IsMemoryManagerSet Function

Syntax

```
function IsMemoryManagerSet: Boolean;
```

Description

The `IsMemoryManagerSet` function returns True if the memory manager is different from Delphi's default memory manager. You can set a different memory manager by calling `SetMemoryManager`.

`IsMemoryManagerSet` is a real function.

Tips and Tricks

If you are implementing a new memory manager, presumably you know whether your code calls `SetMemoryManager`. The utility of `IsMemoryManagerSet` is to know whether functions such as `GetHeapStatus` are meaningful. If `IsMemoryManagerSet` returns True, you should assume that `GetHeapStatus` will not return any useful information. Consult the documentation for the new memory manager to learn what function, if any, replaces `GetHeapStatus`.

See Also

GetHeapStatus Function, GetMemoryManager Procedure, SetMemoryManager Procedure

---

IsMultiThread Variable

Syntax

```
var IsMultiThread: Boolean;
```

Description

Delphi automatically sets `IsMultiThread` to True when you create a thread using `BeginThread` or with the `TThread` class in the `Classes` unit. You can test `IsMultiThread` and avoid some thread-protection overhead when it is False.

Tips and Tricks

- Delphi's memory manager checks `IsMultiThread` and uses critical sections to protect the integrity of its internal data structures. Therefore, if you create a thread by calling the Windows API function `CreateThread`, you must explicitly set `IsMultiThread` to True.

- Delphi also sets `IsMultiThread` to True for web servers and COM servers that don't force single threading (`tmSingle` threading model).

- If you write your own DLL that might be loaded by a multithreaded application, set `IsMultiThread` to True. If you use `DllProc` to learn when more than one thread attaches to the DLL, you must realize the application might start multiple threads before loading the DLL.

See Also

BeginThread Function, DllProc Variable, ThreadVar Keyword

IUnknown Interface

Syntax

```
type IUnknown = interface
  ['{00000000-0000-0000-C000-000000000046}']
  function QueryInterface(const IID: TGUID; out Obj): HResult; stdcall;
  function _AddRef: Integer; stdcall;
  function _Release: Integer; stdcall;
end;
```

Description

The `IUnknown` interface is the base for all interfaces in Delphi. Every class that implements any interface must implement `IUnknown` also. For your convenience, Delphi declares the `TInterfacedObject` class, which implements `IUnknown`.

Delphi calls `_AddRef` when an interface is assigned to a variable or passed as an argument to a subroutine. It calls `_Release` automatically when an interface-type variable goes out of scope.

Tips and Tricks

- `IUnknown` is the base interface in COM, which means any Delphi class can implement any COM interface. A Delphi program can use COM objects the same way it uses any other interface. COM is entirely optional, though. Many uses of interfaces are completely unrelated to COM.

- Although the convention is that `_AddRef` and `_Release` manage a reference count, you are free to implement these methods any way you wish. If you want to take advantage of interfaces without using reference counting, you can implement these methods as stubs. Return a non-zero value because a zero result means the object's reference count has reached zero.

- Delphi implements the **as** operator for interfaces by calling `QueryInterface`. The most logical implementation of `QueryInterface` calls `GetInterface`, but you are free to implement it any way you want. Be sure to return S_OK (zero) for success; any other result from `QueryInterface` tells Delphi's as operator to raise runtime error 23 (`EIntfCastError`).

- If you just want to test whether an interface is supported, and you don't want the overhead of raising an exception, call `QueryInterface` directly instead of using the as operator, or call `Supports` in the `SysUtils` unit.

See Also

As Keyword, Interface Keyword

JITEnable Variable

Syntax

```
var JITEnable: Byte;
```

Description

`JITEnable` determines which exceptions enable the just-in-time debugger.

Tips and Tricks

- The default value is 0, which means only unhandled exceptions start the just-in-time debugger.
- A value of 1 means non-Delphi exceptions trigger the just-in-time debugger.
- A value of 2 or more means any exception starts the just-in-time debugger.

See Also

DebugHook Variable, ErrorProc Variable, ExceptionClass Variable, ExceptProc Variable, Raise Keyword

---

Label Keyword

Syntax

```
label Digits, Identifier, ...;
```

Description

The `label` keyword declares one or more labels. A label can be a digit string with up to four digits (as in standard Pascal) or an identifier (an extension to standard Pascal). A label can be used later in the same block to identify a statement as the target of a goto statement. You can also use a label as the target of a JMP instruction in an assembler block. See the goto statement for more information.

Tips and Tricks

In an assembler block, you can avoid declaring your labels by prefacing the label with an at (@) sign. Such labels are local to the subroutine.

See Also

Asm Keyword, Goto Keyword

Length Function

Syntax

```
function Length(const S: String): Integer;
function Length(const A: array): Integer;
```

Description

Length returns the number of elements in a string or array. It is not a real function.

Tips and Tricks

- Although Length is most often used to learn the length of a dynamic array, you can also call Length to find the length of an open array parameter or even a static array.

- For an array, Length(A) always returns Ord(High(A)) - Ord(Low(A)) + 1. For a ShortString, however, Length returns the value stored in the length byte, which might be shorter than the string size.

Example

```
// Toggle case of a string.
procedure ToggleCase(var S: string);
var
  I: Integer;
begin
  for I := 1 to Length(S) do
    if S[I] in ['a'..'z'] then
      S[I] := UpCase(S[I])
    else if S[I] in ['A'..'Z'] then
      S[I] := DownCase(S[I]);
end;
```

See Also

High Function, Low Function, SetLength Procedure, SizeOf Function

---

LibModuleList Variable

Syntax

```
var LibModuleList: PLibModule;
```

Description

LibModuleList points to the head of a singly linked list of TLibModule records. Each node in the list represents a module, that is, the application or library and the packages and other DLLs that it loads.

Tips and Tricks

- Don't mess with the LibModuleList variable. Delphi provides a number of procedures to manipulate the list for you: EnumModules, EnumResource-Modules, RegisterModule, and UnregisterModule.

- Delphi automatically inserts a node in the list when it loads a package or DLL. To examine the contents of the list, call **EnumModules**, or to examine the associated resource modules, call **EnumResourceModules**.

See Also

EnumModules Procedure, EnumResourceModules Procedure, Package Directive, PLibModule Type, RegisterModule Procedure, TLibModule Type, UnregisterModule Procedure

Library Keyword

Syntax

```
library Name;
  Declarations...
Block.
```

Description

A library project defines a dynamically linked library (DLL). When Windows loads the library, Delphi first executes the initialization sections of all units. Then Delphi executes the library's block.

Tips and Tricks

- If your library passes strings, dynamic arrays, or **Variants** as arguments or return values between modules (the application or other libraries), you must use **ShareMem** as the first unit. See Chapter 2 for details.

- If your library allocates memory (such as objects) freed by the application or another library, or if your library frees objects allocated by a different module, you must use the **ShareMem** unit.

- If you pass object references as arguments or return values between modules, be aware that the **is** and **as** operators will not work correctly. Each module (program or library) keeps its own copy of every class's RTTI. The **is** and **as** operators rely on RTTI to test class types, so different RTTI implies different types. If this is a problem, use packages instead of libraries. Chapter 3 explains RTTI in detail.

Example

```
library FontNames;

// Delphi lets you extend the IDE by loading packages or DLLs
// that use the Open Tools API. This rather trivial IDE extension
// must be compiled with the VCL50 runtime package. To install the
// extension, add a registry value under
// HKEY_CURRENT_USER\Software\Borland\Delphi\5.0\Experts
// The entry name is a unique string, and the value is the path
// of this DLL.
//
// After compiling this DLL, creating the registry entry, and
// restarting Delphi, open the Object Inspector and choose
// the Font.Name property. Drop down the list of font names
```

```
// and watch what happens. If you have a lot of fonts installed,
// this will take a long time. Delete the registry entry and
// restart Delphi to remove the IDE extension.

uses ShareMem, DsgnIntf, ToolsAPI;

function Init(const BorlandIDEServices: IBorlandIDEServices;
  RegisterProc: TWizardRegisterProc;
  var Terminate: TWizardTerminateProc): Boolean; stdcall;
begin
  FontNamePropertyDisplayFontNames := True;
  Result := True;
end;

exports Init name WizardEntryPoint;

end.
```

See Also

Asm Keyword, Begin Keyword, DllProc Variable, Exports Keyword, External Directive, Package Directive, Program Keyword

---

Ln Function

Syntax

```
function Ln(X: Floating-point type): Extended;
```

Description

Ln returns the natural logarithm of X. The Ln function is built-in.

Tips and Tricks

- Delphi automatically converts Integer and Variant arguments to floating point. To convert an Int64 argument to floating point, add 0.0.
- If X is a signaling NaN or negative (including negative infinity), Delphi reports runtime error 6 (EInvalidOp).
- If X is zero, Delphi reports runtime error 7 (EZeroDivide).
- If X is positive infinity, the result is positive infinity.
- If X is a quiet NaN, the result is X.

See Also

Exp Function

Lo Function

Syntax

```
function Lo(Value: Integer): Byte;
```

Description

The Lo function returns the least significant byte of an integer. The Lo function is not a real function, but is expanded inline by the compiler.

Tips and Tricks

The Lo function is equivalent to the following function:

```
function Lo(Value: Integer): Byte;
begin
  Result := Value and $FF;
end;
```

See Also

Hi Function

LoadResourceModule Function

Syntax

```
function LoadResourceModule(ModuleName: PChar): LongWord;
```

Description

Delphi automatically calls LoadResourceModule to load a language-specific DLL for an application. If no such DLL is found, the function returns zero; otherwise, it loads the DLL as a data file and returns the DLL's instance handle.

When Delphi loads a module (application, DLL, or package), it automatically calls LoadResourceModule to look for a DLL whose name is the same as the module name, but with an extension that specifies a locale. LoadResourceModule looks for the locale extension in three places. At each step, it tries to load the locale-specific DLL, and if it fails, it tries the next step in the sequence:

1. First, it checks the registry. It looks for the application's full pathname under two registry keys:

   - HKEY_CURRENT_USER\Software\Borland\Delphi\Locales
   - HKEY_CURRENT_USER\Software\Borland\Locales

   If the application has an entry under either key, the value of that entry is the locale extension. If the application does not have an entry, but the key has a default value, the default value is the locale extension.

2. Next, it looks for a DLL whose extension is the local language and country code.

3. Finally, it looks for a DLL whose extension is just a language code.

If LoadResourceModule finds a DLL with the locale extension, it loads the DLL and returns the resource DLL's instance handle. It also saves the instance handle so FindResourceHInstance will look for resources in the localized DLL.

LoadResourceModule is a real function.

LoadResString Function

Syntax

```
function LoadResString(Rec: PResStringRec): string;
```

Description

The LoadResString function loads a string resource. When you declare a string with the resourcestring keyword, Delphi automatically creates a string table resource and assigns a unique identifier to the string. The compiler generates code to call LoadResString to look up the string, given the resource identifier.

LoadResString is a real function.

Tips and Tricks

Delphi handles the string resource automatically, so you have no reason to call this function. If you must, you can pass the address of a resourcestring identifier as the argument.

See Also

LoadResourceModule Function, PResStringRec Type, ResourceString Keyword, TResStringRec Type

LongBool Type

Syntax

```
type LongBool;
```

Description

The LongBool type is a logical type whose size is the same as the size of a LongWord. A LongBool value is False when its ordinal value is zero, and it is True when its ordinal value is any non-zero value. LongBool uses -1 as the ordinal value for True constants, e.g., LongBool(True).

Tips and Tricks

- You can use a LongBool value anywhere you can use a Boolean. It is most useful when interfacing with C and C++, where any non-zero integer is considered True.

- LongBool is especially useful as a return type for many Windows API functions, which are documented to return zero for failure and any non-zero value for success.

- ByteBool and WordBool are similar to LongBool, but they have different sizes.

And Keyword, Boolean Type, ByteBool Type, Not Keyword, Or Keyword, WordBool Type, Xor Keyword

---

LongInt Type

Syntax

```
type LongInt = -2147483648..2147483647;
```

Description

LongInt is a 32-bit signed integer. Even if the size of Integer changes in a future version of Delphi, LongInt will remain the same. See the Integer type for more information about this type and other integer types.

See Also

Integer Type, LongWord Type, MaxLongInt Constant

LongWord Type

Syntax

```
type LongWord = 0..4294967295;
```

Description

LongWord is a 32-bit unsigned integer type. Even if the size of Integer changes in a future version of Delphi, LongWord will remain the same.

See Cardinal for caveats on using this type. See the Integer type for more information about this type and other integer types.

See Also

Cardinal Type, Integer Type

Low Function

Syntax

```
function Low(Type or variable): Ordinal type;
```

Description

The Low function returns the smallest value of an enumerated type, the lower bound of an array index, or the same information for a variable of ordinal or array type.

Low is built into the compiler and is not a real function.

Tips and Tricks

• In a for loop, subrange type declaration, or any other situation where you use the limits of an ordinal or array type, always use the Low function instead

---

of referring explicitly to the low ordinal value. A future version of your code might change the type, and you don't want to scramble through all your code looking for explicit references to an enumerated literal that should really have been calls to the Low function.

- Calling Low for a ShortString returns zero, which is the index of the length byte. You cannot call Low for an AnsiString or WideString, so use 1 because long strings always have an origin of 1.

- Low for an open array parameter is always zero, regardless of the type or range of the actual array argument.

Example

See the High function for an example.

See Also

Dec Procedure, High Function, Inc Procedure, Length Function, Pred Function, Succ Function

---

MainInstance Variable

Syntax

```
var MainInstance: LongWord;
```

Description

The MainInstance variable stores the instance handle of the main program (.*exe* file).

Tips and Tricks

- Any unit in a package can refer to MainInstance to obtain the handle of the main application. Even packages loaded into separate DLLs can use MainInstance.

- A library that does not use the *vcl50* package, however, cannot use MainInstance, which is zero in this case.

Example

```
// The MAINICON resource is stored in the project's resource file,
// which is in the main module. To load the icon resource, you
// must use the main module's instance handle. This function
// loads the MAINICON resource and returns its handle.
function LoadMainIcon: HICON;
begin
  Result := LoadIcon(MainInstance, 'MAINICON');
end;
```

See Also

FindClassHInstance Function, FindHInstance Function, HInstance Variable, ModuleIsLib Variable, ModuleIsPackage Variable

---

MainThreadID Variable

Syntax

```
var MainThreadID: LongWord;
```

Description

The `MainThreadID` variable stores the Windows thread ID for the application's main thread. Use `MainThreadID` if you need to send a message to the main thread, for example.

See Also

BeginThread Function, IsMultiThread Variable

MaxInt Constant

Syntax

```
const MaxInt = High(Integer);
```

Description

`MaxInt` is the largest possible value of type `Integer`. The constant is a convenient shorthand for `High(Integer)`. The exact value of `MaxInt` can change from one release of Delphi to another. Currently, it has the value 2,147,483,647.

Tips and Tricks

A common idiom when writing code that must interface with C or C++ libraries (including the Windows API) is to declare an array with the largest possible dimensions. A separate function parameter or record member holds the true array size. The maximum array dimension depends on the size of the base type, so you can declare the array type as follows:

```
type CArray = array[0..MaxInt div SizeOf(BaseType) - 1] of BaseType;
```

See Also

Integer Type, MaxLongInt Constant

MaxLongInt Constant

Syntax

```
const MaxLongInt = High(LongInt);
```

Description

The `MaxLongInt` constant is a convenient shorthand for `High(LongInt)`, which has the value 2,147,483,647.

See Also

Integer Type, LongInt Type, MaxInt Constant

Message Directive

Syntax

```
procedure Name(var Msg); message Constant;
```

Description

A method can be a message handler when you use the **message** directive. A message handler must take one **var** argument; usually this argument is of type **TMessage** or one of the similar types in the **Messages** unit. The only requirement Delphi imposes is that the message argument be at least as big as a **Word**. Delphi checks the first **Word** of the message parameter to decide which message handler to call.

The message handler must specify a constant message number. The message number is stored in the class's RTTI.

Tips and Tricks

- Message handlers and dynamic methods are stored in the same RTTI table. Delphi assigns small negative numbers to dynamic methods. To avoid conflicts with dynamic methods, do not use message handler numbers with the most significant bit set, that is, use numbers under $8000 (32,768).

- Any class—not just controls and components—can define message handlers. Visual controls map Windows messages to Delphi messages, and the **Dispatch** method of **TObject** calls the appropriate message handler. In the past, messages were necessary to implement cross-type polymorphism, where objects could respond to a message regardless of base class. Interfaces have replaced this mechanism, so the only need for message handlers in new code is to handle Windows messages.

- Delphi defines many messages in its **Controls** unit. Anyone writing new controls or components should be aware of these messages and decide which ones a new control should handle and which ones it should send.

Example

```
// Control that displays the time of day in a clock face.
// If Windows changes the system time, it broadcasts Wm_TimeChange
// to all top-level windows. The form, in turn, broadcasts
// Cm_TimeChange to all controls. This control has a message
// handle to redisplay the time.
type
  TClock = class(TCustomControl)
  private
    fTime: TDateTime;
    procedure CmTimeChange(var Msg: TWmTimeChange);
        message Cm_TimeChange;
  ...
  end;
```

See Also

Class Keyword, Dynamic Directive, Procedure Keyword, TObject Type

MkDir Procedure

Syntax

```
procedure MkDir(const Directory: string)
```

Description

Call MkDir to create a directory. If the directory cannot be created, Delphi reports an I/O error using the Windows error code, such as Error_Already_Exists if the directory already exists.

You can include or omit a trailing backslash character in the directory name.

MkDir is not a real procedure.

Example

```
// Create a directory, but only if it does not already exist.
procedure MakeDirectory(const Directory: string);
var
  Search: TSearchRec;
begin
  if FindFirst(Directory, faDirectory, Search) = 0 then
    FindClose(Search)
  else
    MkDir(Directory);
end;
```

See Also

ChDir Procedure, GetDir Procedure, IOResult Function, RmDir Procedure

---

Mod Keyword

Syntax

```
Integer expression mod Integer expression
```

Description

The mod operator performs an integer modulus or remainder operation. The result of A mod B is A - (A div B) * B.

Tips and Tricks

- If A and B are positive, the modulus and the remainder are identical.

- A mod B has the same absolute value regardless of the sign of A and B. The sign of A mod B is the same as the sign of A.

- If B = 0, Delphi reports runtime error 3 (EDivByZero).

See Also

Div Keyword

ModuleIsCpp Variable

Syntax

```
unit SysInit;
var ModuleIsCpp: Boolean;
```

Description

`ModuleIsCpp` is True for a module that was compiled and linked in C++ Builder, and False for a module that was compiled and linked in Delphi.

Tips and Tricks

Unlike most other system variables, `ModuleIsCpp` is not shared among all packages in an application.

ModuleIsLib Variable

Syntax

```
unit SysInit;
var ModuleIsLib: Boolean;
```

Description

`ModuleIsLib` is True for a unit that is part of a DLL or package, and False for a unit linked statically with an application.

Tips and Tricks

Unlike most other system variables, `ModuleIsLib` is not shared among all packages in an application. This makes it more useful than the `IsLibrary` variable.

See Also

HInstance Variable, IsLibrary Variable, Library Keyword, ModuleIsPackage Variable, Package Directive

ModuleIsPackage Variable

Syntax

```
unit SysInit;
var ModuleIsPackage: Boolean;
```

Description

`ModuleIsPackage` is True for a unit in a package, and False for a unit linked statically with a library or application.

Tips and Tricks

Unlike most other system variables, `ModuleIsPackage` is not shared among all packages in an application.

HInstance Variable, ModuleIsLib Variable, Package Directive

ModuleUnloadList Variable

Syntax

```
var ModuleUnloadList: PModuleUnloadRec;
```

Description

The `ModuleUnloadList` variable points to the head of a singly linked list of `TModuleUnloadRec` records. Each record keeps track of a procedure that is called when a module (application, library, or package) is unloaded.

Tips and Tricks

*   Add new procedures to the start of the list by calling `AddModuleUnloadProc`. Remove procedures from the list by calling `RemoveModuleUnloadProc`. Delphi automatically walks the list and calls every procedure when you unload a package, free a library, or when the application exits.

*   Most programs never need to examine `ModuleUnloadList`.

See Also

AddModuleUnloadProc Procedure, PModuleUnloadRec Type, RemoveModuleUnloadProc Procedure, TModuleUnloadRec Type, UnregisterModule Procedure

Move Procedure

Syntax

```
procedure Move(const Source; var Dest; Count: Integer);
```

Description

The `Move` procedure copies `Count` bytes from `Source` to `Dest`. `Move` is a real procedure.

Tips and Tricks

*   `Source` and `Dest` are not pointers, so pass the actual variables, or dereference pointers to dynamically allocated memory.

*   `Move` can handle overlapping memory correctly.

Example

```
// Insert an item into the middle of an array. Discard the
// value that is currently at A[High(A)].
procedure ArrayInsert(var A: array of Integer; Value, Index: Integer);
begin
  Assert((Low(A) <= Index) and (Index <= High(A)));
  // First make room for the new value.
  Move(A[Index], A[Index+1], (High(A)-Index) * SizeOf(Integer));
```

```
// Then save the value in the array.
A[Index] := Value;
end;
```

See Also

FillChar Procedure

Name Directive

Syntax

```
exports Subroutine signature name String, ... ;
subroutine declaration; external DllName name String;
```

Description

A unit or library can export any subroutine and supply a different name for it in a DLL. Without the name directive, Delphi uses the function or procedure name. The name directive lets you use names that include non-alphanumeric characters, or just use a different name.

Tips and Tricks

- If you export overloaded subroutines, you must use the name directive to ensure the overloaded routines are exported with unique names.
- You can use the index and name directives for the same exported routine (in that order).
- For more information and an example, see the exports keyword.
- To export a subroutine by index only, use an empty string for the name.

See Also

Exports Keyword, External Directive, Index Directive, Name Directive

---

Near Directive

Syntax

```
Subroutine header; near;
```

Description

The near directive has no meaning. It exists for backward compatibility with Delphi 1.

See Also

Far Directive

New Procedure

Syntax

```
procedure New(var P: Pointer-type);
procedure New(var P: ^object; Constructor);
```

Description

The New procedure allocates a new variable of pointer or old-style object type.

The most common case is setting a pointer variable to point to dynamically allocated memory. New calls GetMem to allocate the memory, and then it calls Initialize to initialize the strings, dynamic arrays, interfaces, or Variants in the new value. Note that other fields, such as scalar values, static arrays, and short strings, are not initialized.

You can also create an old style object by calling New. The first parameter is a pointer variable, and the optional second argument is the constructor name and its optional arguments. Delphi calls the constructor, allocates the memory for the object, initializes the memory to all zeros, and sets the pointer to refer to the newly allocated memory. New is not a real procedure.

Tips and Tricks

- Unlike standard Pascal, Delphi Pascal uses a plain call to New to allocate a variant record. Do not supply values for the variant tags. New always allocates the maximum amount of memory needed for all combinations of variant tags.

- If you need to allocate a variably sized array, use GetMem. If you need to allocate a single record or a fixed-size array, use New.

Example

```
type
  PEmployee = ^TEmployee;
  TEmployee = record
    Name: string;
    TIN: string[9];
    Salary: Currency;
  end;
var
  E: PEmployee;
begin
  New(E);
  try
    E.Salary := 0; // Initialize to zero until a proper value is set.
    AbuseByPointyHairBoss(E);
  finally
    Dispose(E);
  end;
end;
```

See Also

Dispose Procedure, GetMem Procedure, Initialize Procedure, IsMultiThread Variable, Object Keyword

Nil Keyword

Syntax

```
const nil = Pointer(0);
```

Description

The `nil` keyword is a special `Pointer` value that is guaranteed to be distinct from any real pointer.

The numeric value of `nil` is zero. When you create a new object, therefore, and Delphi initializes all the object's fields to zero, you can rely on pointer, class, interface, and method type fields to be initialized to `nil`.

Tips and Tricks

- You can also assign `nil` to method-type variables or fields, in which case Delphi stores `nil` for the code and data pointers. When comparing a method with `nil`, Delphi checks only the code pointer. In other words, the following two examples are equivalent:

```
if Notify = nil then ...
if (TMethod(Notify).Code = nil then ...
```

- The most common use for `nil` is to mark pointer and method-type variables with a "not-a-pointer" value. For example, an event property that does not have an event handler assigned to it has the value `nil`.

- Assigning `nil` to an interface-type variable causes Delphi to call `_Release` on the old value of the variable (if the variable was not `nil` to start with).

- Delphi represents an empty dynamic array, long string, or wide string as a `nil` pointer.

- Many Delphi programmers prefer the `Assigned` function over a comparison with `nil`. It is primarily a style issue, but see the `Assigned` function for more information.

See Also

Assigned Function, Pointer Type

Nodefault Directive

Syntax

```
property Declaration nodefault;
```

Description

The `nodefault` directory tells Delphi that the property does not have a default value and that the *.dfm* file should always contain the property value.

Tips and Tricks

- Only ordinal-type properties can have default values, so the `nodefault` directive has meaning only for these properties. String, floating-point, class,

Variant, Int64, and interface-type properties have a hardcoded default value of "zero" (empty string, nil, Unassigned, etc.).

- Delphi stores the smallest integer as the marker for nodefault, so nodefault is almost the same as default -2147483648. ("Almost" because properties of enumerated, character, or set type cannot have an integer constant as a default value, which is one reason Delphi uses the most negative integer as the nodefault marker value.)

- The nodefault directive is optional. If you omit it, Delphi assumes nodefault. You should use nodefault in your property declarations as a reminder to the person who must read and maintain your code that the property has no default value.

- Delphi always constructs new objects with zero for all fields. If you want to use zero as the default value for a property, you must explicitly declare zero as the default value in the property declaration. You do not need to do anything special in the constructor.

Example

```
property Color nodefault;
property Area: Integer read fArea write SetArea nodefault;
```

See Also

Default Directive, Property Keyword, Stored Directive

NoErrMsg Variable

Syntax

```
var NoErrMsg: Boolean;
```

Description

When a GUI application exits due to an error, it displays a message dialog box with the error message and address. If the NoErrMsg flag is True, the message box is not displayed. The default value is False. In a console application, the error message is always printed, regardless of the value of NoErrMsg.

See Also

ErrorAddr Variable, ErrorProc Variable, Halt Procedure, RunError Procedure

---

Not Keyword

Syntax

```
not Boolean expression
not Integer expression
```

Description

The not operator performs a negation. If the operand has type Boolean, the negative is a logical negation (not False = True and not True = False). If the

---

operand is an integer, the not operator performs a bitwise negation of each bit in the integer value. In other words, it performs a complement operation.

Tips and Tricks

The ByteBool, LongBool, and WordBool types interpret any non-zero ordinal value as True. When not returns True, it always returns an ordinal value of –1. In other words, not not X does not always have the same ordinal value as X. If the ordinal value of a logical variable matters, you should use an integer type and not a logical type.

See Also

> And Keyword, Boolean Type, False Constant, Integer Type, Or Keyword, True Constant, Xor Keyword

---

Null Variable

Syntax

```
var Null: Variant;
```

Description

The Null variable is the Null Variant value. You should not change its value.

Tips and Tricks

- Variant variables are initialized to Unassigned. When you want to assign a value to a Variant, but are unable to assign a specific, known value, use Null to represent an unknown or missing value. In particular, TField-derived components use the Null value to represent SQL NULL values (when you want the field value as a Variant).

- Variant expressions that use Null as an operand produce a Null result.

- Attempting to convert a Null value to a number raises runtime error 15 (EVariantError).

- Refer to nil for the equivalent of NULL in C and C++.

Example

```
// In the Variant array Data, compute the average of all
// non-Null values.
function ComputeAverage(Data: Variant): Variant;
var
  Sum: Double;
  Count: Integer;
  I: Integer;
begin
  Sum := 0.0;
  Count := 0;
  for I := VarArrayLowBound(Data) to VarArrayHighBound(Data) do
    if not VarIsNull(Data[I]) then
    begin
      Sum := Sum + Data[I];
      Inc(Count);
```

```
      end;
    if Count = 0 then
       Result := Null
    else
       Result := Sum / Count;
end;
```

See Also

EmptyParam Variable, Unassigned Variable, Variant Type, VarIsNull Function

---

Object Keyword

Syntax

```
type Name = Subroutine header of object;

type Name = object
   Declarations...
end;

type Name = object(Base class)
   Declarations...
end;
```

Description

The `object` keyword has two distinct and unrelated uses: to declare method types and to declare old-style classes.

* Delphi Pascal lets you declare a procedure or function type as a plain subroutine or as a method. When you declare a plain procedural type, the type is a plain pointer type. You can assign pointers to subroutines whose signatures match the type, and the pointer value is an ordinary code pointer.

  Using the `of object` syntax, the procedural type becomes a method type. Methods have two parts: a code pointer and a data pointer. When you take a method's address, you are capturing the code pointer for the method's code (which is similar to a plain procedural pointer) and a data pointer (which is the object reference or class reference for a class method).

* Object-type declarations are obsolete and have been replaced by `class` declarations. The old-style `object` declarations exist primarily for backward compatibility with Turbo Pascal. New Delphi programs should use `class` declarations instead.

Tips and Tricks

* Properties of method type are called *events*.

* The TMethod type is a record that holds a generic method pointer. You can cast TMethod to a particular type, such as TNotifyEvent to call the method.

Examples

```
type
   TNotifyEvent = procedure(Sender: TObject) of object;
```

```
TSimpleComponent = class(TComponent)
private
  fOnChange: TNotifyEvent;        // Save a method reference here.
protected
  procedure Changed; virtual;
published
  property OnChange: TNotifyEvent read fOnChange write fOnChange;
end;
...
procedure TSimpleComponent.Changed;
begin
  if Assigned(fOnChange) then     // Test whether the method is nil.
    fOnChange(Self);              // This is how you call the method.
end;
```

See Also

Class Keyword, Dispose Procedure, Function Keyword, New Procedure, Packed Keyword, Procedure Keyword, Record Keyword, TMethod Type, Type Keyword, $A Compiler Directive, $Align Compiler Directive

---

Odd Function

Syntax

```
function Odd(Value: Integer): Boolean;
function Odd(Value: Int64): Boolean;
```

Description

The standard Pascal Odd function returns True if Value is odd, that is, it is not evenly divisible by 2. It returns False if the number is even. Odd is not a real function.

See Also

Boolean Type, Integer Type

Of Keyword

Syntax

```
type Name = array[Index type] of Base type;

type Name = Subroutine header of object;

case Expression of
  Selector: ...
end;
```

Description

The of keyword serves many roles in Delphi, but is always subservient to another keyword. See the array, object, and case keywords for details.

Array Keyword, Case Keyword, Function Keyword, Object Keyword, Procedure Keyword, Type Keyword

OleStrToString Function

Syntax

```
function OleStrToString(OleStr: PWideChar): string;
```

Description

The `OleStrToString` function converts a Unicode string into a multibyte string. `OleStrToString` is a real function.

Tips and Tricks

See the `WideString` type for a discussion of Unicode and multibyte character sets.

See Also

OleStrToStrVar Procedure, PWideChar Type, String Keyword, StringToOleStr Function, StringToWideChar Function, WideChar Type, WideCharLenToString Function, WideCharLenToStrVar Procedure, WideCharToString Function, WideCharToStrVar Procedure, WideString Type

OleStrToStrVar Procedure

Syntax

```
procedure OleStrToString(OleStr: PWideChar; var Dest: string);
```

Description

The `OleStrToStrVar` procedure converts a Unicode string into a multibyte string. `OleStrToStrVar` is a real procedure.

Tips and Tricks

See the `WideString` type for a discussion of Unicode and multibyte character sets.

See Also

OleStrToString Function, PWideChar Type, String Keyword, StringToOleStr Function, StringToWideChar Function, WideChar Type, WideCharLenToString Function, WideCharLenToStrVar Procedure, WideCharToString Function, WideCharToStrVar Procedure, WideString Type

OleVariant Type

Syntax

```
type OleVariant;
```

Description

The `OleVariant` type is the same as the `Variant` type, except that an `OleVariant` can store only OLE-compatible types. In particular, an `OleVariant` cannot store a Delphi string, but must store a wide string instead.

Tips and Tricks

When you assign a value to an `OleVariant`, Delphi automatically converts its value to an OLE-compatible value, that is, it converts an `AnsiString` (`varString`) to a wide string (`varOleStr`).

See Also

AnsiString Type, PWideChar Type, String Keyword, VarCast Procedure, VarCopy Procedure, Variant Type, WideString Type

On Directive

Syntax

```
try
  Statements...
except
  on Variable: Class name do Statement;
  on Class name do Statement;
  else Statements...
end;
```

Language
Reference

Description

The on directive introduces an exception handler in a **try-except** statement. You can have any number of exception handlers. Each one introduces an exception class, possibly with a variable name.

Delphi tests the exception object against each exception class, in order of appearance. The search stops with the first handler where the exception object's class matches the handler's class or is derived from the handler's class (the is operator returns True). Delphi then executes the associated statement (or block), and if that statement does not raise another exception, execution continues with the statement following the **end** keyword for the **try-except** statement.

If the handler includes a variable name, Delphi assigns the exception object to that variable. The variable's lexical scope is the exception handler, so you cannot refer to the variable in a different handler or outside the **try-except** statement.

If no classes match the exception object, and an **else** clause appears, Delphi executes the statements following the **else**. If no classes match, and the **try-except** has no **else** clause, the same exception is raised, giving another **try-except** statement an opportunity to handle the exception.

At the end of the exception handler, Delphi frees the exception object unless the handler raises the same exception with the plain **raise** statement.

Tips and Tricks

- An exception handler can raise an exception, in which case control immediately leaves the **try-except** statement, and Delphi searches for another exception handler, farther back in the call stack.

- Because Delphi searches the exception handlers in order, you should always put the most specific exception classes first.

- Any object can be an exception object. By convention, Delphi uses classes that inherit from **SysUtils.Exception**. Most exception classes are declared in the **SysUtils** unit. Appendix B, *The SysUtils Unit*, lists the standard exception classes.

Example

See the **except** keyword for an example.

See Also

Else Keyword, Except Keyword, ExceptClsProc Variable, ExceptObjProc Variable, Raise Keyword, Try Keyword

---

OpenString Type

Syntax

```
Subroutine declaration(...; var Param: OpenString; ...);
```

Description

OpenString declarations are let you pass a **ShortString** argument to a subroutine when the subroutine does not know the exact string size. Ordinarily, a **var** string parameter's type must match exactly with an actual argument's type. In the case of short strings, the maximum string length is part of the type and must match, to ensure that the subroutine does not try to store more characters in the string than can fit.

An OpenString parameter relaxes the restriction and lets you pass any size string to the subroutine. Delphi passes an additional, hidden parameter that contains the maximum string size. References to **Param** in the subroutine, therefore, are type safe.

Tips and Tricks

- The $OpenStrings compiler directive makes **var ShortString** parameters behave as OpenString parameters. This directive is enabled by default. The only time you need to declare a parameter as type OpenString is when you are disabling the $OpenStrings compiler directive.

- If you disable the $LongStrings compiler directive, the string type is a short string, so **var string** parameters are like OpenString (unless you also disable the $OpenStrings compiler directive).

- If you are using long strings, you have no need for OpenString parameters.

AnsiString Type, ShortString Type, String Keyword, Var Keyword, $H
Compiler Directive, $LongStrings Compiler Directive, $OpenStrings Compiler
Directive, $P Compiler Directive

Or Keyword

Syntax

```
Boolean expression or Boolean expression
Integer expression or Integer expression
```

Description

The or operator performs a logical *or* if the operands are of Boolean type or a
bitwise *or* if the operators are integers. Integer operands can be of any integer
type, including Int64. A logical *or* is False only if both operands are False and is
True if either operand is True.

Tips and Tricks

• Unlike standard Pascal, if the left-hand operand is True, Delphi does not evaluate the right-hand operand because the result must be True. You can avoid
  this shortcut operation and return to standard Pascal with the $BoolEval or
  $B compiler directives.

• An integer or operates on each bit of its operands, setting the result bit to 1 if
  either operand has a 1 bit, and sets a bit to 0 if both operands have 0 bits. If
  one operand is smaller than the other, Delphi extends the smaller operand
  with 0 in the leftmost bits. The result is the size of the largest operand.

Examples

```
var
  I, J: Integer;
  S: string;
begin
  I := $25;
  J := $11;
  WriteLn(I or J); // Writes 53 (which is $35)
...
  // The short-circuit behavior of OR in the next example prevents
  // Delphi from referring to the nonexistent string element at
  // the end of the string, in case the string is empty.
  if (Length(S) = 0) or (S[Length(S)] <> '\') then
    S := S + '\';
```

See Also

And Keyword, Boolean Type, ByteBool Type, LongBool Type, Not Keyword,
Shl Keyword, Shr Keyword, WordBool Type, Xor Keyword, $B Compiler
Directive, $BoolEval Compiler Directive

Ord Function

Syntax

```
function Ord(A: AnsiChar): Integer;
function Ord(C: Char): Integer;
function Ord(W: WideChar): Integer;
function Ord(E: Enumerated type): Integer;
function Ord(I: Integer): Integer;
function Ord(I: Int64): Int64;
```

Description

The Ord function returns the ordinal value of a character or enumeration as a non-negative integer. Calling Ord on an integer argument is a no-op, returning its argument. Ord is not a real function.

Tips and Tricks

You can cast an ordinal variable to an integer type to get its ordinal value. Calling the Ord function is better because it states clearly and directly what the code is doing.

Example

```
// The TypInfo unit provides the GetEnumName function that returns
// the name of an enumerated value, given its TypeInfo pointer and
// its ordinal value. Using GetEnumName, you can write functions
// such as the following, which converts a Boolean to a string.
function BoolToStr(B: Boolean): string;
begin
   Result := GetEnumName(TypeInfo(Boolean), Ord(B));
end;
```

See Also

AnsiChar Type, Char Type, Chr Function, Type Keyword, WideChar Type

---

Out Directive

Syntax

```
Subroutine header(Parameters...; out Name: Type; ...);
```

Description

The out directive is used in subroutine parameter declarations. It is similar to a var keyword in declaring a parameter the subroutine can change. The difference between var and out is that an out parameter does not pass a meaningful value into the subroutine when the routine is called—it only provides a useful output value when the routine returns.

Tips and Tricks

• Out parameters are often used in COM interfaces.

- Out parameters are useful for reference-counted entities, such as strings, dynamic arrays, and interfaces. Out has slightly improved performance over var because the compiler does not have to increment the reference count when passing the argument to the subroutine. The subroutine must change the value of the variable, and the compiler increments the reference count normally at that time.

- Even if the parameter is not reference counted, you can use the out directive to tell the person who reads or maintains your code that the subroutine does not rely on an input value for that parameter.

Example

```
type
  ICollection = interface
    ...
    // Every collection can have any number of enumerators that
    // enumerate the items in the collection. The Enum function
    // creates a new enumerator and stores it in the Enumerator
    // argument.
    function Enum(out Enumerator: IEnumerator): HResult;
    ...
```

See Also

Const Keyword, Interface Keyword, Var Keyword

Output Variable

Syntax

```
var Output: TextFile;
```

Description

The Output variable is a text file that Delphi automatically opens for writing, but only in console applications. The output file is usually the console, but the user can redirect output from the command shell.

Output is an ordinary TextFile, and you can close it or open a different file. Opening a file without a name is the same as opening the console file. For example, Delphi always performs the following when a console application starts running:

```
AssignFile(Output, '');
Rewrite(Output);
```

Calling Write and WriteLn without a file reference as the first argument is the same as calling Write and WriteLn using Output as the first argument.

See Also

AssignFile Procedure, Input Variable, TextFile Type, Write Procedure, WriteLn Procedure

---

Overload Directive

Syntax

Subroutine declaration; overload; *other directives...*

Description

The overload directive tells Delphi that you will declare another subroutine with the same name but with different parameters.

Tips and Tricks

• If you use the overload directive in a method declaration, it must appear before the virtual, dynamic, or abstract directives.

• You can declare any function, procedure, or method with the overload directive.

• You can overload a method in a derived class even if the method with the same name is in a base class and does not use the overload directive.

• An alternative to using overloaded methods is to use default parameters. For parameters with simple types, default parameters usually result in less code to write and maintain. For complex parameters, such as objects, you might find it easier to write overloaded subroutines that call each other.

• The compiler uses the type and number of the actual arguments to determine which overloaded routine to call. To distinguish between different integer types, it uses the narrowest type possible. If the compiler cannot decide which overloaded routine to call, it issues an error.

Example

```
// If the Time parameter is zero, record the current date and time
// as a time stamp.
// Write a message to a debug log file.
procedure Log(const Message: string; Time: TDateTime = 0); overload;
// Write a formatted message to a debug log file.
procedure Log(const Fmt: string; const Args: array of const;
    Time: TDateTime = 0); overload;

// The compiler chooses which Min function based on the argument.
function Min(I, J: Integer): Integer; overload;
function Min(I, J: Int64): Int64; overload;
function Min(I, J: Extended): Extended; overload;

X := Min(10, 100);        // Calls Min(I, J: Integer)
Y := Min(10, 10000000000); // Calls Min(I, J: Int64);
Z := Min(10, 100.0);       // Calls Min(I, J: Extended);
```

See Also

Function Keyword, Procedure Keyword

Override Directive

Syntax

Subroutine declaration; override;

Description

Use the override directive to declare a method that overrides a virtual or dynamic method declared in a base class. Refer to Chapter 2 for a discussion of virtual methods and polymorphism.

Example

```
type
  // Tile a bitmap.
  TTile = class(TGraphicControl)
  private
    fBitmap: TBitmap;
    procedure SetBitmap(NewBitmap: TBitmap);
    procedure BitmapChanged(Sender: TObject);
  protected
    procedure Paint; override;
  public
    constructor Create(Owner: TComponent); override;
    destructor Destroy; override;
  published
    property Align;
    property Bitmap: TBitmap read fBitmap write SetBitmap;
    property OnClick;
    // Many other properties are useful, but were omitted to save space.
    // See TControl for a full list.
  end;
```

See Also

Class Keyword, Dynamic Directive, Function Keyword, Inherited Keyword, Procedure Keyword, Reintroduce Directive, Virtual Directive

---

Package Directive

Syntax

```
package Name;
requires
  Names...;
contains
  Names...;
end.
```

Description

The package directive introduces a package source file. A package is a special kind of DLL that contains units that can be linked dynamically into another project.

Tips and Tricks

- A package source file has the extension *.dpk* (for Delphi package). A single file contains a single package declaration.

- You can edit the package source file by hand, but usually you will use the Package Manager in Delphi's IDE.

- If you edit the package source file manually, make sure the syntax is correct. Delphi's compiler is not always graceful when it encounters syntax errors in a package source file.

See Also

Contains Directive, Requires Directive

PackageInfo Type

Syntax

```
type PackageInfo = ^PackageInfoTable;
```

Description

The PackageInfo type is a pointer to a PackageInfoTable record.

See Also

GetPackageInfoTable Type, PackageInfoTable Type, PUnitEntryTable Type, UnitEntryTable Type

---

PackageInfoTable Type

Syntax

```
type
  PackageInfoTable = packed record
    UnitCount: Integer;
    UnitInfo : PUnitEntryTable;
  end;
```

Description

Every package has a PackageInfoTable record, which points to a list of unit entry table records, each of which points to the initialization and finalization section of that unit. Every unit contained in a package has a unit entry table. When Delphi loads or unloads a package, it uses the package information table to initialize or finalize the units in the package.

Delphi takes care of packages automatically. You rarely need to use the package information directly.

See Also

Finalization Keyword, GetPackageInfoTable Type, Initialization Keyword, Package Directive, PackageInfoTable Type, PUnitEntryTable Type, Unit Keyword, UnitEntryTable Type

---

PackageUnitEntry Type

Syntax

```
type
  PackageUnitEntry = packed record
    Init, FInit: procedure;
  end;
```

Description

The PackageUnitEntry record holds a pointer to the code for the initialization and finalization sections of a unit. Delphi automatically creates this record for each unit, and every application, library, and package keeps a table of all of its units' records.

Delphi takes care of units automatically. You rarely need to use the unit information directly.

See Also

Finalization Keyword, GetPackageInfoTable Type, Initialization Keyword, PackageInfoTable Type, PUnitEntryTable Type, Unit Keyword, UnitEntryTable Type

---

Packed Keyword

Syntax

```
type Name = packed record ... end;
type Name = packed class ... end;
type Name = packed object ... end;
type Name = packed array[...] of ...;
```

Description

Delphi aligns record and object fields on natural boundaries to improve performance. If you use the packed directive, Delphi does not insert any padding to align fields within the object or record.

An aligned record is also padded so its size is a multiple of 4 bytes. A packed record does not have any extra padding, but Delphi aligns and pads variables and dynamically allocated memory on 4-byte boundaries, so the size of a packed record is meaningful only if you are creating an array of records or using records as fields in other structured types.

The unpacked alignment for a field depends on the size of the field:

- Byte-sized fields and sets of any size are aligned on byte boundaries.

- Word-sized fields are aligned on word (2-byte) boundaries.

- LongWord-sized fields (including Single) are aligned on long word (4-byte) boundaries.

- Other types (Comp, Currency, Double, Extended, Int64, Real48, Variant) are aligned on 8-byte boundaries.

- Arrays are aligned according to the alignment of the array's base type.

- Records are aligned according to the largest alignment used by a member in the record.

Tips and Tricks

- Accessing a packed field is slower than accessing an aligned field. Use the packed keyword only when the need to conserve memory outweighs the performance penalty.

- Delphi does not pack Boolean fields into single bits, the way some Pascal compilers do.

- Arrays are always packed. You can supply the packed keyword in an array declaration for compatibility with standard Pascal, but it has no effect.

Example

```
type
  Big = record     // SizeOf(Big) = 16
    B1: Byte;
    W: Word;         // Align W on a word boundary by inserting a pad byte
    B2: Byte;
    L: LongWord;     // Align L on a 4-byte boundary by inserting 3 bytes
    B3: Byte;        // Record size is aligned to a long word boundary
  end;
  Small = packed record // SizeOf(Small) = 9
    B1: Byte;
    W: Word;         // Align W on a byte boundary: no padding
    B2: Byte;
    L: LongWord;
    B3: Byte;        // Record size is not padded.
  end;
```

See Also

Array Keyword, Class Keyword, Object Keyword, Record Keyword

PAnsiChar Type

Syntax

```
type PAnsiChar = ^AnsiChar;
```

Description

The PAnsiChar type is a pointer to AnsiChar and with Delphi's extended syntax, it can also be treated as an AnsiString or a pointer to an array of AnsiChar.

Tips and Tricks

- PAnsiChar is used most often as a parameter type for DLLs written in C or C++, such as the Windows API.

- You can treat a PAnsiChar pointer as a pointer to an array of AnsiChar. The array index is an Integer subrange, starting from zero. Delphi does not provide any bounds checking for the array. The convention is that the end of the string is denoted by the presence of the #0 character.

- Perform pointer arithmetic on a PAnsiChar pointer by adding and subtracting integers similar to the way the Inc and Dec procedures work.

- Delphi's extended syntax is enabled by default. Use the $X or $ExtendedSyntax compiler directive to disable this feature and revert to behavior closer to standard Pascal.

See Also

AnsiChar Type, AnsiString Type, Array Keyword, Char Type, PChar Type, String Keyword, PWideChar Type, $ExtendedSyntax Compiler Directive, $X Compiler Directive

PAnsiString Type

Syntax

```
type PAnsiString = ^AnsiString;
```

Description

The PAnsiString type is a convenience type for a pointer to an AnsiString. Note that AnsiString is a pointer, so PAnsiString is rarely used.

See Also

AnsiString Type, String Type, PString Type, PWideString Type

ParamCount Function

Syntax

```
function ParamCount: Integer;
```

Description

The ParamCount function returns the number of command-line parameters available to the application. This value is zero in a library. ParamCount is a real function.

Example

See ParamStr for an example.

See Also

CmdLine Variable, ParamStr Function

ParamStr Function

Syntax

```
function ParamStr(Number: Integer): string;
```

Description

The `ParamStr` function returns the Numberth command-line parameter. `ParamStr` is a real function.

Tips and Tricks

- Parameter number zero is the application pathname.

- Parameters are numbered from 1 to `ParamCount`. If Number is invalid, `ParamStr` returns an empty string.

- When breaking a command line into parameters, Delphi uses white space characters as separators. Use double quotes around text that contains space characters to include the spaces as part of the parameter (e.g., long filenames).

- To look for command-line switches, call the `FindCmdLineSwitch` function from the `SysUtils` unit.

Example

```
program Echo;
// Echo command-line arguments, separated by spaces.
{$AppType Console}
var
  I: Integer;
begin
  if ParamCount > 0 then
    Write(ParamStr(1));
  for I := 2 to ParamCount do
    Write(' ', ParamStr(I));
  WriteLn;
end.
```

See Also

CmdLine Variable, ParamCount Function

Pascal Directive

Syntax

Subroutine declaration; pascal;

Description

The `pascal` directive tells the compiler to use Pascal calling conventions for the function or procedure. The caller of the subroutine pushes arguments onto the stack, starting with the leftmost argument. Before the subroutine returns, the subroutine pops the arguments from the stack.

Functions return ordinal values, pointers, and small records or sets in EAX and floating-point values on the FPU stack. Strings, dynamic arrays, Variants, and large records and sets are passed as a hidden var parameter. If the subroutine is a method, Self is the first parameter, and the hidden var parameter is the second, so these parameters are pushed first onto the stack.

Tips and Tricks

Don't be deceived by the name. Delphi's default calling convention is `register`, not `pascal`. The `pascal` convention is for backward compatibility, and should not be used except to interface with an archaic DLL.

See Also

CDecl Directive, Function Keyword, Procedure Keyword, Register Directive, SafeCall Directive, StdCall Directive

---

PChar Type

Syntax

```
type PChar = ^Char;
```

Description

The `PChar` type is a pointer to `Char` and with Delphi's extended syntax, it can also be treated as a `string` or a pointer to an array of `Char`.

Tips and Tricks

- `PChar` is used most often as a parameter type for DLLs written in C or C++, such as the Windows API.

- You can treat a `PChar` pointer as a pointer to an array of `Char`. The array index is an `Integer` subrange, starting from zero. Delphi does not provide any bounds checking for the array. The convention is that the end of the string is denoted by the presence of the #0 character.

- Perform pointer arithmetic on a `PChar` pointer by adding and subtracting integers similar to the way the `Inc` and `Dec` procedures work.

- Delphi's extended syntax is enabled by default. Use the `$X` or `$ExtendedSyntax` compiler directive to disable this feature and revert to behavior closer to standard Pascal.

See Also

AnsiChar Type, AnsiString Type, Array Keyword, Char Type, PAnsiChar Type, PWideChar Type, String Keyword, $ExtendedSyntax Compiler Directive, $X Compiler Directive

---

PCurrency Type

Syntax

```
type PCurrency = ^Currency;
```

Description

The `PCurrency` type is a convenience type for a pointer to type `Currency`.

See Also

Currency Type

PDateTime Type

Syntax

```
type PDateTime = ^TDateTime;
```

Description

The PDateTime type is a convenience type for a pointer to type TDateTime.

See Also

TDateTime Type

PExtended Type

Syntax

```
type PExtended = ^Extended;
```

Description

The PExtended type is a convenience type for a pointer to type Extended.

See Also

Extended Type

PGUID Type

Syntax

```
type PGUID = ^TGUID;
```

Description

The PGUID type is a convenience type for a pointer to type TGUID.

See Also

TGUID Type

Pi Function

Syntax

```
function Pi: Extended
```

Description

The Pi function returns an approximation for the mathematical value of π. The compiler expands this function inline so it can treat the Pi function as a constant and evaluate constant expressions that use Pi. The compiler also recognizes the context and uses the appropriate type and precision for its approximation (that is, Single, Double, or Extended). As a result, you get a better approximation of π than you could get by writing a decimal constant.

Double Type, Extended Type, Single Type

PInt64 Type

Syntax

```
type PInt64 = ^Int64;
```

Description

The `PInt64` type is a convenience type for a pointer to type `Int64`.

See Also

Int64 Type

PInterfaceEntry Type

Syntax

```
type PInterfaceEntry = ^TInterfaceEntry;
```

Description

The `PInterfaceEntry` type is a convenience type for a pointer to type `TInterfaceEntry`.

See Also

Class Keyword, Interface Keyword, PInterfaceTable Type, TInterfaceEntry Type, TInterfaceTable Type, TObject Type, TypeInfo Function

---

PInterfaceTable Type

Syntax

```
type PInterfaceTable = ^TInterfaceTable;
```

Description

The `PInterfaceTable` type is a convenience type for a pointer to type `TInterfaceTable`.

See Also

Class Keyword, Interface Keyword, TInterfaceEntry Type, TInterfaceTable Type, TObject Type, TypeInfo Function

---

PLibModule Type

Syntax

```
type PLibModule = ^TLibModule;
```

Description

The `PLibModule` type is a convenience type for a pointer to type `TLibModule`.

See Also

EnumModules Procedure, EnumResourceModules Procedure, LibModuleList Variable, RegisterModule Procedure, TLibModule Type, UnregisterModule Procedure

---

PMemoryManager Type

Syntax

```
type PMemoryManager = ^TMemoryManager;
```

Description

The `PMemoryManager` type is a convenience type for a pointer to type `TMemoryManager`.

See Also

GetMemoryManager Procedure, IsMemoryManagerSet Function, SetMemoryManager Procedure, TMemoryManager Type

---

PModuleUnloadRec Type

Syntax

```
type PModuleUnloadRec = ^TModuleUnloadRec
```

Description

The `PModuleUnloadRec` type is a convenience type for a pointer to type `TModuleUnloadRec`.

See Also

AddModuleUnloadProc Procedure, ModuleUnloadList Variable, RemoveModuleUnloadProc Procedure, TModuleUnloadProcLW Type

---

Pointer Type

Syntax

```
type Pointer;
```

Description

The `Pointer` type is a generic pointer type. Without using type casts, you can assign any pointer-valued expression to a `Pointer`-type variable or assign a `Pointer`-type expression to a variable with a specific pointer type.

Tips and Tricks

- Because object references are actually pointers, you can freely type cast an object reference to a `Pointer` and back again.

- Good programming style is to use typed pointers as much as possible. Types help prevent errors and provide documentation to the person reading and maintaining the code. A common source of errors is typecasting a pointer incorrectly.

Example

```
// The TList type stores a list of Pointers. Delphi automatically
// converts typed pointers and object references to Pointer.
// Retrieving items from the list is also simple.
procedure TForm1.FormCreate(Sender: TObject);
var
  List: TList;
  I: Integer;
  P: ^Integer;
  F: TForm;
begin
  List := TList.Create;
  List.Add(@I);       // Add takes an argument of type Pointer
  List.Add(Self);

  P := List[0];       // List[0] returns type Pointer
  P^ := 10;
  F := List[1];
  F.Show;

  List.Free;
end;
```

See Also

Addr Function, Nil Keyword, Ptr Function, $T Compiler Directive, $TypedAddress Compiler Directive, @ Operator

---

POleVariant Type

Syntax

```
type POleVariant = ^OleVariant;
```

Description

The `POleVariant` type is a convenience type for a pointer to type `TOleVariant`.

See Also

OleVariant Type, PVariant Type, Variant Type

Pos Function

Syntax

```
function Pos(const SubStr, Str: string): Integer;
```

Description

The Pos function returns the index of the first occurrence of SubStr in Str, or zero if SubStr never occurs in Str. Pos is not a real function.

Tips and Tricks

- String indices start at 1.

- The search is case sensitive.

- Pos does not handle multibyte characters. You should use AnsiPos, in the SysUtils unit, instead of Pos.

Example

```
// Environment variables such as PATH store a list of directories
// separated by semicolons. The SplitPath function takes such a string
// as an argument and splits the string into separate filenames.
// The filenames are stored in the FileList argument.
// Note that filenames can contain multibyte characters, so this
// function should call AnsiPos instead of Pos. Nonetheless, it is
// a demonstration of using either function.
procedure SplitPath(const Path: string; FileList: TStrings);
var
  Semicolon: Integer;
  FileName: string;     // First filename in the remaining path
  Remaining: string;    // The rest of path after the first filename
begin
  Remaining := Path;
  FileList.BeginUpdate;
  try
    FileList.Clear;
    while Remaining <> '' do
    begin
      Semicolon := Pos(';', Remaining);
      if Semicolon = 0 then
        Semicolon := MaxInt;
      FileName := Copy(Remaining, 1, Semicolon-1);
      Delete(Remaining, 1, Semicolon);
      FileList.Add(FileName);
    end;
  finally
    FileList.EndUpdate;
  end;
end;
```

See Also

AnsiString Type, Copy Function, Delete Procedure, Insert Procedure, ShortString Type, String Type

---

Pred Function

Syntax

```
function Pred(const Value): Ordinal type;
```

Description

The Pred function returns the predecessor of an ordinal value, usually an enumerated value. That is, it returns the enumerated value whose ordinal value is one less than Value. Pred is not a real function.

Tips and Tricks

- Dec, Pred, and subtraction by one have similar performance, so choose the one that you find most clear and easy to read.

- Calling Pred(Low(SomeType)) raises runtime error 4 (ERangeError). Without overflow checking, though, Pred returns a value with the desired ordinal value, even though that value is not valid for the type.

Example

```
type TDay =
  (Sunday, Monday, Tuesday, Wednesday, Thursday, Friday, Saturday);
var
  Day: TDay;
begin
  ...
  Day := Pred(Day);
  ...
```

See Also

Dec Procedure, High Function, Inc Procedure, Low Function, Succ Function, $OverflowChecks Compiler Directive, $Q Compiler Directive

---

PResStringRec Type

Syntax

```
type PResStringRec = ^TResStringRec;
```

Description

The PResStringRec type is a convenience pointer to a TResStringRec record. The address of a resourcestring identifier is a PResStringRec pointer.

See Also

LoadResString Function, ResourceString Keyword, String Keyword, TResStringRec Type

Private Directive

Syntax

```
type Class declaration
private
  Field declarations...
  Property and method declarations...
end;
```

Description

The **private** directive introduces the private section of a class declaration. **Private** fields, methods, and properties are not accessible by other classes and subroutines, except in the same unit.

Tips and Tricks

- Declare all fields as private, and declare properties to access the fields at higher access levels: protected, public, or published. That gives you the flexibility to change the way a field is accessed, say by changing a direct field reference to a method reference. Such changes affect only the implementation of the class, and not its use.

- The **private** directive prevents you from calling the method directly, but the class might have other ways to call the method. The private method can be a message handler, support a public property, or implement an interface's method.

Example

See the **class** keyword for an example.

See Also

Class Keyword, Protected Directive, Public Directive, Published Directive

---

Procedure Keyword

Syntax

```
procedure Name;
procedure Name(Parameters...);

type Name = procedure(Parameters...);
type Name = procedure(Parameters...) of object;
```

Description

The **procedure** keyword declares a subroutine that does not have a return type. You can also declare a procedural type.

In the interface section of a unit, only the procedure header (its name, parameters, and directives, but not the body) can appear.

In the implementation section, you must provide a complete definition for every procedure declared in the interface section. (See the **external** directive to learn how to define a procedure without providing a body.) You can omit the parameters in the implementation section if the procedure is not overloaded. If you provide the parameters, they must match exactly (including the parameter names) with the procedure header in the interface section.

A procedure's implementation should not repeat the directives that appeared first with the procedure header.

Tips and Tricks

- Although it seems like an additional maintenance burden to keep a copy of the header in the procedure's implementation, it is a great benefit to the person who maintains the code. It is inconvenient to have to jump to the procedure's declaration just to learn about its parameters.

- You can declare multiple procedures with the same name by using the overload directive.

- A procedure can be declared in a class declaration, in which case it is called a method. A method can be declared with the dynamic or virtual directives to declare a virtual method. A virtual method can be declared with the abstract directive, in which case, you must not provide a procedure implementation.

- The default calling convention is register. You can choose a different calling convention with the cdecl, pascal, safecall, or stdcall directives.

- Directives are optional, but if you include them, you must use the following order for methods:
  - reintroduce
  - overload (cannot mix with message)
  - virtual, dynamic, override, message
  - cdecl, pascal, register, safecall, stdcall
  - abstract (only if virtual, dynamic, or override appears earlier)

Example

```
type
  TRandProc = procedure(var Rand: Integer; Max: Integer);
  TRandMethod = procedure(var Rand: Integer) of object;
  TRandClass = class
  private
    fMin, fMax: Integer;
  public
    constructor Create(Min, Max: Integer);
    procedure GetRand(var Rand: Integer);
    property Min: Integer read fMin;
    property Max: Integer read fMax;
  end;

procedure TestRand(var Rand: Integer; Max: Integer);
begin
  Rand := Random(Max);
end;
```

```
procedure TRandClass.GetRand(var Rand: Integer);
begin
  Rand := Random(Max - Min + 1) + Min;
end;

var
  P: TRandProc;
  M: TRandMethod;
  O: TRandClass;
  I: Integer;
begin
  O := TRandClass.Create(1, 6);
  try
    P := RandProc;
    P(I, 100);
    WriteLn(I);
    M := O.GetRand;
    M(I);
    WriteLn(I);
  finally
    O.Free;
  end;
end.
```

See Also

Abstract Directive, CDecl Directive, Class Keyword, Dynamic Directive, External Directive, Function Keyword, Message Directive, Object Keyword, Overload Directive, Pascal Directive, Register Directive, Reintroduce Directive, SafeCall Directive, StdCall Directive, Type Keyword, Virtual Directive

---

Program Keyword

Syntax

```
program Name;
Declarations...
Block.
```

Description

The program keyword begins an application. The file extension for a program's source file is .dpr (for "Delphi project").

Tips and Tricks

*   Delphi accepts program parameters, for compatibility with standard Pascal, but it ignores them.

*   When the program starts, it first runs the initialization sections of all units, then it runs the program's statement block. After the block ends, the program calls the ExitProc procedure, then runs the finalization section of each unit.

*   Initialization sections run in the order of appearance in the program's uses declaration, traversing each unit's uses declaration. Finalization sections run in reverse order of the initialization sections. In other words, the first unit

listed in the program's **uses** declaration is the first unit to be initialized. Then, the first unit's used units are initialized one at a time, each unit initializing its used units before its initialization code runs.

- The *Block* can be a simple **end** statement if the program has no code to run. In that case, immediately after every initialization section runs, the program ends by calling **ExitProc** and the finalization sections.

Example

```
program Echo;
// Echo command-line arguments, separated by spaces.
{$AppType Console}
var
  I: Integer;
begin
  if ParamCount > 0 then
    Write(ParamStr(1));
  for I := 2 to ParamCount do
    Write(' ', ParamStr(I));
  WriteLn;
end.
```

See Also

Asm Keyword, Begin Keyword, ExitProc Variable, Initialization Keyword, InitProc Variable, Library Keyword, Uses Keyword, $AppType Compiler Directive

---

Property Keyword

Syntax

```
property Name: Type read Getter write Setter;
property Name: Type read Getter write Setter
    index Constant default Constant stored Stored;
property Name[Index: IndexType]: BaseType read Getter write Setter;
    default;
property Name;

property Name: Type;              // in dispinterface declarations only
property Name: Type readonly;
property Name: Type writeonly;

property Name: Type read Getter implements Interfaces...;
```

Description

The **property** keyword begins a property declaration in a **class**, **interface**, or **dispinterface** declaration. A property can be invoked from an object or interface reference using the same syntax as a field, but you can use a method to implement access to the property. This gives you the best of both worlds: convenient syntax and flexible semantics, without sacrificing performance.

In a dispinterface declaration, a property can be declared as readonly or writeonly. The default (if both these directives are omitted) is read and write access.

A property can also provide the implementation of one or more interfaces. See the implements keyword for more information about this use of properties.

Tips and Tricks

- Delphi lets you declare default and stored values for any property, but these directives are meaningful only for published properties. The compiler generates RTTI for the published property, including the values of the default and stored directives. These directives have no other impact on the language or the compiler, but the IDE reads the RTTI to decide which properties to store in a *.dfm* file.

- Note that the default directive has two uses: to specify a default value for a scalar property and to identify a default array property. The position of the default directive (before or after the semicolon) determines its interpretation.

- Directives are optional, but if you use them, they must appear in the following order: index, read, write, default or nodefault, stored, implements.

- The *Getter* and *Setter* are optional, but you must include at least one or the other. A published property must have both. The *Getter*, *Setter*, or *Stored* references can be a field reference or a method name. The method can be virtual, but not dynamic or a message handler. The *Stored* value can also be a constant Boolean expression. See the read, stored, and write directives for more information.

- You can redeclare a property that is inherited from a base class by listing only the property keyword followed by the property name. The property retains the same directives it inherits from the base class. When you redeclare a property, you can redeclare it with a higher access level than what the base class uses. This technique is commonly used in components, where a customizable base class declares properties as protected, and customized derived classes redeclare the same properties as public or published.

Example

```
{
  Red-black trees:
  Each node is colored Red or Black. The tree is balanced by
  maintaining certain rules about red nodes and black nodes.
}

type
TRbColor = (rbBlack, rbRed);
TRbNode = class
private
  fLeft, fRight: TRbNode;
  fItem: ICollectible;
  fParent: Integer;
  function GetParent: TRbNode;
```

```
      procedure SetParent(Parent: TRbNode);
  protected
      constructor Create(Item: ICollectible; Leaf, Parent: TRbNode;
                         Color: TRbColor);
      function IsRed: Boolean;
      function IsBlack: Boolean;
      function GetColor: TRbColor; virtual;
      procedure SetColor(Color: TRbColor); virtual;

      property Left: TRbNode read fLeft write fLeft;
      property Right: TRbNode read fRight write fRight;
      property Item: ICollectible read fItem write fItem;

      Property Color: TRbColor read GetColor write SetColor;
      Property Parent: TRbNode read GetParent write SetParent;

  end;
```

See Also

Class Keyword, Default Directive, Dispinterface Keyword, Implements
Directive, Index Directive, Interface Keyword, NoDefault Directive, Read
Directive, Readonly Directive, Stored Directive, Write Directive, Writeonly
Directive

Protected Directive

Syntax

```
type Class declaration
protected
    Field declarations...
    Method and property declarations...
end;
```

Description

The protected directive introduces the protected section of a class declaration.
Protected fields, methods, and properties are accessible only by methods of the
class and its descendants. Classes and subroutines declared in the same unit can
also access the protected declarations.

Tips and Tricks

- Most methods or properties that are not part of the public interface should
  usually be made protected. When you declare a method as private, or do not
  have a protected property to access a private field, you are limiting the ways
  your class can be reused. You cannot predict the ways in which a class will
  be used in other projects, and hiding important declarations in a private section only frustrates would-be users of your class.

- On the other hand, details of the implementation of a class must sometimes
  be kept private so you can be free to change the implementation in a future
  revision. Be sure to define appropriate protected methods to allow reuse of
  your class, even if the protected method merely calls a private method.

- Many protected methods should be virtual. Because it is difficult to know how a subclass might want to extend or alter the behavior of an ancestor class, it is usually better to err on the side of too much flexibility. Make a protected method static only when you have a reason to do so.

Example

See the **class** keyword for an example.

See Also

Class Keyword, Private Directive, Public Directive, Published Directive

---

PShortString Type

Syntax

```
type PShortString = ^ShortString;
```

Description

The PShortString type is a convenience type for a pointer to a ShortString.

See Also

PAnsiString Type, PString Type, ShortString Type

PString Type

Syntax

```
type PString = ^string;
```

Description

The PString type is a convenience type for a pointer to a string. Note that the string type is a pointer, so PString is rarely used.

See Also

PAnsiString Type, PShortString Type, String Keyword, PWideString Type

---

Ptr Function

Syntax

```
function Ptr(Value: Integer): Pointer;
```

Description

The Ptr function type casts the Value to an untyped Pointer. The Ptr function is not a real function.

Calling `Ptr` is just like casting a value to a `Pointer`. If you can, you should cast to a specific pointer type, such as `PInt64` instead of using an untyped `Pointer`. Typed pointers provide more type safety.

See Also

Addr Function, Assigned Function, Pointer Type

Public Directive

Syntax

```
type Class declaration
public
    Field declarations...
    Method and property declarations...
end;
```

Description

The `public` directive introduces the public section of a class declaration. Public fields, methods, and properties are accessible from any other subroutines or method in the same unit or in any unit that uses the declaring unit (provided the class declaration is in the unit's interface section).

Tips and Tricks

- Fields should never be made public. Instead, declare fields in the private section, and declare public properties to access the fields. Properties are more flexible than fields, and they give you more opportunity to change the class declaration without affecting uses of the class.

- Public methods and properties define the external behavior of a class and its objects. Once a class is in use, refrain from making changes to the public methods and properties if at all possible. Instead of changing a method, declare a new method with new behavior. Public changes have a way of propagating and upsetting other code in a project.

- A class declaration can begin with an initial, unnamed section. The default access level for the unnamed section is public unless the class uses the `$M` or `$TypeInfo` compiler directives to enable RTTI, or if the class inherits from a class that has RTTI enabled. `TPersistent` in Delphi's `Classes` unit enables RTTI, so all persistent classes (including all components, controls, and forms) have RTTI. The initial, unnamed section is published for classes with RTTI.

Example

See the `class` keyword for an example.

See Also

Class Keyword, Private Directive, Protected Directive, Published Directive, $M Compiler Directive, $TypeInfo Compiler Directive

Published Directive

Syntax

```
type Class declaration
published
    Field declarations...
    Method and property declarations...
end;
```

Description

The published directive introduces the published section of a class declaration. Just like public declarations, published fields, methods, and properties are accessible from any other subroutines or method in the same unit or in any unit that uses the declaring unit (provided the class declaration is in the unit's interface section).

Tips and Tricks

- The difference between public and published is that published declarations tell the compiler to store runtime type information about the published fields, methods, and properties.

- The compiler treats a published section like public unless RTTI is enabled with the $M or $TypeInfo compiler directives, or if the class inherits from a class with RTTI enabled. TPersistent in Delphi's Classes unit enables published RTTI, so all persistent classes (including all components, controls, and forms) have RTTI. The initial, unnamed section is published for classes with RTTI.

- Delphi's IDE relies on the initial, unnamed section of a form class for storing its fields and methods. Although the compiler will let you move these declarations to any published section of the class, the IDE requires the declarations be in the unnamed section. Because forms and data modules have TPersistent as an ancestor, the initial, unnamed section is published.

- Published fields must be of class type, and that class must also have RTTI enabled.

- Published properties cannot be array properties. The type of a published property is limited to ordinal types, set types that fit in an Integer (currently 32 or fewer elements), class types where the class has RTTI enabled, Variants, floating-point types except for Real48, or all kinds of strings, but not arrays, pointers, records, or old-style objects.

Example

See the class keyword for an example.

See Also

Class Keyword, Private Directive, Protected Directive, Public Directive, $M Compiler Directive, $TypeInfo Compiler Directive

PUnitEntryTable Type

Syntax

```
type PUnitEntryTable = ^UnitEntryTable;
```

Description

The PUnitEntryTable type is a convenience pointer to a UnitEntryTable record.

See Also

Finalization Keyword, Initialization Keyword, PackageInfo Type, PackageInfoTable Type, Unit Keyword, UnitEntryTable Type

PVarArray Type

Syntax

```
type PVarArray = ^TVarArray;
```

Description

The PVarArray type is a convenience type for a pointer to a TVarArray record. The TVarData record for a Variant array stores a PVarArray value. See TVarData for more information.

See Also

TVarArray Type, TVarArrayBound Type, TVarData Type, Variant Type

PVarData Type

Syntax

```
type PVarData = ^TVarData;
```

Description

The PVarData type is a convenience type for a pointer to a TVarData record.

See Also

TVarData Type, Variant Type

PVariant Type

Syntax

```
type PVariant = ^Variant;
```

Description

The PVariant type is a convenience type for a pointer to a Variant.

Variant Type

PVarRec Type

Syntax

```
type PVarRec = ^TVarRec;
```

Description

The **PVarRec** type is a convenience type for a pointer to a **TVarRec** record. The **TVarRec** type is used to interpret a variant open array (**array of const**) in a subroutine.

See Also

Array Keyword, Variant Type

PWideChar Type

Syntax

```
type PWideChar = ^WideChar;
```

Description

The **PWideChar** type is a pointer to **WideChar** and with Delphi's extended syntax, it can also be treated as a **WideString** or a pointer to an array of **WideChar**.

Tips and Tricks

- **PWideChar** is used most often as a parameter type for DLLs written in C or C++, such as the Windows API.

- You can treat a **PWideChar** pointer as a pointer to an array of **WideChar**. The array index is an **Integer** subrange, starting from zero. Delphi does not provide any bounds checking for the array. The convention is that the end of the string is denoted by the presence of the #0 character.

- Perform pointer arithmetic on a **PWideChar** pointer by adding and subtracting integers similar to the way the **Inc** and **Dec** procedures work.

- Delphi's extended syntax is enabled by default. Use the **$X** or **$ExtendedSyntax** compiler directive to disable this feature and revert to behavior closer to standard Pascal.

See Also

AnsiChar Type, AnsiString Type, Array Keyword, Char Type, PAnsiChar Type, PChar Type, String Keyword, WideString Type, $ExtendedSyntax Compiler Directive, $X Compiler Directive

PWideString Type

Syntax

```
type PWideString = ^WideString;
```

Description

The PWideString type is a convenience type for a pointer to a WideString. Note that a WideString is a pointer, so PWideString is rarely used.

See Also

PAnsiString Type, PShortString Type, PString Type, String Keyword, WideString Type

---

Raise Keyword

Syntax

```
raise Object reference
raise Object reference at Pointer
raise
```

Description

The **raise** statement raises an exception. The exception object is passed to an exception handler, and Delphi will automatically free the object when the exception handler finishes. Usually, the object reference creates a new instance of an exception object, and the exception class usually inherits from the Exception class in the SysUtils unit, but you are free to raise any object reference as an exception.

By default, Delphi stores the code address of the **raise** statement as the exception address. You can specify a different address with the **at** directive.

Inside an exception handler, you can use a plain **raise** statement to reraise the current exception. In this case, Delphi refrains from freeing the exception object until the next exception handler in the stack gets its chance to handle the exception.

Tips and Tricks

- Low-level code and utilities should report exceptional conditions by raising exceptions. High-level and user interface code should use **try-except** or **TApplication.OnException** to catch and handle exceptions in a user-friendly manner.

- Raising and handling an exception takes time and processor resources. Do so only for exceptional conditions. Do not use exceptions as a normal way to return information. For example, a collection class might implement the Contains method to return True if the collection contains an item, and False if the item is not in the collection. The normal return status is True or False, so this method does not raise an exception. On the other hand, the Delete method deletes an item. If the item is not in the collection, that is an exceptional condition, and the `Delete` method should raise an exception.

- Define new exception classes as needed. The exception class conveys information to the exception handler, and the handler might use the exception class to take actions that are specific to certain exceptions.

- Be sure to use a `resourcestring` for the exception message, so the application can be localized more easily.

Example

```
// Raise a generic exception at the caller's address.
procedure Error(const Fmt: string; const Args: array of const);
  function Caller: Pointer;
  asm
    // Get the caller's address from the stack. The details
    // might change, depending on compiler version and options.
    MOV EAX, [ESP+4]
  end;

begin
  raise Exception.CreateFmt(Fmt, Args) at Caller;
end;

// Delete a file, raising an exception for any failure,
// including file not found.
procedure RemoveFile(const FileName: string);
begin
  if not DeleteFile(FileName) then
    raise Exception.CreateFmt('Cannot delete %s: %s',
      [FileName, SysErrorMessage(GetLastError)]);
end;
```

See Also

At Directive, Except Keyword, Finally Keyword, IOResult Function, Try Keyword

---

RaiseList Function

Syntax

```
function RaiseList: Pointer;
```

Description

The `RaiseList` function returns a pointer to the current exception frame, which might be the first node in a list of exceptions. The `System` unit does not declare the type of the exception frame; the record is shown in the example.

The first frame in the list is the current exception. If an exception handler raises an exception, you can have multiple frames in the exception list.

`RaiseList` is a real function.

Tips and Tricks

- Usually, the **try-except** statement provides the necessary functionality for handling exceptions. You shouldn't need to call **RaiseList** unless you are trying to handle exceptions in a non-standard way.

- Each thread has its own separate exception list.

Example

```
type
  PRaiseFrame = ^TRaiseFrame;
  TRaiseFrame = packed record
    NextRaise: PRaiseFrame;
    ExceptAddr: Pointer;
    ExceptObject: TObject;
    ExceptionRecord: PExceptionRecord; // Type defined in Windows unit.
  end;
...
try
  ...
except
  Code := PRaiseFrame(RaiseList).ExceptionRecord.ExceptionCode;
  if Code = Exception_BreakPoint then
    ...
end;
```

See Also

ErrorProc Variable, Except Keyword, ExceptProc Variable, Raise Keyword, SetRaiseList Procedure, Try Keyword

---

Random Function

Syntax

```
function Random: Extended;
function Random(Limit: Integer): Integer;
```

Description

The **Random** function returns a pseudorandom number. Without arguments, it returns a floating-point number in the range $0 \leq \text{Result} < 1$. The second form takes an integer argument and returns an integer in the range $0 \leq \text{Result} < \text{Limit}$. **Random** is not a real function.

Tips and Tricks

- Delphi uses a pseudorandom number generator (PRNG) with a cycle of 2^{32}. Although adequate for simple simulations, it is not suitable for use in encryption or other areas where you need a high-quality PRNG.

- Call **Randomize** once to start the sequence of pseudorandom numbers at a different number each time you run the program.

Example

```
type
  TDieRoll = 1..6;
  TDiceRoll = 2..12;

// Simulate a roll of one ordinary die. Note that Random
// returns a value in the range [0, 5], so add 1 to get [1, 6].
function Die: TDieRoll;
begin
  Result := Random(6) + 1;
end;

// Simulate the roll of two ordinary dice.
function Dice: TDiceRoll;
begin
  Result := Die + Die;
end;
```

See Also

Randomize Procedure, RandSeed Variable

Randomize Procedure

Syntax

```
procedure Randomize;
```

Description

Call Randomize once at the start of a program to start the sequence of pseudo-random numbers at a different number each time you run the program. Randomize sets the RandSeed variable to a value based on the time of day. Randomize is a real procedure.

Tips and Tricks

- When testing a program, do not call Randomize. That way, you will get the same sequence of pseudorandom numbers every time you run the program, and you can compare results between runs. After testing, add the call to Randomize so that each time the program runs, it starts the sequence of pseudorandom numbers differently.

- Do not call Randomize more than once in the same program. Doing so destroys the randomness of the pseudorandom numbers.

- Randomize uses the time of day to initialize RandSeed. If the program runs at the same time every day, you should find a different way to initialize RandSeed.

Example

```
unit RandomDice;
interface
...
function Die: TDieRoll;
```

```
function Dice: TDiceRoll;
implementation
...
initialization
  Randomize;
end.
```

See Also

Random Function, RandSeed Variable

RandSeed Variable

Syntax

```
var RandSeed: LongInt;
```

Description

RandSeed contains the seed for the pseudorandom number generator. If you do not call Randomize, RandSeed starts at zero.

Example

```
// Initialize RandSeed with a less predictable initial value.
// This version incorporates the time of day, process ID,
// and elapsed time since boot. It is unlikely that all three
// will be the same from one run of the program to another.
procedure MyRandomize;
begin
  Randomize; // Start with the time of day.
  RandSeed := ((RandSeed shl 8) or GetCurrentProcessID) xor
    GetTickCount;
end;
```

See Also

Random Function, Randomize Procedure

Read Directive

Syntax

```
property Name: Type ... read Getter ...;
```

Description

A property's read directive tells Delphi how to get the property's value. The *Getter* can be the name of a field or a method in the class or in an ancestor class.

If the *Getter* is a field, the field's type must be the same as the property's type. The usual access rules apply, so the field cannot be a private field of an ancestor class unless the ancestor class is in the same unit. Typically, the field is a private field of the same class that declares the property. The field can be an aggregate (record or array), and the *Getter* must specify a record member or array element (at a constant index) of the appropriate type. Records and arrays can be nested.

If the *Getter* is a method, the method must be a function whose return type is the same as the property type. The method can be static or virtual, but it cannot be a dynamic method.

If the property is indexed or an array property, the *Getter* must be a method. The first parameter is the index value, which is an Integer. Subsequent arguments are the array indices. The type of each *Getter* argument must match the type of the corresponding array index.

When the user reads the property value, Delphi gets the value from the *Getter* field or by calling the *Getter* method.

Tips and Tricks

- If you use a *Getter* field, Delphi compiles all property references into direct field references, so there is no performance penalty for using a property instead of a field.

- A good programming style is to make all fields private and declare protected, public, or published properties to access the fields. If you need to modify the class at a later date, you can change the field to a method without affecting any code that depends on the class and its property.

Example

See the **property** keyword for examples.

See Also

Class Keyword, Index Directive, Property Keyword, Write Directive

---

Read Procedure

Syntax

```
procedure Read(var F: File; var Variable; ...);
procedure Read(var F: TextFile; var Variable; ...);
procedure Read(var Variable; ...);
```

Description

The Read procedure reads data from a binary or text file. It is not a real procedure.

To read from a typed binary file, the *Variable* must be of the same type as the base type of the file. Delphi reads one record from the file into *Variable* and advances the file position in preparation for reading the next record. If the file is untyped, Delphi reads as many bytes as specified for the record size when the file was opened with Reset. You can list more than one variable as arguments to Read, in which case, Read will read multiple records and assign each one to a separate variable.

When reading from a TextFile, Read performs a formatted read. Delphi reads characters from the input file and interprets them according to the type of each *Variable*. Read skips over white space characters (blanks, tabs, and ends of lines) when reading a number, and stops reading when it gets to another white space character.

When reading strings and characters, Read does not skip over white space. If *Variable* is a long string, Read reads the entire line into the string, but not the end-of-line characters. If *Variable* is a short string, Read stops at the end of the line or the size of the string, whichever comes first.

Errors

- If the file has not been assigned, Read reports I/O error 102.

- If the file is not open for read access, Read reports I/O error 103.

- If the input is not formatted correctly (e.g., trying to read 3.14 as an Integer), Read reports I/O error 106.

- If the read fails for another reason (say, a network error), Read reports the Windows error code as an I/O error.

- If an input value is out of range for its type (say, 257 when reading a Byte), Read silently casts the value to the correct type without raising an exception or reporting a runtime error.

Tips and Tricks

- Delphi does not buffer input from a binary file, so you probably want to call BlockRead to read many records at one time.

- Reading past the end of file raises I/O error 100 for a binary file. For a text file, the read always succeeds in reading the character #26. Reading a number or string results in zero or an empty string.

- Without a file as the first argument, Read reads from the text file Input.

Example

```
var
  I: Integer;
  D1, D2: Double;
  S1, S2: string;
begin
  Read(S1); // Reads entire line, but not end of line.
  Read(S2); // Always reads end of line.
  Read(I);  // Skips over end of line and spaces to read a number.
  Read(D1, D2);  // Spaces also terminate and separate numbers.
```

See Also

BlockRead Procedure, File Keyword, Input Variable, IOResult Function, ReadLn Procedure, TextFile Type, Write Procedure

---

ReadLn Procedure

Syntax

```
procedure ReadLn(var F: TextFile; var Variable; ...);
procedure ReadLn(var Variable; ...);
```

```
procedure ReadLn(var F: TextFile);
procedure ReadLn;
```

Description

ReadLn is just like Read, but after it finishes reading into all the *Variables*, ReadLn skips the rest of the line and prepares to read the next line. Without any *Variable* arguments, ReadLn skips the rest of the line.

ReadLn cannot read a binary file. It is not a real procedure.

Tips and Tricks

- To ReadLn, a line ends when it reads a carriage return (#13) or reaches the end of file. The carriage return can optionally be followed by a linefeed (#10) or end of file.

- When reading strings, you almost certainly want to use ReadLn instead of Read. Calling Read to read a long string reads everything up to but not including the line ending. If you call Read again to read a string, it will read everything up to but not including the line ending, which means it reads an empty string. ReadLn reads the string and then skips the line ending, so you can read the next line of text into the next string.

- Without a TextFile as the first argument, ReadLn reads from Input.

Example

```
program bmindex;
// Compute a Body-Mass Index, given a person's height in centimeters
// and weight in kilograms. A BMI greater than 26 means a person
// is overweight.
var
  Height, Weight: Single;
  BMI: Integer;
begin
  WriteLn('Enter your height in centimeters: ');
  ReadLn(Height);
  WriteLn('Enter your weight in kilograms: ');
  ReadLn(Weight);
  BMI := Round((Weight * 10000) / (Height * Height));
  Write('Your body-mass index is ', BMI, '.');
  if BMI > 26 then
    WriteLn(' I recommend losing some weight.')
  else
    WriteLn;

  WriteLn('Press ENTER to exit.');
  ReadLn;
end.
```

See Also

BlockRead Procedure, Input Variable, IOResult Function, Read Procedure, TextFile Type, Write Procedure, WriteLn Procedure

Readonly Directive

Syntax

```
property Name: Type readonly;
```

Description

The `readonly` directive applies only to properties in a **dispinterface** declaration. See the **dispinterface** keyword for details.

See Also

Dispinterface Keyword, Property Keyword, Writeonly Directive

Real Type

Syntax

```
type Real = Double;
```

Description

The `Real` type is another name for `Double`; this name exists for compatibility with standard or Turbo Pascal programs. If you have a file that stores Turbo Pascal `Real` values, you must use the `Real48` type to read those values from the file. The `$RealCompatibility` compiler directive lets you treat all uses of the `Real` type as `Real48`.

See Also

Double Type, Real48 Type, $RealCompatibility Compiler Directive

Real48 Type

Syntax

```
type Real48;
```

Description

The `Real48` type exists for backward compatibility with Turbo Pascal. It defines a 6-byte floating-point type. `Real48` values must be converted to **Extended** before using them in any computations, so they are slower than using `Double` or `Extended`.

The Real48 type has an 8-bit exponent and a 39-bit normalized mantissa. It cannot store denormalized values, infinity, or not-a-number. If the exponent is zero, the number is zero.

See Also

Extended Type, Real Type, $RealCompatibility Compiler Directive

ReallocMem Procedure

Syntax

```
procedure ReallocMem(var P: Pointer; NewSize: Integer);
```

Description

ReallocMem changes the size of a dynamically allocated block, preserving as much of the previous contents as possible.

If P is nil, ReallocMem is just like GetMem. If NewSize is zero, it is just like FreeMem, which means P is not changed, so it contains an invalid pointer after ReallocMem returns.

When possible, ReallocMem tries to adjust the size of the current memory block, but if it cannot, it allocates an entirely new block of the desired size and copies the old data into the new block. In either case, if NewSize is bigger than the current size, the extra memory is not initialized.

ReallocMem is not a real procedure.

Tips and Tricks

- If you have a block that grows incrementally, anticipate future growth. Instead of frequently increasing the block size in small steps, increase the size by larger steps less often. Try to call ReallocMem as little as possible because ReallocMem often fails to reuse the current block. As the block size grows, the performance penalty for copying the old block to the new block also grows.

- ReallocMem in Delphi's default memory manager is thread-safe, that is, you can call ReallocMem from multiple threads simultaneously, but only if IsMultiThread is True.

- Delphi's memory manager assumes that the program will frequently allocate and free blocks of varying sizes. Most programs fit this pattern, but a few don't. If your program often calls ReallocMem to incrementally increase the size of a large block, you might run into performance problems and excessive wasted memory. The solution is to call ReallocMem less often, or if you must call it frequently, substitute your own memory manager that does a better job at increasing a block's size without needing to allocate new, larger blocks.

Example

```
// A trivial list that grows by bounds, not steps.
type
  TObjectArray = array[0..MaxInt div SizeOf(TObject) - 1] of TObject;
  PObjectArray = ^TObjectArray;
  TWholeNumber = 0..MaxInt;
  TArray = class
  private
    fList: PObjectArray;
    fCapacity: TWholeNumber;
    fCount: TWholeNumber;
```

```
      procedure Grow;
   public
      constructor Create;
      procedure Add(Obj: TObject);
      procedure Remove(Obj: TObject);
      property Items[Index: TWholeNumber]: TObject
          read GetItem write SetItem;
      property Count: TWholeNumber read fCount;
      property Capacity: TWholeNumber read fCapacity;
   end;

procedure TArray.Add(Obj: TObject);
begin
   if Count = Capacity then
      Grow;
   fList[Count] := Obj;
   Inc(fCount);
end;

procedure TArray.Grow;
begin
   // When small, grow by 100%, when larger grow by only 50%.
   if Capacity < 64 then
      fCapacity := Capacity * 2
   else
      fCapacity := Capacity + Capacity div 2;
   ReallocMem(fList, Capacity * SizeOf(TObject));
end;
```

See Also

FreeMem Procedure, GetMem Procedure, ReallocMemory Function, SysReallocMem Function

---

ReallocMemory Function

Syntax

```
function ReallocMemory(Ptr: Pointer; Size: Integer): Pointer; cdecl;
```

Description

The ReallocMemory function calls Delphi's memory manager to reallocate a block of memory with a new size. ReallocMemory returns a pointer to the start of the block.

ReallocMemory is for use by C++ Builder. If you are writing a memory manager in Delphi, you should call SysReallocMem.

ReallocMemory is a real function.

See Also

FreeMemory Function, GetMemory Function, IsMultiThread Variable, ReallocMem Procedure, SysReallocMem Function

Record Keyword

Syntax

```
type Name = record Members... end;
type Name = packed record Members... end;
type Name = record Members...
                case Selector of Case, ...: (Members...;);
                ...
            end;
type Name = packed record Members...
                case Name: Selector of Case, ...: (Members...;);
                ...
            end;
```

Description

A record in Delphi is the same as a record in standard Pascal. A record is a structured type that contains zero or more *members*. Each member is like a variable, consisting of a name and a type. A record-type variable has space for all of the record's members, and you can refer to individual members of a record.

By default, record members are aligned so they start on natural boundaries. A packed record eliminates the padding between members, which can result in a smaller record size, but at the expense of increased access time. See the packed keyword for details.

Variant Records

A record can be a variant record (equivalent to a union in C or C++), where members can share the same space within the record. The variant part of a record must follow all the non-variant members. The *Selector* can be just a type name or it can declare an additional member. The selector member tells you which variant case to use. Without a selector member, you must use another technique to know which variant case is correct.

Each case specifies one or more constants whose type is the selector type. After the colon, the case lists zero or more member declarations inside parentheses.

You cannot have long string, dynamic array, interface, or Variant members in the variant part of a record. Delphi cannot tell which variant members are currently active, so the compiler cannot tell when to initialize or finalize the memory for strings, dynamic arrays, interfaces, and Variants.

Variant records can be packed. Each variant case is packed without regard to the other variant cases. The size of a variant record is the largest size of all the variant cases.

Tips and Tricks

Records have less overhead than classes, so they are often used in situations where you must allocate many records, but you don't need to do much with them.

Example

See TVarRec and TVarData for additional examples.

```
type
  TEmployeeKind = (ekGrunt, ekBoss, ekSlacker);
  PEmployee = ^TEmployee;
  TEmployeeArray = array[0..MaxEmployee] of PEmployee;
  TEmployee = record
    Name, ID: string;
    Salary: Currency;
    case Kind: TEmployeeKind of
    ekGrunt: (Boss: PEmployee;);
    ekBoss: (Group: TEmployeeArray;
             GroupSize: 0..MaxEmployee;);
    ekSlacker: ();
  end;
```

See Also

Case Keyword, Packed Keyword, Type Keyword, $A Compiler Directive, $Align Compiler Directive

---

RefAnyProc Variable

Syntax

```
var RefAnyProc: Pointer;

procedure RefAny(var V: Variant);
RefAnyProc := @RefAny;
```

Description

The RefAnyProc variable points to a procedure that creates a reference to a varAny Variant. If you must maintain a reference count, RefAny increments the reference count. If each varAny keeps a unique copy, you can make a copy of the varAny data in the RefAnyProc procedure. The default value is a procedure that raises runtime error 15 (EVariantError).

Tips and Tricks

The CorbaObj unit sets this variable to point to a procedure that supports CORBA's Any type. If you are not using CORBA, you can use varAny values for your own purposes.

Example

See the ChangeAnyProc variable for an explanation of this example.

```
// Each varAny Int64 value has its own unique Int64 value.
// When Delphi makes a reference, it sets V to a copy of
// the original. This procedure gives V a unique Int64 value.
procedure RefVarInt64(var V: Variant);
var
  Value: Int64;
begin
  if TVarData(V).VType = varAny then
  begin
    Value := PInt64(TVarData(V).VAny)^;
```

```
      SetVarInt64(V, Value);
   end;
end;
...
```

RefAnyProc := @RefVarInt64;

See Also

ChangeAnyProc Variable, ClearAnyProc Variable, TVarData Type, Variant Type

---

Register Directive

Syntax

```
Subroutine declaration; register;
```

Description

The **register** directive tells the compiler to use Borland's fast register calling convention for the function or procedure. The caller stores the first three arguments in the registers EAX, EDX, and ECX, and pushes the remaining arguments onto the stack, starting with the leftmost argument. Parameters that do not fit into a 32-bit register (such as Double) are pushed onto the stack, so the registers contain the first three arguments that are not on the stack. Before the subroutine returns, it pops the arguments from the stack.

Functions return ordinal values, pointers, and small records or sets in EAX and floating-point values on the FPU stack. Strings, dynamic arrays, Variants, and large records and sets are passed as a hidden var parameter. This hidden parameter is the last parameter. If the subroutine is a method, Self is passed in EAX.

Tips and Tricks

- Borland's register calling convention is different from Microsoft's register calling convention. For maximum compatibility in a DLL or COM object, use stdcall or safecall conventions.

- The **register** calling convention is the default.

See Also

CDecl Directive, Function Keyword, Pascal Directive, Procedure Keyword, SafeCall Directive, StdCall Directive

---

Register Procedure

Syntax

```
procedure Register;
begin
   ...
end;
```

Description

When you write a design-time package, you will usually write a `Register` procedure in one or more units that the package contains. When Delphi loads the design-time package in the IDE, it searches for a procedure named `Register` and calls that procedure, if it exists. It calls the procedures in the order in which the units appear in the package source file.

Tips and Tricks

- The procedure name must follow the capitalization shown here: an initial capital R, followed by a lowercase `egister`. This restriction is unusual for Pascal, but it provides compatibility with C++ Builder, which is a case-sensitive language. You can write a package in Delphi and load it in C++ Builder, or vice versa.

- The `Register` procedure is optional.

- Delphi's IDE calls the `Register` procedure when it loads design-time packages. If you load the same package in an application, the `Register` procedure is not called automatically.

See Also

Package Directive

RegisterModule Procedure

Syntax

```
procedure RegisterModule(LibModule: PLibModule);
```

Description

`RegisterModule` adds `LibModule` to the head of the module list. Delphi automatically calls `RegisterModule` for the packages it loads when the application starts. Delphi also registers the packages your program loads dynamically.

`RegisterModule` is a real procedure.

Tips and Tricks

To examine the contents of the list, call `EnumModules`, or to enumerate the associated resource modules, call `EnumResourceModules`.

See Also

EnumModules Procedure, EnumResourceModules Procedure, LibModuleList Variable, PLibModule Type, TLibModule Type, UnregisterModule Procedure

---

Reintroduce Directive

Syntax

```
Method declaration; reintroduce;
```

Description

A derived class uses the `reintroduce` directive to hide the name of a virtual or dynamic method that was declared in a base class. Without the directive, the compiler warns you that the derived class is hiding the ancestor's method. Hiding, in this context, means that you cannot call the ancestor method if you have an object reference whose type is the derived class. Any attempt to call the method actually calls the derived class's method.

Tips and Tricks

The `reintroduce` directive, if it appears, must be the method's first directive.

Example

```
type
  TVector = class
  public
    procedure Add(Item: Integer); virtual;
  end;
  TSingleVector = class
  public
    // The TSingleVector.Add method hides TVector.Add, so the compiler
    // warns you about this. If you are hiding the method deliberately,
    // say so with the reintroduce directive.
    procedure Add(Item: Single); reintroduce;
  end;
```

See Also

Dynamic Directive, Function Keyword, Override Directive, Procedure Keyword, Virtual Directive

---

RemoveModuleUnloadProc Procedure

Syntax

```
procedure RemoveModuleUnloadProc(Proc: TModuleUnloadProc);

procedure YourProcedure(HInstance: Integer);
begin ... end;
RemoveModuleUnloadProc(YourProcedure);
```

Description

`RemoveModuleUnloadProc` removes your module unload procedure from the list. Delphi keeps a list of packages that comprise an application. When Delphi unloads a package, it calls a series of unload procedures, passing the DLL's instance handle to each one.

To add a procedure to the list, call `AddModuleUnloadProc`.

`RemoveModuleUnloadProc` is a real procedure.

AddModuleUnloadProc Procedure, ModuleUnloadList Variable, PModuleUnloadRec Type, TModuleUnloadRec Type, UnregisterModule Procedure

Rename Procedure

Syntax

```
procedure Rename(var F: File; const NewName: string);
procedure Rename(var F: TextFile; const NewName: string);
```

Description

The Rename procedure renames a file. You must call **AssignFile** first to assign the current filename. If the file cannot be renamed, the Windows error code is reported as an I/O error.

See Also

AssignFile Procedure, Erase Procedure, File Keyword, IOResult Function, TextFile Type

Repeat Keyword

Syntax

```
repeat
    Statements...
until Boolean expression
```

Description

Delphi's **repeat** statement works the same way as that of standard Pascal. The *Statements* are executed repeatedly until the *Boolean expression* is True.

Tips and Tricks

- The *Statements* always execute at least once.
- You don't need **begin** and **end** to define a block because the **repeat** and **until** keywords delimit the statement list.

Example

```
if FindFirst(Path, faAnyFile, Search) = 0 then
try
  repeat
    MungFile(Path + Search.Name);
  until FindNext(Search) <> 0;
finally
  FindClose(Search);
end;
```

Boolean Type, Break Procedure, Continue Procedure, For Keyword, Until Keyword, While Keyword

Requires Directive

Syntax

```
package Name;
requires
  OtherName, ...;
end.
```

Description

The `requires` directive begins a list of package names that are required to build package *Name*. The package names are separated by commas.

Tips and Tricks

* When Delphi compiles a package, it must locate every unit contained in the package and every unit used by the contained units. All the units are partitioned into two groups: units contained in the required packages, and all others. The latter units are the ones that Delphi compiles into the new package. If you don't want a unit to be contained in a package, that unit must be contained in a different package, which is required by the package you are compiling.

* Usually, you will use Delphi's package editor to add or remove required packages. You can edit the package source manually, but doing so does not update the package editor. Close and reopen the project or project group to force Delphi to read the new package source file.

* Delphi's IDE does not always treat a package as a project. If you have difficulties with the IDE, try creating a new project group, then add the package to the project group.

* Packages are DLLs, so Windows finds a package file the same way it finds any DLL. You cannot specify a complete path when listing a required package—only the package name.

See Also

Contains Directive, Package Directive

Reset Procedure

Syntax

```
procedure Reset(var F: TextFile);
procedure Reset(var F: File);
procedure Reset(var F: File; RecordSize: Integer);
```

Description

The Reset procedure opens an existing file. If the file is a TextFile, Reset opens the file for read-only access. If the file is a binary file, the file is opened to allow read and write function calls, but the FileMode variable dictates how the operating system opens the file. Reset is not a real procedure.

If the file is a typed binary file (e.g., file of *something*), use the second form of Reset, that is, pass the file variable only. If the file is an untyped binary file (just file), you can optionally supply the second argument to tell Delphi the record size. If you omit the record size, Delphi uses 128 bytes.

Errors

* Reset reports I/O error 102 if you fail to call AssignFile prior to calling Reset.

* If Reset cannot open the file, it reports the Windows error code as an I/O error.

Tips and Tricks

* If the file is already open, it is closed first.

* By default, Reset opens a binary file to allow reading and writing. Set the FileMode variable to 0 before calling Reset to open a file for read-only access.

* To use Reset to append to a binary file, open the file, seek to the end of the file, and then begin writing.

* When using an untyped file, it is usually simplest to supply a record size of 1 when calling Reset, and then call BlockRead and BlockWrite to read and write as much data as you want. Alternatively, create a type for File of Byte, so you don't need to set the record size in Reset.

Example

```
// Copy a file.
procedure CopyFile(const Source, Dest: string);
const
  BufferSize = 8192;
var
  SourceFile, DestFile: File of Byte;
  Buffer: PByte;
  Count: LongInt;
begin
  AssignFile(SourceFile, Source);
  AssignFile(DestFile, Dest);
  Buffer := nil;
  try
    GetMem(Buffer, BufferSize);
    FileMode := 0;
    Reset(SourceFile);
    Rewrite(DestFile);
    repeat
      BlockRead(SourceFile, Buffer^, BufferSize, Count);
```

```
        BlockWrite(DestFile, Buffer^, Count);
      until Count = 0;
    finally
      CloseFile(SourceFile);
      CloseFile(DestFile);
      FreeMem(Buffer);
    end;
  end;
```

See Also

Append Procedure, CloseFile Procedure, FileMode Variable, IOResult
Function, Rewrite Procedure

Resident Directive

Syntax

```
exports Name resident;
```

Description

The **resident** directive has no meaning. It exists for backward compatibility with
Delphi 1.

See Also

Exports Directive

Resourcestring Keyword

Syntax

```
resourcestring Name = String; ... ;
```

Description

A **resourcestring** declaration is similar to a **const** declaration for a string,
except that the string value is stored in a string table resource. You use the *Name*
in your code the same way you would use any string-type constant. The compiler
replaces the string constant with a call to **LoadResString** to load the resource at
runtime.

Tips and Tricks

- Use **resourcestring** declarations for any string that can be localized: error
  messages, prompts, and so on. This is especially important if you are writing
  components or other third-party software. You should expect your component to be used in an application that requires localization, and plan ahead.
  Delphi automatically loads the string from the locale-specific resource DLL, if
  one is available.

- If you create a **resourcestring** that is used as a format string (say, for the
  SysUtils.Format function), always include position specifiers. This helps
  the translator who might need to rearrange the order of the parameters when
  translating the string to a foreign language.

- Delphi assigns the resource identifiers automatically. This means you can use resourcestrings in any unit without worrying about conflicts of resource identifiers. It also means that the resource identifiers can change every time you rebuild the project.

- The address of a resourcestring is a PResStringRec pointer, which you can use at runtime to obtain the resource identifier.

Example

```
// Copy a file.
procedure CopyFile(const SourceName, DestName: string);
resourcestring
  CantCopy = 'Cannot copy %0:s to %1:s: %2:s';
var
  SourceStream, DestStream: TFileStream;
begin
  SourceStream := nil;
  DestStream := nil;
  try
    try
      SourceStream := TFileStream.Create(SourceName, fmOpenRead);
      DestStream := TFileStream.Create(DestName, fmCreate);
      SourceStream.CopyFrom(DestStream);
    finally
      SourceStream.Free;
      DestStream.Free;
    end;
  except
    on E: Exception do
      raise Exception.CreateFmt(CantCopy,
                                [SourceName, DestName, E.Message]);
  end;
end;
```

See Also

Const Directive, LoadResString Function, PResStringRec Type, TResStringRec Type

---

Result Variable

Syntax

```
var Result: Function return type;
```

Description

Delphi automatically creates a variable named Result in every function. The variable's type is the return type of the function. The value that Result has when the function returns is the function's return value.

In standard Pascal, a function specifies its return value by assigning to a pseudo-variable whose name is the same as the function's. The Result variable works similarly, but because it behaves as a real variable, you can use it in expressions— something you cannot do with the function name.

Functions return ordinal values, pointers, and small records or sets in EAX, and floating-point values on the FPU stack. Strings, dynamic arrays, Variants, and large records and sets are passed as a hidden var parameter.

Tips and Tricks

- Think of the Result variable as a var parameter. It does not have any valid value when the function begins, so you must initialize it or otherwise ensure that it has a meaningful value.

- Delphi declares the Result variable even if you do not use it. If you try to declare a local variable named Result, the compiler issues an error (Identifier redeclared) message.

Example

```
// Return a reversed copy of S.
function Reverse(const S: string): string;
var
  I, J: Integer;
begin
  I := 1;
  J := Length(S);
  SetLength(Result, J);
  while I <= J do
  begin
    Result[I] := S[J];
    Result[J] := S[I];
    Inc(I);
    Dec(J);
  end;
end;
```

See Also

Function Keyword, Out Directive

Rewrite Procedure

Syntax

```
procedure Rewrite(var F: TextFile);
procedure Rewrite(var F: File);
procedure Rewrite(var F: File; RecordSize: Integer);
```

Description

The Rewrite procedure opens a new file for writing. If the file already exists, its contents are discarded before opening the file. A TextFile is opened for write access only. A binary file is opened for read and write access. Rewrite is not a real procedure.

If the file is a typed binary file (e.g., file of *something*), use the second form of Reset, that is, pass the file variable only. If the file is an untyped binary file (just file), you can optionally supply the second argument to tell Delphi the record size. If you omit the record size, Delphi uses 128 bytes.

Errors

- Rewrite reports I/O error 102 if you fail to call **AssignFile** prior to calling Rewrite.

- If Rewrite cannot open the file, it reports the Windows error code as an I/O error.

Tips and Tricks

- If the file is already open, it is closed first.

- When using an untyped file, it is usually simplest to supply a record size of 1 when calling Rewrite, and then call **BlockRead** and **BlockWrite** to read and write as much data as you want. Alternatively, create a type for **File of Byte**, so you don't need to set the record size in Rewrite.

Example

See Reset for an example.

See Also

Append Procedure, AssignFile Procedure, CloseFile Procedure, IOResult Function, Reset Procedure

---

RmDir Procedure

Syntax

```
procedure RmDir(const Directory: string);
```

Description

RmDir removes a directory. If RmDir cannot delete the directory, it reports the Windows error code as an I/O error. In particular, if the directory is not empty, the error code is Error_Dir_Not_Empty (145). RmDir is not a real procedure.

Example

```
// Delete a directory and its contents.
procedure DestroyDir(const Directory: string);
var
  Path: string;
  Search: TSearchRec;
begin
  Path := IncludeTrailingBackslash(Directory);
  if FindFirst(Path + '*.*', faAnyFile, Search) = 0 then
  try
    repeat
      if (Search.Attr and faDirectory) <> 0 then
        DestroyDir(Path + Search.Name)
      else
        DeleteFile(Path + Search.Name);
    until FindNext(Search) <> 0;
  finally
    FindClose(Search);
  end;
```

```
    RmDir(Path);
end;
```

See Also

ChDir Procedure, GetDir Procedure, IOResult Function, MkDir Procedure

---

Round Function

Syntax

```
function Round(X: Floating-point type): Int64;
```

Description

The Round function rounds off a floating-point value to an integer. Round is not a real function.

Tips and Tricks

- The Round function uses the prevailing round mode in the floating-point control word. By default, Delphi sets this to round-towards-even, also known as "banker's rounding." Numbers are rounded to the closest integer, and numbers that fall exactly between two integers are rounded off to an even number.

- If you change the floating-point control word, you also change the behavior of Round and all functions that depend on Round. If you want to choose a different round-off mode, change the floating-point control word temporarily, as shown below.

```
// Round up towards positive infinity.
function RoundUp(X: Extended): Int64;
const
  RoundUpCW: Word = $1B32; // same as Default8087CW, except round up
var
  OldCW: Word;
begin
  OldCW := Default8087CW;
  try
    Set8087CW(RoundUpCW);
    Result := Round(X);
  finally
    Set8087CW(OldCW);
  end;
end;
```

- If X is an integer, the compiler eliminates the call to Round and simply returns X.

- If X is a Variant, Delphi automatically converts it to a floating-point number and rounds it off.

- The compiler does not accept an Int64 argument, but there is no reason to call Round for Int64.

- If X is infinity or NaN, Round reports runtime error 6 (EInvalidOp).

See Also

Int Function, Trunc Function

RunError Procedure

Syntax

```
procedure RunError(ErrorCode: Integer = 0);
```

Description

The RunError procedure halts the program with an error status. RunError is not a real procedure.

Tips and Tricks

- When a runtime error occurs, if ErrorProc is nil, Delphi calls RunError to print an error message and stop the program. In a GUI application, Delphi shows the error message in a dialog box. In a console application, Delphi prints the error message to the console.

- If you write your own ErrorProc procedure, you can call RunError to halt the program and display a brief error message, but most likely you will want your ErrorProc procedure to do something different, such as raise an exception or print a different error message.

- The ExitProc procedure and units' finalization sections get to run before the program terminates.

- Like Halt, RunError is a quick way to terminate a program, but not usually the right way for a GUI application. Instead, you should close the main form to terminate the application.

Example

```
// Report a run-time error. The address of the call to RunError
// is the error address. The address passed to ErrorProc is
// the address of the call to ErrorProc, which is close to,
// but not quite the same as, the address of the call to
// RunError. You can adjust the value returned by Caller,
// but that would be highly dependent on Delphi's code generator.

procedure ReportError(ErrorCode: Integer);
  function Caller: Pointer;
  asm
    MOV EAX, [ESP]
  end;
type
  TErrorProc = procedure(Code: Integer; Addr: Pointer);
begin
  if ErrorProc <> nil then
    TErrorProc(ErrorProc)(ErrorCode, Caller);
  RunError(ErrorCode);
end;
```

Language
Reference

See Also

ErrorAddr Variable, ErrorProc Variable, ExitCode Variable, ExitProc Variable, Finalization Keyword, Halt Procedure, NoErrMsg Variable, SetInOutRes Procedure

---

SafeCall Directive

Syntax

```
Subroutine declaration; safecall;
```

Description

The **safecall** directive tells the compiler to use the safe calling convention for the function or procedure.

Like **stdcall**, the caller pushes the arguments onto the stack, starting with the rightmost argument. Before the subroutine returns, it pops the arguments from the stack.

If the routine is a function, Delphi passes an extra argument to store its return value. Functions and procedures are converted internally to functions that return an HResult value. If the subroutine is a method, **Self** and the hidden function result parameter are last, so they are pushed first onto the stack.

The compiler automatically wraps the subroutine body in an exception handler, so Delphi catches all exceptions, and the **safecall** method never raises an exception that is visible to the caller. If the subroutine returns normally, Delphi stores zero in the hidden HResult return value. If the **safecall** routine is a method that raises an exception, Delphi calls the object's **SafeCallException** method to map the exception to an HResult value. If the **safecall** routine is a plain function or procedure, Delphi maps every exception to **E_Unexpected**. Schematically, calling a **safecall** routine looks like the following:

```
type
  TSomething = class
    function Divide(I, J: Integer): Integer; safecall;
  end;

// If you write Divide as follows:
function TSomething.Divide(I, J: Integer): Integer;
begin
  Result := I div J;
end;

// Delphi compiles it into something that looks like this:
function TSomething.Divide(I, J: Integer; var Rtn: Integer): HResult;
begin
  try
    Rtn := I div J;
    Result := S_OK;
  except
```

```
        Result := Self.SafeCallException(ExceptObject, ExceptAddr);
      end;
    end;
```

The compiler generates the subroutine call using the **stdcall** calling convention, and also checks the **HResult** that the function returns. If the status indicates an error, Delphi calls the procedure stored in **SafeCallErrorProc**. In other words, calling a **safecall** routine looks like the following:

```
// If you write this:
X := Something.Divide(10, 2);

// Delphi actually calls the method this way:
ErrorCode := Something.Divide(X, 10, 2));
if Failed(ErrorCode) then
begin
  if SafeCallErrorProc <> nil then
    SafeCallErrorProc(ErrorCode, EIP); // EIP=instruction pointer
  ReportError(24);
end;
```

Tips and Tricks

- You must use **safecall** for dual-dispatch interfaces.

- Delphi takes care of the safe calling automatically, so you don't usually need to concern yourself with the details. Write the **safecall** method the way you would any other method.

See Also

CDecl Directive, Function Keyword, Interface Keyword, Pascal Directive, Procedure Keyword, Register Directive, SafeCallErrorProc Variable, StdCall Directive

---

SafeCallErrorProc Variable

Syntax

```
var SafeCallErrorProc: Pointer;

procedure SafeCallError(ErrorCode: Integer; ErrorAddr: Pointer);
begin ... end;
SafeCallErrorProc := @SafeCallError;
```

Description

Delphi calls the procedure that **SafeCallErrorProc** points to when a **safecall** routine returns an **HResult** that indicates an error. If **SafeCallErrorProc** is nil, or if the procedure does not raise an exception (so it returns normally), Delphi reports runtime error 24 (**ESafeCallException**).

Tips and Tricks

- The **ComObj** unit sets this variable to a procedure that tries to get **IErrorInfo** information, and raise an **EOleException** exception using the **ErrorCode** and **IErrorInfo** data.

- When you implement a COM server in Delphi, any Delphi exceptions raised in a `safecall` method are handled by the object's `SafeCallException` method and mapped to an `HResult`. The `SafeCallErrorProc` procedure is called only for runtime errors and non-Delphi exceptions.

See Also

Function Keyword, Interface Keyword, Procedure Keyword, Safecall Directive, TObject Type

---

Seek Procedure

Syntax

```
procedure Seek(var F: File; RecordNumber: LongInt);
```

Description

The `Seek` procedure moves the file position to *RecordNumber*. `Seek` is not a real function.

Tips and Tricks

- You cannot call `Seek` for a `TextFile`. If you must seek to a specific position, use the Windows API:

```
// Seek to a byte position in a text file. See SetInOutRes for the
// same procedure with error-handling. Assume the buffer is empty.
procedure TextSeek(var F: TextFile; Pos: LongInt);
begin
  SetFilePointer(TTextRec(F).Handle, Pos, nil, File_Begin);
end;
```

- The start of the file is record number 0.
- If F is an untyped `File`, the record size is set when you open the file with `Reset` or `Rewrite`.

Example

```
// Rewind a file to the beginning.
Seek(F, 0);

// Jump to the end of a file.
Seek(F, FileSize(F));
```

See Also

File Keyword, FilePos Function, IOResult Function

SeekEof Function

Syntax

```
function SeekEof(var F: TextFile = Input): Boolean
```

Description

SeekEof skips over white space characters and then returns True if the text file is at the end of file or False if there is more text to read. SeekEof is not a real function.

Errors

- If the file F is not open, SeekEof reports runtime error 103.
- The file must have been opened by calling Reset. If the file F was opened by calling Rewrite or Append, SeekEof reports runtime error 104.
- SeekEof is allowed only for text files.

Example

```
var
   CmdLine: string;
begin
   while not SeekEof do
   begin
     ReadLn(CmdLine);
     DoCommand(CmdLine);
   end;
end;
```

See Also

Eof Function, IOResult Function, Reset Procedure, SeekEoln Procedure

---

SeekEoln Function

Syntax

```
function SeekEoln(var F: Text = Input): Boolean
```

Description

SeekEoln skips over white space characters and then returns True if the text file is at the end of file or end of line. Eoln interprets a carriage return (#13) as the end of line. It returns False if there is more text to read and the next character is not a carriage return. SeekEoln is not a real function.

Errors

- If the file F is not open, SeekEoln reports runtime error 103.
- The file must have been opened by calling Reset. If the file F was opened by calling Rewrite or Append, SeekEoln reports runtime error 104.

Example

```
// Read a series of numbers on one line of text.
// Return the sum of those numbers.
function SumLine: Double;
var
  X: Double;
begin
```

```
    Write('Number list: ');
    Result := 0.0;
    while not SeekEoln do
    begin
      Read(X);
      Result := Result + X;
    end;
end;
```

See Also

Eoln Function, IOResult Function, Reset Procedure, SeekEof Procedure,
TextFile Type

Self Variable

Syntax

```
var Self: Class type;
```

Description

In every method, Delphi declares the Self variable as a hidden parameter. In a
method, the value of the Self variable is the object reference. In a class method,
Self is the class reference.

Tips and Tricks

- A constructor can assign a new value to Self, which becomes the value the
  constructor returns. Usually, though, you should override the NewInstance
  method instead of assigning to Self.

- In ordinary methods, assigning to Self has no effect outside the method.

- A method also has an implicit with Self do for the method's body. In other
  words, all of the fields, methods, and properties are in scope, and you can
  refer to them without the explicit reference to Self.

- In the register calling convention, Self is the first argument, so it is passed
  in the EAX register.

- In the pascal calling convention, Self is the last argument, so it is pushed
  last onto the stack, after all other arguments.

- In the cdecl, safecall, and stdcall calling conventions, Self is the last
  argument to a procedure, so it is pushed first onto the stack. If a function
  must return a string, dynamic array, Variant or large record result, a pointer
  to the result is pushed after Self, as a hidden var parameter.

Example

```
procedure TForm1.FormCreate(Sender: TObject);
var
  Button: TButton;
begin
  Button := TButton.Create(Self);
  Button.Parent := Self;
```

```
        // Center the button on the form. Note that Self.ClientWidth
        // and plain ClientWidth are the same property.
        Button.Left := (Self.ClientWidth - Button.Width) div 2;
        Button.Top  := (ClientHeight - Button.Height) div 2;
        Button.Caption := 'Click me!';
        Button.OnClick := ButtonClick;    // or use Self.ButtonClick
    end;
```

See Also

CDecl Directive, Class Keyword, Pascal Directive, Register Directive, Safecall Directive, StdCall Directive, TObject Type

Set Keyword

Syntax

```
type Name = set of Ordinal type;
```

Description

A set type is defined in terms of a base type, which must be an ordinal type: enumeration, integer, or character. Delphi implements the set type using a bit mask, where each member of the base type is assigned a corresponding bit in the set type. Set types are limited to 256 elements, and the ordinal values of the base type are likewise limited to the range 0 to 255.

The set's bit mask is stored as an array of bytes. The ordinal value of a set member determines which bit of which bytes the member occupies: ordinal value 0 is the least significant bit of the first byte, and 255 is the most significant bit of the 32nd byte. Storage for a set does not include any bytes that have no members, but if a byte contains at least one member, the set includes the entire byte. The representation for a set ensures that the same ordinal value always occupies the same bit position, regardless of the set's actual type.

For example, set of 5..10 takes up 2 bytes. The first byte stores members 5..7 at bits 5 to 7 and the next byte stores members 8..10 at bits 0 to 2.

Tips and Tricks

- Sets are often easier to use than bit masks.

- Programmers coming to Delphi from other languages are unaccustomed to Pascal's set operators. Familiarize yourself with the operators described in Chapter 7, *Operators.*

- You can type cast a small set to an integer bit mask. The type cast must use an integer type that is the same size as the set. To type cast a font style, for example, use Byte(Font.Style). Use Word for a set with up to 16 members and LongWord for sets of up to 32 members.

Example

```
    // The Windows API function, GetFileAttributes, returns a bitmask,
    // but using a bitmask is clumsier than using a set. Define a
    // wrapper function that returns the same file attributes as a set.
    type
```

```
TWindowsFileAttribute =
    (wfaReadonly, wfaHidden, wfaSystem, wfaReserved,  wfaDirectory,
     wfaArchive, wfaEncrypted, wfaNormal, wfaTemporary, wfaSparse,
     wfaReparsePoint, wfaCompressed, wfaOffline);
  TWindowsFileAttributes = set of TWindowsFileAttribute;

function FileAttributes(const FileName: string): TWindowsFileAttributes;
var
  Attributes: DWORD;
begin
  Attributes := GetFileAttributes(PChar(FileName));
  if Attributes = $FFFFFFFF then
    Result := []
  else
    Result := TWindowsFileAttributes(Word(Attributes));
end;
...
if wfaDirectory in FileAttributes(Path) then
  RmDir(Path);
...
if ([wfaHidden,wfaSystem] * FileAttributes(Path)) <> [] then
  ShowMessage(Path + ' is a system file');
```

See Also

In Keyword, Type Keyword

Set8087CW Procedure

Syntax

```
procedure Set8087CW(ControlWord: Word);
```

Description

The Set8087CW procedure sets the floating-point control word and saves the value of the ControlWord variable in Default8087CW. Set8087CW is a real procedure.

Tips and Tricks

- See the Intel architecture manuals to learn more about the floating-point control word.

- Common uses for Set8087CW are to change the floating-point precision, exception mask, and rounding mode. Make sure you do not reduce the floating-point precision if you are using the Comp or Currency types.

Example

```
type
  TRoundMode = (rmNearest, rmDown, rmUp, rmZero);
  TPrecisionMode = (pmSingle, pmReserved, pmDouble, pmExtended);
  TExceptionMask = (emInvalid, emDenormalized, emZeroDivide,
                    emOverflow, emUnderflow, emPrecision);
  TExceptionMasks = set of TExceptionMask;

  TFpuControl = record
```

```
      RoundMode: TRoundMode;
      Precision: TPrecisionMode;
      ExceptionMask: TExceptionMasks;
   end;
const
  RoundShift = 10;
  PrecisionShift = 8;

// Set the floating-point control word in a structured manner.
procedure SetFpuCW(const FpuCW: TFpuControl);
var
  CW: Word;
begin
  CW := Byte(FpuCW.ExceptionMask);
  CW := CW or (Ord(FpuCW.Precision) shl PrecisionShift);
  CW := CW or (Ord(FpuCW.RoundMode) shl RoundShift);
  Set8087CW(CW);
end;
```

See Also

Comp Type, Currency Type, Default8087CW Variable, Extended Type, Int Function, Round Function, Trunc Function

---

SetInOutRes Procedure

Syntax

```
procedure SetInOutRes(Code: Integer);
```

Description

The SetInOutRes procedure sets the I/O error code to Code. Calling IOResult returns this error code and then resets the code to zero.

Tips and Tricks

- Each thread keeps its own I/O error code. Be sure to call SetInOutRes in the context of the correct thread.

- Delphi reserves error codes 100–106 for its own I/O errors. (See IOResult for a description of these error codes.) For all other errors, use the standard Windows error codes.

- Calling SetInOutRes does not raise the runtime error—it only stores the error code. If you want to report the I/O error, you must do that separately. See ErrorProc and RunError for examples of how to do this.

Example

```
// Implement Seek on a text file.
procedure TextSeek(var F: TextFile; Position: Integer);
var
  Handle: Integer;
  NewPosition: DWORD;
begin
  // A TextFile is actually a record whose first value is a handle.
```

```
Handle := PInteger(@F)^;
NewPosition := SetFilePointer(Handle, Position, nil, File_Begin);
if NewPosition = $FFFFFFFF then
begin
  SetInOutRes(GetLastError);
  ReportError(0); // zero means I/O error
end;
end;
```

See Also

ErrorProc Variable, File Keyword, IOResult Function, RunError Procedure, TextFile Type

---

SetLength Procedure

Syntax

```
procedure SetLength(var S: string; Length: Integer);
procedure SetLength(var A: Array type; Length: Integer);
procedure SetLength(var A: Array type; Len1: Integer; Len2...);
```

Description

The SetLength procedure changes the size of a string or dynamic array. If the new length is longer than the current length, the extra space is not initialized, unless the array contains strings, interfaces, other dynamic arrays, or Variants, in which case they are properly initialized.

SetLength is not a real procedure.

Tips and Tricks

- The Length is in logical units (array elements, characters). In particular, if S is a WideString, the Length is in characters, not bytes.

- If the string or array has multiple references, SetLength always creates a unique instance and sets its length, even if the new length is the same as the current length.

- If A is a multidimensional dynamic array, you can pass one or more lengths to SetLength. The first length is for the leftmost dimension, and subsequent lengths initialize successive dimensions. The default length is zero for any dimension that you omit from SetLength.

Example

```
// Return a string of length Length, filled with repetitions
// of the given character.
function FillString(Length: Integer; Fill: Char): string;
begin
  SetLength(Result, Length);
  FillChar(Result[1], Length, Fill);
end;

// Create a square identity matrix of size N.
type
```

```
  TIntMatrix = array of array of integer;
procedure SetIdentityMatrix(var M: TIntMatrix; N: Integer);
var
  I, J: Integer;
begin
  SetLength(M, N, N);
  for I := 0 to N-1 do
  begin
    for J := 0 to N-1 do
      M[I, J] := 0;
    M[I, I] := 1;
  end;
end;
```

See Also

AnsiString Type, Array Keyword, SetString Procedure, ShortString Type, String Keyword, Type Keyword, UniqueString Procedure, WideString Type

---

SetMemoryManager Procedure

Syntax

```
procedure SetMemoryManager(const NewMgr: TMemoryManager);
```

Description

SetMemoryManager installs a new memory manager to handle dynamic memory allocations from GetMem, New, object creation, and all other needs for dynamic memory, including long strings, dynamic arrays, and Variants.

SetMemoryManager is a real procedure.

Tips and Tricks

- When setting a new memory manager, the unit that calls SetMemoryManager must be the first unit in the project. If not, the first unit most likely allocates memory from Delphi's default memory manager, but after your memory manager is installed, the new manager will be the one to free the memory even though it did not allocate that memory.

- For the same reason, you should not save and restore the original memory manager. Delphi allocates memory at unpredictable times, and you cannot rely on the order of initializing and finalizing units to ensure that all memory allocated with one manager will be freed by the same manager. The only safe approach is to use one memory manager exclusively.

- If you are using DLLs, you need to be careful about memory allocated by a DLL that is not freed before the DLL is unloaded. This can easily happen if you pass long strings, dynamic arrays, or Variants across DLL boundaries. The solution is to direct all dynamic memory requests to a separate DLL. Delphi's ShareMem unit does this with *borlndmm.dll,* and you can do the same with your custom memory manager. See Chapter 2 for more information and examples.

Example

```
// The debugging memory manager allocates a guard word around
// each allocated chunk of memory. If a guard word is overwritten,
// you know you have a problem. Allocated and free blocks use
// different guard words, to check for double-frees. When a block is
// freed, its contents are overwritten with FreeFill, which helps catch
// errors where the program refers to a freed block.
const
  AllocatedGuard = $0AC0ACDC;
  FreeGuard      = $0FC0FCEE;
  FreeFill       = $42FE;
  GuardSize      = SizeOf(LongInt);
  MaxArraySize   = MaxInt div 4 - 1;
type
  TIntegerArray = array[0..MaxArraySize] of LongInt;
  PIntegerArray = ^TIntegerArray;

// Round up Size to a multiple of the guard word size
function RoundUpSize(Size: Integer): Integer;
begin
  Result := (Size + GuardSize - 1) div GuardSize * GuardSize
end;

procedure SetDebugManager;
var
  Mgr: TMemoryManager;
begin
  Mgr.GetMem := DebugGet;
  Mgr.FreeMem := DebugFree;
  Mgr.ReallocMem := DebugRealloc;
  SetMemoryManager(Mgr);
end;
```

See Also

FreeMemory Function, GetMemory Function, GetMemoryManager Procedure,
IsMemoryManagerSet Function, ReallocMemory Function, SysFreeMem
Function, SysGetMem Function, SysReallocMem Function, TMemoryManager
Type

SetRaiseList Function

Syntax

```
procedure SetRaiseList(RaiseList: Pointer);
```

Description

SetRaiseList sets the pointer to the exception list that RaiseList returns. See
the RaiseList function for the format of the raise list data.

SetRaiseList is a real procedure.

- Each thread maintains its own raise list.

- There is rarely any reason to call this function. Delphi automatically creates the raise list when an exception is raised.

See Also

Raise Keyword, RaiseList Function

SetString Procedure

Syntax

```
procedure SetString(var Str: string; Buffer: PChar; Length: Integer);
```

Description

The SetString procedure sets the length of Str to Length, then copies Length characters from Buffer to the string. SetString is not a real procedure.

Tips and Tricks

- If Str is a long string, SetString always allocates a new string, so Str is set to a unique string.

- Str can be a ShortString, in which case the Length must be less than 256.

- Buffer can be nil, in which case the string length is set, but its contents are left uninitialized. In the case of a ShortString, the previous string contents are left untouched.

Example

```
// Given an instance or module handle, return the corresponding
// filename. Note that Delphi will automatically convert
// a PChar to a string, but it must scan the PChar to learn
// its length. GetModuleFileName returns the length, so there is
// no need to let Delphi rescan the string.
function GetModuleName(Instance: THandle): string;
var
  Len: Integer;
  Buffer: array[0..MAX_PATH] of Char;
begin
  Len := GetModuleFileName(HInstance, Buffer, SizeOf(Buffer));
  SetString(Result, Buffer, Len);
end;
```

See Also

AnsiString Type, SetLength Procedure, ShortString Type, String Keyword, WideString Type

SetTextBuf Procedure

Syntax

```
procedure SetTextBuf(var F: TextFile; var Buffer);
procedure SetTextBuf(var F: TextFile; var Buffer; Size: Integer);
```

Description

The SetTextBuf procedure sets a new text buffer to use for future I/O. Buffer is the new file buffer, and Size is its size in bytes. If Size is omitted, SetTextBuf uses SizeOf(Buffer).

Binary files do not have buffers, so SetTextBuf works only for the TextFile type.

You can set the text buffer for any open TextFile. Do not set the buffer after you have already performed I/O, or you may lose the contents of the old buffer. If the buffer is dynamically allocated, do not free the buffer until after you have closed the file.

SetTextBuf is not a real procedure.

Tips and Tricks

Every TextFile has a small built-in buffer. For console I/O and other ordinary uses, the small buffer is adequate. If you find that file I/O is a performance bottleneck, try using a larger buffer.

Example

```
// Read a list of numbers from a file and return the sum.
function SumFile(const FileName: string): Double;
var
  Number: Double;
  F: TextFile;
  Buffer: array[0..8191] of Char;
begin
  Result := 0.0;
  AssignFile(F, FileName);
  Reset(F);
  try
    SetTextBuf(F, Buffer);
    while not SeekEof(F) do
    begin
      ReadLn(F, Number);
      Result := Result + Number;
    end;
  finally
    CloseFile(F);
  end;
end;
```

See Also

IOResult Function, Reset Procedure, Rewrite Procedure, TextFile Type

---

Shl Keyword

Syntax

```
Value shl Bits
```

Description

The shl operator performs a left shift of an integer *Value* by *Bits* bit positions. Vacated bits are filled in on the right with zero bits.

The *Bits* operand is interpreted as an unsigned integer, modulo the size of the *Value*. That is, if *Value* is a LongInt, *Bits* is interpreted modulo 32, and if *Value* has type Int64, *Bits* is interpreted modulo 64. In other words, only the least significant few bits of *Bits* are used to determine the shift amount.

Tips and Tricks

- Remember that the size of the Integer and Cardinal types can change with new versions of Delphi. Use the fixed-size types if you need a specific number of bits, such as 32 for LongInt and LongWord.

- Do not use the shl operator instead of multiplying by a power of two. If you mean multiplication, you should write multiplication. The shl operator does not check for overflow errors. Let Delphi's compiler decide the best instruction to use.

Example

```
// Measure the size of an integer, which can vary between versions.
function BitsPerInteger: Integer;
var
  Test: Integer;
begin
  Test := 1;
  Result := 0;
  while Test <> 0 do
  begin
    Test := Test shl 1;
    Inc(Result);
  end;
end;
```

See Also

And Keyword, Not Keyword, Or Keyword, Shr Keyword, Xor Keyword

ShortInt Type

Syntax

```
type ShortInt = -128..127;
```

Description

The ShortInt type defines an 8-bit signed integer.

Tips and Tricks

- C, C++, and Java programmers must take care because ShortInt is not equivalent to the short type in these other languages. The short type is more closely akin to Delphi's SmallInt type.

- See Integer for more information about integer types.

See Also

Byte Type, Integer Type

ShortString Type

Syntax

```
type ShortString;
type Name = string[Constant];
```

Description

A ShortString is a counted string with a maximum length of 255 characters. You can declare a short string with the ShortString type or with the string keyword and a maximum length. The maximum length must be a constant expression in the range 0 to 255. If you use the $H or $LongStrings compiler directive, you can change a plain use of the string keyword to mean ShortString instead of the default AnsiString.

Delphi stores a short string as a character array with a reserved byte to store the string's length. If you take the address of a short string, Delphi returns a pointer to the length byte.

Tips and Tricks

- As with all strings in Delphi, string indices start at 1, but you can also refer to element 0 of a short string, which returns the length, as a Char. Instead of referring to the zeroth element, though, you should use the Length function and SetLength procedure to get or set the string's length.

- Most strings in new Delphi programs use the more convenient AnsiString type, but short strings are useful for reading and writing data. See the File keyword for an example.

See Also

AnsiString Type, File Keyword, Length Function, SetLength Procedure, SetString Procedure, String Keyword, WideString Type, $H Compiler Directive, $LongStrings Compiler Directive

---

Shr Keyword

Syntax

```
Value shr Bits
```

Description

The shr operator performs a right shift of an integer *Value* by *Bits* bit positions. Vacated bits are filled in on the left with zero bits.

The *Bits* operand is interpreted as an unsigned integer modulo the size of the *Value*. That is, if *Value* is a LongInt, *Bits* is interpreted modulo 32, and if *Value* has type Int64, *Bits* is interpreted modulo 64. In other words, only the least significant few bits of *Bits* are used to determine the shift amount.

Tips and Tricks

- Remember that the size of the Integer and Cardinal types can change with new versions of Delphi. Use the fixed-size types if you need a specific number of bits, such as 32 for LongInt and LongWord.

- Do not use the shr operator instead of dividing by a power of two. If you mean division, you should write division. The shr operator does not check for range errors and does not propagate the sign bit. Let Delphi's compiler decide the best instruction to use.

Example

```
// Measure the size of an integer, which can vary between versions.
function BitsPerInteger: Integer;
var
  Test: Integer;
begin
  Test := -1;
  Result := 0;
  while Test <> 0 do
  begin
    Test := Test shr 1;
    Inc(Result);
  end;
end;
```

See Also

And Keyword, Not Keyword, Or Keyword, Shl Keyword, Xor Keyword

---

Sin Function

Syntax

```
function Sin(Number: Floating-point type): Extended;
```

Description

The Sin function computes and returns the sine of Number, which is an angle in radians. The Sin function is built-in.

Tips and Tricks

- Delphi automatically converts Integer and Variant arguments to floating point. To convert an Int64 argument to floating point, add 0.0.

- If Number is a signaling NaN, positive infinity, or negative infinity, Delphi raises runtime error 6 (EInvalidOp).

- If Number is a quiet NaN, the result is Number.

See Also

ArcTan Function, Cos Function

Single Type

Syntax

```
type Single;
```

Description

The Single type is an IEEE standard floating-point type that uses 4 bytes to store a sign bit, an 8-bit exponent, and a 23-bit mantissa. The mantissa is usually normalized, that is, it has an implicit 1 bit before the most significant bit. If the exponent is zero, however, the mantissa is denormalized—without the implicit 1 bit. Thus, the numerical value of 0.0 is represented by all zero bits. An exponent of all 1 bits represents infinity (mantissa is zero) or not-a-number (mantissa is not zero).

The limits of Single are roughly 1.18×10^{-38} to 3.40×10^{38}, with about seven decimal digits of precision. Table 5-3 shows the detailed format of finite and special Single values.

Table 5-3: Format of Single Floating-Point Numbers

Numeric class	Sign	Exponent	Mantissa
Positive			
Normalized	0	0...1 to 1...10	0...0 to 1...1
Denormalized	0	0...0	0...1 to 1...1
Zero	0	0...0	0...0
Infinity	0	1...1	0...0
Signaling NaN	0	1...1	0...1 to 01...1
Quiet NaN	0	1...1	1...0 to 1...1
Negative			
Normalized	1	0...1 to 1...10	0...0 to 1...1
Denormalized	1	0...0	0...1 to 1...1
Zero	1	0...0	0...0
Infinity	1	1...1	0...0
Signaling NaN	1	1...1	0...1 to 01...1
Quiet NaN	1	1...1	1...0 to 1...1

Tips and Tricks

- The Single type corresponds to the float type in Java, C, and C++.

- Single is usually used when memory is at a premium. It does not usually offer a performance advantage over Double, and it suffers from a limited range and restricted precision.

- Refer to the Intel architecture manuals (such as the *Pentium Developer's Manual*, volume 3, *Architecture and Programming Manual*) or IEEE standard 754 for more information about infinity and NaN (not a number). In Delphi, use of a signaling NaN raises runtime error 6 (EInvalidOp).

Example

```
type
  TSingle = packed record
    case Integer of
    0: (Float: Single;);
    1: (Bytes: array[0..3] of Byte;);
    2: (Words: array[0..1] of Word;);
    3: (LongWords: array[0..0] of LongWord;);
  end;
  TFloatClass = (fcPosNorm, fcNegNorm, fcPosDenorm, fcNegDenorm,
            fcPosZero, fcNegZero, fcPosInf, fcNegInf, fcQNaN, fcSNan);

// Return the class of a floating-point number: finite, infinity,
// not-a-number; also positive or negative, normalized or denormalized.
// Determine the class by examining the exponent, sign bit,
// and mantissa separately.
function fp_class(X: Single): TFloatClass; overload;
var
  XParts: TSingle absolute X;
  Negative: Boolean;
  Exponent: Byte;
  Mantissa: LongInt;
begin
  Negative := (XParts.LongWords[0] and $80000000) <> 0;
  Exponent := (XParts.LongWords[0] and $7F800000) shr 23;
  Mantissa :=  XParts.LongWords[0] and $007FFFFF;

  // The first three cases can be positive or negative.
  // Assume positive, and test the sign bit later.
  if (Mantissa = 0) and (Exponent = 0) then
    // Mantissa and exponent are both zero, so the number is zero.
    Result := fcPosZero
  else if Exponent = 0 then
    // If the exponent is zero, but the mantissa is not,
    // the number is finite but denormalized.
    Result := fcPosDenorm
  else if Exponent <> $FF then
    // Otherwise, if the exponent is not all 1, the number is normalized.
    Result := fcPosNorm
  else if Mantissa = 0 then
    // Exponent is all 1, and mantissa is all 0 means infinity.
    Result := fcPosInf

  else
  begin
```

```
    // Exponent is all 1, and mantissa is non-zero, so the value
    // is not a number. Test for quiet or signaling NaN.
    if (Mantissa and $400000) <> 0 then
      Result := fcQNaN
    else
      Result := fcSNaN;
    Exit; // Do not distinguish negative NaNs.
  end;

  if Negative then
    Inc(Result);
end;
```

See Also

Double Type, Extended Type

SizeOf Function

Syntax

```
function SizeOf(const Value or type): Integer;
```

Description

The SizeOf function returns the number of bytes that *Value or type* occupies, which can be an expression or a type identifier. SizeOf is not a real function.

Tips and Tricks

- A common use for SizeOf is when calling GetMem, so you know how much memory to request.

- The size of a pointer, object reference, or class reference is 4 because a pointer fits into 4 bytes (but future versions of Delphi might require more memory to store a pointer).

- To learn the number of bytes an object takes up, call the class's InstanceSize method.

Example

```
var
  P: ^Integer;
begin
  // Allocate memory for 32 integers.
  GetMem(P, 32 * SizeOf(Integer)); /
```

See Also

GetMem Procedure, Length Function, TObject Type, Type Keyword

---

Slice Function

Syntax

```
function Slice(var A: array; Count: Integer): array;
```

Description

Slice returns the first Count elements of the array A as an argument for an open array parameter. The only time you can use Slice is when passing an array to a subroutine. The Slice function is a convenient way to use a dynamically allocated static array and still keep the advantages of Delphi arrays.

Slice is not a real function.

Example

```
// A drawing package stores a polygon with up to MAX_POINTS points.
// A TPolygon record stores the array of vertices and the number
// of points in the polygon. DrawPolygon draws the polygon on a canvas.
type
  TPolygon = record
    NumPoints: 0..MaxInt;
    Points: array[1..MAX_POINTS] of TPoint;
    end;
procedure DrawPolygon(Canvas: TCanvas; const Polygon: TPolygon);
begin
  Canvas.Polygon(Slice(Polygon.Points, Polygon.NumPoints));
end;
```

See Also

Array Keyword, Copy Function, Type Keyword

SmallInt Type

Syntax

```
type SmallInt = -32768..32767
```

Description

The SmallInt type is a signed, 16-bit integer.

See Integer for more information about integer types.

See Also

Integer Type, Word Type

Sqr Function

Syntax

```
function Sqr(X: Floating-point type): Extended;
function Sqr(X: Integer): Integer;
function Sqr(X: Int64): Int64;
```

Description

The Sqr function returns the square of its argument. It is not a real function, but is expanded inline by the compiler.

Tips and Tricks

- If Number is negative or positive infinity, the result is positive infinity.
- If Number is negative zero, the result is positive zero.
- If a floating-point result is too large, Delphi raises runtime error 8 (EOverflow).
- If an integer result is too large, Delphi 5 truncates the answer without checking for integer overflow.
- If Number is a signaling NaN, Delphi raises runtime error 6 (EInvalidOp).
- If Number is a quiet NaN, the result is Number.

Example

```
function Hypotenuse(X, Y: Double): Double;
begin
  Result := Sqrt(Sqr(X) + Sqr(Y));
end;
```

See Also

Extended Type, Integer Type, Sqrt Function

Sqrt Function

Syntax

```
function Sqrt(Number: Floating-point type): Extended;
```

Description

The Sqrt function returns the positive square root of its argument. It is not a real function, but is expanded inline by the compiler.

Tips and Tricks

- Delphi automatically converts Integer and Variant arguments to floating point. To convert an Int64 argument to floating point, add 0.0.
- If Number is positive infinity, the result is positive infinity.
- If Number is negative zero, the result is negative zero.
- If Number is negative non-zero, negative infinity, or a signaling NaN, Delphi raises runtime error 6 (EInvalidOp).
- If Number is a quiet NaN, the result is Number.

Example

```
function Hypotenuse(X, Y: Double): Double;
begin
  Result := Sqrt(Sqr(X) + Sqr(Y));
end;
```

See Also

Extended Type, Sqr Function

StdCall Directive

Syntax

```
Subroutine declaration; stdcall;
```

Description

The `stdcall` directive uses the Windows standard calling convention: arguments are pushed onto the stack, starting with the rightmost argument. The subroutine is responsible for popping the arguments from the stack.

Functions return ordinal values, pointers, and small records or sets in `EAX` and floating-point values on the FPU stack. Strings, dynamic arrays, `Variants`, and large records and sets are passed as a hidden `var` parameter. This hidden parameter is the last parameter, so it is pushed first onto the stack. If the subroutine is a method, `Self` is pushed just before the function's `var` result (if one is needed).

Tips and Tricks

- Use `stdcall` for subroutines you export from a DLL that will be called by other languages.

- Use `stdcall` for Windows callback functions.

Example

```
// Make a list of all the top-level windows.
function Callback(Handle: HWND; List: TStrings): LongBool; stdcall;
var
  Caption: array[0..256] of Char;
  Len: Integer;
  Text: string;
begin
  Len := GetWindowText(Handle, Caption, SizeOf(Caption)-1);
  SetString(Text, Caption, Len);
  List.Add(Text);
  Result := True;
end;
...
EnumWindows(@Callback, LParam(ListBox1.Items));
```

See Also

CDecl Directive, Function Keyword, Pascal Directive, Procedure Keyword, Register Directive, SafeCall Directive

Stored Directive

Syntax

```
property Name: Type Directives... stored Boolean;
```

Description

The `stored` directive takes a Boolean value: a method that returns a Boolean result, a Boolean-type field reference, or a constant expression of Boolean type.

The property's RTTI records the field offset, method reference, or constant value, and Delphi's IDE uses this information to decide whether to omit the property from the *.dfm* file.

The IDE calls the method, checks the field's value, or uses the constant Boolean value, and if the value is `False`, the property is not saved to the *.dfm* file. If the stored value is `True`, the default behavior occurs, namely, that the property is stored if its value is different from the default value.

Tips and Tricks

- The **stored** directive is often misunderstood. Setting **stored** to `True` does not force Delphi to store the property value in the *.dfm* file. `True` is the default value of the **stored** directive. Instead, all you can do is omit the property from the *.dfm* file by setting **stored** to `False`.

- You can use **stored** with properties at any access level, but it has meaning only for published properties.

- If you use a method name, the method can be static or virtual, but not dynamic or a message handler.

- A field reference can be a field name, a record member, or an array element with a constant index. The field reference must have a Boolean type.

Example

Delphi's `TFont` class lets you specify a font's size in points or pixels. The `Height` property is the font's height in pixels, and the `Size` property is the font's size in points. Only the `Height` is stored in the *.dfm* file, and the `Size` is calculated from the `Height`. Thus, the `Size` property uses **stored** `False`, as you can see in the example:

```
type
  TFont = class(TGraphicsObject)
  ...
  published
    property Charset: TFontCharset read GetCharset write SetCharset;
    property Color: TColor read FColor write SetColor;
    property Height: Integer read GetHeight write SetHeight;
    property Name: TFontName read GetName write SetName;
    property Pitch: TFontPitch read GetPitch write SetPitch
        default fpDefault;
    property Size: Integer read GetSize write SetSize stored False;
    property Style: TFontStyles read GetStyle write SetStyle;
  end;
```

See Also

Default Directive, NoDefault Directive, Property Keyword, Published Directive

---

Str Procedure

Syntax

```
procedure Str(const Value; var S: string);
```

```
procedure Str(const Value:Width; var S: string);
procedure Str(const Value:Width:Precision; var S: string);
```

Description

The Str procedure formats a number as a string, similar to Write, except that it "writes" to the string S. The Value can be any numeric or Boolean expression. The string S can be a long string, short string, or zero-based character array. Str is not a real procedure.

Width and Precision can be any integer expressions. Width specifies the minimum size of the string representation of Value, and Precision specifies the number of places after the decimal point of a floating-point number.

Str uses as many characters as it needs, so Width is just the suggested minimum width. If the number requires fewer than Width characters, Str pads the string on the left with blanks. If you do not supply a Width, Delphi uses 1 as the minimum width for integers and it prints floating-point numbers as 26 characters in the following form:

```
'-1.12345678901234567E+1234'
```

If the Value is a floating-point number, Str reduces the number of decimal places to fit the value into a string that uses at most Width characters. Str always uses at least one digit after the decimal place, though. You can also supply a Precision, which tells Str how many decimal places to use after the decimal point. If you supply a Precision, Str uses fixed-point notation instead of exponential notation.

Tips and Tricks

- The SysUtils unit has several functions that provide more flexibility than Str.

- If the ShortString is too short to represent the entirety of Value, Str stops when it fills the string and does not report an error.

Example

```
procedure ShowInfo;
var
  S: string;
begin
  Str(List.Count, S);
  ShowMessage(S + ' items in the list.');
end;
```

See Also

String Type, Val Procedure, Write Procedure

String Keyword

Syntax

```
type string;
type Name = string[Constant];
```

Description

The `string` keyword represents the string type, which is either `AnsiString` or `ShortString`, depending on its use and the `$H` or `$LongStrings` compiler directive.

Without a maximum length in square brackets, `string` is the same as `AnsiString` (unless you use the `$H` or `$LongStrings` compiler directive). With a maximum length, `string` is a short string type. The maximum string length must be in the range 0 to 255.

See `AnsiString` and `ShortString` for more details.

See Also

AnsiChar Type, AnsiString Type, Char Type, Length Function, OleStrToString Function, OleStrToStrVar Procedure, PChar Type, PWideChar Type, SetLength Procedure, SetString Procedure, ShortString Type, StringToOleStr Function, StringToWideChar Function, WideChar Type, WideCharLenToString Function, WideCharLenToStrVar Procedure, WideCharToString Function, WideCharToStrVar Procedure, WideString Type, $H Compiler Directive, $LongStrings Compiler Directive

---

StringOfChar Function

Syntax

```
function StringOfChar(Ch: Char; Count: Integer): string;
```

Description

`StringOfChar` creates and returns a string that contains `Count` occurrences of the character `Ch`. `StringOfChar` is not a real function.

If `Count` ≤ 0, `StringOfChar` returns an empty string.

See Also

Char Type, FillChar Procedure, String Keyword

StringToOleStr Function

Syntax

```
function StringToOleStr(const Str: string): PWideChar;
```

Description

The `StringToOleStr` function converts a string to a wide string suitable for passing to OLE and COM routines.

`StringToOleStr` is a real function.

Tips and Tricks

The wide string is dynamically allocated, and you must make sure you free it by calling the Windows API function `SysFreeString`.

```
procedure Demo;
var
  OleStr: PWideChar;
begin
  OleStr := StringToOleStr(S);
  try
    SomeOLEProcedure(OleStr);
  finally
    SysFreeString(OleStr);
  end;
end;
```

See Also

OleStrToString Function, OleStrToStrVar Procedure, PWideChar Type, String
Keyword, StringToWideChar Function, WideChar Type, WideCharLenToString
Function, WideCharLenToStrVar Procedure, WideCharToString Function,
WideCharToStrVar Procedure, WideString Type

StringToWideChar Function

Syntax

```
function StringToWideChar(const Str: string; Result: PWideChar;
                          Size: Integer): PWideChar;
```

Description

The StringToWideChar function converts Str to a wide string. It copies at most
Size-1 characters from Str to Result, appending #0 to the result string. It
returns a pointer to Result.

StringToWideChar is a real function.

Example

```
procedure Demo;
var
  OleStr: PWideChar;
begin
  GetMem(OleStr, (Length(S)+1) * SizeOf(WideChar));
  try
    StringToWideChar(S, OleStr, Length(S)+1);
    SomeOLEProcedure(OleStr);
  finally
    FreeMem(OleStr);
  end;
end;
```

See Also

OleStrToString Function, OleStrToStrVar Procedure, PWideChar Type, String
Keyword, WideChar Type, WideCharLenToString Function,
WideCharLenToStrVar Procedure, WideCharToString Function,
WideCharToStrVar Procedure, WideString Type

Succ Function

Syntax

```
function Succ(const Value): Ordinal type;
```

Description

The Succ function returns the successor of an ordinal value, usually an enumerated value. That is, it returns the enumerated value whose ordinal value is one more than *Value*. Succ is not a real function.

Tips and Tricks

- Inc, Succ, and addition by one have similar performance, so choose the one that you find most clear and easy to read.

- Calling Succ(High(*SomeType*)) raises runtime error 4 (ERangeError). Without overflow checking, though, Succ returns a value with the desired ordinal value, even though that value is not valid for the type.

Example

```
type TDay =
  (Sunday, Monday, Tuesday, Wednesday, Thursday, Friday, Saturday);
var
  Day: TDay;
begin
  Day := Succ(Day);
  ...
```

See Also

Dec Procedure, High Function, Inc Procedure, Low Function, Pred Function, $OverflowChecks Compiler Directive, $Q Compiler Directive

---

Swap Function

Syntax

```
function Swap(Value: Integer): Integer;
```

Description

The Swap function swaps the bytes in the least significant word of Value. It leaves the high order 16 bits alone. If Value is of type Int64, Swap silently ignores the most significant 32 bits, leaves the next most significant 16 bits alone, and performs the swap of the low order 16 bits. It returns the resulting 32-bit value (having discarded completely the original high-order 32 bits).

Swap is not a real function, but is expanded inline.

Tips and Tricks

- This function is provided for backward compatibility. It has little use in its current incarnation.

- Swapping bytes is a common activity when moving files or data through a network. Intel processors use little-endian order for data (least significant bytes at higher addresses), and some other processors use big-endian order (most significant bytes at higher addresses).

Example

```
// Reverse the bytes in a 32-bit integer, suitable for moving
// a LongWord between Intel and Sun, for example.
function Swap32(Value: LongWord): LongWord;
begin
  Result := Swap(Value shr 16) or (Swap(Value) shl 16);
end;

// If you really need to reverse the bytes in a 32-bit integer,
// say to convert bit-endian to little-endian, don't use Swap
// at all, but use the BSWAP instruction.
function FastSwap(Value: LongWord): LongWord; register; overload;
asm
  bswap eax
end;

// To swap an Int64 value, the argument is passed on the stack,
// but the return value is in EAX:EDX.
function FastSwap(Value: Int64): Int64; register; overload;
asm
  mov edx, [esp+8]
  bswap edx
  mov eax, [esp+12]
  bswap eax
end;
```

See Also

Hi Function, Lo Function, Shl Keyword, Shr Keyword

SysFreeMem Function

Syntax

```
function SysFreeMem(P: Pointer): Integer;
```

Description

SysFreeMem uses Delphi's built-in memory manager to free the memory that P points to. It returns zero for success and a non-zero error code if P is invalid or nil.

SysFreeMem is a real function.

Tips and Tricks

- SysFreeMem is useful if you are writing your own memory manager as a filter and want to call Delphi's memory manager from your custom memory manager.

- If you are not implementing a memory manager, use `Dispose` or `FreeMem`, not `SysFreeMem`, to free memory.

- `FreeMem` and `Dispose` already check for a `nil` pointer, so `SysFreeMem` doesn't have to.

Example

```
// See SetMemoryManager for an explanation of this memory manager.

// Return True if the memory pointed to by PArray is a valid heap block
// and the guard words are intact. Return false for any error.
function GuardsAreOkay(PArray: PIntegerArray; Fill: Boolean): Boolean;
const
  DelphiInUseFlag = 2;
  MemMgrFlags = 7;
var
  Size: LongWord;
begin
  // First get the block size. The size is the long word before
  // the start of the block. Delphi sets the size and stores flags
  // in the 3 LSBits. Delphi's format is subject to change in future
  // releases. The middle bit is set for an allocated block.
  PArray := PIntegerArray(PChar(PArray) - SizeOf(Size));
  Size := PArray[0];
  PArray := PIntegerArray(PChar(PArray) + SizeOf(Size));

  if (Size and DelphiInUseFlag) <> DelphiInUseFlag then
  begin
    Result := False;
    Exit;
  end;

  // Remove Delphi's flag from the size, and subtract the size of
  // Delphi's header.
  Size := Size and not MemMgrFlags - SizeOf(Size);

  // Check the guard words.
  if PArray[0] <> AllocatedGuard then
    Result := False

  // The size includes the 2 guard words, so the last guard word
  // is at the size-1 index.
  else if PArray[Size div GuardSize - 1] <> AllocatedGuard then
    Result := False

  else
  begin
    // If we made it this far, the block looks okay.
    Result := True;

    // If the caller requests it (DebugFree does), fill the entire
    // block with the special FreeFill bit pattern, which helps
    // detect problems caused by referring to freed memory.
```

```
  if Fill then
    FillChar(PArray^, Size div 2, FreeFill);

  // Change the guard words to FreeGuard even if the caller doesn't
  // want the entire block filled.
  PArray[0] := FreeGuard;
  PArray[Size div GuardSize - 1] := FreeGuard;
  end;
end;

// Return zero for success, non-zero for failure.
function DebugFree(Mem: Pointer): Integer;
var
  PArray: PIntegerArray;
begin
  // Get the pointer to the true start of the memory block.
  PArray := PIntegerArray(PChar(Mem) - GuardSize);

  if not GuardsAreOkay(PArray, True) then
    Result := 1
  else
    Result := SysFreeMem(PArray);
end;
```

See Also

Dispose Procedure, FreeMem Procedure, FreeMemory Function,
GetMemoryManager Procedure, IsMemoryManagerSet Function, IsMultiThread
Variable, SetMemoryManager Procedure, SysGetMem Function,
SysReallocMem Function, TMemoryManager Type

SysGetMem Function

Syntax

```
function SysGetMem(Size: Integer): Pointer;
```

Description

SysGetMem allocates Size bytes of memory using Delphi's built-in memory
manager. It returns a pointer to the newly allocated memory or nil for an error.
The memory is not initialized.

SysGetMem is a real function.

Tips and Tricks

- If you write your own memory manager, you can call SysGetMem to perform
  the memory allocation.

- If you are not implementing a new memory manager, use New or GetMem, not
  SysGetMem, to allocate memory.

Example

```
// See SetMemoryManager for an explanation of this memory manager.

// Allocate Size bytes and return a pointer to the new memory.
// Return nil for errors, and Delphi will raise an exception.
// Allocate extra bytes for debugging.
function DebugGet(Size: Integer): Pointer;
var
  PArray: PIntegerArray;
begin
  Size := RoundUpSize(Size);

  // Allocate enough room for 2 guard words: at the start and end
  // of the block.
  PArray := SysGetMem(Size + 2*GuardSize);
  if PArray = nil then
    Result := nil
  else
  begin
    // Store the guard words.
    PArray[0] := AllocatedGuard;
    PArray[Size div GuardSize + 1] := AllocatedGuard;
    // Return a pointer to the memory just past the first guard.
    Result := @PArray[1];
  end;
end;
```

See Also

GetMem Procedure, GetMemory Function, GetMemoryManager Procedure, IsMemoryManagerSet Function, IsMultiThread Variable, New Procedure, SetMemoryManager Procedure, SysFreeMem Function, SysReallocMem Function, TMemoryManager Type

SysReallocMem Function

Syntax

```
function SysReallocMem(P: Pointer; NewSize: Integer): Pointer;
```

Description

The SysReallocMem function calls Delphi's built-in memory manager to reallocate a block of memory with a new size. The new block might be at the same address as the old block, or it might be copied to a new address. In either case, SysReallocMem returns a pointer to the start of the block.

If the new size is larger than the old size, the extra memory is uninitialized. If the request cannot be fulfilled, SysReallocMem leaves the old block alone and returns nil. SysReallocMem is a real function.

Example

```
// See SetMemoryManager for an explanation of this memory manager.
// See SysFreeMem for the GuardsAreOkay function.
```

```
// See SetMemoryManager for the RoundUpSize function.

// Reallocate the block to the new size. Return a pointer to the
// new memory block or nil for failure.
function DebugRealloc(Mem: Pointer; Size: Integer): Pointer;
var
  PArray: PIntegerArray;
begin
  // Get the pointer to the true start of the memory block.
  PArray := PIntegerArray(PChar(Mem) - GuardSize);

  if not GuardsAreOkay(PArray, False) then
    ReportError(2); // invalid pointer

  // Round up Size to a multiple of the guard word size
  Size := RoundUpSize(Size);

  PArray := SysReallocMem (PArray, Size);
  if PArray = nil then
    Result := nil
  else
  begin
    // Store the guard words.
    PArray[0] := AllocatedGuard;
    PArray[Size div GuardSize + 1] := AllocatedGuard;
    // Return a pointer to the memory just past the first guard.
    Result := @PArray[1];
  end;
end;
```

See Also

GetMemoryManager Procedure, IsMemoryManagerSet Function, IsMultiThread Variable, ReallocMem Procedure, ReallocMemory Function, SetMemoryManager Procedure, SysFreeMem Function, SysGetMem Function, TMemoryManager Type

---

TClass Type

Syntax

```
type TClass = class of TObject;
```

Description

TClass is the root metaclass type. You can use TClass any time you need a generic class reference.

Tips and Tricks

- You can call any class method by invoking the method from a class reference.

- You cannot use the is and as operators on a class reference, but you can call the InheritsFrom class method to test whether a class reference inherits from another class.

- Delphi represents a class reference as a pointer to the class's VMT. Thus, the size of a TClass reference is the same size as a Pointer.

Example

```
// Map class names to class references.
type
  TClassMap = class
  private
    fList: TStrings;
    function GetClass(const Name: string): TClass;
    procedure PutClass(const Name: string; Value: TClass);
  public
    procedure Add(ClsRef: TClass);
    property Classes[const Name: string]: TClass
        read GetClass write SetClass; default;
  end;

procedure TClassMap.Add(ClsRef: TClass);
begin
  // TStrings takes TObject as the associated data,
  // so cast TClass to TObject.
  fList.AddObject(ClsRef.ClassName, TObject(ClsRef));
end;

function TClassMap.GetClass(const Name: string): TClass;
begin
  Result := TClass(fList.Objects[fList.IndexOf(Name)]);
end;

procedure TClassMap.SetClass(const Name: string; Value: TClass);
var
  Index: Integer;
begin
  Index := fList.IndexOf(Name);
  if Index < 0 then
    fList.AddObject(Name, TObject(Value))
  else
    fList.Objects[Index] := TObject(Value);
end;
...
var
  Map: TClassMap;
  Cls: TClass;
...
Map.Add(TObject);
Map.Add(TComponent);
Map.Add(TForm);
Cls := Map['TButton'].ClassParent; // Cls := TButtonControl
```

See Also

Class Keyword, Of Keyword, Self Variable, TObject Type, Type Keyword

TDateTime Type

Syntax

```
type TDateTime = type Double;
```

Description

The TDateTime type stores a date and time as the number of days since the start of the day on December 30, 1899, which is the standard used in OLE automation. The integer part is the number of days, and the fractional part specifies the time of day.

Tips and Tricks

- TDateTime does not store a time zone, so if you want to record a date and time in a file or database, you should convert the local time to UTC (Coordinated Universal Time). When loading the date and time from the file or database, convert back to local time. That lets users work in different time zones without running into problems.

- You can count the number of days between two TDateTime values by subtracting, and converting the result to an integer. Whether you round off or truncate depends on the circumstances. Do you want to count the number of "days" between 1:00 A.M. on March 3 to 11:00 P.M. on March 4 as one day (truncate) or two days (round off)?

- Unix represents a date and time as the number of seconds since midnight January 1, 1970 UTC. If a file or database contains a Unix time, you can convert it to a Delphi TDateTime by dividing by SecsPerDay and then adding 25569. That gives you the UTC date and time; you must convert this to a local date and time before using it in most Delphi programs.

Example

```
// Convert a local time to UTC by adding the time zone bias.
// To convert from UTC back to local, subtract the bias.
function LocalToUTC(DateTime: TDateTime): TDateTime;
var
  Info: TTimeZoneInformation;
  Bias: LongInt;
begin
  case GetTimeZoneInformation(Info) of
  Time_Zone_Id_Standard, Time_Zone_Id_Daylight:
  begin
    // The value returned by GetTimeZoneInformation is for the current
    // date and time, not for DateTime. Determine whether DateTime
    // is in standard or daylight savings time.
    if IsDaylightSavingsTime(DateTime, Info) then
      Bias := Info.Bias + Info.DaylightBias
    else
      Bias := Info.Bias + Info.StandardBias;

    Result := DateTime + Bias / MinutesPerDay;
  end;
  Time_Zone_Id_Unknown:
```

```
      Result := DateTime + Info.Bias / MinutesPerDay;
    else
      RaiseLastWin32Error;
      Result := DateTime; // turn off Delphi's warning
    end;
  end;
```

See Also

Double Type, Frac Function, Int Function, Round Function, Trunc Function, Type Keyword

---

TEnumModuleFuncLW Type

Syntax

```
type TEnumModuleFuncLW =
    function (HInstance: LongWord; Data: Pointer): Boolean;
```

Description

The EnumModules and EnumResourceModules functions call a programmer-supplied callback function for each module. The callback function's signature must match the TEnumModuleFuncLW type.

Tips and Tricks

For backward compatibility, EnumModules and EnumResourceModules are over-loaded and can use callback functions that declare the first argument as type LongInt instead of LongWord. New code should use LongWord (or the DWORD type from the Windows unit, which is the same thing).

Example

See EnumModules for an example.

See Also

EnumModules Procedure, EnumResourceModules Procedure

Test8086 Variable

Syntax

```
var Test8086: Byte;
```

Description

The Test8086 variable is always 2. It exists for backward compatibility only.

Test8087 Variable

Syntax

```
var Test8087: Byte;
```

Description

The `Test8087` variable is always 3. It exists for backward compatibility only.

TestFDIV Variable

Syntax

```
var TestFDIV: ShortInt;
```

Description

The `TestFDIV` variable tells whether the floating-point processor has a correct implementation of the FDIV instruction.

If you use the `$U` or `$SafeDivide` compiler directive, all floating-point division operations call a function that tests the floating-point processor for the infamous Pentium FDIV bug. If the bug is present, future divisions will be performed by a software subroutine that gives the correct answer. If the bug is not present, future divisions will be performed by the floating-point hardware.

The `TestFDIV` variable contains one of the following values:

−1   The processor is flawed and will be bypassed.

0   The processor has not yet been tested.

1   The processor has been tested and is correct.

Tips and Tricks

`TestFDIV` exists for backward compatibility only. Windows handles this problem in the operating system.

See Also

$SafeDivide Compiler Directive, $U Compiler Directive

Text Type

Syntax

```
type Text;
```

Description

The `Text` type is the same as `TextFile`. New programs should use `TextFile` to avoid conflicts with the commonly used property named `Text`.

See Also

TextFile Type

TextFile Type

Syntax

```
type TextFile;
```

Description

The `TextFile` type represents a text file. A text file is different from a binary file in that a text file contains lines of text, where the size of each line can vary. Unlike standard Pascal, the `TextFile` type is unrelated to `File of Char`.

The actual encoding of a line ending is not relevant in a Delphi program. The `ReadLn` and `WriteLn` procedures and the `Eoln` and `SeekEoln` functions automatically handle line endings. A text file ends at the end of the file or at the first occurrence of the #26 character (Ctrl-Z).

Tips and Tricks

- By default, text files are buffered with a 128-byte buffer. You can choose a different size buffer by calling `SetTextBuf`.

- The `TextFile` type is equivalent to the following record. The `SysUtils` unit has a declaration of this type, or you can copy the declaration to your own unit.

```
type
  PTextBuf = ^TTextBuf;
  TTextBuf = array[0..127] of Char;
  TTextRec = packed record
    Handle: Integer;
    Mode: Integer;          // fmInput or fmOutput
    BufSize: Cardinal;      // Size of Buffer.
    BufPos: Cardinal;       // Current position in Buffer.
    BufEnd: Cardinal;       // Last position of data in Buffer.
    BufPtr: PChar;          // Pointer to the start of the data in Buffer.
    OpenFunc: Pointer;      // Pointers to functions that take a
    InOutFunc: Pointer;     // var TextFile argument and return an
    FlushFunc: Pointer;     // integer result: zero for success and an
    CloseFunc: Pointer;     // error code for an error.
    UserData: array[1..32] of Byte;  // For your use.
    Name: array[0..259] of Char;     // Filename.
    Buffer: TTextBuf;
  end;
const
  // Values for Mode. Defined in SysUtils.
  fmClosed = $D7B0;
  fmInput  = $D7B1;
  fmOutput = $D7B2;
  fmInOut  = $D7B3;
```

- You can write your own text file driver by filling in a `TTextRec` record with your own buffer and function pointers. Write a function to assign the text file (equivalent to `AssignFile`) by initializing the record. Set `Mode` to `fmClosed` and `Name` to the filename or an empty string (if the "file" is not mapped to a real file). Initialize the buffer by setting `BufSize` and `BufPtr`. (Usually `BufPtr` points to `@Buffer`.) Set `OpenFunc` to point to your custom open function.

When the user opens the file, Delphi sets the `Mode` member and calls the `OpenFunc` function. Delphi sets `Mode` according to the following rules.

If the user calls...	Mode is set to...
Reset	fmInput
Rewrite	fmOutput
Append	fmInOut

If Mode is fmInOut, you must change it to fmOutput before your open function returns. Set the InOutFunc member to point to your custom input or output function. Use the Mode to determine whether you will need to perform input or output. The CloseFunc member points to a function that closes the file and sets the Mode back to fmClosed. The Flush function is called after each Write. You can flush all output immediately to disk or wait until the buffer fills. Before closing an output file, Delphi automatically calls InOutFunc to write the last buffer to the file.

Example

```
// Create a text file driver that maps a TextFile to a TStream,
// from the Classes unit. Streams are a flexible, object-oriented
// approach to I/O that is used widely in the VCL.

const
  fmClosed = $D7B0;              // Modes copied from SysUtils
  fmInput  = $D7B1;
  fmOutput = $D7B2;
  fmInOut  = $D7B3;
type
  TTextBuf = array[0..127] of Char;
  TTextRec = packed record
    Handle: THandle;
    Mode: Integer;
    BufSize: Integer;
    BufPos: Integer;
    BufEnd: Integer;
    BufPtr: PChar;
    OpenFunc: Pointer;
    InOutFunc: Pointer;
    FlushFunc: Pointer;
    CloseFunc: Pointer;

    // User data must fit into 32 bytes. The first part of the user
    // data stores the stream reference. The rest is not used.
    Stream: TStream;
    Unused: array[1..32-SizeOf(TStream)] of Byte;

    Name: array[0..259] of Char;
    Buffer: TTextBuf;
  end;

// Read a buffer from the stream.
function Input(var F: TTextRec): Integer;
begin
  F.BufPos := 0;
  F.BufEnd := F.Stream.Read(F.BufPtr^, F.BufSize);
```

```
    Result := 0;
end;


// Write the buffer to the stream. If the write fails,
// return the Windows error code.
function Output(var F: TTextRec): Integer;
begin
  if F.BufPos = F.Stream.Write(F.BufPtr^, F.BufPos) then
    Result := 0
  else
    Result := GetLastError;
  F.BufPos := 0;
end;


// Don't flush data after every write.
function Flush(var F: TTextRec): Integer;
begin
  Result := 0;
end;


// Nothing to do when closing a file.
function Close(var F: TTextRec): Integer;
begin
  Result := 0;
end;


// Open a text file on a stream.
function Open(var F: TTextRec): Integer;
begin
  case F.Mode of
  fmInput:
    begin
      // Read from an existing file.
      F.Stream.Position := 0;
      F.BufEnd := 0;
      F.InOutFunc := @Input;
      Result := 0;
    end;
  fmInOut:
    begin
      // Append to the end of an existing file.
      F.Mode := fmOutput;
      F.BufEnd := F.BufSize;
      F.Stream.Position := F.Stream.Size;
      F.InOutFunc := @Output;
      Result := 0;
    end;
  fmOutput:
    begin
      // Write a new file.
      F.Stream.Position := 0;
      F.BufEnd := F.BufSize;
      F.InOutFunc := @Output;
      Result := 0;
    end;
```

```
  else
    Result := Error_Invalid_Parameter;
  end;
end;

// Assign a stream to a text file.
procedure AssignStream(var AFile: TextFile; Stream: TStream);
var
  F: TTextRec absolute AFile;
begin
  F.Handle := Invalid_Handle_Value;
  F.Mode := fmClosed;
  F.BufSize := SizeOf(F.Buffer);
  F.BufPtr := @F.Buffer;
  F.BufPos := 0;
  F.OpenFunc := @Open;
  F.CloseFunc := @Close;
  F.FlushFunc := @Flush;
  F.Stream := Stream;
  F.Name[0] := #0;
end;
...

// To open a TextFile on a stream, call AssignStream instead of
// AssignFile, for example.
Stream := TMemoryStream.Create;
AssignStream(Output, Stream);
Rewrite(Output);
... Call Write and WriteLn to write to the standard output file.
CloseFile(Output);

// Display the stream contents.
Memo1.Lines.LoadFromStream(Stream);
```

See Also

Append Procedure, Eof Function, Eoln Function, File Keyword, IOResult
Function, Read Procedure, ReadLn Procedure, Reset Procedure, Rewrite
Procedure, SeekEof Function, SeekEoln Function, SetTextBuf Procedure, Write
Procedure, WriteLn Procedure

TGUID Type

Syntax

```
type
  TGUID = packed record
    D1: LongWord;
    D2: Word;
    D3: Word;
    D4: array[0..7] of Byte;
  end;
```

Description

The TGUID type stores a Globally Unique Identifier (GUID). When Windows generates a new GUID, it guarantees that the GUID is unique among all the GUIDs generated throughout the world. Delphi uses GUIDs to identify and look up interfaces.

Tips and Tricks

- Delphi automatically casts an interface name to its GUID, so you can use the interface name in calls to QueryInterface, for example.

- In an interface declaration, write a GUID in square brackets, e.g.:

```
type IUnknown = interface
  ['{00000000-0000-0000-C000-000000000046}']
```

- To generate a new GUID in the IDE, press Ctrl-Shift-G.

- GUIDs are optional in interface declarations, but you usually need them. Without a GUID, you cannot cast an interface to another type.

See Also

Interface Keyword, IUnknown Interface, PGUID Type

THeapStatus Type

Syntax

```
type
  THeapStatus = record
    TotalAddrSpace: Cardinal;
    TotalUncommitted: Cardinal;
    TotalCommitted: Cardinal;
    TotalAllocated: Cardinal;
    TotalFree: Cardinal;
    FreeSmall: Cardinal;
    FreeBig: Cardinal;
    Unused: Cardinal;
    Overhead: Cardinal;
    HeapErrorCode: Cardinal;
  end;
```

Description

The GetHeapStatus function returns a THeapStatus record. This record provides information about Delphi's internal memory manager. If you install a custom memory manager, all of the heap status values, which are shown in the following list, will probably be zero.

TotalAddrSpace
    The total number of bytes being managed by the memory manager. Delphi starts out with 1MB of virtual memory. The address space grows as needed:

    TotalAddrSpace = TotalUncommitted + TotalCommitted.

TotalUncommitted

The total number of bytes being managed that have not been allocated space in the swap file.

TotalCommitted

The total number of bytes being managed that have been allocated space in the swap file:

TotalCommitted = TotalAllocated + TotalFree + Overhead

TotalAllocated

The total number of bytes currently allocated and being used by your program.

TotalFree

The total number of bytes free to be allocated by your program. When the available free memory is too small to fulfill an allocation request, the memory manager gets additional memory from Windows.

TotalFree = FreeSmall + FreeBig + Unused

FreeSmall

The total number of bytes in the lists of free small blocks. The memory manager keeps lists of free blocks at certain "small" sizes. Each list holds blocks of a single size. Most memory requests in an average program are for small blocks, so the manager can fulfill these requests quickly by returning the address of a small block from the appropriate list. "Small" is under 4KB.

FreeBig

For blocks larger than 4KB, Delphi keeps a single list of large blocks. Large memory requests come from the list of big blocks. The first block big enough to meet a request is carved into two pieces: the part that is allocated and returned, and the remainder, which goes back into the free list.

Unused

The number of bytes that are under control of the memory manager but have not yet been allocated by your program.

Overhead

The number of bytes of overhead imposed by the memory manager to keep track of its allocated blocks.

HeapErrorCode

An internal error code, which should be zero. A non-zero value means the memory manager's internal data structures are damaged. The program's behavior will be unpredictable, but you should expect an access violation or similar error. If you want to know about the specific error codes, and you have the Professional or better version of Delphi, see *Source\Rtl\GetMem.inc*.

See Also

GetHeapStatus Function, IsMemoryManagerSet Function, SetMemoryManager Procedure

Then Keyword

Syntax

```
if Expression then Statement
```

Description

The then keyword is part of an if statement. See the if statement for details.

See Also

Else Keyword, If Keyword

Threadvar Keyword

Syntax

```
threadvar Name = Type; ...
```

Description

The threadvar keyword starts a variable declaration in the same manner as the var keyword, except that threadvar can be used only at the unit level. Variables declared using threadvar have distinct values in each thread. Ordinary variables, on the other hand, are shared among all threads in a process.

Tips and Tricks

- If you are using the TThread class (Classes unit), you will probably find it more convenient to use fields to store per-thread data.

- If you are writing a reusable subroutine or class that might be used in multiple threads, you can use threadvar variables to keep track of per-thread information.

- Threadvar declarations apply only to the variable itself. If the variable is a pointer or encapsulates a pointer (e.g., object, long string, dynamic array, Variant), the data might be accessible from multiple threads.

- Threadvar variables use Windows thread-local storage (TLS). Every variable access requires a function call, so another reason to use the TThread class is that access to the object's fields is faster than using threadvar variables.

- Every module that uses a threadvar variable requires a TLS slot, but Windows has a small number of TLS slots available. A large project should use packages to ensure the availability of this limited resource.

  Every module (application, DLL, package) that contains a threadvar variable needs its own, separate TLS slot. If you link a DLL statically, the DLL contains its own copy of the System unit and its IOResult and RaiseList variables (which are threadvar variables). A project with a large number of DLLs can run out of TLS slots even if they don't have their own threadvar variables.

  If you use packages, the vcl50 package contains the shared instance of the System unit and its threadvar variables. That means the project needs only one TLS slot, no matter how many DLLs and packages it loads. If any DLL or package needs its own **threadvar** variables, only that module would need another TLS slot.

- Do not use **threadvar** variables in the finalization section of a unit that might be used in a DLL. Delphi frees the TLS memory when it unloads the DLL, but before it calls the finalization sections.

Example

```
// Each thread has a separate List variable, but it is up to the
// programmer to assign a unique TList object to each List variable.
threadvar
  List: TList;

procedure ThreadFunc(Param: Pointer);
begin
  List := TList.Create;
  ...
end;

procedure StartThread;
begin
  Handle := BeginThread(nil, 0, ThreadFunc, nil, 0, Id);
end;
```

See Also

BeginThread Function, IsMultiThread Variable, TlsIndex Variable, TlsLast Variable

---

TInterfacedClass Type

Syntax

```
type TInterfacedClass = class of TInterfacedObject;
```

Description

The **TInterfacedClass** type is a convenience type for the metaclass of **TInterfacedObject**.

See Also

Class Keyword, TInterfacedObject Type

TInterfacedObject Type

Syntax

```
type
  TInterfacedObject = class(TObject, IUnknown)
  protected
    FRefCount: Integer;
    function QueryInterface(const IID: TGUID; out Obj): HResult; stdcall;
    function _AddRef: Integer; stdcall;
```

```
      function _Release: Integer; stdcall;
   public
      procedure AfterConstruction; override;
      procedure BeforeDestruction; override;
      class function NewInstance: TObject; override;
      property RefCount: Integer read FRefCount;
   end;
```

Description

The TInterfacedObject class implements the IUnknown interface with the reference counting semantics that Delphi and COM expect. It also implements
QueryInterface to call GetInterface. In other words, TInterfacedObject
provides useful implementations of IUnknown's methods, so you can and should
use TInterfacedObject as a base class for any class that must implement one or
more interfaces.

Tips and Tricks

* If you are using COM, you probably want to use one of the classes derived
  from TInterfacedObject or TAggregatedObject, which you can find in
  the ComObj and ComServ units.

* If you are not using COM, TInterfacedClass provides the minimum functionality you need to take full advantage of Delphi's interfaces.

* You don't have to use TInterfacedObject. Any class can implement the
  methods of IUnknown. When implementing IUnknown in another class, you
  might want to copy the implementation of the _AddRef, _Release, and
  QueryInterface methods from TInterfacedObject.

Example

```
type
   // Interface for accessing an object
   IObject = interface
   ['{618977EA-1ADA-11D3-B1A8-00105AA9C2AD}']
      function GetValue: TObject;
      procedure SetValue(Value: TObject);
      property Value: TObject read GetValue write SetValue;
   end;

   TObjectWrapper = class(TInterfacedObject, IObject)
   private
      fObject: TObject;
      function GetValue: TObject;
      procedure SetValue(Value: TObject);
   public
      constructor Create(ObjRef: TObject);
      property Value: TObject read GetValue write SetValue;
   end;
```

See Also

Interface Keyword, TObject Type

TInterfaceEntry Type

Syntax

```
type
  TInterfaceEntry = packed record
    IID: TGUID;
    VTable: Pointer;
    IOffset: Integer;
    ImplGetter: Integer;
  end;
```

Description

Every class that implements one or more interfaces has a table of interface entries in its RTTI. The **TInterfaceEntry** record stores the necessary information for the interface. See Chapter 3 for more information about RTTI.

Tips and Tricks

- An object can implement an interface using a property (with the **implements** directive). The property is implemented with a field or method reference, which is stored in the **ImplGetter** member as the field offset, virtual method offset, or static method pointer. Usually, the class implements the interface by implementing all the methods of the interface and **ImplGetter** is zero.

- If the class implements the interface directly, the compiler generates a virtual method table for the interface and stores a pointer to the vtable in the **VTable** field. The compiler also generates a hidden field to store the interface. The field's offset in the object is **IOffset**. When you create a new object, Delphi automatically initializes the hidden interface fields.

- See the **TObject** type and its **GetInterfaceTable** and **GetInterface** methods to see how Delphi looks up interfaces.

See Also

Implements Directive, Interface Keyword, PInterfaceEntry Type, Property Keyword, TGUID Type, TInterfaceTable Type, TObject Type

---

TInterfaceTable Type

Syntax

```
type
  TInterfaceTable = packed record
    EntryCount: Integer;
    Entries: array[0..9999] of TInterfaceEntry;
  end;
```

Description

Every class that implements one or more interfaces has a table of interface entries in its RTTI, as represented by a **TInterfaceTable** record. See Chapter 3 for more information.

- **EntryCount** is the actual number of interface entries in the **Entries** array.
- See the **TObject** type and its **GetInterfaceTable** and **GetInterface** methods to see how Delphi looks up interfaces.

See Also

Interface Keyword, PInterfaceTable Type, TInterfaceEntry Type, TObject Type

TLibModule Type

Syntax

```
type
  TLibModule = record
    Next: PLibModule;
    Instance: LongWord;
    CodeInstance: LongWord;
    DataInstance: LongWord;
    ResInstance: LongWord;
    Reserved: Integer;
  end;
```

Description

The **TLibModule** type stores information about the project module and every package that the project loads. The records are stored in a singly linked list, where the **Next** member points to the next module in the list.

Instance is the module's instance handle. **ResInstance** is the module's resource instance handle. If the module has a separate resource library, Delphi automatically loads the language-specific library and saves the instance handle in **ResInstance**. Otherwise, **ResInstance** is the same as **Instance**.

CodeInstance and **DataInstance** are used by C++ Builder for libraries.

See Also

LibModuleList Variable, PLibModule Type, RegisterModule Procedure, UnregisterModule Procedure

TlsIndex Variable

Syntax

```
unit SysInit;
var TlsIndex: Integer;
```

Description

Each module keeps track of its thread-local storage (TLS) slot for implementing **threadvar** variables. When the module is loaded, it checks **TlsLast** to see if the module has any **threadvar** variables. If so, it requests a TLS slot from Windows and saves the index in **TlsIndex**. Do not change the value of this variable. If the module cannot get a free TLS slot, it raises runtime error 226.

See Also

ThreadVar Keyword, TlsLast Variable

TlsLast Variable

Syntax

```
unit SysInit;
var TlsLast: Byte;
```

Description

The address of **TlsLast** denotes the amount of memory required for storing **threadvar** variables. When a thread starts up, Delphi allocates that much memory in the thread-local storage (TLS) for storing **threadvar** variables. The address is **nil** if the program, library, or package does not use any **threadvar** variables, in which case the module does not allocate a TLS slot.

See Also

ThreadVar Keyword, TlsIndex Variable

TMemoryManager Type

Syntax

```
type
  TMemoryManager = record
    GetMem: function(Size: Integer): Pointer;
    FreeMem: function(P: Pointer): Integer;
    ReallocMem: function(P: Pointer; Size: Integer): Pointer;
  end;
```

Description

The **TMemoryManager** type stores the three function pointers needed to implement a memory manager.

Example

See **SetMemoryManager** for an example.

See Also

GetMemoryManager Procedure, IsMemoryManagerSet Function, PMemoryManager Type, SetMemoryManager Procedure

TModuleUnloadProcLW Type

Syntax

```
type
  TModuleUnloadProcLW = procedure(HInstance: LongWord);
```

Description

You can register a callback procedure that Delphi calls when it unloads a package or project module. The procedure signature must match the TModuleUnload-ProcLW type, that is, take a handle as an argument.

Tips and Tricks

For backward compatibility, Delphi overloads the AddModuleUnloadProc and RemoveModuleUnloadProc procedures to accept a callback procedure with a LongInt argument. For new code, be sure to use LongWord (or the Windows equivalents DWORD or THandle).

Example

See AddModuleUnloadProc for an example.

See Also

AddModuleUnloadProc Procedure, RemoveModuleUnloadProc Procedure, TModuleUnloadRec Type

---

TModuleUnloadRec Type

Syntax

```
type
  TModuleUnloadRec = record
    Next: PModuleUnloadRec;
    Proc: TModuleUnloadProcLW;
  end;
```

Description

Delphi keeps a singly linked list of TModuleUnloadRec records. Each record stores a pointer to a callback procedure. When Delphi unloads a package or when the project unloads itself, Delphi calls all the procedures in the list, passing the module's instance handle as an argument.

Example

See AddModuleUnloadProc for an example.

See Also

AddModuleUnloadProc Procedure, ModuleUnloadList Variable, PModuleUnloadRec Type, RemoveModuleUnloadProc Procedure, TModuleUnloadProcLW Type

---

To Keyword

Syntax

```
for Variable := Expr1 to Expr2 do Statement
```

Description

The to keyword is part of a for loop that counts up. See the explanation of the for loop for details.

See Also

Downto Keyword, For Keyword

TObject Type

Syntax

```
type
  TObject = class
    constructor Create;
    procedure Free;
    class function InitInstance(Instance: Pointer): TObject;
    procedure CleanupInstance;
    function ClassType: TClass;
    class function ClassName: ShortString;
    class function ClassNameIs(const Name: string): Boolean;
    class function ClassParent: TClass;
    class function ClassInfo: Pointer;
    class function InstanceSize: LongInt;
    class function InheritsFrom(AClass: TClass): Boolean;
    class function MethodAddress(const Name: ShortString): Pointer;
    class function MethodName(Address: Pointer): ShortString;
    function FieldAddress(const Name: ShortString): Pointer;
    function GetInterface(const IID: TGUID; out Obj): Boolean;
    class function GetInterfaceEntry(const IID: TGUID):PInterfaceEntry;
    class function GetInterfaceTable: PInterfaceTable;
    function SafeCallException(ExceptObject: TObject;
      ExceptAddr: Pointer): HResult; virtual;
    procedure AfterConstruction; virtual;
    procedure BeforeDestruction; virtual;
    procedure Dispatch(var Message); virtual;
    procedure DefaultHandler(var Message); virtual;
    class function NewInstance: TObject; virtual;
    procedure FreeInstance; virtual;
    destructor Destroy; virtual;
  end;
```

Description

TObject is the root class from which all other classes descend. It has no explicit fields, but it stores a pointer to its VMT in a hidden field. It also defines a number of useful methods that all classes inherit.

Class Methods

This section describes the class methods of TObject.

ClassInfo Function

ClassInfo returns a pointer to the class's TTypeInfo table. It is similar to calling TypeInfo(ClassRef), except that the TypeInfo function works only

---

with a type name, but you can call ClassInfo with respect to any class or object reference, including metaclass variables.

ClassName Function

The ClassName function returns the name of the class, which is stored in the class's RTTI.

ClassNameIs Function

The ClassNameIs function tests whether a given string matches the class name. Class names are not case sensitive, so the comparison ignores case differences. The function returns True if Name is the same as the class name, and False if Name is different.

ClassParent Function

The ClassParent function returns the metaclass for the immediate base class. TObject.ClassParent returns nil because it has no base class.

Create Constructor

Create does nothing. It exists so you can safely call inherited Create from any constructor, and so you can construct an instance of any class. When you write a derived class and implement its constructor, always call the inherited constructor.

Destroy Destructor

Although Delphi lets you declare multiple destructors, you shouldn't. Instead, you should override Destroy. TObject.Destroy does nothing, but it is always wise to call inherited Destroy in your destructors.

GetInterfaceEntry Function

GetInterfaceEntry looks up a GUID and returns a pointer to the matching TInterfaceEntry record, or nil if the class and its ancestors do not support the requested interface. If the receiving class does not support the interface, GetInterfaceEntry checks the base classes to see if they support the interface.

GetInterfaceTable Function

GetInterfaceTable returns a pointer to the TInterfaceTable record that stores the interfaces that the class supports. If the class does not implement any interfaces, the function returns nil. This function simply returns the pointer from the class's RTTI.

InheritsFrom Function

InheritsFrom tests whether a class is the same class as AClass or is a descendent of AClass; if so, it returns True. The function returns False if AClass is not a base class of the receiving class. The is and as operators call InheritsFrom to perform the same check.

InitInstance Function

The InitInstance function takes a pointer to the memory that has been allocated for an object and initializes it. It returns the same pointer, but as an object reference. The object's memory is initialized to zero, any interfaces that the class implements are initialized, and the class's VMT pointer is stored as the object's first (hidden) field.

If you override the `NewInstance` method to change the way objects are allocated, you should call `InitInstance` to initialize the object.

InstanceSize Function

`InstanceSize` returns the number of bytes that instances of the class require. Do not use `SizeOf`, because class references and object references are pointers, so `SizeOf(AClass)` or `SizeOf(AnObject)` return the same as `SizeOf(Pointer)`. If you override `NewInstance` to allocate memory for the object in a nonstandard way, be sure to allocate at least `InstanceSize` bytes.

MethodAddress Function

The `MethodAddress` function looks up a method name in the RTTI table of published methods, and returns the code pointer for the method. The search is not sensitive to case. If the class does not implement the method, `MethodAddress` searches the RTTI tables of the ancestor classes. If no ancestor class implements the method as a published method, the function returns `nil`.

You can construct a `TMethod` (in the `SysUtils` unit) record by assigning the `MethodAddress` value to the `Code` member and an object reference to the `Data` member. You can then cast the `TMethod` record to an event type, such as `TNotifyEvent`, as shown here:

```
var
  Notify: TNotifyEvent;
begin
  TMethod(Notify).Code := Form.MethodAddress('Button1Click');
  TMethod(Notify).Data := Form;
  Notify(Button1);
end;
```

MethodName Function

The `MethodName` function gets the name of a published method, given its code pointer. If the method is not found, it returns an empty string. Delphi calls `MethodName` when writing a *.dfm* file, so it can record method names in the form description.

NewInstance Function

The `NewInstance` function creates a new instance of a class and initializes the object. It returns the new object reference. The method is virtual, so you can override it and change the way Delphi creates objects of a particular class. If you do, be sure to call `InitInstance` to initialize the object, and override `FreeInstance` to free the memory for the object.

Object Methods

This section describes the static and virtual methods of `TObject`.

AfterConstruction Procedure

Delphi calls `AfterConstruction` after the constructors finish their work and return. You can override this method to perform any actions that must wait until after the object has been entirely constructed. This is especially useful if you are writing classes for use in Delphi and C++ Builder. The two languages have different semantics for constructors, but you can bypass the differences by overriding `AfterConstruction`.

BeforeDestruction Procedure

Delphi calls `BeforeDestruction` when an object is about to be destroyed, but before any of the destructors have been called. You can clean up the object or take care of other details that require a valid object to function correctly. This is especially useful if you are writing classes for use in Delphi and C++ Builder. The two languages have different semantics for destructors, but you can bypass the differences by overriding `BeforeDestruction`.

ClassType Function

The `ClassType` function returns the object's metaclass reference, which is just a pointer to the VMT.

CleanupInstance Procedure

The `CleanupInstance` procedure cleans up strings, `Variants`, dynamic arrays, and interfaces. If you override `FreeInstance`, be sure to call `CleanupInstance` before freeing the object's memory.

DefaultHandler Procedure

`DefaultHandler` is the default message handler. Delphi calls `DefaultHandler` when it tries to dispatch a message but cannot find a handler for the message. `TObject` implements `DefaultHandler` to do nothing. Derived classes can and do override this method to implement other behavior. For example, `TWinControl` forwards the message to the control's window procedure.

Dispatch Procedure

The `Dispatch` procedure dispatches a message. `Dispatch` looks at the first two bytes of its argument, and interprets the `Word` as a message number. It looks up the message in the class's RTTI, and if the class has a message handler, `Dispatch` calls that method. Otherwise, it searches the RTTI of the ancestor classes. If `Dispatch` cannot find a message handler for the message, it calls `DefaultHandler`.

FieldAddress Function

The `FieldAddress` function looks up the name of a field in the class's RTTI table of published fields, and returns a pointer to the object's field or `nil` if the class and its ancestors do not publish a field of that name. The search is not sensitive to case. Published fields must be of class type, so you know that the field stores a class reference.

Free Procedure

Call the `Free` procedure to free an object. Do not call the destructor directly. `Free` tests whether an object reference is `nil`, and calls `Destroy` only for non-nil references.

FreeInstance Procedure

The `FreeInstance` procedure cleans up an object (by calling `CleanupInstance`) and frees the object's memory. You can override this method to implement custom behavior. If you override `FreeInstance`, be sure to call `CleanupInstance`. If you override `NewInstance`, you should also override `FreeInstance`.

GetInterface Function

GetInterface looks up a GUID and fetches a matching interface. It returns True if an interface was found and assigned to Obj, and it returns False if the object does not support the requested interface. If the interface is not supported, Obj is set to nil.

SafeCallException Function

Delphi wraps every safecall method in a try-except block to catch all Delphi exceptions. It then calls the object's SafeCallException method to map the exception to a standard Windows error code. TObject always returns E_Unexpected.

TComObject is a little smarter and uses IErrorInfo to report the exception error message, if it can. Delphi automatically handles the details for you, and if you want more control over how your COM server reports errors to its clients, you can set the ServerExceptionHandler property.

Tips and Tricks

The virtual methods of TObject are special in that they are stored at negative offsets in the virtual method table. The "first" method in the VMT is the first virtual method of a derived class. See Chapter 3 for more information about the VMT.

See Also

Class Keyword, FreeMem Procedure, Function Keyword, GetMem Procedure, Interface Keyword, Message Directive, Procedure Keyword, Property Keyword, SafeCall Directive, SafeCallErrorProc Variable, Self Variable, TClass Type, Type Keyword

TResStringRec Type

Syntax

```
type
  TResStringRec = packed record
    Module: ^LongInt;        // resource module
    Identifier: Integer;     // string table resource identifier
  end;
```

Description

Delphi compiles a resourcestring declaration into a TResStringRec record and a call to LoadResString. The Module points to the handle of the resource module that contains the string table resource, and the Identifier is the resource identifier for the string resource. The linker automatically assigns a unique identifier to each resourcestring.

See Also

LoadResString Function, PResStringRec Type, ResourceString Keyword

Trunc Function

Syntax

```
function Trunc(X: Floating-point type): Int64;
```

Description

The Trunc function truncates a floating-point value by discarding the fractional part (round towards zero). Unlike Int, Trunc returns an integer result. Trunc is not a real function.

Tips and Tricks

- The Trunc function temporarily sets the floating-point control word, then truncates the number, and restores the control word.

- If X is an integer, the compiler eliminates the call to Trunc and simply returns X.

- If X is a Variant, Delphi automatically converts it to a floating-point number and truncates it.

- The compiler does not accept an Int64 argument, but there is no reason to call Trunc for Int64.

- If X is infinity or NaN, Trunc reports runtime error 6 (EInvalidOp).

See Also

Int Function, Round Function

Truncate Procedure

Syntax

```
procedure Truncate(var F: file);
procedure Truncate(var F: TextFile);
```

Description

Truncate truncates a file so its current position becomes the end of the file. Truncate is not a real procedure.

If the file is not open, Truncate reports I/O error 103.

See Also

Eof Function, File Keyword, FilePos Function, FileSize Function, IOResult Function, Seek Procedure, SeekEof Function, TextFile Type

Try Keyword

Syntax

```
try Statements... finally Statements... end;
```

```
try Statements... except Statements... end;

try Statements... except Handlers... end;
```

Description

The try keyword introduces a try-except statement or a try-finally statement. The two statements are related but serve different purposes.

The try-finally statement is used to manage memory and other resources. It performs the statements first in the try part of the statement, then in the finally part of the statement. The statements in the finally part are executed no matter how control leaves the try part: exception, returning from a subroutine with the Exit procedure, or exiting a loop with the Break procedure.

The try-except statement handles errors and exceptional conditions. It first performs the statements in the try part of the statement. If an exception is raised, control transfers to the except part of the statement, where Delphi searches for a matching exception handler. If the except part contains plain statements, Delphi executes those statements, and then control continues after the end of the try-except statement. If the except part contains one or more exception handlers (which start with the on directive), Delphi searches for a matching handler. If it cannot find a matching handler, control continues with the next try-except statement in the call stack.

Tips and Tricks

- Use try-finally to free temporary objects and other resources and to perform related cleanup activities. Typically, you should not need more than one try-finally statement in a subroutine or method.

- Use try-except to handle exceptional cases. In utilities and reusable classes, you should rarely use try-except. Instead, an application uses try-except to catch specific exceptions and do something useful with them, such as log them in an error log, send email to the vendor, or create a friendly dialog box.

- Low-level code might use try-except to catch a low-level exception, add information, and raise a higher-level exception.

Example

```
// Copy a file.
procedure CopyFile(const DestFile, SourceFile: string);
const
  ReadFlags = fmOpenRead or fmShareDenyWrite;
resourcestring
  sSourceError = 'Cannot open source file: %s';
  sDestError = 'Cannot open destination file: %s';
  sCopyError = 'Cannot copy %1:s to %2:s: %0:s';
var
  DestStream, SourceStream: TStream;
begin
  DestStream := nil;
  SourceStream := nil;
```

```
try
  try
    SourceStream := TFileStream.Create(SourceFile, ReadFlags);
    DestStream := TFileStream.Create(DestFile, fmCreate);
    DestStream.CopyFrom(SourceStream);
  except
  // EFCreateError and EFOpenError derive from EStreamError,
  // so check the derived classes first. Raise a new exception
  // that provides additional information. If any other kind
  // of exception is raised, the exception propagates to the
  // caller and its caller, until Delphi finds another exception
  // handler.
  on Ex: EFCreateError do
    raise EFCreateError.CreateFmt(sDestError, [Ex.Message]);
  on Ex: EFOpenError do
    raise EFOpenError.CreateFmt(sSourceError, [Ex.Message]);
  on Ex: EStreamError do
    raise EStreamError.CreateFmt(sCopyError,
              [Ex.Message, SourceFile, DestFile]);
  end;
  finally
    // Even if the try-except raises an exception, the finally
    // part executes, so the stream objects can be freed.
    DestStream.Free;
    SourceStream.Free;
  end;
end;
```

See Also

Except Keyword, Finally Directive, On Directive, Raise Keyword

---

TThreadFunc Type

Syntax

```
type
  TThreadFunc = function(Parameter: Pointer): Integer;
```

Description

The BeginThread function takes a thread function as one of its arguments. The function's signature must match the TThreadFunc type. BeginThread passes its Param argument to the thread function. The thread function's return value becomes the thread's exit code.

Example

See BeginThread for an example.

See Also

BeginThread Function, EndThread Procedure, IsMultiThread Variable, ThreadVar Keyword

---

TVarArray Type

Syntax

```
type
  TVarArray = packed record
    DimCount: Word;
    Flags: Word;
    ElementSize: Integer;
    LockCount: Integer;
    Data: Pointer;
    Bounds: array[0..255] of TVarArrayBound;
  end;
```

Description

The TVarArray record stores the information used to implement a Variant array. TVarData stores a pointer to a TVarArray record when the Variant type includes the varArray bit.

DimCount

Stores the number of dimensions, which is always in the range 1..64.

Flags

Feature flags that Windows uses to keep track of the array's memory and how to manage it.

ElementSize

The size in bytes of each element of the array. The element size depends on the element type, as stored in the VType field of TVarData.

LockCount

The lock count is usually zero. It is incremented when you call VarArrayLock and decremented when you call VarArrayUnlock. The only time you can resize an array is when its LockCount is zero.

Data

A pointer to the array's data. The actual contents of the array are stored in a single dimensional array, where the leftmost subscript varies fastest (row-major order).

Bounds

An array of TVarArrayBound records to keep track of the bounds for each array dimension. The Bounds member is allocated dynamically, so it actually contains DimCount records.

See TVarData to see how a Variant stores the pointer to the TVarArray record.

See Also

PVarData Type, TVarArrayBound Type, TVarData Type, VarArrayCreate Function, VarArrayDimCount Function, VarArrayHighBound Function, VarArrayLock Function, VarArrayLowBound Function, VarArrayOf Function, VarArrayRedim Procedure, VarArrayRef Function, VarArrayUnlock Function, Variant Type, VarIsArray Function, VarType Function

TVarArrayBound Type

Syntax

```
type
  TVarArrayBound = packed record
    ElementCount: Integer;
    LowBound: Integer;
  end;
```

Description

A Variant array keeps track of its array bounds with a **TVarArrayBound** record for each dimension. The record stores the lower bound and the number of elements in the array. A **Variant** array's **TVarArray** data stores an array of **TVarArrayBound** records.

See Also

TVarArray Type, TVarData Type, VarArrayCreate Function, VarArrayDimCount Function, VarArrayHighBound Function, VarArrayLock Function, VarArrayLowBound Function, VarArrayOf Function, VarArrayRedim Procedure, VarArrayRef Function, VarArrayUnlock Function, Variant Type, VarIsArray Function, VarType Function

TVarData Type

Syntax

```
type
  TVarData = packed record
    VType: Word;
    Reserved1, Reserved2, Reserved3: Word;
    case Integer of
      varSmallint: (VSmallint: Smallint);
      varInteger:  (VInteger: Integer);
      varSingle:   (VSingle: Single);
      varDouble:   (VDouble: Double);
      varCurrency: (VCurrency: Currency);
      varDate:     (VDate: Double);
      varOleStr:   (VOleStr: PWideChar);
      varDispatch: (VDispatch: Pointer);
      varError:    (VError: LongWord);
      varBoolean:  (VBoolean: WordBool);
      varUnknown:  (VUnknown: Pointer);
      varByte:     (VByte: Byte);
      varString:   (VString: Pointer);
      varAny:      (VAny: Pointer);
      varArray:    (VArray: PVarArray);
      varByRef:    (VPointer: Pointer);
  end;
```

Description

The TVarData record is Delphi's implementation of the Variant type. You can cast any Variant to TVarData to examine the internal workings of the Variant.

The VType field stores the variant type (as returned by VarType). The other fields store type-specific information. Values up to 8 bytes in size are stored directly in the TVarData record. Larger items are stored separately; the TVarData record holds a pointer to the actual data (such as VArray, which points to a TVarArray record).

Tips and Tricks

- VString is actually a string type, but Delphi does not let you store a string in a variant record because it cannot initialize or finalize the record properly. Instead, the code that manages the Variant takes care of initializing or finalizing the string.

- VUnknown is actually an IUnknown interface, and VDispatch is an IDispatch interface. As with strings, Delphi does not permit interfaces in a variant record.

- VAny is an opaque pointer. You can assign procedures to the ChangeAnyProc, ClearAnyProc, and RefAnyProc variables to implement the varAny type. Delphi uses varAny to implement the Any type in CORBA.

- VPointer is a pointer to variant data. If a Variant's VarType includes the varByRef bit, the Variant value stores an additional level of indirection, and sets VPointer to point to the data. If you want to access the VPointer field, cast it to the type that is appropriate for the variant type, e.g., PDateTime for varDate, PInteger for varInteger.

Example

```
// Store an Int64 value in a Variant by using varAny.
procedure SetVarInt64(var V: Variant; Value: Int64);
begin
  // Ensure that the old value is cleaned up.
  V := Unassigned;
  // Save the Int64 value in dynamically allocated memory
  // and store the pointer in the Variant.
  TVarData(V).VType := varAny;
  GetMem(TVarData(V).VAny, SizeOf(Int64));
  PInt64(TVarData(V).VAny)^ := Value;
end;
```

See Also

ChangeAnyProc Variable, ClearAnyProc Variable, Currency Type, Double Type, Integer Type, Pointer Type, PWideChar Type, RefAnyProc Variable, Single Type, SmallInt Type, String Keyword, TDateTime Type, Type Keyword, TVarArray Type, Variant Type, VarType Function

TVarRec Type

Syntax

```
type
  TVarRec = record
    case Byte of
      vtInteger:     (VInteger: Integer; VType: Byte);
      vtBoolean:     (VBoolean: Boolean);
      vtChar:        (VChar: Char);
      vtExtended:    (VExtended: PExtended);
      vtString:      (VString: PShortString);
      vtPointer:     (VPointer: Pointer);
      vtPChar:       (VPChar: PChar);
      vtObject:      (VObject: TObject);
      vtClass:       (VClass: TClass);
      vtWideChar:    (VWideChar: WideChar);
      vtPWideChar:   (VPWideChar: PWideChar);
      vtAnsiString:  (VAnsiString: Pointer);
      vtCurrency:    (VCurrency: PCurrency);
      vtVariant:     (VVariant: PVariant);
      vtInterface:   (VInterface: Pointer);
      vtWideString:  (VWideString: Pointer);
      vtInt64:       (VInt64: PInt64);
  end;
```

Description

A subroutine parameter of type **array of const** is actually an array of **TVarRec** records. Delphi converts each open array element to a **TVarRec** record, filling in the **VType** member with the type code and the appropriate member with the actual value.

Tips and Tricks

* Delphi uses open arrays and **TVarRec** values to implement subroutines that take a variable number of arguments, while preserving complete type safety.

* **TVarRec** and **TVarData** are entirely unrelated. They look similar because they do similar things, but they are not interchangeable.

* **TVarRec** can handle more types than a **Variant**, but it cannot handle all Delphi types. In particular, arrays, records, and enumerations are not supported.

Example

```
// Compute the sum of an arbitrary number of values.
function Sum(const Data: array of const): Double;
var
  I: Integer;
begin
  Result := 0.0;
  for I := Low(Data) to High(Data) do
    case Data[I].VType of
    vtInt64:    Result := Result + Data[I].VInt64^;
    vtCurrency: Result := Result + Data[I].VCurrency^;
    vtInteger:  Result := Result + Data[I].VInteger;
```

```
      vtExtended: Result := Result + Data[I].VExtended^;
      vtVariant:  Result := Result + Data[I].VVariant^;
      else
        raise Exception.Create('Non-numeric value in Sum');
      end;
  end;
```

See Also

Array Keyword, Const Keyword, TVarData Type, Variant Type

Type Keyword

Syntax

```
type Name = Type declaration; ...
type Name = type Type declaration;

type Name1 = Name2;
type Name = (Identifier, ...);
type Name = Expr1..Expr2;
type Name = ^Type;
type Name = array[...] of Name;
type Name = class ... end;
type Name = class of ...;
type Name = dispinterface ... end;
type Name = file of Type;
type Name = function ...;
type Name = interface ... end;
type Name = object ... end;
type Name = procedure ...;
type Name = record ... end;
type Name = set of Ordinal type;
```

Description

The **type** keyword begins a type declaration, as it does in standard Pascal.

If the type declaration begins with another occurrence of the **type** keyword, Delphi generates unique RTTI for the type, even if the type is just a synonym for an existing type. It also makes the type a distinct type with regard to **var** parameters.

Tips and Tricks

- A common convention in Delphi programs is to begin type names with the letter T, except for exception classes (which begin with E), interfaces (which begin with I), and pointer types (which begin with P).

- A forward class declaration must be resolved in the same type block where it is declared. For example:

```
type
  TExample = class; // forward declaration
  TOther = class
    procedure Example(E: TExample);
```

```
      end;
      // Full class declaration without using another "type" keyword,
      // which starts a new type block.
      TExample = class
        procedure Example(Other: TOther);
      end;
```

* A class declaration in the interface section of a unit must have definitions for all of the class's non-abstract methods in the implementation section of the same unit.

Example

```
type
    TSuit = (Diamond, Club, Heart, Spade);
    PCard = ^TCard;   // pointer to TCard;
    TCard = record
      Suit: TSuit;
      Rank: 1..13;
    end;
    Deck = array[1..52] of TCard;
    TSuits = set of TSuit;

    TCardFunc = function(const Card: TCard): Integer;
    TCardProc = procedure(const Card: TCard);
    TCardMethodFunc = function(const Card: TCard): Integer of object;
    TCardMethodProc = procedure(var Card: TCard) of object;

    IGame = interface
    ['{6164F471-5E41-11D3-B1B6-00105AA9C2AD}']
      procedure Play;
      procedure Draw(var Card: TCard);
    end;
    TGame = class(TInterfacedObject, IGame)
    public
      procedure Play;
      procedure Draw(var Card: TCard);
    end;
```

See Also

Array Keyword, Class Keyword, Dispinterface Keyword, File Keyword, Function Keyword, Integer Type, Interface Keyword, Object Keyword, Packed Keyword, Procedure Keyword, Record Keyword, Set Keyword, TClass Type, TextFile Type, TObject Type, TypeInfo Function

---

TypeInfo Function

Syntax

```
function TypeInfo(Type name): Pointer;
```

Description

The **TypeInfo** function returns a pointer to a type's runtime type information. The pointer is actually a **PTypeInfo** pointer, which is a pointer to a **TTypeInfo** record. These types are declared in the **TypInfo** unit.

See Chapter 3 for more information about runtime type information.

Example

```
// Convert a set to a string representation, e.g.,
// '[fsBold,fsItalic]'.
function SetToString(Info: PTypeInfo; const Value): string;
var
  I: Integer;
  Data: PTypeData;         // set's type data
  EnumInfo: PTypeInfo; // set's base type info
  EnumData: PTypeData;     // set's base type data
begin
  if Info.Kind <> tkSet then
    Result := ''
  else
  begin
    Data := GetTypeData(Info);
    EnumInfo := Data^.CompType^;
    EnumData := GetTypeData(EnumInfo);

    Assert(EnumInfo.Kind in [tkEnumeration,tkInteger]);

    Result := '[';
    for I := EnumData.MinValue to EnumData.MaxValue do
      if I in TIntegerSet(Value) then
      begin
        // The element is in the set, so add its name to the string.
        if Length(Result) > 1 then
          Result := Result + ',';  // Separate items with commas.
        Result := Result + GetEnumName(EnumInfo, I);
      end;
    Result := Result + ']';
  end;
end;
...
S := SetToString(TypeInfo(TFontStyles), Control.Font.Style);
```

Unassigned Variable

Syntax

```
var Unassigned: Variant;
```

Description

The **Unassigned** variable is a **Variant** value that represents an uninitialized variable. Delphi automatically initializes every **Variant** variable to **Unassigned**. If you attempt to use an **Unassigned** value in an expression, Delphi reports runtime error 16 (**EVariantError**).

Tips and Tricks

- Calling VarClear is the same as assigning Unassigned to a Variant variable.
- VarIsEmpty returns True for Unassigned.

See Also

Null Variable, VarClear Procedure, Variant Type, VarIsEmpty Function

---

UniqueString Procedure

Syntax

```
procedure UniqueString(var Str: string);
```

Description

The UniqueString procedure ensures that Str has a reference count of one. If Str has no other references, UniqueString leaves it alone; otherwise, UniqueString allocates a new copy of the string and assigns that unique copy to Str.

UniqueString is a real procedure.

Tips and Tricks

- You do not usually need to call UniqueString. Delphi uses copy-on-write semantics for strings, so if you have multiple references to a string and you modify the string through one reference, Delphi automatically creates a unique string to modify, so the other references continue to refer to the original string.

- If you cast a string to PChar, Delphi also ensures that the PChar points to a unique instance of the string. If you modify the string through the PChar pointer, the other references to the original string are safe.

See Also

String Keyword

Unit Keyword

Syntax

```
unit Name;
interface
  Declarations...
implementation
  Declarations...
initialization
  Statements...
finalization
  Statements...
end.

unit Name;
interface
```

```
  Declarations...
implementation
  Declarations...
begin
  Statements...
end.
```

Description

The unit keyword introduces a unit, which is Delphi's basic module for building programs. A unit's name must match the filename (with a *.pas* extension). Chapter 2 has more information about units.

Tips and Tricks

- The interface or implementation sections can each have a uses declaration. If so, the uses declaration must appear first in the section.

- The initialization and finalization sections are optional. If a unit has a finalization section, it must have an initialization section, even if the initialization section is empty.

- You can use the begin keyword instead of initialization, but if you do, the unit cannot have a finalization section.

See Also

Begin Keyword, End Keyword, Finalization Keyword, Implementation Keyword, Initialization Keyword, Interface Keyword, Uses Keyword

Language Reference

UnitEntryTable Type

Syntax

```
type UnitEntryTable = array[0..9999999] of PackageUnitEntry;
```

Description

Every package has a UnitEntryTable, which stores the PackageUnitEntry records for the units contained in the package.

See Also

GetPackageInfoTable Function, PackageInfoTable Type, PackageUnitEntry Type, PUnitEntryTable Type, Unit Keyword

UnregisterModule Procedure

Syntax

```
procedure UnregisterModule(LibModule: PLibModule);
```

Description

UnregisterModule removes a module from Delphi's list of registered modules. Delphi automatically calls UnregisterModule when it unloads a package or when the program exits.

Tips and Tricks

You can call `UnregisterModule` to remove a module from the list, but doing so prevents Delphi from finalizing the module.

See Also

EnumModules Procedure, EnumResourceModules Procedure, LibModuleList Variable, PLibModule Type, RegisterModule Procedure, TLibModule Type

---

Until Keyword

Syntax

```
repeat
  Statements...
until Boolean expression
```

Description

The `until` keyword marks the end of a **repeat-until** statement.

See Also

Boolean Type, Break Procedure, Continue Procedure, Repeat Keyword

---

UpCase Function

Syntax

```
function UpCase(C: Char): Char;
```

Description

The `UpCase` function converts an ASCII character to uppercase. If C is not a lower-case character, `UpCase` returns C. `UpCase` is a real function.

Tips and Tricks

- `UpCase` does not handle international characters—it handles only "a" through "z".

- Delphi does not have a corresponding `DownCase` function.

Example

```
function DownCase(Ch: Char): Char;
begin
  if Ch in ['A'..'Z'] then
    Result := Chr(Ord(Ch) - Ord('A') + Ord('a'))
  else
    Result := Ch;
end;

// Convert an identifier to canonical form, i.e., initial uppercase
// character followed by all lower case characters.
function Canonical(const S: string): string;
var
```

```
    I: Integer;
begin
  SetLength(Result, Length(S));
  if Length(S) > 0 then
    Result[1] := UpCase(S[1]);
  for I := 2 to Length(S) do
    Result[I] := DownCase(S[I]);
end;
```

See Also

AnsiChar Type, Char Type, WideChar Type

Uses Keyword

Syntax

```
uses Unit name, ...;
uses Unit name in File name, ...
```

Description

The **uses** keyword lists the names of units that are imported into the surrounding unit, program, or library. The **uses** declaration is optional, but if you use it, it must be the first declaration in a program, library, or in the interface and implementation sections of a unit.

Tips and Tricks

- In a program or library, the syntax can follow the second form, where the *File name* is a string literal that specifies the path to the file that contains the unit's source code. The compiler uses the path information to locate the file for compiling it, and the IDE uses the path to manage the project.

- Any changes made to a unit's interface section may cause all dependent units to be recompiled. A dependent unit is recompiled if it uses any of the declarations that changed in the original unit's interface section. In a large project, you can save yourself some recompilation time by using units in the implementation section as much as possible.

- The symbols a unit exports in its interface section are available to any other unit that uses the first unit. Delphi searches the used units in order from last to first. Thus, units listed later in a **uses** declaration take precedence over units listed earlier. If you need to use a symbol from a unit listed earlier, you can qualify the symbol name with the unit name followed by a dot (.).

Example

```
uses SysUtils, Windows;

// Windows and SysUtils both define DeleteFile. Because Windows comes
// later in the uses list, its DeleteFile takes precedence over the
// one in SysUtils. You can call the DeleteFile in SysUtils by
// prefacing the function name with the unit name, e.g.,
procedure RemoveFile(const FileName: string);
begin
```

```
      SysUtils.DeleteFile(FileName);
   end;
```

See Also

Implementation Keyword, Interface Keyword, Library Keyword, Program
Keyword, Unit Keyword

Val Procedure

Syntax

```
procedure Val(const S: string; var Result; var Code; Integer);
```

Description

Val converts a string to a numeric value. The Result argument can be an integer,
Int64, or floating-point variable. If the conversion is successful, Code is zero.
Otherwise, the value of Code is the string position where Val first detected a
format error. Val is not a real procedure.

Tips and Tricks

To convert a string to a floating-point number, use the string conversion functions
in the SysUtils unit instead of Val. The problem is that Val does not heed the
local settings for the decimal separator, making the procedure useless in an international setting.

Example

```
// Prompt the user for a number, and return the number that the
// user enters. If the user enters invalid input, show what
// the user mistyped and try again.
function GetNumber(const Prompt: string): Int64;
var
  S: string;
  Code: Integer;
begin
  repeat
    Write(Prompt);
    ReadLn(S);
    Val(S, Result, Code);
    if Code <> 0 then
    begin
      WriteLn(S);
      WriteLn('^':Code, ' invalid input');
    end;
  until Code = 0;
end;
```

See Also

Str Procedure

Var Keyword

Syntax

```
var
  Name: Type;
  Name: Type = Expression;
  ...
```

Description

The **var** keyword declares one or more variables. If you use the **var** keyword at the unit level, it declares global variables whose lifetime is that of the entire unit. If you use the **var** keyword in a subroutine, you are declaring local variables whose scope and lifetime are limited to that subroutine.

You can also supply an initial value for a global variable, but not for a local variable.

Tips and Tricks

- Without an initial value, a global variable is initialized to zero (empty string, nil pointer, etc.), and a local variable is not initialized.

- Local variables are not usually initialized, but Delphi ensures that memory-managed variables, such as strings, dynamic arrays, **Variants**, and interfaces are properly managed.

- The Result variable is special. It is initialized by the caller, not the subroutine, and the initial value is not necessarily zero.

Example

```
unit Debug;
interface
var
  FileName: string = 'c:\debug.txt';
procedure Log(const Msg: string);
implementation
uses SysUtils;

procedure Log(const Msg: string);
var
  F: TextFile;
  TimeStamp: string;
begin
  AssignFile(F, FileName);
  if FileExists(FileName) then
    Append(F)
  else
    Rewrite(F);
  try
    TimeStamp := DateTimeToStr(Now);
    WriteLn(F, '[', TimeStamp, '] ', Msg);
  finally
    CloseFile(F);
  end;
```

```
end;
end.
```

See Also

Const Keyword, Function Keyword, Library Keyword, Procedure Keyword, Program Keyword, Result Variable, Self Variable, ThreadVar Keyword, Unit Keyword

---

VarArrayCreate Function

Syntax

```
function VarArrayCreate(const Bounds: array of Integer;
    VarType: Integer): Variant;
```

Description

The `VarArrayCreate` function creates a `Variant` array. The first argument specifies the number of dimensions and the bounds for each dimension. The second argument is the `Variant` type of each array element.

The array bounds are specified as pairs of integers: the lower and upper bounds of each dimension. The array can have up to 64 dimensions. If you try to create an invalid array, `VarArrayCreate` reports runtime error 24 (`EVariantError`).

`VarArrayCreate` is a real function.

Tips and Tricks

- Create a heterogeneous array by specifying `varVariant` as the element type. That way, each element of the array can be of any `Variant` type.

- You cannot create an array of `varEmpty` or `varNull` types.

Example

```
// Return a Variant array of 12 random numbers.
function RandomDozen: Variant;
var
  I: Integer;
begin
  Result := VarArrayCreate([1, 12], varDouble);
  for I := VarArrayLowBound(Result) to VarArrayHighBound(Result) do
    Result[I] := Random;
end;
```

See Also

TVarArray Type, TVarArrayBound Type, VarArrayDimCount Function, VarArrayHighBound Function, VarArrayLock Function, VarArrayLowBound Function, VarArrayOf Function, VarArrayRedim Procedure, VarArrayRef Function, VarArrayUnlock Function, Variant Type, VarIsArray Function, VarType Function

---

VarArrayDimCount Function

Syntax

```
function VarArrayDimCount(const V: Variant): Integer;
```

Description

VarArrayDimCount returns the number of dimensions of a Variant array. If V is not a Variant array, the function returns zero.

VarArrayDimCount is a real function.

Example

```
var
  V: Variant;
begin
  V := VarArrayCreate([1, 12], varDouble);
  WriteLn(VarArrayDimCount(V)); // Writes 1
```

See Also

TVarArray Type, TVarArrayBound Type, VarArrayCreate Function, VarArrayHighBound Function, VarArrayLock Function, VarArrayLowBound Function, VarArrayOf Function, VarArrayRedim Procedure, VarArrayRef Function, VarArrayUnlock Function, Variant Type, VarIsArray Function, VarType Function

---

VarArrayHighBound Function

Syntax

```
function VarArrayHighBound(const V: Variant; Dim: Integer): Integer;
```

Description

VarArrayHighBound returns the upper bound of dimension Dim for the Variant array V. Dim must be in the range 1 to VarArrayDimCount. If Dim is out of range or if V is not a Variant array, the function reports runtime error 20 (EVariantError).

VarArrayHighBound is a real function.

Example

See VarArrayCreate for an example.

See Also

TVarArray Type, TVarArrayBound Type, VarArrayCreate Function, VarArrayDimCount Function, VarArrayLock Function, VarArrayLowBound Function, VarArrayOf Function, VarArrayRedim Procedure, VarArrayRef Function, VarArrayUnlock Function, Variant Type, VarIsArray Function, VarType Function

VarArrayLock Function

Syntax

```
function VarArrayLock(var V: Variant): Pointer;
```

Description

VarArrayLock locks the Variant array's dimensions so it cannot be resized, and returns a pointer to a simple array of the Variant array's contents. The data array is organized such that the leftmost index varies first (row-major order). Note that ordinary Pascal arrays are stored in column-major order, so the rightmost index varies first.

VarArrayLock is a real function.

Tips and Tricks

- If you need to perform an operation on all the elements of the Variant array, lock the array first to enhance performance.

- The data array contains the actual values of each element of the Variant array. Verify that the array element type is what you expect, and cast the data pointer to the correct data type.

- While an array is locked, you cannot change its size, but you can change its contents. Changes to the array elements are reflected in the raw data array that VarArrayLock returns.

- You can lock an array more than once. To unlock the array, you must call VarArrayUnlock once for every time you call VarArrayLock.

Example

```
// Swap two doubles.
procedure DSwap(var A, B: Double);
var
  Tmp: Double;
begin
  Tmp := A;
  A := B;
  B := Tmp;
end;

// Transpose a 2D matrix of varDouble values. For maximum performance,
// lock the Variant array and access the raw data.
procedure Transpose(var M: Variant);
type
  TDoubleArray = array[0..MaxInt div SizeOf(Double)-1] of Double;
  PDoubleArray = ^TDoubleArray;
var
  I, J: Integer;
  Data: PDoubleArray;
  Dim1: Integer;
  Low1, Low2: Integer;
  High1, High2: Integer;
begin
```

```
      Assert(VarType(M) = varArray or varDouble);
      Data := VarArrayLock(M);
      try
        Low1 := VarArrayLowBound(M, 1);
        Low2 := VarArrayLowBound(M, 2);
        High1 := VarArrayHighBound(M, 1);
        High2 := VarArrayHighBound(M, 2);
        Dim1 := High1 - Low1 + 1;

        // The raw data array is a 1D vector, but the data values are
        // still organized as a matrix. Swap the M[J, I] and M[I, J]
        // elements of the matrix, using the Data array.
        for I := Low1 to High1 do
          for J := I to High2 do
              DSwap(Data[J-Low2 + (I-Low1)*Dim1],
                    Data[I-Low2 + (J-Low1)*Dim1]);
      finally
        VarArrayUnlock(M);
      end;
    end;
```

See Also

TVarArray Type, TVarArrayBound Type, VarArrayCreate Function,
VarArrayDimCount Function, VarArrayHighBound Function,
VarArrayLowBound Function, VarArrayOf Function, VarArrayRedim
Procedure, VarArrayRef Function, VarArrayUnlock Function, Variant Type,
VarIsArray Function, VarType Function

VarArrayLowBound Function

Syntax

```
function VarArrayLowBound(const V: Variant; Dim: Integer): Integer;
```

Description

VarArrayLowBound returns the lower bound of dimension Dim for the Variant
array V. Dim must be in the range 1 to VarArrayDimCount. If Dim is out of range
or if V is not a Variant array, the function reports runtime error 20
(EVariantError).

VarArrayLowBound is a real function.

Example

See VarArrayCreate for an example.

See Also

TVarArray Type, TVarArrayBound Type, VarArrayCreate Function,
VarArrayDimCount Function, VarArrayHighBound Function, VarArrayLock
Function, VarArrayOf Function, VarArrayRedim Procedure, VarArrayRef
Function, VarArrayUnlock Function, Variant Type, VarIsArray Function,
VarType Function

VarArrayOf Function

Syntax

```
function VarArrayOf(const Values: array of Variant): Variant;
```

Description

VarArrayOf creates a one-dimensional Variant array that contains the same values as the open array argument. The resulting array has a lower bound of zero and an upper bound of the array size minus 1.

VarArrayOf is a real function.

Example

```
// The following two examples do the same thing.
V := VarArrayOf([1.0, 20, 'Testing']);

V := VarArrayCreate([0, 2], varVariant);
V[0] := 1.0;
V[1] := 20;
V[2] := 'Testing';
```

See Also

TVarArray Type, TVarArrayBound Type, VarArrayCreate Function, VarArrayDimCount Function, VarArrayHighBound Function, VarArrayLock Function, VarArrayLowBound Function, VarArrayRedim Procedure, VarArrayRef Function, VarArrayUnlock Function, Variant Type, VarIsArray Function, VarType Function

---

VarArrayRedim Procedure

Syntax

```
procedure VarArrayRedim(var V: Variant; HighBound: Integer);
```

Description

VarArrayRedim resizes the rightmost dimension of the Variant array V. The upper bound of the highest dimension is changed to HighBound.

VarArrayRedim is not a real function.

Tips and Tricks

- You cannot resize a Variant array while the array is locked.

- Resizing an array preserves as many array elements as possible. If the array grows larger, the new elements are initialized to zero if the array element type is a numeric type, Unassigned for varVariant elements, and an empty string for string elements.

- You cannot change the size of an array reference (that is, the result of calling VarArrayRef). You must pass the actual array to the VarArrayRedim procedure.

Example

```
// Read numbers from the user into a growing array.
// This function is inefficient, but a good demonstration
// of VarArrayRedim.
function GetArray: Variant;
var
  Number: Integer;
begin
  Result := VarArrayCreate([1, 0], varInteger);
  while not Eof do
  begin
    ReadLn(Number);
    VarArrayRedim(Result, VarArrayHighBound(Result, 1) + 1);
    Result[VarArrayHighBound(Result, 1)] := Number;
  end;
end;
```

See Also

TVarArray Type, TVarArrayBound Type, VarArrayCreate Function,
VarArrayDimCount Function, VarArrayHighBound Function, VarArrayLock
Function, VarArrayLowBound Function, VarArrayOf Function, VarArrayRef
Function, VarArrayUnlock Function, Variant Type, VarIsArray Function,
VarType Function

VarArrayRef Function

Syntax

```
function VarArrayRef(const V: Variant): Variant;
```

Description

VarArrayRef creates a new Variant array with the varByRef bit set in the
Variant's VarType. The new Variant refers directly to the array data in V. Any
changes to the dimensions or contents of V are also reflected in the new array.

VarArrayRef is a real function.

Tips and Tricks

- Once you have created the reference, you must take care not to let the reference outlive the original array. If both Variants are in the same scope, you are fine, but do not return the reference array from a function where the original array is local to the function.

- You cannot redimension an array reference.

Example

```
var
  Orig, Ref: Variant;
begin
  Orig := VarArrayCreate([1, 10], varInteger);
  Ref := VarArrayRef(Orig);
  Orig[1] := 42;
```

```
      WriteLn(Ref[1]);                       // Writes 42
      VarArrayRedim(Orig, 5);                 // Also affects Ref
      WriteLn(VarArrayHighBound(Ref, 1));     // Writes 5
    end;                                      // Ref and Orig are cleaned up
```

See Also

TVarArray Type, TVarArrayBound Type, VarArrayCreate Function,
VarArrayDimCount Function, VarArrayHighBound Function, VarArrayLock
Function, VarArrayLowBound Function, VarArrayOf Function, VarArrayRedim
Procedure, VarArrayUnlock Function, Variant Type, VarIsArray Function,
VarType Function

VarArrayUnlock Procedure

Syntax

```
procedure VarArrayUnlock(var V: Variant);
```

Description

VarArrayUnlock unlocks a Variant array that was previously locked by
VarArrayLock.

You can lock an array more than once. To unlock the array, you must call
VarArrayUnlock once for every time you call VarArrayLock.

VarArrayUnlock is a real function.

Example

See VarArrayLock for an example.

See Also

TVarArray Type, TVarArrayBound Type, VarArrayCreate Function,
VarArrayDimCount Function, VarArrayHighBound Function, VarArrayLock
Function, VarArrayLowBound Function, VarArrayOf Function, VarArrayRedim
Procedure, VarArrayRef Function, Variant Type, VarIsArray Function, VarType
Function

VarAsType Function

Syntax

```
function VarAsType(const V: Variant; VarType: Integer): Variant;
```

Description

VarAsType performs a typecast of V to a new Variant type. VarType must not
contain the varArray or varByRef bits. If V cannot be converted to the desired
type, VarAsType reports runtime error 15 (EVariantError).

VarAsType is a real function.

Tips and Tricks

- `VarAsType` is a functional version of `VarCast`. If you want to assign the result to an `OleVariant`, you should use `VarCast` instead, because it performs additional type checking.

- If the type of `Source` is already `VarType`, `VarAsType` performs a simple copy.

Example

```
Int := 1;
Float := VarAsType(Int, varDouble);
```

See Also

OleVariant Type, TVarData Type, VarCast Procedure, VarCopy Procedure, Variant Type, VarIsArray Function, VarIsEmpty Function, VarIsNull Function

---

VarCast Procedure

Syntax

```
procedure VarCast(var Dest: Variant; const Source: Variant;
                  VarType: Integer);
procedure VarCast(var Dest: OleVariant; const Source: Variant;
                  VarType: Integer);
```

Description

`VarCast` performs a typecast of `Source` to a new `Variant` type, storing the result in `Dest`. `VarType` must not contain the `varArray` or `varByRef` bits.

If `Dest` is an `OleVariant`, the new type must be an OLE-compatible type. In particular, you cannot cast to `varString`, but must use `varOleStr` instead. Otherwise, `VarCast` reports runtime error 15 (`EVariantError`).

`VarCast` is not a real procedure.

Tips and Tricks

- `VarCast` is similar to `VarAsType`. The difference is that `VarCast` performs additional tests when casting to an `OleVariant`.

- If the type of `Source` is already `VarType`, `VarCast` performs a simple copy.

Example

```
var
  V: Variant;
  O: OleVariant;
begin
  V := 'This is a test';     // VarType(V) = varString
  VarCast(O, V, varOleStr);
```

See Also

OleVariant Type, TVarData Type, VarAsType Function, VarCopy Procedure, Variant Type, VarIsArray Function, VarIsEmpty Function, VarIsNull Function

---

VarClear Procedure

Syntax

```
procedure VarClear(var V: Variant);
```

Description

VarClear disposes of the old value of V and sets its type to **varEmpty**.

VarClear is not a real function.

Example

```
// The following two statements do the same thing:
VarClear(V);
V := Unassigned;
```

See Also

ClearAnyProc Variable, Unassigned Variable, Variant Type, VarIsEmpty Function

---

VarCopy Procedure

Syntax

```
procedure VarCopy(var Dest: Variant; const Source: Variant);
```

Description

VarCopy clears Dest and assigns a copy of Source to Dest.

VarCopy is not a real function.

Tips and Tricks

- Assigning Dest := Source ends up calling the VarCopy procedure, but assignment is sometimes more efficient.

- If Dest is an OleVariant, and Source is a Variant of type varString, VarCopy automatically converts the type to varOleStr.

See Also

OleVariant Type, Variant Type

VarDispProc Variable

Syntax

```
var VarDispProc: Pointer;

procedure Invoke(Result: PVariant; const Instance: Variant;
  CallDesc: PCallDesc; Params: Pointer); cdecl;
VarDispProc := @Invoke;
```

Description

VarDispProc points to a procedure that invokes an IDispatch method from a Variant reference. When a Variant refers to a COM server, it is actually storing an IDispatch interface and has the VarType of varDispatch. When your program calls a method or uses a property of the COM server, the Variant object must call the IDispatch.Invoke method. Delphi relies on the VarDispProc procedure to do this.

Result is a pointer to a Variant where a function result should be stored, or it is nil if no result is expected. Instance is the Variant that contains the IDispatch interface invoking the method or property. CallDesc points to a record that describes the method to be invoked, and Params points to an array that describes the method arguments.

Tips and Tricks

- Do not assign nil to VarDispProc. Unlike similar procedure pointers in Delphi, if VarDispProc is nil, Delphi does not have a default behavior, and you get an access violation instead.

- The initial value of VarDispProc points to a procedure that reports runtime error 17 (EVariantError).

- The ComObj unit defines this procedure to handle all the details for you. It also declares the PCallDesc type.

See Also

DispCallByIDProc Variable, Dispinterface Keyword, IDispatch Interface, Interface Keyword, OleVariant Type, Variant Type

---

VarFromDateTime Function

Syntax

```
function VarFromDateTime(DateTime: TDateTime): Variant;
```

Description

VarFromDateTime creates a varDate Variant for the given TDateTime value. VarFromDateTime is a real function.

Tips and Tricks

- You must call VarFromDateTime to convert a TDateTime value to a Variant. If you try to assign a TDateTime to a Variant, Delphi creates a varDouble Variant because TDateTime is really a floating-point type.

- Delphi's format for TDateTime values is the OLE standard, so if you create a varDate Variant by directly assigning the member of a TVarData record, you can assign a TDateTime value to the VDate member.

- If you want extra control over the string formatting of a TDateTime, you can call VarToDateTime and then use the functions in SysUtils to format the string. Casting the varDate to a varString value always uses a short date and time format.

Example

```
// The following two examples do the same thing.
V := VarFromDateTime(Now);

VarClear(V);
TVarData(V).VType := varDate;
TVarData(V).VDate := Now;
```

See Also

TDateTime Type, VarClear Procedure, Variant Type, VarToDateTime Function

---

Variant Type

Syntax

```
type Variant;
```

Description

The `Variant` type is a dynamic type. A `Variant` variable can change type at runtime, sometimes storing an integer, other times a string, and other times an array.

Delphi automatically casts numbers, strings, interfaces, and other types to and from `Variants` as needed. You can also use a number of functions to further manipulate and work with `Variants`.

Chapter 6, *System Constants*, lists all the possible types for a `Variant`.

Tips and Tricks

- Variants offer flexibility, but you pay a performance price. Even simple arithmetic with `Variants` is much more complicated and time-intensive than arithmetic with typed variables. Every reference to a `Variant` must be checked at runtime, which can be costly if your program often uses `Variants`.

- Variants are usually easy to understand and use, but they have some subtleties. For example, `Unassigned` and `Null` represent distinctly different `Variant` values and concepts. One way to think of the difference is to imagine a `Variant` as a box that contains a piece of paper. On the paper is written the `Variant`'s value: a number, a string, the time of day, etc. `Null` is a blank piece of paper. `Unassigned` is an empty box.

- To convert a `TDateTime` to or from a `Variant`, you must use the functions `VarFromDateTime` and `VarToDateTime`.

- The most common use for `Variants` is calling an OLE automation server when you don't have a `dispinterface` at compile time. You call the server's methods, but Delphi cannot look up the methods at compile time, so it checks them at runtime. Ordinarily, you could not call a method without having a base class or interface to declare the method's name, arguments, and return type, but using a `Variant`, you can defer these details until runtime, when Delphi uses the server's `IDispatch` interface to look up the method and its signature.

Example

```
var
  WordApp: Variant;
  A, X: Variant;
begin
  WordApp := CreateOleObject('Word.Basic');
  WordApp.FileNew;

  X := Pi;
  X := X / 2.0;   // Mix Variants and numbers in expressions.
  ShowMessage(X); // Delphi automatically converts to a string.

  // Create a 3x3 matrix.
  A := VarArrayCreate([1, 3, 1, 3], varDouble);
  for I := 1 to 3 do
    for J := 1 to 3 do
      A[I, J] := I + J;
end;
```

See Also

ChangeAnyProc Variable, ClearAnyProc Variable, EmptyParam Variable, Null
Variable, OleVariant Type, RefAnyProc Variable, TVarData Type, Unassigned
Variable, VarArrayCreate Function, VarArrayDimCount Function,
VarArrayHighBound Function, VarArrayLock Function, VarArrayLowBound
Function, VarArrayOf Function, VarArrayRedim Procedure, VarArrayRef
Function, VarArrayUnlock Procedure, VarAsType Function, VarCast Procedure,
VarClear Procedure, VarCopy Procedure, VarDispProc Variable,
VarFromDateTime Function, VarIsArray Function, VarIsEmpty Function,
VarIsNull Function, VarToDateTime Function, VarToStr Function, VarType
Function

VarIsArray Function

Syntax

```
function VarIsArray(const V: Variant): Boolean;
```

Description

VarIsArray returns True if the Variant V is an array, and it returns False otherwise. A Variant array has the varArray bit set in its VarType.

VarIsArray is a real function.

Example

```
// Return the sum of all the numbers in a 1D array, or if the
// argument is not an array, return its numeric value.
function Sum(const V: Variant): Variant;
var
  I: Integer;
begin
  if VarIsArray(V) then
  begin
```

```
      Result := 0.0;
      Assert(VarArrayDimCount(V) = 1);
      for I := VarArrayLowBound(V, 1) to VarArrayHighBound(V, 1) do
        Result := Result + V[I];
    end
    else
      Result := V + 0.0; // Ensure that the result is numeric.
  end;
```

See Also

TVarArray Type, TVarArrayBound Type, VarArrayCreate Function,
VarArrayDimCount Function, VarArrayHighBound Function, VarArrayLock
Function, VarArrayLowBound Function, VarArrayOf Function, VarArrayRedim
Procedure, VarArrayRef Function, VarArrayUnlock Function, Variant Type,
VarIsArray Function, VarType Function

VarIsEmpty Function

Syntax

```
function VarIsEmpty(const V: Variant): Boolean;
```

Description

VarIsEmpty returns True if the Variant V has the varEmpty type, and it returns
False for any other kind of Variant. A Variant's initial type is varEmpty.

VarIsEmpty is a real function.

Example

```
// Convert a Variant to a TDateTime, but if the Variant
// does not have a value, return the current date and time.
function GetDate(V: Variant): TDateTime;
begin
  if VarIsEmpty(V) or VarIsNull(V) then
    Result := Now
  else
    Result := VarToDateTime(V);
end;
```

See Also

Unassigned Variable, VarClear Procedure, Variant Type, VarIsNull Function,
VarType Function

VarIsNull Function

Syntax

```
function VarIsNull(const V: Variant): Boolean;
```

Description

VarIsNull returns True if the Variant V has the varNull type, and it returns
False for any other kind of Variant. VarIsNull is a real function.

Example

See Null and VarIsEmpty for examples.

See Also

Null Variable, Variant Type, VarIsEmpty Function, VarType Function

---

VarToDateTime Function

Syntax

```
function VarToDateTime(const V: Variant): TDateTime;
```

Description

VarToDateTime converts a Variant to a TDateTime. If the Variant cannot be converted to varDate, the function reports runtime error 15 (EVariantError).

VarToDateTime is a real function.

Tips and Tricks

• Assigning a Variant to a TDateTime variable does not work. Because TDateTime is a floating-point type, the assignment would try to convert the Variant to a varDouble, not a varDate.

• VarToDateTime eventually calls the Windows API function VariantChangeTypeEx to parse the string and interpret the date and time. See the Platform SDK documentation for details. VarToDateTime accepts many more formats than StrToDateTime.

Example

```
// Parse a string as a date and time.
function StringToDateTime(const S: string): TDateTime;
var
  V: Variant;
begin
  V := S;
  Result := VarToDateTime(V);
end;
```

See Also

TDateTime Type, VarFromDateTime Function, Variant Type

VarToStr Function

Syntax

```
function VarToStr(const V: Variant): string;
```

Description

VarToStr converts a Variant to a string. If V is Null, VarToStr returns an empty string. VarToStr is a real function.

Tips and Tricks

The only difference between calling `VarToStr` and simply assigning a `Variant` to a string variable occurs if the `Variant` is `Null`. Assigning `Null` to a string would result in runtime error 15 (`EVariantError`).

See Also

Null Variable, String Keyword, Variant Type, VarIsNull Function

---

VarType Function

Syntax

```
function VarType(const V: Variant): Integer;
```

Description

`VarType` returns a `Variant`'s type code. The type code determines the actual data type of the `Variant` value, and whether the `Variant` is an array or a reference.

See Chapter 6 for a list of variant type codes.

`VarType` is a real function.

Tips and Tricks

The type code is a bit mask. The low-order 12 bits specify a type code, and the higher bits specify additional type information. Use the **varTypeMask** constant to find the actual type code. The possible modifiers are **varArray** for an array and **varByRef** for indirect data.

Example

```
// Calling VarType is the same as accessing the VType field of the
// TVarData record. The following two examples do the same thing.
// (Accessing the field is slightly faster, but is harder to read.)
I := VarType(V);

I := TVarData(V).VType;

if VarType(V) = varDateTime then
   TVarData(V).VDate := Now;
```

See Also

TVarData Type, Variant Type, VarIsArray Function, VarIsEmpty Function, VarIsNull Function

---

Virtual Directive

Syntax

```
Method declaration; virtual;
```

Description

You can declare a virtual method in a base class by using the `virtual` directive or the `dynamic` directive. The semantics of both directives is the same. The only difference is the implementation of the method and how it is called. For details, see Chapter 3.

Derived classes must use the `override` directive to override the method.

Tips and Tricks

- You should almost always use the `virtual` directive instead of `dynamic`. In most cases, `virtual` methods are faster and take up less memory than `dynamic` methods.

- The `virtual` directive must follow the `reintroduce` and `overload` directives and precede the calling convention and `abstract` directives (if the declaration uses any of these directives).

Example

```
type
  WholeNumber = 0..MaxInt;
  TIterator = function(Item: Pointer): Boolean of object;
  // Abstract base class for a variety of collection classes.
  // Derived classes must override several methods to implement
  // the detailed behavior.
  TCollection = class
  protected
    constructor Create; virtual;
    function Add(Item: Pointer): WholeNumber; virtual; abstract;
    function GetCount: WholeNumber; virtual; abstract;
    function Delete(Index: WholeNumber): Pointer; virtual; abstract;
  public
    procedure Remove(Item: Pointer); virtual;
    procedure ForEach(Iterator: TIterator); virtual;
  end;
  // Abstract class for several different binary trees.
  // Implements the binary-tree methods, but leaves some of the
  // details to derived classes.
  TBinaryTree = class(TCollection)
  private
    fRoot: TBinaryNode;
    fCount: Integer;
    constructor Create; override;
  public
    function Add(Item: Pointer): WholeNumber; override; abstract;
    function GetCount: WholeNumber; override;
    function Delete(Index: WholeNumber): Pointer; override; abstract;
    procedure ForEach(Iterator: TIterator); override;
  end;
  // Balanced binary tree. Notice the public constructor.
  // All abstract methods have been implemented.
  TBalancedBinaryTree = class(TBinaryTree)
  public
    constructor Create; override;
```

```
    function Add(Item: Pointer): WholeNumber; override;
    function Delete(Index: WholeNumber): Pointer; override;
  end;
```

See Also

Abstract Directive, Class Type, Dynamic Directive, Overload Directive,
Override Directive, Reintroduce Directive

While Keyword

Syntax

```
while Expression do Statement
```

Description

The while statement is the same as it is in standard Pascal. While the *Expression*
is True, Delphi repeatedly executes the *Statement*. If the *Expression* is False
the first time it is tested, the *Statement* never executes.

See Also

Boolean Type, Break Procedure, Continue Procedure, Do Keyword, For
Keyword, Repeat Keyword

WideChar Type

Syntax

```
type WideChar = #0..#65535;
```

Description

The WideChar type represents a 16-bit Unicode character. Unicode is a superset of
the AnsiChar type: values between #0 and #255 are the same in both character
sets, but Unicode has many additional characters to support a variety of international languages.

See Also

AnsiChar Type, Char Type, Chr Function, OleStrToString Function,
OleStrToStrVar Procedure, Ord Function, PWideChar Type, String Keyword,
StringToOleStr Function, StringToWideChar Function, WideCharLenToString
Function, WideCharLenToStrVar Procedure, WideCharToString Function,
WideCharToStrVar Procedure, WideString Type

WideCharLenToString Function

Syntax

```
function WideCharLenToString(Source: PWideChar; Len: Integer): string;
```

Description

WideCharLenToString converts a Unicode string of Len characters (not bytes) to a multibyte character string. See WideString for more information about Unicode and multibyte strings.

See Also

OleStrToString Function, OleStrToStrVar Procedure, PWideChar Type, String Keyword, StringToOleStr Function, StringToWideChar Function, WideChar Type, WideCharLenToStrVar Procedure, WideCharToString Function, WideCharToStrVar Procedure, WideString Type

WideCharLenToStrVar Procedure

Syntax

```
procedure WideCharLenToStrVar(Source: PWideChar; Len: Integer;
    var Dest: string);
```

Description

WideCharLenToStrVar converts a Unicode string of Len characters (not bytes) to a multibyte character string, which it stores in Dest. See WideString for more information about Unicode and multibyte strings.

See Also

OleStrToString Function, OleStrToStrVar Procedure, PWideChar Type, String Keyword, StringToOleStr Function, StringToWideChar Function, WideChar Type, WideCharLenToString Function, WideCharLenToStrVar Procedure, WideCharToStrVar Procedure, WideString Type

WideCharToString Function

Syntax

```
function WideCharToString(Source: PWideChar): string;
```

Description

WideCharToString converts a #0-terminated Unicode string to a multibyte character string. See WideString for more information about Unicode and multibyte strings.

See Also

OleStrToString Function, OleStrToStrVar Procedure, PWideChar Type, String Keyword, StringToOleStr Function, StringToWideChar Function, WideChar Type, WideCharLenToString Function, WideCharLenToStrVar Procedure, WideCharToStrVar Procedure, WideString Type

WideCharToStrVar Procedure

Syntax

```
procedure WideCharToStrVar(Source: PWideChar; var Dest: string);
```

Description

WideCharToStrVar converts a #0-terminated Unicode string to a multibyte character string, which is stores in Dest. See WideString for more information about Unicode and multibyte strings.

See Also

OleStrToString Function, OleStrToStrVar Procedure, PWideChar Type, String Keyword, StringToOleStr Function, StringToWideChar Function, WideChar Type, WideCharLenToString Function, WideCharLenToStrVar Procedure, WideCharToString Function, WideString Type

WideString Type

Syntax

```
type WideString;
```

Description

WideString is similar to AnsiString, but instead of storing a string of AnsiChar characters, it stores a Unicode string of WideChar (16-bit) characters. WideString keeps track of its length and automatically appends a #0 character to the end of the string so you can easily cast it to PWideChar.

Internally, Delphi stores a WideString as a pointer to a record, except that the pointer actually points to the Data member, and the Length is stored in the four bytes preceding the WideString pointer.

```
type
  // This is the logical structure of an WideString, but the
  // declaration below is descriptive and cannot be compiled.
  TWideString = record
    Length: LongWord;
    Data: array[1..Length+1] of WideChar;
  end;
```

Tips and Tricks

- Like AnsiString, Delphi automatically manages the memory for WideString variables. Unlike AnsiString, WideString does not have a reference count, so every assignment of a WideString value results in a complete copy of the string. Thus, using WideString is less efficient than using AnsiString.

- Delphi automatically converts between AnsiString and WideString, from PWideChar to WideString, and from a zero-based array of WideChar to WideString.

- You can cast a WideString to PWideChar, which is often required for calling Windows API functions, but you must take the same care you take when casting an AnsiString to PChar. Delphi automatically frees the string when the string is no longer needed, but this also invalidates the PChar or PWideChar pointer. As long as nothing is still using the pointer, you are fine. Thus, you can use a PWideChar cast when calling an API function, but don't save the PWideChar pointer for future use.

- When converting a WideString to an AnsiString, Delphi uses the ANSI code page and lets Windows perform the default mapping for non-ANSI characters. If you want more control over the conversion process, call the Windows API function WideCharToMultiByte directly.

- After converting a wide string to a narrow string, the narrow string might contain multibyte characters. The SysUtils unit contains a number of functions to work with multibyte strings. See Appendix B for details.

- The VCL does not use Unicode. If you want to use the Unicode controls in Windows NT, you must create your own components or find third-party solutions.

See Also

AnsiString Type, Length Function, OleStrToString Function, OleStrToStrVar Procedure, PWideChar Type, SetLength Procedure, SetString Procedure, String Keyword, StringToOleStr Function, StringToWideChar Function, WideChar Type, WideCharLenToString Function, WideCharLenToStrVar Procedure, WideCharToString Function, WideCharToStrVar Procedure

---

With Keyword

Syntax

```
with Expression do Statement
```

Description

The with statement adds a record, object, class, or interface reference to the scope for resolving symbol names. Delphi searches for names in the following order:

1. Members of records, objects, classes, or interfaces listed in the with statement, starting with the last or innermost with statement, and continuing with earlier or outer with statements.

2. Local variables and subroutine parameters, including implicitly defined variables, such as Result and Self.

3. Members of Self (if the subroutine is a method). You can think of every method as having an implicit with Self do before the method body.

4. Global variables in the same unit as the reference.

5. Global variables declared in other units, starting with the last unit named in the uses declaration.

Tips and Tricks

- Be careful using the with statement. Indiscriminate use of the with statement obscures the meaning of code and makes it harder to identify the object references that are the targets of methods and properties. Changes to the referenced record, object, class, or interface can cause an identifier to be interpreted in a different scope. If you are fortunate, the change will cause a syntax error; if you are not, the change will not be noticed until your program performs incorrectly.

- Nonetheless, with has its uses. It can be a convenient way to avoid creating a temporary variable when adding such a variable does not contribute to the clarity of your code.

Example

```
// When the user clicks the button, add an item to the list,
// and edit the caption so the user can assign a useful name.
procedure TMyForm.Button1Click(Sender: TObject);
begin
  with ListView1.Items.Add do
  begin
    Caption := 'New Name'; // Refers to the new list view item Caption
    EditCaption;           // not Self.Caption.
  end;
end;
```

See Also

Do Keyword, Self Variable

Word Type

Syntax

```
type Word = 0..65535;
```

Description

The Word type represents unsigned, 16-bit integers.

See Integer for more information about integer types.

See Also

Integer Type, SmallInt Type

WordBool Type

Syntax

```
type WordBool;
```

Description

The WordBool type is a logical type whose size is the same as the size of a Word. A WordBool value is False when its ordinal value is zero, and it is True when its ordinal value is any non-zero value. `WordBool` uses –1 as the ordinal value for `True` constants, e.g., `WordBool(True)`.

Tips and Tricks

- You can use a `WordBool` value anywhere you can use a `Boolean`. It is most useful when interfacing with C and C++, where any non-zero integer is considered `True`.

- `ByteBool` and `LongBool` are similar to `WordBool`, but they have different sizes.

See Also

And Keyword, Boolean Type, ByteBool Type, LongBool Type, Not Keyword, Or Keyword, Xor Keyword

---

Write Directive

Syntax

```
property Name: Type ... write Setter;
```

Description

A property's `write` directive tells Delphi how to change the property's value. The `Setter` can be the a field reference or a method name in the class or in an ancestor class.

If the `Setter` is a field, the field's type must be the same as the property's type. The usual access rules apply, so the field cannot be a private field of an ancestor class unless the ancestor class is in the same unit. Typically, the field is a private field of the same class that declares the property.

The field can be an aggregate (record or array), and the `Setter` must specify a record member or array element (at a constant index) of the appropriate type. Records and arrays can be nested.

If the `Setter` is a method, the method must be a procedure whose argument type is the same as the property type. The method can be static or virtual, but it cannot be a dynamic method or message handler.

If the property is indexed or an array property, the `Setter` must be a method. The first parameter is the index value, which is an `Integer`. Subsequent arguments are the array indices. The type of each `Setter` argument must match the type of the corresponding array index. The last argument is the new property value.

When the user assigns to the property value, Delphi assigns the value to the `Setter` field or calls the `Setter` method.

Tips and Tricks

- If you use a `Setter` field, Delphi compiles all property references into direct field references, so there is no performance penalty for using a property instead of a field.

- If a published property has a class type (other than TComponent or one of its descendants), you should define a *Setter* method that calls the object's Assign method:

```
type
  TDemo = class(TComponent)
  private
    Font: TFont;
    procedure SetFont(NewFont: TFont);
  public
    constructor Create(Owner: TComponent); override;
    destructor Destroy; override;
  published
    property Font: TFont read fFont write SetFont;
  end;

procedure TDemo.SetFont(NewFont: TFont);
begin
  Font.Assign(NewFont);
end;
```

- A good programming style is to make all fields private and declare protected, public, or published properties to access the fields. If you need to modify the class at a later date, you can change the field to a method without affecting any code that depends on the class and its property.

Example

See the property keyword for examples.

See Also

Class Keyword, Index Directive, Property Keyword, Read Directive

---

Write Procedure

Syntax

```
procedure Write(var F: File; var Value; ...);
procedure Write(Expr:Width:Precision; ...);
procedure Write(var F: TextFile; Expr:Width:Precision; ...);
```

Description

The Write procedure writes text or other values to a file. If you are writing to a binary file, you must supply a variable of the same type as the file's base type. You can write multiple records by listing multiple variables as arguments to the Write procedure.

When writing to a TextFile, you can write strings, numbers, characters, and Boolean values. Each value can be followed by the *Width* and *Precision* expressions, separated by colons. *Width* and *Precision* can be any integer expressions. *Width* specifies the minimum size of the string representation of *Expr*, and *Precision* specifies the number of places after the decimal point of a floating-point number.

Write uses as many characters as it needs, so *Width* is just the suggested minimum width. If the number requires fewer than *Width* characters, Write pads the string on the left with blanks. If you do not supply a *Width*, Delphi uses 1 as the minimum width for integers and it prints floating-point numbers as 26 characters in the following form:

```
'-1.12345678901234567E+1234'
```

If *Expr* is a floating-point number, Write reduces the number of decimal places to fit the value into a string that uses at most *Width* characters. Write always uses at least one digit after the decimal place, though. You can also supply a *Precision*, which tells Write how many decimal places to use after the decimal point. If you supply a *Precision*, Write uses fixed-point notation instead of exponential notation.

Tips and Tricks

- If the file has not been assigned, Write reports I/O error 102.

- If the file is not open for write access, Write reports I/O error 104.

- When the write fails because the disk is full, sometimes Write reports the Windows error Error_Disk_Full (112); sometimes it reports I/O error 101.

- If no file is given as the first argument, Write writes to the text file Output.

- The Str procedure does the same thing as Write, except that it "writes" a single value to a string instead of a file.

Example

```
var
   D1, D2: TSomeRecord;
   F: File of TSomeRecord;
begin
   ...
   Write(F, D1, D2);
```

See Also

BlockWrite Procedure, File Keyword, IOResult Function, Output Variable, Read Procedure, Str Procedure, TextFile Type, WriteLn Procedure

---

WriteLn Procedure

Syntax

```
procedure WriteLn(Expr:Width:Precision; ...);
procedure WriteLn(var F: TextFile; Expr:Width:Precision; ...);
```

Description

WriteLn is just like the Write procedure, except it prints a line ending after printing its arguments. A line ending is a carriage return followed by a line feed (#13#10). With no arguments, or only a TextFile argument, WriteLn prints only a line ending.

Tips and Tricks

- If the file has not been assigned, `Write` reports I/O error 102.

- If the file is not open for write access, `Write` reports I/O error 104.

- When the write fails because the disk is full, sometimes `Write` reports the Windows error `Error_Disk_Full` (112); sometimes it reports I/O error 101.

- If no `TextFile` is given as the first argument, `WriteLn` writes to `Output`.

- See the `Write` procedure for a description of how to format the output.

Example

```
// Print a table of square roots.
WriteLn('Num   Square root');
for I := 1 to 10 do
  WriteLn(I:3, '':2, Sqrt(I):18:15);
```

See Also

BlockWrite Procedure, IOResult Function, Output Variable, ReadLn Procedure, TextFile Type, Write Procedure

---

Writeonly Directive

Syntax

```
property Name: Type writeonly;
```

Description

The `writeonly` directive applies only to properties in a `dispinterface` declaration. See the `dispinterface` keyword for details.

See Also

Dispinterface Keyword, Property Keyword, Readonly Directive

Xor Keyword

Syntax

```
Boolean expression xor Boolean expression
Integer expression xor Integer expression
```

Description

The `xor` operator performs an exclusive or on its operands. If the operands are of Boolean type, it returns a Boolean result: True if the operands are different and False if they are the same.

An integer `xor` operates on each bit of its operands, setting the result bit to 1 if the corresponding bits in both operands are different, and to 0 if both operands have identical bits. If one operand is smaller than the other, Delphi extends the smaller operand with 0 in the leftmost bits. The result is the size of the largest operand.

Tips and Tricks

- With Boolean operands, **xor** is just like comparing for inequality. In most cases, the <> operator is easier to understand than using **xor**.

- The **xor** operation is reversible, which leads some people to use it for encrypting passwords. Using **xor** to encrypt passwords is like using bubble gum to lock a door. It doesn't work, and it's easy to break in. Search the World Wide Web to find free, reusable solutions for securely encrypting passwords.

Examples

```
var
  I, J: Integer;
begin
  I := $25;
  J := $11;
  WriteLn(I xor J); // Writes 52 (which is $34)
  ...
```

See Also

And Keyword, Boolean Type, ByteBool Type, LongBool Type, Not Keyword, Or Keyword, Shl Keyword, Shr Keyword, WordBool Type, Xor Keyword, $B Compiler Directive, $BoolEval Compiler Directive

CHAPTER 6

System Constants

This chapter is separate from Chapter 5, *Language Reference*, to make it easier to find the information you need. Instead of cluttering Chapter 5 with all the individual identifiers, this chapter organizes the system constants logically. All the constant literals described in this chapter are defined in the System unit, so they are available at all times.

Variant Type Codes

The VarType function returns the type code of a Variant. The type code is a small integer that contains a type identifier with the optional modifiers varArray and varByRef. Any type except varEmpty and varNull can have the varArray modifier. Delphi automatically takes care of the varByRef modifier. For more information, see the discussion of the Variant type in Chapter 5. Table 6-1 lists the type identifiers, and Table 6-2 lists the optional modifiers.

Table 6-1: Variant Type Identifiers

Literal	Value	Description
varEmpty	$0000	Variant not assigned
varNull	$0001	Null value
varSmallint	$0002	16-bit, signed integer
varInteger	$0003	32-bit, signed integer
varSingle	$0004	32-bit floating-point number
varDouble	$0005	64-bit floating-point number
varCurrency	$0006	64-bit fixed point number with four decimal places
varDate	$0007	64-bit floating-point date and time
varOleStr	$0008	#0-terminated wide string
varDispatch	$0009	IDispatch interface

Table 6-1: Variant Type Identifiers (continued)

Literal	Value	Description
varError	$000A	32-bit error code
varBoolean	$000B	Logical True or False
varVariant	$000C	Pointer to another Variant
varUnknown	$000D	IUnknown interface
varByte	$0011	8-bit, unsigned integer
varStrArg	$0048	Not used in Variants, but describes a string parameter to an IDispatch method
varString	$0100	Delphi AnsiString
varAny	$0101	Opaque pointer, used for CORBA Any values
varTypeMask	$0FFF	Mask to extract type identifier from VarType

Table 6-2: Variant Type Modifiers

Literal	Value	Description
varArray	$2000	Variant is an array.
varByRef	$4000	Additional level of indirection to access data.

Open Array Types

When a subroutine parameter is a variant open array (array of const), Delphi passes the array argument by converting each array element to a TVarRec record. Each record's VType member identifies the member's type. For more information, see the discussion of the array keyword in Chapter 5. Table 6-3 lists the VType values for a TVarRec record.

Table 6-3: Possible Values for TVarRec.VType

Literal	Value	Element Type
vtInteger	0	Integer
vtBoolean	1	Boolean
vtChar	2	Char
vtExtended	3	Extended
vtString	4	ShortString
vtPointer	5	Pointer
vtPChar	6	PChar
vtObject	7	TObject
vtClass	8	TClass
vtWideChar	9	WideChar
vtPWideChar	10	PWideChar
vtAnsiString	11	AnsiString
vtCurrency	12	Currency
vtVariant	13	Variant

Table 6-3: Possible Values for TVarRec.VType (continued)

Literal	Value	Element Type
vtInterface	14	IUnknown
vtWideString	15	WideString
vtInt64	16	Int64

Virtual Method Table Offsets

Chapter 3, *Runtime Type Information*, describes the format of a class's virtual method table (VMT). Delphi does not provide a convenient record for accessing a VMT, but it does define the offsets (in bytes) of the various parts of a VMT. The offsets are relative to the class reference (TClass). Note that the offsets change from one version of Delphi to the next. Table 6-4 lists the offset names and values.

Table 6-4: Offsets in a Class's Virtual Method Table

Literal	Value	Description
vmtSelfPtr	−76	Pointer to the start of the VMT
vmtIntfTable	−72	Pointer to the interface table
vmtAutoTable	−68	Pointer to the automation table
vmtInitTable	−64	Pointer to the initialization and finalization table
vmtTypeInfo	−60	Pointer to the class's TTypeInfo record
vmtFieldTable	−56	Pointer to the published field table
vmtMethodTable	−52	Pointer to the published method table
vmtDynamicTable	−48	Pointer to the dynamic method and message table
vmtClassName	−44	Pointer to the class name as a ShortString
vmtInstanceSize	−40	Instance size in bytes
vmtParent	−36	Pointer to a pointer to the base class VMT
vmtSafeCallException	−32	Address of the SafeCallException method
vmtAfterConstruction	−28	Address of the AfterConstruction method
vmtBeforeDestruction	−24	Address of the BeforeDestruction method
vmtDispatch	−20	Address of the Dispatch method
vmtDefaultHandler	−16	Address of the DefaultHandler method
vmtNewInstance	−12	Address of the NewInstance method
vmtFreeInstance	−8	Address of the FreeInstance method
vmtDestroy	−4	Address of the Destroy destructor

Runtime Error Codes

Delphi does not export literals for its runtime errors. Instead, it defines a number of literals in the implementation section of the System and SysInit units, and other error codes are defined implicitly in the System code. For your convenience, the following tables list all the runtime error numbers that are built into Delphi's System unit.

The internal error codes are used internally to the System unit. If you implement an ErrorProc procedure, these are the error codes you must interpret.

The ErrorProc procedure in the SysUtils unit maps internal error codes to exceptions. Table 6-5 lists the internal error codes and the exception class that the SysUtils unit uses for each error.

If you do not use the SysUtils unit, or if an error arises before the SysUtils unit is initialized or after it is finalized, the ErrorProc procedures in the System unit maps internal error codes to external error codes. Some memory and pointer errors do not produce immediate access violations, but instead corrupt memory in a way that does not let Delphi shut down cleanly. These errors often manifest themselves as runtime errors when the program exits. Table 6-6 lists the external error codes.

Table 6-7 lists the I/O error codes, which are reported with an internal error code of zero. Note that any Windows error code can also be an I/O error code. (SysUtils raises EInOutError for all I/O errors.)

Table 6-5: Internal Error Codes

Error Number	Description	SysUtils Exception Class
0	I/O error; see Table 6-7	EInOutError
1	Out of memory	EOutOfMemory
2	Invalid pointer	EInvalidPointer
3	Integer divide by zero	EDivByZero
4	Array bounds error	ERangeError
5	Integer or enumerated range error	EIntOverflow
6	Invalid floating-point operation	EInvalidOp
7	Floating-point divide by zero	EZeroDivide
8	Floating-point overflow	EOverflow
9	Floating-point underflow	EUnderflow
10	Invalid object type cast	EInvalidCast
11	Access violation	EAccessViolation
12	Stack overflow	EPrivilege
13	Control+Break interrupt	EControlC
14	Privileged instruction	EStackOverflow
15	Invalid Variant type cast	EVariantError
16	Invalid Variant operation	EVariantError

Table 6-5: Internal Error Codes (continued)

Error Number	Description	SysUtils Exception Class
17	No Variant method call dispatcher	EVariantError
18	Unable to create Variant array	EVariantError
19	Array operation on a non-array Variant	EVariantError
20	Variant array bounds error	EVariantError
21	Assertion failed	EAssertionFailed
22	SysUtils external exception	EExternalException
23	Invalid interface type cast	EIntfCastError
24	Error in safecall method	ESafeCallException

Table 6-6: External Error Codes

Error Number	Description
200	Divide by zero
201	Array bounds error
202	Stack overflow
203	Out of memory
204	Invalid pointer
205	Floating-point overflow
206	Floating-point underflow
207	Invalid floating-point operation
210	Call to an abstract method
215	Integer or enumerated bounds error
216	Access violation
217	Unhandled exception
218	Privileged instruction
219	Invalid class type cast
220	Invalid Variant type cast
221	Invalid Variant operation
222	No Variant method call dispatcher
223	Unable to create Variant array
224	Array operation on a non-array Variant
225	Variant array bounds error
226	Cannot initialize thread local storage
227	Assertion failed
228	Invalid interface type cast
229	Error from a safecall method

Table 6-7: I/O Error Codes

Error Number	Description
100	Read past end of file.
101	Disk is full.
102	`AssignFile` has not yet been called.
103	The file is closed.
104	File not open for input.
105	File not open for output.
106	Incorrectly formatted input for `Read`.

CHAPTER 7

Operators

This chapter describes the symbolic operators, their precedence and semantics. Chapter 5, *Language Reference*, describes the named operators in depth, but not the symbolic operators, because it's hard to alphabetize symbols. This chapter describes the symbolic operators in depth.

Delphi defines the following operators. Each line lists the operators with the same precedence; operator precedence is highest at the start of the list and lowest at the bottom:

```
@ not ^ + - (unary operators)
* / div mod and shl shr as
+ - or xor
> < >= <= <> = in is
```

A Variant can be a string, number, Boolean, or other value. If an expression mixes Variant and non-Variant operands, Delphi converts all operands to Variant. If the Variant types do not match, Delphi casts one or both operands as needed for the operation, and produces a Variant result. See the Variant type in Chapter 5 for more information about Variant type casts.

Unary Operators

@ *operator*

Returns the address of its operand. The address of a variable or ordinary subroutine is a Pointer, or if the $T or $TypedAddress compiler directive is used, a typed pointer (e.g., PInteger).

The address of a method has two parts: a code pointer and a data pointer, so you can assign a method address only to a variable of the appropriate type, and not to a generic Pointer variable. If you take the address of a method using a class reference instead of an object reference, the @ operator returns just the code pointer. For example:

```
Ptr := @TObject.Free;
```

When assigning the address of a subroutine to a procedural-type variable, if the subroutine's signature matches the variable's type, you do not need the @ operator. Delphi can tell from the assignment that you are assigning the subroutine's address. If the types do not match, use the @ operator to take the subroutine's address. For example, to assign an error procedure to Delphi's `ErrorProc` variable, which is an untyped `Pointer`, you must use the @ operator:

```
function GetHeight: Integer;
begin
  Result := 42;
end;

procedure HandleError(Code: Integer; Addr: Pointer);
begin
  ...
end;

type
  TIntFunction = function: Integer;
var
  F: TIntFunction;
  I: Integer;
begin
  // Do not need @ operator. Assign GetHeight address to F.
  F := GetHeight;
  // Call GetHeight.
  I := F;

  // Need the @ operator because the type of ErrorProc is Pointer.
  ErrorProc := @HandleError;

  // Call GetHeight via F, and compare integer results
  if F = GetHeight then
    ShowMessage('Heights are equal');
  // Compare pointers to learn whether F points to GetHeight.
  if @F = @GetHeight then
    ShowMessage('Function pointers are equal');
```

You can also use the @ operator on the left-hand side of an assignment to assign a procedural pointer that does not have the correct type. For example, the value returned from the Windows API function `GetProcAddress` is a procedure address, but it has the generic `Pointer` type. A type cast is usually the best way to solve this problem, but some people prefer to use the @ operator on the left-hand side of an assignment, for example:

```
type
  TIntFunction = function: Integer;
var
  F: TIntFunction;
begin
  // The following two statements do the same thing:
  @F := GetProcAddress(DllHandle, 'GetHeight');
  F := TIntFunction(GetProcAddress(DllHandle, 'GetHeight'));
```

To take the address of a procedural-type variable, repeat the @ operator, for example, @@Variable:

```
var
   F: TIntPointer;
   P: Pointer;
begin
   F := GetHeight;      // F points to GetHeight.
   P := @@F;            // Store address of the variable F in P.
```

Not *operator*

Logical negation. See the not keyword in Chapter 5 for details.

^ *operator*

Pointer dereference. This postfix operator follows a pointer-type expression and returns the value it points to. The type of the result is the base type of the pointer.

When accessing a record member or array element via a pointer, Delphi automatically supplies one level of indirection if needed. For example:

```
type
   TRecord = record
      Member: PInteger;
   end;
   PRecord = ^TRecord;
var
   P: PRecord;
   I: Integer;
begin
   New(P);
   P.Member := @I;      // Implicit P^.Member
   P.Member^ := 10;     // Need explicit ^ without record member reference
```

+ *operator*

Sign identity. The + operator can be used before any numeric expression. It has no effect, that is, +7 = 7.

– *operator*

Arithmetic negation. The – operator can be used before any numeric expression to change the sign of the expression, e.g., – (X + Y). Note that Delphi parses a negative constant as the – operator applied to a positive constant. That means you cannot write the most negative integer in decimal. You can use Low(Integer) instead.

Multiplicative Operators

* *operator*

The multiplication operator is also the set intersection operator. When the operands are sets of the same type, the result is a set that contains all members that are in both operand sets. For example:

```
var
   A, B, C: set of 0..7;
begin
   A := [0, 1, 2, 3];
```

```
B := [2, 3, 4, 5, 6];
C := A * B;          // C := [2,3]
A := [1, 0];
C := A * B;          // C := []
```

/ operator

Floating-point division. Dividing two integers converts the operands to floating point. Division by zero raises runtime error 7.

Div operator

Integer division. See Chapter 5 for details.

Mod operator

Modulus (remainder). See Chapter 5 for details.

And operator

Logical or bitwise conjunction. See Chapter 5 for details.

Shl operator

Left shift. See Chapter 5 for details.

Shr operator

Right shift. See Chapter 5 for details.

As operator

Type check and cast of object and interface references. See Chapter 5 for details.

Additive Operators

+ operator

Addition, string concatenation, set union, and **PChar** pointer offset. If both operands are strings, the result is the string concatenation of the two strings. If the operands are sets with the same type, the result is a set that contains all the elements in both operand sets.

If one operand has type **PChar** or **PWideChar** and the other is an integer, the result is a pointer whose value is offset by the integer in character units (not bytes). The integer offset can be positive or negative, but the resulting pointer must lie within the same character array as the **PChar** or **PWideChar** operand. For example:

```
var
  A, B, C: set of 0..7;
  Text: array[0..5] of Char;
  P, Q: PChar;
begin
  A := [0, 1, 2];
  B := [5, 7, 4];
  C := A + B;          // C := [0, 1, 2, 4, 5, 7];

  Text := 'Hello';
  P := Text;
  Q := P + 3;
  WriteLn(Q);          // Writes 'lo'
  WriteLn('Hi' + Q);   // Writes 'Hilo'
```

- operator

Subtraction, set difference, `PChar` pointer offset, and `PChar` difference. If the operands are sets with the same type, the result is a set that contains the elements that are in the left-hand operand set but not in the right-hand operand.

If one operand has type `PChar` or `PWideChar` and the other is an integer, the result is a pointer whose value is offset by the integer, in character units (not bytes). The integer offset can be positive or negative, but the resulting pointer must lie within the same character array as the `PChar` or `PWideChar` operand.

If both operands are of type `PChar` or `PWideChar` and both pointers point into the same character array, the difference is the number of characters between the two pointers. The difference is positive if the left-hand operand points to a later character than the right-hand operand, and the difference is negative if the left-hand operand points to a character that appears earlier in the character array:

```
var
  A, B, C: set of 0..7;
  Text: array[0..5] of Char;
  P, Q: PChar;
begin
  A := [0, 1, 2, 4, 5, 6];
  B := [5, 7, 4];
  C := A - B;        // C := [0, 1, 2, 6];
  C := B - A;        // C := [7];

  Text := 'Hello';
  P := Text;
  Q := P + 3;
  WriteLn(Q);        // Writes 'lo'
  P := Q - 2;
  WriteLn(P);        // Writes 'ello'
  WriteLn(Q - P);    // Writes 2
```

Or *operator*

Logical or bitwise disjunction. See Chapter 5 for details.

Xor *operator*

Logical or bitwise exclusive or. See Chapter 5 for details.

Comparison Operators

The comparison operators let you compare numbers, strings, sets, and pointers.

= *operator*

Equality. Compare numbers, strings, pointers, and sets for exact equality.

Note that comparing floating-point numbers for exact equality rarely works the way you think it should. You should use a fuzzy comparison that accounts for floating-point imprecision. See D. E. Knuth's *Seminumerical Algorithms* (third edition, Addison Wesley Longman, 1998), section 4.2.2, for an excellent discussion of this problem and suggested solutions.

<> *operator*

Inequality. Compare numbers, strings, or character pointers, and sets. Returns the logical negation of the = operator.

> *operator*

Greater than; compares numbers, strings, or character pointers. When you compare PChar or PWideChar values, you are comparing pointers. The operator returns True if the left-hand operand points to a later position than the right-hand operand. Both operands must point to locations in the same character array. Strings are compared by comparing their characters' ordinal values. (The SysUtils unit contains functions that compare strings taking into account the Windows locale. Most applications should use these functions instead of a simple string comparison. See Appendix B, *The SysUtils Unit*, for details.) For example:

```
var
   Text: array[0..5] of Char;
   P, Q: PChar;
begin
   Text := 'Hello';
   P := Text;
   Q := P + 3;
   WriteLn(Q > P);     // True because Q points to a later element than P
   if Text > 'Howdy' then
      // string comparison is False
```

< *operator*

Less than; compares numbers or strings, or character pointers. When you compare PChar or PWideChar values, you are comparing pointers. The operator returns True if the left-hand operand points to an earlier position than the right-hand operand. Both operands must point to locations in the same character array. Strings are compared by comparing their characters' ordinal values. (The SysUtils unit contains functions that compare strings taking into account the Windows locale. Most applications should use these functions instead of a simple string comparison. See Appendix B for details.) For example:

```
var
   Text: array[0..5] of Char;
   P, Q: PChar;
begin
   Text := 'Hello';
   P := Text;
   Q := P + 3;
   WriteLn(Q < P);     // False because Q points to a later element than P
   if Text < 'Howdy' then
      // string comparison is True
```

>= *operator*

Greater than or equal, or superset. For numbers, strings, and PChar or PWideChar pointers, the >= operator is True when > is True or = is True. For sets, the >= operator tests whether all members of the right-hand operand are also members of the left-hand operand.

For example:

```
var
  A, B: set of 0..7;
begin
  A := [0, 1, 2, 4, 5, 6];
  B := [5, 7, 4];
  if A >= B then
    // False because (7 in A) is False
  B := [1, 2, 0]
  if A >= B then
    // True because all members of B are in A
```

<= operator

Less than or equal, or subset. For numbers, strings, and PChar or PWideChar pointers, the <= operator is True when < is True or = is True. For sets, the <= operator tests whether all members of the left-hand operand are also members of the right-hand operand. For example:

```
var
  A, B: set of 0..7;
begin
  A := [4, 5, 6];
  B := [5, 7, 4];
  if A <= B then
    // False because (6 in A) is False
  B := [5, 7, 6, 4]
  if A <= B then
    // True because all members of A are in B
```

In operator

Tests whether an element is a member of a set. See Chapter 5 for details.

Is operator

Tests the type of an object reference. See Chapter 5 for details. Note that is does not work on interfaces; call QueryInterface instead. (See also the Supports function in Appendix B.)

CHAPTER 8

Compiler Directives

Compiler directives are special comments that control the compiler and its behavior, similar to #pragma directives in C++. This chapter discusses compiler directives and lists all the compiler directives Delphi supports.

A directive comment is one whose first character is a dollar sign ($). You can use either kind of Pascal-style comment:

```
{$AppType GUI}
(*$AppType GUI*)
```

You cannot use a C++ style comment (//$Apptype) for a compiler directive.

If the first character of a comment is not a dollar sign, the comment is not a compiler directive. A common trick to deactivate or "comment out" a compiler directive is to insert a space or other character just before the dollar sign, for example:

```
{ $AppType GUI}
(**$AppType GUI*)
```

Delphi has three varieties of compiler directives: switches, parameters, and conditional compilation. A switch is a Boolean flag: a feature can be enabled or disabled. A parameter provides information, such as a filename or stack size. Conditional compilation lets you define conditions and selectively compile parts of a source file depending on which conditions are set. Conditions are Boolean (set or not set).

The names and parameters of compiler directives are not case-sensitive. You cannot abbreviate the name of a compiler directive. Delphi ignores extra text in the comment after the compiler directive and its parameters (if any). You should refrain from including extra text, though, because future versions of Delphi might introduce additional parameters for compiler directives. Instead of including commentary within the directive's comment, use a separate comment.

You can combine multiple directives in a single comment by separating them with commas. Do not allow any spaces before or after the comma. If you use a long directive name, it must be the last directive in the comment. If you have multiple long directives, or any parameter directive, you must use separate comments for each one:

```
{$R+,Q+,C+,Align On}
{$O+,M 1024,40980}
```

Some directives are global for a project. These directives usually appear in the project's source file (*.dpr* file). Some apply only to packages and must appear in the package source file (*.dpk* file). Other directives apply to the entire file in which they appear. That file can be a project, package, or unit source file. If you use the same project or file directive more than once, Delphi keeps the last one it sees.

Some directives are local in scope. You can enable and disable them multiple times in the same file. A few local directives apply to an entire subroutine, using the directive in force at the end of the subroutine.

Some directives have two names, a single character and a long name. Long names are easier to read, and they are also helpful when the single letter is both a switch and a parameter. For example, the $I switch is equivalent to $IOChecks, and the $I parameter means $Include. By using the long name, you avoid any possibility of mistakes, such as {$I -}, which includes the file named "-" instead of disabling the $I switch (because of the space between the I and the -).

Usually compiler directives appear in the source file, but you can also supply directives on the command line. (See Appendix A, *Command-Line Tools*, for details.) Most compiler options also have equivalent settings in the project options, so you can set the options in the IDE. These options apply to all the units in the project, but you can override the project options with directives in the unit source files. For your convenience, the IDE also creates a compiler configuration file (*.cfg*), which contains roughly the same configuration information, but in a format suitable for use with the command-line compiler.

Using project options in the IDE is convenient. If you do so, be sure to store the Delphi options file (*.dof*) with the project's source files in your version control system. If you are not storing the *.dof* file with your source files, or if you are selling source code and don't want to include the *.dof* files, you should include the compiler options in the source files. Not everyone uses the same options, and several of the options affect the syntax and semantics of the compiler. Without knowing the correct options to use, you cannot recompile most Delphi programs.

Some of the compiler directives apply to C++ Builder, not Delphi. Delphi ignores these directives. C++ Builder uses them to guide how it generates the *.hpp* file for a Pascal unit.

$A Compiler Directive

See

$Align Compiler Directive

$Align Compiler Directive

Syntax

```
{$A+}          // default
{$Align On}    // default
{$A-}
{$Align Off}
```

Scope

Local

Description

When enabled, the $A or $Align directive aligns class, object, and record fields. When disabled, all structured types are packed. Alignment helps a program run faster, but at the expense of additional memory.

Use the $Align directive at the beginning of a file to affect all declarations in that file. For individual declarations, it's better to use the packed modifier.

Example

```
type
{$Align On}
  TPadded = record
    A: Byte;
    B: Integer; // Delphi inserts padding between A and B to align B
  end;
  TPacked = packed record
    A: Byte;
    B: Integer; // no padding because the record is packed
  end;
{$Align Off}
  TUnaligned = record
    A: Byte;
    B: Integer; // no padding because the record is not aligned
  end;
```

See Also

Packed Keyword

$AppType Compiler Directive

Syntax

```
{$AppType GUI}      // default
{$AppType Console}
```

Scope

Project

Description

The $AppType compiler directive tells the linker to create a GUI or console application. In a console application, Delphi opens the Input and Output files to read from and write to the console. When compiling a console application, Delphi defines the CONSOLE conditional symbol in all units that make up the project. The default is a GUI application.

See Also

Input Variable, IsConsole Variable, Output Variable, Program Keyword

$Assertions Compiler Directive

Syntax

```
{$C+}            // default
{$Assertions On} // default
{$C-}
{$Assertions Off}
```

Scope

Local

Description

$C or $Assertions enables or disables the Assert procedure. When enabled (the default), the compiler generates code to test assertions. When disabled, the compiler ignores all calls to the Assert procedure and does not generate any code for them.

Tips and Tricks

A common misconception is that assertions are primarily for debugging, and that they should be disabled for release. Assertions ensure the proper functioning of your program. If an assertion fails, that means the state of your program is different from anything you anticipated. If the program were to continue running, its behavior would be completely unpredictable. The results might include corruption of the user's data or other dire consequences. It is better to report the assertion violation and terminate the program.

If an assertion in an inner loop causes performance problems, you can disable just that assertion by using conditional compilation with the $Assertions compiler directive.

Example

```
Assert(List.Count > 0, 'Internal error: List must not be empty');
for I := 0 to List.Count-1 do
begin
{$ifndef DEBUG}
  {$Assertions Off}
{$endif}
  Assert(IsValid(List[I]));
{$ifndef DEBUG}
```

```
  {$Assertions On}
{$endif}
  DoSomething(List[I]);
end;
```

See Also

Assert Procedure, $IfDef Compiler Directive, $IfNDef Compiler Directive

---

$B Compiler Directive

See

$BoolEval Compiler Directive

$BoolEval Compiler Directive

Syntax

```
{$B-}          // default
{$BoolEval Off} // default
{$B+}
{$BoolEval On}
```

Scope

Local

Description

By default, the and and or operators do not evaluate their right-hand operands if the expression result is known from the left-hand operand. This is known as *short-circuiting* the expression. C, C++, and Java programmers are familiar with short-circuit logical operators.

If you prefer the traditional Pascal use of the and and or operators, you can disable short-circuit operators with the $BoolEval compiler directive. Note that most Delphi programmers prefer using short-circuit operators because they produce code that is easier to read.

 Most Delphi programs work correctly only when $BoolEval is disabled. Do not enable this option unless you know the code does not rely on short-circuit operators.

Example

```
// Ensure that a path ends with a backslash.
// The first approach uses the short-circuit AND operator.
{$BoolEval Off}
if (Length(Path) > 0) and (Path[Length(Path)] <> '\') then
  Path := Path + '\';
```

```
// This is how you must write the same expression without
// using the short-circuit operator.
{$BoolEval On}
if Length(Path) > 0 then
  if Path[Length(Path)] <> '\' then
    Path := Path + '\';
```

See Also

And Keyword, Boolean Type, Or Keyword

$C Compiler Directive

See

$Assertions Compiler Directive

$D Compiler Directive

See

$DebugInfo Compiler Directive, $Description Compiler Directive

---

$DebugInfo Compiler Directive

Syntax

```
{$D+}           // default
{$DebugInfo On} // default
{$D-}
{$DebugInfo Off}
```

Scope

File

Description

When $DebugInfo is enabled, the compiler generates line number information to help you debug the unit. Without the line number information, the only way you can debug the unit is from the CPU view.

To take maximum advantage of the debugger, you should also use the $LocalSymbols directive to store information about the types, variables, and subroutines in the unit.

The debug information is stored in the unit's *.dcu* file and does not affect performance or the size of the final *.exe* or *.dll* file. The most common reason to disable $DebugInfo is when you are releasing *.dcu* files without the source code. In very large projects, you might save a little bit of time and disk space by disabling $DebugInfo, but in most cases, the savings are minuscule.

See Also

$DefinitionInfo Compiler Directive, $LocalSymbols Compiler Directive, $ReferenceInfo Compiler Directive

---

$Define Compiler Directive

Syntax

```
{$Define Name}
```

Scope

File

Description

The $Define directive defines *Name* as a conditional symbol, for use in conditional compilation. Subsequent uses of the $IfDef directive for *Name* test positive. You can define the same name more than once in a file. See the $IfDef for an example. Conditional symbol names are not case sensitive.

Unlike macro definitions in C and C++, a definition in Delphi is a simple flag. A name is defined or not defined. Test whether a name is defined by using the $IfDef and $IfNDef compiler directives. You can use the same name as a conditional symbol and as an identifier in the same file.

See Also

$Else Compiler Directive, $Endif Compiler Directive, $IfDef Compiler Directive, $IfNDef Compiler Directive, $IfOpt Compiler Directive, $Undef Compiler Directive

---

$DefinitionInfo Compiler Directive

Syntax

```
{$YD}                // default
{$DefinitionInfo On} // default
{$Y+}
{$Y-}
{$DefinitionInfo Off}
```

Scope

File

Description

By default, the compiler records information about the definition of each symbol—type, variable, and subroutine—in a unit. The project browser and code explorer in the IDE let you browse and examine that information, peruse the symbols in a unit, or jump straight to the definition of a symbol.

Compiler
Directives

With $DefinitionInfo off, you cannot use the browser or code explorer, but compile times and *.dcu* file sizes are reduced slightly. Definition information has no impact on the performance or size of the final *.exe* or *.dll* file.

The $DefinitionInfo and $ReferenceInfo directives define three possible states of browser information. The $Y directive provides a shortcut for the three states:

- The $YD directive is equivalent to enabling definitions and disabling references. This is the default.

- The $Y+ directive is equivalent to enabling definitions and references.

- The $Y- directive is equivalent to disabling definitions and references.

- You cannot enable references without also enabling definitions, so there is no fourth state.

In order to use definition info, you must also enable the $DebugInfo and $LocalSymbols compiler directives.

See Also

$DebugInfo Compiler Directive, $LocalSymbols Compiler Directive, $ReferenceInfo Compiler Directive

---

$DenyPackageUnit Compiler Directive

Syntax

```
{$DenyPackageUnit Off} // default
{$DenyPackageUnit On}
```

Scope

File

Description

If you enable the $DenyPackageUnit compiler directive, Delphi prevents you from using the unit in a package. Some units might perform special initialization or finalization services for an application and cannot be used in a package (which is really a DLL). For example, Delphi's ComServ unit uses the $DenyPackageUnit directive. It implements several methods for managing a COM server DLL, and those methods must reside in the DLL itself, and not in a package DLL.

See Also

Package Directive, $WeakPackageUnit Compiler Directive

$Description Compiler Directive

Syntax

```
{$Description String}
{$D String}
```

Scope

Project

Description

The $Description string can be up to 256 characters, enclosed in single quotes. Delphi stores the description string in the *.exe* or *.dll* file.

Most applications should use a version information resource instead of a description string. You can provide much more detailed information. Descriptions are most useful for design-time packages because Delphi displays the description as the package name in the Install Packages dialog box.

See Also

$D Compiler Directive, $E Compiler Directive

$DesignOnly Compiler Directive

Syntax

```
{$DesignOnly Off} // default
{$DesignOnly On}
```

Scope

Project

Description

Use the $DesignOnly directive in a package's *.dpk* file to mark the package as being a design-time package. You cannot link the package with an application or library. You can only install the package in the IDE of Delphi or C++ Builder.

When you write a component, put the component's unit in a runtime package, and put the property and component editors in a design-time package. That way, an application can link with the component's runtime package and avoid the overhead of linking the design-time code, which the application doesn't need.

See Also

Package Directive, $RunOnly Compiler Directive

$E Compiler Directive

Syntax

```
{$E Extension}
```

Scope

Project

Description

The $E directive specifies the filename extension used for a library. The default extension is *.dll*. You can include or omit an initial dot (.), but do not enclose the extension in quotes.

Use the $E directive when compiling a screen saver, control panel applet, or other special DLL.

Example

```
{$e CPL}  { control panel applet }
{$e .scr} { screen saver }
```

See Also

$Description Compiler Directive, Library Keyword

$Else Compiler Directive

Syntax

```
$Else
```

Scope

Local

Description

The $Else compiler directive starts the else part of a conditional. If the condition is True, the compiler skips the code between the $Else and the $EndIf compiler directives. If the condition is False, the compiler compiles source code in the else part.

See $IfDef for an example.

See Also

$Define Compiler Directive, $EndIf Compiler Directive, $IfDef Compiler Directive, $IfNDef Compiler Directive, $IfOpt Compiler Directive, $Undef Compiler Directive

---

$EndIf Compiler Directive

Syntax

```
$Endif
```

Scope

Local

Description

$Endif ends a conditional compilation section. See $IfDef for an example.

See Also

$Else Compiler Directive, $IfDef Compiler Directive, $IfNDef Compiler Directive, $IfOpt Compiler Directive, $Undef Compiler Directive

$ExtendedSyntax Compiler Directive

Syntax

```
{$X+}               // default
{$ExtendedSyntax On} // default
{$X-}
{$ExtendedSyntax Off}
```

Scope

Local

Description

If $ExtendedSyntax is enabled, the compiler extends the syntax of standard Pascal in a few ways:

- The value returned from a function call does not have to be assigned to a variable. Sometimes functions return a result, but the result is not important. Delphi's extended syntax lets you call the function as though it were a procedure and ignore the function's result.

- Functions can assign a return value to the implicit Result variable.

- An array of Char whose index is an integer type with a zero origin can be treated as a string. The string must be #0 terminated. You can also use such an array in any context that calls for a PChar type, and the compiler automatically passes the address of the first element of the array.

Delphi does not have any compiler directives for most of its other extensions to standard Pascal, but see the $BoolEval compiler directive for an exception.

See Also

$BoolEval Compiler Directive, Function Keyword, PChar Type

$ExternalSym Compiler Directive

Syntax

```
{$ExternalSym Identifier}
```

Scope

Local

Description

The $ExternalSym compiler directive tells C++ Builder that *Identifier* is an external symbol that should not be defined in the C++ header file (.hpp) it generates for the Pascal unit.

Sometimes a symbol you must define in the Pascal unit is already defined elsewhere in C++ Builder. Use the $ExternalSym compiler directive to prevent C++ Builder from writing the symbol in the *.hpp* file. Note that the compiler uses the unit name as a namespace name. When you use $ExternalSym, you are telling the compiler that the symbol is defined outside the namespace. Contrast this behavior with the $NoDefine directive, where the symbol is defined in the unit's namespace.

Example

```
type
  size_t = LongWord;
  {ExternalSym size_t} {C++ already defines this type}
var
  S: size_t;
```

See Also

$HppEmit Compiler Directive, $NoDefine Compiler Directive, $NoInclude Compiler Directive

---

$G Compiler Directive

See

$ImportedData Compiler Directive

$H Compiler Directive

See

$LongStrings Compiler Directive

$Hints Compiler Directive

Syntax

```
{$Hints On} // default
{$Hints Off}
```

Scope

Local, applies to entire subroutine

Description

The $Hints compiler directive enables or disables compiler hints. The compiler issues hints for code that seems suspect or likely to be an error. For example, the compiler issues a hint if a class has an unused private method. You might have written the method knowing that it is not currently used, but planning to use it in a future version. You can suppress the hint with the $Hints directive.

Tips and Tricks

Do not disable compiler hints globally in a file or project. The compiler hints are useful and can warn you about numerous common errors. Disable hints only when you know it is safe, and then disable them only for the subroutine in question.

Example

```
type
  TExample = class
  private
  {$Hints off}  { I know it's not used now, but I will use it later. }
    procedure Unused;
  {$Hints on}
    ...
  end;
```

See Also

$Warnings Compiler Directive

$HppEmit Compiler Directive

Syntax

```
(*$HppEmit String*)
```

Scope

Local

Description

Use the $HppEmit compiler directive to write *String* in the *.hpp* file for C++ Builder. The string is written to the user-supplied section at the top of the file. All the $HppEmit strings appear in the same order as their appearance in the *.pas* file.

You can use $HppEmit to include any text you want in the *.hpp* file, from additional #include directives to type declarations.

Example

```
type
  TComplex = record
    Re, Im: Double;
  end;

// Define the structure differently in C++.
// Note the use of { and } in the HppEmit code, which would interfere
// in Pascal comments that use { and } because the comments do not
// recognize quoted strings. Use (* and *) instead.

{$ExternalSym TComplex}
(*$HppEmit 'struct TComplex {'*)
(*$HppEmit '  double Re;'*)
(*$HppEmit '  double Im;'*)
```

Compiler Directives

```
(*$HppEmit '  TComplex(double r=0, double i=0) : Re(r), Im(i) {}'*)
(*$HppEmit '};'*)
```

See Also

$ExternalSyms Compiler Directive, $NoDefine Compiler Directive, $NoInclude
Compiler Directive

$I Compiler Directive

See

$Include Compiler Directive, $IOChecks Compiler Directive

$IfDef Compiler Directive

Syntax

```
{$IfDef Name}
   ...
{$Else}
   ...
{$Endif}
```

Scope

Local

Description

$IfDef starts a conditional compilation section. If *Name* is defined (by a prior
occurrence of $Define), the source code after the $IfDef directive is compiled,
up to the corresponding $Else or $EndIf compiler directive. The use of $Else is
optional. You can nest conditional compilation sections.

A common use for conditional compilation is to test the version of Delphi.
Table 8-1 lists the symbols predefined by the compiler with the version of the
compiler that defines each symbol.

Table 8-1: Predefined Symbols

Symbol	Compiler Version
CONSOLE	Defined for {$AppType Console}
CPU386	All versions
VER80	Delphi 1
VER90	Delphi 2
VER93	C++ Builder 1
VER100	Delphi 3
VER110	C++ Builder 3
VER120	Delphi 4
VER125	C++ Builder 4
VER130	Delphi 5

Table 8-1: Predefined Symbols (continued)

Symbol	Compiler Version
WINDOWS	Delphi 1
WIN32	Delphi 2, 3, 4, 5; C++ Builder 1, 3, 4

Example

```
{$IfOpt D+} // Debugging is enabled.
  {$define DEBUG}
  {$Assertions On}
  {$RangeChecks On}
  {$OverflowChecks On}
{$else}
  {$undef DEBUG} // Just in case it's defined in the project options
{$endif}
...
{$ifdef DEBUG}
  Log('Debug message');
{$endif}
```

See Also

$Define Compiler Directive, $Else Compiler Directive, $Endif Compiler Directive, $IfNDef Compiler Directive, $IfOpt Compiler Directive, $Undef Compiler Directive

---

$IfNDef Compiler Directive

Syntax

```
{$IfNDef Name}
   ...
{$Endif}
```

Scope

Local

Description

$IfNDef is similar to $IfDef except that it tests whether *Name* is *not* defined. See $IfDef for an explanation and example.

See Also

$Define Compiler Directive, $Else Compiler Directive, $Endif Compiler Directive, $IfDef Compiler Directive, $IfOpt Compiler Directive, $Undef Compiler Directive

---

$IfOpt Compiler Directive

Syntax

```
{$IfOpt Switch+}
   ...
```

Compiler
Directives

```
{$Endif}
{$IfOpt Switch-}
   ...
{$Endif}
```

Scope

Local

Description

$IfOpt is similar to $IfDef, except that it tests the state of a switch compiler directive. Only single-letter switches can be tested. If the directive is enabled, the *Switch+* test is True and *Switch-* is False. If the directive is disabled, *Switch+* is False and *Switch-* is True.

See $IfDef for more information.

Example

```
// Temporarily disable Range checks, then revert to the original switch.
{$IfOpt R+}
  {$define RangeChecks}
{$else}
  {$undef RangeChecks}
{$endif}
{$R-}
... // code that requires range checks be disabled
{$ifdef RangeChecks}
  {$R+}
{$endif}
```

See Also

$Define Compiler Directive, $Else Compiler Directive, $Endif Compiler Directive, $IfDef Compiler Directive, $IfNDef Compiler Directive, $Undef Compiler Directive

---

$ImageBase Compiler Directive

Syntax

```
{$ImageBase Integer}
```

Scope

Project

Description

The image base is the address at which Windows loads a module. The default image base is $00400000, which is the Windows default. You don't need to change this for programs, but you should change it for libraries and packages.

Windows must load every module at a unique address. It tries to load the module at the image base address, but if that address conflicts with another module in the

---

same process, Windows must relocate the module to a different virtual address. Relocating increases the time needed to load a module.

Delphi's standard packages use image bases starting at $40000000. Microsoft system DLLs start at $70000000. There are no standards for third-party packages and DLLs, so do your best to choose addresses that do not conflict.

$ImplicitBuild Compiler Directive

Syntax

```
{$ImplicitBuild On}    // default
{$ImplicitBuild Off}
```

Scope

File

Description

By default, Delphi automatically rebuilds packages when it needs to. Disable the $ImplicitBuild directive to prevent Delphi from checking whether a package needs to be rebuilt.

During development of a package, it is best to enable implicit building, especially if you are working on multiple, interrelated packages. It is easy to forget which units have changed and which packages need to be recompiled, so let Delphi figure it out for you.

Once you have finished development of a package, you can disable implicit rebuilding to reduce the overhead of determining what needs to be rebuilt.

Tips and Tricks

- The default setting applies only when the directive is omitted from a package source file. The package editor in Delphi's IDE has its own default, and when it creates a new package, it inserts $ImplicitBuild Off in the package source file.

- Note also that implicit building happens only when the source file changes. If you change only the form (that is, the *.dfm* file), the package is not rebuilt, even if the $ImplicitBuild directive is enabled.

See Also

Package Directive

$ImportedData Compiler Directive

Syntax

```
{$G+}                  // default
{$ImportedData On}     // default
{$G-}
{$ImportedData Off}
```

Scope

Local

Description

The $ImportedData compiler directive is not implemented.

A reference to a global variable in a different unit ordinarily requires an extra level of indirection in case the other unit resides in a separate package. The theory is that disabling the $ImportedData directive eliminates this indirection. In practice, this directive has no effect. The compiler automatically determines whether the indirection is needed and compiles references to global variables accordingly.

$Include Compiler Directive

Syntax

```
{$Include FileName}
{$I FileName}
```

Scope

Local

Description

The $Include compiler directive tells the compiler to read *FileName* and include its entire contents where the $Include directive appears.

The best way to use $Include is to import conditional definitions and compiler directives. You should use units to import type, variable, and subroutine declarations.

Use quotes around *FileName* to protect spaces and other special characters.

See Also

Unit Keyword

$IOChecks Compiler Directive

Syntax

```
{$I+}            // default
{$IOChecks On}   // default
{$I-}
{$IOChecks Off}
```

Scope

Local

Description

When $IOChecks is enabled, Delphi checks the results of all I/O functions and reports an I/O runtime error if a function fails. With $IOChecks disabled, you must call the IOResult function to learn whether an I/O operation succeeded.

Example

```
// Return True if the named file is a PostScript file,
// and False if the file does not exist or is not a PostScript file.
// A PostScript file starts with the characters '%!'.
function IsPostScript(const FileName: string): Boolean;
type
  TPair = array[0..1] of Char;
const
  PostScript: TPair = '%!';
var
  F: File of TPair;
  Pair: TPair;
begin
  AssignFile(F, FileName);
  FileMode := 0;
{$IOChecks Off}
  Reset(F);
  Read(F, Pair);
{$IOChecks On}
  Result := (IOResult = 0) and (Pair = PostScript);
  CloseFile(F);
end;
```

See Also

IOResult Function

$J Compiler Directive

See

$WriteableConst Compiler Directive

$L Compiler Directive

See

$Link Compiler Directive, $LocalSymbols Compiler Directive

$Link Compiler Directive

Syntax

```
{$L FileName}
{$Link FileName}
```

Scope

Local

Description

The $Link compiler directive links a relocatable object file (.*obj*) with the Delphi project. The object file can provide the implementation of subroutines declared with the **external** directive. The object file must use the Intel object file format (OMF), so you cannot use the COFF files that Visual C++ and most other C and C++ compilers produce. You can use an object file produced by Borland C++ and Borland TASM (Turbo assembler), but not by C++ Builder.

Use quotes for filenames that contain spaces or other funny characters. The default extension for *FileName* is .*obj*.

See Also

External Directive

$LocalSymbols Compiler Directive

Syntax

```
{$L+}               // default
{$LocalSymbols On} // default
{$L-}
{$LocalSymbols Off}
```

Scope

File

Description

If $DebugInfo is enabled, you can also enable $LocalSymbols to store information about subroutines, types, variables, and source line numbers in a unit. The symbol information is stored in the .*dcu* file and has no impact on the performance or size of the final .*exe* or .*dll* file. Delphi ignores the $LocalSymbols compiler directive when $DebugInfo is disabled.

In very large projects, you might save a little bit of time and disk space by disabling $LocalInfo, but in most cases, the savings are minuscule and not worth the effort to disable the directive.

See Also

$DebugInfo Compiler Directive, $DefinitionInfo Compiler Directive, $ReferenceInfo Compiler Directive

---

$LongStrings Compiler Directive

Syntax

```
{$H+}               // default
{$LongStrings On} // default
```

```
{$H-}
{$LongStrings Off}
```

Scope

Local

Description

By default, Delphi interprets the **string** type to mean **AnsiString**. If you disable the **$LongStrings** compiler directive, Delphi reverts to the Delphi 1 behavior where **string** is a **ShortString**.

Most new Delphi programs rely on long strings, which are much easier to use than short strings. Disable **$LongStrings** only to preserve compatibility with Delphi 1.

See Also

AnsiString Type, ShortString Type, String Keyword

$M Compiler Directive

Syntax

```
{$M MinStackSize,MaxStackSize}
```

Scope

Project

Description

The **$M** compiler directive sets the minimum and maximum stack size. The default minimum size is 16 KB and the default maximum size is 1 MB. For clarity, use **$MinStackSize** and **$MaxStackSize** instead of **$M**.

Example

```
// Default stack sizes in hexadecimal
{$M $4000,$100000}
```

See Also

$MaxStackSize Compiler Directive, $MinStackSize Compiler Directive, $TypeInfo Compiler Directive

---

$MaxStackSize Compiler Directive

Syntax

```
{$MaxStackSize Integer}
```

Scope

Project

Description

$MaxStackSize set the program's maximum stack size in bytes. A library ignores this compiler directive because a DLL does not have its own stack. The default maximum stack size is 1 MB (1048576 bytes), which is more than adequate for most programs.

Windows creates the stack with the minimum stack size specified with the $MinStackSize directive, and the stack grows as needed, up to the maximum size. If the stack size reaches the maximum size, Delphi reports runtime error 12 (EStackOverflow).

In most programs, if you get a stack overflow error, it is due to a software defect, such as unbounded recursion. Check closely for mistakes before you increase the maximum stack size.

See Also

$M Compiler Directive, $MinStackSize Compiler Directive

$MinEnumSize Compiler Directive

Syntax

```
{$Z1}            // default
{$MinEnumSize 1} // default
{$Z2}
{$Z4}
{$MinEnumSize 2}
{$MinEnumSize 4}
{$Z-} // obsolete, means {$Z1}
{$Z+} // obsolete, means {$Z4}
```

Scope

Local

Description

The $MinEnumSize compiler directive sets the smallest size (in bytes) that Delphi uses for an enumerated type. The default is 1 byte, which means Delphi uses the size that is most appropriate. An enumeration with up to 256 literals fits in 1 byte, and an enumeration with up to 65,568 literals fits into 2 bytes.

If you have an enumerated type that must be compatible with an enum in a C or C++ program, you can adjust the size of the enumerated type for compatibility. Usually, that means setting the minimum enumeration size to 4.

Example

```
{$MinEnumSize 4}  // Increase the size for C compatibility.
type
  TCEnum = (cRed, cBlack);
{$MinEnumSize 1} // Restore the default.

function GetColor: TCEnum; external 'cdemo.dll';
```

$MinStackSize Compiler Directive

Syntax

```
{$MinStackSize Integer}
```

Scope

Project

Description

$MinStackSize set the program's initial stack size in bytes. A library ignores this compiler directive because a DLL does not have its own stack. The default minimum stack size is 16 KB (16384 bytes), which is suitable for most programs.

Windows increases the stack size as needed, up to the maximum size established with the $MaxStackSize compiler directive.

See Also

$M Compiler Directive, $MaxStackSize Compiler Directive

$NoDefine Compiler Directive

Syntax

```
{$NoDefine Identifier}
```

Scope

Local

Description

The $NoDefine compiler directive prevents C++ Builder from writing the definition of *Identifier* to the unit's *.hpp* file. Unlike $ExternalSym, the compiler assumes that you will provide an alternate definition of *Identifier* by using the $HppEmit directive. When you do so, you must be sure to define the symbol in the unit's namespace.

Example

```
unit Complex;
interface
type
  TComplex = record
    Real, Imag:  Double;
  end;
  {NoDefine   TComplex}
  (*$HppEmit  'namespace Complex  {*)
  (*$HppEmit  '  class TComplex  {' *)
  (*$HppEmit  '  public: ' *)
```

```
(*$HppEmit  '      TComplex() : m_real(0), m_imag(0) {} ' *)
(*$HppEmit  '    private: ' *)
(*$HppEmit  '      double m_real, m_imag; ' *)
(*$HppEmit  '    }; ' *)
(*$HppEmit  '};' *)
```

See Also

$ExternalSym Compiler Directive, $HppEmit Compiler Directive, $NoInclude Compiler Directive

---

$NoInclude Compiler Directive

Syntax

{$NoInclude UnitName}

Scope

Local

Description

The $NoInclude compiler directive prevents C++ Builder from adding #include "UnitName.hpp" in the unit's .*hpp* file. By default, C++ Builder includes a header file for all of the user-defined units that appear in the **uses** declarations.

Use $NoInclude when you know that a unit's declarations are provided by a different .*hpp* file. You might need to combine $NoInclude with $HppEmit to include a different .*hpp* file.

See Also

$ExternalSym Compiler Directive, $HppEmit Compiler Directive,. $NoDefine Compiler Directive

---

$O Compiler Directive

See

$Optimization Compiler Directive

$ObjExportAll Compiler Directive

Syntax

{$ObjExportAll Off} // default
{$ObjExportAll On}

Scope

File

Description

The `$ObjExportAll` compiler directive tells C++ Builder to export all symbols when compiling the unit as an *.obj* file. You might want to use this directive when using a Pascal unit in a C++ DLL or package to avoid creating a *.def* file.

See Also

Exports Keyword

$OpenStrings Compiler Directive

Syntax

```
{$P+}             // default
{$OpenStrings On} // default
{$P-}
{$OpenStrings Off}
```

Scope

Local

Description

The `$OpenStrings` compiler directive treats all `string`-type parameters as `OpenString` parameters. If `$LongStrings` is enabled, Delphi ignores `$OpenStrings`.

The `$OpenStrings` directive affects only parameters declared with the `string` type, and only when long strings are disabled. Even if `$OpenStrings` is enabled, you can use the `OpenString` type to declare an open string parameter.

`$OpenStrings` exists for backward compatibility. New Delphi programs should use long strings instead of short strings.

See Also

OpenString Type, String Keyword

$Optimization Compiler Directive

Syntax

```
{$O+}             // default
{$Optimization On} // default
{$O-}
{$Optimization Off}
```

Scope

Local, applies to entire subroutine

Description

With `$Optimization` enabled, the compiler produces more efficient code. Delphi's optimizations are safe and do not affect the semantics of the code. Sometimes, debugging is more difficult with optimization enabled, but unless you are having a specific problem with the optimizer, you should usually leave the $Optimization switch enabled.

Tips and Tricks

Some optimizations can be confusing if you are running your program in the debugger. The most common optimizations that make debugging more difficult are:

- Eliminating redundant or unneeded code. You cannot set a breakpoint on a statement if the optimizer determines that the statement serves no purpose.

- For loops run backwards. If you do not refer to the loop control variable of a for loop, Delphi optimizes the loop control to count down to zero.

- Rearranging branches. Break, Continue, Exit and goto statements might be optimized and rearranged. Most often, this is seen when a Break statement in a subroutine is optimized into an immediate return from the subroutine.

- Sometimes, case statements are compiled as jump tables. The tables look like code, but are really offsets to the code for different cases. The jump tables make the code hard to read. The compiler might generate a jump table even if optimizing is disabled.

If you have difficulty setting a breakpoint at a specific location because of the optimizer, temporarily insert a breakpoint assembler instruction. A hardcoded breakpoint is better than disabling the optimizer because it affects only the single point you are interested in. Another possibility is to call a subroutine that does nothing. For example:

```
procedure Example;
var
  I: Integer;
begin
  for I := 1 to 10 do
    if SomeCondition then
      Break;         // Optimizer eliminates the Break so you cannot
  end;               // set a breakpoint on that statement.

...

    if SomeCondition then
    begin
      asm int 3 end;  // One workaround is to force a breakpoint.
      Break;
    end;

procedure Empty;
begin
end;

...

    if SomeCondition then
    begin
      Empty;  // Another is to call a do-nothing procedure and use the
      Break;  // debugger to set a breakpoint here.
    end;
```

See Also

$StackFrames Compiler Directive

$OverflowChecks Compiler Directive

Syntax

```
{$Q-}                   // default
{$OverflowChecks Off}   // default
{$Q+}
{$OverflowChecks On}
```

Scope

Local

Description

The $OverflowChecks directive tells the compiler to generate code that checks the result of integer and enumerated operations to ensure the results are within the bounds of the integer or enumerated type. If an operation produces an out-of-range result, Delphi reports runtime error 5 (EIntOverflow).

Tips and Tricks

You should always enable the $OverflowChecks directive because it can catch numerous errors in your code. A common misconception is that the checks should be disabled in released programs. If an integer or enumerated overflow occurs, you want to catch the error as soon as possible, and not wait for the error to propagate in unknown and unpredictable ways through your program, possibly corrupting your user's data along the way. Do not disable the overflow checks unless you have a specific performance problem, and then disable the checks only in the performance-critical parts of your code.

See Also

$RangeChecks Compiler Directive

$P Compiler Directive

See

$OpenStrings Compiler Directive

$Q Compiler Directive

See

$OverflowChecks Compiler Directive

$R Compiler Directive

See

$RangeChecks Compiler Directive, $Resource Compiler Directive

$RangeChecks Compiler Directive

Syntax

```
{$R-}              // default
{$RangeChecks Off} // default
{$R+}
{$RangeChecks On}
```

Scope

Local

Description

The $RangeChecks directive tells the compiler to generate code that checks array operations to ensure that the array index is within the array bounds. If an index is out of bounds, Delphi reports runtime error 4 (ERangeError).

Tips and Tricks

- You should always enable the $RangeChecks directive because it can catch numerous errors in your code. A common misconception is that the checks should be disabled in released programs. If an array bounds error occurs, you want to catch the error as soon as possible, and avoid referring to an invalid array location, which can result in memory corruption. Do not disable the range checks unless you have a specific performance problem, and then disable the checks only in the performance-critical parts of your code.

- Many Internet security breaches are due to array bounds errors. The programs were mostly written in C, which never checks array bounds, but when using Delphi, you have no excuse not to take advantage of the security features that the language offers.

- When $RangeChecks is enabled, Delphi also checks string references to make sure they are between 1 and the string length, but if a long string is empty, Delphi raises an access violation instead of a runtime error (because Delphi represents an empty string with a nil pointer). Thus, you should always check for an empty string before using a string subscript:

```
if (Length(S) > 0) and (S[1] = '#') then
  ShowMessage('S starts with #');
```

See Also

$OverflowChecks Compiler Directive

$RealCompatibility Compiler Directive

Syntax

```
{$RealCompatibility Off} // default
{$RealCompatibility On}
```

Scope

Local

Description

When you enable the $RealCompatibility directive, the compiler makes the Real type equivalent to Real48. By default, Real is equivalent to Double. This directive exists for backward compatibility. New programs should use the new floating-point types (Single, Double, and Extended). If you must read an old Real value from a file, you can use Real48.

See Also

Double Type, Extended Type, Real Type, Real48 Type, Single Type

---

$ReferenceInfo Compiler Directive

Syntax

```
{$YD}              // default
{$Y+}
{$Y-}

{$ReferenceInfo Off} // default
{$ReferenceInfo On}
```

Scope

Local

Description

By default, the debugging information for a unit includes the definitions of all symbols declared in the unit. With the $ReferenceInfo directive, you can also store references to the symbols. With the reference information, the project browser can show you every use of a type, variable, subroutine, or other symbol.

You must enable $DefinitionInfo in order to use $ReferenceInfo. The $DefinitionInfo and $ReferenceInfo directives define three possible states of browser information. The $Y directive provides a shortcut for the three states:

- The $YD directive is equivalent to enabling definitions and disabling references. This is the default.

- The $Y+ directive is equivalent to enabling definitions and references.

- The $Y- directive is equivalent to disabling definitions and references.

- You cannot enable references without also enabling definitions, so there is no fourth state.

Definitions and references require that $DebugInfo and $LocalSymbols be enabled.

See Also

$DebugInfo Compiler Directive, $DefinitionInfo Compiler Directive, $LocalSymbols Compiler Directive

---

$Resource Compiler Directive

Syntax

```
{$R FileName}
{$Resource FileName}
{$R 'Filename.res' 'FileName.rc'}
{$Resource 'FileName.res' 'FileName.rc'}
```

Scope

Local

Description

The $Resource directive includes an external resource file in a project or package. When the project or package is linked, Delphi includes the resource file in the final *.exe*, *.dll*, or *.bpl* file. The resource file does not have to exist when the unit is compiled—only when the project is linked. A source file can load any number of resource files.

If the *FileName* is an asterisk (*), Delphi uses the source file's base name, substituting the extension that appears in the directive. For example, form units must include the directive {$R *.DFM}, which loads the form's description as a resource file. (To maintain compatibility with Delphi 1, binary *.dfm* files are 16-bit resource files. Delphi converts them to 32-bit resources when linking the project.)

The two-parameter form of the $Resource directive applies only to *.dpr* files. If the directive appears at the start of a project's *.dpr* file and it lists two filenames, the first file is linked into the project, and the second appears in the project manager. When Delphi's IDE builds the project, it also compiles the resource script (*.rc* file) into a *.res* file so it can link the *.res* file with the project. Compiling the resource script is a feature unique to the IDE. The command-line compiler does not compile the resource script. (For more information on the command-line compiler, see Appendix A.)

Put the filenames in single quotes if the name includes spaces or other unusual characters, or if you are using the two-filename version of this directive.

$RunOnly Compiler Directive

Syntax

```
{$RunOnly Off}  // default
{$RunOnly On}
```

Scope

Project

Description

Use the $RunOnly directive in a package's *.dpk* file to mark the package as a runtime package. You cannot load the package into Delphi's IDE. You can only link the package with an application or library.

When you write a component, put the component's unit in a runtime package, and put the property and component editors in a design-time package. That way, an application can link with the component's runtime package and avoid the overhead of linking the design-time code, which the application doesn't need.

See Also

$DesignOnly Compiler Directive

$SafeDivide Compiler Directive

Syntax

```
{$U-}              // default
{$SafeDivide Off}  // default
{$U+}
{$SafeDivide On}
```

Scope

Local

Description

When you enable the $SafeDivide directive, Delphi ensures that the infamous Pentium FDIV bug does not bite your program. With the $SafeDivide directive, floating-point division is carried out by a special function. The first time your program calls the function, it tests for the presence of the bug. If the floating-point hardware is defective, subsequent divisions are carried out by software. If the hardware is correct, subsequent divisions are carried out by the hardware. The test subroutine sets the TestFDIV variable to –1 if the hardware is defective or 1 if the hardware is correct.

The FDIV error affects only older Pentium processors and only certain division operations. Most programs can safely ignore this problem today.

See Also

TestFDIV Variable

$StackFrames Compiler Directive

Syntax

```
{$W-}               // default
{$StackFrames Off}  // default
```

```
{$W+}
{$StackFrames On}
```

Scope

Local

Description

The $StackFrames directive causes the compiler to generate a stack frame for
every subroutine call (except for subroutines you write in assembly language). The
default is that stack frames are created only when they are needed for local
variables.

Some debugging tools require stack frames. If you are not using such a tool, you
can leave the default setting, which results in slightly more efficient code.

$T Compiler Directive

See

$TypedAddress Compiler Directive

$TypedAddress Compiler Directive

Syntax

```
{$T-}               // default
{$TypedAddress Off} // default
{$T+}
{$TypedAddress On}
```

Scope

Local

Description

When $TypedAddress is enabled, the @ operator returns a typed address of a
variable or subroutine. The default is that the @ operator returns a generic
Pointer type. Even when $TypedAddress is enabled, assignments of a typed
pointer to the Pointer type are still allowed as are assignments from Pointer to
a specific pointer type.

Tips and Tricks

* Enable $TypedAddress because it encourages good programming practices
  and careful use of pointers. Unsafe pointer assignments can be caught at compiler time.

* The Addr function always returns an untyped Pointer. If you enable
  $TypedAddress, use Addr when you need an untyped pointer and use @
  when you want a type-safe address.

Example

```
var
  P: PInteger;
  Q: ^Double;
  I: Integer;
begin
{$TypedAddress On}
  P := @I;
  Q := @I; // not allowed because types don't match
{$TypedAddress Off}
  Q := @I; // allowed, even though types don't match
```

See Also

@ Operator, Addr Function, Pointer Type

$TypeInfo Compiler Directive

Syntax

```
{$M-}           // default
{$TypeInfo Off} // default
{$M+}
{$TypeInfo On}
```

Scope

Local

Description

When the $TypeInfo directive is enabled, classes are compiled with runtime type information. This means the class can have a published section, and the compiler stores additional information about the class in the class's virtual method table.

Any class that inherits from a class with RTTI also has RTTI, so you need the $TypeInfo directive only for the base class. Delphi compiles the TPersistent class with $TypeInfo, so all derived classes (including TComponent, TForm, and all the VCL controls and related classes) have RTTI.

See Also

Class Keyword

$U

See

$SafeDivide Compiler Directive

$Undef Compiler Directive

Syntax

```
{$Undef Name}
```

Compiler
Directives

Scope

Local

Description

$Undef removes the definition of *Name*, so subsequent uses of {$IfDef *Name*} are False.

See Also

$Define Compiler Directive, $Else Compiler Directive, $Endif Compiler Directive, $IfDef Compiler Directive, $IfNDef Compiler Directive, $IfOpt Compiler Directive

---

$V Compiler Directive

See

$VarStringChecks Compiler Directive

$VarStringChecks Compiler Directive

Syntax

```
{$V+}                  // default
{$VarStringChecks On}  // default
{$V-}
{$VarStringChecks Off}
```

Scope

Local

Description

Ordinarily, the type of an argument for a **var** parameter must match the parameter's type exactly. This restriction ensures type safety when the subroutine modifies the **var** parameter. If the $VarStringChecks directive is disabled, Delphi loosens the restriction for short strings, letting you pass any short string argument to a subroutine with any type of **var** short string parameter.

If you disable $VarStringChecks, you must take care that the subroutine does not exceed the size of the short string argument. One way to ensure this is to pass only arguments of maximum possible length (e.g., string[255] or ShortString types). Even better is to use long strings instead of short strings.

Tips and Tricks

Disable $VarStringChecks only when needed for backward compatibility. In new code, you should usually use long strings, but if you must use short strings, try using type OpenString instead of disabling $VarStringChecks.

See Also

AnsiString Type, OpenString Type, ShortString Type, String Keyword

---

$W Compiler Directive

See

$StackFrames Compiler Directive

$Warnings Compiler Directive

Syntax

```
{$Warnings On}   // default
{$Warnings Off}
```

Scope

Local, applies to entire subroutine

Description

The $Warnings compiler directive enables or disables compiler warnings. The compiler issues warnings for code that appears to be incorrect without actually violating any of the syntax rules for Delphi Pascal. For example, the compiler issues a warning if a subroutine uses a variable before the variable is assigned any value. Or a subroutine might not return a value in all situations. If you know the warning is unfounded, you can suppress it with the $Warnings directive.

Tips and Tricks

- You should not disable compiler warnings globally in a file or project. The compiler warnings are useful and can warn you about numerous common errors. Disable warnings only when you know it is safe, and then disable them only for the subroutine in question.

- Instead of disabling warnings, try to rewrite the code so the compiler does not generate a warning. Sometimes this means writing code that you know is dead and will never be executed, but the alternative is usually worse. When you disable warnings, you might be hiding a warning for an error you don't know about.

Example

```
// Disable the warning about Result being undefined.
{$Warnings off}
function RunProgram(const Path: string): DWORD;
var
  Code: DWORD;
  StartupInfo: TStartupInfo;
  ProcessInfo: TProcessInformation;
begin
  FillChar(StartupInfo, SizeOf(StartupInfo), 0);
  StartupInfo.cb := SizeOf(StartupInfo);
  if not CreateProcess(PChar(Path), nil, nil, nil, False, 0, nil, nil,
                       StartupInfo, ProcessInfo)
  then
    RaiseLastWin32Error
```

```
     // Raises an exception, so the function never returns, and the
     // result doesn't matter.
     // Using $Warnings is one solution; another is to set Result here.
     // The dead code satisfies the compiler and doesn't have the problem
     // of disabling warnings for the entire function.
   else
   begin
     WaitForSingleObject(ProcessInfo.hProcess, Infinite);
     GetExitCodeProcess(ProcessInfo.hProcess, Code);
     Result := Code;
   end;
 end;
 {$Warnings on}
```

See Also

$Hints Compiler Directive

$WeakPackageUnit Compiler Directive

Syntax

```
{$WeakPackageUnit Off}
{$WeakPackageUnit On}
```

Scope

File

Description

Use $WeakPackageUnit in a unit that is contained in a package when the following criteria are true:

- The package will be used in a variety of applications.

- The unit is not used by most of those applications.

- The unit requires a DLL that most users do not already have.

Ordinarily, the package requires the DLL because the unit requires it. This means an application that uses the package also requires the DLL. In other words, the application vendor must ship the DLL with the application even though the application does not use the DLL.

$WeakPackageUnit solves this problem by linking the unit "weakly" with the package. Specifically, the unit is not actually linked into the package's *.bpl* file. Instead, the unit is contained entirely in the *.dcp* file, which usually stores only the interface part of a unit. If an application does not use the unit, the unit is not linked with the application, and the application does not require the unit's associated DLL. If the application does use the unit, the unit is linked statically with the application, and the application requires the unit's DLL.

If the package contains another unit (Unit2) that uses the weak unit (Unit1), Unit2 breaks the "weakness" constraints. An application that uses the package always links with Unit2 (because Unit2 is always in the package), which requires

---

Unit1, which requires the DLL. Thus, a weak unit must stand alone in the package so the weak linking can work correctly.

A weak unit cannot contain any global variables, an initialization section, or a finalization section.

$WeakPackageUnit has a lot of limitations, and its use is limited. In the few cases where it is needed, though, it is absolutely necessary. If you are not writing packages to sell to other Delphi developers, you don't need to concern yourself with this directive at all.

See Also

Package Directive

$WriteableConst Compiler Directive

Syntax

```
{$J+}                  // default
{$WriteableConst On}   // default
{$J-}
{$WriteableConst Off}
```

Scope

Local

Description

When you declare a const with a type, Delphi allocates memory for the constant. The program can change the value of the "constant," just as though it were a variable. The difference between a typed constant and a local variable is that a typed constant in a subroutine keeps its value across subroutine calls.

If you disable the $WriteableConst directive, you can prevent any assignments to a typed constant, thereby making the constant truly constant. There is no substitute for typed constants in a subroutine, though, so disable $WriteableConst with care. Disable only specific constants whose value you want to protect, and do not disable this directive globally in a project or an entire file.

```
const
  {$WriteableConst off}
  BoolNames: array[Boolean] of string = ('No way', 'As you wish');
  {$WriteableConst on}
```

See Also

Const Keyword

$X Compiler Directive

See

$ExtendedSyntax Compiler Directive

$Y Compiler Directive

See

$DefinitionInfo Compiler Directive, $ReferenceInfo Compiler Directive

$Z Compiler Directive

See

$MinEnumSize Compiler Directive

APPENDIX A

Command-Line Tools

Interactive development environments are great, but don't throw away that command line yet. Compiling a big project is often easier using the command-line compiler than compiling the same project in the IDE. This chapter tells you how to use the command-line compiler and other tools effectively.

Compiler, dcc32.exe

Usage

```
dcc32 [-Aunit=alias] [-B] [-CC] [-CG] [-Dsyms] [-Edirectory]
    [-Faddress] [-GD] [-GP] [-GS] [-H] [-Ipaths] [-J] [-JP] [-Kaddr]
    [-LEdirectory] [-LNdirectory]
    [-LUpackage] [-M] [-Ndirectory] [-Opaths] [-P] [-Q] [-Rpaths] [-TXext]
    [-Upaths] [-V] [-VN] [-VR] [-W] [-Z] [-$A+|-] [-$B+|-] [-$C+|-]
    [-$D+|-] [-$G+|-] [-$H+|-] [-$I+|-] [-$J+|-] [-$L+|-]
    [-$M+|-|minStackSize[,maxStackSize]] [-$O+|-] [-$P+|-]
    [-$Q+|-] [-$R+|-] [-$T+|-] [-$U+|-] [-$V+|-] [-$W+|-]
    [-$X+|-] [-$Y+|-YD] [-$Z+|-|1|2|4] file... [options...]
```

Description

dcc32.exe is Delphi's command-line compiler. It uses the same compiler as the IDE, but you run the program from a command prompt. To control the compiler, you must supply options on the command line or in a configuration (*.cfg*) file. The IDE automatically creates a configuration file for every project, so it is easy to compile a project or unit from the command line using the same options you use in the IDE.

You can mix options and filenames in any order on the command line. The compiler reads all the options before it starts to compile any of the files. The filenames can be any program, library, unit, or package source files. Unlike the IDE, with the command-line compiler, you can compile a single unit (*.pas*) source file.

If a filename is that of a project, library, or package, the compiler also links the necessary units into the final *.exe*, *.dll*, or *.bpl* file. If you omit the extension from a source filename, Delphi tries *.pas*, then *.dpr*. To compile a package, you must supply the *.dpk* extension.

If you do not list any filenames on the command line, the compiler prints a brief summary of its options and usage.

The compiler gets options from four places. It checks all four sources, in order, so later sources can override earlier ones:

- The global configuration file, *dcc32.cfg*, is in Delphi's *bin* directory. You can modify this file to store options that apply to all projects. For example, you might use –u to list directories where Delphi should look for *.dcu* files.

- The local configuration file, *dcc32.cfg*, is in the current directory.

- The project configuration file resides in the same directory as the project source file. Its filename is the project filename, with the *.cfg* extension. Note that the IDE automatically creates a *.cfg* file for each project, saving the project's options in the configuration file.

- You can override the options in the configuration files by specifying additional or different options on the command line. The options can precede or follow the source filename.

A configuration file can contain any number of command-line options on any number of lines. For maximum clarity, it is best to put separate options on separate lines.

Each option switch can start with a hyphen (–) or a slash (/). If you use a slash, you can concatenate options into a single command-line argument, but if you use a hyphen, you must separate options with spaces. In either case, you can use single-letter compiler directive switches as command-line switches, e.g., –$A+. Combine compiler directive switches by separating them with commas, e.g., -$A+,B+,M–. Switches are not case sensitive, so /H is the same as /h.

 Be careful when using directive switches with the command-line compiler. Unlike compiler directives that are embedded in source code, directive switches on the command line and in *.cfg* files are not subject to error checking. Any letter is allowed as a switch name, and invalid switches are ignored. Any character is allowed after the switch letter, and most characters mean the same as +.

You can list any number of filenames on the command line. The compiler compiles the source files one at a time. If a source file uses other units, the compiler ensures that those units are up to date and compiles them first, if necessary.

Unlike the IDE, the command-line compiler does not compile resource scripts listed in $R and $Resource compiler directives. You must run the resource compiler separately. (The next section covers the resource compiler.)

The rest of this section lists all the command-line options:

-A*unit=alias;...*

Create a unit alias so any use of *unit* in a unit's uses declaration is actually a reference to *alias*. This option is used most often when a new version of a unit has a different name than an earlier version of the unit. You can list multiple unit-alias pairs by separating them with a semicolon, for example, **-AWinTypes=Windows;WinProcs=Windows**.

-B

Build all used units even if the *.dcu* files are up to date. Another way to force Delphi to compile all the units in a project is to delete the project's *.dcu* files first.

-CC

Create a console application (**$AppType Console** compiler directive).

-CG

Create a GUI application (**$AppType GUI** compiler directive).

-D*sym1;sym2;...*

Define *sym1*, *sym2*, and so on, as conditional compilation symbols. Define multiple symbols by separating them with a semicolon (;). The **-D** option is equivalent to using the **$Define** compiler directive.

-E*directory*

Store the output *.exe* or *.dll* file in *directory*. The default is the current directory.

-F*address*

Find the source line that corresponds to the *address* you get from a runtime error dialog box. If your application reports an error at an address, and you want to locate the source of the error, rebuild the project with the exact same options as you used earlier, but with the **-F** switch. The compiler requires debug information (**-$D+**) in order to locate the source line number.

-GD

Create a detailed *.map* file that lists the segments, public symbols, and code addresses for every line number of every unit that has debug information enabled (**$DebugInfo** compiler directive). The map file is stored in the project's output directory (**-E** or **-LE** option) and has the same name as the project, but with the *.map* extension.

-GP

Create a medium-sized *.map* file that lists all segments and public symbols. The map file is stored in the project's output directory (**-E** or **-LE** option) and has the same name as the project, but with the *.map* extension.

-GS

Create a small *.map* file that lists only the segments, that is, the starting address and size for each unit's code and data segments. The map file is stored in the project's output directory (**-E** or **-LE** option) and has the same name as the project, but with the *.map* extension.

-H

Generate compiler hints (**$Hints** compiler directive).

-I*paths*

Search for source files in the directories listed in ***paths***. Separate directory names with semicolons.

-J

Generate a C *.obj* file in addition to a *.dcu* file for each unit.

-JP

Generate a C++ *.obj* file in addition to a *.dcu* file for each unit.

-K*addr*

Set the image base to the integer ***addr*** ($ImageBase compiler directive). For example, -K$400000.

-LE*directory*

Store output *.bpl* files in ***directory***. The default is the current directory.

-LN*directory*

Store output *.dcp* files in ***directory***. The default is the current directory.

-LU*package*

Link using the runtime package ***package***. The project links dynamically with the units in ***package*** and does not include a copy of the units in the project's *.exe* or *.dll* file.

-M

Make the unit files, that is, compile them only if needed.

-N*directory*

Store output *.dcu* files in ***directory***. The default is the current directory.

-O*paths*

Search for *.obj* files in the directories listed in ***paths***. Separate directory names with semicolons.

-P

Search for a unit by its short (8.3) filename in addition to its long name. Use this option if the files are stored on a filesystem that does not support long filenames, such as an old NetWare file server.

-Q

Compile quietly and do not list filenames as they are compiled.

-R*paths*

Search for *.res* files in the directories listed in ***paths***. Separate directory names with semicolons.

-TX*ext*

Set the extension of the output file to ***ext***. Unlike the $E compiler directive (which works only for libraries), the -TX option applies to programs and libraries. If you omit a leading dot (.) in ***ext***, the compiler automatically inserts one. For example, -TXscr.

-U*paths*

Search for *.dcu* files in the directories listed in ***paths***. Separate directory names with semicolons.

-V

Store Turbo Debugger information in the *.exe*, *.dll*, or *.bpl* file. Delphi's integrated debugger does not use this information—only Turbo Debugger does. Using this option increases the size of the file considerably, but does not impact runtime performance.

-VN

Generate C++ namespaces. Use this option only if you intend to use the Delphi unit in a C++ project, because it increases the size of the output file and compile time.

-VR

Generate remote debugger symbols (*.rsm* file). Using this option does not affect the project's *.exe* or *.dll* file, but the *.rsm* file can be large. Use this option only when you are using Borland's remote debugger.

-W

Generate compiler warnings ($Warnings compiler directive).

-Z

Disable implicit building of low-level packages ($ImplicitBuild compiler directive).

-$A-
-$A+

Align record, class, and object fields ($Align compiler directive). Default is -$A+.

-$B-
-$B+

Evaluate Boolean expressions without using short-circuiting ($BoolEval compiler directive). Default is -$B-.

-$C-
-$C+

Compile assertions ($Assertions compiler directive). Default is -$C+.

-$D-
-$D+

Generate debug information to store in the *.dcu* file ($DebugInfo compiler directive). Default is -$D+.

-$G-
-$G+

This option is not implemented (see the $ImportedData compiler directive for an explanation). Default is -$G+.

-$H-
-$H+

The string type means AnsiString. Disable this option to make string be the same as ShortString ($LongStrings compiler directive). Default is -$H+.

`-$I-`
`-$I+`

Enable I/O checking so failures of input and output subroutines cause runtime errors (`$IOChecks` compiler directive). Default is `-$I+`.

`-$J-`
`-$J+`

Typed `const` declarations are writable at runtime (`$WriteableConst` compiler directive). Default is `-$J+`.

`-$L-`
`-$L+`

Store local symbol information as part of a *.dcu* file's debug information (`$LocalSymbols` compiler directive). Default is `-$L+`.

`-$M-`
`-$M+`

Generate runtime type information for all class declarations (`$TypeInfo` compiler directive). Default is `-$M-`.

`-$MminStackSize`
`-$MminStackSize,maxStackSize`

Set the minimum stack size (`$MinStackSize` compiler directive) and optionally the maximum stack size (`$MaxStackSize` compiler directive). Default is 16384 and 1048576 bytes (`-$M$4000,$100000`).

`-$O-`
`-$O+`

Enable compiler optimization (`$Optimizations` compiler directive). Default is `-$O+`.

`-$P-`
`-$P+`

`ShortString` subroutine parameters are treated as `OpenString` parameters (`$OpenStrings` compiler directive). Default is `-$P+`.

`-$Q-`
`-$Q+`

Enable integer and enumeration overflow checking (`$OverflowChecks` compiler directive). Default is `-$Q-`.

`-$R-`
`-$R+`

Enable array bounds checking (`$RangeChecks` compiler directive). Default is `-$R-`.

`-$T-`
`-$T+`

The @ operator returns a typed pointer (`$TypedAddress` compiler directive). Default is `-$T-`.

`-$U-`
`-$U+`

Perform safe floating-point division, avoiding the infamous Pentium FDIV bug (`$SafeDivide` compiler directive). Default is `-$U-`.

-$V-
-$V+

When disabled, loosens restrictions on `var` string parameters to allow short string arguments whose maximum size does not match the parameter's maximum size ($VarStringChecks compiler directive). Default is -$V+.

-$W-
-$W+

Generate stack frames ($StackFrames compiler directive). Default is -$W-.

-$X-
-$X+

Enable Pascal syntax extensions ($ExtendedSyntax compiler directive). Default is -$X+.

-$Y-
-$Y+
-$YD

Generate debug and reference information ($ReferenceInfo and $DebugInfo compiler directives). Default is -$Y+.

-$Z-
-$Z+
-$Z1
-$Z2
-$Z4

Set the minimum size of enumerated types to 1, 2, or 4 bytes ($MinEnumSize compiler directive). -$Z- means -$Z1, and -$Z+ means -$Z4. Default is -$Z1.

Resource Compiler, brcc32.exe

Usage

```
brcc32 [-16] [-31] [-32] [-w32] [-ccodepage] [-dname[=string]
   [-fofilename] [-h] [-?] [-ipaths] [-llanguage] [-m] [-r]
   [-v] [-x] file
```

Description

The resource compiler compiles a resource script (*.rc*) into a resource file (*.res*). The command-line resource compiler can be more convenient than using the Project Manager in the IDE when you want to automate builds.

See the Microsoft Platform SDK documentation for the format of a resource script. This information is available online from *msdn.microsoft.com* and on the Microsoft Developer Network CDs.

Options are not case sensitive. Each option can begin with a hyphen (–) or a slash (/). Unlike the command-line compiler, you cannot concatenate any options, even if you use a slash.

The rest of this section describes the command-line options.

-16
-31

Build a 16-bit *.res* file (for compatibility with Windows 3.*x*).

-32
-w32

Build a 32-bit *.res* file (for Windows 9*x*, Windows NT, Windows 2000). This is the default.

-c*codepage*

Set the default code page to *codepage*. The code page controls the interpretation of multibyte characters. See the Windows API documentation for a list of supported code pages.

-d*name*[=*string*]

Define *name* as though it appeared in a #define directive in the source file. The default definition for *name* is 1. You can supply a different definition after an equal sign.

-fo*filename*

Set the output filename to *filename*. The default is a file with the same name as the input file, but with the extension *.res*. If *filename* has no extension, *.res* is used.

-h
-?

Display a brief help message listing the command-line options.

-i*paths*

Search for #include files in the directories in *paths*. Separate directory names with semicolons.

-l*language*

Set the default language to *language*. See the Windows API documentation for a list of supported languages.

-m

Enable multibyte character support. The resource script contains 8-bit ANSI characters, but some resources call for Unicode. You can use multibyte characters to create Unicode characters.

-r

Ignored, for compatibility with older versions of the resource compiler.

-v

Verbose mode: lists the filenames and all the resources as they are compiled. Unlike the other options, -V in uppercase is ignored and is not the same as -v in lowercase.

-x

Ignore the INCLUDE environment variable. By default, the resource compiler checks the INCLUDE environment variable for #include paths (like the -i option).

DFM Converter, convert.exe

Usage

```
convert [-b] [-i] [-s | -t] filenames... | @filelist
```

Description

Delphi can store a form description (*.dfm* file) in a binary format or textual format. The IDE lets you choose which format you prefer. You can also run the *convert. exe* program to change from binary to text or text to binary.

 Windows NT also has a program named *convert.exe*. Make sure you are running the right *convert* utility.

---

convert.exe processes each file by reading it, converting it, and writing a new file. If the input file has the extension *.dfm*, it must be in binary format and *convert.exe* writes a textual file with the extension *.txt*. If an input file has the extension *.txt*, it must be a text file, which is converted to binary and written to a *.dfm* file of the same name.

If a *.dfm* file is in text format, or a *.txt* file is binary, *convert.exe* prints an error message and skips that file.

You can list any number of files and wildcards, and *convert.exe* processes the files one at a time. If you have many files to convert, list the files or wildcards in a separate text file, and name the file list on the command line after an at sign (@).

Without any switches, *convert.exe* works the same way it worked in Delphi 4 and earlier. New in Delphi 5 are command-line switches to control the conversion process. Option switches are not case sensitive. Each option can begin with a hyphen (–) or a slash (/). Unlike with the command-line compiler, you cannot concatenate any options, even if you use a slash.

The rest of this section describes the command-line options:

–b

Always convert to binary, regardless of the file's extension.

–i

Convert in place. Instead of copying a *.dfm* file to a *.txt* file or vice versa, each file is converted in place and its contents are overwritten with the conversion results. Without the –b or –t option, the –i option toggles the format of each file from binary to text or from text to binary.

–s

Convert files in subdirectories. For each file named on the command line or in a file list, *convert* searches for files with the same name but in subdirectories of the directory that contains the file. If a filename does not contain a directory or drive letter, *convert* uses the current working directory.

`-t`

Always convert to text, regardless of the file's extension.

Object File Dumper, tdump.exe

Usage

```
tdump [-a] [-a7] [-boffset] [-C] [-d] [-e] [-ea[:v]] [-ed]
    [-ee[=symbol]] [-eiid] [-el] [-em[=symbol] [-em.[module]]
    [-ep] [-er] [-ex] [-h] [-iid] [-l] [-le[=symbol]] [-li[=symbol]]
    [-m][-o] [-oiid] [-oxid] [-q] [-r] [-R]
    [-s[number | boffset | eoffset | f | s | u ] [-?] [=str]]
    [-um] [-v] [-xid]
    [inputfile [listfile]] [options...]
```

Description

The *tdump.exe* program displays useful information about binary files, especially *.exe*, *.dll*, *.bpl*, *.obj*, and *.lib* files. The first file named on the command line is the input file to examine. (You cannot use wildcards to specify more than one file.) The second filename is the output filename. If you do not supply a `listfile`, *tdump* writes to the standard output. The output from *tdump* is usually voluminous, so a `listfile` is usually a good idea. Options and filenames can be mixed in any order.

Unlike switches for the other command-line tools, switches for *tdump* are case sensitive. You can start a switch with a hyphen (-) or slash (/). Unlike when using the compiler, you cannot concatenate switches, even if you use a slash.

Object files can be in COFF (Common Object File Format) or OMF (Intel's Object Module Format). COFF is used by Visual C++ and other compilers, but not by any Borland product. OMF is used by Delphi, Borland C++, and other compilers. If you use the wrong options with the wrong file, *tdump* prints an error message and exits.

For more information about OMF, visit Intel's developer web site (*http://developer. intel.com/*). Intel also has information about the PE (portable executable) format, which is used for Win32 programs and DLLs. For a good discussion of the Win32 PE file format and the COFF object file format used in Windows, see *Windows 95 System Programming Secrets*, by Matt Pietrek (IDG books, 1995).

With no switches, *tdump* prints the contents of `inputfile` in a format that is appropriate for the file type, e.g., DOS executable, PE (Win32) executable or DLL, OMF object or library file, COFF object or library file. If *tdump* cannot determine the file type, it dumps the file's contents in hexadecimal (-h option).

`-a`

Display the contents of `inputfile` as 8-bit ANSI characters. Control characters are printed as dots (`.`).

`-a7`

Display the contents of `inputfile` as 7-Bit ASCII characters. Unprintable and control characters are printed as dots (`.`).

-b*offset*

Start reading *inputfile* at byte number *offset*.

-C

The *inputfile* is a COFF file. The filename must end with *.obj* or *.lib*. You can use this option to examine the object and library files from Visual C++ or other compilers.

-d

Display 32-bit debug information in OMF object and library files. The filename must end with *.obj* or *.lib*.

-e

Display *inputfile* as an executable file. The file can be an executable or DLL file for Windows, DOS, or OS/2. The output includes the file's header, section headers, imported symbols, exported symbols, and resources.

-ea[:v]

Include all exported symbols in an *.exe* or *.dll* file. The default is to list only symbols that are named, sorted in alphabetical order. With the **-ea** switch, the list is unsorted; with **-ea:v**, the list is sorted in address order, that is, by relative virtual address (RVA).

-ed

Do not display the debug information in an *.exe* or *.dll* file.

-ee[=*symbol***]**

List only the exported symbols in an *.exe* or *.dll* file. With an optional *symbol*, list only that symbol if it is exported from the file.

-ei*id*

List only table *id* in an LE or LX format file (OS/2 *.exe* or Windows 3.*x* VxD). The *id* can be HDR, OBJ, FIX, NAM, or ENT (*id* is case sensitive).

-el

Do not type line numbers from the *.exe* file.

-em[=*symbol***]**

List only the imported symbols in an *.exe* or *.dll* file. With an optional *symbol*, list only that symbol if it is imported.

-em.[*module***]**

List only the imported modules in an *.exe* or *.dll* file. With an optional *module*, list only that module if it is imported.

-ep

Do not display the PE header of an *.exe* or *.dll* file.

-er

Do not display the relocation records of an *.exe* or *.dll* file.

-ex

Do not display any new executable header of an *.exe* or *.dll* file.

-h

Display the contents of the *inputfile* in hexadecimal.

-i*id*

Include the 16-bit Turbo Debugger tables specified by *id.* Use a question mark (?) to print on the standard output (not the *listfile*) a list of debug table letters. Each table is identified by a single letter (e.g., A for symbol table, B for module table, C for source file tables, and so on). Type multiple tables by listing multiple letters.

-l

Interpret the *inputfile* as an OMF library. The file must have the extension *.lib.* Borland's C and C++ compiler produce OMF libraries, but not all compilers use OMF.

-le[=*symbol***]**

Display the export definition record (EXPDEF) for all symbols whose name contains *symbol.* If you do not supply a symbol name, *tdump* prints all EXPDEF records.

-li[=*symbol***]**

Display the import definition record (IMPDEF) for all symbols whose name contains *symbol.* If you do not supply a symbol name, *tdump* prints all IMPDEF records.

-m

Disable C++ name demangling. Note that Delphi mangles names for compatibility with C++.

-o

Interpret *inputfile* as an OMF object file. The file should have the extension *.obj.* Delphi can produce OMF *.obj* files, as can Borland's C and C++ compilers.

-oi*id*

Display the OMF record name *id.* Use a question mark (?) as the *id* to print on the standard output (not the *listfile*) a list of the OMF record names.

-ox*id*

Exclude the OMF record name *id.* Use a question mark (?) as the *id* to print on the standard output (not the *listfile*) a list of the OMF record names.

-q

Do not type the copyright message that *tdump* usually shows as the first list of its output.

-r

Include a raw (hexadecimal) dump of the contents of OMF records.

-R

Display the PE relocation table of an *.exe* or *.dll* file.

-s[*number* **|** *boffset* **|** *eoffset* **|** f **|** s **|** u] **[=***str***]**

Search for human-readable strings. If you specify a search string, only strings that contain *str* are printed. Otherwise, all strings that contain at least *number* printable characters are printed. You can combine search options, e.g., -s8ufb100f1000=unit.

-s*number*[=*str*]
> Search for strings that contain at least number printable *characters*. The default is four.

-sb*offset*[=*str*]
> Begin the search at byte position *offset*.

-se*offset*[=*str*]
> End the search at byte position *offset*.

-sf[=*str*]
> Format long strings by wrapping them.

-ss[=*str*]
> Perform a case-sensitive search.

-su[=*str*]
> Print matches without a leading byte offset (Unix style).

-s[=*str*]
> Perform a case-insensitive search.

-um
> Read *inputfile* and find all mangled symbol names. Unmangle each name and print the names one name per line in the output file.

-v
> Type more verbose information for resources, COFF files, PE format files, and string dumps.

-x*id*
> Exclude the 16-bit Turbo Debugger tables specified by *id*. Use a question mark (?) to type on the standard output (not the *listfile*) a list of debug table letters. Each table is identified by a single letter (e.g., A for symbol table, B for module table, C for source file tables, and so on). Exclude multiple tables by listing multiple letters.

-?
> Display a summary of the command-line switches.

IDE, delphi32.exe

Usage

```
delphi32 [-attach:process;event] [-b] [-d file arguments] [-hhostname] [-hm] [-hv] [-m] [-np] [-ns] [-opath] [-sdpaths] [-td] [file]
```

Description

The IDE is not a command-line tool, but it can be treated as a command-line compiler with the −b and −m switches (described in this section). It takes other switches to start a debugging session or display debugging information about Delphi itself.

Options are not case sensitive. Each option can begin with a hyphen (−) or a slash (/). Unlike when using the command-line compiler, you cannot concatenate any options, even if you use a slash.

The rest of this section describes the command-line options:

-attach:*process;event*

Start Delphi by debugging the running process whose process ID is *process*. When attaching to the process, pass *event* as the event ID. Delphi uses this option to enable its just-in-time debugger. You cannot generate an *event* manually, so you cannot use this option in other situations.

-b

Build the project named on the command line and exit. Error, warning, and hint messages are written to a file with the project's filename and the extension *.err*. The error file is deleted if the project is compiled with no messages.

-d*file arguments*...
-d *file arguments*...

Start by loading *file* in the debugger. Any command-line arguments that follow the filename are passed to the program when it starts.

-h*hostname*

Start a remote debugging session on *hostname*.

-hm

Display heap statistics in Delphi's main window caption. The heap statistics show how much memory the IDE is using. See `AllocMemCount` and `AllocMemSize` for information about the numbers. The numbers are updated when the IDE is idle.

-hv

Check the heap for validity and display the heap status in Delphi's main window caption. The heap validity is tested when the IDE is idle.

-m

Make the project named on the command line and exit. Error, warning, and hint messages are written to a file with the project's filename and the extension *.err*. The error file is deleted if the project is compiled with no messages.

-np

Do not load any project or desktop when starting.

-ns

Do not display a splash screen when starting.

-o*path*

When compiling with the −b or −m switches, write error, warning, and hint messages to the file *path* instead of the default (project filename with extension *.err*).

-sd*paths*

Search for debug source files in the directories listed in *paths*. Separate directories with semicolons.

-td

Enable some Turbo Debugger features in the IDE debugger.

    −   The CPU and FPU view remain open after a process exits.

- Run → Program Reset resets the program being debugged and then reloads it in the debugger. If no process is running, the last program that was debugged is loaded into the debugger.

- If no project is open, breakpoints and watch points are saved in the default desktop.

APPENDIX B

The SysUtils Unit

The SysUtils unit contains many utility classes, types, variables, and subroutines. They are so central to Delphi programming that many Delphi users forget that the SysUtils unit is not built in and is optional. Because it is not built into the Delphi Pascal language, the SysUtils unit is not covered in this book's main text. On the other hand, it plays such a central role in almost every Delphi program, package, and library, omitting it would be a mistake—hence this appendix.

Errors and Exceptions

This section lists the classes and subroutines to help you handle errors and exceptions. The most important role SysUtils plays is assigning values to the error-handling procedure pointers the System unit declares, namely:

- AbstractErrorProc raises an EAbstractError exception.

- AssertErrorProc raises an EAssertionFailed exception.

- ErrorProc maps runtime errors to exceptions.

- ExceptClsProc maps Windows and hardware exceptions to Delphi exception classes.

- ExceptionClass is set to Exception.

- ExceptObjProc maps Windows and hardware exceptions to Delphi exception objects.

- ExceptProc displays exception information and calls Halt.

If an error or exception occurs before the SysUtils unit is initialized or after it is finalized, you don't get the advantage of its error-handling procedures, and must rely on the simple approach of the System unit. This problem occurs most often when an application shuts down: an application corrupts memory by freeing already-freed memory, overrunning a buffer, etc., but the problem is not detected immediately. After the `SysUtils` unit is finalized, the heap corruption is detected and another unit reports runtime error 217. Sometimes a unit raises an exception, in which case you get runtime error 216. You can improve this situation by moving the `SysUtils` unit to earlier in the project's **uses** declaration. Try listing it first in the project's main source file (but after `ShareMem`). That forces other units to finalize before `SysUtils` cleans up its error handlers.

Exception Classes

The other major role `SysUtils` plays in handling errors is declaring a hierarchy of exception classes. The `Exception` class is the root of the exception class hierarchy. The `SysUtils` unit sets the `ExceptionClass` variable to `Exception`, so the IDE stops when any exception that inherits from `Exception` is raised.

Every exception object has an associated string message. When you raise an exception, you provide the message in the exception constructor. `Exception` declares several different constructors, as you can see in Example B-1, which shows the public methods and properties of `Exception`. The overloaded constructors let you specify a static string as the message, load a string resource by identifier, or load a `resourcestring` by taking its address (`PResStringRec`). You can use a simple string or a format string and associated arguments. You can also provide a help context number (which is zero by default). Instead of using the resource forms of the constructor, it is best to use a `resourcestring` and call `Create`, `CreateFmt`, `CreateHelp`, or `CreateFmtHelp`. The resource forms of the constructor exist for compatibility with older versions of Delphi.

Example B-1: Public Interface of the Exception Class

```
type
  Exception = class(TObject)
  public
    constructor Create(const Msg: string);
    constructor CreateFmt(const Msg:string; const Args:array of const);
    constructor CreateRes(Ident: Integer); overload;
    constructor CreateRes(ResStringRec: PResStringRec); overload;
    constructor CreateResFmt(Ident: Integer;
        const Args: array of const); overload;
    constructor CreateResFmt(ResStringRec: PResStringRec;
        const Args: array of const); overload;
    constructor CreateHelp(const Msg: string; AHelpContext: Integer);
    constructor CreateFmtHelp(const Msg: string;
        const Args: array of const; AHelpContext: Integer);
    constructor CreateResHelp(Ident: Integer; AHelpContext: Integer);
        overload;
    constructor CreateResHelp(ResStringRec: PResStringRec;
        AHelpContext: Integer); overload;
    constructor CreateResFmtHelp(ResStringRec: PResStringRec;
        const Args: array of const; AHelpContext: Integer); overload;
    constructor CreateResFmtHelp(Ident: Integer;
        const Args: array of const; AHelpContext: Integer); overload;
    property HelpContext: Integer read FHelpContext write FHelpContext;
    property Message: string read FMessage write FMessage;
  end;
```

All exception classes inherit from **Exception**. Table B-1 shows the class hierarchy. When writing an application, you should derive your own exception classes from one of the standard ones. That way, you can easily customize and extend the exceptions in future versions of your application.

Table B-1: Exception Classes

Exception Class	Description
Exception	Base class.
EAbort	"Silent" exception raised from **Abort** procedure.
EAbstractError	Call to abstract method.
EExternal	Hardware or Windows exception.
EAccess-Violation	Access violation.
EControlC	User interrupt.
EExternal-Exception	Other external exception.
EIntError	Integer math error.
EDivByZero	Integer divide by zero.
EIntOverflow	Integer or enumeration range overflow.
ERangeError	Array bounds error.
EMathError	Floating-point math error.
EInvalidOp	Invalid floating-point operand or operation.
EOverflow	Floating-point overflow.
EUnderflow	Floating-point underflow.
EZeroDivide	Floating-point divide by zero.
EPrivilege	Windows privilege violation.
EStackOverflow	Execution stack overflow.
EAssertionFailed	Call to **Assert** failed.
EConvertError	Data conversion error.
EHeapException	Dynamic memory error.
EInvalidPointer	Invalid pointer in memory manager.
EOutOfMemory	Memory manager out of memory.
EInOutError	Input or output error.
EIntfCastError	Interface casting error (**as** operator).
EInvalidCast	Object typecasting error (**as** operator).
EInvalidContainer	(Not used in the VCL.)
EInvalidInsert	(Not used in the VCL.)
EPackageError	Cannot load or unload a package.
EPropReadOnly	(Not used in the VCL.)
EPropWriteOnly	(Not used in the VCL.)
ESafeCallException	**Safecall** method returned a failure status.
EVariantError	Any error with **Variant** or **OleVariant**.
EWin32Error	Windows error code.

Most exception classes are trivial derivations from a base class. For example, the declaration of **EOverflow** is shown in Example B-2.

Example B-2: Example of a Trivial Exception Class, EOverflow

```
type
  EOverflow = class(EMathError);
```

A few exception classes declare additional methods or fields:

EExternal Class

```
type
  EExternal = class(Exception)
  public
    ExceptionRecord: PExceptionRecord;
  end;
```

Stores a pointer to the Windows exception record. Read about the details of the exception record format in the Windows Platform SDK documentation.

EHeapException Class

```
type
  EHeapException = class(Exception)
  public
    procedure FreeInstance; override;
  end;
```

Overrides **FreeInstance** to control whether the exception object is actually freed. The **SysUtils** unit allocates a singleton exception object for each class that inherits from **EHeapException**. That way, it doesn't have to try to allocate an exception object after Windows runs out of memory or after the heap becomes corrupt.

EInOutError Class

```
type
  EInOutError = class(Exception)
  public
    ErrorCode: Integer;
  end;
```

Stores the I/O error code in **ErrorCode**. The error code can be one of the built-in Delphi error codes or a Windows error code. The Delphi error codes are described at the end of Chapter 6, *System Constants*. To obtain the text of a Windows I/O error, call **SysErrorMessage**, described later in this section.

EWin32Error Class

```
type
  EWin32Error = class(Exception)
  public
    ErrorCode: DWORD;
  end;
```

Stores the Windows error code in **ErrorCode**, and sets the exception message to the text of the Windows error message.

Error-Handling Support

The SysUtils unit also declares some types and subroutines to provide additional support for handling errors and exceptions:

Abort Procedure
```
procedure Abort;
```
Raises an EAbort exception. A GUI application ignores an EAbort exception, so you can call Abort to raise an exception that is not visible to the user.

AddExitProc Procedure
```
procedure AddExitProc(Proc: TProcedure);
```
You should use finalization sections instead of exit procedures, but older programs might still use exit procedures. The System unit has a single variable, ExitProc, to store a pointer to an exit procedure. The SysUtils unit goes one better and keeps a chain of exit procedures. Instead of assigning a value to ExitProc, call AddExitProc. SysUtils sets ExitProc to its own exit handler, which calls all the exit procedures in last-in-first-called order.

AddTerminateProc Procedure
```
type TTerminateProc = function: Boolean;
procedure AddTerminateProc(TermProc: TTerminateProc);
```
Adds a procedure to a list of termination procedures. A GUI application calls the termination procedures when it is about to exit. If any of the procedures returns False, the application does not exit.

Beep Procedure
```
procedure Beep;
```
Calls the Windows API function MessageBeep(0), which plays the system default sound.

CallTerminateProcs Function
```
function CallTerminateProcs: Boolean;
```
A GUI application calls the CallTerminateProcs function when it receives the Wm_QueryEndSession message. CallTerminateProcs calls each termination function and if any one function returns False, it returns False immediately, and the application does not exit. If every termination function returns True, CallTerminateProcs returns True.

ExceptAddr Function
```
function ExceptAddr: Pointer;
```
When an exception is raised, the code address is saved in ExceptAddr. You can use it when reraising an exception or use the information to log or display the exception.

ExceptionErrorMessage Function
```
function ExceptionErrorMessage(ExceptObject: TObject;
    ExceptAddr: Pointer; Buffer: PChar; Size: Integer): Integer;
```
Call ExceptionErrorMessage to format a string for an exception. Pass the exception object and address as the first two arguments. The string buffer and its size are the next two arguments. The function returns the length of the

formatted string. The exception message includes the module name, exception address, exception class name, and exception message (if the exception object inherits from **Exception**).

ExceptObject Function

```
function ExceptObject: TObject;
```

The **ExceptObject** function returns a reference to the exception object. Call this function only while handling an exception, because Delphi frees the exception object after the exception handler finishes.

OutOfMemory Procedure

```
procedure OutOfMemoryError;
```

Call **OutOfMemory** to raise an **EOutOfMemory** exception. **SysUtils** preallocates a singleton **EOutOfMemory** object, which **OutOfMemory** reuses. That avoids the problem of trying to allocate a new exception object when there is no more memory to be allocated. When writing a custom memory manager, you do not need to call **OutOfMemory** to report an error—instead, make sure the allocation or reallocation function returns **nil**, and Delphi will take care of the rest.

RaiseLastWin32Error Procedure

```
procedure RaiseLastWin32Error;
```

RaiseLastWin32Error raises an **EWin32Error** exception, using the most recent Windows error code as the exception error code (obtained by calling **GetLastError**). Call **RaiseLastWin32Error** any time a Windows API function fails and you want to report the failure as an exception. See also **Win32Check**, later in this section.

ShowException Procedure

```
procedure ShowException(ExceptObject: TObject; ExceptAddr: Pointer);
```

Call **ShowException** to display an exception message. In a console application, the exception message is written to the **Output** file. In a GUI application, the message is displayed in a dialog box. The text of the message is obtained by calling **ExceptionErrorMessage**.

SysErrorMessage Function

```
function SysErrorMessage(ErrorCode: Integer): string;
```

SysErrorMessage returns the text for a Windows error code. An application should always report a Windows error as a text message instead of a number. The **EWin32Error** class automatically includes the error text in its exception message, but **EInOutError** does not format most Windows error codes. Also, if you handle Windows errors in some other fashion, be sure to call **SysErrorMessage**.

Win32Check Function

```
function Win32Check(RetVal: LongBool): LongBool;
```

Every time you call a Windows API function, you should check the return status to be sure the function call succeeded. An API call can fail for any number of obscure reasons. An easy way to check is to call **Win32Check**, which takes a Boolean argument, and if the argument is False, calls **RaiseLastWin32Error**.

File Management

The SysUtils unit declares a number of useful types, constants, and subroutines for managing files and directories and for parsing filenames. This section describes these utilities.

File Input and Output

The standard Pascal I/O procedures use the Windows API to perform the actual file operations. You can also call the Windows API directly, but you might find it easier to use the SysUtils file I/O functions. These functions are thin wrappers around the Windows API functions, providing the convenience of using Delphi strings, for example, instead of PChar strings.

FileClose Procedure

```
procedure FileClose(Handle: Integer);
```

FileClose closes an open file. If the file is not open, the error is silently ignored.

FileCreate Function

```
function FileCreate(const FileName: string): Integer;
```

FileCreate creates a new file and opens it for read and write access, denying all sharing. If the file already exists, it is recreated. The result is the file handle or –1 for an error.

FileGetDate Function

```
function FileGetDate(Handle: Integer): Integer;
```

FileGetDate returns the modification date of an open file. The modification date is updated when the file is closed, so you might need to close the file first and then call **FileAge** to get the most reliable modification date. FileGetDate returns –1 for an error.

A file date and time are packed into bit fields in a 32-bit integer. The resolution is to the nearest two seconds, and it can represent years in the range 1980 to 2099. Figure B-1 shows the format of a file date and time. See FileDateToDateTime to convert the file date to a TDateTime.

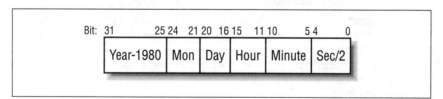

Figure B-1: Format of a file date and time

FileOpen Function

```
function FileOpen(const FileName: string; Mode: LongWord): Integer;
```

FileOpen opens an existing file. The **Mode** combines access and sharing flags, as shown in Table B-2. Choose one access mode and one sharing mode

---

and combine them with addition or an inclusive or. The return value is the file handle or −1 for an error.

Table B-2: File Access and Sharing Modes

Literal	Value	Description
Access Modes		
fmOpenRead	$0000	Read-only access
fmOpenWrite	$0001	Write-only access
fmOpenReadWrite	$0002	Read and write access
Sharing Modes		
fmShareCompat	$0000	Exclusive access
fmShareExclusive	$0010	Exclusive access
fmShareDenyWrite	$0020	Shared reading is permitted
fmShareDenyRead	$0030	Shared writing is permitted
fmShareDenyNone	$0040	Shared reading and writing is permitted

FileRead Function

```
function FileRead(Handle: Integer; var Buffer; Count: LongWord):
    Integer;
```

FileRead reads up to Count bytes into Buffer. Note that Buffer is the actual buffer, not a pointer. The number of bytes actually read is returned, or −1 for errors.

FileSeek Function

```
function FileSeek(Handle, Offset, Origin: Integer): Integer; overload;
function FileSeek(Handle: Integer; const Offset: Int64;
    Origin: Integer): Int64; overload;
```

FileSeek sets the read or write position (in bytes) of an open file and returns the new file position (a byte offset from the start of the file). Table B-3 lists the possible values for the Origin. To learn the current file position, pass an Origin of File_Current and an Offset of 0. The overloaded version of this function lets you seek in files larger than 2 GB.

Table B-3: FileSeek Origin

Literal	Value	Description
File_Begin	0	Offset is relative to the beginning of the file.
File_Current	1	Offset is relative to current file position.
File_End	2	Offset is relative to the end of the file.

If the seek fails, the 32-bit version returns −1 for an error. The 64-bit version returns −1 in the low-order 32-bits of its result. Because this might be a valid return value, call GetLastError to get the error code, which is zero if the seek succeeded.

FileSetDate Function

```
function FileSetDate(Handle: Integer; Age: Integer): Integer;
```

FileSetDate sets the modification time of an open file. Under Windows NT, the file access and creation times are not changed. Zero is returned for success or an error code for failure.

FileWrite Function

```
function FileWrite(Handle: Integer; const Buffer; Count: LongWord):
    Integer;
```

FileWrite writes **Count** bytes from **Buffer** to the file. It returns the number of bytes written or −1 for an error. Note that **Buffer** is the actual data, not a pointer.

TFileRec Type

```
const fmClosed = $D7B0;
const fmInput  = $D7B1;
const fmOutput = $D7B2;
const fmInOut  = $D7B3;
type
  TFileRec = packed record
    Handle: Integer;
    Mode: Integer;
    RecSize: Cardinal;
    Private: array[1..28] of Byte;
    UserData: array[1..32] of Byte;
    Name: array[0..259] of Char;
  end;
```

The standard Pascal **file** type is actually a **TFileRec** record. Cast the **file** variable to **TFileRec** to access the file handle and other fields. For example, get the modification date of a **file** as follows:

```
function GetFileDate(var F: file): TDateTime;
var
  Date: Integer;
begin
  Date := FileGetDate(TFileRec(F).Handle);
  if Date = -1 then
    raise Exception.Create('Cannot get file date');
  Result := FileDateToDateTime(Date);
end;
```

TTextRec Type

```
type
  PTextBuf = ^TTextBuf;
  TTextBuf = array[0..127] of Char;
  TTextRec = packed record
    Handle: Integer;
    Mode: Integer;
    BufSize: Cardinal;
    BufPos: Cardinal;
    BufEnd: Cardinal;
    BufPtr: PChar;
    OpenFunc: Pointer;
```

```
    InOutFunc: Pointer;
    FlushFunc: Pointer;
    CloseFunc: Pointer;
    UserData: array[1..32] of Byte;
    Name: array[0..259] of Char;
    Buffer: TTextBuf;
  end;
```

The standard Pascal Text or TextFile type is actually a TTextRec record. You can cast a TextFile to TTextRec to obtain the file handle or other fields. You can also define your own text file driver by filling in the fields of a TTextRec record. See TextFile in Chapter 5, *Language Reference*, for details.

Managing Files

This section describes other functions for working with files:

DeleteFile Function

```
function DeleteFile(const FileName: string): Boolean;
```

DeleteFile deletes a file and returns True for success or False for failure. Call GetLastError to obtain the error code. Note that the Windows unit also has a DeleteFile function, but it takes a PChar argument. If you get an error regarding a parameter type mismatch, the most likely reason is that the Windows unit appears later than the SysUtils unit in the uses declaration. Move SysUtils so it comes after Windows, or explicitly qualify the function name, as in SysUtils.DeleteFile.

FileAge Function

```
function FileAge(const FileName: string): Integer;
```

FileAge returns the modification date of a file. It returns a file date or –1 for an error. See FileDateToDateTime to convert the file date into a TDateTime. Figure B-1 (earlier in this appendix) shows the format of a file date and time.

FileExists Function

```
function FileExists(const FileName: string): Boolean;
```

FileExists returns True if a file exists or False if the file does not exist or if the user does not have enough privileges to determine whether the file exists.

FileGetAttr Function

```
function FileGetAttr(const FileName: string): Integer;
```

FileGetAttr returns a file's attributes or –1 for an error. The file attributes are returned as a bit mask. Table B-4 describes the file attributes that might be returned. SysUtils declares constants for some of the attributes, but for the other attributes, you must use the literals declared in the Windows unit. For more information about Windows file attributes, see the Microsoft Platform SDK documentation, in particular, the GetFileAttributes function. (Some of these attributes apply only to Windows 2000.)

FileSearch Function

```
function FileSearch(const Name, DirList: string): string;
```

Table B-4: File Attributes

Windows Literal	SysUtils Literal	Description
File_Attribute_Archive	faArchive	File is marked for backup.
File_Attribute_Compressed	None	File contents are compressed.
File_Attribute_Directory	faDirectory	File is a directory.
File_Attribute_Encrypted	None	File contents are encrypted.
File_Attribute_Hidden	faHidden	File is hidden from normal directory listings.
File_Attribute_Normal	None	No attributes are set.
File_Attribute_Offline	None	File is not immediately available.
File_Attribute_Readonly	faReadonly	File is read-only.
File_Attribute_Reparse_Point	None	File is a reparse point.
File_Attribute_Sparse_File	None	File contents are sparse.
File_Attribute_System	faSysFile	System file.
File_Attribute_Temporary	None	Temporary file.

FileSearch looks in the directories listed in DirList for a filename Name. The search always starts with the current directory before searching the directories listed in DirList. Separate the directory names with semicolons. The Name must be a plain filename or relative path. FileSearch returns the complete path or an empty string if the file is not found.

FileSetAttr Function

```
function FileSetAttr(const FileName: string; Attr: Integer): Integer;
```

FileSetAttr changes a file's attributes and returns zero for success or the error code for failure. Table B-4 lists the file attributes supported by Windows.

FindClose Procedure

```
procedure FindClose(var F: TSearchRec);
```

FindClose ends a directory search that was started with FindFirst. If FindFirst returns a successful result, your program must call FindClose when it is done searching.

FindFirst Function

```
type
  TFileName = type string;
  TSearchRec = record
    Time: Integer;
    Size: Integer;
    Attr: Integer;
    Name: TFileName;
    ExcludeAttr: Integer;
    FindHandle: THandle;
    FindData: TWin32FindData;
```

```
  end;
function FindFirst(const Path: string; Attr: Integer;
    var Rec: TSearchRec): Integer;
```

FindFirst starts a directory search. The search looks for files that match the Path specifier. The Path can include wildcard characters (* and ?). If Attr is zero, all regular files are found. You can specify a bitmask of faHidden, faSysFile, and faDirectory to find special files and directories, too. Use faAnyFile to find all files and directories. FindFirst returns zero for success or an error code for failure. If it returns zero, you must eventually call FindClose to free the resources allocated by FindFirst.

If FindFirst returns zero, it fills in Rec with information about the first matching file. The following fields are for your use. The other fields are reserved for use by FindFirst, FindNext, and FindClose.

Attr

> The file's attributes. See Table B-4 for a list of Windows file attributes.

FindData

> You can get more detailed information in the Windows data record. This record is documented under WIN32_FIND_DATA in the Platform SDK. In particular, you can get the short (8.3) name of a file, get the size of a file that is larger than 2 GB, or get the file access and creation dates and times.

Name

> The file's long name. See the FindData member for the short filename.

Size

> The size of the file in bytes. If the file is larger than 2 GB, the Size contains the low-order 32-bits of the file's true size; get the complete file size from the FindData member.

Time

> The file's modification date and time as a file date. See FileDateToDateTime to convert this value to a TDateTime. Figure B-1 (earlier in this appendix) shows the format of a file date and time.

FindNext Function

```
function FindNext(var F: TSearchRec): Integer;
```

After FindFirst returns zero, call FindNext to find the next matching file. Pass the same search record as the sole argument to FindNext. The return value is zero for success or an error code for any error. If FindNext cannot find any more matching files, the error is Error_No_More_Files. Be sure to call FindClose after you are done using FindFirst and FindNext.

RenameFile Function

```
function RenameFile(const OldName, NewName: string): Boolean;
```

RenameFile changes a file or directory name and returns True for success or False for failure. Call GetLastError to learn the error code. You can rename a file to a different directory or drive. You can rename a directory, but only on the same drive.

Managing Directories

This section lists the functions for working with directories. If any of these functions returns False, call GetLastError to get the error code.

CreateDir Function

```
function CreateDir(const Dir: string): Boolean;
```

CreateDir creates a directory and returns True for success or False for failure. Call CreateDir instead of MkDir when you want to have the convenience of a Boolean result instead of messing around with I/O results.

GetCurrentDir Function

```
function GetCurrentDir: string;
```

GetCurrentDir returns the current working drive and directory. The returned value is the same as the string obtained by calling GetDir with a first argument of zero, but GetCurrentDir is more convenient.

RemoveDir Function

```
function RemoveDir(const Dir: string): Boolean;
```

RemoveDir deletes an empty directory and returns True for success or False for failure. Call RemoveDir instead of RmDir if you do not want to mess around with I/O results.

SetCurrentDir Function

```
function SetCurrentDir(const Dir: string): Boolean;
```

SetCurrentDir sets the working drive and directory. It returns True for success or False for failure. Call SetCurrentDir instead of ChDir when you don't want to mess around with I/O results.

Managing Disks

DiskFree Function

```
function DiskFree(Drive: Byte): Int64;
```

DiskFree returns the number of free bytes on a drive. The Drive parameter is 1 for drive A:, 2 for B:, and so on. If Drive is 0, DiskFree gets information about the default drive. DiskFree correctly handles drives larger than 2 GB, except on Windows 95a, which does not have support for large disk partitions. DiskFree returns −1 if the drive is invalid.

DiskSize Function

```
function DiskSize(Drive: Byte): Int64;
```

DiskSize returns the size of a drive in bytes. The Drive parameter is 1 for drive A:, 2 for B:, and so on. If Drive is 0, DiskSize gets information about the default drive. DiskSize correctly handles drives larger than 2 GB, except on Windows 95a, which does not have support for large disk partitions. DiskSize returns −1 if the drive is invalid.

Managing Filenames

The SysUtils unit has several functions to help you parse and manipulate filenames. These functions are all multibyte aware, that is, they correctly handle multibyte character strings.

ChangeFileExt Function

```
function ChangeFileExt(const FileName, Extension: string): string;
```

ChangeFileExt changes a file extension, that is, the part of a filename after the last dot (.). If the filename has no extension, Extension is appended to the end. The new filename is returned. The Extension can be any string, including an empty string. By convention, non-empty extensions start with a dot (.).

ExcludeTrailingBackslash Function

```
function ExcludeTrailingBackslash(const S: string): string;
```

ExcludeTrailingBackslash returns a copy of S, but if the last character of S is a backslash (\), that character is deleted from the result. The most common use for this function is to prepare a directory name for use with functions such as SetCurrentDir.

ExpandFileName Function

```
function ExpandFileName(const FileName: string): string;
```

ExpandFileName returns the absolute path for a file, including drive and directory.

ExpandUNCFileName Function

```
function ExpandUNCFileName(const FileName: string): string;
```

ExpandUNCFileName returns the fully expanded, absolute path for a file. Drive letters are expanded into their UNC (universal naming convention) paths (e.g., \\server\sharename).

ExtractFileDir Function

```
function ExtractFileDir(const FileName: string): string;
```

ExtractFileDir returns the path part of a filename, without a trailing backslash. You can use the result as the argument to any of the directory functions (described earlier in this appendix).

ExtractFileDrive Function

```
function ExtractFileDrive(const FileName: string): string;
```

ExtractFileDrive returns the drive or UNC host and share name part of a filename. If the filename does not contain a drive specifier, this function returns an empty string.

ExtractFileExt Function

```
function ExtractFileExt(const FileName: string): string;
```

ExtractFileExt returns the extension part of a filename, including its leading dot (.). If the filename has no extension, this function returns an empty string.

ExtractFileName Function

```
function ExtractFileName(const FileName: string): string;
```

`ExtractFileName` returns the plain filename part of a path, including the extension, without any drive or directory. If `FileName` ends with a colon or backslash, this function returns an empty string.

ExtractFilePath Function

```
function ExtractFilePath(const FileName: string): string;
```

`ExtractFilePath` returns the path part of a filename—everything that `ExtractFileName` does not return. Note that the returned path might end with a backslash. See `ExtractFileDir` to get the directory name without the trailing backslash (which is usually more useful).

ExtractRelativePath Function

```
function ExtractRelativePath(const BaseName, DestName: string): string;
```

`ExtractRelativePath` returns a pathname that identifies the file named `DestName`, relative to the directory in `BaseName`.

ExtractShortPathName Function

```
function ExtractShortPathName(const FileName: string): string;
```

`ExtractShortPathName` converts a filename to a short (8.3) pathname. If the `FileName` is already in its short form, the same filename is returned. If the file does not exist, an empty string is returned.

Note that there is no `ExtractLongPathName` function because most Windows operating systems do not have any API function to obtain a long pathname. Instead, you can use the `GetLongPathName` function in Example B-3.

Example B-3: GetLongPathName Function

```
// Separate a path into the drive and directory part and the trailing
// filename part. If the path is a UNC name, leave the sharename
// as part of the drive and directory.
procedure ExtractFileParts(const Path: string;
                           var Directory, Name: string);
var
  I: Integer;
begin
  // Get the drive letter or UNC host and share name.
  // SysUtils doesn't have a function to do this...
  I := LastDelimiter('\:', Path);
  Name := Copy(Path, I + 1, MaxInt);
  if (I > 1) and
     (Path[I] = '\') and
     (not (Path[I - 1] in ['\', ':']) or
         (ByteType(Path, I - 1) = mbTrailByte))
  then
    Dec(I);
  Directory := Copy(Path, 1, I);

  // If the Directory is a UNC host only, we went too far and extracted
  // the share name as Name.
  if (Length(Directory) > 2) and
     (Directory[1] = '\') and
```

```
     (LastDelimiter('\', Directory) = 2) then
  begin
    Directory := Path;
    Name := '';
  end;
end;

function GetLongPathName(const PathName: string): string;
var
  Directory, FileName, FullName: string;
  LongName: string;
  Info: TShFileInfo;
begin
  FullName := ExcludeTrailingBackslash(PathName);
  repeat
    ExtractFileParts(FullName, Directory, FileName);
    if FileName = '' then
      // When the path gets down to the drive only, there's no need
      // to expand any further.
      LongName := IncludeTrailingBackslash(Directory)
    else if ShGetFileInfo(PChar(FullName), 0, Info, SizeOf(Info),
                          Shgfi_DisplayName) = 0 then
    begin
      // Cannot expand the filename.
      Result := '';
      Exit;
    end
    else
      LongName := Info.szDisplayName;

    // Make sure the backslash delimiters are included in the result.
    if Result = '' then
      Result := LongName
    else
      Result := IncludeTrailingBackslash(LongName) + Result;
    FullName := Directory;
  until FileName = '';
end;
```

IncludeTrailingBackslash Function

```
function IncludeTrailingBackslash(const S: string): string;
```

IncludeTrailingBackslash returns a copy of S, but guarantees that the last character of S is a backslash (\\). If one is not already present, it is appended. Call IncludeTrailingBackslash when building a path from separate directory and filenames.

String Management

This section lists subroutines related to AnsiString and PChar strings. An AnsiString can also store a multibyte string, that is, a string where a single character might occupy more than one byte. The functions listed in the following sections handle multibyte strings correctly. Unlike `PChar` strings, an `AnsiString` can contain any character, including #0. However, some string-handling functions assume that the string does not contain any #0 characters (except the #0 that appears after the end of the string). These functions are so noted in their descriptions.

For an example of working with strings that might be multibyte strings, see Example B-4, at the end of this section.

ANSI String Functions

The ANSI string functions use `AnsiString` arguments and results, but more important, they recognize the Windows locale to handle ANSI characters, such as accented letters. They also handle multibyte strings.

AdjustLineBreaks Function

```
function AdjustLineBreaks(const S: string): string;
```

`AdjustLineBreaks` converts the string `S` into DOS format by converting single carriage return (#13) and line feed (#10) characters into CR-LF pairs. Existing CR-LF line endings are untouched. Files that are copied from Unix or Macintosh systems use different line break characters, which can confuse some Windows and DOS programs. (Macintosh uses a lone carriage return for a line break; Unix uses a lone line feed character.)

AnsiCompareFileName Function

```
function AnsiCompareFileName(const S1, S2: string): Integer;
```

`AnsiCompareFileName` is similar to `AnsiCompareText`, but it works around a problem with full-width Japanese (Zenkaku) filenames, where the ASCII characters take up two bytes instead of one. Always call `AnsiCompareFileName` to compare two filenames.

AnsiCompareStr Function

```
function AnsiCompareStr(const S1, S2: string): Integer;
```

`AnsiCompareStr` compares two strings and returns an integer result, as listed in Table B-5.

Table B-5: Results of AnsiCompareStr

Result	Description
-1	S1 < S2
0	S1 = S2
+1	S1 > S2

The comparison is case sensitive and takes into consideration the Windows locale and multibyte strings.

AnsiCompareText Function

```
function AnsiCompareText(const S1, S2: string): Integer;
```

`AnsiCompareText` compares two strings and returns an integer result in the manner of `AnsiCompareStr`. The comparison is *not* case sensitive and takes into consideration the Windows locale and multibyte strings.

AnsiLastChar Function

```
function AnsiLastChar(const S: string): PChar;
```

AnsiLastChar returns a pointer to the last character of S, which might not be the last byte of a multibyte string. If the string is empty, `nil` is returned.

AnsiLowerCase Function

```
function AnsiLowerCase(const S: string): string;
```

AnsiLowerCase converts the string S to lowercase, taking into account the Windows locale to map accented characters and multibyte characters.

AnsiLowerCaseFileName Function

```
function AnsiLowerCaseFileName(const S: string): string;
```

AnsiLowerCaseFileName converts the filename S to lowercase, taking into account the Windows locale to map accented characters and multibyte characters. **AnsiLowerCaseFileName** works around a problem with full-width Japanese (Zenkaku) filenames, where the ASCII characters take up two bytes instead of one.

AnsiPos Function

```
function AnsiPos(const Substr, S: string): Integer;
```

AnsiPos returns the position of the first occurrence of SubStr in S or zero if S does not contain SubStr. This function assumes S does not contain any #0 characters (except the #0 that appears after the end of the string).

AnsiQuotedStr Function

```
function AnsiQuotedStr(const S: string; Quote: Char): string;
```

AnsiQuotedStr returns a copy of S enclosed in quotes. The quote character is Quote. Occurrences of Quote in S are repeated in the result string. This function assumes S does not contain any #0 characters (except the #0 that appears after the end of the string).

AnsiSameStr Function

```
function AnsiSameStr(const S1, S2: string): Boolean;
```

AnsiSameStr returns True if the strings S1 and S2 are identical, and False otherwise. The comparison is case sensitive.

AnsiSameText Function

```
function AnsiSameText(const S1, S2: string): Boolean;
```

AnsiSameText returns True if the strings S1 and S2 are identical, and False otherwise. The comparison is *not* case sensitive.

AnsiUpperCase Function

```
function AnsiUpperCase(const S: string): string;
```

AnsiUpperCase converts the string S to uppercase, taking into account the Windows locale to map accented characters and multibyte characters.

AnsiUpperCaseFileName Function

```
function AnsiUpperCaseFileName(const S: string): string;
```

AnsiUpperCaseFileName converts the filename S to uppercase, taking into account the Windows locale to map accented characters and multibyte characters. **AnsiUpperCaseFileName** works around a problem with full-width

Japanese (Zenkaku) filenames, where the ASCII characters take up two bytes instead of one.

ByteToCharIndex Function

```
function ByteToCharIndex(const S: string; Index: Integer): Integer;
```

ByteToCharIndex returns the character index that corresponds to byte position Index in string S. In a multibyte string, the character index might be less than the byte index. If the byte index is invalid, zero is returned.

ByteToCharLen Function

```
function ByteToCharLen(const S: string; MaxLen: Integer): Integer;
```

ByteToCharLen returns the number of characters in the string S, considering at most MaxLen bytes. In a multibyte string, the character length might be less than the byte length.

ByteType Function

```
type TMbcsByteType = (mbSingleByte, mbLeadByte, mbTrailByte);
function ByteType(const S: string; Index: Integer): TMbcsByteType;
```

ByteType returns the kind of byte at position Index in string S. The byte types are listed in Table B-6.

Table B-6: Values for ByteType

Literal	Description
mbSingleByte	Ordinary, single-byte character
mbLeadByte	First byte of a multibyte character
mbTrailByte	Second byte of a multibyte character

Unlike other string functions, ByteType does not do any range checking of its arguments. If Index is out of bounds, ByteType will not detect the error and the results are unpredictable.

CharToByteIndex Function

```
function CharToByteIndex(const S: string; Index: Integer): Integer;
```

CharToByteIndex returns the byte index for the character at logical position Index in the string S. In a multibyte string, the byte index might be greater than the character index. If the character index is invalid, zero is returned.

CharToByteLen Function

```
function CharToByteLen(const S: string; MaxLen: Integer): Integer;
```

CharToByteLen returns the number of bytes in S, considering at most MaxLen characters of S. In a multibyte string, the character length can be smaller than the byte length.

FindCmdLineSwitch Function

```
function FindCmdLineSwitch(const Switch: string;
    SwitchChars: TSysCharSet; IgnoreCase: Boolean): Boolean;
```

FindCmdLineSwitch returns True if the command line contains Switch. The SwitchChars parameter specifies which characters mark the start of a switch (usually '-/'). If IgnoreCase is False, the switch name must match Switch exactly; if it is True, the command-line switch can appear in uppercase, lowercase, or a mixture.

IsDelimiter Function

```
function IsDelimiter(const Delimiters, S: string; Index: Integer):
    Boolean;
```

IsDelimiter returns True if the character that starts at byte position Index of S is one of the characters in Delimiters. False is returned if the character is not in Delimiters, if Index is out of bounds, or if the character at Index is the leading or trailing byte of a multibyte character. Delimiters cannot be a multibyte string, and you cannot use #0 as one of the delimiters.

IsPathDelimiter Function

```
function IsPathDelimiter(const S: string; Index: Integer): Boolean;
```

IsPathDelimiter returns True if the character that starts at position Index of S is a backslash (\), which is the Windows path separator.

IsValidIdent Function

```
function IsValidIdent(const Ident: string): Boolean;
```

IsValidIdent returns True if Ident holds a valid Delphi Pascal identifier, that is, a string whose first character is a letter or underscore and whose subsequent characters are letters, digits, or underscores.

LastDelimiter Function

```
function LastDelimiter(const Delimiters, S: string): Integer;
```

LastDelimiter returns the index of the last (rightmost) occurrence in S of any of the characters in Delimiters. If none of the Delimiters characters appears in S, LastDelimiter returns zero. Delimiters cannot be a multibyte string, and you cannot use #0 as one of the delimiters.

StringReplace Function

```
type TReplaceFlags = set of (rfReplaceAll, rfIgnoreCase);
function StringReplace(const S, OldSubStr, NewSubStr: string;
    Flags: TReplaceFlags): string;
```

StringReplace returns a copy of S, where OldSubStr is replaced by NewSubStr. If Flags include rfReplaceAll, every occurrence of OldSubStr is replaced; otherwise, only the first occurrence is replaced. The search for OldSubStr is case sensitive unless you include the rfIgnoreCase flag.

WrapText Function

```
function WrapText(const Line, BreakStr: string;
    BreakChars: TSysCharSet; MaxCol: Integer): string; overload;
function WrapText(const Line: string; MaxCol: Integer = 45): string;
    overload;
```

WrapText returns a copy of Line broken into multiple lines, MaxCol columns wide. Each line is broken when a line reaches MaxCol characters. To create a line break, BreakStr is inserted in the string after a series of BreakChars characters at the end of the line. (In Delphi 5, existing line breaks are assumed to use #13 and #10 as line break characters, regardless of BreakStr.)

The second form of WrapText uses [' ', '-', #9] (space, hyphen, tab) for BreakSet and #13#10 (carriage return, line feed) for BreakStr.

PChar Functions

Delphi can automatically convert a PChar string into an AnsiString, but there are times when you do not want the overhead of the conversion. Instead, you can call the various PChar-related functions to work with a PChar string in its native format. Note that using a PChar string can be slower than using an AnsiString because the length of an AnsiString is known beforehand, but in a PChar, the function must scan the string to locate its end.

When working with PChar strings, make sure you do not overflow the memory allocated for the string. Delphi cannot help you because a PChar is just a pointer, not a true array, so Delphi does not know the size of the memory allocated for the string. Whenever possible, use the L version of these functions, as in AnsiStrLComp instead of AnsiStrComp.

Unless noted otherwise, the functions described in this section all handle multibyte strings correctly.

AnsiExtractQuotedStr Function

```
function AnsiExtractQuotedStr(var Src: PChar; Quote: Char): string;
```

AnsiExtractQuotedStr parses the Src string for a quoted string. The first character of Src must be Quote or else the function returns an empty string immediately. If the first character is Quote, the string enclosed by the quote characters is copied and returned. Repeated quote characters in the string are reduced to a single quote. Src is updated to point to the character immediately after the closing quote. If Src has no closing quote, it is updated to point to the terminating #0 byte, and the quoted text up to the end of the string is returned.

AnsiStrComp Function

```
function AnsiStrComp(S1, S2: PChar): Integer;
```

AnsiStrComp compares S1 and S2 and returns an integer result in the manner of AnsiCompareStr. The comparison is case sensitive and uses the Windows locale.

AnsiStrIComp Function

```
function AnsiStrIComp(S1, S2: PChar): Integer;
```

AnsiStrIComp compares S1 and S2 and returns an integer result in the manner of AnsiCompareStr. The comparison is not case sensitive and uses the Windows locale.

AnsiStrLastChar Function

```
function AnsiStrLastChar(S: PChar): PChar;
```

AnsiStrLastChar returns a pointer to last character in the string S before the trailing #0 byte. In a multibyte string, the last character is not necessarily the last byte.

AnsiStrLComp Function

```
function AnsiStrLComp(S1, S2: PChar; MaxLen: Cardinal): Integer;
```

AnsiStrLComp compares up to **MaxLen** characters of **S1** and **S2**, returning an integer result in the manner of **AnsiCompareStr**. The comparison is case sensitive and uses the Windows locale.

AnsiStrLIComp Function

```
function AnsiStrLIComp(S1, S2: PChar; MaxLen: Cardinal): Integer;
```

AnsiStrLIComp compares up to **MaxLen** characters of **S1** and **S2**, returning an integer result in the manner of **AnsiCompareStr**. The comparison is not case-sensitive and uses the Windows locale.

AnsiStrLower Function

```
function AnsiStrLower(Str: PChar): PChar;
```

AnsiStrLower converts **Str** in place to all lowercase. It returns the value of **Str**. The conversion uses the Windows locale to properly convert non-ASCII characters.

AnsiStrPos Function

```
function AnsiStrPos(Str, SubStr: PChar): PChar;
```

AnsiStrPos searches for the first occurrence of **SubStr** in **Str** and returns a pointer to the start of the substring in **Str**, or **nil** if the substring is not found.

AnsiStrRScan Function

```
function AnsiStrScan(Str: PChar; Chr: Char): PChar;
```

AnsiStrRScan searches for the last (rightmost) occurrence of the character **Chr** in **Str** and returns a pointer to the character in **Str** or **nil** if the character is not found.

AnsiStrScan Function

```
function AnsiStrScan(Str: PChar; Chr: Char): PChar;
```

AnsiStrScan searches for the first occurrence of the character **Chr** in **Str** and returns a pointer to the character in **Str** or **nil** if the character is not found.

AnsiStrUpper Function

```
function AnsiStrUpper(Str: PChar): PChar;
```

AnsiStrUpper converts **Str** in place to all uppercase. It returns the value of **Str**. The conversion uses the Windows locale to properly convert non-ASCII characters.

StrAlloc Function

```
function StrAlloc(Size: Cardinal): PChar;
```

StrAlloc allocates a **PChar** string that can hold up to **Size – 1** bytes. The memory is not initialized. To free the memory, you must call **StrDispose**.

StrBufSize Function

```
function StrBufSize(const Str: PChar): Cardinal;
```

StrBufSize returns the number of bytes allocated by **StrAlloc** or **StrNew**. It does not work for any other **PChar** string.

StrByteType Function

```
function StrByteType(Str: PChar; Index: Cardinal): TMbcsByteType;
```

StrByteType returns the type of the byte at position Index in Str. You must ensure that Index is a valid index for the string. The byte type can be a single byte character, or the leading or trailing byte of a multibyte character. See ByteType, earlier in this appendix, for the details of the TMbcsByteType enumeration

StrCat Function

```
function StrCat(Dest: PChar; const Source: PChar): PChar;
```

StrCat copies Source onto the end of Dest. You must ensure that Dest has enough room for the copy of Source. Consider using StrLCat to help make sure Dest does not suffer a buffer overflow. StrCat returns a pointer to the start of the destination string (Dest).

StrCopy Function

```
function StrCopy(Dest: PChar; const Source: PChar): PChar;
```

StrCopy copies Source to Dest. You must make sure Dest has enough room for Source. Most programs should call StrLCopy to ensure Dest does not suffer a buffer overflow. StrCopy returns a pointer to the start of the destination string (Dest).

StrDispose Procedure

```
procedure StrDispose(Str: PChar);
```

StrDispose frees a PChar string that was allocated by StrNew or StrAlloc. If Str is nil, StrDispose returns without doing anything. Do not confuse this procedure with DisposeStr.

StrECopy Function

```
function StrECopy(Dest: PChar; const Source: PChar): PChar;
```

StrECopy copies Source to Dest just like StrCopy, but StrECopy returns a pointer to the #0 character at the end of Dest.

StrEnd Function

```
function StrEnd(const Str: PChar): PChar;
```

StrEnd returns a pointer to the #0 character at the end of Str.

StrLCat Function

```
function StrLCat(Dest: PChar; const Source: PChar; MaxLen: Cardinal):
    PChar;
```

StrLCat copies at most MaxLen bytes from Source to the end of Dest. StrLCat returns a pointer to the start of the destination string (Dest). If Source is a multibyte string, you must make sure that MaxLen does not fall in the middle of a multibyte character.

StrLCopy Function

```
function StrLCopy(Dest: PChar; const Source: PChar; MaxLen: Cardinal):
    PChar;
```

StrLCopy copies at most MaxLen bytes from Source to Dest. If Source is a multibyte string, you must make sure that MaxLen does not fall in the middle of a multibyte character.

StrLen Function

```
function StrLen(const Str: PChar): Cardinal;
```

StrLen returns the length of **Str** in bytes. Note that a multibyte string can have fewer characters than bytes.

StrMove Function

```
function StrMove(Dest: PChar; const Source: PChar; Count: Cardinal):
   PChar;
```

StrMove copies exactly **Count** bytes from **Source** to **Dest**. Unlike **StrCopy**, **StrMove** does not stop at the end of the **Source** string. The source and destination buffers can overlap. **StrMove** returns the value of **Dest**. **Move** (described in Chapter 5) and **StrMove** do the same thing; choose the one that is most convenient for a particular use.

StrNew Function

```
function StrNew(const Str: PChar): PChar;
```

StrNew allocates a new copy of **Str** and returns a pointer to the start of the new string. You must call **StrDispose** to free the string. Do not confuse this function with **NewStr**.

StrPCopy Function

```
function StrPCopy(Dest: PChar; const Source: string): PChar;
```

StrPCopy copies an **AnsiString** into a **PChar** string. You must ensure that the **Dest** buffer is big enough for the **Source** string. You might want to use **StrPLCopy** to make sure you do not overflow the **Dest** buffer. **StrPCopy** returns a pointer to the start of **Dest**.

StrPLCopy Function

```
function StrPLCopy(Dest: PChar; const Source: string;
   MaxLen: Cardinal): PChar;
```

StrPLCopy copies at most **MaxLen** bytes from the **Source** ANSI string to **Dest**. It returns a pointer to the start of **Dest**. If **Source** is a multibyte string, you must make sure that **MaxLen** does not fall in the middle of a multibyte character.

Obsolete String Subroutines

The string subroutines and variables described in this section are obsolete and should not be used in new code. They exist only for backward compatibility.

AppendStr Procedure

```
procedure AppendStr(var Dest: string; const S: string);
```

AppendStr appends **S** to the end of **Dest**. New code should use simple string assignment:

```
Dest := Dest + S;
```

AssignStr Procedure

```
procedure AssignStr(var P: PString; const S: string);
```

AssignStr performs a simple string assignment, i.e., **P^ := S**.

CompareStr Function

```
function CompareStr(const S1, S2: string): Integer;
```

`CompareStr` compares two strings and returns an integer result as shown in Table B-7. The comparison is case sensitive and does not consider the Windows locale. New programs should use `AnsiCompareStr`.

Table B-7: Results of CompareStr

Result	Description
Negative	`S1 < S2`
Zero	`S1 = S2`
Positive	`S1 > S2`

CompareText Function
```
function CompareText(const S1, S2: string): Integer;
```
`CompareText` compares two strings and returns an integer result in the same manner as `CompareStr`, but the comparison is not case sensitive. The Windows locale is not used, so only ASCII characters are compared without regard to case. New programs should use `AnsiCompareText`.

DisposeStr Procedure
```
procedure DisposeStr(P: PString);
```
`DisposeStr` frees a string that was allocated by `NewStr`. Do not confuse this procedure with `StrDispose`.

EmptyStr Variable
```
var EmptyStr: string = '';
```
`EmptyStr` is a global variable that stores an empty string. Do not change its value. This variable exists solely for backward compatibility. Delphi represents an empty string with a `nil` pointer, and you are better off using an explicit empty string (`''`) instead of referring to this global variable.

LowerCase Function
```
function LowerCase(const S: string): string;
```
`LowerCase` converts a string to lowercase, but only ASCII characters are converted. New programs should use `AnsiLowerCase`.

NewStr Function
```
function NewStr(const S: string): PString;
```
`NewStr` allocates a new string as a copy of `S`, and returns a pointer to the string. Long strings are now implemented as pointers, so there is no reason to use an extra level of indirection. To free the string, you must call `DisposeStr`. Do not confuse this function with `StrNew`.

NullStr Variable
```
var NullStr: PString = @EmptyStr;
```
`NullStr` is a pointer to an empty string. Do not change its value.

QuotedStr Function
```
function QuotedStr(const S: string): string;
```
`QuotedStr` returns a copy of `S` enclosed in single quotes (`'`). Single quote characters in `S` are repeated, following the rules of Pascal. The implementation

of `QuotedStr` has poor performance if `S` contains many single quotes. New programs should use `AnsiQuotedStr`.

SameText Function

```
function SameText(const S1, S2: string): Boolean;
```

`SameText` returns True if `S1` and `S2` have identical contents without regard to case differences, that is, if `CompareText` returns zero. New programs should call `AnsiSameText`.

StrComp Function

```
function StrComp(const Str1, Str2: PChar): Integer;
```

`StrComp` compares `Str1` and `Str2`, returning an integer result in the manner of `CompareStr`. New programs should call `AnsiStrComp`.

StrIComp Function

```
function StrIComp(const Str1, Str2: PChar): Integer;
```

`StrIComp` compares `Str1` and `Str2` without regard to case differences or the Windows locale, returning an integer result in the manner of `CompareStr`. New programs should call `AnsiStrIComp`.

StrLComp Function

```
function StrLComp(const Str1, Str2: PChar; MaxLen: Cardinal): Integer;
```

`StrLComp` compares at most `MaxLen` characters in `Str1` and `Str2`, returning an integer in the manner of `CompareStr`. Case is significant, but the Windows locale is not. New programs should use `AnsiStrLComp`.

StrLIComp Function

```
function StrLIComp(const Str1, Str2: PChar; MaxLen: Cardinal): Integer;
```

`StrLIComp` compares up to `MaxLen` bytes in `Str1` and `Str2`, returning an integer in the manner of `CompareStr`. The comparison is not case sensitive and does not use the Windows locale. New programs should call `AnsiStrLIComp`.

StrLower Function

```
function StrLower(Str: PChar): PChar;
```

`StrLower` converts `Str` in place to all lowercase and returns a pointer to the start of the string. Only ASCII characters are converted and the Windows locale is not used. New programs should use `AnsiStrLower`.

StrPas Function

```
function StrPas(const Str: PChar): string;
```

`StrPas` converts a `PChar` string to an `AnsiString`. Delphi does this automatically, so there is no need for new programs to call `StrPas`.

StrPos Function

```
function StrPos(const Str, SubStr: PChar): PChar;
```

`StrPos` searches for the first occurrence of `SubStr` in `Str` and returns a pointer to the first byte of the substring in `Str`. If the substring is not found, `nil` is returned. New programs should use `AnsiStrPos`.

StrRScan Function

```
function StrRScan(const Str: PChar; Chr: Char): PChar;
```

StrRScan searches for the last (rightmost) occurrence of the character **Chr** in the string **Str** and returns a pointer to the character in **Str** or **nil** if the character is not found. New programs should call **AnsiStrRScan**.

StrScan Function

```
function StrScan(const Str: PChar; Chr: Char): PChar;
```

StrScan searches for the first occurrence of the character **Chr** in the string **Str** and returns a pointer to the character in **Str** or **nil** if the character is not found. New programs should call **AnsiStrScan**.

StrUpper Function

```
function StrUpper(Str: PChar): PChar;
```

StrUpper converts **Str** in place to all uppercase and returns a pointer to the start of the string. Only ASCII characters are converted and the Windows locale is not used. New programs should use **AnsiStrUpper**.

Trim Function

```
function Trim(const S: string): string;
```

Trim returns a copy of **S** without any leading or trailing control or space characters. A control character is any character whose ordinal value is less than that of the ANSI space character (#32). Unlike the other obsolete functions, Delphi does not have an **AnsiTrim** function. Example B-4 shows one way to write such a function.

Example B-4: ANSI Version of Trim

```
type
  TTrimType = (ttLeft, ttRight);
  TTrimTypes = set of TTrimType;
// Trim space and control characters.
// Handle multibyte strings correctly.
function AnsiTrim(const S: string;
    TrimType: TTrimTypes = [ttLeft, ttRight]): string;
var
  Left, Right: 0..MaxInt;
  I: 0..MaxInt;
begin
  Left := 1;
  Right := Length(S);
  if ttLeft in TrimType then
  begin
    I := 1;
    while I <= Length(S) do
    begin
      if S[I] in LeadBytes then
        Inc(I)
      else if Ord(S[I]) > Ord(' ') then
        Break;
      Inc(I);
    end;
    Left := I;
  end;
  if ttRight in TrimType then
```

Example B-4: ANSI Version of Trim (continued)

```
begin
  I := Length(S);
  while I >= Left do
  begin
    if ByteType(S, I) = mbTrailByte then
      Dec(I)
    else if Ord(S[I]) > Ord(' ') then
      Break;
    Dec(I);
  end;
  Right := I;
  end;
  Result := Copy(S, Left, Right-Left+1);
end;

function AnsiTrimLeft(const S: string): string;
begin
  Result := AnsiTrim(S, [ttLeft]);
end;

function AnsiTrimRight(const S: string): string;
begin
  Result := AnsiTrim(S, [ttRight]);
end;
```

TrimLeft Function

```
function TrimLeft(const S: string): string;
```

TrimLeft returns a copy of S without any leading control or space characters. A control character is any character whose ordinal value is less than that of the ANSI space character (#32).

TrimRight Function

```
function TrimRight(const S: string): string;
```

TrimRight returns a copy of S without any trailing control or space characters. A control character is any character whose ordinal value is less than that of the ANSI space character (#32).

UpperCase Function

```
function UpperCase(const S: string): string;
```

UpperCase returns a copy of S, where lowercase ASCII characters are converted to uppercase. See AnsiUpperCase to handle ANSI characters using the Windows locale.

Numeric Conversion

This section lists types, constants, and subroutines that help you convert integers, currency, and floating-point numbers to text and to convert text to numbers.

CurrencyDecimals Variable

```
var CurrencyDecimals: Byte;
```

`CurrencyDecimals` is the default number of digits to the right of the decimal point when formatting money in a call to `Format` and its related functions. The default value is taken from the Windows locale.

CurrencyFormat Variable

```
var CurrencyFormat: Byte;
```

`CurrencyFormat` specifies how to format a positive `Currency` amount by positioning the currency symbol relative to the numeric currency amount. The default value is taken from the Windows locale. The possible values are listed in Table B-8.

Table B-8: Values for CurrencyFormat

Value	Description	Example
0	\<symbol>\<amount>	$1.00
1	\<amount>\<symbol>	1.00$
2	\<symbol>\<space>\<amount>	$ 1.00
3	\<amount>\<space>\<symbol>	1.00 $

CurrencyString Variable

```
var CurrencyString: string;
```

`CurrencyString` is the symbol that identifies a currency value, such as `'$'` for U.S. dollars. The default value is taken from the Windows locale.

CurrToStr Function

```
function CurrToStr(Value: Currency): string;
```

`CurrToStr` converts a `Currency` value to a string, using the local currency symbol and general format. The formatted string has no minimum number of decimal places after the decimal separator (that is, it does not heed `CurrencyDecimals`).

CurrToStrF Function

```
function CurrToStrF(Value: Currency; Format: TFloatFormat;
    Digits: Integer): string;
```

`CurrToStrF` converts a `Currency` value to a string using the given `Format` (usually `ffCurrency`) and `Digits` places after the decimal point. See `FloatToStrF` for more information about the `Format` parameter.

DecimalSeparator Variable

```
var DecimalSeparator: Char;
```

`DecimalSeparator` is the character that separates the integer part from the fractional part of a floating-point number. The default value is obtained from the Windows locale.

FloatToDecimal Procedure

```
type
  TFloatRec = packed record
    Exponent: Smallint;
    Negative: Boolean;
    Digits: array[0..20] of Char;
  end;
```

```
TFloatValue = (fvExtended, fvCurrency);
procedure FloatToDecimal(var Result: TFloatRec; const Value;
    ValueType: TFloatValue; Precision, Decimals: Integer);
```

FloatToDecimal is a low-level formatting procedure. Other formatting functions call it, but applications rarely do. FloatToDecimal stores the exponent and sign in the Result record and formats the mantissa as a string of decimal digits. Precision is the minimum number of significant digits, and Decimals is the number of digits before the decimal point. The Value must be Currency or Extended, and you must specify the type accordingly in ValueType (that is, fvCurrency or fvExtended). If the ValueType and the type of Value do not match, the results are unpredictable.

FloatToStr Function

```
function FloatToStr(Value: Extended): string;
```

FloatToStr converts a floating-point number to a string using the general format with 15 places of precision.

FloatToStrF Function

```
type TFloatFormat = (ffGeneral, ffExponent, ffFixed, ffNumber,
                     ffCurrency);
function FloatToStrF(Value: Extended; Format: TFloatFormat;
    Precision, Digits: Integer): string;
```

FloatToStrF returns the floating-point Value as a formatted string. The Format argument determines how the number is formatted. Precision is the number of significant figures, and Digits is usually the number of places after the decimal separator. The formatted string uses the DecimalSeparator and ThousandSeparator characters as needed.

The maximum precision for FloatToStrF is 18 decimal places, but the maximum precision of the Extended, Currency, and Comp types is 19 decimal places. Computation using these types will carry the full precision correctly, but if you try to display or print the largest or smallest Currency and Comp values, the last decimal place will not be correct, and the Extended values will not be formatted to their full precision.

Regardless of the Format, positive infinity is always formatted as the string INF, and negative infinity is -INF. Quiet NaNs are formatted as NAN. (The strings INF and NAN cannot be localized.) For finite values, the Format parameter works as follows:

ffCurrency
    Format the number using CurrencyFormat or NegCurrFormat (e.g., $31,415.00). Digits specifies the number of places after the decimal point. If Digits is zero, no decimal separator appears.

ffExponent
    Format the number using scientific notation (e.g., -3.14E+01). One digit always precedes the decimal separator, and Precision determines the

total number of digits formatted. `Digits` specifies the number of digits in the exponent, which should be in the range 1 to 4. The exponent always starts with a plus or minus sign. The entire number starts with a minus sign if necessary.

ffFixed

Format the number using fixed decimal notation (e.g., `-3141.59`). At least one digit always precedes the decimal separator. If more than `Precision` digits are needed to the left of the decimal separator, the format is automatically changed to `ffExponent`.

ffGeneral

Format the number in fixed or exponential notation: fixed is used if possible, otherwise exponential is used. Numbers less than 0.00001 use exponential notation. Trailing zeros are removed, and if no digits appear after the decimal separator, the separator character is also removed.

ffNumber

Format the string in fixed format, but using the `ThousandSeparator` character to separate thousands, millions, and so on (e.g., `-314,159.26535`).

FloatToText Function

```
function FloatToText(Buffer: PChar; const Value; ValueType:TFloatValue;
   Format: TFloatFormat; Precision, Digits: Integer): Integer;
```

`FloatToText` is a low-level function that converts a floating-point value to a character array, storing the result in `Buffer`. The length of the formatted string is returned. Note that the string does *not* have a #0 character appended. You must make sure that `Buffer` is large enough to store the formatted string. `Value`, `ValueType`, `Format`, `Precision`, and `Digits` have the same interpretation as in `FloatToDecimal`.

FloatToTextFmt Function

```
function FloatToTextFmt(Buffer: PChar; const Value;
   ValueType: TFloatValue; Format: PChar): Integer;
```

`FloatToTextFmt` is a low-level function that formats a floating-point number according to the format string in `Format`. The result is stored in `Buffer`, which must be large enough for the formatted string. The length of the string is returned. Note that the string does *not* have a #0 character appended. The `Value` can be `Currency` or `Extended`, and `ValueType` specifies the type, as described under `FloatToDecimal`.

The `Format` string specifies how to format the string. It contains up to three parts separated by semicolons. The first part specifies the format for positive numbers, the second for negative numbers, and the third for zero. If any part is missing, the positive format is used. If the positive part is empty, the general format of `FloatToStrF` is used. Each part contains format specifiers. The specifiers describe the format or picture for a single value. The value is rounded off to the number of decimal places that appear after the decimal separator. The number and position of the 0 specifiers dictate the number of places before and after the decimal separator that will always appear in the formatted string.

Format a digit if the number requires a digit in this place.

0 Format a digit if the number requires a digit in this place; otherwise, use `'0'`.

. *(dot)*

Format a decimal separator (the `DecimalSeparator` variable). The second and subsequent uses of this specifier in a single part are ignored. If the format does not contain the decimal point specifier, the value is rounded off to an integer.

, *(comma)*

Format a thousand separator (the `ThousandSeparator` variable) between each group of three digits to the left of the decimal separator. This specifier can appear anywhere in a format part.

E+
E-
e+
e-

Format the number using scientific notation. The case of the specifier determines the case of the exponent character (**E**) in the formatted string. The **E+** and **e+** specifiers produce a plus sign for positive exponents. The **E-** and **e-** specifiers omit the plus sign for positive exponents.

'xxx'
"xxx"

Characters in quotes are copied verbatim to the formatted string (after removing the quotes). You can use other formatting characters in the quotes.

; A semicolon separates the positive, negative, and zero parts of a format specifier.

(anything else)

Any other characters are copied to the formatted string.

Table B-9 shows some examples of format specifiers.

Table B-9: Examples of Format Strings for FloatToTextFmt

Format String	Value	Result
#.00	–31.456	–31.47
,0.##	3141592	3,141,592
#;(#);'0.'	0	0.
#;(#)	–31.456	(31)

FmtLoadStr Function

```
function FmtLoadStr(Ident: Integer; const Args: array of const):string;
```

FmtLoadStr loads a string resource and uses that string as the format string in a call to **Format**. New programs should use a **resourcestring** and call **Format** directly.

FmtStr Procedure

```
procedure FmtStr(var Result: string; const Format: string;
    const Args: array of const);
```

FmtStr formats a string in the same manner as Format, but instead of returning the formatted string, it stores it in Result.

Format Function

```
function Format(const Format: string; const Args: array of const):
    string;
```

Format returns a formatted string. The Format argument specifies how to produce the string by formatting the arguments in the Args variant open array. The Format string is copied to the result string, expanding format specifiers, which start with a percent sign (%). To format a literal percent sign, repeat it: %%.

Each format specifier has the following form:

% [index :] [-] [width] [.precision] type

The *index* is an index into the Args array, where zero is the first argument. Without an index specifier, each format specifier corresponds to successive elements in the Args array. Using an index specifier, you can reuse the same argument multiple times in a single format string. When you plan to localize an application, you should use an index specifier for all arguments because a different language might require a different order for the arguments.

The *width* specifies the minimum number of characters for the formatted field. If the actual formatted value is smaller than *width* characters, it is padded on the left with blanks. If you use a minus sign before the *width*, the number is left-aligned and padded on the right.

Different format types use the *precision* differently. See the discussions for each type for details.

You can hardcode the *index, width,* and *precision* numbers in the format string (e.g., %1:10.2f), or you can use an asterisk for any or all of these values (e.g., %*:*.*f). The asterisk means the next argument from the Args array supplies the value. The Args value must be an integer.

The *type* is a single letter in uppercase or lowercase:

d   Format a signed decimal integer. The *precision* specifies the minimum number of digits to display, padding with zero if necessary. The Args value must be an integer.

e   Format a floating-point number in exponential notation. The *precision* specifies the total number of digits in the formatted string. The default is 15. The Args value must be a floating-point number or Currency.

f   Format a floating-point number in fixed-point notation. The *precision* specifies the number of digits after the decimal separator. The default is 2. The Args value must be a floating-point number or Currency.

g   Format a floating-point number in general notation. The *precision* specifies the number of significant digits. The Args value must be a floating-point number or Currency.

m   Format a `Currency` value. The precision specifies the number of places
     after the decimal point. The default is given by the `CurrencyDecimals`
     variable. The currency format is dictated by the `CurrencyFormat` and
     `NegCurrFormat` variables. The `Args` value must be a floating-point
     number or `Currency`.

n   Format a floating-point number in number notation, that is, using fixed
     notation with `ThousandSeparator` to separate groups of three digits.
     The `Args` value must be a floating-point number or `Currency`.

p   Format a pointer as a hexadecimal number. The `Args` value must be a
     pointer.

s   Format a character or string. The *precision* specifies the maximum
     number of characters to display. The `Args` value must be an `AnsiChar`,
     `AnsiString`, `PChar`, `PWideChar`, `ShortString`, `Variant`, or
     `WideString`. `WideChar` is not allowed. A `Variant` is converted to a
     string and then formatted.

u   Format an unsigned decimal integer. The *precision* specifies the
     minimum number of decimal digits to display, padding with zero if
     necessary. The `Args` value must be an integer.

x   Format an unsigned hexadecimal integer. The case of the *type* deter-
     mines the case of the letters used in the hexadecimal number. The
     precision specifies the minimum number of decimal digits to display,
     padding with zero if necessary. The `Args` value must be an integer.

If the format string contains any errors or if the format *type* does not match
the type of the corresponding argument in the `Args` array, `Format` raises an
`EConvertError` exception.

FormatBuf Function
```
function FormatBuf(var Buffer; BufLen: Cardinal; const Format;
    FmtLen: Cardinal; const Args: array of const): Cardinal;
```

`FormatBuf` formats a string and stores the result in `Buffer`. Up to `BufLen`
bytes are written to `Buffer`, including a trailing #0 byte. The length of the
format string is given in `FmtLen`. The length of the resulting string is returned.
See `Format` for more information.

FormatCurr Function
```
function FormatCurr(const Format: string; Value: Currency): string;
```

`FormatCurr` formats a `Currency` value as a string, according to the `Format`
argument. See `FloatToTextFmt` for more information.

FormatFloat Function
```
function FormatFloat(const Format: string; Value: Extended): string;
```

`FormatFloat` formats a floating-point value as a string, according to the
`Format` argument. See `FloatToTextFmt` for more information.

HexDisplayPrefix Variable
```
var HexDisplayPrefix: string;
```

`HexDisplayPrefix` is the string used to preface hexadecimal integers. In
Delphi programs, this is `'$'`. In C++ Builder programs, it is `'0x'`. Do not

change the value of this variable—several units in the VCL check it to determine whether the application is a Delphi project or a C++ Builder project. (See the `ModuleIsCpp` variable in Chapter 5 for the proper way to perform this test.)

IntToHex Function

```
function IntToHex(Value: Int64; Digits: Integer): string; overload;
function IntToHex(Value: Integer; Digits: Integer): string; overload;
```

`IntToHex` formats an integer as a string in hexadecimal, with `Digits` number of decimal places. The resulting string is *not* prefaced with the `HexDisplayPrefix`.

IntToStr Function

```
function IntToStr(Value: Int64): string; overload;
function IntToStr(Value: Integer): string; overload;
```

`IntToStr` formats an integer as a string.

NegCurrFormat Variable

```
var NegCurrFormat: Byte;
```

`NegCurrFormat` specifies how a negative Currency value is formatted. It is similar in spirit to `CurrencyFormat`, but has many more options. The default value is taken from the Windows locale. The possible values are shown in Table B-10.

Table B-10: Values for NegCurrFormat

Value	Description	Example
0	(<symbol><amount>)	($1.00)
1	–<symbol><amount>	-$1.00
2	<symbol>–<amount>	$-1.00
3	<symbol><amount>–	$1.00-
4	(<amount><symbol>)	(1.00$)
5	–<amount><symbol>	-1.00$
6	<amount>–<symbol>	1.00-$
7	<amount><symbol>–	1.00$-
8	–<amount><space><symbol>	-1.00 $
9	–<symbol><space><amount>	-$ 1.00
10	<amount><space><symbol>–	1.00 $-
11	<symbol><space><amount>–	$ 1.00-
12	<symbol><space>–<amount>	$ -1.00
13	<amount>–<space><symbol>	1.00- $
14	(<symbol><space><amount>)	($ 1.00)
15	(<amount><space><symbol>)	(1.00 $)

StrFmt Function

```
function StrFmt(Buffer, Format: PChar; const Args: array of const):
    PChar;
```

StrFmt formats a string and stores the result in `Buffer`. You must make sure `Buffer` is large enough to store the result. `Buffer` is returned. To avoid buffer overruns, use `StrLFmt` instead.

StrLFmt Function

```
function StrLFmt(Buffer: PChar; MaxLen: Cardinal; Format: PChar;
    const Args: array of const): PChar;
```

StrLFmt formats a string and stores the result in `Buffer`. At most `MaxLen` bytes are written to `Buffer`, not including the trailing `#0` byte that is always appended to the formatted string. `Buffer` is returned.

StrToCurr Function

```
function StrToCurr(const S: string): Currency;
```

StrToCurr converts a string to a `Currency` value. It raises an `EConvertError` exception if the string cannot be converted. See `TextToFloat` for more information.

StrToFloat Function

```
function StrToFloat(const S: string): Extended;
```

StrToFloat converts a string to a floating-point value. It raises an `EConvertError` exception if the string cannot be converted. See `TextToFloat` for more information.

StrToInt64 Function

```
function StrToInt64(const S: string): Int64;
```

StrToInt64 converts a string to an `Int64` integer. Leading and trailing white space is ignored. The string can start with a sign (`'+'` or `'-'`) and be decimal or hexadecimal (prefaced by `'$'` or the C++-style prefixes `'0x'` or `'0X'`— that's a zero followed by the letter *x* in either case). If the string is empty or is not a valid integer, an `EConvertError` exception is raised.

StrToInt Function

```
function StrToInt(const S: string): Integer;
```

StrToInt converts a string to an integer. Leading and trailing white space is ignored. The string can start with a sign (`'+'` or `'-'`) and be decimal or hexadecimal (prefaced by `'$'` or the C++-style prefix, `'0x'`). If the string is empty or is not a valid integer, an `EConvertError` exception is raised.

StrToInt64Def Function

```
function StrToInt64Def(const S: string; Default: Int64): Int64;
```

StrToInt64Def converts a string to an `Int64` integer. Leading and trailing white space is ignored. The string can start with a sign (`'+'` or `'-'`) and be decimal or hexadecimal (prefaced by `'$'` or the C++-style prefix, `'0x'`). If the string is empty or is not a valid integer, `Default` is returned.

StrToIntDef Function

```
function StrToIntDef(const S: string; Default: Integer): Integer;
```

StrToIntDef converts a string to an integer. Leading and trailing white space is ignored. The string can start with a sign (`'+'` or `'-'`) and be decimal or hexadecimal (prefaced by `'$'` or the C++-style prefix, `'0x'`). If the string is empty or is not a valid integer, `Default` is returned.

TextToFloat Function

```
function TextToFloat(Buffer: PChar; var Value; ValueType: TFloatValue):
   Boolean;
```

TextToFloat parses a string to find a floating-point value. **ValueType** must be **fvCurrency** or **fvExtended** and must match the type of **Value**. The string cannot have any currency symbols or thousand separators. The decimal separator character (if one appears in the string) must be equal to the **DecimalSeparator** variable. The number can be in fixed or exponential notation and can have a leading plus or minus sign. **TextToFloat** returns True for success or False if the string could not be converted to a number.

ThousandSeparator Variable

```
var ThousandSeparator: Char;
```

ThousandSeparator is the character used to separate thousands in a formatted number or currency value. The default value is obtained from the Windows locale.

Dates and Times

This section lists types, constants, and subroutines related to dates and times. Delphi has five different ways to keep track of a date and time:

- The **TDateTime** type is the most common way to store a date and a time. See its description in Chapter 5 for details.

- DOS stores the modification date of a file using a simple file date format, which fits in an integer. Convert a file date to a **TDateTime** type or vice versa.

- The **TTimeStamp** type is a record that keeps the date and time in separate fields, so **TTimeStamp** is harder to use than **TDateTime**. You can convert between these two types.

- You can also keep track of the year, month, day, hour, minute, second, and millisecond as separate values. Convert between discrete values and a **TDateTime** value with the encode and decode subroutines.

- Windows stores the separate components of a date and time in the **TSystemTime** record. Delphi has convenience functions to convert between **TSystemTime** and **TDateTime**.

Date Function

```
function Date: TDateTime;
```

Date returns the current date in the local time zone. The time is set to midnight (zero).

DateDelta Constant

```
const DateDelta = 693594;
```

DateDelta is the number of days between January 1, 0001 and December 31, 1899. The former is the initial date used for **TTimeStamp**, and the latter is the initial date used for **TDateTime**.

DateSeparator Variable

```
var DateSeparator: Char;
```

DateSeparator is the character used to separate the month, day, and year in the short format for a date. The default value is taken from the Windows locale.

DateTimeToFileDate Function

`function DateTimeToFileDate(DateTime: TDateTime): Integer;`

DateTimeToFileDate converts a **TDateTime** value to a file date, which you can use in a call to **FileSetDate**. Figure B-1 (earlier in this appendix) shows the format of a file date and time. The time is truncated to a two-second time. If the year is out of the range of a file date (1980 to 2099), zero is returned.

DateTimeToStr Function

`function DateTimeToStr(DateTime: TDateTime): string;`

DateTimeToStr formats a **TDateTime** value as a string, formatting the date with **ShortDateFormat**, followed by a blank, followed by the time, formatted with **LongTimeFormat**. The time is omitted if it is zero (midnight).

DateTimeToString Procedure

`procedure DateTimeToString(var Result: string; const Format: string;`
`    DateTime: TDateTime);`

DateTimeToString formats a **TDateTime** value as a string, using **Format** to control the formatting. The string is stored in **Result**. If you try to format a string longer than 256 characters, **DateTimeToString** silently truncates the string.

The **Format** string determines how the date and time are formatted by interpreting successive characters in the format string. The result string is built by appending the desired formatted date or time in the same order as the format string. Characters that are not format specifiers are copied to the result string. Repeating a format character a different number of times than is shown in this section is usually harmless, but may have unpredictable results. The **Format** string is not case sensitive (except for the **AM/PM** and **A/P** specifiers). If **Format** is an empty string, the default format is `'C'`. Following are the date and time format specifiers:

c   Use **ShortDateFormat**, a blank, and **LongTimeFormat**. The time is omitted if it is zero (midnight).

d   Formats the day of the month (1–31).

dd   Formats the day of the month padded to two places (01–31).

aaa
ddd
      Formats the day of the week using **ShortDayNames**.

aaaa
dddd
      Formats the day of the week using **LongDayNames**.

ddddd
      Formats the date using **ShortDateFormat**.

dddddd
      Formats the date using **LongDateFormat**.

g   Formats the short era name for Japanese and Taiwanese locales.

gg   Formats the full era name for Asian locales.

e   Formats the year in the current era without a leading zero.

ee   Formats the year in the current era padding with a leading zero to a minimum of two places.

m   Formats the month number (1–12). If m follows immediately after an h or hh specifier, formats the minute (0–59).

mm   Formats the month number padded to two places (01–12). If mm follows immediately after an h or hh specifier, formats the minute (00–59).

mmm
     Formats the month using ShortMonthNames.

mmmm
     Formats the month using LongMonthNames.

yy   Formats the year as a two-digit number (00–99).

yyyy
     Formats the year as a four-digit number (0000–9999).

h   Formats the hour (0–23). The hour uses a 12-hour clock if the format includes one of the AM/PM specifiers.

hh   Formats the hour padded to two places (00–23). The hour uses a 12-hour clock if the format includes one of the AM/PM specifiers.

n   Formats the minute (0–59).

nn   Formats the minute padded to two places (00–59).

s   Formats the second (0–59).

ss   Formats the second padded to two places (00–59).

z   Formats the millisecond (0–999).

zzz
     Formats the millisecond padded to three places (000–999).

t   Formats the time using ShortTimeFormat.

tt   Formats the time using LongTimeFormat.

am/pm
     Formats 'am' for midnight and times before noon and 'pm' for noon and times after noon. A preceding h or hh specifier uses a 12-hour clock (0–11). The case of the string exactly matches the case of the format specifier.

a/p Formats 'a' for midnight and times before noon and 'p' for noon and times after noon. A preceding h or hh specifier uses a 12-hour clock (0–11). The case of the string exactly matches the case of the format specifier.

ampm

Formats `TimeAMString` for midnight and times before noon and `TimePMString` for noon and times after noon. A preceding h or hh specifier uses a 12-hour clock (0–11).

/ Formats the `DateSeparator` character.

: Formats the `TimeSeparator` character.

'xxx'
"xxx"

Formats exactly the contents of the quoted string (without the quotes).

DateTimeToSystemTime Procedure

```
procedure DateTimeToSystemTime(DateTime: TDateTime; var SystemTime: TSystemTime);
```

`DateTimeToSystemTime` converts a `TDateTime` value to a Windows system time.

DateTimeToTimeStamp Function

```
function DateTimeToTimeStamp(DateTime: TDateTime): TTimeStamp;
```

`DateTimeToTimeStamp` converts a `TDateTime` value to a `TTimeStamp` record.

DateToStr Function

```
function DateToStr(Date: TDateTime): string;
```

`DateToStr` formats the date part of a `TDateTime` as a string, using `ShortDateFormat`.

DayOfWeek Function

```
function DayOfWeek(Date: TDateTime): Integer;
```

`DayOfWeek` returns the day of the week for a date, where 1 represents Sunday, and 7 represents Saturday.

DecodeDate Procedure

```
procedure DecodeDate(Date: TDateTime; var Year, Month, Day: Word);
```

`DecodeDate` extracts the year, month, and day of month from a `TDateTime`. The month is the range 1–12 for January to December.

DecodeTime Procedure

```
procedure DecodeTime(Time: TDateTime; var Hour, Min, Sec, MSec: Word);
```

`DecodeTime` extracts the hour, minute, second, and millisecond time from a `TDateTime`.

EncodeDate Function

```
function EncodeDate(Year, Month, Day: Word): TDateTime;
```

`EncodeDate` creates a `TDateTime` for the given year, month, and day of month. The time part of the result is zero. The month must be in the range 1–12. If any argument is invalid, an `EConvertError` exception is raised.

EncodeTime Function

```
function EncodeTime(Hour, Min, Sec, MSec: Word): TDateTime;
```

EncodeTime creates a TDateTime for the given parts of a time. The date part of the result is zero. If any argument is invalid, an EConvertError exception is raised.

EraNames Variable

```
var EraNames: array[1..7] of string;
```

EraNames stores the names for up to 7 eras, corresponding to the eras in EraYearOffsets. Eras are used in some Asian locales to format dates.

EraYearOffsets Variable

```
var EraYearOffsets: array[1..7] of Integer;
```

EraYearOffsets stores the year offsets for up to 7 eras. Each era has an associated name in EraNames.

FileDateToDateTime Function

```
function FileDateToDateTime(FileDate: Integer): TDateTime;
```

FileDateToDateTime converts a file date and time to a TDateTime value. Figure B-1 (earlier in this appendix) shows the format of a file date and time.

FormatDateTime Function

```
function FormatDateTime(const Format: string; DateTime: TDateTime):
    string;
```

FormatDateTime formats a date and a time as a string. See DateTimeToString for details about the Format parameter.

IncMonth Function

```
function IncMonth(const Date: TDateTime; NumberOfMonths: Integer):
    TDateTime;
```

IncMonth adds NumberOfMonths to the month of Date and returns the resulting TDateTime. If the day of the month is greater than the number of days in the resulting month, it is adjusted to the last day of the month.

IsLeapYear Function

```
function IsLeapYear(Year: Word): Boolean;
```

IsLeapYear returns True if the Year is a leap year or False for other years.

LongDateFormat Variable

```
var LongDateFormat: string;
```

LongDateFormat is the format used by DateTimeToString and the dddddd format specifier. The default value is taken from the Windows locale.

LongDayNames Variable

```
var LongDayNames: array[1..7] of string;
```

LongDayNames stores the full names for the days of the week. The first day in the array is Sunday and the last is Saturday. The default values are taken from the Windows locale.

LongMonthNames Variable

```
var LongMonthNames: array[1..12] of string;
```

LongMonthNames stores the full names for the months (in order from January to December). The default values are taken from the Windows locale.

LongTimeFormat Variable
```
var LongTimeFormat: string;
```

LongTimeFormat is the format used by **DateTimeToString** and the **c** and **tt** format specifiers. The default value is taken from the Windows locale.

MonthDays Constant
```
type PDayTable = ^TDayTable;
type TDayTable = array[1..12] of Word;
const MonthDays: array [Boolean] of TDayTable;
```

MonthDays stores the number of days in a month. The array is two-dimensional, with a **Boolean** first dimension: True for a leap year and False for non-leap years. The second dimension is the month number, in the range 1–12 (January to December).

MSecsPerDay Constant
```
const MSecsPerDay = SecsPerDay * 1000;
```

MSecsPerDay is a convenient constant for the number of milliseconds in a day.

MSecsToTimeStamp Function
```
function MSecsToTimeStamp(MSecs: Comp): TTimeStamp;
```

MSecsToTimeStamp converts a number of milliseconds to a **TTimeStamp** record.

Now Function
```
function Now: TDateTime;
```

Now returns the current date and time in the local time zone.

ReplaceDate Procedure
```
procedure ReplaceDate(var DateTime: TDateTime; const NewDate: TDateTime);
```

ReplaceDate changes the date part of **DateTime** to **NewDate** without affecting the time part.

ReplaceTime Procedure
```
procedure ReplaceTime(var DateTime: TDateTime; const NewTime: TDateTime);
```

ReplaceTime changes the time part of **DateTime** to **NewTime** without affecting the date part.

SecsPerDay Constant
```
const SecsPerDay = 24 * 60 * 60;
```

SecsPerDay is a convenient constant for the number of seconds in a day.

ShortDateFormat Variable
```
var ShortDateFormat: string;
```

ShortDateFormat is the format used by **DateTimeToString** and the **c** and **ddddd** format specifiers. The default value is taken from the Windows locale.

ShortDayNames Variable
```
var ShortDayNames: array[1..7] of string;
```

ShortDayNames stores the shortened names for the days of the week. The first day in the array is Sunday and the last is Saturday. The default values are taken from the Windows locale.

ShortMonthNames Variable

```
var ShortMonthNames: array[1..12] of string;
```

ShortMonthNames stores the shortened names for the months (in order from January to December). The default values are taken from the Windows locale.

ShortTimeFormat Variable

```
var ShortTimeFormat: string;
```

ShortTimeFormat is the format used by **DateTimeToString** and the **t** format specifier. The default value is taken from the Windows locale.

StrToDate Function

```
function StrToDate(const S: string): TDateTime;
```

StrToDate parses a string to obtain a date. The string must contain a date in the format specified by **ShortDateFormat**, and the parts of the date must be separated by the **DateSeparator** character. If the string contains only two numbers, they are interpreted as the month and day in the current year. If the string is not in the correct format, an **EConvertError** exception is raised. If the year contains only two digits, the year is expanded to four digits according to the value of the **TwoDigitYearCenturyWindow** variable.

StrToDateTime Function

```
function StrToDateTime(const S: string): TDateTime;
```

StrToDateTime parses a string to obtain a date and a time. The string can start with a date in the format required by **StrToDate**. If the date is omitted, **StrToDateTime** uses the current local date. The date and the time are separated by one or more blanks. The time must be in the format required by **StrToTime**. If the string is not in the correct format, an **EConvertError** exception is raised.

StrToTime Function

```
function StrToTime(const S: string): TDateTime;
```

StrToTime parses a string to obtain a time. The string must contain at least one number (the hour). Minutes, seconds, and milliseconds are optional. The parts of a time must be separated by the **TimeSeparator** character. The time string can begin or end with an AM or PM specifier, which must be one of the following: **TimeAMString**, **TimePMString**, **'AM'**, or **'PM'** (case is not significant). If the string is not in the correct format, an **EConvertError** exception is raised.

SystemTimeToDateTime Function

```
function SystemTimeToDateTime(const SystemTime: TSystemTime): TDateTime;
```

SystemTimeToDateTime converts a Windows system time to the equivalent **TDateTime**.

Time Function

```
function Time: TDateTime;
```

Time returns the current time in the local time zone with a date of zero.

TimeAMString Variable

```
var TimeAMString: string;
```

TimeAMString is the string that marks times before noon. Its default value is taken from the Windows locale.

TimePMString Variable

```
var TimePMString: string;
```

TimePMString is the string that marks times after noon. Its default value is taken from the Windows locale.

TimeSeparator Variable

```
var TimeSeparator: Char;
```

TimeSeparator is the character that separates parts of a time. Its default value is taken from the Windows locale.

TimeStampToDateTime Function

```
function TimeStampToDateTime(const TimeStamp: TTimeStamp): TDateTime;
```

TimeStampToDateTime converts a **TTimeStamp** record to a **TDateTime** value.

TimeStampToMSecs Function

```
function TimeStampToMSecs(const TimeStamp: TTimeStamp): Comp;
```

TimeStampToMSecs converts a **TimeStamp** record to a number of milliseconds. The result is type **Comp**, not **Int64**, so you need to be sure that the floating-point precision is set to full extended precision. See **Comp** in Chapter 5 for details.

TimeToStr Function

```
function TimeToStr(Time: TDateTime): string;
```

TimeToStr formats the time part of a **TDateTime** as a string, using the short time format.

TTimeStamp Type

```
type
  TTimeStamp = record
    Time: Integer;
    Date: Integer;
  end;
```

TTimeStamp stores a date and a time in separate parts. The **Time** member stores the number of milliseconds since midnight, and the **Date** member stores one more than the number of days since January 1, 0001. Although **TTimeStamp** is harder to use than **TDateTime**, it has the advantage of storing the time exactly, so you can avoid problems with floating-point precision.

TwoDigitYearCenturyWindow Variable

```
var TwoDigitYearCenturyWindow: Word = 50;
```

When converting a string to a date, if the year has only two digits, Delphi uses **TwoDigitYearCenturyWindow** to determine whether the year refers to the current century, the previous century or the next century. The window is a range of 100 years around the current year, starting with the current year minus **TwoDigitYearCenturyWindow**. **StrToDate** picks the year in the window that has the same last two digits as the two-digit year it wants to convert. If `TwoDigitYearCenturyWindow` is zero, the two digit year is always in the same century as the current century. Table B-11 lists some examples.

Table B-11: Examples of Interpreting Two-Digit Years

TwoDigitYearCenturyWindow	Current Year	2-Digit Year	StrToDate Year
50	1998	47	2047
50	1998	48	1948
0	1998	97	1997
0	1998	98	1998
50	2001	50	2050
50	2001	51	1951

Localization

Every Delphi programmer who distributes components must understand localization issues, because you never know who will use your component or where they will use it. To allow for various users, `resourcestring` should be used for all string constants that might be translated to a different language. `Format` strings should use index specifiers in case the translated format must rearrange the order of the arguments.

Formatting of dates, time, and numbers must heed the local specifications for `DecimalSeparator`, `CurrencyFormat`, and so on. The user can use the Regional Settings applet in the Windows Control Panel to change these settings. If the user wants to separate the parts of a date with question marks, your program or component should heed that setting (which is stored in the `DateSeparator` variable) and not arbitrarily use a hardcoded separator.

Strings might contain non-ASCII accented characters or even be multibyte strings. For information about the specific formatting functions, see their descriptions elsewhere in this appendix. This section lists additional types, constants, and subroutines related to localization.

For more information about locales and Windows, see the Microsoft Platform SDK documentation. In particular, read about National Language Support.

GetFormatSettings Procedure
```
procedure GetFormatSettings;
```

`GetFormatSettings` loads the local settings from Windows for the variables listed in Table B-12. A GUI application automatically calls this procedure when the format settings change (that is, when the application receives a `Wm_WinIniChange` message).

Table B-12: Variables Set by GetFormatSettings

Variable	Description
CurrencyDecimals	Number of decimal places for Currency
CurrencyFormat	Format for positive Currency values

Table B-12: Variables Set by GetFormatSettings (continued)

Variable	Description
CurrencyString	Symbol to denote Currency values
DateSeparator	Character to separate parts of a date
DecimalSeparator	Character to separate integer from fraction
EraNames	Names of Asian eras
EraYearOffsets	Years for Asian eras
ListSeparator	Character to separate items in a list
LongDateFormat	Long format for dates
LongDayNames	Full names for days of the week
LongMonthNames	Full names for months
LongTimeFormat	Long format for times
NegCurrFormat	Format for negative Currency values
ShortDateFormat	Brief format for dates
ShortDayName	Abbreviated names for days of the week
ShortMonthNames	Abbreviated names for months
ShortTimeFormat	Brief format for times
ThousandSeparator	Character to separate groups of thousands
TimeAMString	String for times before noon
TimePMString	String for times after noon
TimeSeparator	Character to separate parts of a time

GetLocaleChar Function

```
function GetLocaleChar(Locale, LocaleType: Integer;
    Default: Char): Char;
```

GetLocaleChar looks up the value of LocaleType in the Windows locale Locale and returns the first character of the result. If the Locale or LocaleType is invalid, Default is returned. GetFormatSettings calls this function to load some of its localization variables.

GetLocaleStr Function

```
function GetLocaleStr(Locale, LocaleType: Integer;
    const Default: string): string;
```

GetLocaleStr looks up the value of LocaleType in the Windows locale Locale and returns the string result. If the Locale or LocaleType is invalid, Default is returned. GetFormatSettings calls this function to load some of its localization variables.

Languages Function

```
function Languages: TLanguages;
```

Languages returns a TLanguages object that contains information about all the locales supported by the local Windows installation. See TLanguages later in this section for more information.

LeadBytes Variable

```
var LeadBytes: set of Char = [];
```

The LeadBytes variable contains a set of characters that can be the leading byte of a multibyte character. Western locales use an empty set, but Far East locales set LeadBytes to the appropriate set according to the local code page.

ListSeparator Variable

```
var ListSeparator: Char;
```

ListSeparator is a character you should use to separate items in a list when displaying information to the user. The default value is set from the Windows locale.

SysLocale Variable

```
var SysLocale: TSysLocale;
```

SysLocale stores the local default locale. See TSysLocale later in this section for details.

TLanguages Type

```
type TLanguages = class
 public
    constructor Create;
    property Count: Integer read ...;
    function IndexOf(ID: LCID): Integer;
    property Name[Index: Integer]: string read ...;
    property NameFromLocaleID[ID: LCID]: string read ...;
    property NameFromLCID[const ID: string]: string read ...;
    property ID[Index: Integer]: string read ...;
    property LocaleID[Index: Integer]: LCID read ...;
    property Ext[Index: Integer]: string read ...;
 end;
```

TLanguages stores information about all the locales supported by the local Windows installation. The SysUtils unit creates a TLanguages instance, so there is no need to create additional instances.

Count returns the number of locales. IndexOf returns the index in TLanguages of a locale identifier. The other properties return information about each locale:

Ext Returns the short language name, which Delphi uses as the filename extension for a resource DLL.

ID Returns the locale identifier formatted as a hexadecimal string.

LocaleID
Returns the locale identifier.

Name
NameFromLCID
NameFromLocaleID
Returns the name of a locale. These properties differ only in the index for looking up the name. The index can be a raw index in TLanguages, a locale identifier, or a locale identifier string.

TSysLocale Type

```
type
   TSysLocale = packed record
     DefaultLCID: LCID;
```

```
  PriLangID: LANGID;
  SubLangID: LANGID;
  FarEast: Boolean;
  MiddleEast: Boolean;
end;
```

TSysLocale stores information about a Windows locale, specifically, the
locale identifier (DefaultLCID), the primary language identifier (PriLangID),
and the secondary language identifier (SubLangID). If the locale requires
multibyte character support, FarEast is True. If Windows is enabled for
Hebrew and Arabic languages, MiddleEast is True.

Modules

Every module (program, library, or package) exports two procedures named
Initialize and Finalize, which invoke the initialization sections and finalization sections for all the units contained in the module. Packages especially rely on
this feature because you can easily load a package DLL (thereby initializing its
units) and unload the DLL (after finalizing the units). The SysUtils unit has a
number of constants, types, and subroutines to help you get information about a
module and to load and unload packages.

Although the names contain the word "Package," most of the subroutines
described in this section work for any kind of module.

FinalizePackage Procedure

```
procedure FinalizePackage(Module: HMODULE);
```

FinalizePackage calls the finalization section for all the units in a loaded
module. UnloadPackage calls FinalizePackage, so you have little reason
to call this procedure yourself. If the module does not have a finalization
section, FinalizePackage raises an EPackageError exception.

GetPackageDescription Function

```
function GetPackageDescription(ModuleName: PChar): string;
```

GetPackageDescription returns the description string for the module
whose path is given by ModuleName. If the file does not exist or cannot be
loaded, EPackageError is raised. If the module does not have a description,
an empty string is returned. The description is specified by the $D or
$Description compiler directive, which the compiler stores as an RCDATA
resource named DESCRIPTION.

GetPackageInfo Procedure

```
type
  TNameType = (ntContainsUnit, ntRequiresPackage);
  TPackageInfoProc = procedure (const Name: string;
    NameType: TNameType; Flags: Byte; Param: Pointer);

procedure GetPackageInfo(Module: HMODULE; Param: Pointer;
    var Flags: Integer; InfoProc: TPackageInfoProc);
```

GetPackageInfo calls InfoProc for every unit in a loaded module (which
can be a package, program, or DLL) and for every required package. Param is
an opaque pointer that is passed directly to InfoProc. The procedure sets

Flags to the package flags, which are described in Table B-13. Note that pfExeModule is wrong in Delphi 5: its value should be $C0000000. If the module is not a Delphi or C++ Builder module, GetPackageInfo raises an exception.

Table B-13: Package Flags

Literal	Value	Description
pfNeverBuild	$00000001	Explicit build.
pfDesignOnly	$00000002	Design-time only.
pfRunOnly	$00000004	Runtime only.
pfIgnoreDupUnits	$00000008	Don't check for duplicate units.
pfModuleTypeMask	$C0000000	Mask for the module kind.
pfExeModule	$00000000	(Literal is wrong in Delphi 5.)
pfPackageModule	$40000000	Package DLL.
pfLibraryModule	$80000000	Other DLL.
	$C0000000	Executable program.
pfProducerMask	$0C000000	Mask for compiler that built the package.
pfV3Produced	$00000000	Delphi 3 or C++ Builder 3.
pfProducerUndefined	$04000000	Unknown compiler.
pfBCB4Produced	$08000000	C++ Builder 4 or later.
pfDelphi4Produced	$0C000000	Delphi 4 or later.

The arguments Delphi passes to InitProc are the unit or package name, the type (unit or required package), some flags, and the Param argument that was passed to GetPackageInfo. The flags describe additional information about the unit, as shown in Table B-14.

Table B-14: Unit Flags

Literal	Value	Description
ufMainUnit	$01	Main unit of package or project.
ufPackageUnit	$02	Package source unit (.dpk file).
ufWeakUnit	$04	Unit is weakly linked.
ufOrgWeakUnit	$08	Weakly linked unit in its original, defining package.[a]
ufImplicitUnit	$10	Unit is implicitly linked.

[a] According to the SysUtils unit, the ufOrgWeakUnit flag is set only for the unit in the package that originally defines it. In practice, it is set for every use of the weakly linked unit.

InitializePackage Procedure

```
procedure InitializePackage(Module: HMODULE);
```

InitializePackage calls the initialization section for all the units in a loaded module. LoadPackage calls InitializePackage for you. If the module does not have an initialization section, an exception is raised.

LoadPackage Function

```
function LoadPackage(const Name: string): HMODULE;
```

LoadPackage loads a package DLL and initializes it by running the initialization section of every unit in the package. It returns the module handle of the newly loaded DLL. If the **Name** does not specify a package, **LoadPackage** raises an **EPackageError** exception.

In order to use the package, you will usually arrange for the package to register itself upon loading. Delphi's IDE does this by having each unit declare a **Register** procedure. The IDE calls the **Register** procedure of each unit after loading the package. Another approach is for the package to be proactive and for each unit's initialization section to call a registration procedure defined in a unit contained in another package. The application also loads the registration package to get the list of registered units. Example B-5 shows one way to do this.

Example B-5: One Way to Register a Dynamically Loaded Package

```
unit Registration;
// Put this unit in its own package. The application adds this
// package to its list of runtime packages. All dynamically loaded
// packages add this package to their lists of required packages.
interface

// You are probably interested in more than just the unit name.
// Add whatever information you feel is important.
procedure RegisterUnit(const Name: string);
procedure UnregisterUnit(const Name: string);

implementation

uses Windows, SysUtils, Classes;

var
  UnitList: TStringList;           // list of unit information
  CritSect: TRtlCriticalSection;   // multithread protection

procedure RegisterUnit(const Name: string);
begin
  EnterCriticalSection(CritSect);
  try
    UnitList.Add(Name);
  finally
    LeaveCriticalSection(CritSect);
  end;
end;

procedure UnregisterUnit(const Name: string);
begin
  EnterCriticalSection(CritSect);
  try
    UnitList.Delete(UnitList.IndexOf(Name));
  finally
```

Example B-5: One Way to Register a Dynamically Loaded Package (continued)

```
      LeaveCriticalSection(CritSect);
    end;
end;

initialization
  UnitList := TStringList.Create;
  InitializeCriticalSection(CritSect);
finalization
  DeleteCriticalSection(CritSect);
  FreeAndNil(UnitList);
end.

// Example of how the Registration unit can be used.
unit Example;

interface
  ...
implementation
  uses Registration;
  ...
initialization
  RegisterUnit('Example');
finalization
  UnregisterUnit('Example');
end.
```

UnloadPackage Procedure

```
    procedure UnloadPackage(Module: HMODULE);
```

UnloadPackage finalizes every unit in the package and then unloads the DLL. It is the programmer's responsibility to ensure that the application does not have any dangling pointers, e.g., references to classes, events, or methods in the package.

Windows

This section describes variables and functions for working with the Windows API.

GetDiskFreeSpaceEx Variable

```
    var GetDiskFreeSpaceEx: function (Directory: PChar; var FreeAvailable,
    TotalSpace: TLargeInteger; TotalFree: PLargeInteger): Bool stdcall;
```

The first release of Windows 95 does not support the **GetDiskFreeSpaceEx** API function, but the OSR2 release does, as does Windows 98 and Windows NT. Delphi hides this difference by setting the **GetDiskFreeSpaceEx** variable to point to the Windows API function if it exists or to a Delphi function on Windows 95a. See the **DiskFree** function earlier in this appendix for the easy way to obtain the free space on a drive.

SafeLoadLibrary Function

```
    function SafeLoadLibrary(const Filename: string;
        ErrorMode: UINT = SEM_NoOpenFileErrorBox): HMODULE;
```

Some DLLs change the floating-point control word, which can affect the precision of Delphi's Comp and Currency types. The SafeLoadLibrary function is just like the Windows API function LoadLibrary, except that it ensures the floating-point control word is not disturbed. The optional second argument is passed to SetErrorMode, so you can control whether file open failures or similar errors are shown to the user.

TMultiReadExclusiveWriteSynchronizer Type

```
type
  TMultiReadExclusiveWriteSynchronizer = class
  public
    constructor Create;
    destructor Destroy; override;
    procedure BeginRead;
    procedure EndRead;
    procedure BeginWrite;
    procedure EndWrite;
  end;
```

Use TMultiReadExclusiveWriteSynchronizer when multiple threads must read a shared resource without changing it. A critical section allows only one thread to access a shared resource, even if that thread will not change it. TMultiReadExclusiveWriteSynchronizer, on the other hand, improves performance by allowing multiple simultaneous readers.

Each reader calls BeginRead to gain read access and EndRead when it is finished. When a thread wants to modify the resource, it calls BeginWrite, which waits until all readers have called EndRead, then it gets exclusive write access. Call EndWrite to give up the exclusive write lock. If a thread locks the synchronizer for write access, all calls to BeginRead in other threads block until the writer thread finishes.

 A thread should relinquish read access before trying to gain write access, otherwise deadlock can occur when two threads sit in their BeginWrite methods, each waiting for the other to call EndRead first.

Win32BuildNumber Variable

```
var Win32BuildNumber: Integer;
```

Win32BuildNumber stores the operating system build number. On Windows 95 and 98, the low order Word is the build number and the high order Word stores the major and minor version numbers (the same values as Win32MajorVersion and Win32MinorVersion).

Win32CSDVersion Variable

```
var Win32CSDVersion: string;
```

Win32CSDVersion stores additional information about the operating system, such as the NT service pack level. The actual text depends on the operating system.

Win32MajorVersion Variable

```
var Win32MajorVersion: Integer;
```

Win32MajorVersion stores the major part of the operating system version number, e.g., 4 for Windows NT 4.0 or Windows 9*x*.

Win32MinorVersion Variable

```
var Win32MinorVersion: Integer;
```

Win32MinorVersion stores the minor part of the operating system version number, e.g., 0 for Windows NT 4.0 or Windows 95, or 10 for Windows 98.

Win32Platform Variable

```
var Win32Platform: Integer;
```

Win32Platform stores the platform, which is one of the values in Table B-15 (the literals are declared in the **Windows** unit).

Table B-15: Values for Win32Platform

Literal	Description
Ver_Platform_Win32s	Win32s for Windows 3.1
Ver_Platform_Win32_NT	Windows NT or Windows 2000
Ver_Platform_Win32_Windows	Windows 95 or Windows 98

To identify the Windows operating system, try the following:

```
function GetOS: string;
begin
  case Win32Platform of
  Ver_Platform_Win32_NT:
    Result := Format('Windows NT %d.%d (Build %d %s)',
      [Win32MajorVersion, Win32MinorVersion,
       Win32BuildNumber, Win32CSDVersion]);
  Ver_Platform_Win32_Windows:
    if Win32MinorVersion = 0 then
      Result := Format('Windows 95 %s (%d.%2.2d.%d)',
          [Win32CSDVersion, Win32MajorVersion, Win32MinorVersion,
           Win32BuildNumber and $FFFF])
    else
      Result := Format('Windows 98 %s (%d.%2.2d.%d)',
          [Win32CSDVersion, Win32MajorVersion, Win32MinorVersion,
           Win32BuildNumber and $FFFF]);
  Ver_Platform_Win32s:
    Result := 'Win32s';
  else
    Result := Format('Windows %d.%2.2d.%d %s',
        [Win32MajorVersion, Win32MinorVersion,
         Win32BuildNumber, Win32CSDVersion])
  end;
end;
```

Miscellaneous

This section lists everything that doesn't fit in the other categories.

AllocMem Function

```
function AllocMem(Size: Cardinal): Pointer;
```

The **AllocMem** function is just like **GetMem**, except that it initializes the allocated memory to all zero. If you call **AllocMem** to allocate a record that contains long strings, interfaces, or **Variants**, you do not need to call **Initialize**. Free the memory with **FreeMem**.

CompareMem Function

```
function CompareMem(P1, P2: Pointer; Length: Integer): Boolean;
```

CompareMem compares **Length** bytes pointed to by P1 and P2 for equality. It returns True if the two memory regions contain identical contents, and False if any byte is different.

FreeAndNil Procedure

```
procedure FreeAndNil(var Obj);
```

When an object reference is stored in a variable or field, pass the object reference to **FreeAndNil** instead of calling the object's **Free** method. The **FreeAndNil** procedure calls **Free** and sets the variable or field to nil.

FreeAndNil is particularly useful in a multithreaded or reentrant situation because it guarantees that the variable is set to nil before the object is freed. In other words, the variable never holds an invalid reference.

Int64Rec Type

```
type
  Int64Rec = packed record
    Lo, Hi: LongWord;
  end;
```

Int64Rec makes it easier to access the high and low long words in an **Int64** or other 64-bit type (such as **Double**).

LoadStr Function

```
function LoadStr(Ident: Integer): string;
```

LoadStr returns a string resource (or an empty string if no resource exists with identifier **Ident**). It exists for backward compatibility. New code should use **resourcestring** declarations.

LongRec Type

```
type
  LongRec = packed record
    Lo, Hi: Word;
  end;
```

LongRec makes it easier to access the high and low words in a **LongWord** or other 32-bit type (such as **Single**).

PByteArray Type

```
type PByteArray = ^TByteArray;
type TByteArray = array[0..32767] of Byte;
```

The most common use of **PByteArray** is in a type cast to treat a region of memory as a raw byte array.

PWordArray Type

```
type PWordArray = ^TWordArray;
type TWordArray = array[0..16383] of Word;
```

The most common use of PWordArray is in a type cast to treat a region of memory as a raw array of words.

Supports Function

```
function Supports(const Instance: IUnknown; const Intf: TGUID;
    out Inst): Boolean; overload;
function Supports(Instance: TObject; const Intf: TGUID;
    out Inst): Boolean; overload;
```

The Supports function is another way to cast an object or interface reference to a different GUID or interface type. In many cases, Supports is more convenient to use than QueryInterface. If Instance is not nil and if it supports the interface Intf, the function sets Inst to the desired interface and returns True. Otherwise, it sets Inst to nil and returns False.

TIntegerSet Type

```
type TIntegerSet = set of 0..SizeOf(Integer) * 8 - 1;
```

Sets are usually easier to use than bit masks. The TIntegerSet type is a set of the integers from 0 to 31. Thus, to test whether the most significant two bits are set in an integer, try the following:

```
if ([30,31] * TIntegerSet(IntValue)) = [30,31] then
  TwoMostSignificantBitsAreSet(IntValue);

// The same thing using integer bit masks is harder to read:
if (IntValue and $C0000000) = $C0000000 then
  TwoMostSignificantBitsAreSet(IntValue);
```

TMethod Type

```
type
  TMethod = record
    Code, Data: Pointer;
  end;
```

All method references are stored in the format described by the TMethod type. You can cast a method to or from TMethod, or cast an event property to or from TMethod.

TProcedure Type

```
type TProcedure = procedure;
```

TProcedure is a simple, parameterless, procedural type.

TSysCharSet Type

```
type TSysCharSet = set of Char;
```

TSysCharSet is a set of all the ANSI characters.

TWordRec Type

```
type
  WordRec = packed record
    Lo, Hi: Byte;
  end;
```

WordRec makes it easier to access the high and low bytes in a Word or other 16-bit type (such as SmallInt).

Index

Delete procedure, 177
Delphi
    language features, compared, 32
    versions, testing, 448
delphi32.exe, 485–487
$DenyPackageUnit compiler directive,
    442
$Description compiler directive, 443
$DesignOnly compiler directive, 443
Destroy destructor, 376
destructor keyword, 177
destructors, 43–44
    Destroy, 376
    prior to calling, 378
DFM converter, 481
directives, 39, 127
    compiler (see compiler directives)
    default, 294
    (see also individual directive names)
directories
    creating, 260
    managing, 500
directory paths, 260
    changing, 160
    files in, 476
    removing, 323
    returning, 220
disks, managing, 500
dispatch interfaces, 180
dispatch methods, 179
Dispatch procedure, 61, 378
DispCallByIDProc variable, 178
dispid directive, 179
dispinterface keyword, 180
Dispose procedure, 70, 103, 181
div keyword, 182
DllProc variable, 6, 182–183
DLLs, 1, 5–7, 247
    functions
        exporting, 201
        implementing, 205
    language-specific, 214, 254
    library modules, 261
    loading/unloading, 182–183
        by multithreaded applications, 249
    memory, 67–68, 133–134, 335
    packages, 7, 318
    parameter types, 280, 283, 300
    (see also libraries)

do keyword, 184
Double type, 184–185
double-byte character sets (see strings,
        multibyte)
DoubleToComp procedure, 186
downto keyword, 187
drives, changing, 160
dynamic arrays, 137, 172
dynamic directive, 39, 187
dynamic link libraries (see DLLs)

E

$E compiler directive, 444
EExternal class, 491
EHeapException class, 491
EInOutError class, 491
$Else compiler directive, 444
else keyword, 188
EmptyParam variable, 188
EncodeDate function, 527
EncodeTime function, 527
end keyword, 189
$Endif compiler directive, 444
EndThread function, 108–109
enumerated types, 82, 153
    ordinal values, 289
    smallest value of, 256
EnumModules procedure, 189–190
EnumResourceModules procedure, 190
Eof function, 26, 191
Eoln function, 191
EraNames variable, 528
Erase procedure, 26, 192
EraYearOffsets variable, 528
error codes, 24
    abstract, 131
    runtime, 425–427
    Windows API, 229
error handling, 327, 488
    AssertErrorProc variable, 144
    ErrorProc variable, 193
    ExceptProc variable, 197
    overflow checks, 461
    SysUtils unit, 492–493
    try keyword, 380
error messages, 193, 245, 320, 325
    addresses in, 192
    displaying, 266

functions (*continued*)
   protected, 295
   return types, 290
   return values, 321
   returning from, 199
   VarToStr, 409
   virtual, 411
   Windows API, return types, 255
   (see also individual function names)
futures, 119–126

G

$G compiler directive, 446
GetDir function, 220
GetDiskFreeSpaceEx variable, 538
GetEnumName function, 82
GetEnumProp function, 82
GetEnumValue function, 82
GetFloatProp function, 82
GetFormatSettings procedure, 532–533
GetHeapStatus function, 220
GetInt64Prop function, 82
GetInterface function, 379
GetInterfaceEntry function, 376
GetInterfaceTable function, 376
GetLocaleChar function, 533
GetLocaleStr function, 533
GetMem procedure, 58, 103, 221–222
GetMemory function, 222
GetMemoryManager procedure, 223
GetMethodProp function, 82
GetObjectProp function, 82
GetObjectPropClass function, 83
GetOrdProp function, 83
GetPackageDescription function, 535
GetPackageInfo procedure, 535–536
GetPackageInfoTable type, 223
GetPropInfo function, 83
GetPropInfos procedure, 83
GetPropList function, 83
GetPropValue function, 84
GetSetProp function, 84
GetStrProp function, 84
GetTypeData function, 79, 84
GetVariantProp function, 84
global variables
   declaring, 395
   finalization sections, 211
   freeing, 35
      objects stored in, 178
Globally Unique Identifiers, storing, 366
goto keyword, 224
GUI builder, 2
GUIDs, storing, 366

H

$H compiler directive, 446
Halt procedure, 225
headers
   declaring, 215
   procedure, 290–291
HeapAllocFlags variable, 226
HexDisplayPrefix variable, 521
Hi function, 226
High function, 12, 226
HInstance variable, 227
$Hints compiler directive, 446, 475
$HppEmit compiler directive, 447
HPrevInst variable, 228
HResult type, 229

I

I/O errors, 193, 333, 491
   opening/closing files, 319, 323
   Read procedure, 307
I/O operations, 245, 453, 478
   performance bottlenecks, 338
   (see also file I/O)
IDE, 2, 5, 485–487
   class declarations, 46, 298
   component references, storing, 51
   exception handling, 174, 196
   methods, published, 73
   packages, 7, 318
IDispatch interface, 229
if keyword, 230
$IfDef compiler directive, 441, 448
$IfNDef compiler directive, 441, 449
$IfOpt compiler directive, 450
image base addresses, 7–8, 450, 476
$ImageBase compiler directive, 450
implementation keyword, 230
implementation sections, 3, 230
   declarations, 33, 244
   procedure headers, 291
   uses declaration, 391

About the Author

Ray Lischner is well known in the Delphi community as an author and speaker. He wrote *Secrets of Delphi 2*, *Hidden Paths of Delphi 3*, and numerous articles for *Delphi Informant*, *Dr. Dobb's Journal*, and other magazines. His conference appearances include the annual Borland/Inprise conference, and he has spoken to Delphi users' groups across the country. He also wrote *Shakespeare for Dummies*. You can reach Ray at *nutshell@tempest-sw.com*.

Colophon

Our look is the result of reader comments, our own experimentation, and feedback from distribution channels. Distinctive covers complement our distinctive approach to technical topics, breathing personality and life into potentially dry subjects.

The animal on the cover of *Delphi in a Nutshell* is a Canadian lynx. This sturdy and powerful cat hunts rodents and small mammals by night in North American mountain and arctic regions. The lynx has larger paws and hence better mobility in snow than its cousin the bobcat, which cannot survive harsh winter conditions. Its fur is thick, and tufts extend from the tips of its ears and from its jaw, giving the cat a striking, stealthy appearance. Indeed, the lynx is stealthy; it is an agile climber of rocks and trees. It stalks its prey and kills alone.

The lynx is, in turn, preyed upon by cougars and wolves. Humans, however, are responsible for endangering the species' survival. For more than two centuries, hunters have been over-shooting and trapping the lynx for its soft, gray fur, decimating the lynx population in its southernmost habitat—the Rocky Mountains of Colorado. To combat the lynx's disappearance, CLAWS (Colorado Lynx and Wolverine Strategy), a steering group working in cooperation with various federal and state wildlife and forestry agencies, plans to reintroduce the species. Forty lynx from Canada are being released into the protected Weminuche Wilderness of Colorado's San Juan National Forest.

Madeleine Newell was the production editor and copyeditor for *Delphi in a Nutshell*. Maureen Dempsey and Jane Ellin provided quality control. Emily Quill, Anna Kim Snow, and Maeve O'Meara provided production assistance. Nancy Crumpton wrote the index.

Ellie Volckhausen designed the cover of this book, based on a series design by Edie Freedman. Kathleen Wilson produced the cover layout with QuarkXPress 3.32 using Adobe's ITC Garamond font.

Alicia Cech designed the interior layout based on a series design by Nancy Priest. Mike Sierra implemented the design in FrameMaker 5.5. The text and heading fonts are ITC Garamond Light and Garamond Book. The illustrations that appear in the book were produced by Robert Romano and Rhon Porter using Macromedia FreeHand 8 and Adobe Photoshop 5. This colophon was written by Sarah Jane Shangraw.